EUROPEAN CONSTITUTIONALISM THE OTHER WAY ROUND

The key argument of the volume is that post-1989 transformation deeply affected states and societies on both sides of the former Iron Curtain and was mutually constitutive. While post-communist Europe had to re-invent itself to be 'admitted' to the EU, the old member states and the EU changed too – less visibly, but no less profoundly. This volume examines these transformations from a new perspective, defined by scholars from post-communist Europe, who set the agenda of the volume in a series of workshops. Their colleagues from the 'West' were invited to reflect on the experience of their countries in the light of the questions and concerns defined in those workshops. The authors include scholars from a variety of backgrounds: established and young, coming from all parts of the continent and having different views on the politics of European integration. This title is also available as open access on Cambridge Core.

Jan Komárek is Professor of EU Law at the University of Copenhagen (on leave) and currently holds the Donatio Universitatis Carolinae Chair (2025–2027) at the Faculty of Law, Charles University in Prague. He was the Principal Investigator of the IMAGINE project (2019–2025).

Birgit Aasa is a qualified lawyer in Estonia and holds a PhD from the European University Institute. She was a postdoctoral research fellow at the IMAGINE project, the University of Copenhagen. She is currently a civil servant in the European Parliament.

Marina Bán has a PhD in Law from the University of Amsterdam and was a postdoctoral research fellow at the IMAGINE project, the University of Copenhagen.

Michał Krajewski holds a PhD from the European University Institute and was a postdoctoral research fellow at the IMAGINE project, the University of Copenhagen. He is currently an inquiries officer at the Office of the European Ombudsman in Brussels.

European Constitutionalism the Other Way Round

FROM THE PERIPHERY TO THE CENTRE

Edited by

JAN KOMÁREK

University of Copenhagen/Charles University in Prague

BIRGIT AASA

European Parliament

MARINA BÁN

Independent Researcher

MICHAŁ KRAJEWSKI

Office of the European Ombudsman

CAMBRIDGE UNIVERSITY PRESS

CAMBRIDGE
UNIVERSITY PRESS

Shaftesbury Road, Cambridge CB2 8EA, United Kingdom

One Liberty Plaza, 20th Floor, New York, NY 10006, USA

477 Williamstown Road, Port Melbourne, VIC 3207, Australia

314–321, 3rd Floor, Plot 3, Splendor Forum, Jasola District Centre, New Delhi – 110025, India

103 Penang Road, #05-06/07, Visioncrest Commercial, Singapore 238467

Cambridge University Press is part of Cambridge University Press & Assessment, a department of the University of Cambridge.

We share the University's mission to contribute to society through the pursuit of education, learning and research at the highest international levels of excellence.

www.cambridge.org
Information on this title: www.cambridge.org/9781009604079

DOI: 10.1017/9781009604093

First published 2025

Cover image: Prague, Czech Republic. October 2016. - stock photo / mgs / Getty Images

A catalogue record for this publication is available from the British Library

A Cataloging-in-Publication data record for this book is available from the Library of Congress

ISBN 978-1-009-60407-9 Hardback

Contents

List of Contributors — *page* ix
Acknowledgements — xi

1 **Imagining Statehood and Constitutionalism in Europe: Introduction** — 1
Jan Komárek, Birgit Aasa, Marina Bán and Michał Krajewski

PART I NATION STATES, MEMBER STATES AND THEIR OTHERS

2 **Vicarious Sovereignty: Becoming European the Estonian Way** — 41
Maria Mälksoo

3 **From Federation to External Constraint: Europe in the Italian Constitutional Imagination** — 61
Marco Goldoni

4 **Sovereignty and the Misery of Small Eastern European Nations** — 83
Hent Kalmo

5 **Ruling Britannia** — 110
Martin Loughlin

6 **The Power of Concepts: From 'Self-Management' to 'Sovereignty' in Soviet Estonia (1987–1988)** — 131
Juhan Saharov

7 **European Integration: Ineffable Aspiration or the Object of Concern? About the Ambiguity of Europe in the Polish Constitutional Imaginary** — 144
Aleksandra Kustra-Rogatka

8 The Constitutionalised Image of Enemy in the Hungarian Fundamental Law 171
Attila Antal

PART II BRINGING BACK THE PAST (TO SERVE OR UNDERSTAND THE PRESENT?)

9 Political Integration through Constitutional Memory? Historical Constitution and Community Building in Hungary 193
Kálmán Pócza

10 The Constitutional Concept of the Historical Constitution and Illiberalism: The Case of Hungary 208
Tímea Drinóczi

11 Estonians' European Imaginaries: The Soviet and Pre-Soviet Legacy 226
Epp Annus

12 Czechoslovakia: Remembering and Forgetting the Failures of a State 250
Mary Heimann

13 A Constitution without Qualities? Three Narratives about Austrian Constitutional Law 266
Ulrich Wagrandl

PART III THE VARIETIES OF LIBERALISM IN EUROPE

14 Rule of What Law? Authoritarian Pasts, Liberal Politics and Constitutional Imagination in Early Post-Communist East Central Europe 297
Michal Kopeček

15 From the Façade to Solid Foundation? The Evolution of the Polish Constitutional Law Discourse in 1944–1989 329
Wojciech Zomerski

16 Nordic Democratic Exceptionality after the End of History: A Neoliberalized Constitutional Imaginary? 357
Johan Strang

17 **Fifty Years of Democratic Constitutionalism in Portugal: Between Constitutional Aspirations and the European Path** 372
Mariana Canotilho

18 **Constitutional Drift: Exploring the Deeper Roots of Polish Constitutional Crisis** 390
Karol Muszyński and Paweł Skuczyński

19 **On the French Constitutional Imaginary: The Erosion of the Long-standing Republican Tradition** 409
François-Xavier Millet

20 **From Legal Impossibilism to the Rule of Law Crisis: Transitional Justice and Polish Counter-Constitutionalism** 429
Michał Krotoszyński

Index 457

Contributors

Birgit Aasa is a Lawyer Linguist at the European Parliament; in 2021–2023 she was a postdoctoral researcher at the IMAGINE project, the University of Copenhagen.

Epp Annus is an associate professor, Tallinn University School of Humanities, and lecturer, Department of Slavic and East European Languages and Cultures, Ohio State University.

Attila Antal is an assistant professor, Eötvös Loránd University Faculty of Law, Institute of Political Science, Hungary.

Marina Bán is an independent researcher; in 2020–2023 they were a postdoctoral researcher at the IMAGINE project, the University of Copenhagen.

Mariana Canotilho is a researcher, University of Coimbra, University of Coimbra Institute for Legal Research, Faculty of Law and Judge of the Portuguese Constitutional Court.

Tímea Drinóczi is a Senior Researcher, Mykolas Romeris University, Lithuania, Research Affiliate, CEU Democracy Institute, Hungary and Faculty of Law, Federal University of Minas Gerais, Brazil.

Marco Goldoni is Professor of Philosophy of Law, School of Law, University of Glasgow.

Mary Heimann is Chair in Modern History and Director of the Central and East European Research Centre, Cardiff University.

Hent Kalmo is a research fellow, Johan Skytte Institute of Political Studies at the University of Tartu.

Jan Komárek is Professor of EU Law (on leave), University of Copenhagen, where he was the Principal Investigator of the IMAGINE project (2019–2025), and currently holds Donatio Universitatis Carolinae Chair (2025–2027) at the Faculty of Law, Charles University in Prague.

Michal Kopeček is a senior researcher, Institute of Contemporary History, Czech Academy of Sciences.

Michał Krajewski is an inquiries officer at the European Ombudsman Office, Brussels; in 2020–2022 he was a postdoctoral researcher at the IMAGINE project, the University of Copenhagen.

Michał Krotoszyński is an assistant professor, Department of Theory and Philosophy of Law, Faculty of Law and Administration, Adam Mickiewicz University in Poznań.

Aleksandra Kustra-Rogatka is an associate professor, Nicolaus Copernicus University in Toruń.

Martin Loughlin is Emeritus Professor of Public Law, London School of Economics and Political Science.

Maria Mälksoo is Professor of International Relations, Department of Political Science, University of Copenhagen.

François-Xavier Millet is Professor of Public Law at the University of the Antilles (Guadeloupe, French West Indies) and the holder of the Jean Monnet Chair on Comparative Regional Integration.

Karol Muszyński is an assistant professor, Faculty of Sociology, University of Warsaw, and a research associate, Centre for Sociological Research, KU Leuven.

Kálmán Pócza is a senior research fellow at the Ludovika University of Public Service and Head of the MCC Center for Constitutional Politics.

Juhan Saharov is a research fellow in political theory, Johan Skytte Institute of Political Studies, University of Tartu.

Paweł Skuczyński is an assistant professor, Faculty of Law and Administration, University of Warsaw.

Johan Strang is Professor of Nordic Studies at the University of Helsinki.

Ulrich Wagrandl is a postdoctoral research and teaching fellow, Institute of Austrian and Europan Public Law, Department of Public Law and Tax Law, Vienna University of Economics and Business.

Wojciech Zomerski is a Max Weber fellow, European University Institute and associated researcher, Centre for Legal Education and Social Theory, University of Wroclaw.

Acknowledgements

The volume forms part of the Project IMAGINE, which has received funding from the European Research Council (ERC) under the European Union's Horizon 2020 research and innovation programme (grant agreement No. 803163). More information on IMAGINE can be found at www.imagine-const.eu. IMAGINE was carried out at the University of Copenhagen, Faculty of Law, *iCourts* – the Danish National Research Foundation's Centre of Excellence for International Courts and Governance.

The co-editing of this volume by Birgit Aasa and Michał Krajewski was unrelated to their current functions at the European Parliament and the European Ombudsman, respectively. The views expressed in the chapters are solely those of the authors and cannot be attributed to the European Parliament or the European Ombudsman.

1

Imagining Statehood and Constitutionalism in Europe

Introduction

Jan Komárek, Birgit Aasa, Marina Bán and Michał Krajewski

1.1 IMAGINING EUROPE AND 'BEYOND'

How is Europe imagined in national constitutions and their conceptual frameworks? And how does Europe influence these very frameworks, or, as we call them, constitutional imaginaries? These are the key questions explored in this volume, which forms part of a collective project *IMAGINE: European Constitutional Imaginaries: Utopias, Ideologies and the Other.*[1]

The first book in the project, published in 2023,[2] examined constitutional imaginaries underpinning European integration: the sets of ideas and beliefs that help to motivate and justify European integration in constitutional terms. Scholars of various disciplinary backgrounds addressed questions raised by the ideological – and at the same time utopian – character of the EU's constitutionalism. The present volume turns the perspective around and puts emphasis on the EU member states, bringing together views from Western and Central Eastern Europe.[3] It explores what

Jan Komárek is Professor of EU Law at the University of Copenhagen (on leave) and currently holds Donatio Universitatis Carolinae Chair (2025–2027) at the Faculty of Law, Charles University in Prague. Birgit Aasa, Marina Bán and Michał Krajewski were post-doctoral research fellows at the University of Copenhagen in 2020–2022 or 2023. Birgit Aasa and Michał Krajewski are currently, respectively, a lawyer linguist at the European Parliament and an inquiries officer at the European Ombudsman in Brussels, but the sections they authored express their personal views only; nothing in this introduction and the book can be attributed to the European Parliament or the European Ombudsman. While all the authors exchanged ideas and feedback in the writing process, Jan Komarek is the author of Section 1.1, the beginning of Section 1.2, and Section 1.3; Birgit Aasa is the author of Section 1.2.1, based on the Estonian study; Marina Bán is the author of Section 1.2.2, based on the Hungarian study; and Michał Krajewski is the author of Section 1.2.3, based on the Polish study.

[1] ERC Starting Grant No 803163. More information on the project can be found at www.imagine-const.eu/ (last accessed 2 April 2025).

[2] Jan Komárek (ed.), *European Constitutional Imaginaries: Between Ideology and Utopia* (Oxford University Press, 2023).

[3] We also use the distinction between the 'old' and 'new' Europe, or 'the West' and 'the East' in the text.

both the mainstream and non-mainstream debates can contribute to European constitutional imaginaries. The volume introduces different themes emerging in national contexts in post-communist Europe and provokes reflections on them from the other side – the EU member states from before 2004.

This means rethinking the way we look at European law and politics: we do not start with questions raised in the centre of the EU (such as 'how to best implement "our" "common" values in the "new" member states?', or, 'why there is democratic "backsliding"'?). Instead, we identify concerns that emerge on the periphery of the EU in order to shed light on European integration and its constitutional imaginary as a whole. Through this exercise we seek to enhance the ambition called for by one of us in the article 'Waiting for the existential revolution in Europe':[4]

> Europe has a much better hope of overcoming its current crisis if it becomes spiritually united. Yet this cannot happen through East Central Europe trying to 'return' to the West or becoming the West. Rather, it lies in the recognition of its unique experience, which is not to be overcome or, even worse, forgotten, but used as a reservoir for Europe's future flourishing.[5]

Section 1.1.1 explains what we mean by 'constitutional imaginaries'. Second, in Section 1.1.2, we discuss how this concept can be employed to better understand the stakes behind the 'constitutionalisation' of the EU. Finally, we suggest what the contribution of post-communist Europe may consist of in Section 1.1.3.

Section 1.2 presents the three themes emerging from post-communist Europe: first, Section 1.2.1 shows how the nature of statehood transforms when the state integrates into a supranational structure and how the imagined 'other' (for example, the enemy, the Soviet Union or even Europe) influences the key concepts of national constitutional law, such as sovereignty, peoplehood or citizenship. The second theme, in Section 1.2.2, concerns the uses and misuses of history in the construction of constitutional imaginary. Finally, there have been varieties of liberalism at play in the period of post-communist transformation (which, from the perspective of the West, was the 'end of history'). These need to be analysed separately, before the hegemonic 'liberal ideology' can be criticised (Section 1.2.3).

Each theme is briefly introduced by the member of our project team who conducted a case study focused on one country: Estonia (Birgit Aasa), Hungary (Marina Bán) and Poland (Michał Krajewski). As will be seen, while it is true that each of these case studies gave rise to a particular theme, similar concerns can be found in other member states of the EU as well. It was precisely the point of our project to identify these similarities and at the same time put them into the common conceptual framework. This introduction explains how we tried to organise our

[4] Jan Komárek, 'Waiting for the Existential Revolution in Europe' (2014) 12 *International Journal of Constitutional Law* 190.

[5] Ibid., 212.

work so that each of the chapters speaks to another and the volume offers (much) more than a mere collection of isolated reflections on a particular member state.

1.1.1 *Constitutional Imaginaries: An Expanding Concept*

Constitutional imaginaries refer to the set of ideas and beliefs that help to motivate and justify the practice of government and collective self-rule.[6] Such imaginaries are as important as institutions and officeholders formally embedded in constitutions. They draw their intellectual basis from broader social imaginaries, which include 'symbolic collections of self-understandings – carried in images and stories and ways of thinking – that reflect crucial facts of social life, and also normative expectations about how that social life ought to be lived'.[7]

Constitutional imaginaries provide political action (anchored in the constitution and getting expression through the medium of law) with an overarching sense and purpose recognised by those governed as legitimate. It is these imaginaries that construct the past and the future of the polity and the political identity of its citizens.[8] Participants in the constitutional practice and everyday politics usually do not reflect on these imaginaries; they remain as background assumptions and framings of everyday political and constitutional thought and action. However, from time to time, imaginaries get to the surface and form the heart of public debate: especially when a momentous step is to be taken by the polity, for example, during the establishment of a new constitutional settlement, such as entering the EU, or when a crisis shatters the existing arrangements.

In some sense constitutional imaginaries can be understood as ideologies in (the post-)Marxist terms as 'means of domination'.[9] However, contrary to such negative connotations, we argue that imaginaries/ideologies are indispensable for political rule. They integrate individual subjects and their beliefs into a common whole.[10] There is a complex relationship between reality and ideology – 'ideologies are

6 On the concept of 'constitutional imaginary', see Jan Komárek, 'European Constitutional Imaginaries: Utopias, Ideologies and the Other', in Jan Komárek (ed.), *European Constitutional Imaginaries: Between Ideology and Utopia* (Oxford University Press, 2023), chapter 1, and Martin Loughlin, 'Constitutional Imagination' (2015) 78 *Modern Law Review* 1. The present chapter builds on and develops the ideas presented in Komárek, 'European Constitutional Imaginaries'.

7 Paul Linden Retek, 'History, System, Principle, Analogy: Four Paradigms of Legitimacy in European Law' (2021) 26 *Columbia Journal of European Law* 1, 8, referring to Charles Taylor, *Modern Social Imaginaries* (Duke University Press, 2003) and Cornelius Castoriadis, *The Imaginary Institution of Society* (MIT Press, 1987), 145.

8 Ulrich Haltern, 'Pathos and Patina: The Failure and Promise of Constitutionalism in the European Imagination' (2003) 9 *European Law Journal* 14, 20.

9 For a critique of such reductive understanding of ideology, see e.g. Susan Marks, *The Riddle of all Constitutions: International Law, Democracy, and the Critique of Ideology* (Cambridge University Press 2000), chapter 1.

10 See Loughlin, 'Constitutional Imagination', 12–13.

neither true nor false but are a set of socially conditioned ideas that provide a truth that people . . . want to hear'.[11]

Constitutional imaginaries thus conceal structures of domination, making conscious choices, distribution and redistribution appear as natural, fixed and incontestable, or at least objectively good. This can be carried out through different means, including through presenting economic choices with significant social costs as objectively unavoidable given the economic situation (the economic emergency rhetoric), by relying on an existential fear of enemies that can be addressed only by joining a powerful alliance, or even by characterising constitutional law and the input of experts (legal, economic or others) as an apolitical and scientific endeavour, offering a universal blueprint for the just ordering of society. As such, ideologies can shape law, and so do constitutional imaginaries – they have a transformative function.

Even though constitutional imaginaries that emerged in post-1989 Central and Eastern Europe – or in any other time and anywhere else in Europe – have been ideological inasmuch as they offered a system of belief indispensable for political rule, it does not mean that alternatives (such as a return to the nation-state and radical 'sovereignty' based on the glorious historical experience – 'making country XY great *again*') are any less ideological. In a way, ideologies are inescapable in politics – and constitutional law alike.

Constitutional imaginaries also form utopias. Utopias provide an external vantage point from which we can criticise ideologies.[12] 'Only those orientations transcending reality' can be referred to as 'utopian' which, 'when they pass over to conduct, tend to shatter, either partially or wholly, the order of things prevailing at the time'.[13] Utopias preserve opposition to the status quo as aspirational schemes that seek actualisation.[14] Therefore, inquiring into the constitutional imaginaries of European states means also inquiring into their fundamental hidden or unhidden aspirations and expectations.

Admittedly, the nation-states usually stem from organic national communities and, as such, constitute 'nomocracies' – communities based on the public good of being able to live and govern in common. In contrast to 'teleocracies' (like the EU), they are not primarily concerned with pursuing specific goals or public goods.[15] However, the constitutional imaginaries emerging before and after 1989 in Europe do manifest specific goals and public goods that constitute fundamental

[11] Christine Sypnowich, 'Law and Ideology', in Edward N. Zalta (ed.), *The Stanford Encyclopedia of Philosophy* (Summer 2019 ed.), https://plato.stanford.edu/archives/sum2019/entries/law-ideology/ (last accessed 2 April 2025).

[12] Loughlin, 'Constitutional Imagination', 13.

[13] Karl Mannheim, *Ideology and Utopia* (Routledge, 1936), 173.

[14] Loughlin, 'Constitutional Imagination', 13.

[15] On this point, see Neil Walker, 'The European Public Good and European Public Goods', in Jan Komárek (ed.), *European Constitutional Imaginaries: Between Ideology and Utopia* (Oxford University Press, 2023), chapter 11.

constitutional principles – oftentimes remaining in opposition, such as sovereignty and security, individual freedom and social justice, the rule of law and transitional justice. Understanding these utopias is crucial for orienting political action towards change and reconciling the political order with the desires of its subjects.

1.1.2 *Constitutionalism and Imaginaries in the EU*

Constitutional imaginaries of Europe in general and in the post-communist Europe in particular have received relatively little to no scholarly attention.[16] There have been numerous interesting and engaging inquiries into bordering subject-matters, which are worth mentioning for a fuller understanding of the broader range of topics at hand when talking about constitutional imaginaries.

In recent years, prominent scholarship has emerged on the 'varieties of constitutionalism'[17] in Europe and how this variety affects the production of constitutional imaginaries in both sites – (nation/member) states and the EU. Nevertheless, the published works primarily concern conflicts between national highest courts and the European Court of Justice.[18] The most recent (and admirably ambitious) project studied constitutional doctrine and theory,[19] whereas the broader intellectual debate on the foundational ideas underpinning constitutionalism(s) among constitutional scholars and other intellectuals in the member states (who very often have engaged in public and policy debates) has still remained unexplored.[20] Our volume seeks to fill this gap with studies on both how Europe is being imagined from national vantage points as well as how Europe affects the shape of constitutional law and theory in the member states.

This analysis is necessary because we lack thorough and internationally accessible exploration of national debates about the changes brought to local constitutionalisms by European integration and how these constitutionalisms conceive of the statehood and its relationship to Europe. In particular, we need to acquire a more

[16] Besides Komárek, *European Constitutional Imaginaries*, see Jiří Přibáň, *Constitutional Imaginaries: A Theory of European Societal Constitutionalism* (Routledge, 2022), which, however, does not take the comparative perspective offered by our volume. Our volume takes a post-communist perspective as a starting point for a reflection on Europe as a whole.

[17] Signe Rehling Larsen, 'Varieties of Constitutionalism in the European Union' (2021) 84 *Modern Law Review* 477 and Bruce Ackerman, 'Three Paths to Constitutionalism: And the Crisis of the European Union' (2015) 45 *British Journal of Political Science* 705.

[18] See Anne-Marie Slaughter, Alec Stone Sweet and Joseph Weiler (eds.), *The European Court and National Courts, Doctrine and Jurisprudence: Legal Change in Its Social Context* (Hart, 1998) and Giuseppe Martinico and Oreste Pollicino (eds.), *The National Judicial Treatment of the ECHR and EU Laws: A Comparative Constitutional Perspective* (Europa Law Publishing, 2010).

[19] Stefan Griller, Lina Papadopoulou and Roman Puff (eds.), *National Constitutions and EU Integration* (Hart, 2022).

[20] See, however, Marco Dani, Marco Goldoni and Agustín José Menedéz (eds.), *The Legitimacy of European Constitutional Orders: A Comparative Inquiry* (Edward Elgar, 2023).

profound understanding of those constitutional imaginaries existing alongside the mainstream liberal paradigm, sometimes supporting and sometimes challenging it. In this sense, an important question tackled in this book is to what extent the non-mainstream imaginaries have been accommodated within the constitutional settlement. Have they been simply relegated to the sphere of anachronistic ideas, waiting for the right time to re-emerge and put in question the constitutional status quo? Inquiring into these debates is an urgent scholarly task given the emerging and mounting challenges to European integration. Notably, these challenges manifesting as illiberal and populist parties are no longer characteristic of only post-communist Europe.

1.1.3 *Learning from Post-Communist Europe*

As a distinctive feature, the volume puts particular emphasis on post-communist Europe. European constitutionalism has so far been interpreted as a Western invention with the post-communist states trying to catch up and 'return to Europe'. In consequence, most research on European constitutionalism, even research that includes the Eastern perspective, examines it through 'Western lenses'. Our goal has been to reverse this dynamic. It stems from the idea to identify influential discussions around constitutional imaginaries in Central and Eastern Europe and invite scholars from the 'West' to reflect on these imaginaries through the lenses of their own national constitutional experience. This way, we sought to avoid a certain hegemonic (and homogenising) tendency in European constitutional scholarship, which often defines the concerns and issues to be debated through the perspective of the West (or the 'old') and its legal traditions - for example, how the rule of law or democracy are understood in the liberal-legalist constitutional thought or how the social question has been addressed by the Western welfare state – and abandoned when neoliberalism took over. The experience of communism and post-communist transformation that begun in the 1990s, but certainly did not end with the entry of many post-communist countries to the EU, is neglected, or worse, taken as a threat to the achievements of the old Europe.[21]

Rather than painting broad-brush analyses of constitutionalism in Central and Eastern Europe, including its similarities or dissimilarities with the Western blueprint, this book suggests a different approach. We have sought to identify and shed light on distinct, perhaps even idiosyncratic but, at any rate, influential constitutional imaginaries in several states of Central and Eastern Europe relating to these states' position in Europe, especially those 'others' that have departed from mainstream liberal constitutionalism and the narrative of the return to Europe. We believe that studying these imaginaries enables a clearer understanding of the dynamics underpinning the constitutional transformation of post-communist

[21] On this, see e.g., the reactions to Damjan Kukovec, 'Law and the Periphery' (2015) 21 *European Law Journal* 406.

member states, including conventionally considered 'achievements' as well as those termed 'backsliding' or 'departure from European values'. But it also provides a fuller picture of *European* constitutional imaginaries in its totality: as it is not only Western European states that form Europe, but the Eastern counterparts as well.

The experience of the 'Other Europe' from *both before and after* 1989 suggests more inventive and fruitful avenues than otherwise explored and expected.[22] Most often, the mainstream picture focuses on the process of transformation of post-communist states into future members of the Union, seeking to comply with the political and economic criteria of EU membership.[23]

Crucially, the fall of communism in 1989 was also transformative for the 'old' Europe. The image of the Union as a guarantee of democracy and freedom from foreign domination, widespread in the Other Europe, incited changes in the deep structure of the Union *as a whole*.[24] The concepts of the 'rule of law' and European values appeared during the conditionality process to prepare the EU enlargement of 2004. As noted by de Witte, the enlargement was a 'constitutional agenda-setter for the EU'.[25] However, the EU institutions were criticised for prioritising 'legal and institutional checklists', while neglecting 'socio-political and socio-cultural realms',[26] as well as failing to engage with local constitutional traditions of, among other things, civil engagement.[27] We believe that national constitutional imaginaries in Central and Eastern Europe have still not received the attention they deserve; something that the present volume seeks to begin remedying.

In addition to the aforementioned analyses, states from the 'Other Europe' have recently received attention due to the much debated 'rule-of-law crisis', manifesting in the undermining of judicial independence, the protection of fundamental rights, media freedom and civil society, while reinforcing proto-authoritarian or authoritarian regimes. The subsequent newer strands of literature focus on the enforcement of EU legal principles towards such states[28] and the process for dismantling

[22] See Komárek, 'Waiting for the Existential Revolution in Europe'.

[23] See particularly, Adam Łazowski (ed.), *The Application of EU Law in the New Member States: Brave New World* (T. M. C. Asser Press, 2010) and Michal Bobek (ed.), *Central European Judges under the European Influence: The Transformative Power of the EU Revisited* (Hart, 2015).

[24] See Wojciech Sadurski, *Constitutionalism and the Enlargement of Europe* (Oxford University Press, 2012).

[25] Bruno de Witte, 'The Impact of Enlargement on the Constitution of the European Union', in Marise Cremona (ed.), *The Enlargement of the European Union* (Hart, 2003), 209.

[26] Kalypso Nicolaidis and Rachel Kleinfeld, 'Rethinking Europe's "Rule of Law" and Enlargement Agenda: The Fundamental Dilemma' (2012) *Jean Monet Working Paper* 08/2012, 2–3, https://jeanmonnetprogram.org/paper/rethinking-europes-rule-of-law-and-enlargement-agenda-the-fundamental-dilemma/ (last accessed 2 April 2025).

[27] Paul Blokker, *New Democracies in Crisis? A Comparative Constitutional Study of the Czech Republic, Hungary, Poland, Romania and Slovakia* (Routledge, 2014).

[28] See, for instance, Carlos Closa and Dimitry Kochenov, *Reinforcing Rule of Law Oversight in the European Union* (Cambridge University Press, 2016).

constitutional safeguards.[29] While deeper cultural, historical and economic reasons underpinning the crisis have also been explored,[30] the internal dynamics between constitutional imaginaries of the 'Other Europe' have yet to be properly considered within the context of European integration and the rule of law crisis. This must, however, be done because post-communist member states have brought with them the legacies that have been supressed to a certain point: essentially, until they stood in the way of the successful 'return to Europe'. They re-emerged quickly after these states had joined the Union and now, *they become internal to its constitutional imaginary*. This presents the current challenges to the authority of EU law as something that comes from without, not from within the Union, and most existing constitutional law scholarship does not capture this aspect of Central and Eastern European constitutionalism.[31] Understanding whether and how European consensus on liberal constitutionalism has dominated the mainstream and superseded national constitutional imaginaries of Europe can be emancipatory, in and of itself, and also instrumental to advancing a genuinely European constitutionalism.

And, on the other hand, among the Central and Eastern European countries, there are also some of the most 'Euro-friendly' and open to EU law states in the Union. This also begs attention – why has such 'Euro-enthusiasm' taken root in that specific part of Europe and how it is related to existential questions of security and the very essence of *being* in the first place. And how does the EU system of law and governance provide replies and remedies to this predicament. All in all, the 'East' is a deep source of idiosyncrasies and novelties in the Union, which deserve more attention.

We need to engage with all the aforementioned aspects of constitutional imaginaries: (1) as indispensable for political rule, but at the same time potentially oppressive ('ideological' in the critical sense); and (2) as a means of justification and contestation. It is crucial to understand and seriously consider national constitutional imaginaries regarding Europe to uncover the reformist potential of the constitutionalist project – its utopia – or its ultimate failure.

1.2 THE STRUCTURE AND THE CONTENTS OF THE VOLUME

The structure of the volume derives from our work on the IMAGINE project throughout three years (2020–2023). A series of workshops, which took place in

[29] Wojciech Sadurski, *Poland's Constitutional Breakdown* (Oxford University Press, 2019).

[30] For instance, Martin Krygier, 'The Challenge of Institutionalisation: Post-Communist "Transitions", Populism, and the Rule of Law' (2019) 15 *European Constitutional Law Review* 544.

[31] For an exception, see Luuk Van Middelaar, *The Passage to Europe: How a Continent became a Union* (Yale University Press, 2013), 181–201; compare to e.g. Christopher J. Bickerton, *European Integration: From Nation-States to Member States* (Oxford University Press, 2012), which also has a historical ambition but does not examine the relevance of 1989 for its thesis.

three post-communist EU member states (Estonia, Hungary and Poland) have identified several overarching issues. These issues were later discussed at a conference in Copenhagen.[32] The volume has subsequently integrated the reflections on these imaginaries coming from authors from other countries, especially from 'old' Europe, who participated at the conference. The following sections introduce the volume's contributions, explaining links between the three case studies and the actual content of the respective part of the volume.

The Estonian workshop inspired Part I of the volume, *Nation States, Member States and Their Others*, presented in Section 1.2.1. The workshop focused on the specific imaginary of national *sovereignty* that can be sustained only by, paradoxically, sacrificing parts of it for the benefit of the Union due to the constant threat from further East. We found similar dynamics of identifying one's own identity in opposition to the 'other' as well as tensions between the imaginaries of complete sovereignty and participation in European integration in Hungary and Poland, but also Italy and the UK. It is the presence of the constant threat from the East (or West) that still informs the constitutional imaginary of most post-communist member states. However, as is clear from the contributions by the authors from the two old member states mentioned, the idea of a 'threat' that lies behind the national border is not something unique to the former part of Europe.

The Hungarian case study focused on the imaginary of *history* and how it shapes national constitutionalism. It gave rise to Part II of the volume, entitled *Bringing Back the Past (to Serve or Understand the Present?)*, presented in Section 1.2.2. The constitutional memory of glorious imperial past is visible both in Hungary and Austria. On the contrary, in Estonia, such a glorious (imperial) past had never existed since the country was the subject of different colonial enterprises throughout its history, especially the Soviet Union. But the Soviet legacy also speaks to the ways in which history matters for national cultural and constitutional understandings of Europe. Again, only by combining insights from these various countries can we see what member states imaginaries of history share and what gives rise to their specific constitutional experiences.

Finally, Section 1.2.3 presents Part III of this volume, *The Varieties of Liberalism in Europe*, which emerged from the Polish workshop. It focused on the origins of *liberal constitutional* imaginary, which presented itself as an apolitical and scientific blueprint for a just ordering of the State, and some alternatives to it, especially those emphasising the need for *transitional and social justice*. The tension between the liberal constitutionalism and alternative imaginaries resonated well in contributions regarding Czechia, Portugal, France or the Nordic countries. By putting these

[32] The workshops were preceded by several internal seminars and one IMAGINE workshop devoted to the history of political and constitutional ideas in Central and Eastern Europe. For information on these events, see IMAGINE website, www.imagine-const.eu/category/events/imagine_events/ (last accessed 2 April 2025).

perspectives together, we see that, through the transformation of the East, the West could transform itself too. The two processes have been linked far more than is usually understood and the flow of ideas and ideologies went in both directions.

1.2.1 *Nation States, Member States and Their Others*

Part I revolves around the questions of sovereignty and identity of different nation states and examines how these issues have shaped the understanding of and belonging to Europe. It also asks how nation states transformed into member states[33] and what were the processes, conflicts, compromises and subjugations made on the way. This part also reflects on the identitarian questions that different member states have gone through and experienced during their time as a nation state and a member state (the UK's experience is instructive in this respect, but other contributions map these changes as well). 'Their Others' in the title of this part refers in the UK's case to Europe, while for most post-communist member states it was the Soviet Union, which figured as the Enemy. Europe has been seen as the positive 'Other', through which states could hope to realise their sovereignty (as Chapter 2 illustrates). The chapter dealing with Hungary, which concludes this part, shows how the figure of an Enemy can be transformed into something else, such as liberal constitutionalism or even the EU and the values it represents.

1.2.1.1 The Estonian Inspiration: Rendering Sovereignty for the Purposes of Security?

The initial theme of this part was discussed at the Estonian workshop, which took place in Tartu in December 2021. The participants of the workshop delivered a multitude of papers on the broader theme of 'Searching for Estonian European constitutional imaginaries – sovereignty in context'.[34] The chapters written by Estonian authors therefore focus mostly on the concept of sovereignty, its different understandings and the particular application practices of it in the Estonian context.

Sovereignty is not an unequivocal or easy concept and it brings with it a certain amount of theoretical and conceptual baggage. Writing in the context of European integration, the Scottish philosopher Neil MacCormick has emphasised that the key idea of sovereignty is power without restriction.[35] This annotation brings along some conceptions of power, authority and territoriality. These can be observed in a particular setting – in the current case, Estonia.

[33] Bickerton, *European Integration*.

[34] For the programme of the workshop, see www.imagine-const.eu/workshop-searching-for-the-estonian-european-constitutional-imaginaries-sovereignty-in-context-tartu-9-december-2021/ (last accessed 2 April 2025).

[35] Neil MacCormick. *Questioning Sovereignty* (Oxford University Press, 1999), 127.

In order to start unpacking the concept of sovereignty in the Estonian imaginaries, some contextual clarifications are due. Firstly, sovereignty has a particularly strong conceptual and celebratory meaning in the context of the Estonian Constitution. The Constitution of the Republic of Estonia incorporates a particularly strong sovereignty clause in its §1(2): 'The independence and sovereignty of Estonia are *timeless* and *inalienable*'.[36] This has been called 'one of the strongest accentuations of sovereignty in Europe and perhaps even in the world'.[37] It has been said that 'the fear of a rollback to a Soviet Union-type organisation was the main consideration behind the wording of this provision'.[38]

According to the Estonian Supreme Court (SC), 'the core essence of sovereignty is the right of discretion in all matters, irrespective of external influences'.[39] Despite this, the SC's approach in particular cases has been much more liberal and accommodating. There the SC treated sovereignty as a principle that is open to restrictions and weighing against other principles.[40]

Secondly, Estonia has a notable 'unconditionally EU-friendly approach'[41] to EU primacy claims, being an example of exceptionless EU law primacy or even adhering to a doctrine of absolute primacy.[42] It has been described as an unconditional acceptance of the standpoint of the Court of Justice of the European Union (CJEU) on primacy,[43] an unprecedented submissiveness to the EU that has no counterparts in other EU Member States.[44]

What might explain such an open approach to EU and international law and a disregard of national sovereignty claims? A small state dimension and a post-imperial sense of ontological insecurity of the very existing as a sovereign state arguably cause this unprecedented Euro-fondness. In other words, in order to be a state, you must

36 The Constitution of the Republic of Estonia – RT 1992, 26, 349; RT I, 15.05.2015, 1, emphasis added.

37 Madis Ernits et al., 'The Constitution of Estonia: The Unexpected Challenges of Unlimited Primacy of EU Law' in Anneli Albi and Samo Bardutzky (eds.), *National Constitutions in European and Global Governance: Democracy, Rights, the Rule of Law* (TMC Asser Press, 2019), 902. See also, Anneli Albi, 'Estonia's Constitution and the EU: How and to What Extent to Amend It?' (2002) 7 *Juridica International* 39, 42.

38 Ernits et al., 'The Constitution of Estonia', 902, referring to Viljar Peep and Lennart Meri (eds.), *Põhiseadus Ja Põhiseaduse Assamblee: Koguteos* (Juura, 1997), 68.

39 Estonian Supreme Court 3-4-1-6-12, para 127.

40 See Estonian Supreme Court 3-4-1-6-12, para 130.

41 Ernits et al., 'The Constitution of Estonia'.

42 Anneli Albi and Hent Kalmo, 'Estonia: From Rules to Pragmatism', in Stefan Griller, Papadopoulou Lina and Puff Roman (eds.), *National Constitutions and EU Integration* (Bloomsbury Publishing, 2021), 4, 21.

43 Damian Chalmers, Gareth Davies and Giorgio Monti, *European Union Law: Cases and Materials*, 2nd ed. (Cambridge University Press, 2010), 190–191. Also see discussion in Tatjana Evas, 'Judicial Reception of EU Law in Estonia', in Bruno de Witte et al. (eds.), *National Courts and EU Law: New Issues, Theories and Methods* (Edward Elgar, 2016), 154

44 Julia Laffranque, 'A Glance at the Estonian Legal Landscape in View of the Constitution Amendment Act' (2007) 7 *Juridica International* 55, 63.

give away some of the very 'stateness' to exist in the first place. Underlying the Estonian acceptance of the supremacy of EU law is an existential fear against its Eastern neighbour. One might consider it a result of a fairly straightforward and perfectly reasonable cost-benefit analysis: the security-related benefits of international cooperation outweigh the loss of sovereignty.

When talking of history, one particularity sets the Estonian chapters apart from others included in this volume. Namely, Estonia was not merely a satellite state of the Soviet Union, but part of the Union itself as it stood in the designated period of history. This perhaps sets out specific visions and imaginaries of Europe generally and of the European Union particularly, but also of the Eastern neighbour – Russia. Is it somehow different to be stepping almost straight from one Union to another, from being the West of the East to being the East of the West, without broader contemplation and societal discussion of the idiosyncrasies and potential differences and similarities these Union-memberships and transformations entail. The Estonian reflections of it were rather poor or even non-existent, but that in itself also reveals something, some deeply rooted ideological and existential understandings of the meaning of Europe and Estonia's place in it. Namely, Estonia has always regarded itself as part of Europe, as the inherent borderlining component of it, something of an outpost between East and West[45] with a strong feeling of belonging to Europe.

All in all, Central and Eastern European distinctiveness from its Western counterpart is overt. History should not be underestimated in this equation and it plays a part in establishing the polities and societies which we today call Central Eastern Europe. History and size of the nation thus is featured in how sovereignty is perceived and performed in the region. History and size matter. Also for sovereignty.

1.2.1.2 Contributions

All contributions show the prominence of the concept of sovereignty from the existence and regaining of the state from the Soviet occupation in the first place to the securitised practice of it in contemporary law and politics. Sovereignty also has a transformative aspect in the current and historical perspective. The current sovereignty undertones allow a state like Estonia to still engage in deep forms of international and regional cooperation – such as the European Union – whereas the past connotations and usages of sovereignty operationalise it for the anti-imperial struggle. Here manifests the great transformability of the concept and its many practical usages.

These questions are well captured in Maria Mälksoo's Chapter 2, entitled 'Vicarious Sovereignty: Becoming European the Estonian Way'. Mälksoo proposes

[45] Heiko Pääbo, 'Estonian Transformation: From an Eastern Outpost in the West to a Western Outpost in the East', in Barbara Törnquist-Plewa and Krzysztof Stala (eds.), *Cultural Transformations after Communism: Central and Eastern Europe in Focus* (Nordic Academic Press, 2011).

a new concept – 'vicarious sovereignty' – to understand and explain the way in which Estonia positions itself vis-à-vis Europe and its national constitution.

Mälksoo defines vicarious sovereignty as 'living through another'. One lives through another by treating their 'achievements and experiences', as Mälksoo puts it, as their own. Like in the case of many other states in the region, 'becoming European', or rather joining the EU and other European and international organisations, was Estonia's purpose, constitutive for its identity. However, the case of Estonia shows an interesting paradox, which is also evident in the Polish case, as described by Kustra-Rogatka in Chapter 7. On the one hand, Estonia's 'vicarious identification with Europe' has made it easier for this state to transfer parts of its sovereignty to the EU. On the other hand, the Constitution of Estonia proclaims a very strong commitment to absolute sovereignty which, again, is also characteristic for Poland. How can one reconcile two such conflicting commitments? Perhaps the states in the region, having barely regained their hard-fought independence, had no choice but to undertake this arduous task and hammer out their identity in-between sovereignty and integration *somehow*. In particular, Estonia had to accept this trade-off for the sake of its 'ontological security', in the words of Mälksoo. She illustrates how Estonia has sought to be 'independent', 'sovereign' and 'European' all at once and in the context of the described permissiveness of the Estonian model of EU membership.

Mälksoo explores 'Estonia's sovereignty-sharing with the EU through the lens of the vicarious identification concept' and the visions of Europe presented by the Estonian constitutional 'map-makers', as she calls them, at the time of the Convention on the Future of Europe: Lennart Meri and Toomas Hendrik Ilves. She specifically investigates the question of restrictions of sovereignty and the boundaries of the European constitution in the imagination of the Estonian influential thinkers and decision-makers during the Convention on the Future of Europe. She examines how these thinkers and decision-makers understood 'becoming European' not just in reference to the EU accession but also in terms of recognising the 'Europeanness' of Central and Eastern Europe by the West of the continent.

Mälksoo's contribution also addresses a phenomenon well-known from most member states: Europe, or the EU, becomes a space of political action that is instrumentalised by various forces at the national level. Marco Goldoni's Chapter 3, 'From Federation to External Constraint: Europe in the Italian Constitutional Imagination', is path-breaking in several respects. First, it shows how the imaginary of Europe has been changing in a single member state, from the period when European integration was only imagined in a quite literal sense by the members of resistance, to the establishment of the European Communities in the 1950s, followed (possibly paradoxically) by a period of ignorance until today, when the EU is seen as a source of external constraint. This story has been told several times already; however, Goldoni does not stop short at that. The second remarkable contribution he makes concerns the kind of actors he looks at in his analysis of Italian constitutional imagination. Inspired by the renewed interest in the study of political parties in political science and theory, Goldoni brings about an original study of Italian political parties relationship to Europe, highlighting the dependency of their imaginaries on what Europe 'offers' for them. In that, Chapter 3 nicely connects to the other chapters in this part, not only that of Mälksoo (Chapter 2), but particularly Kustra-Rogatka's Chapter 7 (dealing with Poland) and Saharov's Chapter 6, offering a conceptual history of the idea of 'self-management', which quickly transformed, after its introduction into official discourse, into a debate on sovereignty.

But does sovereignty in Central Eastern Europe have a different meaning than sovereignty in the Western part of the continent? Some have argued it does.[46] Do other concepts such as democracy, liberalism or rule of law perhaps then too have a different connotation? This brings to the question: is Central Eastern Europe's current predicament different because its history is different?

This is the main question to be answered in Hent Kalmo's Chapter 4, 'Sovereignty and the Misery of Small Eastern European Nations', which broadly speaking tackles the concept of sovereignty and puts it into the context of small Central Eastern European states. It also touches upon the issues of the East Europeans' 'Europeanness' among other things. Kalmo's thesis is that Eastern and Central Europe is not uniformly *souverainiste* in the sense that the constitutional rules of all the countries in this region are not always strongly protective of sovereignty.

Kalmo argues that it has been a certain representation or rather a set of conflicting representations related to the idea of being a small nation which has engendered the ambivalent attitude to national sovereignty observable in Eastern and Central Europe. This ambivalence is illustrated particularly well by Estonia, where the already mentioned strong symbolic commitment to national sovereignty has coincided with the ambition of international integration, as manifested with the openness of Estonia's legal system to international law. Kalmo's central concept – the smallness of the nation – is not so much a single idea, or a theory, but a recurring cultural theme, an unresolved problem and an axis of debate. It still generates legal contradictions and conflicting constitutional doctrines. When the national security may be endangered, sovereignty may either offer protection or, quite to the contrary, hinder seeking assistance from a larger political community. This 'small nationess' has thus hung over the region and can be seen as a common constitutional imaginary.

Kalmo also presents his 'misery thesis', which is kind of an idea of an 'Eastern *Sonderweg*'. According to this thesis, the history of Western and Eastern Europe have been different, so their essential characteristics must be different too, including political culture or even nationalism. The roots of these difference can be traced to the Middle Ages or beyond.

[46] Chris J. Bickerton, 'From Brezhnev to Brussels: Transformations of Sovereignty in Eastern Europe' (2009) 46 *International Politics* 732, 734.

Kalmo draws the misery thesis from István Bibó's famous essay 'The Miseries of East European Small States'[47] for whom the key puzzle of the causes of the Second World War lied in Eastern Europe since it was there that most critical territorial disputes had flared up in the late 1930s. Also, according to Tony Judt, while 'northern and western European peoples formed states by expansion from a core',[48] the countries of modern Eastern Europe were born from the collapse of empires – Russian, Turkish, Austrian and German. The Eastern identity, for Kalmo, who refers to Judt, necessarily thus consists of 'an all-or-nothing claim to territory and power at the expense of a neighbour making an identical claim. This resulted in the great misfortune of the eastern half of Europe. the division into states came late and all at once'.[49] The misery thesis also explains the post-war difficulties of Central Eastern Europe by the simple fact that the region had remained on the wrong side of the Iron Curtain: its problems resulted from Soviet domination, not from something indigenous.

Martin Loughlin's Chapter 5, on 'Ruling Britannia', discusses the key features of Britain's constitutional identity, as they developed throughout history, and argues that they 'ensured that Britain could never become an active participant in the European federal project'.[50] In this respect, the chapter provides an interesting counterpoint to the other contributions in this part, not only those concerning Estonia, but also Goldoni's chapter on Italy. Europe is always perceived as the Other, which threatens rather than protects or extends sovereignty of a member state.

The British constitutional identity consists of several narratives, which all together provide for a constitutional imaginary of a nation, but also define the framework of its government. First, the doctrine of the ancient constitution, according to which it was already the early Saxons (the Goths) who had created an ancient, pre-feudal and liberty-preserving constitution. No great constitutional documents of English (and British) constitutional history (including the Magna Carta) instituted freedom for the English, as it existed long before them in the form of this 'ancient constitution'. Loughlin mentions how the modern constitutional scholarship avoided closer examination of the founding principles and instead relied on the Whig interpretation of history, which 'present[ed] a story about the triumph of liberty over absolute sovereign power, evidenced by the increasing importance of representative institutions in the British system'.[51]

The other narratives of the British constitutional identity relate to this mythology, especially those concerning the pivotal importance of local self-government in the English system and the rule of law. The persistence of the Crown and its paradoxical

47 István Bibó, *The Art of Peacemaking: Political Essays by Istvan Bibo* (Yale University Press, 2015).
48 Tony Judt, *A Grand Illusion? An Essay on Europe* (Penguin Books, 1996), 56.
49 Ibid.
50 See Chapter 5.
51 Ibid.

(perhaps) relationship to Parliamentary sovereignty have remained unresolved, also when the British state was formed and 'Britons' came into existence.

In the penultimate part of his chapter, Loughlin discusses the difficult relationship between the British Constitution and the European integration project, which led to the contemporary crisis of constitutional identity of Britain. For an external observer it may seem that Loughlin's 'best hope' – 'the advancement of radical reforms to the system of government, which might incrementally provide an institutional foundation for a renewal of faith'[52] was lost at the moment when the United Kingdom decided to leave the European Union.

The next Estonian contribution to the volume combines the concept of sovereignty and the Soviet era. It shows that imaginaries can also acquire a formal content and meaning, as was the case in the mid-perestroika Estonia when a contest for 'future scenarios' for economic development in Estonia was held. Juhan Saharov's Chapter 6, 'The Power of Concepts: From "Self-management" to "Sovereignty" in Soviet Estonia (1987–1988)', takes its grounding in these historical events, which he calls the finest hour for imagining alternative futures for the republic. He shows how the imagination of futures takes place in the late totalitarian system which has opened its society to radical reforms. He considers the period of 1987–1988 to be the period of different imaginaries – could Estonia become an economically independent republic within the Soviet Union, a sovereign socialist republic or an independent republic or be restored as a continuation of the pre-war Republic? As the ultimate outcome was the latter, he puts particular importance on the power of specific concepts and languages within the 1989 revolutions, including their impact on the Soviet collapse.

The central concepts in Saharov's 'conceptual revolution' are 'sovereignty' and 'self-management'. The contest for 'future scenarios' created the concept of 'self-management' in the economic sphere in Estonia in 1987, which continued its independent development to the final language of political sovereignty in 1988. This resulted in the fact that the politically and legally more useful term 'sovereignty' replaced the term 'self-management' as the central concept in reformists' tactics and an eventual declaration of sovereignty on 16 November 1988 by the Supreme Soviet of the Estonian Soviet Socialist Republic (ESSR) which initiated the 'Parade of Sovereignties' across the Soviet Union with its ultimate dissolution. Just like that, 'sovereignty' killed the Soviet Union[53], and it happened first in Estonia due to the conceptual revolution of 'self-management' to develop into the concept of 'sovereignty' in 1987–1988. As such, Saharov shows the identification of 'specific conceptual processes in pre-revolutionary periods through which specific and technical concepts, derived from an expert-language framework, acquire broader resonance

[52] Ibid.

[53] Edward D. Walker, *Dissolution: Sovereignty and the Breakup of the Soviet Union* (Rowman & Littlefield, 2003), 1.

and meaning in society, thus contributing to the rise of a revolutionary situation'.[54] At the same time, they were also imaginaries of the future form of the republic, which transformed quickly from the economic visions into political ones in 1988. Thus, the role of the 'future scenarios' methodology should not be underestimated, and the method was a way to reform socialism, to imagine new models for a union republic and ultimately a sovereign independent republic.

Furthermore, a telling example of the transformations and tensions in the sovereignty concept has emerged from Poland around the interpretive difficulties encountered by the Constitutional Tribunal in highly controversial and political cases, in which it was expected to provide 'objective' and 'apolitical answers'. These tensions are analysed in detail by Aleksandra Kustra-Rogatka in Chapter 7, 'European Integration: Ineffable Aspiration or the Object of Concern? About the Ambiguity of Europe in the Polish Constitutional Imaginary'. Her doctrinal analysis demonstrates the struggles of legal constitutionalism in Poland operating in a difficult political context. The author depicts European integration as remaining in constant tension in Polish constitutional imaginary with the aspiration of retaining complete sovereignty. European integration and complete sovereignty acted as ideologies and utopias that Polish constitutionalism tried to mix like water with fire. The author analyses this shaky constitutional imaginary on three levels mentioned by Loughlin in Chapter 5: the level of thought (the constitution-making process), that of the text (the Constitution of 1997) and that of the constitutional practice (how the EU Treaties were ratified and what conditions and limits upon the European integration were imposed by the Constitutional Tribunal). The Constitutional Tribunal's at least partly conflicting doctrines of absolute constitutional supremacy coupled with simultaneous openness to European integration – aimed at satisfying the left, the centre and the right – must have ultimately failed. Kustra-Rogatka argues that the balance was recently clearly tilted towards 'sovereignty'.[55]

In addition, links can be discovered between the Central-European national constitutional imaginaries as well, particularly in the area of enemy-making, discussed in Chapter 8, 'The Constitutionalised Image of the Enemy in the Hungarian Fundamental Law' by Attila Antal.

Creating and joining 'United Europe' meant, for a long time, supressing the image of enemy and not using its affective power when mobilising people around the constitution. This, of course, does not mean that enemies disappeared from the constitutional imaginary of Europe – they were rather only partially shifted to its subconscious, un-reflected layer. In many states, however, these buried images have been gradually emerging again – either as political narratives with

[54] Juhan Saharov, *From Economic Independence to Political Sovereignty: Inventing 'Self-Management' in the Estonian SSR* (University of Tartu Press, 2021), 60.

[55] Wojciech Sadurski and Aleksandra Gliszczyńska-Grabias, 'Is It Polexit Yet? Comment on Case K 3/21 of 7 October 2021 by Constitutional Tribunal of Poland' (2023) 19 *European Constitutional Law Review* 163.

constitution-changing ambitions, as arguments in the case-law of constitutional courts or even as full-fledged constitutional reform projects.

In relation to this, a Hungarian constitutional and historical intersection is revealed through the reliance on history in order to guard and maintain independence and sovereignty. This is also rooted in the idea of Hungary's historical constitution and has played a significant role in the building of identity in a legal manner through the case law of the Constitutional Court, ultimately rejecting mainstream European narratives.[56] This connection draws from medieval sources, as well as the narrative of Hungary being the defender of Christian Europe from invasion, which has been identified in the early nineteenth century, and reflects back to the Ottoman times between 1526 and 1686.[57] In addition, the current approach of the current Hungarian political regime to the historical constitution as the reason why Hungary is entitled to autonomy and independence have drawn from various historical struggles such as the 1848 revolution, the 1867 compromise with Austria, the resistance to the communist regime and, very propagandistically, since the 2010s against the EU.[58]

This type of identity formation through the incorporation of history in constitutionalism reflects further on the legacy of the democratic transition, particularly around the presence and relationship of the historical constitution and the invisible constitution. This doctrine was created by the Constitutional Court of the early 1990s as an exact opposite of using historical narratives, instead relying on supposedly universal democratic values.[59] Therefore, the idea of the invisible constitution made use of the same idea and motto as the transition itself – catching up and copying Western European democracies. The current constitutional system rejects this idea completely, throwing away the idea of the invisible constitution, favouring the integration of the historical constitution into the legal system instead. This shows how the legacy of the transition in constitutionalism is mixed. It can be criticised for leaning too much into European integration and lacking consideration of other aspects and developments of Hungary's past, such as the evolution of the country's role in Imperial Austria–Hungary.[60] While, at the time of its inception in 1867, Hungary was the economically and politically weaker member of the union, thanks

[56] Miklós Könczöl and István Kevevári, 'History and Interpretation in the Fundamental Law of Hungary' (2020) 5 *European Papers* 161, 166–167.

[57] Gábor Halmai, 'Fidesz and Faith: Ethno-Nationalism in Hungary', *Verfassungsblog* (29 June 2018), https://verfassungsblog.de/fidesz-and-faith-ethno-nationalism-in-hungary/ (last accessed 2 April 2025).

[58] Tímea Drinóczi, 'The Identity of the Constitution and Constitutional Identity: Opening up a Discourse between the Global North and the Global South' (2018) 21 *Iuris Dictio* 63, 68–70.

[59] László Sólyom, 'The Role of Constitutional Courts in the Transition to Democracy with Special Reference to Hungary' (2003) 18 *International Sociology* 133, 152; Ildikó Szabó, 'Rendszerváltás és nemzeti tematika' (2005) 2 *Politikatudományi Szemle* 89, 95–96.

[60] Gábor Halmai, 'Restoring Constitutionalism in Hungary: How Should Constitution Making Be Different from What Happened in 1989?', *Verfassungsblog* (13 December 2021), https://verfassungsblog.de/restoring-constitutionalism-in-hungary/ (last accessed 2 April 2025).

to the economic development of the immediately following decades, the state has managed to strengthen its position as Austria's equal in the arrangement.

Chapter 8 reveals this misuse and abuse of identity creation, particularly reflecting on the idea of enemy-making. He connects the ideas of history, constitution and imagination in the Fundamental Law itself. He explains how the misuse of history and identity in the Hungarian legal system becomes dangerous in creating a constitutionalised image of an enemy. This construction can then be relied on in political debates and even be used for propaganda purposes. Relying on a primary lens of politics, he delves deep into the polarities of the NER system and the process of enemy-making in the Fundamental Law. He shows how otherisation works in this system, how the Hungarian government has otherised different communities, somewhat ironically similar to how the country itself is otherised on the European scene. He reflects on the images of political enemies evolving as aspects of the Hungarian government's identity and how, through these identities, the antagonising of the EU mainstream becomes possible.

1.2.2 *Bringing Back the Past (to Serve or Understand the Present?)*

Part II examines how history and the way it is narrated forms part of constitutional imaginary. The uses (and abuses) of history in the context of European integration have not been sufficiently explored and, if so, the focus tends to be on Hungary. However, there are many more interesting questions reaching beyond the present 'rule of law crisis' in that country. In particular, constitutional lawyers have rarely reflected on the way they tell the story of their state – and there is much to be said about European integration beyond the usual story of how the 'Founding Fathers' secured peace and prosperity for the European continent after WWII.

1.2.2.1 The Hungarian Inspiration: History and Constitutionalism

In November 2021, the Institute of Legal Studies of the Hungarian Academy of Sciences hosted the IMAGINE workshop, 'History, Constitution and Identity in Hungary', inviting experts from the fields of law, history and political science to reflect on the intersection of these fields, specifically on the emergence and re-occurrence of historical narratives in constitutional debates.[61] The workshop was built on the hypothesis of tracking the extensive differences between the approaches towards constitutional imaginaries as they relate to the historical past between the EU and Hungary. It aimed to exemplify and address these differences through the examination and analysis of Hungary's constitutional debates through a historical–political lens.

[61] For the programme of the workshop, see www.imagine-const.eu/history-constitution-and-identity-in-hungary-18-november-2021-centre-of-social-sciences-institute-for-legal-studies-hungarian-academy-of-sciences/ (last accessed 2 April 2025).

The study of Hungarian constitutional imaginaries presents an opportunity to evaluate the complicated story of the use and misuse of history in Central and Eastern European constitutional debates. Not only is this a prominent feature of Hungarian constitutionalism but it directly relates to the strand in European legal scholarship that engages history of European integration – including its 'darker legacies'.[62]

To critically study the role of history in European constitutional imaginaries is important because the EU's efforts of fostering European unity and integration and ideas of democracy originate from a 'historical escapism' – to ensure the brutal crimes committed and constant (political and sometimes violently military) warring between neighbouring countries in the first half of the twentieth century should cease and never happen again.[63]

However, the EU, by virtue of being a supranational institution, gives rise to a conflict and a potential hierarchy between its member states over whose historical–constitutional visions and imaginaries prevail, and how to settle the disagreements that result from their differences – meaning which Member State will be able to better integrate their constitutional ideas into the EU's institutional structure.[64] The recent crises within the EU have revealed that the roots, basis and nature of constitutional imaginaries differ fundamentally between the Western and Central-Eastern part of the EU. As the building of the primary European constitutional imaginaries happened through mostly unspoken agreement of the old, Western Member States, Hungary's rule of law backsliding has exposed this divide and its much more far-reaching roots in the constitutional debate. This happened because the Hungarian developments involved a noticeable transformation of the approach to national and international history, ultimately posing the country against EU initiatives and values on the basis of Hungary's past.

The workshop was organised at a pivotal time as both national and international commentators have noted the prevalence of historical narratives and attempted to explain its expansive inclusion in the Hungarian Fundamental Law.[65] Such inclusion was part and parcel of Hungary's new political system, the System of National Cooperation (NER), as conceptualised by the Fidesz government after their 2010 landslide election victory. Noticeably, this system is markedly different,

62 For a pioneering study in this context, see Christian Joerges and Navraj Singh Ghaleigh (eds.), *Darker Legacies of Law in Europe: The Shadow of National Socialism and Fascism over Europe and Its Legal Traditions* (Hart, 2003). More recently the debate on the legacies of colonialism in European integration also started among legal scholars (somewhat belatedly): see Signe Rehling Larsen, 'European Public Law after Empires' (2022) 1 *European Law Open* 6.

63 Kalypso Nicolaidis, 'European Demoicracy and Its Crisis' (2013) 51 *Journal of Common Market Studies* 351, 352.

64 Larsen, 'Varieties of Constitutionalism', 478.

65 Gábor Halmai, 'Memory Politics in Hungary: Political Justice without Rule of Law', *Verfassungsblog*, 10 January 2018. https://verfassungsblog.de/memory-politics-in-hungary-political-justice-without-rule-of-law/ (last accessed 2 April 2025).

especially from the Hungary of the transitional decades (1990–2010), as it seems to have incorporated and developed a strange imitation and mix of previous Hungarian historical eras and echoes, sometimes with politically-driven intentions, sometimes less openly, several pre-1990 historical regimes. In its international political behaviour, nostalgia and reliance on civic transformation, the NER system relies on the legacy of imperial Austria–Hungary. In its treatment of memory politics and the shaping of Hungary's image and the meaning of Hungarian-ness, it takes from the policies of the interwar Horthy-regime. In its economic policy, the NER is inspired by the communist regime, particularly its post-1956 period – the decades of 'goulash communism'.

Reflecting on these ideas, the workshop differed from similar events because it relied on an interdisciplinary perspective, discussing the historical periods to which the NER refers: the imperial civic age, the interwar conservative–nationalist age and the post–WWII communist period.

The participants have traced and discussed the roots of Hungarian constitutionalism in the nineteenth century by dissecting the concept and development of the *historical constitution* of the country, by revealing how the period of Austria–Hungary is reflected in the NER system through the rhetoric of civic transformation.[66] The NER's entire state organisational system is aimed at boosting Hungary's further civic developments. In terms of policy, the dismantled system of the Austro-Hungarian age has been rebuilt by Fidesz. This includes a complete reform of the judicial system and the municipal system, bringing back parallels to the previous nineteenth century arrangements.[67]

Presentations at the workshop further situated the intersection of history and constitutionalism during twentieth century Hungary, including the interwar conservative–nationalist and post–WWII communist periods. The role of the interwar Horthy-regime in the NER system is a lot less transparent and more influential than the impact of the imperial civic age. Unlike the Austria–Hungary allusions, which are less present in the Fundamental Law but can be detected in the legal

[66] The civic transformation of Hungary consists of legal measures enacted around and particularly in the immediate aftermath of the 1867 Austro-Hungarian Compromise Treaty, throughout the 1870s. These laws were the last symbolic and practical steps in shedding the feudal framework of state organisation, including the freedom of the peasantry, the reform of the tax and election system and the act on nationalities and the compromise treaty with Croatia. They are regarded as the stepping-stone in Hungary's late nineteenth century economic development helping the country to become a leader not only within the Empire but an international political factor as well. Therefore, the Austro-Hungarian period, particularly between the years of 1867 and the turn of the century, are known as Hungary's civic age. See: Norbert Csibi and Ádám Schwarczwölder (eds.) *Modernizáció és nemzetállam-építés: Haza és/vagy haladás dilemmája a dualizmus kori Magyarországon* (Kronosz Kiadó, 2018), 8–9; Csaba Fazekas, 'Történelem a politika hátterében: A rendszerváltás utáni magyarország politikai rendszere, valamint 19–20. századi előzményei' (2021) 11 *Multidiszciplináris tudományok* 329.

[67] Marina Bán, 'The Governance of History via Law: An Overview' (2022) 63 *Hungarian Journal of Legal Studies* 315.

system, the Fundamental Law and the NER's historical memory-related policies fully lean into the much-criticised legacy of the Horthy-regime. The idea of strengthening nationalism, protecting of Hungarian identity internally and abroad, with the simultaneous prosecution of other minorities alludes to the Horthy-regime quite openly. This can be traced in the glorification of the Hungarian past in the Fundamental Law, the whitewashing of the more controversial aspects of the Horthy-regime and the continuous references to the Treaty of Trianon and its postWWIIWWI arrangement.[68] On the one hand, internally, this has brought about a nationalistic reframing of the education system and the rejection of minorities found not to have roots in the Hungarian past, or found not to adhere to the idealised version and meaning of belonging to the Hungarian nation. On the other hand, internationally, the system quite forcefully steps up to gift rights and privileges to the Hungarian community living beyond the border, specifically aimed at those living in the territories that had belonged to Hungary before the Treaty of Trianon.

The Kádár era of the communist regime reflects in the NER's economic policy, albeit much less openly, as the rejection of the communist past is a central part in the NER system. Nevertheless, the recent decades' economic measures reflect the nature of the communist regime very carefully in several aspects. In its systemic aspect, the NER brings back nationalisation and bulk buying of companies and estates, thus fostering corruption and the appearance of oligarchs. In its more personal aspects, several policy decisions particularly favour the upper middle class of society. This includes a very favourable tax system and measures aimed at fostering marriages and children, which not only adheres to a nationalist policy but also affords significant financial support to young couples and families.[69] In this way, the NER alludes to the times of goulash communism, involving policy decisions that economically benefit the population (or at least some groups of it) and guarantee them a comfortable life. In exchange, they are inclined to overlook other, deficient parts of the system as they are not implicated in it.

Therefore, the Hungarian workshop's reflections on the differences in historical outlook between mainstream Europe are complemented with the contributions of this volume. They reveal different blind spots on the both sides of the former Iron Curtain – and the legacy of the Habsburg Empire – for its successor states, but for the Union as well, have not been examined thus far. World War II, or, what the historian Tony Judt saw as the 'European civil war that had begun in 1914'[70] and finished only with the fall of communism, lies at the heart of the European constitutional imaginary. Schuman Declaration proclaimed in 1950 that 'World peace

68 Andrea Pető, 'The Illiberal Memory Politics in Hungary' (2021) 24 *Journal of Genocide Research* 86; Domonkos Sik, 'Memory Transmission and Political Socialization in Post-Socialist Hungary' (2015) 63 *The Sociological Review* 53, 59.

69 Mitchell A. Orenstein and Bojan Bugarič, 'Work, Family, Fatherland: The Political Economy of Populism in Central and Eastern Europe' (2022) 29 *Journal of European Public Policy* 176.

70 Tony Judt, *Postwar: A History of Europe Since 1945* (Penguin Press 2005), 749.

cannot be safeguarded without the making of creative efforts proportionate to the dangers which threaten it' and warns, at the same time, that 'A united Europe was not achieved and we had war'. However, the contributions to this volume tell a different story.

1.2.2.2 Contributions

Chapters 9 and 10, which deal with Hungary, attempt to understand how the incorporation of historical narratives in constitutionalism can be situated within the current system of democratic backsliding in this country. Kálmán Pócza's Chapter 9, 'Political Integration through Constitutional Memory? Historical Constitution and Community Building in Hungary', poses the question of what role Hungary's historical constitutionalism plays in the development and expansion of the constitutional imagination of Hungary. Despite the problematic nature of the Fundamental Law, where such recent historical–constitutional musing has been codified, and the chequered past of the historical constitution itself, its continuous prevalence presents an apt opportunity for Pócza to engage in the past, present and future of Hungarian historical constitutionalism. His analysis is timely because, while ample disagreement exists among Hungarian and international scholars on the place and use of the historical constitution in a modern legal system, its relevance cannot be denied and therefore should not be set aside as merely a political tool of an authoritarian regime.

However, while the historical constitution should not be set aside as only a political tool, Pócza's approach to the Fundamental Law remains mostly theoretical and figurative and, thus, does not really consider the political implications of the historical constitution concept in the NER and how it can be used and misused by the Hungarian government and by the Constitutional Court.[71] His analysis presupposes the use of the historical constitution in post-2010 Hungary as politically contextless, as a simple re-emergence of an essentially historical concept.

In contrast, this lack of consideration is addressed in Chapter 10, 'The Constitutional Concept of the Historical Constitution and Illiberalism: The Case of Hungary', by Tímea Drinóczi. Drinóczi examines the historical constitution and its place, use and misuse in the current Hungarian political system. She takes a legal approach and she reflects on the practical consequences of the inclusion of the historical constitution in the NER's legal system. She connects the misuse of the historical constitution to Hungary's budding illiberal authoritarianism and points out the dangers of too extensive reliance on historical narratives, particularly the potential mistakes and misinterpretation their legalisation can result in. While she

[71] Gábor Halmai, 'National(ist) Constitutional Identity? Hungary's Road to Abuse Constitutional Pluralism', *EUI Working Papers* 2017/8, 8–12, https://hdl.handle.net/1814/46226 (last accessed 2 April 2025).

does take the historical development of the concept into account, she focuses her analysis on the post-2010 evolution of the idea, aptly pointing out how the NER abuses the concept of the historical constitution for political means. She does not posit any use or present relevance of the historical constitution in modern times, which, due to the undoubted prominence of this concept throughout Hungarian history of the last two centuries, may be a slight oversight but remains a question well-addressed by Pócza.

In consequence, these two contributions function as opposites and complements. Through two different methods, they approach the controversial but absolutely necessary analysis of the place and importance of the historical constitution in the Hungarian legal system and its relationship to modern democracy, coming to completely different conclusions. Hence, they reveal the core of engaging with the interplay of historical and constitutional narratives in Hungary and the underlying imaginaries that shape them.

The works of Pócza and Drinóczi are further complemented by Epp Annus' analysis on the imaginaries of history and the feeling of 'Europeanness' in Estonia. In Chapter 11, 'Estonians' European Imaginaries: The Soviet and Pre-Soviet Legacy', she delves deep into the questions of the Estonian European (self-)images and the Soviet impact on them. She juxtaposes the 'Soviet question' in relation to the 'European question' and tackles the ultimate question of how the Soviet rule impacted the national imaginary of Europe and Europeanness. She takes a 'pluriscalar' approach: she analyses the sense of belonging at different scales, that is, the scale of the ESSR within the USSR as well as within Europe and even the larger 'West'. The author discusses how Estonia was 'relocated' from 'Europe' to the 'colonial matrix of control' exerted by Moscow and Leningrad within the Soviet Union and then again to 'Europe', and what it meant in practical terms for the society and the social imaginaries. Somewhat paradoxically, the Soviet Union's centre might have served for a time as an access point but also a gatekeeper to Europe. And yet, the author claims that earlier cultural traditions and values connected to Europe were preserved and, after the fall of the Soviet Union, contributed to the new hybrid imaginaries, as she demonstrated relying on rich literary sources. What might have helped in the process of retaining the distinct Estonian imaginary was that Estonia has always felt a somewhat culturally superior 'West' of the Soviet Union. Nonetheless, the 'return to Europe', as the popular rhetoric framed it, also raised challenging identitarian questions, such as 'exactly how European are we?' The related challenging questions are the relation to the former Soviet sphere and the Russian minority. Overall, Chapter 11 shows how the category of 'Europeanness' depends on its relations with other overlapping identitarian categories.

All in all, the Soviet experience can inform Estonia's understanding of Europe and the EU. The different scalar categories and imperatives at play have had the force to subjugate the rhetorically strong claims of sovereignty under the open and liberal claims to be open to the EU and the West in general, thereby supporting unconditional belonging to Europe assertions. Both the conceptual apparatus at play in the critical years of pre- and re-independence and the predominant European imaginaries during and after Soviet occupation exemplify the leap from colonised subjugated state to the re-strengthened pronouncements of national agency and sovereignty with a hint of post-colonial mentality.

In addition, Mary Heimann's Chapter 12, 'Czechoslovakia: Remembering and Forgetting the Failures of a State', provides an interesting reflection by the author of a monograph that provoked severe criticism in the country it studied, despite rather positive reception among academic historians. Heimann argues that today's Czech Republic succeeded to a series of failed constitutional imaginaries, polities which proved unable, for a variety of reasons, to endure in the forms in which they had first been conceived and created.

Although factually accurate, this is not the way in which the 75-year history of Czechoslovakia is usually told, commemorated or remembered. Chapter 12 looks at the highly emotive, polarised reception of *Czechoslovakia: The State That Failed* from its first publication in English (Yale University Press, 2009) until its eventual publication in Czech, with the support of former Czechoslovak dissident leaders. This case-study of how one revisionist history came to be written, received, blocked, championed and republished, sheds light on narratives of victimisation and exceptionalism which dominated official Czech memory after the overthrow of Communism in 1989 but which are increasingly being challenged by modern historians.

Finally, Ulrich Wagrandl's Chapter 13 explores the 'background stories' of Austrian constitutional law, especially one of which celebrates its greatest historical achievements of the rule of law and giving to the world constitutional review. This author takes inspiration from the famous Robert Musil's novel for the title of his chapter, which deals with Austria: 'A Constitution without Qualities? Three Narratives about Austrian Constitutional Law'. Wagrandl presents three narratives of the Austrian constitution, each of them faithful for the Central European sense for irony: first, that the Austrian constitution is in ruins, referring to its lacking aesthetic, especially if compared to its German counterpart. However, as Wagrandl shows, more recently the constitution became the subject of appraisal, when the first-ever crisis of government ensued after chancellor Sebastian Kurz was faced with the first successful parliamentary vote of no confidence in Austria in reaction to the corruption scandal in his party. Suddenly, Wagrandl notes, 'the Austrian president praised the "elegance" and "beauty" of the constitution'.[72]

The second narrative submits that the Austrian constitution is value-neutral and formalist. Again, Wagrandl carefully digs under the surface to find that it holds no more– even if it 'took a German law professor teaching in Austria to tell the truth'.[73]

[72] Chapter 13.
[73] Ibid.

Finally, the third narrative provides that the Austrian constitution is a role model for European integration and that, from the historical perspective, it gave the world judicial review. From the perspective of this volume this is the most interesting one: especially as the Habsburg Empire, remembered – with no nostalgia – in some of its once subjected countries as the 'prison of nations', is suddenly taken as a model for the constitutional architecture of European integration. For Wagrandl, two features of the Austrian constitution stand out: the openness towards international law (EU law and the ECHR in particular) and the institution of a specialised constitutional court, brought to life by Hans Kelsen (although one must remember that the first-ever specialised constitutional court was established by the Czechoslovak constitution in 1920).

1.2.3 *The Varieties of Liberalism in Europe*

Part III starts from a now common diagnosis: liberal constitutionalism is in crisis. That much is agreed by both those who want to save it for our times and others who look for alternatives. This part examines how liberalism and some of its central tenets, such as the rule of law, the emphasis on legal institutions and principles or the strong role of experts, became dominant ideological constraints on developing alternatives.

As will be seen, Europe and European integration have played an important role in this process, especially with its emphasis on integration through the market, which tends to be conceived as something separate from democracy or the rule of law. As the chapters in this part show, the relationship between the political and economic dimension of liberalism is much more complicated than had been thought at the 'end of history' and the reign of the Washington consensus.

1.2.3.1 The Polish Inspiration: Liberal Constitutionalism as a Sign of Belonging to Europe

The Polish workshop was held in Warsaw in December 2021. The starting point for the reflection on Polish constitutionalism was an ongoing debate about the status of liberal legal constitutionalism as a 'scientific' and supposedly apolitical endeavour. Liberal legal constitutionalism marked Poland's return and belonging to Europe and it was perceived as providing a blueprint for the rational organisation of the State. The Polish participants to the workshop reflected on the origins of this imagination, its operation in constitutional and political practice until its recent breakdown and alternative imaginations that it might have overshadowed (or not).

The debate is related to what has been termed in the literature as the 'constitutional crisis' or 'rule-of-law backsliding' in Poland. Scholars saw the symptoms of the crisis in the political capture of the Constitutional Tribunal and subsequent systemic undermining of judicial independence safeguards.[74] Some researchers have explained this crisis as resulting from the relatively superficial transplant of the Western legal institutions and principles during the political transformation in the late 1980s and 1990s, uncoupled from a deeper internationalisation of the rule-of-law values by the society and neglect of democratic civic engagement.[75] Factors related to the reality of economic transformation, culture and history might have played a role in resisting the rule-of-law values. The law was conceived of as an instrument of economic transformation subordinated to the goal of socio-economic change and generally enjoyed low authority within society from the communist times.[76] Also, Poles generally prefer non-institutional and extra-legal conflict resolution.[77]

However, other researchers have interpreted the crisis as a breakdown of the epistemic hegemony of liberal and legal constitutionalism, especially the belief in its apolitical, objectively rational and scientific nature.[78] This constitutional imaginary might have been in constant tension with the nature and origin of the constitutional text. The integrating objective of legal constitutionalism in Poland, thus understood, has been challenging to attain since the Constitution of 1997 was a complex political compromise, excluding the right-wing forces internally divided at that time and subsequently contesting the constitutional settlement.[79] The Constitution of 1997 ended up being a melting pot of ideas drawn from liberal ideology, patriotic narratives, the social teaching of the Catholic Church, the post-socialist belief in the welfare State and the ordo-liberal constraints upon the public finances, among other things. The Constitutional Tribunal and constitutional scholarship faced the arduous task of solving constitutional disputes and concretising constitutional standards based on the hybrid and ambiguous text. According to some researchers, the cracking belief in the possibility of deriving objectively rational standards from such a text pushes the Polish political system towards political

[74] Sadurski, *Poland's Constitutional Breakdown*.

[75] Krygier, 'The Challenge of Institutionalisation', 557–558. See also, Bojan Bugarič, 'A Crisis of Constitutional Democracy in post-Communist Europe: "Lands in-between" Democracy and Authoritarianism' (2015) 13 *International Journal of Constitutional Law* 219, 238; Sadurski, *Poland's Constitutional Breakdown*, chapter 7; Blokker, *New Democracies in Crisis?*

[76] Grażyna Skąpska, 'The Legacy of Anti-legalism', in Martin Krygier (ed.), *Marxism and Communism: Posthumous Reflections on Politics, Society, and Law* (Rodopi, 1994).

[77] Jacek Kurczewski and Małgorzata Fuszara, 'Patterns of Preference for Dispute Resolution in Poland' (2017) *Polish Sociological Review* 505.

[78] A. Czarnota, 'Constitutional Breakdown, Backsliding, or New Post-Conventional Constitutionalism?', in U. Belavusau and A. Gliszczyńska-Grabias (eds.), *Constitutionalism under Stress. Essays in Honour of Wojciech Sadurski* (Oxford University Press, 2020); Adam Sulikowski, 'Trybunał Konstytucyjny a polityczność: O konsekwencjach upadku pewnego mitu' (2016) (No 4) *Państwo i Prawo* 3; Martin Loughlin, *Against Constitutionalism* (Harvard University Press, 2022).

[79] Paul Blokker, 'Building Democracy by Legal Means? The Contestation of Human Rights and Constitutionalism in East-Central Europe' (2020) 18 *Journal of Modern European History* 335, 343–344.

constitutionalism.[80] Increasingly often do we encounter ideas of the return to the parliamentary majority as representing the nation's will and the need to curb the 'excesses of judicial power' and unfolding 'juristocracy'.[81]

Interestingly, researchers specialising in legal philosophy and sociology, rather than the doctrine of constitutional law, had undertaken critical analyses of the epistemic status and legitimation strategy of liberal legal constitutionalism already a few years before the constitutional crisis began in Poland. Some scholars argued that constitutional law is deeply rooted in the Enlightenment, with its belief in individualism and the power of human reason.[82] Sulikowski argued for a 'post-modernisation' of the Polish constitutional scholarship, including critical analyses of the political and ideological foundations of legal doctrines, especially those developed by the Constitutional Tribunal, such as the right to life 'from conception'. In his view, the existing constitutional scholarship was animated by the belief in 'constitutional truth' generated by adjudication and scholarship, exceedingly focused on the doctrinal recycling and systematisation of the arguments and ideas emerging in the case law of the Constitutional Tribunal rather than their critical analysis.[83] Moreover, Dębska and Warczok critically deconstructed how the Constitutional Tribunal legitimised its power by presenting itself as a neutral and scientific institution – primarily, by dint of the recruitment of the constitutional judges mostly from professors of law – which speaks for the apolitical 'sacred law' rather than 'profane politics'. It neutralised its politically controversial appraisals, presenting them as objective legal truth.[84] After the constitutional crisis began, defenders of the positivist constitutional law scholarship saw 'post-modernism' and the resulting breakdown of trust in an objective constitutional truth as contributing to the rule-of-law decay.[85]

80 Czarnota, 'Constitutional Breakdown'.

81 Aleksandra Kustra-Rogatka, 'The Hypocrisy of Authoritarian Populism in Poland: Between the Facade Rhetoric of Political Constitutionalism and the Actual Abuse of Apex Courts' (2023) 19 *European Constitutional Law Review* 25.

82 Adam Sulikowski, 'O możliwościach postmodernizacji nauki prawa konstytucyjnego' (2010) (No 12) *Państwo i Prawo* 3, referring to Krzysztof Wojtyczek, 'Polska nauka prawa konstytucyjnego na przełomie wieków', in M. Zubik (ed.), *Dwadzieścia lat transformacji ustrojowej w Polsce* (Wydawnictwo Sejmowe, 2010), 36–37. See also, Adam Sulikowski, *Konstytucjonalizm a nowoczesność: Dyskurs konstytucyjny wobec tryumfu i kryzysu moderny* (Złota Seria Uniwersytetu Wrocławskiego, 2008).

83 Sulikowski, 'O możliwościach', 12–13; Adam Sulikowski, 'Konstytucjonaliści a postmodernizm' (2011) (No 12) *Państwo i Prawo* 30, 37; Adam Sulikowski and Krysztof Otręba, 'O potrzebie studiów krytycznych nad prawem konstytucyjnym' (2017) (No 3) *Państwo i Prawo* 5.

84 Hanna Dębska, *Władza, Symbol, Prawo: Społeczne Tworzenie Trybunału Konstytucyjnego* (Wydawnictwo Sejmowe, 2014); Hanna Dębska and Tomasz Warczok, 'Sacred Law and Profane Politics: The Symbolic Construction of the Constitutional Tribunal' (2014) 188 *Polish Sociological Review* 461.

85 Marek Zubik, 'O przewrotnych interpretacjach przepisów Konstytucji dotyczących władzy sądzenia' (2017) (No 10) *Państwo i Prawo* 5.

The origins of this dominant constitutional imaginary in Poland can be traced back to the communist period.[86] As argued by Zomerski in Chapter 15, the façade communist constitutionalism began to crack in the 1970s and 1980s. Legal academics started analysing how the previously developed theoretical ideas relating to positivist constitutionalism could be put to practice to unmask and remedy the pathologies of the communist regime. This intellectual process informed the setting up of the Supreme Administrative Court, the Ombudsman and the Constitutional Tribunal a few years before the communist regime collapsed in 1989. Also, this process corresponded to the general strategy of the democratic opposition, which demanded taking communist law seriously to obtain legal protection for dissidents, thereby fundamentally transforming the law's façade nature.

However, liberal and positivist legal constitutional doctrines that helped to dismantle the communist regime and introduce essential legal and political accountability of the holders of public power faced new challenges in the long run. The legitimation strategy based on the supposedly apolitical, objectively rational and scientific nature of liberal and legal constitutionalism – modelled upon the one practised in the West – was increasingly challenging to sustain in the context of the unfolding democratic conflict. During almost thirty years of its operation as an independent institution, the Constitutional Tribunal engaged with several highly controversial political issues, including the settlement with the communist past (lustration),[87] abortion and the freedom of conscience and religion,[88] the equality of men and women,[89] socio-economic reforms during the economic transformation[90] and austerity measures during the global financial crisis undermining the protection of social rights.[91]

In the context of highly controversial political problems put on the Constitutional Tribunal's docket, the Constitutional Tribunal might have been portrayed as siding with the previous liberal government, for instance, regarding their socio-economic reforms.[92] Undoubtedly, liberal constitutionalism created appropriate conditions for neoliberal reforms in the region in the 1990s but its relationship to the problems of

[86] See Chapter 15.

[87] Michał Krotoszyński, 'Transitional Justice and the Constitutional Crisis: The Case of Poland (2015–2019)' (2019) *Archiwum Filozofii Prawa i Filozofii Społecznej* 22.

[88] Karolina Kocemba and Michał Stambulski, 'Divine Decision-making' *Verfassungsblog*, 9 November 2020, https://verfassungsblog.de/divine-decision-making/ (last accessed 30 March 2023); Wojciech Sadurski and Aleksandra Gliszczyńska-Grabias, 'Freedom of Religion versus Humane Treatment of Animals: Polish Constitutional Tribunal's Judgment on Permissibility of Religious Slaughter' (2014) 11 *European Constitutional Law Review* 596.

[89] Dębska, 'Władza, Symbol, Prawo', chapter 4; Anna Śledzińska-Simon, 'Kobiety i płeć w Konstytucji' (2022) (No 10) *Państwo i Prawo* 74.

[90] Jerzy Oniszczuk, *Wolności i Prawa Socjalne oraz Orzecznictwo Konstytucyjne* (Szoła Główna Handlowa, 2005).

[91] Michał Krajewski, 'The Constitutional Quandary of Social Rights: Questions in Times of the Polish Illiberal Turn' (2023) 21 *International Journal of Constitutional Law* 156.

[92] Ibid.

social justice might have been ambiguous.[93] Also, as pointed out by Krotoszyński in Chapter 20, a part of the right wing has criticised the Constitutional Tribunal's decisions relating to the compliance of lustration with the rule-of-law standards as supposedly geared towards protecting the post-communist elites against democratic accountability. The persisting necessity to deal with the communist past, including to revisit the status of former communist elites that transformed in contemporary capitalist elites, remains essential to the political manifesto of this part of the right wing. This is related to the belief in transitional justice being neglected or the absence of systemic regulation for the restitution of property nationalised in Poland after WWII and ensuing judicial failings.[94]

The breakdown of the epistemic status of liberal and legal constitutionalism as laying down objectively rational and apolitical standards for enacting laws, including those related to transitional justice, could explain the conduct of right-wing populist politicians engaged in dismantling the Constitutional Tribunal and judicial independence. However, another reasoning is necessary to explain the relative ambivalence of society towards constitutional backsliding. Although some protests and social movements against dismantling constitutional checks and balances emerged, they did not manage to stop the anti-constitutional changes.

Assuming the rationality of social actors, largely uninterested in stopping the constitutional backsliding, some researchers inquire into the functioning of Polish legal institutions before the crisis. They argue that a factor fostering the rule of law crisis in Poland has been severe failings in access to justice and the inefficient functioning of the judiciary coupled with a preference for extra-legal and informal dispute settlement. They found the general population's relative indifference towards dismantling the rule of law as rational in the short run. 'If the law is inaccessible and irrelevant, why die for it?'[95] Other researchers also highlight the failings of legal culture and lawyers' communication with ordinary citizens. Socialised in the tradition of legal formalism and unequipped with argumentative skills, judges and lawyers try as much as possible to apply narrowly construed statutory text. This way, they diminish their responsibility for 'justice' in individual cases.[96] Overall, it seems that legal constitutionalism might have generated promises

[93] Sulikowski, 'Trybunał Konstytucyjny a polityczność', 13–14.

[94] See Joanna Kusiak, 'Rule of Law and Rules-Lawyering: Legal Corruption and "Reprivatization Business" in Warsaw' (2019) 43 *International Journal of Urban and Regional Research* 589.

[95] Jan Winczorek and Karol Muszyński, 'The Access to Justice Gap and the Rule of Law Crisis in Poland' (2022) 42 *Zeitschrift für Rechtssoziologie* 5.

[96] Marek Zirk-Sadowski, 'Transformation and Integration of Legal Cultures and Discourses: Poland', in Wojciech Sadurski, Adam Czarnota and Martin Krygier (eds.), *Spreading Democracy and the Rule of Law: The Impact of EU Enlargement on the Rule of Law, Democracy and Constitutionalism in Post-communist Legal Orders* (Springer, 2006), 308–311. See also, Marcin Matczak, Matyas Bencze and Zdenek Kühn, 'Constitutions, EU Law and Judicial Strategies in the Czech Republic, Hungary and Poland' (2010) 30 *Journal of Public Policy* 81.

and social expectations of a well-functioning legal system, which were not fulfilled in practice.

In this context, an important question is how the emphasis on legal institutions and principles overshadows the importance of civic engagement and deliberative interactions with the society and its organic organisations. As Muszyński and Skuczyński argue in Chapter 18, in Poland, before 1997, social dialogue operated relatively well, with trade unions collaborating with parliamentary committees to hammer out social policies. However, due to neo-liberal trends of increasing the efficiency and rationalising law-making, social policymaking became top-down, concentrated in the hands of the executive, to efficiently implement the EU acquis prior to the accession. The dominance of the executive branch over parliamentary law-making and social dialogue may create conditions for the emergence of illiberal trends. Legal institutions and principles proved unable, by themselves, to stop these trends.[97]

1.2.3.2 Contributions

The contributions in Part III analyse the currently dominant legal, political and economic ideologies of our time – liberal constitutionalism and neoliberalism – and seek to uncover counter-narratives in the member states. It again puts together the experience of the old and Other Europe to uncover their mutual relationship – how one presupposes the other. Related to the triumph of liberalism as a political doctrine (analyses in the following part), the imaginary of individual freedom that gets best realised in the market where free people enter into transactions prevailed over the idea of freedom as something inevitably social – and having dimension of social justice, which demands more than the liberal idea of 'justice as fairness'. Social question had to be answered through individual responsibility, not collective arrangements. However, constitutions – and, more importantly, constitutional actors – of some member states have resisted such move, which we seek to explore.

The part is introduced by Michal Kopeček's Chapter 14, on 'Rule of What Law? Authoritarian Pasts, Liberal Politics and Constitutional Imagination in Early Post-Communist East Central Europe'. Kopeček reveals the great variety of imaginaries in Central and Eastern Europe behind the seemingly uniform concept of *Rechtstaat* and liberal constitutionalism, as well as related concepts, such as the rule of law, legality or rights. Looking from the historical perspective, he traces the evolution of these concepts in the region, exploring first the main tenets of the socialist legality and how it was challenged by human rights liberalism, with its attempts to empower emerging civil society, leading to the transformation of 1989. Kopeček explains also how human rights liberalism emphasised the cultural transformation of the society, whereas neoliberalism, which came later, aimed at a market transformation. While

97 Chapter 18.

Rechtstaat seems to have been the overarching concept uniting these and other constitutional imaginaries, it was internally differentiated with various imaginaries playing important roles at different stages of the transformation process. Ultimately, the dominant legal constitutionalism emphasised the need to protect democracy from itself by means of legal institutions, thereby institutionalising mistrust in citizens whom it considered to be not yet ready to take charge, which seems at odds with earlier ambitions of human rights liberalism. Simultaneously, neoliberalism prioritised economic growth and foreign investment. For neoliberals, the rule of law was supposed to guarantee, first and foremost, economic freedom and progress. Kopeček also discusses how Western thinkers writing about the role of law and rights and representing different schools of thought emphasising 'negative freedom' or 'substantive justice' influenced thinkers in Central and Eastern Europe. Moreover, he discusses how post-communist legal positivists, with their formal understanding of the rule of law, could relatively easily transition to the new constitutional settlement.

This exceptionally rich intellectual history of the rule of law in the region sketched by Kopeček helps understand that the overwhelming consensus about the importance of the rule of law or *Rechstaat* – fundamentally contested concepts – might in fact have been concealing the great variety of constitutional imaginaries that all seemingly refer to these overarching concepts. Perhaps even more importantly, this history helps understand why the apparent compromise about the rule of law in the region has turned out to be fragile and superficial. With this broad-brush but rich sketch, Kopeček has laid the ground for other chapters in this part of the volume.

Chapter 15, by Wojciech Zomerski, entitled 'From the Facade to Solid Foundation? The Evolution of the Polish Constitutional Law Discourse in 1944–1989' helps uncover the deep origins of Polish liberal and legal constitutional imaginary emphasising the idea of apolitical legal science. Zomerski enquires into why legal constitutionalism was so smoothly transplanted in Poland. Blokker had previously discussed this transplant as resulting from the activities of European organisations, such as the European Union and the Council of Europe.[98] However, Zomerski demonstrates that the grounds were prepared long before. Starting from the 1960s, legal academia in Poland enjoyed some intellectual freedom and began developing modern constitutional law ideas rooted in strict legal positivism to portray them as scientific and apolitical in the context of the communist regime. Initially, legal academics were interested in justifying the legal and justiciable nature of the communist Constitution of 1952 and its Kelsenian supremacy over the entire legal order. They argued against its portrayal as a purely ornamental document disconnected from social and political reality. By discussing this Constitution's limited justiciability and non-judicial enforcement mechanisms, they sought to legitimise the communist regime since constitutional norms stood in

[98] Blokker, *New Democracies in Crisis?*

stark contrast with reality. This legitimation strategy was linked to the general optics adopted in Polish jurisprudence to portray the interpretation of the law as scientific and apolitical to maintain the law's relative autonomy from communist politics.[99] As already mentioned, the façade communist constitutionalism began to crack in the 1970 and 1980s. Legal academics started analysing how the previously developed theoretical ideas relating to positivist constitutionalism could be put to practice to unmask and remedy the pathologies of the communist regime by means of legal institutions such as courts or the ombudsman.

The dominance of liberal and legal constitutionalism and a nascent debate about alternative imaginaries does not seem confined to CEE. In Chapter 16, 'Nordic Democratic Exceptionality after the End of History: A Neoliberalized Constitutional Imaginary?', Johan Strang discusses the transformation of the Nordic constitutional imaginary. While mainstream Western constitutionalism was about constraining democracy in the name of the rights of citizens, as he argues, Nordic constitutionalism favoured unconstrained democracy enabling progressive social policies. However, Strang argues that the very notion of democracy in the Nordics has changed. Having departed from its roots in popular sovereignty, public participation and redistributive social policies, it is now associated – perhaps just as elsewhere in Europe – with the rule of law, human rights, political and economic freedom. Strang is wondering what the causes of this profound transformation of the Nordic constitutional imaginary are and how this transformation could be researched empirically. Perhaps it is connected to Europeanisation and globalisation. Notably, he does not treat it as a negative phenomenon, seeing in it a chance for avoiding the 'abusive paternalism' of the political community and empowering vulnerable minorities.

A reflection on alternatives to liberal constitutionalism and legal institutions was also found in the Portuguese constitutional discourse. In Chapter 17, 'Fifty Years of Democratic Constitutionalism in Portugal: Between Constitutional Aspirations and the European Path', Mariana Canotilho discusses, first, the origin and essential characteristics of the Portuguese constitution of 1976 resulting from the democratic revolution of 1974. In her view, that this Constitution has turned out to be so stable comes from the fact that it resulted from a wide political compromise between conservative and socialist forces, even though the compromise itself resulted from a serious conflict. It is a 'normative constitution', as Canotilho puts it, with a robust system of constitutional review and an exceptionally rich catalogue of fundamental rights, in which even socio-economic rights are justiciable rather than being merely policy principles. Interestingly, Canotilho notes that such elaborate guarantees of fundamental rights might lead to clashes with EU law, where the latter requires uniform conditions for the effectiveness of EU rules without leaving to the national

99 Wojciech Zomerski, 'O wpływie doświadczeń realnego socjalizmu na teorię dogmatyki prawa: W stronę demokratycznej teorii prawa?' (2020) *Przegląd Prawa i Administracji* 221.

constitution the possibility to undermine this effectiveness with standards of fundamental rights higher than those recognised at the EU level. Nonetheless, the Portuguese constitution and constitutional case law is widely open to international and EU law. Another essential feature of the Portuguese constitution is elaborate 'anti-oligarchic' provisions on political pluralism and democracy that is to be pursued at the different levels of society, including especially participation of political and social actors in public decision-making concerning many spheres of social life (such as healthcare and schools) and even the right of workers to participate in the management of companies. Thus, Portuguese democracy should be decentralised, popular and effective, and not only representative. The Constitution also contains the 'economic constitution', which presupposes the political control of the economy and State intervention.

Having characterised the Portuguese Constitution, which indeed seems to differ in important respects from the mainstream liberal constitutions, Canotilho provides an account of the most salient constitutional debates in Portugal. The first one was the constitutional debate regarding the 'directive constitution', that is, the extent to which the Constitution limits the lawmakers in pursuing their policies, especially in the socio-economic sphere, including whether there is a constitutional non-retrogression principle regarding the already achieved degree of social protection. Although the Portuguese Constitutional Court might have seemed to abandon this principle, Canotilho believes that the debate comes back in somewhat different terms. The second, closely related debate concerned a clash of the Portuguese economic constitution with the EU austerity measures during the economic crisis. How would compliance with these measures despite constitutional guarantees affect the Constitution's authority?, asks Canotilho. She argues that, by upholding the social constitutional imaginary, the Constitutional Court gained huge popular support. At the same time, she anticipates further clashes between the Portuguese and European constitutional imaginary. In this context, she argues for mutual openness of both EU and national imaginaries in view of preserving the valuable elements of the national imaginary, especially democracy that is to be pursued at different levels of society and social commitments. This way the EU constitutional imaginary could also be enriched.

Remaining interested in the shortcomings of liberal legal constitutionalism before the constitutional crisis in Poland, Karol Muszyński and Paweł Skuczyński, in Chapter 18, 'Constitutional Drift: Exploring the Deeper Roots of Polish Constitutional Crisis' explore how the dominance of liberal and communitarian constitutional imaginaries in the practice of governance in Poland overshadowed nascent practices of societal constitutionalism, thereby leading to the 'constitutional crisis' in the long run. They argue that an imaginary of societal constitutionalism has long been present in Polish society. According to it, different societal subsystems (labour, healthcare, politics) generate their own normativity and seek to influence the general law-making process. This imaginary corresponds to 'the classic corporate social model characteristic for continental Europe'. Hence, the importance of social dialogue between the executive, the lawmakers and social actors and creating opportunities for them to express their normativity and participate in governance. Otherwise, social actors become alienated, the social authority of law to the hammering out of which these actors could not contribute drops drastically, whereas the social system becomes susceptible to strategic action and control by actors wishing to seize the 'whole power'. They call this process a 'constitutional drift' which, in their view, explains the deep roots of the Polish constitutional crisis.

First, the authors argue that the Polish Constitution of 1997, resulting from a challenging political compromise, was drafted in sufficiently broad terms to accommodate interpretations in the spirit of liberal, communitarian and societal constitutional imaginary alike. The Constitution granted a special status to many types of social organisations and social dialogue. Nonetheless, in the long run, the societal imaginary was overshadowed by the liberal and communitarian imaginaries. In these imaginaries, the Constitution was seen as a vehicle of substantive values (negative freedom or common good) rather than a catalyst of a process in which societal organisations could effectively contribute to the genuinely democratic law-making process with their own normativities. The authors argue that the accession to the EU could play a role in this regard. Although the EU law itself gives an important role to social dialogue, in Poland social dialogue might have been seen as an obstacle to a technocratic Europeanisation of the legal order and an effective absorption of EU funds. In the mid-2000s, the role of social organisations was reduced by the executive to that of providers of technical input and expertise rather than fully-fledged social normativity. At that time, the rise of the executive had already become evident, coupled with the undermining of the parliament and treating it as a 'voting machine'.

In the view of the authors, the subsequent 'constitutional crisis', during which the executive sought to assert dominance over the judiciary, was only a continuation of earlier trends. At the same time, the authors believe that societal constitutionalism must be revived in Poland to stop and reverse the 'constitutional drift', thereby safeguarding the political system against constitutional crises in the future.

François-Xavier Millet's Chapter 19, 'On the French Constitutional Imaginary: The Erosion of the Long-standing Republican Tradition', discusses not so much the tension between liberalism and the social question, but a tension between liberalism and the Republican imaginary that put much more emphasis on the positive or political liberty, the formation of general interest or general will. Nonetheless, the social question and solidarity are still important components of the Republican imaginary.

Millet argues that the Republican imaginary is still evident in many other idiosyncrasies of the French constitutional law and it continues to clash with the Anglo-Saxon liberalism underlying the EU integration, including the law of the European Union and the European Convention of Human Rights. Having traced the deep roots of the Republican thinking in terms of 'common good' to, paradoxically, the monarchic Ancient Regime, Millet subsequently offers a *tour de force* through the French constitutional law. He highlights characteristic constitutional emanations of the Republican thought. He notes that even the French 'unbridled passion for constitution' is an expression of a typical Republican quest for best possible constitutional arrangements securing a perfect political regime and the formation of the general will rather than only a legal framework offering negative and individualistic safeguards *against* the State. He also notes such Republican elements in the French constitutional law as the indivisibility and centralisation of the State, the trust in the ability of the parliament to express the general will and general interest, coupled with the initial absence of mechanisms designed to enforce any supra-legislative individual rights against such general will, as well as *laïcité* (which, in the eyes of a liberal constitutionalist, may disproportionately restrict the freedom of religion), a special body of administrative law protecting public property, or the priority given to fundamental rights that are collective in nature (such as the freedom of the press and association). Certainly, many specific constitutional arrangements identified by Millet cannot be considered exclusively French (for instance, in Chapter 18, Muszyński and Skuczyński mention the elements of a Republican–communitarian constitutional imaginary in the Polish constitution-making process), but their *accumulation* in France clearly shows a distinct and dominant constitutional imaginary.

Subsequently, Millet moves to the French intellectual history, trying to discover any traces of genuine liberal thinkers in France. He admits himself that he fails in this quest, as even in the liberal thought he discusses he finds a distinct Republican flavour. He is also sceptical about any major intellectual turn towards liberalism in the 1970s in France. Coming back to constitutional law, he admits that the Republican constitutional imaginary has been seriously affected because of external factors such as the European Union and the European Convention of Human Rights. Certain Republican concepts, such as sovereignty, have been progressively replaced by their liberal substitutes, such as constitutional identity. Europeanisation is the reason, according to Millet, why the judicial review of legislation has been reinforced in France and encompassed not only the Republican concern for the separation of powers but also the liberal concern for individual fundamental rights.

Finally, Millet discusses how the Republican and liberal constitutional imaginary clash within the French debates as well as legal and political developments concerning Europe, such as the ratification of the Maastricht Treaty, the referendum of the European Constitution and the Yellow Vests movement. Thus, he shows that the clash of the imaginaries regularly resurfaces.

Another tension that legal and liberal constitutionalism may cause concerns the pursuit of transitional justice. In this context, Michał Krotoszyński's 'From Legal Impossibilism to the Rule of Law Crisis: Transitional Justice and Polish Counter-Constitutionalism' (Chapter 20) is a fact-checking exercise. It verifies whether liberal legal constitutionalism formed obstacles towards an alternative constitutional imaginary of transitional justice, especially lustration mechanisms. The author demonstrates that the accusation in this regard against the Constitutional Tribunal remains unjustified on legal grounds. First, he argues that, when it comes to transitional justice standards, Polish constitutionalism was not 'imitative' but 'adaptive', which again provides nuance to Blokker's argument of imitative constitutionalism in post-communist Europe. The Constitutional Tribunal creatively adjusted to the Polish context Western European recommendations (for instance, by the Council of Europe), thereby leaving the politicians with ample leeway to attain the political goals of lustration. Importantly, dissenting judges frequently expressed their expectations of either more transitional justice-oriented or more strictly rule-of-law approaches to the challenged lustration mechanism, proving the Constitutional Tribunal's preference for the middle-ground. Overall, the Constitutional Tribunal was not hostile to transitional justice. Instead, the politicians created the narrative of clashing constitutional imaginaries. They failed to enact efficient mechanisms for dealing with the communist past addressing the constitutional standards, blaming the Constitutional Tribunal.

1.3 INVITATION

The greatest hope we have with this volume is that it will provoke further reflections and debates in *both* the West and East and that the latter will not only mirror the West, but become a true partner in the debate on the current shape and future of Europe.[100] As the war in Ukraine has shown, post-communist member states – the former vassals of the Soviet Union – bring sensitivities that have been long ignored on the part of the continent that was free of foreign aggression for decades.

One such debate concerns the imperial legacies of Europe and their influence on the shape of the continent's integration and its law.[101] It should be clear that 'Europe' is not a hegemonic space that once controlled – sometimes with great violence – the rest of the world (with the possible exclusion of North America). Inside Europe there were also places whose experience is much closer to that of Europe's external colonies than that of the imperium. And their road to freedom has

[100] In that respect, the programme of the 2023 Academy of European Law, organised every year by the European University Institute in Florence, is anything but promising: the specialized course on 'Revisiting the Fundamentals of EU Law' features twelve academics, all of them coming from 'old' Europe.

[101] See Peo Hansen and Stefan Jonsson, *Eurafrica: The Untold History of European Integration and Colonialism* (Bloomsbury Academic, 2014). Larsen, 'European Public Law after Empires' has opened this question in the context of law; see also Komárek's critique in Jan Komárek, 'Why Read the Transformation of Europe Today? On the Limits of a Liberal Constitutional Imaginary', in Jan Komárek (ed.), *European Constitutional Imaginaries: Between Ideology and Utopia* (Oxford University Press, 2023), 143.

begun only very recently – or, if we really talk about Europe as the continent not reduced to the EU, some are currently fighting for it.

The greatest contribution of this book may consist in reminding those, who fight for their European future, that there is no Eden of freedom and prosperity there. Only another struggle, which, nevertheless, is mostly made of words resulting in political agreements rather than through arms and lives lost. Our job is to make our voices heard.

PART I

Nation States, Member States and Their Others

2

Vicarious Sovereignty

Becoming European the Estonian Way

Maria Mälksoo

As Estonia restores and surpasses the statehood enjoyed in the era 1918–1940, a new Estonian is being born: knowledgeable, proud and self-confident, European in outlook, and hungry for achievement in a pioneer kind of way typically associated more with America than the continent. The new Estonian will shape the Estonia of tomorrow; his attitudes will become the national attitude, his sensitivities will become the national sensitivities.

Foreign Minister Toomas Hendrik Ilves at the Institute of International Affairs, Stockholm, January 9, 1997.

2.1 INTRODUCTION

How to be 'independent', 'sovereign' and 'European' – all at once? The opening quote of this chapter by one of the defining foreign ministers and European ideologues in Estonia's post-Soviet journey of 'becoming European' illustrates well how any iteration of identity and belonging is always a performative speech act – that is, it aims to bring something about by the act of saying it.[1] The musings on the emergence of new Estonia and new Estonian are, hence, a politically self-conscious make-believe rather than an objective observation of an unmediated reality. The following inquiry into the Estonian European constitutional imaginaries proceeds from the very methodological premise. I understand the imaginaries in question as political performatives that have been articulated and enacted in a particular historical and political context with a specific political goal in mind. My argument is that the internal paradox of this goal can be captured by the concept of vicarious sovereignty: the Europeanization of a state as a means to practice sovereign agency.

Estonia's model of the European Union (EU) membership is notably permissive, considering the country's constitutionally unequivocal commitment to the

The writing of this chapter was supported by the Volkswagen Foundation grant no. 120221 to the MEMOCRACY consortium project.

[1] John L. Austin, *How to Do Things with Words*, 2nd ed. (Clarendon Press, 1975).

conservative notion of sovereignty.[2] Having restored its sovereignty from the embers of the Soviet Union in 1991,[3] Estonia joined the EU in 2004 along with nine other, mostly Central-Eastern European countries. Striving to be recognized as a 'good European', Estonia's implementation of EU law has been generally without reservations, with primacy granted to EU law over the national constitution.[4]

An apparent paradox of Estonia's constitutionally conservative understanding of sovereignty and its practical sharing with the EU is illustrative of a general aperture between the principle and practice of sovereignty. Classically conceived as indivisible, with the ultimate authority vested in a single sovereign or institution within a political community,[5] sovereignty is 'eminently divisible' in practice, and the idea of indivisible sovereignty is thus indeed an idea in the mind rather than an empirical fact.[6] Further, sovereignty in and of itself has no purposive content: it refers, by default, to some higher order value. For the constructivist International Relations (IR) scholarship, the reference point of sovereignty is accordingly provided by socially recognized identity values.[7]

The mapping of Estonian European constitutional imaginaries is, hence, also an exercise in defining what makes a state a state; the nature and features of sovereignty in the early twenty-first century and, last but not least, the probing of the meaning of the Estonian 'social self' at the time a political window of opportunity opened for its self-(re)enactment as a sovereign state. This chapter explores how political agency has been imagined by a country that has pooled important aspects of its sovereign power with the EU.[8] This question is probed in the context of Estonia's participation

[2] Article 1 of the Constitution, adopted in 1992, states that 'Estonia is an independent and sovereign democratic republic wherein the supreme power of state is vested in the people. The independence and sovereignty of Estonia are timeless and inalienable.'

[3] Estonia's sovereign statehood, which had been illegally taken away by the Soviet Union in the course of WWII, was reinstated on the doctrine of legal continuity, instead of being established anew by seceding from the Soviet Union.

[4] Hent Kalmo and Anneli Albi, 'Estonia', in Stefan Griller, Lina Papadopoulou and Roman Puff (eds.), *National Constitutions and EU Integration* (Hart Bloomsbury, 2022).

[5] For critical engagements with the classical position, see Jens Bartelson, 'On the Indivisibility of Sovereignty' (2011) 2 *Republic of Letters: A Journal for the Study of Knowledge, Politics, and the Arts* 85; John Agnew, 'Sovereignty Regimes: Territoriality and State Authority in Contemporary World Politics' (2005) 95 *Annals of the Association of American Geographers* 437.

[6] David A. Lake, 'Delegating Divisible Sovereignty: Sweeping a Conceptual Minefield' (2007) 2 *The Review of International Organisations* 219, 220.

[7] Christian Reus-Smit, *The Moral Purpose of the State: Culture, Social Identity, and Institutional Rationality in International Relations* (Princeton University Press, 1999), 30.

[8] See Lake, 'Delegating Divisible Sovereignty', 220, 231–234, for a distinction between delegating sovereignty and pooling sovereignty. In the first case, states grant an international organization contingent authority to perform certain limited tasks; whereas pooling occurs when states transfer the authority to a collective decision-making body producing binding decisions for member states. Pooling sovereignty accordingly refers to 'compromising to some extent on their ideal policy to get a policy that actually "works" and solves the problem before them'. Ibid, 232. See, further, Saskia Sassen, *Losing Control? Sovereignty in an Age of Globalization* (Columbia University Press, 1995).

in the discussions of the Convention on the Future of the European Union in the early 2000s – the process which could be legitimately described as the constitutional leg in Estonia's journey of 'becoming European'.[9]

I explore Estonia's sovereignty-sharing with the EU through the lens of the vicarious identification concept. Vicarious identification refers to the subject's attempts to establish and legitimize a vicarious identity – that is, a sense of self-identity, purpose and self-esteem through riding on (and appropriating) the achievements and experiences of others.[10] The dictionary references for 'vicarious' include 'substitute', 'second-hand', 'derivative', 'secondary' and 'surrogate' – in short, 'experienced in the imagination through the feelings or actions of another person'. The other meaning of the word 'vicarious' pertains to 'acting or done for another'. The adjective derives etymologically from the Latin *vicarius*, meaning 'substituted, delegated', and from *vicis*, denoting 'a change, exchange, interchange, succession, alternation, substitution'.[11] As in vicarious relationships, one thing is taken to stand in or substitute for another, there is a 'second hand'-quality about such liaisons. Vicarious identity is then 'one that can be delegated, substituted, or understood as interchangeable with the identity of another'.[12] Coveting such an identity can be considered as a form of ontological security seeking or the subject's desire for continuous self-being in the face of potentially destabilizing existential anxieties.[13] It is not uncommon among states to seek a sense of ontological stability, security and self-esteem 'through locating themselves as members of civilizational communities, seeking to vicariously appropriate elements of a civilizational tradition and its achievements as their own' for the promise of vicarious identity relationships to 'establish, preserve, or even enhance a state's club/positional status'.[14]

Building on the notion of vicarious identity, I conceptualize *vicarious sovereignty*, using Estonia's experience of 'becoming European' post-1991. I refer to the politics of becoming European both in the narrow institutionalist sense of Central and East European (CEE) states' journey from the accession negotiations in 1997 to the EU membership in 2004 and in the deeper identitarian meaning of seeking recognition to Central and East Europeans' 'Europeanness' from the authoritative carriers of contemporary European identity in the western part of the continent.

The argument is structured in three parts. In Section 2.2, the concept of vicarious sovereignty is outlined against the backdrop of the idea of sovereignty as a symbolic

9 Maria Mälksoo, *The Politics of Becoming European: A Study of Polish and Baltic Post-Cold War Security Imaginaries* (Routledge, 2010).

10 Christopher S. Browning, Pertti Joenniemi and Brent J. Steele, *Vicarious Identity in International Relations: Self, Security, and Status on the Global Stage* (Oxford University Press, 2021), 1, 17.

11 *Online Etymology Dictionary*, www.etymonline.com/search?q=vicarious (last accessed 2 April 2025).

12 Browning et al., *Vicarious Identity in International Relations*, 11.

13 Ibid., 184.

14 Ibid., 44–45.

form, a highly ambiguous and contested social structure of international politics. Section 2.3 zooms in on the context of the Estonian European constitutional imaginaries to set the historical background for this chapter's empirical research question, namely: *how were the conditions for sovereignty and the boundaries of the European constitution imagined by the Estonian state-appointed visionaries and spokespeople during the Convention on the Future of Europe?* Such a focus is by default limited and, some might argue, rather outdated, since the Europe and Estonia envisioned twenty years ago are another country compared to today. My claim is not that zooming in on the bygone political discourse on the future of Europe and Estonia's way of blending in with it would point at some deeper continuities in the contemporary Estonian constitutional thought either domestically or at the European level. Nor do I suggest that the originally provided rationale for vicarious practicing of sovereignty through the EU membership remains intact *anno* 2025. The national conservatives of contemporary Estonia, along with considerable segments of the public, would not necessarily subscribe today to the idea that substituting national sovereignty unquestioningly with the European authority is in the interests of Estonia's security. Rather, I propose that the temporal window in the focus of this chapter marks an important (if ultimately not realized) constitutional moment in the European integration process, crystallizing Estonia's political discussions back in the day about its sovereign agency in the European polity (of which it was yet to become a formal part then). This moment thus allowed Estonia to tap into the political reconciliation attempts of becoming a state while – and arguably via – becoming an EU member state. Consequently, in Section 2.4, I offer a discursive breakdown of a set of notable visions of Europe, as articulated by the defining Estonian constitutional 'map-makers' at the time of the Convention (2001/2002–2003), to wit: Lennart Meri and Toomas Hendrik Ilves.[15] While hardly representative of the broader constitutional debate back at the time, such a sample is still evocative of the political discourse in Estonia's run-up to the EU accession. The limited handful of the highlighted political visions is, alas, also indicative of the slender original contributions by the Estonian political elite to 'thinking Europe' in the first place. The chapter concludes with brief reflections on the broader applicability of the vicarious sovereignty concept beyond the (historical) Estonian case.

2.2 THE 'NECESSARY FICTION' OF SOVEREIGNTY

Sovereignty is one of the 'necessary fictions' international relations (are) run by: it is the foundational concept for international law and IR theory, providing both

[15] Meri was the Estonian government's representative at the Convention, whereas Ilves was Estonia's Minister for Foreign Affairs at the time of the Convention's deliberations, providing one of the most noteworthy political interventions in the debate with his Humboldt lecture of 2001.

disciplines with an original *raison d'être*. As 'the paradigmatic symbolic structure of the international system',[16] the 'highly ambiguous' concept of sovereignty has many allusions.[17] Besides being referred to as the constitutive norm of the modern institution of statehood or 'a foundational habit of the modern state system',[18] sovereignty has been denoted as a legal status, an institution, (a bundle of) rights, a bridge between inside/outside of the state and, hence, a constitutive link between the (international) society and states and the list goes on.[19] Jens Bartelson has made a compelling case for sovereignty to be understood as a symbolic form 'by means of which we have come to perceive the political world, but as such it does not stand in any determinate relationship to the world thus perceived'.[20] A symbolic form 'represents a perspective taken of an object rather than a representation of its essence'.[21] The objectivity of symbolic forms consequently stems from their virtue of organizing words and things into meaningful wholes (and rendering the latter accessible to knowledge).[22] Adopting a narrow sense of the concept of symbolic form, sovereignty can be understood as structuring the production of both meaning and experience. According to this line of thinking, drawing on Ernst Cassirer's earlier work on symbolic forms, 'sovereignty is real only by virtue of having been constructed'.[23] Hence, the meaningful question is not to contemplate over the realness or constructed-ness of sovereignty but to probe 'how this symbolic form has been used as a template for organizing political life, and by what means it has been allowed to structure the political world'.[24] Put differently, sovereignty is not either present or absent: rather, sovereignty 'unfolds in legal and political games as meaning production and praxis' in particular ways.[25]

The preceding threads imply, by default, a non-fixed meaning of the sovereignty concept through time. It is precisely the shifting meanings of sovereignty, Cynthia Weber argues, that ought to be studied for 'what counts and/or functions as sovereign is not the same in all times and places'.[26] Taking a cue from her

[16] Charlotte Epstein, Thomas Lindemann and Ole Jacob Sending, 'Frustrated Sovereigns: The Agency That Makes the World Go Around, Introduction to the Special Issue on Misrecognition in World Politics: Revisiting Hegel (2018) 44 *Review of International Studies* 787, 790.

[17] Hent Kalmo and Quentin Skinner, *Sovereignty in Fragments: The Past, Present and Future of a Contested Concept* (Cambridge University Press, 2010).

[18] Sebastian Schmidt, 'Foreign Military Presence and the Changing Practice of Sovereignty: A Pragmatist Explanation of Norm Change' (2014) 108 *The American Political Science Review* 817, 822.

[19] Tanja E. Aalberts, *Constructing Sovereignty between Politics and Law* (Routledge, 2012), 40.

[20] Bartelson, 'On the Indivisibility of Sovereignty', 86.

[21] Jens Bartelson, *Sovereignty as Symbolic Form* (Routledge, 2014), 14–15.

[22] Ibid., 15.

[23] Ibid., 17.

[24] Ibid.

[25] Rebecca Adler-Nissen and Ulrik Pram Gad, 'Introduction: Postimperial Sovereignty Games in the Nordic Region' (2014) 49 *Cooperation and Conflict* 3,17.

[26] Cynthia Weber, *Simulating Sovereignty: Intervention, the State and Symbolic Exchange* (Cambridge University Press, 1995), 2.

exploration of how the meaning of sovereignty has become stabilized historically, the study of Estonian imaginaries of Europe and the constitution thereof is concurrently an inquiry into how the Estonian state has been written with particular capacities and legitimacies within the bounds of the EU as a postmodern or late sovereign in and of itself.[27] Notably, Estonia had just about restored its state sovereignty when it felt compelled to share it with the EU – a post-Westphalian polity in the latter's self-mythology, increasingly focussed on individual sovereignty via the emphasis on fundamental rights already at the time of the enlargement.[28] As an instance of exercising authority functionally, not territorially, the EU has emerged as 'a late-sovereign complex of overlapping claims to sovereignty',[29] decentring the familiar sovereign state imaginary with its distinctive mix of integrated and differentiated authority.[30]

As Bartelson notes, the concept of sovereignty concurrently functions as a source of self-identity and a principle of self-recognition.[31] The recognition granted by international society can be legal-political, pertaining to equal rights and obligations therein, or moral, going 'beyond the mere recognition of rights, and into the thick recognition of social and cultural identities'.[32] Ayse Zarakol has proposed to call the two different IR understandings of the concept of recognition 'legal' and 'existential' recognition, respectively.[33] Whereas the first, legal (or thinly understood) recognition concerns seeking statehood, thick (or existential) understanding of recognition does not see the innate recognition aspiration solved by legal recognition only. Rather, legal recognition can provide a prerequisite for agency, whereas the desire to be recognized as a certain sort of being still persists. Pinning down sovereignty gets further complicated with the modern concept of 'independence' added in the mix. The latter is closely linked to popular or national sovereignty, at the core of which is 'the idea of the self-determining community that constitutes the rules by which a people will be governed'.[34]

Estonian political scientists Eiki Berg and Ene Kuusk have distinguished (and even sought to empirically measure) internal and external aspects of sovereignty on

[27] Cf. Ibid., 29; Rebecca Adler-Nissen, 'Sovereignty', in Rebecca Adler-Nissen (ed.), *Bourdieu in International Relations: Rethinking Key Concepts in IR* (Routledge, 2013), 179.

[28] Today, Poland and Hungary have emerged as vocal critics of such an understanding about the EU, seeing it rather as a projection of the German–French power than a practical utopia of individual empowerment.

[29] Adler-Nissen and Pram Gad, 'Introduction', 20.

[30] Jennifer Mitzen, 'Feeling at Home in Europe: Migration, Ontological Security, and the Political Psychology of EU Bordering' (2018) 39 *Political Psychology* 1373.

[31] Jens Bartelson, 'Three Concepts of Recognition' (2013) 5 *International Theory* 107, 111.

[32] Ibid., 117–118.

[33] Ayse Zarakol, 'Sovereign Equality as Misrecognition' (2018) 44 *Review of International Studies* 848, 850. See also Lisa Strömbom, 'Thick Recognition: Advancing Theory on Identity Change in Intractable Conflicts' (2014) 20 *European Journal of International Relations* 168.

[34] Karin Fierke, 'Introduction: Independence, Global Entanglement and the Co-production of Sovereignty' (2017) 6 *Global Constitutionalism* 167, 171.

the reasoning that 'entities' internal legitimacy and external recognition issues matter most in the praxis to relatively locate them within international society'.[35] Consequently, internal sovereignty is understood in terms of symbolic attributes (such as flag, national holidays), governance (constitution, autonomous government, head of state), monetary system, territorial integrity and permanent population. External sovereignty, in turn, pertains to 'the extent of actorness, the existence of security structures, diplomatic relations with other countries and membership in international organisations'.[36] According to this view, most attributes of statehood and sovereignty are related to symbols, constitutional arrangements and world standing. Estonia's early permissiveness[37] in granting the EU supremacy above its own constitution might appear striking for the temporal proximity of the restoration of the country's long-coveted sovereign agency as a legal subject and the politically articulated vision of the substantiation and execution of that agency emphatically through the membership in the EU. Such politics was underpinned by the general perception of Russia as an existential threat, against which membership in the EU was supposed to provide a political remedy. Having entrusted some of its sovereignty features to the EU's competence, the absolute sovereignty of Estonia (and any other member state, for that matter) is naturally reduced to a degree; yet the benefits from international cooperation were considered to be higher, for instance through enhanced security provisions, than the losses accompanying the waiver of some sovereignty attributes.[38] Whether or not such sovereignty attributes are those 'mainly with symbolic meaning', as Berg and Kuusk maintain,[39] is yet an open question, however.

2.2.1 *Vicarious Sovereignty*

From a classical position on sovereignty, 'vicarious sovereignty' appears as a contradiction in terms. Recalling an ideal–typical vision of sovereignty, the state either is sovereign or it is not.[40] However, whereas theories of sovereignty presuppose that

35 Eiki Berg and Ene Kuusk, 'What Makes Sovereignty a Relative Concept? Empirical Approaches to International Society' (2010) 29 *Political Geography* 40, 42.

36 Ibid.

37 The 2003 constitutional amendments on the basis of which Estonia's entrance to the EU was made legally possible still allow for a pro-sovereignty interpretation as well. Nor should the notable pro-Europeanness of the 2008 Estonian Supreme Court be taken as the last word in this process, as the modification of the Court's initially strongly pro-European interpretation by the successive composition attests to.

38 For a characteristic example, see Märt Rask, 'Suveräänsuse areng Euroopa Nõukogu ja Euroopa Liidu õigusaktide mõjusfääris tuginedes Euroopa Inimõiguste Kohtu ja Euroopa Kohtu pretsedendiõigusele', 28 August 2011, www.riigikohus.ee/sites/default/files/elfinder/dokumendid/m.raski_ettekanne_vene_kk_2011_0.pdf (last accessed 2 April 2025).

39 Berg and Kuusk, 'What Makes Sovereignty a Relative Concept?', 49.

40 See Hans J. Morgenthau, 'The Problem of Sovereignty Reconsidered' (1948) 48 *Columbia Law Review* 341, 365. Notably, international law has historically allowed for various kinds of states: for instance, the practice until 1918 also knew vassal states and protectorates. There were only a

political authority ought to be indivisible, the findings of political science are customarily testing to its actual divisibility.[41] Constructivist International Relations theory, in particular, contests the indivisibility of sovereignty, noting the variability of what having sovereignty means in international society at different times and places.[42] Not unlike Facebook's transfiguration to Meta, the concept of vicarious sovereignty remains tied to 'the symbolic form of sovereignty'[43] while stretching the dogged idea of sovereignty as indivisible to the point of voiding it from its original (if mythical) substance.

Vicarious sovereignty is sovereignty achieved through sovereignty shared – a curious kind of sovereignty that emerges by the act of pooling national authority with other polities and thereby supposedly elevating state's agency in international politics. It is a type of sovereignty that materializes through membership in another polity and a state's willing self-subjugation to the latter's supremacy for the sake of the supposed generation of a sense of ontological security thereby. Vicarious sovereignty can be visually depicted through an image of a Russian doll embedded in a bigger version of its spit image. Vicarious identity entails integrating others' stories as part of one's own autobiography, presenting events not experienced by the self directly precisely *as if* they were. Vicarious sovereignty, in its turn, emerges as a condition of pooled sovereignty where the elevation of sovereign being/status is supposedly achieved by sharing parts of it with a broader community that the actor identifies with and gains its sense of ontological security, order and purpose from.[44]

Vicarious sovereignty has obvious resonance with the earlier notion of 'associated sovereignty', coined to capture the system of governance characterized by the softening of sovereign power via pooling competencies in overlapping domains of power and interest at the European level.[45] Alike associated sovereignty, vicarious sovereignty captures the paradoxical quest to regain national sovereignty through international integration, accompanied by the process of a Europeanization of state identity. Distinct from associated sovereignty, vicarious sovereignty emphasizes the affectively charged ontological security seeking dynamics such pooling of sovereignty in the European polity is imbued with. The assumedly heightened 'bang for the buck' of one's international agency as a result of shared sovereign power is accordingly accompanied by a specific emotive logic of elevated sense of self and status as an important goal in the process. Vicarious sovereignty highlights the affective mobilization of identity concerns in the process of diffusing sovereign

handful of 'sovereign' states in 1913, a number of them, in fact, empires. See, further, Gerry Simpson, *Great Powers and Outlaw States: Unequal Sovereigns in the International Legal Order* (Cambridge University Press, 2004).

41 Bartelson, 'On the Indivisibility of Sovereignty', 93.

42 Aalberts, *Constructing Sovereignty*, 125.

43 Bartelson, 'On the Indivisibility of Sovereignty'.

44 Browning et al., *Vicarious Identity in International Relations*, 2.

45 Peter J. Katzenstein, 'United Germany in an Integrating Europe' in Peter J. Katzenstein (ed.), *Tamed Power: Germany in Europe* (Cornell University Press, 1997), 33.

power in the European system of associated sovereignty. While associated sovereignty has been prominently unfolded against the backdrop of the institutionalized taming of Germany's power in Europe,[46] vicarious sovereignty captures the power dynamics of attempted strengthening and projecting of European identity and belonging by the latecomers to the European polity from its oft-disregarded smaller fringes.[47]

The concept of vicarious sovereignty is further distinct from other restrained types of sovereignty, such as semisovereignty[48] and 'nested' conception of sovereignty.[49] The concept of 'semisovereignty' – albeit 'epitomi[zing] a condition familiar to most small states in world politics'[50] – is internally grounded, with its coiner's original emphasis on largely self-imposed domestic constraints that limited the sovereignty of the West German state.[51] Whereas semisovereignty in its original conception similarly refers to a condition of 'tamed sovereignty' for '[a] semisovereign state is not free to act as it pleases',[52] the notion of vicarious sovereignty is explicitly relational vis-à-vis a polity or polities beyond the state. A wider view of semisovereignty equates it with pooled or shared sovereignty, framed by interdependence and reflexive multilateralism, turning all states effectively semisovereign and sovereignty thus into a bargaining resource.[53]

If sovereignty traditionally refers to a materialization of an idea of the state, ontological security[54] pertains to the securing of the idea of the state – that is, in

46 Peter J. Katzenstein (ed.), *Tamed Power: Germany in Europe* (Cornell University Press, 1997). See also Chapter 7, focusing on a variety of Central European cases between internationalization and institutionalization.

47 Cf. Peter J. Katzenstein (ed.), *Mitteleuropa: Between Europe and Germany* (Berghahn Books, 1997).

48 In Katzenstein's original account, the concept of 'semisovereignty' refers to the organization of power in domestic politics, combining co-operative federalism, powerful societal groups and non-partisan parapublic institutions, rather than the loss of sovereignty due to European integration or external prerogatives. Peter J. Katzenstein, *Policy and Politics in West Germany: The Growth of a Semisovereign State* (Temple University Press, 1987).

49 Simpson's 'nested sovereignty' refers to a situation in settler colonialism where one sovereign political body exists nested within another sovereign political body on the example of indigenous peoples and their political orders in North America. Audra Simpson, *Mohawk Interruptus: Political Life across the Borders of Settler States* (Duke University Press, 2014).

50 Peter J. Katzenstein, 'Conclusion: Semisovereignty in United Germany', in Simon Green and William E. Paterson (eds.), *Governance in Contemporary Germany: The Semisovereign State Revisited* (Cambridge University Press, 2012), 286.

51 William E. Paterson 'European Policy-Making: Between Associated Sovereignty and Semisovereignty', in Simon Green and William E. Paterson (eds.), *Governance in Contemporary Germany: The Semisovereign State Revisited* (Cambridge University Press, 2012), 261.

52 Katzenstein, 'Conclusion', 283.

53 Paterson, 'European Policy-Making', 278.

54 The literature on ontological security in International Relations is voluminous and growing fast. For key inspirations, see Ronald D. Laing, *The Divided Self: An Existential Study in Sanity and Madness* (Penguin Books, 1990 [1960]) and Anthony Giddens, *Modernity and Self-identity: Self and Society in the Late Modern Age* (Stanford University Press, 1991). For path-breaking

case a state is in our focus in the first place, as the concept of ontological security originates from individual and social psychology.[55] The premise of ontological security is that our self-understandings are formulated against the backdrop of our awareness of the profound uncertainties and arbitrariness of human life and our own mortality. Ontological security-seeking is accordingly about strategies of managing that anxiety (for example, via autobiographical narratives and routines vis-à-vis 'significant others') so that we could go on with our everyday life.[56] The ontological security promise and allure of vicarious identification with 'Europe' and its modern-day institutionalized materialization in the EU thus probed the *finalité* of the Estonian state as discussed in the run-up to the EU membership. Estonia's 'sovereignty games' in the EU illustrate the relativity of the concept of sovereignty in the context where the execution of sovereignty is considered to be dependent on its sharing in crucial parts with the vicarious identification object (that is, the EU).[57]

2.3 THE CONSTITUTIONAL PROCESS OF BECOMING EUROPEAN

Estonia was the first of the former USSR republics to start the accession negotiations with the EU in 1998, becoming a member of the Union on 1 May 2004. To enable the accession, the Accession to the EU and the Supplementary Act to the Constitution was passed, following the referendum of 14 September 2003. However, while carefully navigating the formal amendment, supplementation by an independent constitutional act *de facto* still changed, not just supplemented the

accounts in IR, see Jennifer Mitzen, 'Ontological Security in World Politics: State Identity and the Security Dilemma' (2006) 12 *European Journal of International Relations* 341 and Brent J. Steele, *Ontological Security in International Relations: Self-identity and the IR State* (Routledge, 2008). For a good round-up of the literature, see Karl Gustafsson and Nina C. Krickel-Choi, 'Returning to the Roots of Ontological Security: Insights from the Existentialist Anxiety Literature' (2020) 26 *European Journal of International Relations* 875.

55 As with the notion of ontological security, the conceptual 'scaling up' of vicarious identification from individual actor level to state level raises methodological challenges and has been questioned for the potential to result in anthropomorphization of states. Browning, Joenniemi and Steele demonstrate the relevance of vicarious identification at the collective level on multiple grounds, showing how vicarious identification is practiced by states in their respective searches to secure a sense of self-identity and status on the global stage; how an international politics of vicarious identification can occur between individuals at a societal level and how individuals 'live through' and vicariously identify with their nation-states. They further propose a useful distinction between *vicarious identification* and *vicarious identity promotion* for ascertaining suitable methods of analysis. – See Browning et al., *Vicarious Identity in International Relations*, chapter 2.

56 Jennifer Mitzen, 'Anxious Community: EU as (in)Security Community' (2018) 27 *European Security* 393, 396.

57 Or a spin on the claim of integration with Europe making Estonia a state in the first place. See Merje Kuus, 'Sovereignty for Security?: The Discourse of Sovereignty in Estonia' (2002) 21 *Political Geography* 393, 398.

constitution of the republic.[58] The Act's provision that the Constitution 'is applied without prejudice to the rights and obligations arising from the Accession Treaty' has been interpreted in the judgments of the Supreme Court in a way that grants EU law primacy.[59] Due to the intense securitization of the country's belonging to Europe via the coveted EU membership,[60] the issue of shared sovereignty created domestic tensions but remained largely depoliticized top-down in Estonia during the accession period.[61]

In order to explore how and why this became possible, ideas and their authors in Estonian European constitutional thought need to be taken seriously, no matter how sparse the respective record.[62] To map the constitutive ideas about the EU's constitution and for the Union's constitutionalism and, more generally, for the European integration, sovereignty and statehood, as articulated from Estonia, I will turn to the two outstanding political figures among the constitutional 'map-makers' at the time of the Convention on the Future of Europe (February 2002–June 2003): namely, Lennart Meri (as the representative of the government to the Convention) and Toomas Hendrik Ilves (as Estonia's foreign minister in 1999–2002 and a prominent voice in the debates on Europe).[63] This is, by default, a delimited sample, as it represents only a small political fraction of what could be described as the Estonian European constitutional thought, leaving aside the oft-heated juridical debates over the European constitution and its hierarchical relationship to the Estonian constitution among the community of Estonian constitutional lawyers (e.g., Anneli Albi, Madis Ernits, Carri Ginter, Hent Kalmo and Julia Laffranque).[64]

58 Anneli Albi, *EU Enlargement and the Constitutions of Central and Eastern Europe* (Cambridge University Press, 2009), 19, 111; Lauri Mälksoo, 'Eesti suveräänsus 1988–2008', in Hent Kalmo and Marju Luts-Sootak (eds.), *Iganenud või igavene? Tekste kaasaegsest suveräänsusest* (Tartu University Press, 2010), 141.

59 Kalmo and Albi, 'Estonia'.

60 For example, not mincing the existentialist words, President Meri argued in his end-of-the-year interview of 1997 that EU membership was necessary for the continuation of the Estonian state. Lennart Meri, 'Euroopa Uniooni on vaja riigi püsimiseks', *Eesti presidendi aastalõpuintervjuu*, *Luup*, 22 December 1997.

61 See Merje Kuus, 'European Integration in Identity Narratives in Estonia: A Quest for Security' (2002) 39 *Journal of Peace Research* 91; Merje Kuus, 'Toward Cooperative Security? International Integration and the Construction of Security in Estonia' (2002) 31 *Millennium: Journal of International Studies* 297; Kuus, 'Sovereignty for Security?'.

62 Cf. Jan Komárek, 'Constitutional Imaginaries: Utopias, Ideologies and the Other', *iCourts Working Paper Series* (no 172), IMAGINE Paper (no 1), October 2019, 19.

63 Ilves was the main promoter and powerhouse behind the idea of Estonia's EU membership in the 1990s, when the membership prospects in NATO looked dim for the Baltic states. He was further savvy to note early on that the question of the EU institutional reform was one of the issues that defied regional compartmentalization and called for all-Union solutions. See Toomas Hendrik Ilves, 'Estonia, the European Union and the New North' (1999) 4 *European Foreign Affairs Review* 291, 294.

64 For a state–academia collaboration in mapping the distinct political visions and the preferable Estonian scenarios for the EU's future in the context of the Convention's debates, see Külliki

The Convention on the Future of the European Union (aka the European Convention) was a body established by the European Council in 2001, tasked with the purpose to re-order the existing treaty base to sustain the Union's functionality in light of the pending enlargement. The main issues discussed at the Convention concerned the ways of making the Union more democratic and transparent; modes of streamlining the decision-making processes; the division of competencies between the EU institutions, member states and pertinent regional organizations; the inclusion of national parliaments at the EU level, and the ways of making the EU's Common Foreign and Security Policy (CFSP) more effective. The membership of the Convention consisted of the representatives of the European Commission, European Parliament, the delegates of the member and candidate states' governments and national parliaments, each of whom had the right to send one governmental and two parliamentarian representatives to the Convention. In all, 28 states and 217 representatives participated in the work of the Convention, led by the former French president Valéry Giscard d'Estaing. The government of Estonia was represented at the Convention by the former president Lennart Meri, with Henrik Hololei serving as a deputy. The Estonian parliament's representatives were Tunne Kelam and Rein Lang for the latter parliament formation and Tunne Kelam and Peeter Kreitzberg for the former.

For Estonia, as then still a candidate country of the EU, participation in the discussions over the future shape and face of the Union on par with the established member states[65] was a valued opportunity. The Convention enabled Estonia to speak along in imagining the future of the European institutions and member states' division of labour in governance *in spe*. It was an opportunity to practice hands-on 'the politics of becoming European'[66] or 'that paradoxical politics by which new cultural identities are formed out of old energies, injuries, and differences'.[67] For Lennart Meri, the Convention must have felt like a symbolic homecoming – if one thinks of his old adages, according to which '[w]hen creating a new Europe we have to at the same time create a new European';[68] or that '[o]ne is not born European. One becomes European. And no one has a monopoly on Europe'.[69] The Convention on the Future of the European Union provided an opportunity to

Tafel and Erik Terk (eds.), *Euroopa Liidu tulevik ja Eesti: Kolm institutsionaalset tulevikuvisiooni* (Riigikantselei Euroopa Liidu sekretariaat ja Eesti Tuleviku-uuringute Instituut, 2003).

65 Except for the candidate states' inability to block the consensus of the member states.

66 Mälksoo, *Politics of Becoming European*.

67 William E. Connolly, 'Suffering, Justice, and the Politics of Becoming', in David Campbell and Michael J. Shapiro (eds.) *Moral Spaces: Rethinking Ethics and World Politics* (University of Minnesota Press, 1999), 136.

68 Lennart Meri, Address by the Estonian Minister of Foreign Affairs at the Opening Stage of the Helsinki Follow-up Meeting of the Conference on Security and Co-operation in Europe, 25 March 1992.

69 Lennart Meri, Remarks by the Estonian Minister of Foreign Affairs in Strasbourg, at the Council of Europe, 26 November 1991.

practically enact Meri's belief that 'Europe is not a continent, but a … philosophical, ethical, cultural, political and economic programme, of which Estonia … used to be an indivisible part and will be so again in the future'.[70] For the EU, the Convention was an instance of 'taking a deep breath' and discussing 'for the first time in history … how to maintain itself so that everything changes, and changes for the better'.[71]

The Convention's discussions around the division of competencies between the EU institutions and the member states polarized between the larger and smaller member states, with Estonia joining the initiative of sixteen small states against the creation of the European president's position and for sustaining the balance between the EU institutions and member states as provided by the EU foundational treaties. For Estonia's positions in the Convention, the bottom line was an emphasis on the effective and transparent functioning of the Union, along with the principle of equality between the EU's member states, including the rotation of the EU commissioners and the presidency of the Council of the EU.[72] Estonian representatives in the Convention were broadly in favour of the subsidiarity principle;[73] yet argued for the leanness and uncomplicatedness of the decision-making processes of the Union, for instance opposing the enlargement of the competencies of national parliaments, regions or regional committees to turn to the European Court in fear of potentially allowing for the transfer of domestic political issues to the EU level.[74] Estonia also emphatically opposed the qualified majority voting in the realm of taxation policy, along with the EU competencies expansion in this sphere.[75] As Tunne Kelam stressed, the competencies given to the EU institutions were

70 Lennart Meri, Solutions to the Baltic Crisis, Estonian Minister of Foreign Affairs at the 'Baltic Solutions' Conference in Tallinn, 2 March 1991.

71 Lennart Meri, 'Lennart Meri: Euroopa kaitsevõime on ajaloo madalaim', Interview to Tuuli Koch, *Eesti Päevaleht*, 22 February 2002, https://epl.delfi.ee/artikkel/50914857/lennart-meri-euroopa-kaitsevoime-on-ajaloo-madalaim (last accessed 3 April 2025).

72 Keit Kasemets and Elo Tuppits, 'Euroopa Liidu laienemine ja Eesti integratsioon ELi', 12 June 2003, www.digar.ee/arhiiv/et/download/22604 (last accessed 3 April 2025). It is notable that almost two decades post-accession, Central and Eastern Europeans are still severely under-represented in EU institutions. See *Geographical Representation in EU Leadership Observatory* 2021. A survey by European Democracy Consulting, https://eudemocracy.eu/wp-content/uploads/2021/02/Geographical-Representation-in-EU-Leadership-Observatory-2021.pdf (last accessed 3 April 2025).

73 The principle of subsidiarity is laid down in the Treaty on European Union (Art 5(3)), seeking to safeguard the ability of the Member States to take decisions and action in areas in which the EU does not have exclusive competence, as well as authorize intervention by the Union when the objectives of an action cannot be sufficiently achieved by the Member States. The principle essentially stands for powers being exercised as close to the citizen as possible (Art 10(3) of the Treaty on European Union).

74 Viljar Veebel, 'Eesti Euroopa tulevikudebatis', in Andres Kasekamp (ed.), *The Estonian Foreign Policy Yearbook* 2003 (The Estonian Foreign Policy Institute, 2003), 142.

75 Ibid., 147; see further, Viljar Veebel, 'Euroopa Liidu põhiseaduslik leping: Eesti ja Euroopa valikud', https://diplomaatia.ee/euroopa-liidu-pohiseaduslik-leping-eesti-ja-euroopa-valikud/ (last accessed 3 April 2025).

effectively to be understood as delegated or 'on loan' by the member states,[76] arguing against the European super-state and for Estonia's continuation as a 'dignified nation state' in a union of nation-states.[77]

In the meantime, Toomas Hendrik Ilves, in his capacity of the Estonian Minister for Foreign Affairs, maintained his belief that full participation in the Union's Common Foreign and Security Policy (CFSP) would make Estonia's 'national foreign policy stronger', as '[w]ith the weight of the EU behind us, we will be able to do more to pursue issues of vital importance to Estonia'.[78] As he averred,

> I believe that due to our size, history and geographic location, we are much more concerned with our external identity than most countries. And so we should be. As a small country, we must constantly develop our international image. So far, we have been fairly successful in developing a positive external image for ourselves. We are widely recognised as a rapidly developing small country and as a result, we are taken seriously on the international arena. In the coming years, our most pressing goal will be to consolidate this positive image. In my opinion, the most obvious and simple way to do this is to join the EU.[79]

In this quintessential case for vicarious sovereignty, Estonia is deemed to be bound to practice its sovereignty by moving it up to the playing field of the EU – arguably in order 'to be' in the first place.[80] An implicit tension between a 'nation-states-Europe' and a more congealed post-sovereign structure visible from the indicated positions of Kelam and Ilves was characteristic to Estonia's practical sovereignty-dilemmas at the cusp of the EU membership more generally.

In Section 2.4, I will delve in further detail into two exemplary speeches which present distinct political visions for the future of Europe: Lennart Meri's speech at the University of Turku on the role of small nations in the European Union (25 May 2000) and Toomas Hendrik Ilves's lecture on constructing a new Europe at the Humboldt University in Berlin (5 February 2001). Such a choice is motivated by three reasons: first, the two highlighted interventions are among the most

[76] Tunne Kelam,'Euroopa Tuleviku Konvent Euroopa ja Eesti tuleviku kujundamisel' (2001) 5 *Riigikogu Toimetised* 138.

[77] Cited in Ülo Toomsalu, 'Kreitzberg ja Kelam jõuavad viimasel hetkel konventi', *Äripäev*, 27 February 2002, www.aripaev.ee/uudised/2002/02/27/kreitzberg-ja-kelam-jouavad-viimasel-hetkel-konventi (last accessed 3 April 2025).

[78] Toomas Hendrik Ilves, 'EU Enlargement and Estonia's Identity on the International Stage', Remarks by the Minister of Foreign Affairs of Estonia, at the International Conference 'Estonia and the European Union' at the National Library, Tallinn, 5 November 1999. Yet, it should be noted that, in later practice, Estonia has been rather reluctant towards surrendering its competencies in security and defence – the traditional purview of state sovereignty – to the EU, preferring to pool its sovereignty in this sphere with NATO instead.

[79] Ibid.

[80] Cf. Erik Ringmar, 'The Relevance of International Law: A Hegelian Interpretation of a Peculiar 17th-Century Preoccupation' (1995) 21 *Review of International Studies* 87, 95. A critical take of this position would suggest that Estonia never managed to grow into a proper state before the elites hurried to share its newly regained sovereignty with the EU.

systematic and visionary political engagements with the European constitutional future debates in Estonia. Secondly, both engage directly with an earlier speech which marked the launch of the political debate over the future constitution of Europe – namely, the German Foreign Minister Joschka Fischer's 'From Confederation to Federation – Thoughts on the Finality of European Integration' at the Humboldt University in Berlin (12 May 2000).[81] Last but not least, both Meri's and Ilves' interventions were delivered at universities, enabling them to appeal on academic freedom as a cloak for speaking more openly in personal, rather than official, capacity.[82] While these speeches come from a different era compared to today, they illuminate a critical juncture in Estonia's political journey of 'becoming European'.

2.4 EUROPEAN FUTURE THROUGH THE ESTONIAN LOOKING-GLASS

Lennart Meri's speech 'The Role of Small Nations in the European Community', held at the University of Turku on 25 May 2000, makes a strong case for the democracy of Europe and the development potential of the European Community depending on the sustained diversity on the continent. Accordingly, keeping an optimal balance between large and small states appears as the key task for the demiurges of the European future as:

> The survival and development of small nations is the key issue of the future of Europe. Europe needs small nations as much as we need Europe. Because the strength of the European Union does not lie in its size – the strength of Europe comes from its diversity.

In this lecture, Meri focuses on the intensity of cultural and political transfers in the historical European space in order to shed light on this 'little peninsula of the Eurasian continent' having 'managed to become the development engine of the

[81] Fischer's federalist vision of the EU was followed by the takes of the French Prime Minister Lionel Jospin, the German *Bundeskanzler* Gerhard Schröder, the Finnish President Tarja Halonen, the President of the European Parliament Nicole Fontaine, the President of the European Commission Romano Prodi and, *inter alia*, the Foreign Minister of Estonia, Toomas Hendrik Ilves.

[82] 'Politicians also taste academic enjoyment on these rare occasions when they manage to express their experimental thoughts in front of an academic auditorium.' Lennart Meri, 'The Role of Small Nations in the European Community', The President of the Republic of Estonia at the University of Turku, 25 May 2000. Ilves, in his turn, expressed his pleasure 'to be able to speak today at Humboldt University, where a tradition of sorts has been established to offer foreign ministers the chance to speak of their personal visions, unencumbered by the straight-jacket of *ex officio* restrictions or silenced by the implications of their personal views for their government's official position. If Chatham House has given us the "Chatham House Rules", then perhaps we can begin to speak of the "Humboldt University Freedom".' Toomas Hendrik Ilves, 'Constructing a New Europe', *Lecture by the Estonian Minister of Foreign Affairs at Humboldt University*, Berlin, 5 February 2001.

entire world'. Through his trademark cornucopia of metaphoric and allegoric language, Meri's Turku lecture is a powerful hymn to Europe's cultural multitude and diversity, for the potency of Europe is deemed to lie precisely in being 'different next to each other'.[83] The performative power of the Turku speech act reaches a climax in Meri's strong (if implicitly made) riposte to the then mulling ideas about a 'multi-speed' Europe led by a 'core engine' of France and Germany as an answer to the efficiency problem of the institutionalized Europe:

> Europe does not worship quantity, but quality. 'Big is beautiful' is alien to Europe, maybe because Europe itself is small and its greatness is first and foremost spiritual. The sum of the cultural nations and states of our tiny continent creates the miracle that we call Europe. This extraordinary multitude of cultures has without a doubt been the result of the geographical multitude of Europe, a present from nature, like any natural resources. And like in the case of natural resources, it took us until recently to learn how to appreciate them and treat them sparingly. Or, if you wish, to pretend being sparing.[84]

Accordingly, Meri maintains that Joschka Fischer's eurofederalism should remain an 'academic excurse' rather than 'find application in the real world'[85] for, ultimately, 'the ethical imperative of the European Union is in the fact that the common denominator on its diverse cultural palette consists of common values of democracy, *one common goal, but every state will find its own way to achieve these goals and principles*' (emphasis added). Hence, small states should not be 'run over' in the debates over the future constitution and set-up of Europe, nor should the internal reforms of the EU take place on account of the expansion of the Union. Meri's ode to state sovereignty[86] is tempered with a reminder of a special political mission of the small states, to make the voice of this 'silent majority … heard loud and clear in the world and especially in Europe'. This mission has gained renewed significance with the expansion of the EU, for at the end of the day:

> The big ones need the small ones in order to maintain the balance in Europe that drives it further, because there are always certain conflicts between the big ones and the presence of the small ones is needed to overcome them. Small states are the lubricating oil of Europe and the mortar of Europe.[87]

83 Such a proposition has an ironic ring to it today, considering the Commission's infringement procedure against Poland for violations of EU law by its Constitutional Tribunal.

84 Lennart Meri, 'The Role of Small Nations in the European Community', The President of the Republic of Estonia at the University of Turku, 25 May 2000.

85 Note that Germany's 2021 coalition agreement asserts support to the idea of a constitutional convention and further development of the Union towards a federal European state. For a summary in English, see 'Germany's Coalition Agreement for a new federal Government', www2.deloitte.com/dl/en/pages/legal/articles/koalitionsvertrag-deutschland.html (last accessed 3 April 2025).

86 'Every nation has the possibility, the necessity and the obligation of self-determination. Independent statehood is the supreme self-realisation of every nation. This can be done only once. When established once, it is principally inalienable. The Finns and the Estonians have taken this step during the last century.' Ibid.

87 Ibid.

The Turku lecture is, therefore, an important prompt in the debate over the future political design of the EU, in characteristic defiance of what Meri had previously described as the feudal eurocentrism of European enlargement debates.[88] Just as the issue of NATO and the EU enlargement *per se*, Meri's intervention on the role of small states in the EU was to serve as a reminder that 'Estonia is not a geographical object, but a constitutional subject'; nor is Europe (or *should be*) the court of Louis XIV where only the specially selected are invited.[89]

A much more federalism–sympathetic vision for Europe's political future was put forth by the then foreign minister of Estonia, Toomas Hendrik Ilves, in his lecture 'Constructing a new Europe' at the Humboldt University in Berlin, on 5 February 2001. This intervention has remained perhaps the best elaborated Estonian political contribution to the discussion on the European constitutionalism – if emphatically delivered in personal, rather than state representative's capacity.[90] It is also the one most directly engaging in dialogue with Joschka Fischer's inaugural intervention of the high-level political debate on the future of the European constitutionalism. In his Humboldt lecture, Ilves called for building on the eighteenth-century early American federalism as 'the intellectual source ... for the future of EU integration', since:

> It was 18th-century America that grappled with the issues virtually identical to those facing Europe today. These include the need to balance the interests of large and small constituent states; the question of how to distribute competencies, i.e. – what should be the prerogatives of the central government and should not; the creation of a monetary union and mechanisms to ensure a common defence.[91]

Consequently, the lecture took a stab at 'three issues of a fundamental nature': namely, (1) the cultural and psychological adjustment of the old members with the new members, arguably 'differ[ing] fundamentally from those in the present EU Member States as regards their national emotional traditions, experiences, interests and value judgments';[92] (2) small vs. large members; and last not least; and (3) democratic legitimacy vs. effective decision-making. Instead of the deepening vs. widening dilemma of the Union, Europe's future functioning, per Ilves, was solving the 'core issue' of keeping the EU legitimate, yet effective among subjects 'of greatly differing size and economic power'. Ilves's case is for the reconsideration of a federalist approach, to clarify 'a fundamental misunderstanding about the meaning of Federalism and

[88] Lennart Meri, The President of the Republic of Estonia on the Security Policy of Estonia at the St Gallen Forum on Security Policy, 25 January 1995.

[89] Ibid.

[90] '... what I have to say today is my own view, and not necessarily the view of the Government of Estonia. It is a personal view expressed in the same spirit and manner as Joschka Fischer spoke here nine months ago'. Toomas Hendrik Ilves, 'Constructing a New Europe', Lecture by the Estonian Minister of Foreign Affairs at Humboldt University, Berlin, 5 February 2001.

[91] Ibid.

[92] Ilves cites here a past president of the European parliament, German social democrat Klaus Hänsch (originally in *Beitrag für die Frankfurter Rundschau*, 23 February 2000).

Constitutionalism', on the one hand, and acknowledging that 'the solutions offered by a federalist approach resolve rather than create the problems we fear', on the other.

According to Ilves, then, if the EU had taken up issues that once were the sole prerogative of the nation-state by the agreement of all the member states, the citizen-to-state relationship emerged in the focus of the Union as a result. Thus, a move from the Union's 'sole reliance on the community method' was deemed necessary, in order to 'take into account the established norms of democratic decision-making that lie at the core of each democratic nation-state's legitimacy'. To beat the Euroscepticism for the perceived lack of transparency, legal understandability and clarity of decision-making, Ilves made a case for a federalist approach – not in the last order to ease the structural tension between small and large constituent members. For Ilves, 'the crux of the dilemma facing the *finalité* of Europe' was in maintaining a similar sense of democratic legitimacy and transparency in EU decision-making that people were accustomed to within their own countries.

The model according to which to mould the enlarged EU parliament was accordingly to be sought from the first 150 years of the American federalism (or the federalism of John Jay, Alexander Hamilton and James Madison) rather than the contemporary American prototype. Hence, Ilves's case for a two-chamber European Parliament, 'to balance the legitimate democratic concerns of the Large (through a proportionally elected lower chamber) with the justified fears of the Small (by way of equal representation in an upper chamber of the legislature)'. For Ilves, a strong bicameral European parliament was the key to EU's democratic legitimacy – yet remained unachievable as long as the single chamber model with semi-proportional representation was to be maintained.

Ilves further took an issue with subsidiarity (aptly described by Joschka Fischer in his own 2000 Humboldt lecture as 'a subject that is . . . discussed by everyone and understood by virtually no one'). Bothered by the principle's divine allusions to authority 'from above' due to the idea of subsidiarity originating from the Catholic Church, Ilves recalls the EU's ultimate authority coming from the citizen – and, hence, the Union's ability to appeal to the will of the electorate – and nothing but. A 'Lockean-Rousseauan vision of bottom-up legitimacy' was accordingly called for to replace the 'Hegelian, trickle-down theory of government in which the higher body pushes decision-making downwards' in order to 'achieve that noble goal of a Europe of Citizens'. Subsequently, not just nation states, but really the citizens were to accede some decision-making upward to the Union.

In sum, besides engaging with 'the dreaded "F-word", that is to say, "Federalism",' Ilves called for a no-frills approach to the EU constitution:

> you can have a constitution without automatically ending up with a super or supra-state. A constitution is a way to codify the relationship between citizens and the political process. But now the Union, with the consent of its members, has begun to deal with such fundamental issues as the citizen–state relationship, issues that previously were the monopoly of the nation-state. Given this development, we need to formalize and legally enshrine this relation in such a way so that everyone

> understands what he can and cannot do, what rights he enjoys and what the duties of those structures created to make the Union work are.[93]

An EU constitution, codifying the Union decision-making process according to a federalist model, was needed precisely for the aforementioned reasons, maintained Ilves. His Humboldt lecture remains a distinct Estonian contribution to the fleeting utopian moment of the European constitutional imaginary.

2.5 CONCLUSION

This chapter has probed a novel conceptual lens of *vicarious sovereignty* for making sense of the Estonian way of reconciling its long-coveted state sovereignty with its equally desired European belonging. In the wind of searching a secure international home for the Estonian state, vicarious sovereignty or the idea of elevated ontological security and international agency by pooling national sovereignty at the EU level emerged as the Estonian way of 'becoming European'. Such a path was far from prescribed, nor has it been failsafe from the 'neo-Westphalian' backlashes which have recently emerged in the context of varying political sensibilities and responses to the migration pressures on the EU more widely.

The Estonian variety of constitutionalism and its European constitutional imaginaries hence raise the question of the broader applicability of the vicarious sovereignty concept within the CEE region and beyond. If the EU member states arguably feature three distinct varieties of constitutionalism – 'post-fascist constitutionalism', 'evolutionary constitutionalism' and 'post-communist constitutionalism'[94] – how does the concept of vicarious sovereignty fare in the constitutional regimes of other states with similar historical trajectories and their respective relationships to the project of European integration? The post-communist constitutions have been characterized as by and large more protective of sovereignty (hence, '*souverainist*') compared to most of their Western European counterparts.[95] According to a Sigrid Rehling Larsen's trenchant assessment, post-communist constitutionalism beckons the return of ethno-nationalism to European constitutionalism for it is embedded in the notion of the sovereign power of the people (conceived of as the ethnically homogenous nation) as the source of all public authority.[96]

93 Ilves, 'Constructing a New Europe'.

94 These ideal types are distinguished by 'radically different notions of what a constitution is, in what ways it creates and constrains the power of the state, and what the foundational ideas of the constitution of public authority are'. Signe Rehling Larsen, 'Varieties of Constitutionalism in the European Union' (2021) 84 *Modern Law Review* 477, 481.

95 See Albi, *EU Enlargement*, 24–25.

96 'At its heart post-communist constitutionalism celebrates what is feared most within post-fascist constitutionalism, namely, the ideas of nationalism, the nation-state and national sovereignty. … Democracy means *national democracy* celebrating the self-determination of the nation finally liberated from imperial oppression.' Larsen, 'Varieties of Constitutionalism', 496, 497.

The concept of vicarious sovereignty and the Estonian practice of it in the run-up to the EU membership contests such a wholesale diagnosis. Compared to Poland's and Hungary's recent reservations about the limitation of sovereignty entailed in EU membership and thus the occasional viewing of the European project as a new form of foreign dominance,[97] Estonia's pooling of sovereignty has been publicly more effortless and enthusiastic throughout the accession process and membership, not least for the existential fear of Russia. Of course, resonating with the broader concerns over the EU endangering rather than protecting democracy, the Estonian national conservatives have similarly viewed the country's 'scaling up' of its sovereignty to the level of the EU as a worrying sign of provincialization – potentially leading to the loss of sovereignty *in toto* and the collapse of the society in the long-run.[98] Taken together, however, the Estonian interventions in the debate on the form and *finalité* of Europe considerably nuance, and at times disturb, a sweeping reading of the 'imitation imperative' and the 'copycat mind' of post-1989 Central and Eastern Europe.[99]

Nonetheless, the conceptual proposition of vicarious sovereignty calls for further empirical applications across other cases in the region, most immediately on the other two Baltic states. The Estonian case illustrates that small does not have to mean peripheral when envisioning the constitutional future for Europe.[100] At a conceptual level, the idea of vicarious sovereignty in and through the EU could be potentially further explored in relation to Jennifer Mitzen's notion of a 'homespace' – where home is conceived 'as hearth and not container and borders as skin or membrane not wall'.[101] Juxtaposed to the other macropolitical idea of home – that is, homeland – homespace is accordingly conceptualized as 'an articulation of "being with becoming"' which is 'located, but not reducible to its location'.[102] Just as the notion of homespace seeks to 'loosen ... the stranglehold of Westphalian territoriality on our political – and theoretical – imagination',[103] the concept of vicarious sovereignty stretches our understanding of the sovereignty games and paradoxes of a small East European state in the late sovereign European polity at the turn of a millennium.

[97] Wojciech Sadurski, *Constitutionalism and the Enlargement of Europe* (Oxford University Press, 2012), 67.

[98] E.g., Jaak Valge, 'Eesti suveräänsusest ja provintsistumisest', *Objektiiv*, 23 November 2015, https://objektiiv.ee/eesti-suveraansusest-ja-provintsistumisest/ (last accessed 3 April 2025).

[99] See Ivan Krastev and Stephen Holmes, *The Light That Failed. A Reckoning* (Penguin Books, 2019).

[100] Cf. Katzenstein, 'United Germany in an Integrating Europe', 5.

[101] Jennifer Mitzen, 'Feeling at Home in Europe: Migration, Ontological Security, and the Political Psychology of EU Bordering', 39 *Political Psychology* 1373, 1384.

[102] Ibid., 1375.

[103] Ibid., 1384.

3

From Federation to External Constraint

Europe in the Italian Constitutional Imagination

Marco Goldoni

3.1 INTRODUCTION

The aim of this chapter is to offer a study of the role of Europe (and European integration) in the Italian political and constitutional imagination. The argument tracks three discreet moments which have shaped the way European integration (and more generally the horizon of European political unity) has been perceived by Italian constitutional actors.[1] In a first brief, but intense and crucial, phase, the position of the main actors identified 'Europe' as an horizon for political action. In this phase, the majority of Italian political and institutional actors partook an idea of Europe as a project for a federation or confederation for the exercise of collective political action. Central for tracking this commitment is to analyse how the political parties that organised the resistance against the occupying Nazi forces and the Fascists talked about Europe in their writings and newspapers. Europe is not the main or only political priority (any reference to Europe comes together with national and State reconstruction), but it is seen by most political parties as an essential component of collective political action. In brief, there is an implication that it is not possible to realise political freedom unless a constitutional structure (often imagined as federal) is organised at the continental level.

The second phase is marked by a certain level of displacement of Europe from the core of the constitutional imagination, or at least from the narratives that support the programmes of the political parties during the electoral campaign (in 1946) for the Constituent Assembly and (in 1948) for the first general elections. This phase began in 1946, but it provided a framework that would apply until (at least) the Single European Act in 1986. This phase saw the adoption of a neutral (and rather invisible to the public opinion) image of the European Economic Community, but

[1] This tripartite temporal organisation dovetails (with some minor differences) with the interpretation of the trajectory of collective political action in European integration provided by Michael Wilkinson, *Authoritarian Liberalism* (Oxford University Press, 2021).

it is important because it paved the way for the hegemony of a specific way of looking at Europe that would emerge with the fall of the Wall.

The third phase brings Europe back to the centre stage, but this time as an 'external bound' for domestic political power. Collective political agency is limited, when not quashed, by inputs coming from the European Union and its governing staples: the governance of the economic and monetary union. At this stage, in the imagination of the majority of Italian political actors, Europe has nothing to do (anymore) with enabling political agency. It constitutes an important point of reference for the activity of governing society because it is perceived as authoritative and as a vector of modernisation, though it is an essential component of a frightening move toward political passivity. Tellingly, the main act of political resistance, usually coming from the right-wing side of the parliamentary spectrum, becomes one not of political action but of victimisation. As a consequence, the horizon of constitutional imagination shrinks remarkably: either Italy should do its homework as demanded by 'Europe' or Italy is a victim of Eurocrats and can only suffer their diktats.

There are several lessons that can be learned by reconstructing the different narratives that animate Italian constitutional imagination and its relation to Europe. The argument of this chapter is based on the assumption of the material context that breathes life into different political and constitutional imaginations: based on the concept of the material constitution, it entails that the development of a constitutional imagination is based on the struggles around the organisation of social production and reproduction.[2] Furthermore, following recent research on the formation of constitutional imaginations,[3] I will assume that the way we understand the value (and assess the potential) of political action is internal to the constitutional imagination itself. In this sense, the constitutional imagination of Europe is not an ideological supra-structure that emerges out of an already established material organisation. To the contrary, political action is part of the struggle for the formation of the spectrum of constitutional imagination.

3.2 QUESTIONS OF METHOD: NARRATIVES

Before moving to the analysis of the first phase (the resistance and the end of WWII), it is necessary to step back and explain the approach adopted in this chapter. The

[2] For an (historical and theoretical) overview of the notion of material constitution, see Marco Goldoni and Michael Wilkinson (eds.), *Cambridge Handbook on the Material Constitution* (Cambridge University Press, 2023).

[3] See Jan Komárek, 'European Constitutional Imaginaries: Utopias, Ideologies and the Other', in Jan Komárek (ed.), *European Constitutional Imaginaries: Between Ideology and Utopia* (Oxford University Press, 2023). In this programmatic introduction, Komárek also urges constitutional lawyers to study imaginaries by considering the context of the contemporary political economy.

reconstruction of the shifting place of the European Communities (and later the European Union) in the Italian constitutional imagination is indeed premised on some methodological assumptions which can only be briefly sketched out in the following paragraphs.[4]

Constitutional imagination is a way of giving form and meaning to the political order of a society. Martin Loughlin provides an insightful starting point when he notes that '[t]he constitutional imagination refers to the manner in which constitutions can harness the power of narrative, symbol, ritual and myth to project an account of political existence in ways that shape – and re-shape – political reality'.[5] The idea is that perceptions of reality are impacted (and fundamentally organised) by the operations of the faculty of imagination. Constitutional orders are no exception to this rule. The way we tell stories and narratives, or re-interpret myths, about the origins or the directions of a constitutional order are ways of moulding the latter. The struggle around the formation of the constitutional imagination is, therefore, a political struggle by definition. It is possible to push Loughlin's point further: it is not only that constitutional orders can borrow the political energy provided by narratives, symbols and myths. It is also the case that, following Robert Cover's iconic statement, '[f]or every constitution there is an epic, for each decalogue a scripture'.[6] This point brings with it two dimensions. On the anthropological level, narratives and myths are not seen as irrational folklore, but as a necessary component of the social condition. On the level of political action, the immanent presence of narratives and myths is also a source of constant proliferation of competing perspectives. In fact, the origin and development of constitutional orders cannot be severed from their narratives and the conflicts that developed around them.

The reconstruction of the constitutional imagination is a daunting task. As highlighted by the given quotes, the constitutional imagination of a social group cannot be neatly separated from social imagination itself. Moreover, there is nothing like an available and stable monolithic constitutional imagination. Part and parcel of the logic intrinsic to constitutional imagination is that there are, unavoidably, competing visions of how an order ought to be conceived in terms of its past, present and future.[7] As Cover noted, there is a jurisgenetic push behind the proliferation of narratives and myths in the interpretation of constitutional orders. For example, understanding a political order in terms of a system or as a project has profound implications over the operations of constitutional actors.[8] The interpretation of a

4 The approach adopted here is heavily influenced by the following works: Robert Cover, 'Nomos and Narrative' (1983) 94 *Harvard Law Review* 4; Paul Kahn, *Origins of Order* (Yale University Press, 2019); Yves Citton, *Mythocracie* (Editions Amsterdam, 2010); Furio Jesi, *Time and Festivity* (Seagulls Books, 2020).

5 Martin Loughlin, 'Constitutional Imagination' (2015) 78 *Modern Law Review* 1.

6 Cover, 'Nomos and Narrative', 4.

7 For a classic statement that political imagination is perspectival, see Hannah Arendt, *Lectures on Kant's Critique of Judgment* (Chicago University Press, 1982).

8 The reference is to Kahn, *Origins of Order*, 10.

constitutional order might swing between different conceptions according to the age. Furthermore, even in the presence of commonly recognised symbols and values, their interpretation will necessarily generate alternative and often incompatible visions. Let's insist on this point: an inherent component of the constitutional order is the struggle for the formation of its imagination. If constitutional law is a 'bridge' that connects two states of affairs, the imagination constitutes the building material of the bridge. In other words, imagining is an inherent component of ordering.

3.3 QUESTIONS OF METHOD: SUBJECTS

These points suggest that the formation of constitutional imagination is a battlefield with many actors involved and it is not external to the wider social imagination.[9] Given the complexity of the task it is mandatory to narrow down the scope of the investigation. In what follows, I will focus only on narratives put forward by the most important political actors in Italian constitution-making: political parties. A *caveat* has to be inserted at this stage. It is indeed a relatively accepted thesis that mass political parties were crucial players in the reconstruction of Italy after the end of WWII.[10] Parties assumed constitutional relevance as the transmission belt between the State, its apparatuses and civil society. The prominent role of the political party in the Italian constitutional order was already a topic of debate among public lawyers during the Fascist age and the attention paid to their development did not stop with the end of the Fascist regime.[11] Political parties were the crucial actors during the last phase of the war for the establishment of the new Italian government after the armistice with the Allies (September 1943). They were also the point of reference for communication with the Allies. Last but not least, they were the main organising forces of the resistance in the North of Italy after September 1943, where Germany had established a new 'Social republic', with a government based in the Lombardy region, whose head of government was, again, Mussolini (this time, however, imposed by Germany). To cut a long story short, political parties were the main organising force of what was, de facto, a double war: a war of liberation from the foreign occupant and a civil war between the Italian fascist government and Italian partisans undergoing in the North of Italy.[12]

9 Recently, many legal and political theorists have expanded on this point by providing important insights. See, for example, the renaissance of sociological constitutionalism and the attention paid to social imaginaries. Cf Paul Blokker and Chris Thornhill (eds.), *Sociological Constitutionalism* (Cambridge University Press, 2017).

10 See, ex multiplis, the recent reconstruction in Paolo Pombeni, *La questione costituzionale in Italia* (Il Mulino, 2016), chapter 1.

11 For an encompassing analysis, see Massimiliano Gregorio, *Parte totale. Le dottrine costituzionali del partito politico fra Ottocento e Novecento* (Giuffre', 2008).

12 The classic text in support of this interpretation is Claudio Pavone, *Una Guerra civile* (Bollati Boringhieri, 1991).

It should be added that, in 1945, the centrality of political parties is far from being an Italian peculiarity. Indeed, political regimes organised around competition between parties were spreading across Europe, though the crisis of 1929 generated a backlash with the rise of the single party system. Yet, the political party, whether in a single or multiparty political system, provided the centre of gravity of many European political systems. Though political parties were not the only organised collective subjects in the newly established republican political regime (trade unions were also well-organised and effective), they played a crucial role in the constituent process and, later, in the application of the constitution. Rather correctly, the republican political regime has been defined as 'a republic of parties'.[13] The capacity of parties to organise political action was quite successful and effective in different spheres of the Italian society: from the workplace to education and healthcare, from industrial politics to new forms of social security.[14] The political and symbolic capital cumulated through the resistance made possible, at a certain point, to put forward a credible narrative of the new constitutional order as a project (the turning point could be located around 1958) with a set of narratives and myths that would be capable of mobilising ample sectors of the population for a couple of decades.

The transformation of the organisation of political parties into catch-all parties and, later on, into machines for capturing electoral consent and distributing privileges (with the annexed loss of representativity)[15] is a relatively recent development whose consequences for the constitutional order are becoming increasingly visible. Formally speaking, political parties are still the 'bearers' of the constitutional order and, in this sense, their strive for shaping the collective political imagination is still of some relevance. But one can doubt whether they are still capable of generating enough political energy for interpreting the constitutional order as a project. Given the focus of this chapter on Europe, the latter point is of remarkable importance. As we shall see, there is a direct connection between the place of the idea of Europe within the Italian constitutional imagination and the changing function of political parties. An analysis of the place of Europe within that imagination also teaches an important lesson on the subjects that steer the governing function. Post-Maastricht, though political parties retain a crucial role as the main conduit of inputs coming from other sources, they have lost their grip on the constitutional imagination in favour of other (often technocratic, but also economic) elites. A proof of this incapacity is the failure of the two formal attempts to change large parts of the

[13] Cf the influential reconstruction by Pietro Scoppola, *La repubblica dei partiti* (Il Mulino, 1991).

[14] A recent analysis of the role of elites and political parties in the Constituent Assembly sheds a new light on this point: Lucia Rubinelli, 'Elites, Democracies, and Parties in the Italian Constituent Debates, 1946–1947' (2020) 27 *Constellations* 199.

[15] Carlo Invernizzi Accetti and Fabio Wolkestein, 'The Crisis of Party Democracy, Cognitive Mobilization, and the Case for Making Parties more Deliberative' (2017) 111 *American Political Science Review* 97; Piero Ignazi, *Party and Democracy* (Oxford University Press, 2017).

written constitution in 2006 (under the impulse of the Berlusconi government) and in 2016 (under the initiative of the Renzi government). In both cases, the governing parties were not able to convince the citizens to vote, in a constitutional referendum, in favour of the constitutional reform.

The rest of the chapter will focus on the narratives adopted by the main political parties during crucial moments of constitutional development in Italian history. I will look at their political programmes, documents and sometimes official declarations published with a view to track the salience and the function of the relation with Europe and the perspective of political and economic unity on the continent. This investigation is far from exhaustive, but it will allow us to show that the change in the constitutional imagination of political parties corresponded to a change in the self-perception of their role in the national and supranational orders. Accordingly, Europe's place in the constitutional imagination mutated as well. The main thesis guiding this reconstruction is that Europe became a different signifier according to the self-perception of the political system's capacity for agency.

3.4 1943–1945: THE FEDERATION IN THE WRITINGS OF THE RESISTANCE

The obvious starting point for understanding the place of Europe in the Italian constitutional imagination is the resistance organised by the political parties initially ostracised by the Fascist regime, after the armistice in September 1943. The relevance of that resistance for the liberation of Italy and its role in the formation of the republican constitutional order have been subject of academic and political scrutiny for decades.[16] The impact of that movement is still a matter of controversy, and this is not surprising as, among many other things, the legitimacy of the origin of constitutional order is at stake. The thorniest issue concerns the role of the resistance as the main inspirational source of the new republican constitution. It is often said that the crucial function of the resistance for the liberation of the country and the influence over the proceedings of the constituent assembly is a myth (inspirational or evil according to the point of view) because, ultimately, it was only thanks to the intervention of the Allies that the country was liberated from the Nazis and the Fascists. Whatever the assessment, there is no denial that the protagonists of the organised resistance had been the political parties (six, in this specific case) banned by the fascist regime and these will later be the main constitution-making actors. They benefitted from the political capital they cumulated by fighting in the North of Italy and from their organisational capacities. The combination of these two factors made these actors the bearers of the constitutional order and, in that capacity, as steering agents of the public opinion.

[16] One example is represented by Sergio Luzzatto, *'Partigia': Una storia della resistenza* (Mondadori, 2013). Another enlightening analysis is offered by G. Filippetta, L'estate che imparammo a sparare (Feltrinelli, 2018).

The Resistance movements produced (with one important exception) a narrative about Europe through the publication (often clandestine and illegal) of pamphlets, newspapers and journals which would have the task of persuading the population not only of the necessity of fighting Nazi-Fascism, but of the virtues of a politically united Europe. The importance of these writings has been rightly emphasised. They do provide the main materials for tracking how these movements of resistance and political parties would see themselves in the future constitutional order. The importance of the Resistance writings cannot be overestimated in the reconstruction of the role a united Europe played in their constitutional projects. This is valid not only for Italy, but for all European movements of resistance, as noted by an historian of European integration:

> They [the writings of the resistance movements] were not marginal efforts, produced in addition to military actions by a few intellectuals. On the contrary, for years, during which other forms of opposition were hardly possible, their writings *were* the Resistance. The most important function of the movements could only be to formulate ethical and political principles that would help people to live through the totalitarian experience, and that would strengthen their opposition to it. *Most groups began their existence in order to publish and distribute illegal newspapers or leaflets.*[17]

Indeed, the call for a European federation was a transnational phenomenon shared (though not unanimously) across many sectors of the Resistance across the continent. As noted by Walter Lipgens,[18] there were many parallels between the documents produced by the Resistance about Europe and its future. The Italian Resistance was part of wider constellations of movements whose activities and publications presented certain common traits around the question of the future of Europe. It was not only the Italian parties of the Resistance which identified in the political unity of the continent a precondition for the restauration of democracy and the realisation of political freedom. This was a position shared by many movements and parties at least until 1945. It is known that documents and manifestos were circulating among multiple resistance movements, creating a dialogue between national experiences. There were also conferences organised (especially in 1944) for exchanging ideas and putting pressures on the Allies by advocating for the need of a European federation.

An analysis of the documents and key publications by members of the resistance and, most importantly, of the political parties shows that the commitment to

[17] Walter Lipgens, 'European Federation in the Political Thought of Resistance Movements' (1968) 1 *Central European History* 5, 8 (emphasis added). The point made by Lipgens is essential for understanding the analysis of these writings. It is precisely the commitment to the projects advocated in those writings that gave to the parties born (or reconstituted) with the Resistance their constitutional legitimacy.

[18] Walter Lipgens, *Documents on the History of European Integration* (De Gruyter, 1984).

economic and political unity of the continent was a position shared by all non-communist political forces. The source of this conviction is to be found in the common fight against Nazism and Fascism. The opinion of many political actors was that this fight created a bond of solidarity among European peoples that made political unity not only possible but necessary. It is not surprising that the totalising nature of the war was perceived as a turning point and a unique political opportunity.[19]

This narrative (of the necessity of European political unity) is adopted and developed following the same thread in many countries. In Italy, the activity of publication and propaganda in favour of a European federation developed against the background of the drafting of the Ventotene manifesto by Altiero Spinelli, Ernesto Rossi and Eugenio Colorni.[20] It is fair to say that this is the most influential document produced during WWII in support of a European federation and it gave birth to a strong (but, in the long-term, not majoritarian) federalist movement. An investigation into the perception of Europe in the imagination of Italian political parties cannot but begin from here. As known, Spinelli and his co-authors drafted the Manifesto in 1941 while under arrest and in confinement on the small island of Ventotene. The document started with a harsh critique of the national State and claimed that only a supranational federation could provide the institutional architecture for peace and political freedom. In brief, their narrative was based on the displacement of the main conflict between left and right with the conflict between the national and the supranational. However, the Ventotene Manifesto was not the product of an organised political force confident about its constituent capacity. It is for this reason that the Manifesto contains an a-political view of the European federation. Written under the shock of the success of the Nazi army and the collapse of continental democracies, the Manifesto does not convey a particular optimistic message about collective political action. It is probably this cautiousness that later made it into a classic point of reference for the federalist side.

Be that as it may, the manifesto served as catalyst for the rise of a federalist movement which was created in 1943 with the aim of building a transnational network of political forces in support of the creation of a European federation. This aim translated into a specific operative approach: influencing the choices and

[19] Lipgens summarises this perception and its impact on the European political imagination in an effective way: 'it was the prime fact of this war – in contrast to the first World War – that (with the exception of Great Britain and four small nations, which Hitler permitted to remain neutral) all states on the European continent collapsed under Hitler's attack. Regimes of different social and political character were overwhelmed by the Germans, and thus demonstrated that they were no longer able to guarantee their people that minimum of security and independence that is the basic reason for their existence . . . The historical significance and the effect of this violent lesson on the people of continental Europe can hardly be overestimated'. Walter Lipgens, 'European Federation in the Political Thought of Resistance Movements during World War II' (1968) 1 *Central European History* 5, 6.

[20] Altiero Spinelli and Rossi Ernesto, *Il manifesto di Ventotene* [1941] (Mondadori, 2006).

the positions of key political parties, with a special emphasis on their youth sections.[21] The movement also published a (clandestine) journal (*L'Unità Europea*) with interventions from some of the most prominent and respected supporters of the federalist idea. In the second issue, one of the co-authors of the Ventotene Manifesto explained that the solution of the problems affecting Europe was to create political unity on a continental scale and invited all political forces to work together for a 'European Revolution'.[22] Behind the project of a continental political unity there was the idea of a third regional force, relatively autonomous and distant from the two rising super-powers, the United States and Russia.

The cultural and political activity of the Federalist Movement achieved important outcomes in two cultural areas: the leftist liberal and a section of the socialist party. The first one gave rise to the Action Party (Partito D'Azione), which gathered many intellectuals and partisans and adopted from the very beginning a pro-European and federalist position.[23] In several documents, often written by Spinelli, and circulated in 1944, with the fear of an increasing influence of the Allies over the future of European unity, the Action Party proposed to operate the alliance among the resistant political parties on two tracks: a national one, revolving around the administration of the future Italian republic, and a supranational one, with a clause to be inserted in the future constitution of a transferring of sovereignty to a democratic European federation.[24] Part and parcel of the narrative put forward by the Action Party publications was insisting on the timeliness of European political unity but, unlike Spinelli's approach based on the primacy of the supranational, most of the writings maintained that the supranational was functional to national reconstruction.[25]

The impact of the federalist movement was possibly even more felt on socialist political culture. Before 1943, only a few (eclectic and heterodox) members of the party were advocating a federalist outcome.[26] As it could be predicted, socialist international solidarity would not represent a sufficient ground for the autonomous value of a European political federation. For this reason, the fact that, during the period starting from 1943, the publications of the Socialist party addressed the federal question with a certain radicality is quite remarkable and, possibly, a proof of the penetration of the Federalist movement's ideas within the party. Of course, the

21 For a history of the Federalist European Movement and its initiatives until 1954, see Sergio Pistone (ed.), *I movimenti per l'unita' Europea dal 1945 al 1954* (Jaca Book, 1992), 17–61.

22 Ernesto Rossi, 'Premesse sociali del federalismo', *Unità Europea*, August 1943, issue 2, 3.

23 For an influential analysis, see Giovanni de Luna, *Storia del Partito d'Azione 1942–1947* (Feltrinelli, 1982).

24 I follow the reconstruction offered in Raffaella Cinquanta, *Partigiani di tutta Europa, unitevi!* (Il Mulino, 2020), chapter II.

25 Cf Daniela Preda, 'La scelta europea di Ferruccio Parri', in Fabio Zucca (ed.), *Europeismo e federalismo in Lombardia* (Il Mulino, 2007).

26 On debate in the Socialist Party before 1943, cf Gaetano Arfé, 'Il percorso dell'europeismo socialista', in *I socialisti e l'Europa* (Franco Angeli, 1989), chapter 1.

socialist party still considered the socialist revolution as the ultimate end of its political organisation but, from 1943, in many sectors of the party, the European federation came to be seen as a necessary step towards a socialist upheaval. The official position of the party was expressed in the Political declaration of 25 August 1943, published in the clandestine newspaper *L'Avanti*, where we can read the following: 'the Socialist Party rejects policies of political isolation and economic autarchy, and it considers international solidarity of proletarian parties as an essential element of their action. International solidarity is an instrument for the promotion of a politics of peace and it should work toward the transformation of Europe into a free federation of States'.[27] Moreover, the interventions of Eugenio Colorni on the same newspaper during 1944 insisted on the opportunity, for the strategy of the socialist party, of committing to the project of a European political federation. The argument acquired a certain traction within the socialist party because the federation was deemed to be the institutional guarantee for the redemption and autonomy of European peoples in their relationship with the Allies. In other words, for the Socialists, a popular, socialist and European political initiative was the only realistic platform which could not be captured by the reason of State of the Allies. The latter could have allowed the formation of a European unity, but this would have been an operation orchestrated 'from above'.

The third major political force that produced a stimulating activity of publications and political propaganda in favour of a European federation was the Christian Democratic party. Although the elaboration of the party's position on the supranational question came slightly late compared to the other two parties (at the moment of the reconstitution of the party, in 1942, the major concerns were related to the status of the social doctrine of the Church), the Christian Democrats endorsed the prospect of some form of political cooperation or unity early on. Already in the first manifesto of the future programme of the party, the international question was treated as a crucial one (under the auspices of a refoundation of the international order). However, the constitutional form to be given to the cooperation among European states was subject to different proposals within the same party. Publications on clandestine newspapers show an array of options that would go from a fully-fledged political federation to a classic confederation among States, and a different geopolitical identification of the position of a European polity. In certain articles, European political unity is a way of organising the relation between the South of Europe and the wider Mediterranean area; in other proposals (against the Atlantic option supported by the party leader, De Gasperi), aware of the future role of the USSR, the suggestion was to build up a confederation open to the participation of Eastern States (in order to favour cooperation with the Italian Communist Party).[28] Overall, while in the socialist field those who supported a

[27] Gaetano Arfé (ed.), *Storia dell'Avanti!* (Edizioni Avanti!, 1973), 32.
[28] Sergio Pistone, *L'Italia e l'Unita' Europea* (Loescher, 1982), 134.

European federation deemed it necessary for achieving socialism, in the Christian democratic area, the push towards some form of European political unity was dictated by the recognition that security for citizens could not be delivered only at the national level, but required cooperation and concerted action at least at the regional level.[29]

In the context of Italian resistance, the only party that maintained a cautious and often critical stance towards the idea of a European federation was the Communist Party. The questions of national reconstruction and international cooperation were, for the Communists, a priority; and they often saw, in the federalist ideas, a trojan horse for the containment of communist goals.[30] Politically, there were two reasons behind the scepticism towards European unity. First, since 1934 the Communist Party had adopted the position of the Comintern on the fight against Fascism: popular and patriotic fronts with international cooperation. Second, the Communist Party's leaders feared that a United States of Europe would be heavily bending towards the Atlantic. These motives explain why the two main publications (printed in clandestinity) of the party (*L'Unità*, a newspaper founded by Antonio Gramsci, and 'La Nostra Lotta') dealt with the questions concerning Europe with caution. A review of the pages of *L'Unità* shows that not a single article, from 1943 to 1945, is exclusively devoted to the topic of the political future of Europe. When the European question was touched upon, it was in articles devoted to other international topics: the Yalta conference, the recognition of the government of national unity by the USSR, the third Moscow conference held in 1943. Often, these nods to the potential for a European political unity are dismissive of it as a project with a classist basis. Parallel to the marginal space devoted to the European federal question is the extended coverage of Federal Democratic Yugoslavia, the antecedent of the Socialist Federative Republic of Yugoslavia. In the analyses dedicated to Yugoslavia, the federal question is given a social spin: the Federation of Yugoslavia is lauded because it has already advanced on the path towards socialism and, in that case, the federal basis of the constitution protected the equal rights of all peoples.[31] In short, the question of federalism was addressed (in positive terms) only for the constitution of the USSR and Yugoslavia. Overall, the Federalist movement's project for a European federation did not have much of an impact on the leadership of the Communist Party.[32] As we shall see, ultimately the Communist party

[29] There is another party that made up the block of resistant parties: the Republican Party. The party did not enter, at the beginning, in the Committee for National Liberation as, for the party, the priority was the abolition of the monarchy (it should be noted that there were pro-monarchy elements within the political arc of the resistance).

[30] For a recent and accurate reconstruction, see Luca Cangemi, *Il PCI contro L'Europeismo* (DeriveApprodi, 2019).

[31] 'I fondamenti democratici della Jugoslavia', *La Nostra Lotta*, 1944, 10–11, quoted by Cangemi, *Il PCI*, 13.

[32] Of course, there were dissenting voices (for example, Eugenio Curiel): see Marino Panzanelli, *L'attività politica di Eugenio Curiel* (Il Mulino, 1979).

advocated the priority of the issue of national reconstruction within the framework of an international cooperation among peoples.[33]

It is time to take stock. The experience of the Resistance against the German occupants and the Fascists produced a constitutional subject (with constituent legitimacy) comprised of six political parties (those banned by the Fascists in the 1920s). Their clandestine activity during the occupation of the North of Italy suggests that (with the exception of the Communist Party) the ideal of European political unity was part of their vision for the future constitutional order of Italy *and* Europe. Some themes recur in many of the documents circulated by these political parties: the creation of supranational institutions with democratic basis; the strengthening of economic cooperation; in a few cases, even the creation of a European army. The narratives put forward by the Resistance movement suggest that the ideal of European political unity was often treated as an autonomous political and constitutional theme, though sometimes linked to the security of the nation State. Yet, these ideas were developed in a situation where they did not have to be tested against the external context of international relations. This lack of a political test diminished the symbolic legacy of these projects. While it was evident that the partisans' exposure to sacrifice was linked to a project of national liberation from both the German occupant and the Fascist government, it was not equally manifest to all involved actors and the wider public opinion that partisans' activities were symbolically connected to the construction of a European political unity.[34]

Partly because of their abstract formulation, partly because elaborated in a precarious and mutating international context, all these writings and dialogue over European unity did not lead to any political achievement in the short-term (and, for what it is worth, the long-term). They informed the constitutional imagination of the new political system, but they did not have the chance to become 'embodied'. More specifically, the project of European unification did not remain central to the collective imagination of those parties after the end of the war. Already in 1946, the topic was not at the forefront of the concerns of many European political parties. Italy was no exception. We turn now to an analysis of the place of European integration in the Constituent Assembly and during the first decade of the new republican constitutional regime.

3.5 1946–1957: EUROPEAN INTEGRATION BY STEALTH

The end of the war signalled the beginning of a process which would make the European question less visible in the public and political debate. It is difficult to

[33] Paolo Spriano, *Storia del Partito Comunista Italiano, volume III: I fronti popolari, la Guerra, Stalin* (Einaudi, 1977), 274–292.

[34] For a clear analysis of the myth-making properties of narratives of sacrifice, see Paul Kahn, *Putting Liberalism in Its Place* (Princeton University Press, 2004), chapter 4.

track the causes of this process with absolute certainty. A plausible, but not definitive answer, is that the quick mutation of the international context made the difference and frustrated the chances of a European federation. Accordingly, what was at the core of the various parties of the resistance as a constitutional project soon became sidelined in favour of other 'international' themes. As already noted, the communist parties of the resistance mostly adhered to the Soviet interpretation of the strategic value of a European federation. This interpretation seemed to be confirmed by the approval of the Truman doctrine (and the Marshall plan of economic aid) and the rise of centrist political parties in what will be the six founding Member States clarified what was the available political space for a supranational community. We should be clear that it is not the case that these political parties stopped supporting the option of a form of European cooperation. It is just that the latter started to be understood as a union which would solidify the connection with the United States.[35]

In Italy, the sidelining of the European question can be seen in the path that led to the writing of the republican constitution and, especially, on the formulation of the crucial article that regulates the relation of the constitutional order with international law and organisations. The consensus surrounding the writing and final adoption of Article 11 (crucial for the definition of Italian's foreign policy) is telling. Indeed, the division between the Christian democrats and the communists (with the socialists having a slightly more nuanced position) was also reflected on the more general theme of the relation between the Italian constitutional order and international law. In the preparatory committee for the first draft of the constitution (known as the Committee of the 75),[36] the divergences were visible and openly expressed. Communists and socialists were suspicious of an opening of the constitution toward international law for strategic reasons. They were convinced that the international law that was emerging through the United Nations was not favourable to an internationalism of the workers. For this reason, they conceived of international law as a set of treaties signed by sovereign States.[37] For the socialist and the communist parties the political unity of the Continent had to be grounded on the unity of workers.

35 Gabriele D'Ottavio, 'Il discorso politico sull'Europa nell'immediato dopoguerra', in Giovanni Bernardini, Maurizio Cau and Gabriele D'Ottavio (eds.), *L'età costituente. Italia 1945–1948* (Il Mulino, 2017), 404.

36 The committee was helped by two of the most prominent international lawyers of the time, Roberto Ago and Gaetano Morelli. The committee's main task was to identify the competent organ for the declaration of war and the signing of international treaties; the legal modalities of introjection of international legal norms into the constitutional order; and the formulation of the principles that ought to direct foreign policy.

37 For a clear formulation, see the intervention of Palmiro Togliatti (Secretary of the Communist Party) in the constituent assembly during the debate on the articles concerning constitutional law: Palmiro Togliatti, *Discorsi alla Costituente* (Editori Riuniti, 2021).

Although the reasons behind the adoption of Article 11 were different, but all major political forces were able to converge on a highly abstract formulation of a principle of constitutional openness towards the international legal order: 'Italy agrees, on conditions of equality with other States, to the limitations of sovereignty that may be necessary to a world order ensuring peace and justice among the Nations. Italy promotes and encourages international organisations furthering such ends'. Following the advice of the subcommittee, the formulation of the article remained rather vague and it committed the republic to a pacifist approach to international relations and law. The article also expressed a generic favour for membership of international organisation without specifying its nature and telos. Recent research has shown that it was possible to converge on such an abstract formulation and, despite the deep division that was emerging with the incipient Cold War, in virtue of an agreement among all constituent parties to leave international relations outside of constitutional politics (though it would still be a central matter for ordinary politics).[38] A feature of this agreement was that the programmes presented by the majority of political parties remained silent on the international and regional dimension of the future constitution.[39] An exception was represented by the Action Party and the Republican Party which mentioned (again, rather vaguely) the principle of international cooperation. This was, as we have seen, in stark contrast with what the same political forces were advocating between 1943 and 1945.

It should be noted that, both in its first formulation and in the final version, in Article 11 there is no reference to Europe. If this might be thought of as a natural outcome given that the process of integration had not yet started,[40] it is rather surprising when one bears in mind the centrality of European cooperation for the parties of the resistance. In fact, the fate of Europe was still present in the public debate and it was mentioned several times during the debates in the Constituent Assembly. Amendments in favour of an explicit reference to European international organisations were proposed by a member of the Christian Democratic Party and a member of the Socialist Party. Both proposals were rejected on the basis of the argument that the reference to international organisations would cover regional

[38] Antonio Varsori, *L'Italia nelle relazioni internazionali dal 1943 al 1992* (Laterza, 1998), 3–43.

[39] The Christian Democrats' programme for the constituent assembly did not contain a single mention about the international sphere. The electoral manifest of the Socialist Party indeed made reference to a possible 'limitation of national sovereignty for the realisation of international peace' but did not mention Europe. The electoral manifesto of the Communists mentioned the international dimension, but only in a fleeting passage, by rejecting any form of militarism or imperialism, and asking for the rejection of any membership in a block of rival military powers. See, for an analysis of these documents, Gabriele D'Ottavio, 'Il discorso politico sull'Europa nell'immediato dopoguerra', in Giovanni Bernardini, Maurizio Cau and Gabriele D'Ottavio (eds.), *L'età costituente. Italia 1945–1948* (Il Mulino, 2017), 406–408.

[40] For a summary of the traditional explanation of the lack of any reference to Europe, see Marta Cartabia and Joseph Weiler, *L'Italia in Europa: profili istituzionali e costituzionali* (Il Mulino, 2000), 134.

organisations as well. Other references to the possibility of future European integration were made during the debates in the Assembly.[41] One can already track different visions of European integration from these interventions: from the classic reference to the Ventotene Manifesto to a confederal understanding of European unity. In other interventions, a functionalist conception of integration was formulated with a view to advocate the construction of a European market and the abolition of tariffs.

Article 11 was interpreted already by the first republican parliament, whose majority gave a wide scope to its field of application. In this sense, the aim of the article ought to be read in expansive terms, that is, beyond the references to peace and the containment of armed conflicts. The parliamentary majority hinted to the fact that membership in international and supranational organisations had to be seen as a legitimate and constitutionally desirable way of pursuing peace.[42] This constitutional attitude indicated a default position of constitutional openness towards supranational and international norms. Unless convincing evidence was brought to demonstrate the potential dangers of membership in an international organisation, the constitution was interpreted by the political majority as always supportive of international law.

However, one can track a different path for the process of European integration that did not apply to the ratification of other international treaties. It is quite telling to compare the parliamentary reaction to the CECA treaty and the adoption of the ECHR, on one hand, and the NATO treaty on the other hand. In the latter case, the option of adhering to the North Atlantic Treaty was seen as a highly political choice in a world increasingly polarised between loyalty toward the United States and the Soviet Union.

In the context of the political culture of the Italian constitutional order, the position of the PCI (the Communist Party) was rather distinctive and a quick look at it will help in explaining why the path of European integration was judged, at least in the first years, as constitutionally irrelevant. The vote of the communists against the CECA treaty and then the Rome Treaty (instituting a common market) was representative of a significant part of the Italian electorate. It should be added that the Socialist Parties abstained during the vote for the ratification of the Rome Treaty, making the inception of the process of European integration an affair of majority politics rather than a constitutional issue. In fact, the communists were not against the idea of further integration in Europe but they disagreed over two essential issues. First, the idea of Europe underlying the Rome Treaty was judged to be too divisive and, potentially, contrary to the aim of bringing peace to the

41 I follow here the reconstruction of the debate during the session of 15 March 1947 by Pietro Faraguna, 'Costituzione senza confine: Principi e fonti costituzionali tra sistema sovranazionale e diritto internazionale', in Fulvio Cortese and Corrado Caruso (eds.), *Immaginare la repubblica* (Franco Angeli, 2018), 73–74.

42 Sergio Bartole, *Interpretazioni e trasformazioni della costituzione* (Il Mulino, 2004), 282.

continent as stated by Article 11 of the Constitution. In a famous intervention on the Communist newspaper *L'Unità*, the leader of the Communist Party (Palmiro Togliatti) made clear that the idea of Europe promoted by European integration was heavily inclined towards Atlanticism and, for this reason, prone to cause division and conflict among European nations. The Communist Party, he noted,

> does not reject these proposal [of European unity], but we say that Europe has to be understood for what it is. Europe begins at the Urals and ends in the Atlantic Ocean. Let's get closer to all European peoples, let's find a way to collaborate in a closer way with all these countries, from Russia to England, from the countries of recent democratisation to France. It is an important attempt but it cannot be done in the name of a small group of satellites of US imperialism, and it cannot be a means for splitting the Continent into two, preparing in this way for war.[43]

The Communists were worried about the economic impact generated by these treaties. They thought, for example, that the CECA treaty was part of an agreement between monopolistic groups derived from the Schumann plan and that it would have impacted countries like Italy in a negative way. Moreover, the Treaty would exclude the countries under the influence of the Soviet Union, blocking potential economic collaborations between the two rising blocks.

The vote against CECA of the Communist Party was the beginning of a season of opposition of that party against European integration. But the organisation of the discussion in Parliament and the following vote of ratification moulded the perception of European integration within Italian constitutional imagination. The constitutional question of the compatibility of the Treaty with the republican constitution was sidelined by key political actors. The report submitted by the executive in support of the proposal of ratification of the treaty was utterly uninterested in the constitutional basis for the adoption. The document was simply silent on the constitutional question, implying that the ratification of the Treaty was not of constitutional relevance. In the Senate, however, the question of the correct constitutional basis for the ratification was posed by arguing that the ECSC was not pursuing the aims stated in Article 11. Moreover, the political opposition demanded, in the lower chamber, that the ratification should take the form of a constitutional statute and not an ordinary one.[44] In the ensuing debate, the political majority minimised the issue, highlighting that the new international organisation granted conditions of reciprocity to its members and that the birth of every new international organisation would require a loss of sovereignty. The reply in the lower chamber by the spokesperson of the political majority tended to minimise this loss and, more generally, the impact of the Treaty on the Italian constitutional order.[45] Ultimately,

[43] Palmiro Togliatti, 'Fermiamo la mano ai nemici della pace!' *L'Unità*, 25 September 1951.

[44] The point would be that the approval of a constitutional statute required an aggravated procedure.

[45] For an analysis of the debate, see Bartole, *Interpretazioni e trasformazioni*, 278.

this interpretation of the first step of European integration paved the way for two important tenets concerning the position of Europe within the constitutional imagination. First, there was no problem of compatibility between the aims of Article 11 and the rise of a regional organisation based on the common management of certain resources and, later, on a common market. Second, by minimising the impact of European integration (with the aim of de-escalating conflict between political parties), the political majority and the executive built the premises for what would become 'integration by stealth'. In other words, it is thanks to this important antecedent that the constitutional question on the legitimacy of European integration was first minimised and, later, made almost invisible. It is also thanks to this decision (and to the structure of the Italian judiciary) that the process of introjection of European norms was channelled, for several years, by the lower bodies of the judiciary.[46]

The same approach to Article 11 was adopted at the time of ratifying the EEC and Euratom treaties. Although those treaties clearly widened the scope of European integration, their impact on the Italian constitutional order was minimised by the government with the support of the political majority. In both chambers the constitutional question of their legitimacy was briefly discussed, but the answer from the majority was to belittle the significance of the loss of sovereignty requested for the adoption of those treaties. The ratification of the EEC treaty sealed the Italian constitutional approach to European integration and succeeded in excising any questions of constitutionality from the horizon of available political options. Given the opposition of the Communist Party and the scepticism of the socialists, the political majority built around the party of Christian Democracy could not pursue the path of constitutional reform (as the majority required would be two thirds in both parliamentary chambers).[47]

This established practice made European integration so invisible to the eyes of political actors that even the approval of a major transformative treaty like the Maastricht treaty went almost unchallenged. The ratification of the Maastricht Treaty represented both the pinnacle of the introjection of primary EU law by stealth and, at the same time, the beginning of what we have termed the third phase, that of Europe as a benevolent external bound. In the parliamentary debate for the approval of the Treaty, only one objection to the constitutionality of the Treaty was raised (from the extreme right-wing of the parliamentary spectrum) and in relation with the lack of reciprocity in light of the opt-out clauses granted to the United

[46] This is the accepted narrative, but a more nuanced version of the role of lawyers and judges has been put forward in Tommaso Pavone, *The Ghostwriters: Lawyers and the Politics behind the Judicial Construction of Europe* (Cambridge University Press, 2022).

[47] It should be added that, at that point in time, the new institution of the popular referendum had not been introduced. Hence, the only path for constitutional maintenance was the approval of a constitutional norm with a qualified majority: Antonio Varsori, *La cenerentola d'Europa? L'Italia e l'integrazione europea dal 1947 ad oggi* (Rubettino, 2010), 34ff.

Kingdom and Denmark.[48] A few doubts on the capacity of Article 11 of providing the basis for the Maastricht treaty were raised, but once again the strategy of the executive (supported by a wider majority in Parliament as, in the meantime, the former Communist Party had become supportive of European integration) was to promise (in vague terms) to undertake the necessary initiatives for making the Treaty compatible with the Italian constitution. Yet, nothing was done after the ratification of the Treaty. The same happened for the ratification of the Constitutional Treaty and then the Lisbon Treaty. This strategy of internalisation of EU primary and secondary law was also cemented by the silence of the Constitutional Court which never called for the need of a constitutional reform for further integration.[49] But, in terms of the constitutional imagination, something had changed after the Maastricht Treaty. It is worth pausing and unpacking the changing context which brought about the change.

3.6 EUROPE AS AN EXTERNAL CONSTRAINT ('VINCOLO ESTERNO')

While European integration did not often make it into newspapers' headlines and many of the constitutional debates during the first decades of the republican constitution ignored it, the political system and other domestic institutions (like the newly instituted Constitutional Court) had to apply the constitutional document (often in conflicting ways) when they had to relate with European norms. Many important reforms were approved by statutes (that is, by Parliament), often with a lively dialectic between the political majority and the opposition. In certain key areas of societal organisation (labour markets, schools, health care system, social security system), the narrative was one of active implementation of the constitutional project, and the intensity of the conflict during the 1960s conveyed a message far from political passivity, which also actively involved several social movements (labour, students, women).

This period of political mobilisation lasted for a decade. It brought about several social and legal changes which would entrench certain interpretations of the republican constitution (especially on civil and social rights).[50] However, the end of a cycle of remarkable economic growth, the sudden and conspicuous rise of inflation and the emergence of terrorist organisations with their violent attack against institutions and symbols of the republic marked the end of that phase of constitutional development. These material and political changes created the

[48] Faraguna, 'Costituzione senza confini', 87.

[49] The Court supported the option of coping with the penetration of European norms into the constitutional order by the means of constitutional interpretation: Vittorio Barsotti, Marta Cartabia, et al., *Italian Constitutional Justice in Global Context* (Oxford University Press, 2016), 205ff.

[50] Cf, *ex multiplis*, Nadia Urbinati, *Lo scettro senza il re* (Donzelli, 2009), chapter 1; Guido Crainz, *Storia della Repubblica* (Donzelli, 2016), chapters II and III.

conditions for the formation of a new public discourse. By the end of the 1970s, the seeds for a new narrative around the Italian political system had been sewn. Domestically, the analysis of the Italian political system as incapable of deciding became central in the political debate and, in brief, it involved public lawyers as well under the question of how to build a 'deciding democracy'. A narrative initially confined to certain neo-liberal and conservative circles acquired increasing traction in the public debate. The main features of that narrative concern two important points: first, a growing distrust of the political class generated by the diffuse political corruption and the incapacity of political parties to realise major social and economic reforms (under the idea that the Italian economy was stagnating by the end of 1970s and needed an injection of economic reforms); second, the organisation of political institutions and powers as dictated by the constitution was stigmatised as the cause for the perceived absence of the governing capacity. More specifically, the parliamentary basis of the form of government and the plurality of political parties comprising the political system were taken to be the cause of a weak decision-making system. A consequence of the rise of this interpretation of the malfunctioning of the constitutional system was the emergence of a discourse around constitutional reform or, even, a new constituent assembly. The call for a constitutional reform with at its core the strengthening of the executive and in particular of the government was already a symptom of the weakening capacity of traditional political parties to steer the political direction of the government. Several attempts were made for a formal change of the second part of the constitution (on the organisation of powers), but none was successful. Possibly, this failure enhanced the perception of the decreasing political power of parties.

It is at this point that a new narrative element was introduced in the public debate and it will successfully transform the perception of European integration in the constitutional imagination. Revealing of the new forces influencing the political imagination, a new idea was coined by the then President of the Bank of Italy – Guido Carli – and supported by the highest State officials. The idea was to build a narrative about the so-called external constraint ('vincolo esterno').[51] Tapping into a tradition of Italian political thought, often afraid of the foreign imposition of political will over the peninsula, the idea was quite simple: the Italian constitutional order and certain sectors of the State ought to be transformed by binding politics to rules and benchmarks set outside of the ordinary domestic political process.[52] The underlying assumption was that the main political actors and the constitutional organisation of powers could not muster enough political power for achieving changes deemed to be necessary. In other words, according to the ideologues of

[51] In his memoir, Carli was explicit: 'the European Union represented an alternative path for the solution of problems which we were not managing to handle through the normal channels of government and parliament': Guido Carli, *Cinquant'anni di vita italiana* (Laterza, 1993), 5.

[52] For a history of the notion, see Enrico Diodato, *Il vincolo esterno* (Mimesis, 2014).

the external constraints, the political system did not have a full governing capacity anymore.

As was the case for the period after the drafting of the republican constitution, the shaping of the constitutional imagination was heavily influenced by international events. The end of the Cold War, the fall of the Berlin Wall and the inception of a new economic globalisation were among the causes of the collapse of the political parties that wrote and applied the republican constitution. By 1993, the parties that wrote the constitution had almost completely collapsed, new political subjects emerged, the Maastricht Treaty had been voted and the first steps toward a new wave of globalisation had been undertaken and more were developing. While in the first phase of the republican constitution, the external constraint had been operating on the basis of international relations and it was represented by the Atlantic alliance, the new external constraint was now identified in a more integrated European Union. But, while the limits imposed by membership of NATO did not impede domestic political action (or at least, it was not perceived to be directive of domestic political action), in the case of the new European Union and the introduction of the path toward the single currency, the impact on the perceived capacity of acting domestically in an autonomous way was quite remarkable. The trauma of the end of the so-called First Republic was compensated by a new narrative which portrayed political actors as deprived of real political agency even over crucial domestic issues. The conditions attached to the participation in the single currency and then the conditions imposed in order to remain member of the Eurozone shaped the constitutional imagination in profound and remarkable ways.[53] The ideologues of the 'external constraint' inspired the negotiating strategies of the Italian representatives during the process leading to the approval of the new single currency and the creation of the European Central Bank.[54] Many domestic reforms (salary moderation, privatisations, liberalisations, pensions reform) were also voted and implemented quite rapidly during the second half of the 1990s. But the impact of the narrative of the external constraint would be felt even more during the following decade, leading to the formation of technical governments (lead by former central bankers or former European Commission members) when the political system could not deliver on the aims and conditionalities decided at the supranational level and the constitutionalisation of the principle of sound budget after the 2008 crisis (art. 81 of the constitution).

The culture of the external constraint has shaped the imagination of the main political actors by framing the available options on the table. For the moment, the majority of the actors in the political system still support the idea that the political

[53] An enlightening reconstruction is provided in Omar Chessa, *La costituzione della moneta* (Jovene, 2016).

[54] See the seminal account by Kenneth Dyson and Kevin Featherstone, 'Italy and EMU as "Vincolo Esterno": Empowering the Technocrats, Transforming the State' (1996) 1 *South European Society and Politics* 272.

programme coming from the external constraint has to be introjected into the Italian legal order and one of the key tasks of political parties is to make sure that this agenda is pursued. It is not surprising that the hegemony of this attitude generated a perception of inevitability of certain measures and the corresponding decline of political agency (at multiple levels). It is also not surprising that the reaction against the narrative of the external constraint has taken up the form of the victimisation of Italy and its citizens. This is the other side of the coin of a constitutional culture where only guarantee institutions and external powers (e.g., the European Commission, the EMU, Germany) are deemed capable of sending proper inputs into the political process.[55] However, the victim-like pose adopted by certain political actors took up a conspiracy-theory rhetoric rather quickly: it is the Brussels' bureaucracy or elite that wants to dictate to Italians what they should do and how they should live, as if the project behind the external constraint was only a 'supranational' project pursued by obscure bureaucrats for reasons that, ultimately, cannot be easily retrieved.

3.7 CONCLUSIONS

An inquiry into the place and meaning attributed to the ideal of European political unity by the Italian constitutional imagination provides several important insights. The most important one is that the struggle for constitutional imagination over Europe allows one to track a remarkable shift in the conception of Italian collective political action. Europe has moved from being (at least for the majority of constitutional actors) an ideal political space for a politics of self-government to being an external constraint and the source of important political aims for the constitutional order. Narratives and myths over Europe changed as the perception of the political parties' capacity of exercising autonomous political power started to decline. One can observe the trajectory that began with 'Europe' being seen as the optimal political space for the realisation of political freedom. It is a narrative that makes up a constitutional imagination of active and transformative party politics. In the language of Italian constitutional law and doctrine, this was a political system capable of forming and imprinting a political direction onto Italian society. Contextual reasons made the role of Europe rather marginal during constituent debates, but this did not affect the perception of the constituent capacity of the political system. However, the international context and the domestic pressure for a quick economic recovery pushed the question of European political unity aside and made it, increasingly, an ordinarily legal (rather than constitutional) question. By 1957, the perception of European integration as an ordinary process had come

55 For a rare overview of the impact of the external constraint on Italian political culture, see Roberto Gualtieri, 'L'Europa come vincolo esterno', in Piero Craveri and Antonio Varsori (eds.), *L'Italia nella costruzione europea. Un bilancio storico (1957–2007)* (Franco Angeli, 2009), 331ff.

to shape the imagination of the majority of political actors. By the time of the approval of the Maastricht Treaty, a new vision of the role of Europe had come to inform the constitutional imagination of Italian political parties. Almost unanimously (and this time including the left parties), Europe had become an essential external staple for the stabilisation and modernisation (in economic and liberal terms) of Italy. Quite interestingly, it will only be at the turn of the twenty-first century that the impact of this conception of Europe will be felt as a 'constitutional issue'. Yet, quite tellingly, the main reactions against some of the substantive inputs coming from the European Union were either of political passivity (we cannot but do what Europe is asking us to do) or of political victimisation (Europe is ruining Italy and its constitutional achievements). This political stalemate is the product of many factors. But one of the most important can be found in the trajectory of a constitutional imagination whose formation goes back, at least, to the 1950s.

4

Sovereignty and the Misery of Small Eastern European Nations

Hent Kalmo

4.1 INTRODUCTION

One of the idiosyncrasies of the countries in Eastern and Central Europe is supposed to be their especially strong attachment to sovereignty. Ivan Krastev has argued that Europe's East–West divide is also inscribed in political imaginaries, and that this fact was clearly visible at the time of the EU's Eastern enlargement. In contrast to the anti-nationalist postmodern vision that had emerged in the West, 'the Eastern European nation-states that joined the EU in 2004 were rather obsessed with the ideas of national sovereignty and ethnic homogeneity', claims Krastev.[1] Or, as Rogers Brubaker has put it: at the time when Western Europe seemed to be moving *beyond* the nation-state, Eastern Europe was apparently moving *back* to it.[2] Of course, even in Western Europe, it has never been obvious to everyone that the nation-state is on the way out. The ideas of sovereignty and the nation-state have often been questioned in a polemical mode, vis-à-vis those believing that, whatever the innovations in the legal architecture of the EU, these novelties do not call for a fundamental revision of constitutional categories. Others have insisted that the nature of the EU could never be captured without the imagination being expanded beyond the already familiar. As Joseph Weiler memorably said in reference to the Maastricht decision of the *Bundesverfassungsgericht*, to describe the EU without rethinking in creative ways the concept of a polity is to be 'looking backwards, like Lot's wife', to something based on the tired old idea of an ethno-culturally homogenous people.[3] Against the

[1] Ivan Krastev, 'Re-imagining the East–West Divide in Europe', *IWMpost 129: European Boundaries and Divides*, www.iwm.at/publication/iwmpost-article/reimagining-the-east-west-divide-in-europe (last accessed 8 April 2025).

[2] Rogers Brubaker, 'Nationalizing States Revisited: Projects and Processes of Nationalization in Post-Soviet States' (2011) 34 *Ethnic and Racial Studies* 1785.

[3] J. H. H. Weiler, 'Does Europe Need a Constitution? Demos, Telos and the German Maastricht Decision' (1995) 1 *European Law Journal* 219, 223.

background of such discussions of the new and the old in constitutional thinking, East-Central Europe has tended to appear as a site of almost comic archaism. According to Anneli Albi, when the recently restored countries of East-Central Europe began to consider EU membership, they did so from the perspective of a traditional idea of sovereignty, centred on such ideas as independence, ethnically defined nation-state and national self-determination.[4] In a similar vein, Signe Larsen has contended that post-communist countries have retained their own brand of constitutionalism which celebrates 'the ideas of nationalism, the nation-state and national sovereignty'.[5]

When faced with such claims, and reflecting on the role of constitutional imaginaries, the first question that comes to mind is whether it could make sense to ascribe a uniform constitutional ideology to a region as large and variegated as East-Central Europe. But if constitutionalism is not an ideology or a worldview, weaving together a set of consistent beliefs about the nation, the state and sovereignty, then what could be meant by saying that these concepts are nonetheless central to the constitutionalism of East-Central Europe? Needless to say, sovereignty itself can be imagined in various ways. There is a long tradition of portraying sovereignty as a myth – something with no corresponding reality other than the force by which it captures the imagination.[6] Hans Kelsen decried the 'dogma of sovereignty' and accused it of inhibiting the development of international law.[7] Resistance to European integration has sometimes also been explained by the strength of outdated ideas.[8] Indeed, to suppose that some national judiciaries remain in thrall to a conception of sovereignty as an absolute and indivisible power, would this not make it hard for them to see it as shared or parcelled out in a way that European integration is assumed to require? And if this is true, are not countries in East-Central Europe particularly exposed to sovereigntism by their shared constitutional outlook? On the other hand, if their proneness to distinct ways of thinking about the nation and its relation to the state – assuming that such regional idiosyncrasies exist – do not translate directly into any legal doctrines, or even an attachment to some traditional notion of sovereignty, then how could their views about the nation be depicted as *constitutional* ideas or imaginaries, as opposed to more general

[4] Anneli Albi, *EU Enlargement and the Constitutions of Central and Eastern Europe* (Cambridge University Press, 2005), 122; see also Anneli Albi, 'Postmodern Versus Retrospective Sovereignty? Two Different Discourses in the EU and the Candidate Countries?', in Neil Walker (ed.), *Sovereignty in Transition* (Hart Publishing, 2003), 401.

[5] Signe Rehling Larsen, 'Varieties of Constitutionalism in the European Union' (2021) 84 *Modern Law Review* 477, 496.

[6] See, for example, Francis Delaisi, *Political Myths and Economic Realities* (Viking, 1927); Walter G. O'Donnell, 'The Myth of Sovereignty' (1949) 24 *Social Science* 91.

[7] Hans Kelsen, *Das Problem der Souveränität und die Theorie des Völkerrechts: Beitrag zu einer reinen Rechtslehre* (Verlag von J. C. B. Mohr, 1928), 236.

[8] Jacques Ziller, 'Sovereignty in France: Getting Rid of the Mal de Bodin' in Neil Walker (ed.), *Sovereignty in Transition* (Hart Publishing, 2003), 261.

social representations that might be populating the mind of those interpreting the law?

Despite all the diversity encountered in East-Central Europe, there is, in fact, a recurring cultural theme running through this region: the idea of being a small nation that has suffered great historical tragedies. This theme certainly gives rise to an imaginary of sorts, a very rich imaginary even, which loses its subtlety when reduced to such catch-all expressions as 'ethnic nationalism'. A distinction should be made between the general concept of the nation and the particular set of ideas that a group of people entertain about themselves as a nation, such as the idea of being a small afflicted nation situated in a dangerous area.[9] The latter is an example of the kind of social myth that offers an identity to a collective and becomes an essential part of collective imaginaries.[10] Attempts have already been made to find some common themes in the political myths of East-Central Europe (for example, the theme of a civilizational bulwark against the East), and to distinguish their varieties in different countries (aside from such particular national myths as the Holy Crown of Hungary or Polish messianic martyrdom).[11] If the idea of being a long-suffering small nation is to be considered a common regional myth of this sort, then it, too, must be understood in a sufficiently vague manner, allowing for variation in what exactly the predicament of the nation consists in and what historical tragedies it has suffered. Moreover, if this idea is to be taken as a constitutional imaginary, then it must be admitted that it is thoroughly ambiguous in its implications. No political or legal position with respect to sovereignty follows from the mere observation that the nation is small, endangered, and therefore in need of protection.

Contrary to what has been suggested by Benedict Anderson – who famously defined nations as imagined communities – the nation is not always imagined as a sovereign entity, destined to inhabit a sovereign state.[12] The national imaginary may be more open-ended. Depending on the kind of threats that are thought to besiege

9 This crucial distinction has been underlined, for example, in Max Scheler, 'Der allgemeine Begriff von "Nation" und die konkreten Nationalideen', in *Schriften zur Soziologie und Weltanschauungslehre* (Franke Verlag, 1963), 334.

10 On social myths as key elements of collective imaginaries, see Gérard Bouchard, *Social Myths and Colletive Imaginaries* (University of Toronto Press, 2017), 4.

11 Walter Kolarz, *Myths and Realities in Eastern Europe* (Kennikat Press, 1946), 72. On the Holy Crown of Hungary as a myth, see László Péter, 'The Holy Crown of Hungary, Visible and Invisible' (2003) 81 *The Slavonic and East European Review* 15. On Polish messianism: Geneviève Zubrzycki, 'Polish Mythology and the Traps of Messianic Martyrology', in Gérard Bouchard (ed.), *National Myths. Constructed Pasts, Contested Presents* (Routledge, 2013).

12 Anderson wrote that the nation is 'imagined as *sovereign* because the concept was born in an age in which Enlightenment and Revolution were destroying the legitimacy of the divinely-ordained, hierarchical dynastic realm. Coming to maturity at a stage of human history when even the most devout adherents of any universal religion were inescapably confronted with the living *pluralism* of such religions, and the allomorphism between each faith's ontological claims and territorial stretch, nations dream of being free, and, if under God, directly so. The gage and emblem of this freedom is the sovereign state.' Benedict Anderson, *Imagined Communities. Reflections on the Origin and Spread of Nationalism* (Verso, 2006), 7.

the nation, state sovereignty may appear either as an all-important protective shield or, on the contrary, an obstacle precluding membership in some larger political community where the nation could fare better than in solitude. In other words, even supposing that countries in East-Central Europe share a collective mentality centred on the category of the nation, and that this mentality induces them to consider fundamental political problems through a particular lens, it does not follow that they should be especially attached to state sovereignty in any traditional sense. Rather than viewing constitutionalism as an expression of some definite ideology, it might be more helpfully approached from the perspective of the problems that are deemed essential by those who practice it. On this reading, constitutionalism is a language that simultaneously frames and engenders disagreements about issues related to constitutional interpretation. The 'nationalist rhetoric of the small nation', as Siniša Malešević has described it, is an axis of debate which functions by continuing to stir up new, often contradictory ideas that can be built into rivalling constitutional doctrines.[13] When the question of sovereignty is treated in this framework, we realise that East-Central Europe's constitutionalism is actually much less archaic than it might seem. Not merely is it open to revising the concept of national sovereignty; it positively invites questions that lead us to re-imagine nation-statehood in a way that supports European integration.

4.2 THE MISERY THESIS

It is remarkable how consistently descriptions of East-Central Europe have advanced some version of what might be called the misery thesis. All nuances aside, the thesis is broadly about an Eastern *Sonderweg*: the idea that the region is different from Western Europe now because its history has been different. In other words, the thesis has two parts. It asserts, on the one hand, that the region possesses some distinguishing characteristics (a particular political culture, a type of nationalism different from the one current in the West) and, on the other, that this peculiarity is best explained by going back to the past, in some cases to the Middle Ages or beyond. This line of thinking finds its *locus classicus* in the famous essay 'The Miseries of East European Small States' by István Bibó, a Hungarian political theorist who wrote at the time of WWII, attempting to lay bare the deep origins of the catastrophe he had seen unfolding. Contrary to the view that was dominant in Hungary, Poland and Czechoslovakia – the three states he was mostly concerned with, alongside Germany which he also assigned to Eastern Europe – Bibó argued

[13] Jan Komárek has argued similarly that the central concepts forming part of any constitutional imaginary are 'contested truths' around which important political arguments turn. Jan Komárek, 'European Constitutional Imaginaries: Utopias, Ideologies, and the Other', in Jan Komárek (ed.), *European Constitutional Imaginaries: Between Ideology and Utopia* (Oxford University Press, 2023), 2–3. On 'small nation' as a rhetorical category, see Siniša Malešević, *Grounded Nationalisms: A Sociological Analysis* (Cambridge University Press, 2019), 126.

that the neighbourhood's small states had not appeared in pre-war dramas merely in the role of victims but had made a large contribution to international tensions with their chronically maladjusted, at times grossly anti-democratic internal politics. For him, the fundamental question for understanding the catastrophe was this: Why had the region abandoned democracy and political liberalism after hailing them so enthusiastically in the wake of the First World War? Bibó's explanation was that, whilst the cause of freedom and the cause of nationalism had progressed harmoniously in the West, these ideals had drifted apart in the East. A sequence of traumatic collective experiences had led to the conviction that democracy cannot be realised without jeopardising the national community. Not only leaders but the populations of small Eastern European states had come to believe that, if they cared about the fate of their nation, they simply could not afford to implement democracy and political freedoms to the full, however much they may have approved of these values in the abstract.

Bibó's thesis was not only about the predicament resulting from someone imagining (wrongly, he emphasised) that there is an incompatibility between democracy and national welfare or even survival. For understanding how this mistaken conclusion could be drawn, and how it could ensconce itself in the mind of Eastern Europeans as a putative lesson of history – prompting them to develop 'the greatest monstrosity of modern European political development: anti-democratic nationalism'[14] – one had to revisit the process by which nations had first emerged in this region. Bibó claimed that the great divergence between East and West could be traced back to the circumstances of nation-building in various parts of Europe. In the West, nations took shape and had the opportunity to mature within pre-existing states, with the result that national and state boundaries overlapped when masses began to be drawn to nationalism at the time of the French Revolution. The Eastern lands, by contrast, were under the power of great empires in the nineteenth century, so that the smaller nations inhabiting this space, unable to realise their aspiration to statehood, were reduced, *faute de mieux*, to cultivating their language and folk customs – not as an idle pastime but to prove that nations were more real, more solid entities than the existing states. According to Bibó, it was not smallness as such which produced the impasse from which Eastern national movements hoped to escape by a turn to a *völkisch* identity. Small nations also existed in the West, but they fared much better, noted Bibó, pointing to Belgians, Danes and others as examples. The main distinguishing factor in the East was the presence of loosely integrated, semi-fixed political organisations: not sufficiently implanted to create national loyalties corresponding to state boundaries (to swallow up the small nations, as it were), yet strong enough to prevent fragmentation and consolidation along

[14] István Bibó, 'The Miseries of East European Small States', in István Bibó, *The Art of Peacemaking: Political Essays by István Bibó* (Yale University Press, 2015), 151 (emphasis omitted).

national lines (the formation of small nation states). Such conditions prevailed only in Central-Eastern Europe and, for this reason, as Bibó put it, linguistic nationalism became the region's specialty.

Bibó was not the first to emphasise the lack of overlap between national and state borders in Eastern Europe and to remark on the importance of this fact for the mentality of the region's inhabitants. In 1915, at the time of WWI, Tomáš G. Masaryk had told a London audience that, if they wanted to understand Eastern Europe, they needed not a political but an ethnographic map. 'An Englishman, speaking of his nation, identifies the nation and state. Not so the Serb or the Bohemian, because to his experience state and nation do not coincide, his nation being spread over several states, or sharing a state with other nations.'[15] Not that this was a great misfortune, from Masaryk's point of view. Although he spoke of Eastern Europe as an ethnological 'danger zone' ridden with cultural and political conflict, for him, there was no misery in the condition of its small nations. Yes, they were latecomers in staking their claim to statehood, but their prospects were bright. Small nations were no less able to protect themselves if sufficiently determined to resist attacks. Masaryk conceded that the nations of East-Central Europe might suffer from some disadvantages, such as a more limited population and a weaker economy, but these handicaps were the result of imperial oppression. 'Let the smaller nations be free: do not interfere, leave them alone, and these drawbacks will soon disappear.'[16]

Here was an authoritative view of Eastern Europe that underlined the small size of its nations yet was thoroughly optimistic in tenor. How did the misery thesis emerge then? It started to take shape at the time when the 'danger zone' of small nationalities became a scene of many independent states. In the mid-1920s, Edvard Beneš, the foreign minister of Czechoslovakia, could still confidently maintain that most of these states were committed to freedom and democracy. Beneš admitted that the region was beset with the problem of discontented ethnic minorities, but he brushed this difficulty aside and, like Masaryk, depicted current difficulties as a legacy of imperial misrule ('a bad training for the present majorities and minorities alike.').[17] What brought about a crucial change in perspective (reflected in Bibó's later analysis) was the claim that the most fateful legacy of the imperial period was a distortion in how Eastern Europe nations imagined themselves. Outside observers pointed out a discrepancy between the self-understanding of the new countries as 'national states' and the fact that none of these states included only one single nation.[18] Bibó took up this line of reasoning, contending that, when small Eastern

[15] Tomáš G. Masaryk, 'The Problem of Small Nations in the European Crisis', in R. W. Seton-Watson (ed.), *Masaryk in England* (Cambridge University Press, 1943), 142.

[16] Ibid., 148.

[17] Edward Beneš, 'The Problem of the Small Nations after the World War' (1925) 4 *The Slavonic Review* 257, 272.

[18] C. A. Macartney, *National States and National Minorities* (Oxford University Press, 1934), 210.

European nations gained statehood, they remained captivated by the territorial fantasies they had developed under imperial domination, and acted as if these aspirations were somehow more real than the reality. As Walter Kolarz put it in his study of the myths of Eastern Europe (1946), beside every actually existing state, there was a 'shadow State shaped by the nationalist imagination'.[19] To see the potential clashes between these various shadow states, one only needed to draw a graph of the divergent claims.

> The result would be a multitude of intersecting circles in which every intersection would denote a conflict, not between the nations themselves, but between their historical theories of the State. Poles and Czechs can find the way to an understanding; but the notions of the 'Bohemian State Rights' or the 'Historic Poland' could never be brought into one formula. There is no reason why Slovaks, Rumanians and Hungarians should not dwell side by side in amity, but the conceptions of a 'Greater Moravian Empire', of a 'St. Stephen's Empire' and of a 'Dako-Rumanian Empire' can never be reconciled. The same is true of Greater Albania and Greater Greece, Greater Bulgaria and Greater Serbia, Greater Lithuania and the Polish *Rzcezc Pospolita* (Commonwealth). The whole picture of Central and Eastern Europe presents an inextricable skein of conflicting national claims.[20]

Even today, the canonical picture of Eastern Europe's misery is that of a strange nationalist fantasy world saturated with historical memories. The 'demons of the past' appear to be especially active in this region.[21] The main thrust of such arguments is that East-Central Europe's idiosyncrasies cannot be explained by the fact that the region remained on the wrong side of the Iron Curtain. 'If one regards Soviet Communism as a disease, then it seems that Eastern Europe may have had a pre-disposition to the infection', wrote one historian.[22] In the mid-1990s, Tony Judt tried to show that the line dividing Eastern from Western Europe is not an artificial creation dating from the Cold War, 'recently drawn across a single cultural space', but rather something older and more real. Similarly to Bibó, Judt made much of the fact that Eastern European peoples were confronted with a well-formed state system at the time they came to political consciousness. 'To have been formed into a recognized nation and a permanent state in earlier centuries was to have been extraordinarily fortunate', wrote Judt. 'Whereas the northern and western European peoples formed states by expansion from a core, absorbing their own peripheries until constrained by topography or competition, the countries of modern eastern

19 Walter Kolarz, *Myths and Realities in Eastern Europe* (Kennikat Press, 1946), 74.

20 Ibid., 74.

21 See, for example, Roman Krakowsky, *Le populisme en Europe centrale et orientale: Un avertissment pour le monde?* (Fayard, 2019), 244. For example, the prospect of immigration is said to reawaken the painful memory of living as a minority in an empire and the difficulties of dealing with other nationalities in an independent state during the interwar period. S. Kauffmann. 'Europe's Illiberal Democracies', *The New York Times*, 9 March 2016.

22 Philip Longworth, *The Making of Eastern Europe* (Palgrave Macmillan, 1992), 7.

Europe were born and could only be born from the collapse of empires – Russian, Turkish, Austrian, German – a process that is still incomplete ... This is *the* great misfortune of the eastern half of Europe: that its division into states came late and all at once. It is what gives to these lands their common history and their common weakness – and it is what in the end makes them crucially different from the luckier peoples to the west.'[23]

Admittedly, it is not quite obvious why the circumstances of the birth of Eastern European states should be essential for understanding their character today. Why should developments in the nineteenth century and earlier be relevant to an enquiry into the region's present political culture? Bibó offered an answer that has proven extraordinarily influential: the region has acquired a traumatised identity as a result of its history.[24] The theoretical paradigm in which Bibó worked was that of collective psychology.[25] Within this paradigm, it was natural to think that, if past collective experiences have been negative, then the present can literally suffer from history, in the form of a neurosis, for example, or a national inferiority complex that leads to a sense of impotence and a desire of compensation.[26] Bibó described how major shocks (such as revolutions, foreign invasions, military defeats) can make communities behave as if they were hysterical individuals: lose touch with reality, be constantly afraid of conspiracies, display both insecurity and overblown self-assessment. Unable to come to terms with an overwhelming trauma, a community concocts various make-believe solutions in an effort to ensure by all means that the catastrophe will not be repeated. 'These are the situations when a nation behaves as though it were unified while it is not, as though it were independent while it is not, as though it were democratic while it is not, and as though it were involved in revolution while it is only languishing.'[27] Bibó claimed that, although some Western

[23] Tony Judt, *A Grand Illusion? An Essay on Europe* (Penguin Books, 1996), 56. Judt also argued that the collective identity of the region's peoples was formed around the experience of making 'an all-or-nothing claim to territory and power at the expense of a neighbour making an identical claim – in many cases over the same land'. Ibid.

[24] One author has recently spoken of a 'wounded identity'; A. Máté-Tóth, *Freiheit und Populismus: Verwundete Identitäten in Ostmitteleuropa* (Springer, 2019), 101.

[25] Maurice Halbwachs, one of the most prominent representatives of this field, described it as being concerned with 'a collective mentality [that] exists and that is not like a lost, isolated and negligible province, but exerts an influence upon all the functions of individual mentality which cannot be understood or explained without it'. Maurice Halbwachs, 'Individual Psychology and Collective Psychology' (1938) 3 *American Sociological Review* 615, 616.

[26] Oliver Brachfeld, *Inferiority Feelings in the Individual and the Group* (Grune & Stratton, 1951). For a study that seeks to trace the slow historical formation of a national inferiority complex in a particular context, see Paul Johansen, 'Nationale Vorurteile und Minderwertigkeitsgefühle als soziale Faktor im mittelalterlichen Livland', in Alexander Bergengruen and Ludwig Deike (eds.), *Alteuropa und die moderne Gesellschaft. Festschrift für Otto Brunner* (Vandenhoeck & Ruprecht, 1963), 88.

[27] István Bibó, 'On the Balance of Power and Peace in Europe', in István Bibó (ed.), *The Art of Peacemaking. Political Essays by István Bibó* (Yale University Press, 2015), 46–47.

European countries have also suffered from a 'collective hysteria', Eastern Europe is especially susceptible to this condition because of its unique calamity-filled history.

A similar relationship between history and collective mentality emerges from a text that has become another *locus classicus* on regional misery. Milan Kundera's 'The Tragedy of Central Europe' (1984) also described the weight of history and its lasting effect on the mind of those who may not have experienced any great traumas personally. Indeed, Kundera asserted that an element of trauma is part of the very idea of a small nation. 'But what is a small nation?', he asked, after having highlighted the importance of this notion for understanding the identity of Central Europe (an 'uncertain zone of small nations between Russia and Germany').[28] He proceeded to offer his famous definition: 'the small nation is one whose very existence may be put in question at any moment; a small nation can disappear, and it knows it.' Kundera claimed that, for the inhabitants of Central Europe, the possibility of collective extinction is not merely an abstract truth but a harrowing lesson of history. 'A Frenchman, a Russian, or an Englishman is not used to asking questions about the very survival of his nation. His anthems speak only of grandeur and eternity. The Polish anthem, however, starts with the verse: "Poland has not yet perished ..."'. This statement – 'Our nation has not yet perished' – captures Central Europe's particular vision of the world, according to Kundera. The crucial difference from Bibó is that Kundera did not depict this attitude as pathological in any way. When 'the devastating march of History' produces a vision based on distrust and existential fear, the outcome is hard-won wisdom, not a hysteria, he suggested. By contrast to Bibó, who was continually insisting on the distorted character of the imaginaries born out of catastrophes, Kundera seems to have thought that contemporary events were amply justifying the fears of Central Europeans. He described how Russia was again expanding eastward, crushing all cultural variety within the Soviet Union and the satellite countries. On the other hand, it was precisely by such shared experiences of existential peril that nations were drawn together into a regional community. 'Central Europe therefore cannot be defined and determined by political frontiers (which are inauthentic, always imposed by invasions, conquests, and occupations), but by the great common situations that reassemble peoples, regroup them in ever new ways along the imaginary and ever-changing boundaries that mark a realm inhabited by the same memories, the same problems and conflicts, the same common tradition.'[29]

The emphasis on perception in Kundera's definition of smallness is very illuminating for understanding the functioning of imaginaries. If smallness is seen as a collective mentality rather than an objective, numerically quantifiable fact, then it matters little if some nation is actually small, or indeed whether there is such a thing

[28] Milan Kundera, 'The Tragedy of Central Europe', in Milan Kundera (ed.), *A Kidnapped West: The Tragedy of Central Europe* (Faber & Faber, 2023), 31.

[29] Ibid., 29.

as a nation at all outside the cognition of individuals. What matters is that the category of being a small nation is being used to make sense of the world. Moreover, as already mentioned, Kundera situated smallness geographically, speaking of a zone between two large neighbours, Germany and Russia. For the purpose of studying imaginaries, it, again, matters little if *we* designate the relevant area as Central or Eastern Europe, or whether the region defined by reference to national fragility exists at all in some objective sense. The important consideration is that smallness and location are unified into an essential nexus – national vulnerability is perceived geopolitically, against the background of some geographical place that is seen as determining for the nation's prospects. It has been observed that national identity nearly always includes an idea of a homeland.[30] In the case of a 'small nation' as defined by Kundera, this must be true, for existential danger is hard to imagine separately from a 'politico-geographic situation', to use the expression by which Friedrich Ratzel sought to capture all the consequences of belonging to a particular place (climate, borders, size, relations with neighbouring states).[31]

The 'misery of small Eastern European nations' can thus be understood in two very different ways. It can refer to an objective condition of vulnerability or, alternatively, it can denote a collective self-image that foregrounds vulnerability. Consequently, the misery thesis may also be reinterpreted as a claim about the potency of a certain kind of rhetoric in East-Central Europe. This is how Miroslav Hroch approached the problem of 'small nations' in his influential account of nation-formation under foreign domination. Analysing post-communist countries, Hroch argued that the imperial background of East-Central European history resulted in some 'permanent characteristics' that are still present in the collective mentality of its inhabitants. The leaders of dominated national movements idealised smallness, but they also reacted defensively against claims that their nation was a fiction. 'This gave rise to the ensuing feeling of permanent endangerment of the nation – which was later transformed into a lasting stereotype – as well as an urge to prove the legitimacy of one's own national existence.'[32] According to this account, it is thus via stereotypes, such as the tendency to represent the nation as a person with its own history, that the experience of living in a multi-ethnic empire continues to impact the present.[33] 'Identification with a national group includes, as it did in the

[30] See Jan Penrose, 'Nations, States and Homelands: Territory and Territoriality in Nationalist Thought' (2002) 8 *Nations and Nationalism* 277. On the relationship between geography and national identity, see David Hooson (ed.), *Geography and National Identity* (Blackwell, 1994).

[31] Friedrich Ratzel, 'Über die geographische Lage. Eine politisch-geographische Betrachtung', in Hans Helmolt (ed.), *Kleine Schriften von Friedrich Ratzel* (R. Oldenbourg , 906), 257.

[32] Miroslav Hroch, 'An Unwelcome National Identity, or What to Do about "Nationalism" in the Post-Communist Countries?', in Miroslav Hroch (ed.), *Comparative Studies in Modern European History. Nation, Nationalism, Social Change* (Routledge, 2007), 271.

[33] Miroslav Hroch, 'Nationalism and National Movements: Comparing the Past and Present of Central and Eastern Europe' in Miroslav Hroch (ed.), *Comparative Studies in Modern European History. Nation, Nationalism, Social Change* (Routledge, 2007), 38.

last century, the construct of the personified and personalised nation', wrote Hroch in 1992. 'The glorious history of this personified nation is understood as the, or a, personal past of each of its members. Its defeats are understood as personal failures and continue to affect their feelings.'[34] By unifying the past and present, and thereby grounding social identity, the category of the nation exhibits the typical structure of a myth, understood not as a false story but as a narrative employed for particular social purposes.[35] 'When the object of history is the nation', remarked Ladislav Holy in his overview of Czech self-stereotypes, 'it is its imagined existence over time which makes possible the construction of the enduring "we" who imagine "our history" and unproblematically utter, as Czechs do, the phrase "We have suffered for three hundred years"'.[36]

Since myths support social identities, the two may be seen as interchangeable, yet there is clearly no such thing as a single, universally shared national identity, nor should we look for *the* national myth with respect to any collective. Identity politics can take the form of a debate over whether the nation is small or not.[37] Even when this happens, however, the category of smallness is still imposed as a frame of political thought. Of course, we do not have to suppose that all countries in East-Central Europe are equally suitable for an analysis emphasising smallness and fragility, even at the level of perception. As we saw, one version of the misery thesis regarding Eastern Europe is that its national myths are loaded with dangerous megalomania. But a great nation with a heroic past can suddenly become small and vulnerable when the mode of interpretation is switched from glorious to tragic, yielding a retrospective impression that its whole history has been overshadowed by the 'fear of the slow death of a small nation', as Paul Lendvai has said regarding Hungarians.[38] Another important characteristic of a myth is that, rather than something fixed, it is a theme which allows for the emergence of many variants or elaborations as the 'work on myth' progresses.[39] In this way, the idea of being a small endangered nation can be continually updated, adding new subthemes or varieties of existential threat – such as demographic decline, for example – so that it becomes a myth that never ceases to resonate with the times.

[34] Ibid., 270.

[35] For a conception of myth as an origin story which is not inherently opposed to history, see William H. McNeill, *Mythistory and Other Essays* (The University of Chicago Press, 1986), 3.

[36] Ladislav Holy, *The Little Czech and the Great Czech Nation. National Identity and the Post-Communist Transformation of Society* (Cambridge University Press, 1996), 117.

[37] Christian Axboe Nielsen, 'Whoever Says That Serbia Is Small Is Lying!': Serbia, Ontological (in)Security and the Unbearable Smallness of Being', in Samuël Kruizinga (ed.), *The Politics of Smallness in Modern Europe: Size, Identity and International Relations since 1800* (Bloomsbery Academic, 2022), 133.

[38] Paul Lendvai, *The Hungarians: A Thousand Years of Victory in Defeat* (Princeton University Press, 2003), 1.

[39] On the idea that myth is a process that develops by continuous work on a theme, see Hans Blumenberg, *Work on Myth* (The MIT Press, 1985).

4.3 THE IDEA OF POST-TRAUMATIC SOVEREIGNTY

But how exactly should we think about the political implications of such myths?[40] What is the politics of being a small nation? The thesis that perceived national misery of the kind observable in Eastern Europe leads to an obsession with sovereignty has been defended perhaps most comprehensively by Jarosław Kuisz who has introduced the idea of 'post-traumatic sovereignty' to express precisely this nexus. Kuisz starts from Kundera's observation that it can be an essential, identity-forming experience for the inhabitants of some country to realise that their state may be wiped away. Once this possibility is recognised, and seared on the mind, as it were, the reappearance of foreign domination becomes the preeminent, all-embracing fear. For Kuisz, the paradigmatic case of such a traumatised condition is Poland where, as he says, the state's survival is the main consideration in approaching nearly all fundamental political problems (with repeated references being made to the eighteenth-century partitions and other similar calamities, like the *annus terribilis* of 1939, when the country was again carved up by Nazi Germany and Soviet Union). Kuisz claims that, even the dispute over the rule of law that started in 2015 'should be understood and interpreted against the background of the trauma of the disappearance of the Polish state from the map of Europe'.[41] Whilst the connection may not be evident at first sight, it is precisely the idea of sovereignty that provides the link: the effect of past catastrophes has been to engender an obsessive determination never to lose political independence again, so that everything resembling it will henceforth be perceived as anathema. 'The loss-of-sovereignty argument is constantly in play', writes Kuisz, 'although it is sometimes rhetorically re-packaged to better suit the twenty-first-century context'.[42]

Kuisz mostly dwells on Poland and its national imaginaries of doom, but he argues that East-Central Europe as a whole is suffering from a traumatised attitude to sovereignty, since the inhabitants of most, if not all, countries in this region have internalised the condition that Kundera thought is defining for a small nation.[43] Loss-of-sovereignty arguments are also frequently heard elsewhere, of course. But

[40] Attempts have been made to distinguish between myths in general and specifically political myths, relying either on their content or on the close relation that some narratives have to political conditions and actions. See Henry Tudor, *Political Myth* (Macmillan, 1972), 138; Chiara Bottici, *A Philosophy of Political Myth* (Cambridge University Press, 2007), 180. It might be less controversial to speak simply of the politics of myth, without classifying myths into political and non-political, as does Bruce Lincoln, *Discourse and the Construction of Society: Comparative Studies of Myth, Ritual, and Classification* (Oxford University Press, 1989), 27.

[41] Jarosław Kuisz, *The New Politics of Poland: A Case of Post-Traumatic Sovereignty* (Manchester University Press, 2023), 197.

[42] Ibid.

[43] Ibid., 201. Similarly to Kundera, Kuisz also attributes the main role to Russia when uncovering the sources of post-traumatic sovereignty, seeing his interpretation validated in the widely diverging reactions in Eastern and Western Europe to Russia's all-out aggression against Ukraine in 2022. Ibid., 188.

Kuisz maintains that they have particular undertones in East-Central Europe where they are 'fuelled by all sorts of regionally and nationally specific backgrounds from the past'.[44] This claim appears as the latest iteration of a particular kind of misery theme about the political ideology of Eastern Europe. According to a popular view, history has endowed, or infected, this region with a special variety of nationalism centred on ethnicity. Whilst Western civic nationalism is taken to be relatively benign and nice, the Eastern ethnic variety is seen as 'doomed to nastiness by the conditions which gave rise to it'.[45] Another widely-held belief is that 'ethnic nationalism' is not merely an outlook about nationhood but also, implicitly at least, a political worldview prepossessed with sovereignty. Carlton Hayes, an important early figure in the study of nationalism, wrote that it is 'a basic part of the nationalist creed, in which every citizen of a national state is now educated, that absolute sovereignty is a right inherent in his national state and that any impairment or threatened impairment of such sovereignty is a wrong which cries to Heaven – and to himself – for vengeance.'[46] Although Hayes was not talking about any specific form of nationalism, others have argued that, when adherents of 'ethnic nationalism' attain statehood, they, especially, will exalt sovereignty as a high, if not the highest value. In other words, it is thought that 'ethnic nationalism' does not morph into something essentially different when the aim of statehood is achieved. On the contrary, it is the state that is rendered cultural and ethnic in orientation, the leaders of the former national movement now having the ambition to enable the core nation to fully realise its sovereignty by permeating the political organisation that has been created. Rogers Brubaker has argued that all states in Central-Eastern Europe are and will be nationalising (and not civic) in this sense, at least to some degree.[47]

But is this really true? And how could we possibly test the theory that, in East-Central Europe, statehood is imagined according to what Brubaker calls a 'nationalist understanding of the world' which views the political universe as being made

[44] Ibid., 203.

[45] This is how Ernst Gellner has described the views of John Plamenatz on 'Eastern nationalism'; see Ernst Gellner, *Nations and Nationalism* (Cornell University Press, 1983), 99; John Plamenatz, 'Two Types of Nationalism', in Eugene Kamenka (ed.), *Nationalism: The Nature and Evolution of an Idea* (Edward Arnold, 1976), 34.

[46] Carlton J. H. Hayes, *Essays on Nationalism* (Russell & Russell, 1966), 167.

[47] Rogers Brubaker, *Nationalism Reframed: Nationhood and the National Question in the New Europe* (Cambridge University Press, 1996), 104. Trying to establish a contrast between Western and Eastern Europe, Alfred Cobban, another influential historian, wrote in a similar vein in the 1940s: 'Once the ideal identification of cultural nation and political state has become accepted, the state in its own defence tends to act as if it were a single and united nation from the cultural point of view, and if in fact it is not this, it must endeavour to make the facts correspond to the ideal, regardless of the rights and liberties of those among its citizens who do not belong to the majority nation.' Alfred Cobban, *The Nation State and National Self-Determination* (Crowell, 1970), 110. Brubaker has later somewhat qualified his views, see Rogers Brubaker, 'Nationalizing States Revisited: Projects and Processes of Nationalization in Post-Soviet State' (2011) 34 *Ethnic and Racial Studies* 165.

up of 'sovereign, independent and culturally distinctive nation-states'.[48] We can certainly assemble a lot of material that seems to show that states in this region have valued sovereignty in the past. For example, the historian Vojtech Mastny has attempted to demonstrate that East-Central Europe has historically exhibited an aversion to federalism. 'Federal structures of any kind had been exceptional and federal thinking at best marginal in the part of Europe whose modern history had been so prominently shaped by an ethnic quest for self-assertion within national states', writes Mastny.[49] He recalls the words of Edvard Beneš who said that federalism reminded the region's inhabitants of their experience as subject nationalities under imperial domination. Some additional evidence for reluctance to parting with sovereignty could perhaps be derived from the 1950s when a group of exiled politicians and diplomats from nine East-Central European countries (Albania, Bulgaria, Czechoslovakia, Estonia, Hungary, Latvia, Lithuania, Poland and Romania) drew up a joint report assessing the prospect of eventually joining the federal projects that were being launched in Western Europe at the time. The group noted that, even though the countries under Soviet rule realised the need for European integration, they were so attached to their national characteristics and cultural independence that they could only countenance pooling some limited sovereign rights.[50] Many other such examples could be found. To come to the more recent period, is it not the case that some East-Central European countries have been contesting with unmissable vehemence the legitimacy of the EU in the name of sovereignty, sometimes going as far as declaring its core treaties unconstitutional?[51]

The first objection that suggests itself is that sovereigntism is hardly specific to East-Central Europe.[52] The more fundamental problem, however, is that the relationship between 'ethnic nationalism' and sovereignty is, in fact, deeply ambiguous. Theories which associate some sort of general worldview with 'ethnic nationalism' tend to obscure the concrete aspects in the representation of the nation (whether it is seen as small or large, for example), assuming, mistakenly, that such nuances are immaterial in comparison to what is considered typical, namely, that the outlook is ethnic rather than civic. Also, if the nation precedes the state in the imagination of

[48] Rogers Brubaker, 'Populism and Nationalism' (2020) 26 *Nations and Nationalism* 44.

[49] Vojtech Mastny, 'The Historical Experience of Federalism in East Central Europe' (1999) 14 *East European Politics and Societies* 64, 94.

[50] Europe: Nine Panel Studies by Experts from Central and Eastern Europe. An Examination of the Post Liberation Problem of the Position of Central and Eastern European Nations in a Free European Community (Free Europe Committee Inc., 1954), 3.

[51] Nathalie Brack, Ramona Coman and Amandine Crespy, 'Sovereignty Conflicts in the European Union' (2019) 4 *Les Cahiers du Cevipol* 22; Lisa H. Anders and Astrid Lorenz, 'Examining Illiberal Trends and Anti-EU Politics in East Central Europe from a Domestic Perspective: State of Research and Outline of the Book', in Astrid Lorenz and Lisa H. Anders (eds.), *Illiberal Trends and Anti-EU Politics in East Central Europe* (Palgrave, 2021), 2.

[52] For different forms of sovereigntism in Western Europe, see Thomas Guénolé, *Le souverainisme* (Humensis, 2022), 59.

its adherents, in line with the typical scenario envisaged by the category of 'ethnic nationalism', then it means that the nation is separable from the state and can be thought of independently of the legal concept of sovereignty traditionally associated with statehood. To illustrate this fact and show how nations and their political destinies were imagined against the background of empires as they existed in East-Central Europe in the nineteenth century, we can evoke the famous letter that the Czech scholar František Palacký sent to the Frankfurt Parliament in 1848. Palacký said that the Czech nation had a vital interest in the continued existence of a strong multi-national Austrian state because it needed protection from the menacing expansion of Russian power to its east. The disappearance of smaller nations in the Austrian Empire was not a danger, Palacký argued, so long as its constitution was built on the right principles.[53] There was indeed a strand of thinking which presented sovereign statehood as a natural goal for every truly respectable nation – a sign that a nation had reached full personhood.[54] National fragility was sometimes adduced as a consideration for acquiring independent statehood as a form of protection.[55] Yet by no means was this a self-evident position for someone who asked, liked Masaryk, at the end of the nineteenth century: 'how can a small nation survive and remain independent?'[56] If political structures were assessed by their ability to further the intellectual and material flourishing of the nation, then it could be argued that a strong empire is, in fact, preferable to a small nation-state. Given the geopolitical realities at the turn of the twentieth century (as the leaders of national movements saw them), the smallness of the nation could also be a strong argument *against* seeking an independent state.

The notion that all small East-Central European states whose political culture was dominated by the idea of an ethnically or culturally defined nation were obsessed with sovereignty as a result of their having emerged from empires is historically quite inaccurate. Of course, once political independence is achieved,

53 'If the bond which unites a number of diverse nations in a single political entity is to be firm and enduring, no nation can have cause to fear that the union will cost it any of the things which it holds most dear. On the contrary, each must have the certain hope that in the central authority it will find defense and protection against possible violations by neighbours of the principles of equality. Then will every nation do its best to confer upon that central authority such powers as will enable it successfully to provide the aforesaid protection.' František Palacký, 'Letter to Frankfurt, 11/4/1848', in Balázs Trencsényi and Michal Kopeček (eds.), *National Romanticism: The Formation of National Movements* (Central European University Press, 2007), 327.

54 Johann Caspar Bluntschli, *Allgemeines Staatsrecht* (J. G. Cotta, 1863), 88.

55 Notably, Roman Dmowski argued in 1903 that the fragmented Polish nation could perish if it was not brought together again in a restored Polish state. Roman Dmowski, 'Gedanken eines modernen Polen (Myśli noweczesnego Polaka)', in Martin Faber (ed.), *Roman Dmowski: Schriften* (Brill, 2023), 138.

56 Tomáš G. Masaryk, 'The Czech Question', in Ahmet Ersoy, Maciej Górny, and Vangelis Kechriotis (eds.), *Discourses of Collective Identity in Central and Southeast Europe (1770–1945), Modernism: The Creation of Nation-States* (Central European University Press, 2007), 205.

it will tend to become a cherished ideal. The imaginary about nationhood is enriched, becoming multi-layered as it now encompasses ideas about one's own state and, in addition, some conception of how the state and the nation cohere. A process of mixing, compounding and rearrangement quickly starts. Citizens of the new state are likely to be too attached to the idea of their nation enjoying sovereignty for wishing to revert back to older 'ethnic' ideas of merely cultural independence. History will often be re-cast in a way that depicts the state as the crowning achievement of the nation, as if political sovereignty has always been the goal.[57] In reality, as David J. Smith and John Hiden have written about developments in the Habsburg and Russian empires, nation-statehood was mostly thrust upon subject peoples 'as a result of the sudden collapse of the dynasties under the pressures of war and revolution'.[58] Natasha Wheatley has argued that, if the inauguration of the successor states is narrated 'purely within the tracks of nationalist history – as the self-actualization of freestanding national units – we risk obscuring the extent to which their modes of self-presentation and self-understanding might originate not with the "nation" but with the empire they ostensibly shucked off.'[59] Wheatley claims that the states created after WWI transported a whole imperial-constitutional imaginary from their imperial origins into the new world order.[60]

There was also continuity in thinking about the nation, for ideas about imperial constitutionalism were built into national imaginaries, as the case of Palacký shows. The fundamental dilemma of a 'small nation' endured. 'What good is political independence if the nation is not economically independent?', asked Masaryk in 1905. 'Some Balkan states are independent in name only. In reality, decisions about them are made by neighbouring states or only by some large banks.'[61] As we saw, ten years later, when WWI had broken out, Masaryk was extremely sanguine about the prospects of small Eastern European nations, albeit without denying that they had some economic drawbacks. By this time, he had come to embrace the idea of an independent Czech nation-state.[62] Yet this hardly means that the considerations he mentioned earlier – the advantages of a greater economic space, the fact small states

57 The assumption that cultural nations always want to become states has been recently contested in André Liebich, *Cultural Nationhood and Political Statehood: The Birth of Self-Determination* (Routledge, 2022).

58 David J. Smith and John Hiden, *Ethnic Diversity and the Nation State: National Cultural Autonomy Revisited* (Routledge, 2012), 9. For a similar argument, see Aviel Roshwald, *Ethnic Nationalism and the Fall of Empires: Central Europe, Russia and the Middle East 1914–1923* (Routledge, 2001), 2.

59 Natasha Wheatley, *The Life and Death of States: Central Europe and the Transformation of Modern Sovereignty* (Princeton University Press, 2023), 189.

60 Ibid.

61 Tomáš Garrigue Masaryk, *Kroměříž Lectures: Problem of a Small Nation* (TRIGON, 2010), 31.

62 Considering his earlier statements, it is doubtful whether this had happened by 1905, as claimed in Roman Szporluk, *The Political Thought of Thomas G. Masaryk* (Columbia University Press, 1981), 124.

are dominated by great powers – suddenly became irrelevant.[63] When new states were erected on the ruins of empires in East-Central Europe, they could also be considered as being independent in name only. Formal sovereignty was not a guarantee of independence.[64] It is true that, in the mid-1930s, when the League of Nations had proven ineffective, Northern and Eastern European small states adopted neutrality as their official line of policy, agreeing to the watering down of the League's Covenant, preferring greater independence, freedom of action and the absence of any security commitments.[65] This did not result from any abstract conception of sovereignty, however. Neutrality was felt to be the only viable option once it had become clear that all dreams of collective security and federal union had failed.

Before WWII, most governments were reluctant to take on the kind of commitments that multiplied later (the protection of individual rights, the creation of supranational bodies, etc). No Pan-European federation emerged, despite the fact that international and constitutional lawyers began to hail the voluntary limitation of sovereignty as a sign of enlightened thinking.[66] The size of the catastrophe that befell East-Central Europe in the late-1930s, which made any status quo solution impossible there, explains why its politicians were actually among the first to imagine a new political order not merely for their region but for Europe as a whole. 'After this war, Europe must become an entity, political and economic', said Władysław Sikorski, the Prime Minister of Poland, calling for a new approach to cooperation in 1941. 'The State, for example, must begin by relinquishing some of its sovereign rights, if this is necessary in order to reach agreement with a neighbouring State on matters of common interest, especially when the basic problem of security and defence is concerned.'[67] Sikorski was negotiating a federal agreement with the Czechoslovak government, whose representative Edvard Beneš, in spite of his earlier remarks on federalism's lack of appeal to a post-imperial mentality, also claimed that small nations can only improve their economic conditions and strengthen collective

[63] These very same considerations had made the idea of creating a federation attractive in the Balkans. See Janko Sakasoff, 'Neoslawismus, Balkanföderalismus und Sozialdemokratie' (1911) 4 *Der Kampf* 212.

[64] 'Gaining the status of a sovereign state might place a country on the same formal footing as all its peers', the historian Aviel Roshwald has written in reference to the interwar period in East-Central Europe. 'But outside the world of military parades, diplomatic balls, and state dinners lurked the reality of a Hobbesian international system in which big states ate little states for breakfast and then spat out the bones.' Aviel Roshwald, 'The Post-1989 Era as Heyday of the Nation-State?' (2011) 24 *International Journal of Politics, Culture, and Society* 11, 12.

[65] Zara Steiner, *The Triumph of the Dark. European International History* 1933–1939 (Oxford University Press, 1933), 359.

[66] Hent Kalmo, 'Sovereignty and European Exceptionalism', in Anne van Aaken, Pierre d'Argent, Lauri Mälksoo and Johann Justus Vasel (eds.), *The Oxford Handbook of International Law in Europe* (Oxford University Press, 2024).

[67] 'The Post-War World' (1942) 12 *Current Notes on International Affairs* 214.

security by creating a larger bloc.[68] As was noted by commentators, the humiliating fate of Central European countries had caused political thinkers to revise their views on state sovereignty. 'After the last war [i.e. WWI] even the smallest nations aspired to complete independence, but they found it only led to isolation in the face of danger ... Today the idea of closer international associations is coming to the fore, so that nations may combine to resist aggression by their stronger neighbours.'[69]

The conclusion to be drawn is not that past traumas have made East-Central European countries more, rather than less, willing to curb their sovereignty. Decades of Soviet rule certainly established untrammelled independence as a desirable goal. Soviet domination was often compared to colonialism, so that the language of self-determination became a natural idiom for the 'captive nations' of East-Central Europe.[70] Nonetheless, as Jarosław Kuisz is keen to stress, the idea of post-traumatic sovereignty does not posit agreement on where the greatest threat to political independence lies after the shocks that have caused this neurotic condition. It only stipulates that the threat of losing sovereignty is now the fundamental, never-forgotten consideration in approaching political issues. The inevitability of disagreements can be brought home by considering another 'post-' condition: a once-imperial nation seeking to come to grips with its diminished status. In attempts to explain Brexit, references were made to British political culture and history, some arguing that the wish to 'take back control' is 'deeply embedded within the political psyche of a large group of British citizens'.[71] But interpretations of Britain's imperial past shaped arguments both for and against membership in the EU. The EU could be presented in two contrasting ways, either as an obstacle to or a vehicle for Britain's imperial ambitions. As has been said, this ambiguity 'requires us to recognise post-imperial patterns of thought, not as a psychological affliction to which only half the population is subject, but as a common cultural inheritance through which all sides

[68] Edvard Beneš, 'Hitler's New Order and the New European and World Order' (Lecture at Cambridge University, May 1941), cited in: Czechoslovakia Ministry of Foreign Affairs, *Czechoslovakia in Post-War Europe: Problems of Reconstruction* (The New Europe Publishing Co., 1942), 11. For these negotiations, see Piotr S. Wandycz, *Czechoslovak–Polish Confederation and the Great Powers, 1940–1943* (Greenwood Press, 1978), 38.

[69] 'Wiadomości Polskie: "A Central European Confederation"' (1942), in Walter Lipgens (ed.), *Documents on the History of European Integration: Continental Plans for European Union 1939–1945* (Walter de Gruyter, 1985), 636.

[70] On the emergence of the expression 'captive nations', see Anna Mazurkiewicz, *Voice of the Silenced Peoples in the Global Cold War: The Assembly of Captive European Nations, 1954–1972* (De Gruyter, 2021). On the comparison of Soviet rule with colonialism as experienced in Africa and Asia, see James Mark, Bogdan C. Iacob, Tobias Rupprecht and Ljubica Spaskovska (eds.), *1989: A Global History of Eastern Europe* (Cambridge University Press, 2019), 174.

[71] Anand Menon and Alan Wagner, 'Taking Back Control: Sovereignty as Strategy in Brexit Politics' (2020) 8 *Territory, Politics, Governance* 279.

think and argue'.[72] In the case of Britain, we may thus speak of post-imperial sovereignty, not having in mind any doctrine but something crucial about British political culture, namely, that the question of sovereignty is there embedded in particular patterns of thought. These patterns do not yield any consistent set of political views, nor even a belief in the value of sovereignty as traditionally understood. Britain's attitude to European integration has been aptly described as 'Euro-equivocation'.[73]

If we distinguish between general patterns of thought, or political languages, on the one hand, and particular arguments formulated within these languages, on the other, then the idea of post-traumatic sovereignty would belong to the level shared by various political camps existing within a country. This means that it cannot be understood as a worldview with a set of clear-cut beliefs about what endangers sovereignty and how to best protect it. Such beliefs pertain to the level where disagreements appear about the central problem, namely, how to ensure that political independence is not lost. On this reading, it becomes much less problematic to portray the idea of post-traumatic sovereignty as a regional phenomenon. Countries in East-Central Europe cannot be lumped together meaningfully for all purposes. What Kuisz claims is that, despite all the differences between their individual historical experiences, countries in this region are similar in being small nations in the sense used by Kundera – they share a feeling of existential danger derived from these experiences. This does not condition these countries to adopt any single position on the value of retaining unlimited independence as opposed to joining some larger organisation. The imaginary of misery can accommodate a whole variety of positions, depending on how the predicament attributed to the nation is articulated in political and legal terms. Even assuming attachment to national independence as a vague general goal, it leaves open a series of hard problems. What exactly is independence? Is it captured by the legal concept of sovereignty? Can it be hollowed out in a federal organisation? Consensus cannot be expected on such questions, since they express ambiguities in the very idea of sovereignty. When threats are seen to emanate from various sources, not merely from legal limitations on decision making, then the same political position (for example, joining a federation) can be seen as either compromising or protecting

[72] Robert Saunders, 'Brexit and Empire: "Global Britain" and the Myth of Imperial Nostalgia' (2020) 48 *The Journal of Imperial and Commonwealth History* 1140, 1140. Another explanation offered for Brexit was geography and how it has configured Britain's relationship with Europe over a very long period. The historian Ian Morris claimed that, only when facts are out 'into this framework do we see why Brexit seems so compelling to some, so appalling to others'; Ian Morris, *Geography Is Destiny. Britain and the World, a 10 000-Year History* (Profile Books, 2022). Whatever one might think of this explanation specifically, or of the relationship between Brexit and geography, the observation is again that geography explains both the Leave and the Remain vote by suggesting completely different implications to different groups.

[73] Brian Harrison, *Finding a Role? The United Kingdom 1970–1990* (Oxford University Press, 2010), 20.

sovereignty. In the presence of such difficulties, it is surely equivocation we should expect, not consistency and agreement.

4.4 POST-COMMUNISM AND THE 'SOVEREIGNTY CONUNDRUM'

In the light of what has been said, we can also form a better understanding of an apparent inconsistency in the behaviour of post-Soviet countries or what Wojciech Sadurski has called the 'sovereignty conundrum', referring to an irony he noted in the eastern enlargement of the EU. 'Countries with a proud national history', wrote Sadurski in 2004,

> which have only just emerged from several decades of humiliating and oppressive domination by the Soviet Union (at worst being subjected to forceful integration into Soviet statehood as in the case of the Baltic states), and at best suffering all the burdens and disadvantages of 'limited sovereignty', are now about to embark upon the surrender of the sovereignty again, this time for an admittedly benign foreign body, but a foreign body nevertheless.[74]

Indeed, how can this be explained? How to account for the wish of post-communist countries to join the EU when, as several authors have claimed, theirs was an old-fashioned sovereigntist outlook, either because East-Central Europe had missed the aggiornamento of constitutional imagination that the West had experienced since the 1950s or because the Soviet era itself had produced a form of constitutionalism that favours an archaic conception of nation-statehood? According to Signe Larsen, one important effect of the Soviet period was to ingrain the idea that threats to democracy emanate primarily from foreign oppressors (from 'them', not 'us'). Hence the image of a pure, ethnically defined nation, deserving of unlimited freedom, and the 'constitutional emphasis on nationalism and sovereignty'.[75] But, if so, there really is a puzzle. If the mindset of the post-Soviet countries was 'incompatible with the constitutional reality of the Union they were acceding to', as Rehling says,[76] how could these countries not merely join the EU but subscribe to even deeper forms of integration later?

Different explanations have been offered for the 'sovereignty conundrum'. Anneli Albi maintains that it was in virtue of some strange naiveté that lawyers in East-Central Europe failed to make their idea of national sovereignty a serious obstacle to the process of accession to the EU. 'Although constitutional awareness about the EU gained ground as accession drew closer, Central and Eastern European scholars

[74] Wojciech Sadurski, 'The Role of the EU Charter of Rights in the Process of Enlargement', in Georg A. Bermann and Katharina Pistor (eds.), *Law and Governance in an Enlarged European Union* (Hart, 2004), 71.

[75] Signe Rehling Larsen, 'Varieties of Constitutionalism in the European Union' (2021) 84 *Modern Law Review* 477, 497.

[76] Ibid.

tended to devote minimal space to analysing the nature of the EU polity, and to view the Union therefore merely as an international organisation or a confederation of states, finding that it would not significantly affect national sovereignty.'[77] Sadurski detected more strategy in the efforts to show that accession to the EU actually involves no loss of sovereignty. In his view, the role of scholars has been either to back up with constitutional arguments political choices made for other reasons or to influence decisions by helping to convince the political class and the society at large that their traditionalist ideas regarding sovereignty and the nation are not at all incompatible with European integration. Thus, some commentators downplayed the unique character of the EU, pointing out that all international treaties entail a surrender of sovereign rights – this being depicted itself an exercise of sovereignty – and emphasising that the difference is simply one of degree. It was also said that some important powers were retained by Member States or that the transfer was not irrevocable. 'In conclusion', writes Sadurski,

> legal constitutional scholarship in the accession states is working hard to reconcile the state-focused discourse of sovereignty with the legal realities of the EU accession, and in so doing it constructs a legal fiction whereby the transfer of some, even crucial, powers to the supranational level does not amount to a transfer of sovereignty, but only to a transfer of the exercise of some sovereign powers.[78]

One difficulty with such explanations is that they make an assumption about what the reality is with regard to the EU, namely, that it involves a loss of sovereignty, so that there must appear an element of deception or at least artificiality in the work of constitutional lawyers who deny this. As a matter of fact, sovereignty is a contested idea and the multiplicity of its meanings can produce genuine disagreements about its continuing relevance, even in an organisation as deeply integrated as the EU.[79] From the point of view of constitutional imaginaries, the more important point is this, however: such explanations also assume too much about what can be deduced from the kind of lofty rhetoric encountered in constitutional texts. There is little doubt that some of the constitutions in East-Central Europe celebrate sovereignty in exalted terms. For example, the preamble to the Polish constitution (1997) reads: 'Homeland, which recovered, in 1989, the possibility of a sovereign and democratic determination of its fate . . .'. This line conveys a sentiment that can certainly be described as pride and joy in the possession of sovereignty. The late-1980s witnessed an explosion of such rhetoric in East-Central Europe. To illustrate the solemnity that was common at the time, we can recall a speech that Bronislavas Genzelis, a

77 Anneli Albi, *EU Enlargement and the Constitutions of Central and Eastern Europe* (Cambridge University Press, 2005), 123–124.

78 Sadurski, 'The Role of the EU Charter of Rights in the Process of Enlargement', 79.

79 See especially Michel Troper, 'The Survival of Sovereignty', in Hent Kalmo and Quentin Skinner (eds.), *Sovereignty in Fragments: The Past, Present and Future of a Contested Concept* (Cambridge University Press, 2011), 132.

Lithuanian politician, gave in 1989: 'Until a nation does not regain independence, its existence is constantly endangered. If a nation has necessary conditions to develop its culture, it is alive; if it has its own economy, it exists, but without political independence it only vegetates.'[80] When the Lithuanian Constitution was adopted a few years later, its opening words struck a similar note. As if to dispel any prospect that the nation will have to vegetate again, Article 3 provided: 'No one may limit or restrict the sovereignty of the People or make claims to the sovereign powers of the People.'[81] Whilst it would be hard to claim that such statements do not demonstrate an attachment to political independence, they nonetheless tell us very little about how sovereignty is actually understood in the constitutional culture that informs the interpretation of these texts. Fundamental questions persist. What is independence? Is it enhanced or weakened in a federal organisation? Which concept of sovereignty is best able to capture the predicament of a small nation in danger?

The 'sovereignty conundrum' may cease to need an explanation once we discover that there is no objective inconsistency in joining the EU under the cover of independence-minded rhetoric. Let us suppose that the Soviet shock indeed produced, or reinforced, a condition of post-traumatic sovereignty – that is, an obsession with political independence – in post-communist countries. As noted by Jarosław Kuisz, one of the expressions of this condition is a Europeanist position which is quite willing to accept the limitations that membership in the EU brings. These limitations are accepted not because of some theoretical notion of sovereignty or a lack of understanding about the incompatibility of these limitations with a traditional idea of sovereignty. The rationale is that membership in the EU strengthens political independence. From this perspective, there is no conundrum, since it is precisely the experience of foreign domination that is thought to weigh in favour of EU membership. Perhaps too schematically, Kuisz divides Poland into two political camps, sovereigntists and Europeanists, attributing to each a reasonably consistent set of views about how Polish sovereignty should be defended. Both camps are supposedly traumatised by Poland's past. Both are fully committed to the imperative of not allowing Poland's political independence to be taken away again. And unsurprisingly, both believe that their views, not those of the other camp, reflect the correct interpretation of Polish history. Sovereigntists look back to interwar Poland, often idealising it, extracting from it what they see as relevant, and project this vision into the future as a model of maximal sovereignty.

> The opponents of the Polish sovereigntists interpret the events of the traumatic past differently. For the Europeanists, membership of the EU is what guarantees the permanence of the state in a content and form adequate to the twenty-first century.

[80] Bronislavas Genzelis, 'Nation and Sovereignty', in Bronislavas Genzelis (ed.), *The Restitution of Lithuania's Statehood* (Lithuanian National Museum, 2007), 108.

[81] See Anneli Albi, *EU Enlargement and the Constitutions of Central and Eastern Europe* (Cambridge University Press, 2005), 26.

> They accuse their opponents of an anachronistic understanding of the state, inadequate for a globalised world. Europeanists are ready for novelty, including the experiment of building European structures. They invariably regard Russia as the main threat to Polish sovereignty and consider power plays within the EU to be the lesser evil, far better than unrestricted competition of the former nation-states in pre-1939 Europe.[82]

To generalise beyond Poland, rather than ascribing a single constitutional ideology or mind-set to a country, it might be more appropriate to distinguish between several competing outlooks, without thereby denying the existence of a common framework of ideas and representations.[83] The presence of some overarching framework and a multiplicity of views within this structure are both central elements if we wish to recognise the indisputable fact of disagreement and still retain the notion that even fundamental differences of opinion are embedded in a shared collective inheritance. In Poland, the Law and Justice party has directed its loss-of-sovereignty rhetoric mostly against the EU. According to Sadurski, this party possesses a 'worldview' that it shares with Hungary's Fidesz and that it hopes to make dominant in all of East-Central Europe – a vision that 'is primarily based on a suspicion of the outside world, and on the celebration of national sovereignty as the supreme value in a nation's policy, which needs to be forever defended and strengthened'.[84] Kuisz describes the ideology of the Law and Justice party in nearly identical terms but he adds a crucially important caveat: its liberal opponents are similarly attached to national sovereignty, only *they* warn against Poland leaving the EU and finding itself exposed to Russian aggression.[85] Although sovereigntists and Europeanists agree on the importance of preserving sovereignty, they disagree on whether some sort of fundamental equivalence can be established between the threats emanating from Russia and the EU. Those opposing the Law and Justice party are not blind to the imperfections of the EU, nor are they necessarily unable to appreciate the difficulty of reconciling the present configuration of the EU with a traditional notion of sovereignty. What they believe, according to Kuisz, is that these problems are either secondary or merely apparent when compared to the much more serious danger posed to Polish sovereignty by Russia.[86]

The collective self-image of being a small endangered nation can be considered as precisely the kind of overarching structure of meaning which operates by framing an on-going debate, rather than dictating any political positions or legal doctrines.

82 Jarosław Kuisz, *The New Politics of Poland: A Case of Post-Traumatic Sovereignty* (Manchester University Press, 2023), 203.

83 For an attempt to describe different political cultures in France, see Serge Bergstein (ed.), *Les cultures politiques en France* (Éditions du Seuil, 1999).

84 Wojciech Sadurski, *Poland's Constitutional Breakdown* (Oxford University Press, 2019), 12.

85 Jarosław Kuisz, *The New Politics of Poland: A Case of Post-Traumatic Sovereignty* (Manchester University Press, 2023), 197.

86 Ibid., 202.

To insist on ambivalence and equivocation is not to imply that such malleable imaginaries are without effect on constitutional reasoning. Clifford Geertz has observed that some of the most critical decisions concerning the direction of public life are not made in formal institutions such as parliaments but in the unformalised realms of the collective consciousness, at the level of the 'conceptual structures individuals use to construe experience'.[87] Whatever their deep cultural sources, it is undeniable, however, that decisions are also made in parliaments and courts. This begs the question of how exactly do the collective images that swirl in a culture enter the realm of formal decisions. Summing up the literature on why national courts have accepted the jurisprudence of the CJEU, Karen Alter has distinguished between two rival approaches: legalism, which invokes legal logic and reasoning to explain national court behaviour, and neo-realism, which puts the emphasis on politics and the pursuit of national interest. Alter criticises both approaches, legalism mainly for ignoring politics and neo-realism for not offering any clear account of how the 'national interest' is constructed.[88] One way to bring culture into this analysis would be to assert that politicians and judges are indeed seeking to further the national interest, but that they understand it in a pre-conditioned manner, in the light of a concrete, culturally informed view of what is the situation of the 'nation'.[89] But even this line of analysis would yield an excessively simplified picture of judicial reasoning. Legal arguments are mostly not a mere dressing up, devised *ex post* after having latched onto some idea of the national interest. Few constitutional scholars would probably accept the claim that, in assessing whether membership of the EU involves a loss of sovereignty, all they are doing is making some pre-determined decision about the national interest palatable to an audience. On the other hand, it would be equally unconvincing to say that, when engaging in this kind of exercise, their eyes are fixed on some abstract notion of sovereignty which they merely unpack by the rules of logic.

What other frame of mind could there be, then, if legal arguments must retain some force yet also be penetrated by the categories that are used to make sense of collective experience? For clarifying the nature of constitutional imaginaries and their role in legal reasoning, it might be useful to start from Carl Schmitt's famous classification of different types of legal thinking, in particular, the distinction between normativism and concrete-order thinking. Schmitt claims that there exist some socially consecrated images (or 'concrete-order notions', as he calls them) such

87 Clifford Geertz, *Interpretation of Cultures: Selected Essays* (Basic Books, 1973), 314.

88 Karen Alter, 'Explaining National Court Acceptance of European Court Jurisprudence: A Critical Evaluation of Theories of Legal Integration', in Anna-Marie Slaughter, Alec Stone Sweet and J. H. H. Weiler (eds.), *The European Court and National Courts: Doctrine and Jurisprudence: Legal Change and Social Context* (Hart, 1998).

89 It has long been recognised that the national interest which influences decisions is not something objective but a reflection of the images that deciders form of their environment; see Joseph Frankel, *National Interest* (Palgrave Macmillan, 1970), 110.

as brave soldiers, duty-conscious bureaucrats, respectable comrades, and so on, which a strictly normativist understanding ('rule and statute thinking') excludes from the law altogether since it considers that they have no direct legal relevance. Actually, says Schmitt, such concrete notions are central to law as abstract rules never enforce themselves but are applied by people in well-determined situations, against the background of concrete patterns of social order which should be honoured, not ignored, according to Schmitt.[90] Irrespective of whether one agrees with this last point (on the need to respect established social institutions), Schmitt's analysis can be taken as an insightful portrayal of how constitutional reasoning really proceeds. Although this might not be how Schmitt himself viewed it, concrete-order thinking could be seen as being directed by what Hans-Georg Gadamer has described as a 'fore-conception'.[91] Interpretation always starts from some provisional understanding which is later replaced by a more suitable one if the expectations of the interpreter are not met. Like Europeanists and sovereigntists in general, scholars and judges may also be impelled by an impression of where the greatest danger lies given the concrete situation of their nation, without this fore-conception necessarily determining their conclusions about the law. They could have a Europeanist sensibility and believe that military aggression is what really threatens their small nation – much more than any formal limitations within the EU – yet still be swayed by the claim that sovereignty (as enshrined in the constitution) is an obstacle to European integration. Some legal arguments may simply appear irresistible to them. What their fore-conception brings is an articulation of the situation in terms of concrete facts and circumstances. But it also brings something else. Schmitt's insight was to note that, when lawyers practice concrete-order thinking, they do not apprehend society as a factual realm separate from applicable norms. The concrete situation bleeds into law by making some interpretations seem more appropriate than others.

The 'sovereignty conundrum' grows out of the assumption that there is no fundamental difference between the Soviet Union or the EU at the level of the idea of foreignness. As Sadurski remarked, for all its benign character, the EU is also a foreign body. When looking at how courts in East-Central Europe have reasoned on European integration, we see, however, that they do not start from such abstract notions as a 'foreign body'. In several cases, courts have explicitly underlined that the problem of sovereignty should be approached in a particular way if membership in an organisation such as the EU is being considered. In its judgment on the Lisbon Treaty, Poland's Constitutional Tribunal maintained that globalisation and European integration had transformed the character of sovereignty, which 'is no longer perceived as an unlimited possibility of exerting influence on other states or a manifestation of power that is free from external influences'.[92] According to the

90 Carl Schmitt, *On the Three Types of Juristic Thought* (Praeger, 2004), 54–55.

91 Hans-Georg Gadamer, *Truth and Method* (Continuum, 2006), 269–270.

92 Para 2.1 of the judgment of 24 November 2010 (K 32/09).

Tribunal, in protecting the nation's freedom to determine its own fate, the Polish Constitution confirms rather than negates the possibility of accepting international commitments, especially if they have 'the compensatory effect in the form of partaking in the decision-making process in the European Union' or are otherwise beneficial for the nation. 'The accession to the European Union creates unique possibilities, in our history, of carrying out modernisation projects in the conditions of stability arising from the membership in the community of values and traditions, in which the Polish national identity is rooted.'[93] Lithuania's Constitutional Court has described EU membership as a geopolitical choice which ensures better preconditions for achieving constitutional imperatives.[94] The Czech Constitutional Court adopted a similar perspective in reviewing the Lisbon Treaty. It asserted that, in a modern democratic state, sovereignty of the state in not an end in itself but a means at the service of foundational values. After dwelling on the *sui generis* character of the EU, the Court cited the memorandum attached to the Czech Republic's accession application from the 1990s which declared:

> The Czech nation has only recently regained its full national sovereignty. Yet, as the Governments of present Member States have done in the past, the Government of the Czech Republic has irrevocably arrived at the conclusion that, within the context of modern European developments the exchange of a part of its national sovereignty for a shared supranational sovereignty and co-responsibility is an inevitable step to be taken for the benefit of its own country and the whole of Europe.[95]

It might be argued that this passage reveals what is really happening: that courts are presenting an internationalist conception of sovereignty to underwrite a political decision at which governments had 'irrevocably arrived'. Yet there is no reason to suppose that the Czech Constitutional Court was being insincere or cunningly strategic when it insisted that the country's independence can be enhanced rather than diminished by membership in the EU since the latter 'can ultimately lead to protection and strengthening of the sovereignty of member states vis-à-vis external, especially geopolitical and economic factors'.[96] In analysing the Court's judgment, one commentator focused on the doctrinal part regarding sovereignty and set it apart from these 'rather political statements emphasizing the necessity of EU integration

[93] Para 2.2 of the judgment of 24 November 2010 (K 32/09).

[94] Irmantas Jarukaitis and Gintaras Švedas, 'The Constitutional Experience of Lithuania in the Context of European and Global Governance Challenges', in Anneli Albi and Samo Bardutzky (eds.), *National Constitutions in European and Global Governance: Democracy, Rights, the Rule of Law* (Springer, 2019), 1008.

[95] Para 148. Translation in: The Editors and Jan Komarek, 'The Czech Constitutional Court's Second Decision on the Lisbon Treaty of 3 November 2009' (2009) 5 *European Constitutional Law Review* 350–351 (emphasis omitted).

[96] Para 102 of the judgment Pl. ÚS 19/08, cited in: Rike U. Krämer, 'Looking through Different Glasses at the Lisbon Treaty: The German Constitutional Court and the Czech Constitutional Court', in Andreas Fischer-Lescano, Christian Joerges and Arndt Wonka (eds.), *The German Constitutional Court's Lisbon Ruling: Legal and Political Science Perspectives* (Zerp, 2010) 13.

in the globalised world'.[97] Such a line of separation can be drawn, of course, and it almost imposes itself when law is distinguished from politics, as it traditionally is. On the other hand, in so doing, we also cut off a flow of reasoning that somehow appears continuous and follows a curiously similar path in many judicial decisions where membership in the EU is under consideration. Arguments about sovereignty are not derived but rather framed, prepared, set out as appropriate against the background of some picture of the world where the nation or the country supposedly finds itself. Moreover, even the most Europhile judgments have not refrained from caveats. By leaving it to Parliament to list the competences that cannot be transferred to the EU, the Czech Constitutional Court suggested that there are such competences and thus limits to integration. Poland's Constitutional Tribunal stated explicitly that there is a point at which the 'essence of sovereignty' is compromised.[98] This reservation was later invoked to contest the validity of EU law.[99] To explain such reversals, we again need to look beyond abstract legal concepts, not assuming, however, that another political decision must have been taken and is simply being justified in the language of sovereignty. Both pro- and contra-EU arguments were linked to sovereignty at the time of the eastern enlargement of 2004.[100] By studying cultural imaginaries, we are making it easier to understand how such contradictory arguments can still make sense today.

97 Petr Bříza, 'The Czech Republic: The Constitutional Court on the Lisbon Treaty: Decision of 26 November 2008' (2009) 5 *European Constitutional Law Review* 149.

98 Para 2.2 of the judgment of 24 November 2010 (K 32/09).

99 See Adam Ploszka, 'It Never Rains but It Pours: The Polish Constitutional Tribunal Declares the European Convention on Human Rights Unconstitutional' (2022) 6 *Hague Journal on the Rule of Law*.

100 Merje Kuus, *Geopolitics Reframed: Security and Identity in Europe's Eastern Enlargement* (Palgrave, 2007), 63

5

Ruling Britannia

Martin Loughlin

5.1 INTRODUCTION

Britain's constitutional evolution falls within the mainstream of European constitutional traditions, but the gulf between its governing practices and those adopted in the European mainstream has grown progressively wider. While most European nation-states have adopted written constitutions at critical moments of modern history, Britain continues to adhere to the traditional conception of a constitution as a set of laws, customs and practices that continuously evolve in response to social, economic and political change. This is one reason why Britain's involvement in the venture of creating a European Union has always been rather awkward.

In this chapter, I sketch the main constitutional tropes that have emerged in British thought and show how they express a constitutional identity antithetical to the assumptions driving the project of continuing European integration. I first introduce a series of constitutional stories through which the English have sought to explain themselves as a nation and a state and then consider how these accounts have evolved with the expansion of the English state into a British imperial state. Finally, I will indicate how these legacies ensured that Britain could never become an active participant in the European federal project.

5.2 ENGLISH CONSTITUTIONAL NARRATIVES

We live in an age of constitutionalism. With so much ideological power now being invested in that term, it is difficult today to speak of the constitution of a state without there looming over us an image of the constitution as a foundational text that not only establishes the framework of government but also expresses the regime's sense of collective identity. Because of this, it may be less confusing simply to state that Britain does not possess a constitution. This claim was first clearly expressed by Alexis de Tocqueville, who noted in 1835 that 'in England the constitution may change continually or rather it does not in reality exist'.[1] Now that the normative weight invested in that term is so great, it is difficult to discuss the British constitution without this leading to a skewed understanding of the nature of the regime.

The British certainly have a system of government, but those who now invoke 'the constitution' invariably end up investing it with an inappropriate degree of normative authority. Whatever normative power the term carries can only be grasped by immersing ourselves in the sense of the constitution as the inheritance of a long tradition in the practical art of governing. But, because the authority of its practices rests on experience, the type of knowledge these practices embody cannot easily be reduced to formal rules: to codify the practices is to change them. To the extent that constitutional rules exist, they are invariably rules of procedure and precedent rather than of principle. Consequently, the normative force of the practices is best revealed through a series of stories that have grown up around them.

These stories have generated a series of shared beliefs about the formation of not just an imagined community (a people, a nation), but also of the terms on which they are governed (a state). I introduce five related narratives through which the political identity of the English is shaped: the ancient constitution, the tradition of local self-government, the authority of the rule of law, the status of the Crown and the principle of sovereignty.

5.2.1 *The Ancient Constitution*

The English political tradition has been much influenced by a series of claims prominently touted by seventeenth-century common lawyers, which they formalized as the doctrine of the ancient constitution. This asserted that the early Saxons (the Goths) had created an ancient, pre-feudal and liberty-preserving constitution. At its core was the great meeting, the *Witenagemote*, where freeborn Anglo-Saxons met to make law and deliberate over the affairs of the kingdom.

This story of the ancient Gothic constitution supports a series of constitutional claims. First, it underpins the asserted existence of an immemorial common law. Arguing that the common law is a body of unchanging custom that exists 'time out of the mind of man', Chief Justice Coke maintained that, rather than conquering England, William I had vindicated his claim in trial by battle and took the throne subject to these ancient laws.[2] The story, secondly, challenges any Norman claim to absolute sovereignty; English kings, including William, occupy an office of limited authority and are obliged to rule according to the ancient fundamental laws of the land. Thirdly, the story rebuts the standard historical account that Parliament came into existence only in the latter half of the thirteenth century as an instrument of

[1] Alexis de Tocqueville, *Democracy in America* (Vintage Books, 1990).

[2] Edward Coke, 'Institutes', in Steve Sheppard (ed.), *The Selected Writings and Speeches of Sir Edward Coke*, vol 2 (Liberty Fund, 2003).

Norman policy. According to the Gothic narrative, the rights of the Commons derive from the ancient *Witenagemote*: the rights of 'freeborn Englishmen' to meet in Parliament derive directly from the ancient constitution, independent of sanction by kings.[3]

According to this narrative, the continuing quest has been to overthrow 'the Norman Yoke' and restore these ancient liberties. The great constitutional documents of Magna Carta (1215), the Petition of Right (1628) and the Bill of Rights (1689) do not enact anything new. 'In all our great political struggles', proclaimed the nineteenth-century Whig constitutional historian, E. A. Freeman, 'the voice of the Englishman has never called for the assertion of new principles, for the enactment of new laws; the cry has always been for the better observance of the laws which were already in force, for the redress of grievances which had arisen from their corruption or neglect'.[4] English constitutional development is apparently marked not by political struggles of the disenfranchised to assert their modern claims, but by the degree to which these ancient liberties have been restored.

During the seventeenth-century, this doctrine of the ancient constitution was part of the ideological weaponry of the parliamentary forces, who maintained that the true source of governmental power lay not with the king but with 'the people', as expressed by their parliamentary representatives. The failure to resolve this dispute between king and parliament by political negotiation led to civil war, defeat of the royalist cause, execution of the king, formation of the Commonwealth and Protectorate and then, in 1660, restoration of the monarchy. These dramatic events in turn shaped the form of the modern British constitution.

The modern constitutional settlement was forged after the Revolution of 1688 when, once James II had fled the kingdom, a convention Parliament – established without any king to convene it – offered the throne to William and Mary on terms laid down in the Bill of Rights. But the settlement was ambiguous. Was the king above the three estates of lords, bishops and commons as the law of the constitution stated? Should the king now be treated as one of three equal component parts of the sovereign Parliament (king, lords and commons) as the emerging doctrine of parliamentary sovereignty implied? Should the commons, as sole representative voice of the people, now be accorded clear primacy in the constitution, as the emerging principle of popular sovereignty suggested? Such questions had to be fudged both to maintain the stability of the post-1688 state and to strengthen the authority of its governing institutions.

From the outset, the modern settlement was marked by a reluctance to avoid any close examination of its founding principles. Its legacy is to be found in a distinctively English style of constitutional scholarship based on what came to be called the

[3] See J. G. A. Pocock, *The Ancient Constitution and the Feudal Law: A Study of English Historical Thought in the Seventeenth Century* (Cambridge University Press, 1987).

[4] E. A. Freeman, *The Growth of the English Constitution* (Macmillan, 1876), 57.

Whig interpretation of history. The great nineteenth-century Whig historians conceived the English constitution as an elaborate cultural heritage whose study provided a boundless source of prescriptive wisdom. They present a story about the triumph of liberty over absolute sovereign power, evidenced by the increasing importance of representative institutions in the British system. And a central theme of this narrative was a distaste for the lawyer's approach to the subject. Complaining that 'the legal mind' is congenitally incapable of grasping ambiguity, uncertainty, or heterogeneity, the historians argued that the invention of the legal concept of sovereignty had corrupted understanding of this unique constitutional development.[5]

5.2.2 *The Tradition of Local Self-Government*

The arguments of the Whig constitutional historians also bolster a claim about the pivotal importance of local self-government in the English system. England, they maintained, 'is pre-eminently the country of local government', a claim based on the fact that the main outlines of English local government – the township, the hundred and the shire – were drawn long before central government (as distinct from rudimentary political overlordship) came into existence.[6] Central administration was the creation of the Normans and local administration, which 'was probably the unconscious adaptation of primeval Teutonic custom to the conditions of new settlement', was at least 500 years older.[7] Consequently, whenever the centre has devised new local tasks, it has tended to work with the existing fabric.

The hundred has since disappeared, but the township (which became known by its ecclesiastical name of parish) and the shire (better known by its Norman name of county) continued as the institutional framework of local government through centuries of unbroken political development. And, although not forming part of the original Teutonic settlement, by the time of the Conquest, each shire had a borough (*burh*), such that the two formed an integral unit: 'The shire maintains the burh; the burh defends the shire'.[8] By the eleventh century, a distinctive pattern of local government that recognized differences between town and country existed, and it establishes the basis of the modern system.

Within this Whig tradition, local self-government is an important source of English liberties. It was claimed that exclusive responsibility for the management of local affairs under the ancient constitution, including that of taxation, rested with the *gemote* (moot or meeting) of all the freemen of the township. Further, the *gemote* provided the foundation of the entire political structure, since it was the

5 Ibid., 4. See also Herbert Butterfield, *The Whig Interpretation of History* (G. Bell and Sons, 1931); J. W. Burrow, *A Liberal Descent: Victorian Historians and the English Past* (Cambridge University Press, 1981).

6 Edward Jenks, *An Outline of English Local Government*, 5th ed. (Methuen, 1921), 9.

7 Ibid.

8 F. W. Maitland, *Township and Borough* (Cambridge University Press, 1898), 37.

heads of the *gemotes* (the *reeves*) who met collectively in the *Witenagemote*, from which the modern parliament emerged. The structure of political authority thus rested on the will of the people expressed through their local communities. Neither the king nor his government had the power to make law or levy taxes without first obtaining the consent of the nation in parliament.

From this perspective, the great constitutional struggle has been to ensure that these ancient local liberties – the fundamental laws – are not usurped by the central authority. This narrative runs through to the nineteenth century where we find Joshua Toulmin Smith arguing that: 'Local self-government lies at the very basis of free institutions, and is the only effectual guarantee for the responsibility of those in authority'.[9] Local government immunises the regime from a hierarchical order being imposed by the central authority.

Yet how is this liberal order maintained once the concept of sovereignty emerges as the fundamental principle during the eighteenth century? One answer was supplied by the German jurist, Rudolf Gneist, who in the late nineteenth century argued, contrary to Montesquieu, that the real basis of English government was to be found not in separation but in unity. England, Gneist contended, is governed from top to bottom by a class of wealthy landowners, who performed unpaid personal service not only as members of the Lords and Commons but also as Justices of the Peace who administered the counties. Beneath the apparent divisions there existed a deep unity, which Gneist referred to as 'self-government'.[10] Within this network, the Justices of the Peace performed the pivotal role. Being entrusted with the combined tasks of administration and justice free from active control by the central authority, the Justices became the principal organs of local government.

Gneist did not base this scheme on some romantic-historical idea of Teutonic folk-freedom that built authority from the locality upwards. He recognized that the English state was highly centralized and that 'England has to thank the Norman kings for an absolute government which enabled her to develop a consciousness of unity and strength at a time when all the great nations of the Continent were disintegrated by feudalism'.[11] It was precisely because England had centralized so early and no serious challengers to the sovereign authority of the central power existed that it was able to concede local liberties. This evolving practice, in turn, established an organic connection between state and society that permitted the

[9] Joshua Toulmin Smith, *Government by Commission Illegal and Pernicious* (S. Sweet, 1849), 51. Cf. Tocqueville, Democracy in America, 61: 'municipal institutions constitute the strength of free nations. Town meetings are to liberty what primary schools are to science; they bring it within the people's reach, they teach men how to use and how to enjoy it. A nation may establish a free government, but without municipal institutions it cannot have a spirit of liberty.'

[10] Rudolg Gneist's main writings on this subject are: *Self-Government: Communalverfassung und Verwaltungsgerichte im England* (Springer, 1871) and *Englische V erfassungsgeschichte* (Springer, 1882). The latter is translated as *The History of the English Constitution*, trans. P. A. Ashworth (Clowes, 1886).

[11] Josef Redlich and F. W. Hirst, *Local Government in England*, vol 2 (Macmillan, 1903), 395.

emergence of the rule of judicature. And it is this rule of judicature that prevented the Crown from taking direct control over local administration.

This narrative of local self-government presents a distinctive account of English constitutional arrangements. By the end of the eighteenth century, it had been recognized across continental Europe that responsibility for the internal administration of the country was that of the central state. As the tasks of government increased, so a distinction emerged between judgement and the execution of a judgement. From this differentiation, two discrete activities came to be identified: the rule of judicature and the rule of administration. The latter – administrative law – was founded on the power of the sovereign to issue ordinances. Since administration was the peculiar domain of the sovereign, these orders were treated as his law and were equivalent to the laws of the land. It was through this administrative law that the central state regulated and controlled the activities of local institutions.

This continental tradition can be contrasted with the English story of local self-government. Although England has since the Conquest been ruled from the centre, the central authority has not generally sought to administer from the centre. Consequently, the idea that administration is the special preserve of the sovereign, in the sense that disputes concerning administrative issues should be resolved by separate courts in accordance with special principles, has never been accepted. This achievement has been realized by ensuring that the common law formed an undivided system of law. Since no clear distinction could be made between public law and private law, the administration has remained subordinated to the ordinary law and the principle of the rule of law comes to represent the rule of judicature.[12]

In this story, there never emerged in England a hierarchical and undifferentiated concept of 'administration'. Central government exercised no inherent superior jurisdiction over local institutions. Local institutions emerge not simply as creatures of the central authority but as representations of historic communities within a structure of national laws to which both the Crown and the localities are bound. In this sense, the English inheritance is one of local government rather than local administration.

A second, equally important, implication concerns the role of Parliament. The common law, as an undivided system of national laws, could not be altered by the Crown alone, but only with the consent of the people expressed in Parliament. This principle of Parliamentary sovereignty is thus entwined with the idea of the unity of law. There being few significant prerogative powers in the domestic sphere, the Crown-in-Parliament, as a supreme legislature, came to exercise absolute authority over internal administration. The Act of Parliament thus became the form through which was framed, not only all new laws, but also all the ordinances which regulate

[12] See A. V. Dicey, *Introduction to the Study of the Law of the Constitution*, 8th ed. (Macmillan, 1915), chapter 4.

the conduct of administrative activity. Consequently, the institutions of local government become answerable not to central government, but to the courts and, ultimately, to Parliament. In the English tradition, relations between the centre and the localities were worked out through a network of relationships between local government, Parliament and the courts.

In this tradition, the Act of Parliament became the formal method by which the will of the central government was expressed to the localities. The significance of this achievement resides in the fact that central government needed to secure the approval of a Parliament comprising representatives of local communities. Parliament thus provided the localities with a forum within which their interests and grievances could be brought to the attention of the central authority.

This tradition lived on until the mid-nineteenth century when rapid industrialization and consequential urbanization undermined the foundations of the system. But its significance, especially in resisting the claims of bureaucratization and the emergence of administrative law through the ongoing work of Parliament, continued to influence constitutional thought. Until the end of the eighteenth century, the Crown and Parliament had generally left local institutions free to deal with their own responsibilities. When, however, new needs made themselves felt through the demand for new services, the centre inevitably became involved. These demands took the form of petitions from local bodies seeking new powers to act. By retaining control over this process, Parliament was able to assume a jurisdiction which in continental states had become the preserve of the central authority under administrative law. This was achieved primarily through the private Bill procedure, in which Bills were presented on the petition of local bodies and were deliberated upon mainly by the representatives of the localities concerned. It thus gradually came to be recognized that two different activities were being carried out under the general form of an Act: legislating both for the common interests of the country (public general legislation) and for special needs of the locality (private or local Acts). Through the development of this latter instrument, Parliament became the mediating link between central and local government. And, insofar as Parliament assumed an essentially judicial mode in adopting the private Bill procedure, this practice of the High Court of Parliament reinforced the principle of the rule of law.

5.2.3 *The Rule of Law*

The principle of the rule of law is based on this rule of judicature. This meant, first, that every exercise of public power must have a legal basis and, secondly, that, having no system of administrative law, the sole judge of legality is the ordinary courts applying the ordinary (*sc.* common) law. There had been occasions, especially under the Tudors and Stuarts, when attempts were made to fashion a special administrative jurisdiction. Under Henry VIII, for example, proclamations and royal warrants were issued directly to the Justices of the Peace, thus bringing them directly under the authority of the Crown and under the Stuarts the Star Chamber, a committee of the Privy Council, threatened to develop into a supreme administrative authority.[13] But controversy over such measures contributed to the constitutional conflicts of the mid-seventeenth century and after 1660 no further attempt was made to develop a separate administrative jurisdiction.

By the eighteenth century, the courts, through the use of the prerogative writs, had established themselves as the principal agencies for the control of local action. That most of the work of local administration was carried out by Justices of the Peace who were themselves also judicial officers reinforced the idea that government was based on law and administrative duties must be undertaken in a judicial spirit. But cohesion was achieved not only through these institutional mechanisms but also through the shared culture of the governing class. The custom of governing families giving their sons a common education in the public schools and Oxford and Cambridge conferred on them the necessary authority to assume office as a Justice of the Peace and later to represent their community in Parliament. This common culture replaced the need for institutional balancing mechanisms. It also rendered the need for constructing a formal body of 'jurist-law' unnecessary, a feature reinforced by the fact that, unlike their continental counterparts, English judges were not civil servants but were drawn from the ranks of practising barristers who often had also taken some part in public and parliamentary life.

Only in the Victorian era were these arrangements transformed into a formal constitutional principle, labelled 'the rule of law'. This was mainly attributable to the work of A. V. Dicey. For Dicey, the rule of law had three specific meanings. First, no one can be punished except for a 'distinct breach of the law established in the ordinary legal manner before the ordinary Courts of the land', a principle that highlights the tradition of strict legality running through the English system. Secondly, it embodies the principle of equality before the law: 'the universal subjection of all classes to one law administered by the ordinary Courts'. This meant that disputes are to be adjudicated in accordance with a common set of rules, applied to ordinary subjects and Ministers of the Crown alike. The third meaning reflects a belief that the constitution itself comes from the ordinary law of the land. The 'law of the constitution', Dicey states, is 'not the source but the consequence of the rights of individuals'. Civil liberty is achieved not by the formal declaration of rights but by constant struggles leading to outcomes recorded and protected in particular judicial decisions.[14]

This safeguarding of liberty through the workings of the 'rule of law' contrasts with modern constitutional documents which contain formal declarations of rights. Rights then are *deduced* from the constitution. In the English case, however, rights

[13] See, e.g., F. W. Maitland, *The Constitutional History of England* (Cambridge University Press, 1908), 261–264.

[14] Dicey, *Law of the Constitution*, chapter 4.

and liberties are *induced* from various court rulings on personal rights. For Dicey, the English approach is preferable. Being the work of many 'whose labours gradually framed the complicated set of laws and institutions which we call the Constitution', it may form a less than tidy arrangement. But, although the Habeas Corpus Acts 'declare no principle and define no rights', they are 'for practical purposes worth a hundred constitutional articles guaranteeing individual liberty'. Rights enunciated in written constitutions can be suspended or repealed, but where the right is 'part of the constitution because it is part of the ordinary law of the land' it 'can hardly be destroyed without a thorough revolution in the institutions and manners of the nation'.[15]

5.2.4 *The Crown*

From these accounts it is evident that there exists no tidy arrangement of institutions that constitutes an apparatus of 'the state'. In English law, the symbol of state power is that of the Crown. Any inquiry into the status of the Crown quickly takes us deep into medieval legal thought and the question of the king's two bodies. As Southcote J. explained in *Willion* v *Berkley* (1559), the king has both a body natural and a body politic, the latter of which is a corporation that includes all his subjects, wherein 'he is the Head, and they are the Members, and he has the sole Government of them; and this Body is not subject to the Passions as the other is, nor to Death, for as to this Body the King never dies'.[16] Maitland commented that 'I do not know where to look in the whole series of our law books for so marvellous a display of metaphysical – or we might say metaphysiological – nonsense'.[17] But it is this notion that provides the basis of the English concept of the state.

It might be thought that one reason for invoking this metaphor was to bolster the perpetuity of the office of the king, but that principle had already been established by the end of the thirteenth century.[18] In practice, it was the question of the Crown's corporate character that proved most troublesome. A distinction between king and Crown had already been drawn by the end of the twelfth century,[19] and by fourteenth century the coronation oath was requiring kings to swear to maintain

[15] Ibid., 197.

[16] *Willion* v *Berkley* (1559) Plowden 233a. See also *Case of the Duchy of Lancaster* (1561) 1 Plowden 212.

[17] F. W. Maitland, 'The Crown as Corporation' (1901) in H. A. L. Fisher (ed.), *Collected Papers*, vol 3 (Cambridge University Press, 1911), 244, 249.

[18] As Coke reported in *Calvin's case* (1608) 7 Co. Rep 1, at 11a, it appeared 'by infinite precedents … that by the laws of England there can be no *inter regnum*' and that 'by the descent, His Majesty was completely and absolutely King, without any essential ceremony or act to be done *ex post facto*, and that coronation was but a Royal ornament and outward solemnization of the descent'.

[19] See George Garnett, 'The Origins of the Crown', in John Hudson (ed.), *The History of English Law: Centenary Essays on 'Pollock and Maitland'* (Oxford University Press, 1996), 171.

unimpaired the rights of the Crown.[20] In this respect, the concept of the Crown seemed to incorporate the entire body politic. The problem was that different versions tended to present themselves on different occasions. Rather than adopting a concept of the Crown as a corporation aggregate which could emerge as analogous to the modern idea of the state, English jurists tended to employ it as 'a personification in its own right' and, therefore, as 'not only above its members, but also divorced from them'.[21] Their habitual distrust of abstraction led to the failure to draw a clear distinction between king and Crown. What resulted was a persistent 'confusion of tongues'[22] in the language through which the law characterized the structure of English governmental authority. Part of the problem was that any attempt to separate the Crown from the person of the king was held to be a 'damnable and damned opinion' which would lead to 'execrable and detestable consequences'.[23]

This failure has bequeathed a distinctive legacy. In law, the Crown is employed as the symbol of government authority. But thereafter it stubbornly refuses to do much real work. In formal terms, it is the king's fiat which makes laws, it is his sentence which condemns and it is his judgements that determine the rights and liabilities of his subjects. The king, as head of the executive, appoints his ministers, who are the king's servants and do not stand in any legal relation to Parliament. Further, this Parliament is summoned, prorogued and dissolved by the king. And, as the fountain of honour, the king maintains the power of dispensing honours and dignities.

Such prerogatives are sometimes said to be attributes of the monarch's ideal character, which we may assume to mean the king as Crown. So, although the ideal king might be the source of justice, at least since the reign of Henry III the monarch has not been able to disturb the fountain or divert the stream from its proper channel, except through the agency of his judges.[24] Further, in the exercise of these prerogative powers, constitutionally the king is advised, directed and controlled by others.[25] But, notwithstanding these modifications as to how these powers are actually exercised, the legal form, which unites two capacities in one person, persists and, with the extending powers of modern government, it has required piecemeal adjustment by both statutory intervention and common law innovation. These developments include ensuring that ministers and government departments are capable of being held legally accountable for wrongful acts and of

[20] See Ernst H. Kantorowicz, *The King's Two Bodies: A Study in Mediaeval Political Theology* (Princeton University Press, 1957), 354–358.

[21] Ibid., 382.

[22] Francis Bacon, *Works*, vol 7, ed. J. Spedding, R.L. Ellis, & D.D. Heath (Longman, 1852), 651.

[23] *Calvin's Case* (1608) 7 Co.Rep.1, 11a–11b.

[24] For the most celebrated formulation, see Sir Edward Coke, *Twelfth Reports, Prohibitions del Roy* (1607) 12 Co. Rep. 63.

[25] Hence the importance of what Dicey (*Law of the Constitution*, chapter 14) called 'conventions of the constitution'. But these conventions are 'vague and slippery' and 'they cannot be understood "with the politics left out"'. G. H. L. Le May, *The Victorian Constitution*, vol 2 (Duckworth, 1979), 21.

reforming the principles of judicial review to ensure oversight of the exercise of public power.[26]

The general point is that, in this tradition, the legal theory of government has been formulated as a set of royal acts and the English have consequently experienced considerable difficulty in advancing a coherent legal theory of the state. At the beginning of the twentieth century, Maitland commented that: 'We cannot get on without the State, or the Nation, or the Commonwealth, or the Public, and yet that is what we are proposing to do.'[27] Subsequent developments have not fully resolved those difficulties.

5.2.5 *Parliamentary Sovereignty*

The seventeenth-century upheavals, driven by the conflict between the Crown and Parliament for ultimate authority, led to a civil war which was resolved in favour of the parliamentary forces. In 1660, however, the monarchy was restored, and the 1688 revolution produced a modern settlement in which fundamental principles were fudged. During the eighteenth century, the conflict between Crown and Parliament for ultimate authority was sublimated through abstraction. This was achieved by formulating as the basic principle of the constitution the idea that sovereignty vests in a composite entity called 'the Crown-in-Parliament'.

This formulation was most authoritatively presented by Sir William Blackstone, whose *Commentaries on the Laws of England* (1765–1769) was the first modern account of the laws of England. Blackstone acknowledged the disjunction between constitutional law and constitutional practice. The law of the constitution, he noted, still 'ascribes to the king, in his high political character . . . attributes of a great and transcendent nature'. Formally, all governmental authority is exercised in the name of the king but the basic legal principle of the constitution was that of the sovereign authority of parliament. But he was quick to emphasise that here 'parliament' did not mean the people's representatives in the Commons. Parliament is a purely legal construct which denotes the king's convening of the three estates of the realm. This is the Crown-in-Parliament and, far from being an expression of popular sentiment, it is a formal expression of state sovereignty.

The Crown-in-Parliament signified 'that absolute despotic power, which must in all governments reside somewhere, is entrusted by the constitution of these kingdoms'. This power, Blackstone asserted, knows no legal limits. Downplaying the checks and balances provided in practice by the three components of Parliament, he emphasized the conceptual unity of the Crown-in-Parliament. Supplanting the

[26] See, e.g., Martin Loughlin, 'The State, the Crown and the Law', in M. Sunkin and S. Payne (eds.), *The Nature of the Crown: A Legal and Political Analysis* (Oxford University Press, 1999), 56–76.

[27] F. W. Maitland, 'The Crown as Corporation' (1901), in H. A. L. Fisher (ed.), *Collected Papers*, vol 3 (Cambridge University Press, 1911), 244ff, 253.

notion that the common law as immemorial custom was an expression of fundamental law, he presented law as a simple positive entity: the commands of the Crown-in-Parliament.

Blackstone's account was reinforced in the nineteenth century in the work of A. V. Dicey, the high priest of Victorian constitutional orthodoxy. Placing law at the centre of constitutional scholarship, Dicey emphasized that the sovereign authority of the Crown-in-Parliament is the first principle of the constitution. Acknowledging that there exists a secondary principle, that of the rule of law, he sought to show that the two are not contradictory. Parliamentary sovereignty promotes the 'supremacy of law' because Parliament's commands 'can be uttered only through the combined actions of its three constituent parts' and it therefore establishes a regime of rigid legality.[28] Dicey advanced an account of the law of the constitution as an autonomous idea, but, like Blackstone, he also asserted that civilized rule rests on the necessity of maintaining an untrammelled power at the centre.

5.3 THE FORMATION OF THE BRITISH STATE

The narratives of constitutional identity so far examined have been English. With the formation of the modern British state, the influence of these schemes became more qualified. The English, as the largest and most powerful nation on the islands, have always sought a dominating influence over the Irish, the Scots and the Welsh, if only to maintain the security of their state. This policy was first advanced by incorporating Wales into the structure of the English state. This was quickly pursued by the Normans through a brutal practice of subjugation, which was formally concluded by the Statute of Wales of 1535. By this Act, Welsh lands were absorbed into the English shire system and the English common law was then applied throughout England and Wales. In this respect, the English state comprises the territories of England and Wales. The Welsh maintain a distinctive identity but, rather than a political identity indicated by distinctive institutions, it is a cultural identity mainly signified by language.

In the eighteenth century, however, constitutional narratives become more ambiguous. Scholars continued to talk about the English constitution – evident in the works of Blackstone and Dicey in the eighteenth and nineteenth centuries – but in 1707 a new state, that of Great Britain had been formed. This state, encompassing England, Wales and Scotland, was established not through conquest but by treaty. In 1707, Scotland and England were joined by a Treaty of Union to create the United Kingdom of Great Britain.

5.3.1 *The Making of Britons*

The formation of the British state was the culmination of a relatively long process. The seeds of union had been sown in 1603 when James VI of Scotland acceded to

[28] Dicey, Law of the Constitution.

the English throne as James I, a process reinforced by the fact that the Reformation had bound Scotland and England together in the community of Protestant nations. But the eventual union of 1707 came about in inauspicious circumstances, involving England offering access to trade and empire in return for Scots' rejection of the Jacobite succession. The settlement resulted in the creation of a common set of legislative, executive and fiscal – though not judicial – arrangements for the new kingdom of Great Britain.

The Union Treaty gave certain protections relating to Scots identity, especially in relation to law, education and religion. Contrary to recent argument by some Scottish jurists, however, it cannot be regarded as analogous to a modern constitutional settlement.[29] Following the Treaty, 45 Scottish MPs and 16 representative peers simply joined the Westminster Parliament without even a general election being held, unequivocally making the point that Scotland had been incorporated into an Anglo-centric British state.

During the period after 1707 a distinctive British national identity was forged. Invented for the purpose of binding England and Scotland together, this identity built on the fears of a French invasion and the reimposition of Catholicism. Protestantism, explains Linda Colley, 'was the foundation that made the invention of Great Britain possible'.[30] Propagated by Anti-Popery and Francophobia, it was mainly advanced through war, specifically, the long wars with the French between 1688 and 1815. This marked a period in which Britain rose to become a major imperial power: in 1740, when 'Rule Britannia' was composed, Britain was well on the way to having built the world's most powerful navy.[31] This growth in power led to the cultivation of imperialism as a distinctively British cult in which all the home nations participated. As Colley notes, 'the cult of superior and unique British liberty was so powerful and so elastic that for a long time it operated as a cross-border cement and language in common'.[32] It also resulted, for reasons of state, in a deliberate suppression of English nationalism. During this period, the terms 'English' and 'British' constitution were commonly used interchangeably and without specificity, and the English narratives of ancient constitution, local government, the rule of law, and the concept of the Crown were incrementally and informally absorbed into an inchoate sense of 'Britishness'.[33] Of pivotal importance was the concept of sovereignty.

[29] T. B. Smith, *The Union of 1707 as Fundamental Law* (Stevens, 1957); Neil MacCormick, 'Does the United Kingdom Have a Constitution?' (1978) 29 *Northern Ireland Legal Quarterly* 1.

[30] Linda Colley, *Britons: Forging the Nation 1707–1837* (Pimlico, 1992), 54.

[31] Linda Colley, *Acts of Union and Disunion* (Profile Books, 2014), 24–25.

[32] Ibid., 39.

[33] Of particular significance are the works of the great Scottish writers of the eighteenth and nineteenth centuries, such as David Hume, John Millar and Thomas Babington Macaulay, all of whom wrote histories of England which included discussions of Scotland, Wales and Ireland.

From the eighteenth century, asserting parliamentary sovereignty as the dominant characteristic of the constitution became a deliberate policy that underpinned the formation of the British state. As a system of government, the British state has never been as centralized or as unitary as its political elite and jurists have tended to suggest. But the doctrine of parliamentary sovereignty was consciously emphasized for the purpose of advancing the unity and homogeneity of the realm. Only in the eighteenth and nineteenth centuries was a legal doctrine of sovereignty formally articulated and it was then wilfully confused with the pseudo historical doctrine that the maintenance of absolute sovereignty at the centre was the pre-condition for maintaining the political stability of the state. As a legal doctrine, it is purely formal: the Act of Parliament is the highest expression of law. Politically, it was employed for rhetorical purposes. The two were commonly conflated for reasons of state.[34]

In a high-profile Scottish case in 1953, Lord Cooper, Lord President of the Court of Session and Scotland's leading judge, asserted that 'the principle of unlimited sovereignty of Parliament is a distinctively English principle and has no counterpart in Scottish constitutional law'.[35] This was a less than astute analysis. The doctrine is neither English nor Scottish; it is a British creation that came to fruition following the Union as a critical element in a strategy of managing not only the newly-formed British state, but also the rapidly expanding British empire.

5.3.2 *The Irish Question*

Union with Ireland follows an altogether different story. Ireland had long been dominated by England through centuries of conquest and colonization, but it was only after the 1798 Rebellion of United Irishmen, influenced by the republican ideals of the American and French revolutions, that the British determined that the only lasting foundation for security lay in the union of Ireland with Britain. In 1801 the Irish Parliament was dissolved and incorporated into the Westminster Parliament. In a formal sense, a new state – the United Kingdom of Great Britain and Ireland – was created. The Treaty of Union of 1801, marking the apotheosis of the principle of parliamentary sovereignty, unified legal authority from the centre throughout the islands.

But the integration of Ireland was a stillborn affair. Attempts to reconcile the aspirations of Irish nationalism within the framework of the British state became the dominant political issue of the late nineteenth century. Home Rule Bills were introduced and rejected in 1886 and 1893 and when a third Bill eventually passed the Commons in 1912, it was enacted in the face of Lords' opposition only through the special procedures of the Parliament Act 1911. The resulting delay led to its

34 See Martin Loughlin and Stephen Tierney, 'The Shibboleth of Sovereignty' (2018) 81 *Modern Law Review*, 989–1016, 1001–1005.

35 *MacCormick v Lord Advocate* (1953) SC 396.

suspension because of the war, which gave time for Ulster Protestants to organize in opposition. What followed in quick succession was the Easter Rising in 1916, the electoral success of Sinn Féin, the formation of the Dáil, the Irish War of Independence (1919–1921) and then the Anglo-Irish Treaty by which Ireland – with the exception of the six counties of Northern Ireland in which there was a Protestant majority – seceded from the United Kingdom. Consequently, the only part of the Westminster Parliament's Government of Ireland Act 1920 to be implemented was – ironically – home rule for Northern Ireland.

Formally, what was created was the United Kingdom of Great Britain and Northern Ireland. But is there really a UK state? Northern Ireland is evidently part of the UK state from the perspective of international law. Whether in a constitutional sense the six counties of Northern Ireland actually forms part of the British state, however, is debateable: the troubled history of the province, its special governmental and security arrangements, the acknowledgement by the British of its right to re-unite with the rest of Ireland when signalled by a majority of its population, and the unique governing arrangements established in accordance with the peace settlement in 1998 all suggest that the province has not, in a strict sense, been structurally integrated into the formation of the British state. The narratives of ancient constitutional liberties, local self-government, and rule of the ordinary common law here have little resonance. The Crown as an expression of state authority is a divisive symbol and the sovereign authority of the Crown-in-Parliament remains contested.[36]

5.3.3 *The Apotheosis of Sovereignty*

The fixation on sovereignty owes much to Dicey's authoritative treatment. In the *Law of the Constitution* he set in place the centrality of the legal doctrine. But he also wrote three books against Irish home rule, released to mark the occasion of the publication of each home rule Bill. In these, his claims extend beyond the legal doctrine and assert the political claim that beneath 'all the formality, the antiquarianism, the shams of the British constitution, there lies latent an element of power which has been the true source of its life and growth'.[37] That power is 'the absolute omnipotence of Parliament' which is 'nothing else but unlimited power'. Dicey claims that Irish home rule 'would dislocate every English constitutional arrangement', but this is not because the legal doctrine would be qualified. Home rule is a constitutional threat because it would weaken the power of Great Britain. By undermining the sovereignty of Parliament, 'it deprives English institutions of

[36] See Martin Loughlin, 'The British Constitution and the Irish Question' (2024) 35 *King's Law Journal* 395–415.

[37] Albert Venn Dicey, *England's Case against Home Rule* (Murray, 1886), 168.

their elasticity, their strength, and their life; it weakens the Executive at home, and lessens the power of the country to resist foreign attack'.[38]

What Dicey's robust defence makes plain is that sovereignty is essential to the exercise of maintaining effective rule across the nations of the United Kingdom and to the task of governing the Empire. But beyond that specifically political conviction sits an illuminating constitutional argument. Ordinary law rules precisely because it operates under the absolute authority of the Crown-in-Parliament. That is, the rule of law depends for its realization on the doctrine of sovereignty. The British constitution comprises a body of rules, customs and practices that fix the terms on which the activity of governing is carried on. But the rules allocating and regulating the exercise of sovereign powers applied in Scotland and Northern Ireland differ in significant respects from those operating in England and Wales. These differences are authorized through the overarching authority of the Crown-in-Parliament. Dicey believed that home rule would lead to 'the immediate dislocation and the ultimate rebuilding of the whole English Constitution' because it would inevitably result in 'leaving the settlement of constitutional questions to a Court'.[39] And constitutional questions are for Parliament, not the courts.

5.4 THE BRITISH CONSTITUTION AND THE PROJECT OF EUROPEAN UNION

With the coming of democracy and the dramatic extension of government powers in the twentieth century, the traditional narratives of constitutional identity were all eroded. What followed was a decline of faith in this constitutional inheritance and increasing ambiguity about constitutional identity. The conviction that progress rested on restoring ancient liberties (rather than meeting new claims) sounded increasingly hollow. The idea that the tradition of local government might be retained in the face of rapid urbanization could not be sustained and the formation of nationally-organized political parties put an end to the notion that MPs were primarily representatives of their localities. Governmental growth shifted the action from Parliament to government, leading to the emergence of a body of administrative law and the necessity of eliminating Crown immunities. It also required a distinction to be drawn between public and private law matters which eroded the significance of the rule of ordinary law. Sovereignty remains the basic principle binding together the British state but, no longer bolstered by its religious and imperial anchoring, the gulf between legal doctrine and governmental practice grows ever wider.

By the end of the century, there had emerged a relatively broad-based conviction that Britain's inherited constitution had come to the end of its useful life. The need

[38] Ibid., 169, 171, 173, 196.
[39] Ibid., 274 and 271.

for basic reform – for modernization – was touted across the political spectrum, though without much insight as to what that might entail. And, in the background, one powerful impetus of modernization had often been overlooked: the UK's participation in the venture of continuing European integration.

Involvement in the European project has empowered the judiciary to enhance rights-based methods of review and has resulted in the British adopting what is in effect a Bill of Rights without having gone through a process of extensive public deliberation.[40] It has also helped set in place a dynamic scheme for devolving governmental powers to the constituent nations of the UK.[41] And it has bolstered the unique cross-border arrangements that brought about a peace settlement in Northern Ireland.[42] Continuing European integration had enabled governing arrangements to be re-configured and constitutional fundamentals re-ordered so as the bring the UK into closer alignment with the frameworks of modern constitutional democracies.

The British have lived with a tension between myth and reality in these stories of constitutional identity throughout the modern era, but this tension acquired a new dimension with accession to the EU. Because of its imperial legacy and close trading ties to British Commonwealth countries, the UK did not initially seek participation in the European project. By the 1960s, however, views were changing. When first contemplating joining, the Government asked its leading lawyer (Lord Kilmuir, the Lord Chancellor) to assess the constitutional implications. His opinion focused directly on the impact of sovereignty and the rule of law:

> To sign the Treaty of Rome would be to legislate for a loss of national sovereignty in three respects. First, parliament would surrender some of its functions to a Council of Ministers which could by majority vote make regulations that became the law of the land. Second, the crown's treaty making power would in part be transferred to an international organisation. Third, British courts would sacrifice some of their independence by becoming subordinate in some respects to the European Court of Justice.

Kilmuir concluded that it will not be easy to persuade Parliament or the public to accept them.[43] And so it proved. The UK eventually joined in 1973 but controversy over the implications for sovereignty has permeated debate ever since.

The European Communities Act 1972, which gave effect in domestic law to this 'new legal order', was a masterpiece of concise legislative drafting. Stating that all rights and obligations 'from time to time arising by or under the Treaties … are

40 Human Rights Act 1998, which makes the rights protected under the European Convention on Human Rights directly enforceable by British judges.
41 Scotland Act 1998; Wales Act 1998.
42 Belfast Agreement; Northern Ireland Act 1998.
43 Cited in Hugo Young, *This Blessed Plot: Britain and Europe from Churchill to Blair* (Macmillan, 1998), 126.

without further enactment to be given legal effect', few grasped its radical implications. It was commonly felt that, holding a veto over any proposed new powers, the UK retained control. But, as the Union evolved, decision-making was streamlined, with majority voting becoming standard. The claim that Parliament retained final authority over adoption of new social or economic regulations therefore became rather strained.

Furthermore, being immersed in the traditions of law-making by Parliament, British politicians were oblivious to the point that the European Court of Justice (ECJ), quickly establishing itself as the guardian of this 'new legal order', could itself be a major source of law. The Court's rulings, especially in enunciating the principles of the *supremacy of European law* (requiring European law to prevail over any conflict with domestic law), and *direct effect* (conferring rights and obligations that can be directly enforced by individuals in the courts of member states), seriously compromised parliamentary sovereignty. Operating as the constitutional court of the European legal order, the ECJ went about constructing that regime and, after years of avoiding the question of the ECJ's primacy, the point was finally accepted by the British courts in the early 1990s.[44]

Following the completion of the single market programme, in 1992 the EU moved to the next – federalist – stage of the project, which included the launch of a single currency (the euro) in 1999. This was accompanied by a period of growing scepticism within the UK about the project, signified politically by the rising influence of the United Kingdom Independence Party (UKIP) and constitutionally by pledges from all major political parties not to agree to the transfer of new powers to the EU without holding a referendum. 'The essence of the problem', noted Vernon Bogdanor, 'was one of fitting Britain into a continental system whose assumptions about constitutions, politics and economics were so different from those held in Britain'.[45]

These developments eventually came to a head in 2015 when the Conservatives were returned as a majority government, having pledged an in/out referendum on EU membership. Held in June 2016, it resulted in a majority (52%:48%) voting to leave. This led to a protracted period of unsettlement, the constitutional implications of which did not end on 31 January 2020, when the UK formally left the EU.

5.5 THE CONTEMPORARY CRISIS OF CONSTITUTIONAL IDENTITY

In different circumstances, Brexit might have become a constitutional moment, an occasion when the nation, recognizing that a new chapter in the development of the British state was opening, grasped the opportunity to renovate constitutional fundamentals. This is not what happened. Instead, Brexit has come to signify the depth of

[44] *R v Secretary of State for Transport, ex parte Factortame (No 2)* [1991] 1 AC 603.

[45] Vernon Bogdanor, *Britain and Europe in a Troubled World* (Yale University Press, 2020), 54.

cleavage in Britain's constitutional identity. The referendum split the country down the middle, exposing fissures on class and geographical lines. It led to Remainers extolling the virtues of the EU as a symbol of modern, liberal, cosmopolitan values and Brexiters, under the mantra of 'taking back control', claiming the decision would lead to the restoration of traditional practices. Both claims were divorced from reality.

One immediate effect of the referendum result was to highlight the gulf that had emerged between the political class and the popular will: having effectively transferred the decision to the electorate, MPs found themselves saddled with implementing a decision despite the fact that around 75 per cent of them had voted to remain. In these circumstances, the traditional practices of parliamentary government were placed under severe strain and at times entirely broke down.[46] Following the resignation of two Prime Ministers (David Cameron after being on the losing side in the referendum; Theresa May after her negotiated withdrawal deal was thrice voted down by the Commons), Boris Johnson took over in summer 2019, went to the country and was returned with an eighty-seat majority (though he was also obliged to resign for other reasons in the summer of 2022). But, ultimately, the process highlights just how much it is the Government, not the Parliament, that has assumed control.

The longer-term implications are even more unsettling. In the process of negotiating withdrawal, the Government has made determined efforts to bolster the traditional principle of sovereignty. It included in the EU (Withdrawal Agreement) Act of 2020 a provision that '[i]t is recognised that the Parliament of the United Kingdom is sovereign', that 'its sovereignty subsists' notwithstanding any continuing EU law, and that 'nothing in this Act derogates from the sovereignty of the Parliament of the United Kingdom' (s.38). This might be read simply as a technical clause within a complex transitional process, but it also sent a signal. That signal was reinforced by the then Government's apparent intention to replace the Human Rights Act with a Bill of Rights Act. Ostensibly designed to restore the balance of power between the legislature and the courts, in reality it aimed to lessen the influence of the European Court of Human Rights and reinforce the sovereignty principle.

The signal being sent is directed primarily to the judiciary who, building on the modernization theme, over the last few decades have been seeking to reorder constitutional fundamentals by asserting that the rule of law, rather than sovereignty, is the basic principle of the British constitution. This thesis, generally called 'common law constitutionalism', asserts that sovereignty does not lie with 'those who wield governmental power' but rests 'in the conditions under which they are

[46] See Martin Loughlin, 'In Search of the Constitution', in Oran Doyle, Aileen McHarg and Jo Murkens (eds.), *Constitutions under Pressure: The Brexit Challenge for Ireland and the United Kingdom* (Cambridge University Press, 2021), 313–335, 328–332.

permitted to do so' and the role of the judiciary must be to make explicit these conditions as 'a framework of fundamental principles'.[47] It is controversial, not least because it implicitly assumes the primacy of English common law within the British state. Yet it is one on which the judiciary have, in certain landmark decisions, made significant advances.[48] Here we see a struggle between the Government and the judiciary over the fundamentals of British constitutional identity.

But there also looms an even more fundamental problem than this contest between the principles of sovereignty and legality. By exposing significant differences across the UK's territorial regions, Brexit has thrown up certain more basic existential threats to the British state. The various devolution schemes set in place since 1998 have created a governmental mosaic, with the devolved schemes all containing modernizing elements and governing arrangements for each part of the UK now significantly varying. Lip service continues to be paid to the continuing sovereign authority of the Westminster Parliament, but these developments have strained this to breaking point. The catalyst has been the Scottish National Party's (SNP) majority rule in Scotland since 2011. They pushed for a referendum on Scottish independence which was held in 2014 and yielded a majority vote against (55.3% to 44.7%). But the Westminster Parliament felt it necessary to make further concessions, including passing legislation stating that 'the Scottish Parliament and the Scottish Government are a permanent part of the United Kingdom's constitutional arrangements' and 'are not to be abolished except on the basis of a decision of the people of Scotland voting in a referendum'.[49] These developments signal the beginning of the end of Dicey's doctrine of parliamentary sovereignty, and the incremental evolution of an asymmetric federal scheme for the UK.

Brexit has brought a new dimension to these territorial developments. Although the 2016 referendum yielded a majority for leaving the EU, Northern Ireland and Scotland recorded majorities (56%:44% and 62%:38%, respectively) in favour of remaining. This divergence strained territorial relations throughout the negotiating process, including claims that withdrawal without the consent of the devolved legislatures was illegitimate. It has also had serious post-exit consequences. Arguing that Scotland had been removed from the EU against its will, the SNP then pledged to hold a second independence referendum (though this would require Westminster's consent). The situation in relation to Northern Ireland is no less serious. It is the one area of the UK that maintains a land border with an EU member state, yet the erection of customs barriers here was felt to threaten the peace process and accords established in the Good Friday Agreement. Consequently, a Protocol to the Withdrawal Agreement was negotiated, under which Northern

47 Sir John Laws, 'Law and Democracy' (1995) *Public Law*, 72–92.

48 See, e.g., *Jackson v Her Majesty's Attorney-General* [2005] UKHL 56; *R(Miller) v Prime Minister/Cherry v Advocate General for Scotland* [2019] UKSC 41.

49 Scotland Act 2016. Similar constitutional protections were included in the Wales Act 2017.

Ireland would remain in the customs union, with a customs border being established in the Irish Sea. But the working arrangements for this have generated disputes between the UK and EU, are a source of continuing discontent among unionist groups in Northern Ireland and may be signalling the moment at which the holding of a referendum on re-uniting Ireland becomes ever closer.

Ruling Britannia today presents greater challenges than has been faced at any stage in modern history. The idea of British nationhood was formed out of a Protestantism that bound the Anglo–Scottish union, flourished with the expansion of the British Empire and was sustained in the twentieth century by the establishment of a national industrial economy. These ties have since been progressively loosened: first through secularization of public life, then through loss of Empire and most recently with the promotion after 1979 of policies of de-industrialization and privatization.[50] Yet, once the factors enabling the British to identify themselves as a nation and a state have dissipated, the conditions for rejuvenating a common constitutional identity no longer seem propitious. It would require a conscious and determined effort to restore a pan-British sense of patriotism, and that seems a distinctively un-British thing to be contemplating. In this respect, George Orwell's observation that 'England is perhaps the only great country whose intellectuals are ashamed of their own nationality' still rings true.[51] The best hope lies in the advancement of radical reforms to the system of government, which might incrementally provide an institutional foundation for a renewal of faith.

[50] See David Edgerton, *The Rise and Fall of the British Nation: A Twentieth-Century History* (Penguin, 2018).

[51] George Orwell, 'England Your England' (1941), in *Essays* (Doubleday, 1954), 257–283 and 279.

6

The Power of Concepts

From 'Self-Management' to 'Sovereignty' in Soviet Estonia (1987–1988)

Juhan Saharov

6.1 INTRODUCTION

The popular narrative in Estonia says that, during the revolutionary periods, there have never been serious alternatives to political independence. From 1991 onwards, this narrative has not lost its momentum. However, this chapter looks at the period of 1987–1988 and claims that it was the finest hour for imagining alternative futures for Estonia.

In the distant past, there have been several, even utopian visions of how we could 'imagine alternatively' Estonia's future. For instance, socialist revolutionary poet Gustav Suits proposed a dual Finnish–Estonian state in November 1917 and later the 'Estonian Labour Republic' (*Eesti Töövabariik*) in January 1918.[1] In 1972, when Estonia was occupied by the Soviet Union, the Estonian émigré professor Rein Taagepera proposed his 30-year plan for Estonia towards a socialist satellite state status (the 'Hungarian path').[2] Both envisioned Estonia as expanding the internal sovereignty but sharing the united external politics. Both men shared the view that it is important to focus on the available resources at your disposal, to exhaust all the means to survive as a nation, even if it does not severely cut ties with the big neighbour. In 1987–1988, new imaginary scenarios emerged in Estonia. Should Estonia develop itself into an economically independent republic (or at least a free trade zone) in the renewed Soviet Union, to a sovereign socialist republic (which shares its foreign and defence politics with the centre) or an independent republic, restored by the legal continuation of the pre-war Republic?

In a more general sense, this chapter shows how the imagination of alternative futures take place in a state-socialist system which has opened all the channels to

This work was supported by an Estonian Research Council grant (PRG942).

1 See Gustav Suits, 'Soome-Eesti unioon; Eesti Töövabariik', in Gustav Suits, *Vabaduse väraval* (2002 [1918]).

2 Rein Taagepera, 'The History of a Document: A Broad Plan for a Small Nation: "Thirty!"' (1992) 23 *Journal of Baltic Studies* 261.

vision and discuss reforms. In what language and through which concepts are the alternative futures being produced? Taking Soviet Estonia as a case study, the chapter shows the specific concepts during the mid-perestroika (1987–1988) period which opened, facilitated, but also delimited the imagination of Estonian futures. The chapter argues that these concepts were innovated by local reformists, through which the alternative scenarios were constructed, creating the peripheral 'conceptual revolution' during the perestroika.

6.2 CREATING THE REPERTOIRE OF FUTURES

Alexis de Tocqueville wrote in 1856, that 'it is not always that things are going from bad to worse that revolutions break out. On the contrary, it oftener happens when a people suddenly find the government relaxing its pressures.'[3] Relaxation of the top-down planning in the economy but also the media censorship during 1986–1987 became the most visual marker of the change in Soviet society. In retrospect, we can conceptualize this moment as an early revolutionary situation. Nowadays, many scholars confirm Tocqueville's observation, however, less has been said about specific conceptual processes of *how* these 'moments of relaxation' during the pre-revolutionary periods become revolutionary situations. Charles Tilly has defined the nature of 'revolutionary situations' in history by referring to the main two characteristics as 'the appearance of contenders, advancing exclusive competing claims to control the state, or some segment of it' and the 'incapacity or unwillingness of rulers to suppress these contenders'.[4] While these conditions were indeed present in 1988 in the Soviet Union, I am more interested in looking at the more ambiguous start of this situation in which the contenders emerge from the local political and scholarly elite. Which claims, concepts and arguments do these contenders use, and in which forms do they make them? Tilly's concept of 'contentious repertoires' brings us closer to this question.[5] According to Tilly, 'repertoires' refer to 'claim-making routines that apply to the same claimant–object pairs . . . these can include, for instance, petition letters, pamphleteering, strikes, civil disobedience, etc.'[6] Repertoires function as an available structural menu for contenders (to choose their action form), but also limit it, as, according to Tilly, repertoire changes very rarely.

However, Tilly's approach to 'repertoires' as a menu for contentious actions was related to the direct, physical form of action and not so much to intellectual conditions. For instance, although Tilly highlights 'pamphleteering' in France in the eighteenth century before the French Revolution, we are not shown the actors'

3 Alexis de Tocqueville, *The Old Regime and the French Revolution* (Anchor Books, 1983 [1856]), 176.

4 Charles Tilly, *European Revolutions 1492–1992* (Blackwell, 1995).

5 Charles Tilly, 'Contentious Repertoires in Great Britain, 1758–1834' (1993) 17 *Social Science History* 253.

6 Charles Tilly, *Contentious Performances* (Cambridge University Press, 2008), 14.

manipulation in the pamphlets to pursue their political goals, or *whether*, and if so, *how*, some concepts were made oppositional. In this chapter, I view expert concepts, argumentative languages and even scientific methods as potentially open to innovation and manipulation in the political sphere. Thus, I want to expand the concept of repertoire for innovators in revolutionary situations by moving from direct physical forms of contention to more abstract ones, considering many more linguistic aspects. Which kind of 'concepts' and 'languages' can be used in the moments when the regime's pressure has been relaxed, but only a limited array of concepts are at hand? To answer that, I will turn next to the Estonian case, which shows the importance of concepts, including its impact on the Soviet collapse.

6.3 FROM 'FUTURE SCENARIOS' TO 'SELF-MANAGEMENT' IN 1987

Two years before Polish Round Table Talks (February–April 1989), before the Civic Forum and Václav Havel's last arrest by the secret police in Prague in October 1989 and before the first mass demonstration in Romania in December 1989, one of the first revolutionary situations in Eastern Europe after the *Solidarność* movement, where (to use Tilly`s words) 'the contenders advance claims to control some segment of the state', emerged in 1987 in Soviet Estonia. On 26 September 1987, a group of Estonian scientists and experts published a short article entitled 'A Proposal: Estonian SSR to Full Self-Management' (*Ettepanek—kogu Eesti NSV täielikule isemajandamisele*) in the progressive local newspaper *Edasi* (*Forward*).[7] Four men were named in the byline (Siim Kallas, Tiit Made, Edgar Savisaar and Mikk Titma) and, thus, the document was quickly named the 'Four-Man Proposal' (*Nelja mehe ettepanek*). All four men were members of the Communist Party of the Soviet Union (CPSU).[8] The proposal called upon the Estonian government and the scientific community to draft plans to achieve an independently operating economy in the union. The request declared the need for 'a radical rearrangement of the Estonian economy and the society as a whole'. The proposal's main message was that public debate should be started on how to gain 'full self-accounting status' for the republic and how to place the economy (including all-union enterprises) on Estonian territory completely under the jurisdiction of the Estonian SSR. The article also proposed giving the republic its national currency. The novelty of the revolutionary 'Four-Man Proposal' consisted of the quest for financial independence of the republic – the claim for the budgetary control over the all-union enterprises, independent economic foreign relations, taxation and currency on the republic's level was unheard of in the Soviet Union. The proposal was considered a 'utopian'

7 Siim Kallas, Tiit Made, Edgar Savisaar and Mikk Titma, 'Ettepanek – kogu Eesti NSV täielikule isemajandamisele', *Edasi*, 26 September 1987.

8 The Communist Party of Estonia (as a branch of the CPSU) was not an independent Party organization and, therefore, people officially joined the CPSU.

plan by many contemporaries. Siim Kallas (one of the signatories of proposal) later said that, although the project was clearly unreachable, 'it was still very useful and healthy project, which helped [metaphorically] to heat the oven, to present constantly more and more radical claims to Moscow'.[9]

The project was also presented as 'opening up the multiple scenarios', inviting experts and scholars to join the debate. This approach was established in May 1987 through a public contest of 'economic development scenarios' announced by the main activist of the Four-Man Proposal, Edgar Savisaar, who headed the department in the Estonian Plan Committee, the regional branch of Gosplan. Although the scenario method known by the local management school from the 1970s, the contest for 'future scenarios' was the first of its kind in Estonia. The Planning Committee's official manual for contestants stated that:

> The contest aims to receive original, scientifically argued, alternative future scenarios that would consist of well-explained ideas for structural changes and economic innovation in the republic; to deploy new techniques for future visioning that would meet the objective conditions of the modern age, and to form interdisciplinary expert groups of scientists from different fields.[10]

More than 100 teams registered for the contest; although only around 20 proposals were accepted (because of the contest's strict requirements), and 6 of these won prizes.[11] The topics of the scenarios included imagining foreign trade in ESSR in the service sector, the vision for secondary schools, reforms in agriculture and so on. After the contest, Savisaar demanded from the government that the six winning scenarios be made public and debated with scientists. The public discussion (as a pillar for glasnost policy) was supposed to change the political culture. Savisaar wrote, in spring 1988, that is why 'a scenario method is an ideal tool for a dialogue between scientists and the political authorities, helping to present alternative future visions and their probable results'.[12] However, the results of the contest were not taken into account at higher levels of political decision-making. This was one of the reasons why Savisaar organized another brainstorming session with an expert group in the Plan Committee in August 1987. The task for the experts was to continue with the scenarios, this time to work out innovative ideas on how to radically change the whole republic`s economic management. However, fearing that it will stay in the cabinets like the scenario contest, Savisaar decided to publish the new proposal straight away in the popular media and it was made on 26 September 1987. Although the new proposal was worked out by approximately ten members, it was publicly signed by only four men in September.

9 Interview with Siim Kallas. In *Teine Eesti. Eeslava*. Eds. Mart Laar, Urmas Ott, Sirje Endre (SE&JS, 1996), 142.
10 Eesti NSV Riiklik Plaanikomitee, *Stsenaariumivõistlusest osavõtja meelespea* (1987), 3.
11 Erik Terk, *Eestist ja ettepoole* (Tallinna Ülikool, 2012), 148.
12 Edgar Savisaar, 'Majandusmõte 3', *Edasi*, 11 May 1988, 3.

The Four-Man Proposal called the Estonian scientific community to brainstorm the concept of 'territorial self-management' (*isemajandamine*) and to 'release the intellectual resources of the people'. Most importantly, it generated a massive debate from October 1987 until the end of 1988. The discussions on 'what it would take to carry out this project' took place every week, mostly in progressive newspapers, mobilizing reform-minded top officials, intellectuals and academics from very different fields. In the end, the reform-minded vice-chairman of the Council of Ministries of Estonia, Indrek Toome, publicly endorsed the project. The new project was exported to other Baltic republics as well. In the autumn of 1988, the governments of all three Baltic republics established a common platform to begin negotiations with Moscow to gain 'economic independence' from central planning. Two concepts, the 'scenario method' and 'economic self-management', had not only helped to construct a novel political project but also facilitated the scientists' path to politics.

Thus, Estonian experts and scientists entered politics by means of their professional language. How unique was this process in East Central Europe? Although it was an exceptional move in the Soviet republics, we can find similar cases in some other countries. For instance, Czechoslovakian forecasting scholar Miloš Zeman rose to politics with his article *Prognostika and Perestroika*, published in August 1989. While Savisaar in Estonia employed the concept of 'future scenario' in 1987, Zeman used 'prognostika' in 1989 as an important scientific source of critical thinking on the 'plurality of possible futures'.[13] Just like Savisaar, Zeman emphasized the necessity of dialogue and public discussion on both social and economic problems. In both cases, the published texts were arrowed at the ultra-centralist rule. This shows one transnational current in Eastern Europe in the late 1980s, where forecasting experts became politicians with the help of their professional language. Both men eventually became prime ministers of their countries; Savisaar in 1990 and Zeman in 1998.

Month after month, the utopian project of 'self-management' (*isemajandamine*) gradually expanded in Estonia. The meanings that were initially connected only with economic policies permeated the social and political sphere in early spring 1988. The Tartu Group of Self-Management (*Isemajandamise Tartu rühm*), consisting of academics from various fields at the University of Tartu, stated in their first meeting on 15 February 1988, that '*isemajandamine* is not only an economic but also a social and ideological problem ... the hope is that regulating the society's economic base will also reactivate social mechanisms'.[14] A fundamental shift in the rhetoric was the group's statement that 'the economy is only an instrument for the ultimate goals of *isemajandamine*', which were the 'increase of sovereignty and subjectivity, growth of welfare, increase of freedom of choice, etc.'[15] The 'self-

[13] Miloš Zeman, 'Prognostika *a přestavba*' (1989) 32 *Technický magazín* 6.

[14] Aivi Ross, 'Isemajandamise Tartu rühm', *Edasi*, 19 March 1988.

[15] Marju Lauristin, 'Isemajandamisfoorum Tartus', *Edasi*, 29 April 1988.

management' as a concept quickly expanded to self-management in all spheres (culture, environment, regional policy, etc.).

Again, comparing the Estonian case with the developments in East-Central Europe in that period, there is a similarity between this discourse of 'self-management in all social spheres' and the discourse of self-management in the civic society proposed by Czech dissidents in the mid-1980s. In 1985, Czech dissident Petr Uhl, in his essay 'The Alternative Community as Revolutionary Avant-garde', explicitly says that 'social (and not merely economic) self-management is a combination of direct and indirect forms of democracy'.[16] In the same year, another Czech dissident, Rudolf Battěk, argued in favour of 'different forms of self-management' and the need for 'pluralizing sovereignty' in society. According to Battěk, 'social structures can be democratized by expanding the elements of self-management, limiting institutional growth, making allowances for ideas as motivational factor, and strengthening direct democracy by eliminating priorities and privileges'.[17] Paul Blokker has described it as a continuation of 'republican language', as it promoted direct democracy, people's moral responsibility to the state and civic initiative from below.[18] The intriguing part is that, whereas in East-Central Europe this 'language' was kept alive by dissidents, in the Estonian SSR it emerged from the community of social scientists, many of them being members of the Communist Party.

6.4 FROM 'SELF-MANAGEMENT' TO 'SOVEREIGNTY' IN 1988

The Tartu group changed the abbreviation of *isemajandamine* (IM) to IME (*Isemajandav Eesti*) in the spring of 1988. In Estonian, 'IME' literally means 'miracle' (*ime*), which helped to give the movement even more positive, creative, even spiritual image. Reformers saw that, although an (economically) utopistic project, a miracle in that sense, it mobilizes the whole nation. By autumn 1988, IME had multiple simultaneous meanings – it denoted a social movement, economic independence, and social self-regulation, but perhaps most importantly it acquired the meaning of political sovereignty.

Indeed, from the perspective of world politics, the most important by-product of the mushrooming discourse on self-management was the revival of the forgotten concept of 'sovereignty' at the end of 1987. By the constitution of the Soviet Union (1977), every Soviet republic was a 'sovereign socialist Soviet state' (§ 76). The concept of 'sovereignty' (in Estonian, *suveräänsus*) was brought into the IME debate in October 1987 by lawyers who said that the republic's economic independence

[16] Petr Uhl and Paul Wilson (1985), 'The Alternative Community as Revolutionary Avant-Garde' 15 *International Journal of Politics* 188.

[17] Rudolf Battěk, 'Spiritual Values, Independent Initiatives and Politics', in Václav Havel (ed.), *The Power of the Powerless* (Hutchinson, 1985), 108.

[18] Paul Blokker, 'Dissidence, Republicanism, and Democratic Change' (2011) 25 *East European Politics and Societies* 219.

cannot be achieved without the republic's sovereignty. Legal scholar Indrek Koolmeister was the first, who stated in October 1987 that 'speaking of being a master in your country, it is not only an economic but also a political-legal category … to speak about the people as a master at the state level means to talk about the sovereignty of people, about its power, and the ways of its realization'.[19] From there, several lawyers started to argue that 'sovereignty' was a constitutional right of every Soviet republic, as the all-union constitution clearly states. Legal scholars Igor Gräzin and Peeter Kask emphasized in November 1987 that 'the republic`s self-management presumes the sovereignty of the republic to expand its rights … and using the constitutional rights that ensure sovereignty is not only the republic's right but also its duty'.[20] It was a remarkable conceptual transfer of the 'sovereignty' from constitutional law to the public sphere, irrespective of the fact that, only a year earlier, this very concept was not perceived by Estonian reformers applicable on the political arena at all.

In September 1988, the politically and legally more useful term 'sovereignty' replaced 'self-management' in reformists' tactics. During the 11th Plenum of the Estonian Communist Party on 9–10 September 1988, Estonian political scientist Andrus Park invited others 'to pay attention to the legal-political questions to secure the Estonian SSR's economic independence', stressing that 'the keyword for the IME movement from now on should be "sovereignty" and only then "self-management"'.[21] However, the final manoeuvre was made due to a direct constitutional dispute with Gorbachev's team, who demanded in summer 1988 that Estonia should confirm the new amendments in the Soviet Union's constitution. In response, on 16 November 1988, the Supreme Soviet of the Estonian SSR adopted the Declaration of Sovereignty. The declaration asserted the ESSR's 'sovereignty' and Estonian laws' primacy over those promulgated by Moscow's all-union government. This step became a blueprint that was soon followed by virtually all other Soviet republics (including the Russian SFSR) and many autonomous republics in 1989–1990. This process, known as the 'Parade of Sovereignties',[22] put the central government at a serious disadvantage in its efforts to re-establish control over the Soviet Union and led to its dissolution in 1991.

The importance of the 'sovereignty factor' on the dissolution of the Soviet Union has been acknowledged. Edward D. Walker has written the most meticulous study

[19] Indrek Koolmeister, 'Isemajandamine ja ise majandamine', *Edasi*, 25 October 1987.

[20] Igor Gräzin and Peeter Kask, 'Isemajandamisest ja suveräniteedist', *Edasi*, 13 November 1987. See also Indrek Koolmeister, 'Isemajandamine ja ise majandamine', *Edasi*, 25 October 1987; and Gunnar Kuldvere's interview with Urve Nõu, Heino Siigur, Tõnu Anton, Enn Hansberg and Indrek Koolmeister, 'Majanduslik ja õiguslik iseseisvus on lahutamatud', *Edasi*, 8 December 1987.

[21] 'Koos rahvaga, rahva huvides'. *Rahva Hääl*, 11 September 1988, 3.

[22] Jeff Kahn, 'The Parade of Sovereignties: Establishing the Vocabulary of the New Russian Federation' (2000) 16 *Post-Soviet Affairs* 58.

TABLE 6.1 *The 'Parade of Sovereignties' (SSRs)*

1988	1989	1990
Estonia, Nov. 16	Lithuania, May 18 Latvia, July 29 Azerbaijan, Sept. 23 Georgia, Oct. 12 Byelorussia, Dec. 7	Russian SFSR, June 12 Uzbekistan, June 20 Moldavia, June 23 Ukraine, July 16 Turkmenistan, Aug. 22 Armenia, Aug. 23 Tajikistan, Aug. 25 Kazakhstan, Oct. 26 Kirghizia, Oct. 28

on the effect of the factor on the USSR's dissolution. Walker emphasized the importance of the sovereignty declarations adopted in 1988–1990, saying that

> 'Sovereignty' killed the Soviet Union ... The concept of 'sovereignty', more than any other competitor such as 'democracy', 'liberty', or 'markets', was used with great effect by the anti-union opposition in the union's republics to challenge the authority of the USSR's central government.[23]

The political efficiency of the concept was also highly esteemed by Boris Yeltsin, who recalled later that 'as soon as the word "sovereignty" resounded in the air ... the last hour of the Soviet empire was chiming'.[24] Throughout 1990, Boris Yeltsin presented 'sovereignty' as a central concept in his speeches in RSFSR regions, calling on regions to declare their sovereignty. Eventually, all fifteen union republics (SSRs) in the Soviet Union and twenty-six different autonomous regions (including ASSRs) in the Russian SFSR adopted sovereignty declarations between 1988 and 1991 (Table 6.1).

While the importance of the 'sovereignty factor' on the dissolution of the Soviet Union has been recognized, some of its questions remain unanswered. For instance, why did it happen first in Estonia and not in other Soviet republics? Why did the concept of 'sovereignty' rise to prominence in Estonia in late 1987? What was the reason for this particular development in the ESSR on the all-union scale?

Even though in November 1988 the 'sovereignty of the Estonian SSR' was declared on the grounds of the ESSR's constitutional rights, its unexpected 'emergence' in late 1987 was related to something else. The rebirth of 'sovereignty' in Estonia was caused by the need to form a legal basis for the project of territorial self-management. In other words, in 1987–1988, 'sovereignty' was supposed to serve the goal of 'self-management' and not vice versa. 'Self-management' became a central

[23] Edward D. Walker, *Dissolution: Sovereignty and the Breakup of the Soviet Union* (Rowman & Littlefield, 2003), 1.

[24] Boris Yeltsin, *The Struggle for Russia* (Crown, 1994), 112.

political concept in the ESSR from September 1987 onwards, before it was replaced by its local successor, 'sovereignty', in late 1988. It was an unintended conceptual consequence of the gradually expanding debate on self-management in 1987. Thus, to understand the spread of 'sovereignty' in Soviet republics in 1987–1989, one should pay attention not only to constitutional factors (i.e., to the Soviet constitution) but also to *why* and *where* the new claim arose, *what* its relation was to other concepts in the ongoing debate, and *which* contextual resources made it possible to create those preceding claims.

6.5 TWO CONCEPTUAL REVOLUTIONS: CENTRAL AND PERIPHERAL

The Sovietologist Archie Brown was the first, in 1989, to describe the years of the mid-perestroika campaign (1987–1988) as a 'conceptual revolution'. To quote Brown, 'the conceptual revolution, like perestroika in general, was in many respects a revolution from above, stimulated by the new vocabulary of politics Gorbachev used'.[25] Brown pointed out several concepts in Gorbachev`s speeches that 'helped to open space for the new political activity'.[26] During perestroika, in 1989, Archie Brown noted that Gorbachev and his allies used three 'new concepts' in 1987–1988, which, according to Brown, 'deserve special emphasis, as they helped to open space for new political activity and provide a theoretical underpinning for some of the concrete reforms that the more radical interpreters of perestroika were attempting to implement'.[27] These were (1) 'socialist pluralism' (*sotsialisticheskoe plyuralizm*) as a pluralism of opinion; (2) 'state based on the rule of law' (*pravovoe gosudarstvo*); and (3) 'checks and balances' (*sderzhek i protivovesov*) as separation of powers.[28] All three received the endorsement of Gorbachev, which corroborates Brown's claim about 'the revolution from above'. However, as we have seen, there was another, parallel conceptual revolution 'from below' (or 'from the side') happening in the periphery – the cases of 'self-management' and 'sovereignty' in Estonia showed the power of concepts during the perestroika. We saw the miraculous revival of 'sovereignty' in 1988, but the Estonian version of 'self-management' (*isemajandamine*) was similarly remarkable. What is the origin of that particular concept? Next, I will briefly describe the conceptual genealogy of *isemajandamine* in Estonia.

The Estonian term *isemajandamine* was part of the Soviet economic vocabulary. It was a translation from a Russian term *khozrachet* (an acronym of the longer version *khozyaistvennyi raschet*). As a Bolshevist concept, it was coined in the early 1920s, when Lenin and Bukharin explained the basis of the New Economic Policy

[25] Archie Brown, *Seven Years that Changed the World: Perestroika in Perspective* (Oxford University Press, 2007), 264.

[26] Ibid., 264.

[27] Ibid., 112–113.

[28] Ibid., 112.

(NEP) in terms of the 'system of *khozraschet*'.[29] To work 'on *khozraschet*' meant that a given economic unit (factory, enterprise) had achieved self-sufficiency, in which costs were covered from the unit's own profits, that is, independently of state directives. Thus, it was completely different from Marxist concept of workers' 'self-government' (sometimes used as a synonym to 'self-management') which had its own historical roots in East Central Europe (*radnicko samoupravljanje* in Yugoslavia; *samorząd robotniczy* in Poland, etc.). In short, *khozraschet* denoted the economic independence of the unit. In 1941, when the Soviets occupied Estonia, *khozraschet* was translated into Estonian as *isemajandamine*.[30] It was widely used during the late 1950s (related with Khrushchev's Sovnarkhoz reform) and during the Kosygin reform plans in the mid-1960s when the self-sufficiency of the economic system was set as the priority in the reform agenda. In the 1970s, the concept faded from the publicity into a long quiescence everywhere in the Soviet Union, including in Estonia. During the early perestroika, NEP and *khozraschet* returned to the Soviet economic debate, perhaps most powerfully with pro-perestroika economist Nikolai Smelev's article 'Advances and Debts' ('Avansy i dolgi') in *Novyi Mir* in June 1987.[31] From mid-1987 onwards, Gorbachev incorporated the term into his programmatic vocabulary and frequently spoke of the need for 'full cost accounting in enterprises' (*polnyi khozraschet predpriyatii*).[32] For instance, in his June 1987 speech in the CPSU Plenum, Gorbachev proposed that all state enterprises work 'on full self-accounting and self-financing', starting in 1988.

Smelev described *khozraschet* as more than just an accounting term. As he saw it, the NEP marked the transition from 'administrative socialism' to '*khozraschet* socialism'.[33] However, in official Soviet economic discourse, the term still had a very technical meaning. It regulated only the management forms and hierarchical relations within the economic units. For instance, *khozraschet*'s qualifiers were 'internal' (in Russian, *vnutrennyi*; in Estonian, *sisemine*) and 'full' (in Russian, *polnyi*; in Estonian, *täielik*). *Vnutrennyi khozraschet* (internal self-accounting) was a management form in which only a small individual unit within a collective farm or enterprise (such as a brigade) had *khozrachet* status. In contrast, in *polnyi khozraschet* (full self-accounting), the whole enterprise or farm worked as an economically self-managing unit. It was used everywhere in the Soviet Union only as a technical accounting term, referring to the enterprises' obligation to operate without losses and not to anything else. It was also the case with the Estonian SSR until 1987, when the Four-Man Proposal radically

[29] Vladimir Ilyich Lenin, *Polnoe Sobranie Socheneniia* (Moscow, 1984), 342.

[30] *Plaanimajandus. Majanduspoliitiline ajakiri* (1941), 12.

[31] Nikolai Smelev, 'Advances and Debts', in Alexander Dallin and Gail W. Lapidu (eds.), *The Soviet System: From Crisis to Collapse* (Westview Press, 1995 [1987]), 261–271. Many observers have identified Smelev's article as the 'main opener' of the public debate on economic reforms in the Soviet Union.

[32] Mikhail Gorbachev, *Perestroika: New Thinking for Our Country and the World* (Harper and Row, 1987), 88–89.

[33] Smelev, 'Advances ad Debts', 263.

changed the conventional meaning of *khozraschet*. The conceptual change was made on two levels. The first was in September 1987, when the Four-Man Proposal lifted its meaning from the individual-unit (enterprise) level to the territorial (republican) level. The second took place in spring 1988, when the Tartu Group of Self-Management and the IME Council expanded it from the strictly economic level into a much broader social sphere. The aforementioned changes also had a specific linguistic resource. The Estonian term *isemajandamine* had the prefix 'self-' (*ise-*), which made it similar to another Estonian term, *iseseisvus* ('independence'). The prefix was missing not only in the Russian term *khozraschet* but also in its translations to the native languages in other Soviet republics. This particular resource explains (but only partially) why the conceptual innovation of *khozraschet* was so resonant in the Estonian SSR.

The innovation of the *isemajandamine* inadvertently made space for other concepts and subsequent shifts, as it motivated other economists to come up with alternative ideas. In the autumn of 1988, economist Arno Köörna proposed that, instead of being a 'self-managing republic', Estonia should become the first 'free economic zone' in the Soviet Union, based on the Chinese model.[34] The proposal of a 'free economic zone' by Köörna attracted numerous critics discussing how to proceed with the reforms in Soviet Estonia. While Köörna and his supporters emphasized that becoming a special economic zone would be 'concrete, real and radical', the vast majority of economists and intellectuals argued against it, saying that a free economic zone would not be a step forward but rather a step back. In October 1988, the rival working groups of the 'self-management' project (the Economic Institute of the Academy of Sciences and the IME Council) published a joint position paper in which they highlighted all the criticisms of Köörna's idea. The main point was that 'a self-managing republic can only be a sovereign state, whereas an economic zone can exist only as a part of a state but never as a state as a whole'.[35] In other words, the orientation of the political elite was clear – it was not towards economic but to political sovereignty in 1988. In other words, the imagination process was so rapid that visions that might have been welcomed as innovative and appropriate in late 1987 (like a free trade zone) were, in the second half of 1988, interpreted as outdated, unnecessary and even dangerous to the IME project. Within a year, an economic proposal had been changed into a political request for republic's sovereignty. The peripheral 'conceptual revolution' had transformed economic concepts into political ones.

6.6 CONCLUSION

Concepts which derive from an expert-language framework can acquire broader resonance and meaning in society and contribute to the rise of a revolutionary

[34] Arno Köörna, 'Hiina ime ja Eesti IME', *Edasi*, 6 October 1988.

[35] 'Erimajanduspiirkond. Meie seisukoht' [The Special Economy Zone: Our Standpoint], *Rahva Hääl*, 21 October 1988.

situation. This chapter shows the identification of those conceptual processes in pre-revolutionary periods. A specific conceptual process sequentially unfolded in the ESSR in 1987–1988, culminating in the concept of 'sovereignty' rising to prominence in late 1987. First, the conceptual innovation of 'self-management' (*isemajandamine*) in Soviet Estonia enabled new kinds of social and political mobilization at different levels: (1) it opened the public press as a new discussion channel for the academics and experts who became involved in an intense debate about the current economic and political situation in Estonia; (2) official working groups were created to develop the idea at the level of the Communist Party and the Academy of Sciences; and (3) it helped to create a common conceptual platform for the Popular Fronts (and later for the national governments) of the three Baltic republics in their quest for economic independence. Secondly, if we analyse official language and concepts in authoritarian regimes, we have to consider the highly ideologized language, hierarchical discourse, censorship constraints, code words, previous connotations, and so on. The reform-minded scientists who masterfully innovated the old term, *isemajandamine* (which started to signify utopian situation where the whole republic could be financially independent), filled the conceptual void for reform-socialist forces. It became the centre of their language for two years (1987–1988) before it led to 'sovereignty' at the end of 1988 when the new concept took over the lead role in the reformists' agenda. Thus, 'self-management' acted like a vanishing mediator, a utopian project, but at the same time an extremely useful one for the local reformers. Both the project and concept (*isemajandamine*) disappeared in 1991, when Estonia become an independent state, and has not been used in the local political sphere since.

However, it is important to stress that the political development of the 'self-management' project in 1987–1988 was an open-ended process without foreseeable consequences. One of the members in the initial expert group, management scholar Erik Terk, said in 2018 that 'we had no way of knowing how it would end ... we did not imagine independence; the realistic aim back then was to negotiate as many economic rights from Moscow as possible'.[36] The development in the direction of political independence in 1988 was not initially planned as a step-by-step strategy, even if in hindsight it is very tempting to see it this way. We should not underestimate the role of the scenario method, used by the experts in the IME movement. We could illustrate this as a serendipitous process. The invention of 'territorial self-management' in September 1987 inspired the scholarly audience to produce new concepts (that they were not using in the first half of 1987) like 'sovereignty'. Eventually, the concept of 'sovereignty', which was initially meant to serve as a legal empowerment for the self-management project, turned out to be the most powerful concept for all Soviet republics.

[36] Author's interview with Erik Terk (Tallinn, 11 May 2018).

The process of expanding the ESSR's economic-territorial rights, from 'self-management' to 'sovereignty', eventually culminated with the official Declaration of Sovereignty, the first of its kind in the Soviet Union (16 November 1988). In 1989–1990, following the Estonian example, all Soviet republics issued their declarations of sovereignty, including the Russian SFSR in June 1990. This process, known as the Parade of Sovereignties, seriously disadvantaged the position of the central government in its pursuit to rebuild the union and, therefore, led to its dissolution. What initially started as a local territorial innovation plan, almost as an imaginary utopia, ultimately had very serious and unexpected legal consequences for the Soviet empire.

7

European Integration

Ineffable Aspiration or the Object of Concern? About the Ambiguity of Europe in the Polish Constitutional Imaginary

Aleksandra Kustra-Rogatka

7.1 INTRODUCTION

One of the peculiarities of the Polish Constitution of 1997 is its syncretism. The combination of various, often divergent or even mutually contradictory (apparently or actually) elements is visible not only in constitutional arrangements for the political system but also in the provisions for fundamental rights or even the ontology of law. The Constitution combines the chancellery and the presidential systems, economic neoliberalism and the vision of a social state, the positivist structure of the sources of law and a jusnaturalist conception of human dignity. This far-reaching constitutional eclecticism resulted from the fragmentation and polarisation of the Polish political scene during the initial period of the political transformation. A difficult and arduous constitutional compromise must have been 'thrashed out'.[1] Although the work on the new constitution had already commenced in 1989, the Constitution was approved in a national referendum only in 1997.[2] It is therefore a relatively late constitution as compared to those adopted in other post-communist countries. The protracted constitution-making was still in progress when, firstly, European integration had already moved to a new level – marked by the creation of the EU in the Maastricht Treaty – and, secondly, Poland's membership of the EU had become a political goal generally supported by all the political forces that participated in drafting the constitution. European integration was not the main topic of fundamental political disputes at the time. For the politicians involved in the work on the constitution, of greatest importance, inter alia, were the content of the preamble, the separation of the State from the Catholic Church, the

[1] Tadeusz Mazowiecki's phrase used in an interview published in: Zbigniew Bujak, *Konstytucja starsza niż myślisz, czyli o tym co z historycznego dorobku państwa polskiego znajdziemy w naszej Konstytucji* (Wydawnictwo ZB, 2019), 160.

[2] For more on this subject, see Bujak, Konstytucja starsza niż myślisz, Ryszard Mojak, 'Geneza prawnoustrojowe zasady i prawne podstawy procedury tworzenia i uchwalenia Konstytucji Rzeczypospolitej Polskiej z 2 kwietnia 1997 r.' (2018) *Gdańskie Studia Prawnicze* (No 4) 97.

division of powers within the framework of a bicephalous executive (between the President and the Council of Ministers) and the concept of individual freedom. Nevertheless, the content of Article 90 – the Polish 'integration clause' – also aroused controversy, mainly due to the politically and historically sensitive issue of transferring the powers of State authorities to an international organisation. The tension between the will to actively participate in European integration and the fears of losing or limiting sovereignty is thus inscribed in the DNA of the Polish Constitution. Interestingly, the provision that is the constitutional basis for Poland's accession to the EU does not expressly indicate these two fundamental and, to some extent, opposing ideas: sovereignty and European integration.

The purpose of this chapter is to analyse Article 90 of the Constitution (in conjunction with other constitutional provisions on international law) as an element of the Polish constitutional imaginary. The notion of constitutional imaginary as formulated by Martin Loughlin will provide the theoretical framework for these considerations. Loughlin drew attention to the manner in which modern constitutions can harness the power of narrative, symbol, ritual and myth to project an account of political existence in ways that shape and re-shape political reality.[3] Loughlin draws attention to three elements that shape the constitutional imaginary: thought, text and action. He claims that the core of the constitutional imaginary and its meaning is determined by an interaction between the concepts of ideology and utopia.[4] Perceived through the lens of Louglin's constitutional imaginary concept, Article 90 of the Polish Constitution turned out to be the provision that shapes intricate relations of two big ineffable ideas: sovereignty and European integration.

The three elements of Loughlin's constitutional imaginary will be the starting point for organising the analysis on Article 90 as a key constitutional provision related to EU membership (and other important constitutional provisions related, *inter alia*, to the application of international law in the Polish legal order). *Thought*, understood as vision (or visions) of constitutional order,[5] will be identified in this chapter with (rather fragmented) discussion on the vision of Poland's membership of the EU during constitution's drafting. *Text* will be related to academic interpretation of constitutional norms, whereas the dimension of *action* will cover the judicial interpretation of the constitutional text presented in the Constitutional Tribunal case-law regarding Poland's membership of the EU, the constitutional practice of applying (and not applying) Article 90 of the Constitution and the unsuccessful attempts to amend the Constitution and introduce a new 'European chapter' to it.

Loughlin points out that each of the elements that make up the constitutional imaginary are characterised by a tension between ideology and utopia. Ideology orders a pattern of action and is an expression of the fundamental symbolic structure

[3] Martin Loughlin, 'The Constitutional Imagination' (2015) 78 *Modern Law Review* 1, 3.

[4] Ibid., 11.

[5] Ibid., 5.

of the association. The main function of ideology within the political domain is to perform the integrative role of maintaining its identity.[6] The primary function of utopia, in turn, is to present an imaginative variation of the prevailing interpretation of constitutional order.[7] 'Utopia is the "view from nowhere". Its role is to highlight the contingency of the existing order by offering a vision of what might be.'[8] In the constitutional imaginary, then, ideology is a technique of integration and utopia primarily a technique of subversion. Ideology conceals the gap in legitimacy claims, whereas utopian thought exposes it.[9] Loughlin points out that both ideology and utopia have a positive and negative dimension:

> The positive role of ideology is to achieve social and political integration through constitutional ordering, while for utopian thought the positive role seeks to elaborate and promote ideals that are implicit within a constitutional text. But on the negative side, ideology can operate primarily to mask the various forms of domination within constitutional arrangements, and, in striving for constitutional perfection, utopianism might simply amount to a flight from political reality.[10]

In my opinion, this dichotomy is somewhat relative. Indeed, ideology may contain certain utopian elements, and every utopia is to some extent ideological. With regard to the place of Europe and the vision of European integration within the framework of Polish constitutional imaginary, the ideology–utopia dichotomy can be identified, on the one hand, with liberalism and the vision of a 'return to Europe' and, on the other hand, with the idea of classically understood sovereignty and striving for a strong nation state. The lack of coherence between the extensive sphere of thought and the laconic and agonistic nature of the constitutional text has been reflected in the constitutional practice (action). The European integration has been perceived in the constitutional practice as both the ineffable aspiration and the object of serious concerns. Since 2004, for a long time, constitutional practice with regards to the EU was a syncretic collection of cautious friendliness towards EU law, emphasis on (formal) constitutional supremacy and narrowing down the interpretation of 'the conferral of competences'. Nevertheless, until recent years, the constitutional text had tended to be interpreted as facilitating rather than limiting Poland's participation in European integration. Therefore, the observed Eurosceptic turn in the political domain is not justified either in the sphere of thought or in the constitutional text. The recent constitutional practice disturbs the existing balance between ideology and utopia. Instead of promoting political unity and overcoming conflicts of interest, it establishes a new site of political conflict.[11]

6 Ibid., 12.
7 Ibid.
8 Ibid., 12–13.
9 Ibid., 13
10 Ibid., 15.
11 Ibid.

7.2 THOUGHT: EUROPEAN INTEGRATION AND THE CONTESTED CONSTITUTIONAL COMPROMISE

The work on the Constitution commenced at a relatively early stage of the systemic transformation but lasted – for various reasons – an unexpectedly long time. Besides other fundamental issues, the question of Poland's future membership of the EU also turned out to be a subject of discussion and controversy.[12] The constitution-making work intensified in the period when Poland's integration with the EU was considered one of the key goals of State policy. All the major political parties declared their will to join the community structures as soon as possible. The pursuit of this goal was emphasised by the signing and subsequent ratification of the Association Agreement.[13] Nevertheless, the 'return to Europe' was not interpreted uniformly by all political parties. The political dispute mainly revolved around the understanding of State sovereignty.

A more detailed analysis of the constitutional provisions related to Poland's membership in the EU should be preceded by an overview of the political dispute over the Polish Constitution, which will help understand the origin of the current 'Eurosceptic' twist in the constitutional practice. The first freely elected Sejm (the lower chamber of the Polish parliament) did not manage to adopt a constitution (1991–1993).[14] The 1993 elections were won by parties burdened with communist heritage: Sojusz Lewicy Demokratycznej – SLD (Democratic Left Alliance) and Polskie Stronnictwo Ludowe – PSL (Polish People's Party). Nevertheless, they did not gain the two-thirds majority necessary to adopt a constitution. Therefore, they created a 'constitutional coalition' with opposition groups originating from post-Solidarity parties: the central-liberal Unia Wolności (Freedom Union) and the left-wing Unia Pracy (Labour Union). The right wing, divided between many parties, found itself outside the parliament but, before the elections planned for autumn 1997, it managed to unite and run for election under the name of Akcja Wyborcza 'Solidarność' (Electoral Action 'Solidarity').[15]

[12] Aleksandra Kustra, *Przepisy i normy integracyjne w konstytucjach wybranych państw członkowskich UE* (Toruń, 2009), 226; Mirosław Wyrzykowski, 'Konstytucyjne aspekty referendum europejskiego', in Eugeniusz Piontek (ed.), *Prawo polskie a prawo Unii Europejskiej* (Liber, 2003), 51.

[13] Kazimierz Działocha, 'Podstawy prawne integracji Polski z Unią Europejską w pracach nad nową konstytucją' (1996) (No. 4) *Państwo i Prawo* 5.

[14] The political consequence of the vote of no confidence in the minority government of Hanna Suchocka by the Sejm of the first term of office was the dissolution of both chambers of the Polish parliament (the Sejm and the Senate) by President Lech Wałęsa in 1993.

[15] AWS was formed in 1996 as a coalition of over thirty parties, uniting liberal, conservative and Christian-democratic forces. Marian Krzaklewski was its first chairman. After the establishment of AWS in 1996, Jarosław Kaczyński was one of its several vice-presidents (while remaining the chairman of the Christian democratic Porozumienie Centrum [PC – the Centre Agreement]). However, just before the elections in 1997, he left AWS, although the Centre Agreement itself remained in this coalition, and the main activists of his party ran from the Action lists. Jarosław

The post-communist SLD–PSL government was losing in the polls along with the upcoming elections of 1997, and the right-wing parties questioned whether the parliament elected in 1993 had the legitimacy required to adopt a constitution, as they considered it unrepresentative. Moreover, they prepared their own constitutional draft promoted as 'civic'. Although the constitution could have been passed before the 1997 parliamentary elections,[16] the right contested the parliamentary 'constitutional compromise' and called for a boycott of the constitutional referendum scheduled for May 1997 or for a vote against the Constitution. Interestingly, this campaign was quite effective: according to a public opinion poll in February 1997, 34% of Poles and 25% of parliament members would support the 'civic' project. Up to 41% of Poles believed that the parliament should not pass the constitution before the 1997 elections.[17] As a result, the parliament had to lower the threshold for the validity of the constitutional referendum, lifting the minimum 50% turnover requirement. The constitution was accepted by a hair's breadth and with a very low turnout. Only 42.86% of those entitled to participate in the referendum actually voted, and only 53.45% of those who participated voted in favour of the Constitution. In eastern and southern Polish voivodeships (the highest-level administrative division of Poland), the percentage of 'no' votes exceeded 70%.[18] As a result, some right-wing parties, including Prawo i Sprawiedliwość – PiS (Law and Justice), which forms the current government, contested the Constitution as, in their view, passed without sufficient democratic legitimation. Presenting this broader background to the political dispute over the Constitution demonstrates the context of changes that took place in the constitutional practice following 2015. It also explains why European integration, initially of interest to a small section of politicians involved in constitution-drafting, at a certain point became the subject of a fierce debate in the National Constituent Assembly and beyond. This is also a historical aspect that should be accounted for when analysing why the final shape of the Polish 'integration clause' is how it is.

Of the seven drafts of the constitution submitted to the Constitutional Committee of the National Assembly in March and April 1993[19], only the so-called presidential draft contained an integration clause, that is, a provision enabling the conferral of

Kaczyński himself was elected to the Sejm in autumn 1997 from the list of Ruch Odbudowy Polski [Movement for Reconstruction of Poland] – a right-wing party founded in 1995 by Jan Olszewski.

[16] Four hundred and fifty-one members of the National Assembly were in favour of the Constitution; forty were against and six abstained.

[17] Adam Leszczyński, '*Czy konstytucję w 1997 r. uchwalono, nie uwzględniając postulatów prawicy? Sprawdzamy, jak było*' oko.press, 7 May 2017, https://oko.press/konstytucje-1997-r-uchwalono-uwzgledniajac-postulatow-prawicy-sprawdzamy-bylo/.

[18] Ibid.

[19] These were drafts of the Constitution prepared by the Senate, Sojusz Lewicy Demokratycznej (SLD), Unia Demokratyczna (UD), Polskie Stronnictwo Ludowe and Unia Pracy (PSL/UP), the President, Konfederacja Polski Niepodległej (KPN) and Porozumienie Centrum (PC). The Porozumienia Centrum project was withdrawn in May 1994.

State authority competences to an external entity.[20] The draft stated that 'the law may authorise the signing of an international agreement which authorises an international (supranational) organisation or institution to exercise certain powers reserved by the constitution for organs of legislative and executive power. The act ratifying such an agreement requires its acceptance by a 2/3 majority of votes.'[21]

The Constitutional Commission of the National Assembly was composed of representatives of both the parliamentary majority and the remaining political forces represented in the parliament. It also established a team of experts.[22] European integration and the status of international law in the Polish legal system were discussed by two subcommittees: the Subcommittee on the Foundations of the Political and Socio-Economic System and the Subcommittee on Matters of Sources of Law. The main achievement of the former was to indicate the need for an 'integration clause' (i.e., a provision that might form the basis for Poland's membership in the EU). The latter resolved most of the problems concerning the status of international law within the Polish legal system.[23] Notably, the inclusion of an explicit legal basis for Poland's accession to the EU raised doubts within the Constitutional Committee. The Committee pondered whether to work on such a clause at all or whether to leave this issue to the ordinary law-making process for when there would be a real chance of EU accession. In that case, a relevant provision would have to be added via an amendment to the Constitution. The parliamentary majority formed by SLD and PSL opted for not settling this issue in the Constitution. They argued that Poland's accession to the EU could be carried out based on constitutional provisions for the ratification of international agreements without the need to explicitly regulate the 'conferral of competences'. They pointed out that Poland had acceded to the Council of Europe in this way in 1991.[24] Interestingly, K. Skubiszewski – an influential professor of international law and minister of foreign affairs between 1989 and 1993 – also opposed the regulation of issues directly related to Poland's future membership of the EU in the Constitution. In an article published in 1994, he indicated that the new Constitution should not regulate matters related to the law of international organisations and that these issues should be left to the decision of the ordinary law-maker after the accession.[25]

[20] Działocha, 'Podstawy prawne integracji Polski z Unią Europejską', 6.

[21] Article 16(3) of the draft submitted by President Lech Wałęsa. It is worth noting that one of the weaknesses of the proposed provision was that it did not consider the conferral of competences to judicial authorities. Nevertheless, this flaw was removed after the self-amendment was submitted by the chancellery of the President of the Republic of Poland. Kustra, Przepisy i normy integracyjne, 239.

[22] They were professors: Piotr Winczorek, Paweł Sarnecki, Maria Kruk-Jarosz, Wiktor Osiatyńskiego, Marian Grzybowski and Kazimierz Działocha.

[23] Kustra, *Przepisy i normy integracyjne*, 239.

[24] Ibid., 239–240, n. 477.

[25] Krzysztof Skubiszewski, 'Przyszła konstytucja RP a miejsce prawa międzynarodowego w krajowym porządku prawnym' (1994) (No. 3) *Państwo i Prawo* 11, 15.

Within the Subcommittees, experts played a decisive role in shaping the proposals that were subsequently discussed at the Constitutional Committee's plenary sessions.[26] The working material entitled 'Preliminary draft of the catalogue of basic political principles that should be expressed in the Constitution of the Republic of Poland' contained, inter alia, point 9 on 'the transfer of some State sovereignty to international institutions'. Three variants were proposed, reflecting different visions of legitimation required for the EU accession:

> a) the Republic of Poland may, by law, transfer sovereign rights to interstate institutions; b) the Republic of Poland may, by means of a constitutional act, transfer supreme rights to interstate institutions; c) the transfer of the sovereign rights of the Republic of Poland to interstate institutions is allowed only by way of (or on the basis of) a nationwide referendum.

The draft also emphasised that adopting such a provision might be beneficial or even necessary for Poland's ambition to integrate with the EU.[27] Nevertheless, a comprehensive draft of the chapter 'Basics of the Political and Socio-economic System' prepared in December 1994, contained no provisions directly related to European integration but only provisions on the relationship between national and international law. Ultimately, the issue of European integration was undertaken by the second of the aforementioned subcommittees (i.e., the Subcommittee on Matters of Sources of Law). It proposed an integration clause according to which the exercise of certain powers of State authorities might be delegated to an international or supranational organisation by way of international agreement ratified after obtaining 2/3 majority of votes in the parliament or submitted for approval in a national referendum.[28]

Starting from spring 1995, the Constitutional Committee discussed the draft constitutional provisions on the EU accession. A point of contention was where to place the integration clause: in Chapter I, regarding the fundamental political principles or Chapter III, regarding the sources of law. The supporters of Chapter I sought to highlight Poland's pro-European policy,[29] whereas the supporters of Chapter III relied on the link between the place of EU law and other international law in the national legal order and the far-reaching consequences for the principle of State sovereignty. In the latter's opinion, bringing the integration clause to the fore of the Constitution would present 'a certain political awkwardness'.[30] Ultimately, it was decided to leave the integration clause in Chapter III.[31]

[26] Kazimierz Działocha, in an interview published in: Bujak, *Konstytucja starsza niż myślisz*, 198.

[27] Ryszard Chruściak, 'Procedury przystąpienia Polski do Unii Europejskiej w pracach nad Konstytucją' (2003) (No. 5) *Państwo i Prawo* 44, 45.

[28] Ibid., 46.

[29] Działocha, 'Podstawy prawne integracji Polski z Unią Europejską', 9; Kustra, *Przepisy i normy integracyjne*, 231.

[30] Działocha, 'Podstawy prawne integracji Polski z Unią Europejską', 9; Kustra, *Przepisy i normy integracyjne*, 231.

[31] Chruściak, 'Procedury przystąpienia Polski', 47–48.

The Constitutional Committee accepted a version of the integration clause based on a proposal by the Council of Ministers. The ratification of an international agreement based on which Poland would confer competences to an international organisation required the two-thirds majority in both chambers of the parliament or consent by way of a national referendum.[32] The decision as to the mode of ratification was to be made by the Sejm by an absolute majority of votes.[33] Notably, the Committee pondered on making the referendum mandatory.[34] However, ratification by the parliament was considered as the default option due to the principle of the representative democracy in the Constitution and the subsidiary nature of direct democracy.[35]

The axiological rift between the desire to participate in the process of European integration and the fears related to the loss of some sovereignty were reflected in the constitution-making works.

First, a major concern was expressed about the proposed paragraph 2 of Article 9 in Chapter I regarding the observance by the Republic of Poland of binding international law. In the version adopted in the Constitutional Commission on 16 January 1997, this additional paragraph was to become an 'integration clause' under which 'the Republic of Poland may, on the basis of an international agreement, confer to an international organisation or an international body the competences of State authorities in certain matters'. At the final stage of editorial work, right-wing senator P. Andrzejewski submitted a motion to delete it. He stated that this provision raised the issue of 'making the sovereignty in the operation of the highest State authorities in Poland – including legislative, executive and judiciary authorities – dependent on the undefined scope of subordination to an international organisation or international body'.[36] This motion proves the fear held by some of the authors of the Constitution about overstating the 'return to Europe' in the Constitution. A similar motion was formulated by the right-wing non-parliamentary opposition in the 'Position of the Social Constitutional Commission of 26 February 1997 on fundamental issues related to the parliamentary draft of the constitution'. This position stated, inter alia, that 'it is necessary to unequivocally guarantee the sovereignty of the State. Upon cases of conferring some jurisdiction of the State to international bodies and organisations one cannot resign from the supremacy of the constitution, although such situations should be provided for by the constitution by establishing a careful and detailed procedure for making decisions, guaranteeing

[32] Ibid., 48.

[33] Ibid., 48–49.

[34] The supporters of such a solution emphasised that since it was a question of conferring constitutional powers of state authority, society's acceptance should be sought in a referendum, just like with the Constitution, see Ibid., 54.

[35] Ibid., 53–54.

[36] Chruściak, 'Procedury przystąpienia Polski', 51; see also Biuletyn Komisji Konstytucyjnej Zgromadzenia Narodowego [Bulletin of the Constitutional Committee of the National Assembly], vol XLIII, 52 and 79.

that the nation will not diminish its rights and that it will act according to its will. In the version proposed in the parliamentary draft of the Constitution, the provisions of Article 9(2) raise justified concerns regarding the abuse of the conferral of competences to international organisations'.[37] In the second reading of the draft of the Constitution, three amendments were submitted for Article 9, all of which related to the content of Article 9(2). One of them proposed deleting Article 9(2) and this motion was voted through.[38] As stated by then Freedom Union member of parliament, J. Zdrada, the discussion on the content of Article 9 was '... not even emotional, but worse. Many used false arguments in this discussion. They invented fears, as if not realising that the matter is somewhat different in international relations. It was alleged that this provision ... actually sells Poland out, giving up sovereignty, independence, etc.'[39] As mentioned earlier, the 'integration clause' ultimately ended up in Chapter III.

Second, there were numerous proposals for procedural restrictions on the conferral of competences to an international organisation. The authors of the constitution 'opened it up' to European integration but, being aware of the accusation made by the non-parliamentary right-wing opposition regarding a 'loss of sovereignty', they included in the integration clause far-reaching procedural limitations. Although they did not opt for an obligatory referendum, they required a qualified majority of two-thirds of the votes in both houses of the parliament. Notably, this solution meant that the procedure for ratifying the EU accession would be more rigid than that for amending the Constitution (which requires the two-thirds majority in the Sejm and only the absolute majority in the Senate; the referendum limited to the most important amendments is optional).[40] Moreover, if the Sejm was to opt for a referendum regarding the accession, a 50 per cent turnout would be mandatory for its validity. Taking into account the fact that, during the referendum regarding the Constitution, the decision was taken to abandon this requirement (and less than half of those eligible to do so actually participated), the requirements of the procedure for ratifying the EU accession through a referendum could have turned out very difficult to fulfil.

However, an ambivalent attitude towards Article 90 of the Constitution was demonstrated by some members of parliament, as evidenced by a statement issued by R. Bugaj – at the time a member of parliament for the Labour Union. In an interview conducted with Z. Bujak, he stated that

[37] Chruściak, 'Procedury przystąpienia Polski', 51; with reference to Biuletyn Komisji Konstytucyjnej Zgromadzenia Narodowego [Bulletin of the Constitutional Committee of the National Assembly], vol. XLIII, 99–100.

[38] Chruściak, 'Procedury przystąpienia Polski', 51–53.

[39] Jerzy Zdrada, in Bujak, *Konstytucja starsza niż myślisz*, 275.

[40] Article 235 of the Constitution, which regulates the issue of passing the act on amending the Constitution, indicated the requirement to obtain a two-thirds majority in the Sejm and an absolute majority in the Senate (with a quorum of at least half of the statutory number of members of a given chamber of parliament).

> ... in fact, it was not needed and the problem could have been resolved differently. This is also an example of the ideological attitude of the Freedom Party [Unia Wolności]. It was a Freedom Party idea (to include an integration clause), and specifically promoted by Suchocka [a Polish political figure, lawyer and the Prime Minister of Poland between 8 July 1992 and 26 October 1993].[41]

When the interviewer stated that such an attitude was surprising, considering the fact that at the same time in Western Europe states entering the EU were introducing similar provisions to their constitutions, R. Bujak stated,

> Yes, but they're not exactly the same, and in any case we could have managed without this article. It protects sovereignty and makes it easier to seize it at the same time, thus creating a certain precedent. I think that we didn't need it, but also when we accepted it, we didn't think that such a conflict would break out around it, although this war was largely artificial. People were looking for a place to aim and shoot from as large a cannon as possible.[42]

To sum up, the tension between the willingness to participate in the process of European integration and the fear of losing sovereignty was noticeable in the constitution-making work. Europe appeared as an unspoken aspiration but also a subject of concern. Political conflicts within the so-called parliamentary constitutional coalition meant that the ultimately adopted wording of Article 90 was a result of a painstaking compromise. Moreover, the criticism of the Constitution by the non-parliamentary right-wing opposition also applied to the Polish 'integration clause'. Fears of a social reaction and the overarching goal of having the Constitution approved in a referendum prevented a stronger articulation of 'openness' to the EU. The broader formula of 'conferral of competences to an international organisation or body' was chosen and the 'conferral of competences' was removed from Chapter I of the Constitution. Therefore, Article 90 appears as, on the one hand, a provision that 'enables' opening up to Europe. Without it, the EU accession would be practically impossible.[43] On the other hand, the EU accession is in this provision subject to relatively tough procedural requirements geared towards the protection of national sovereignty.

7.3 TEXT: CONSTITUTIONAL SILENCE AND ITS INTERPRETATION

Jerzy Ciemieniewski, MP in the 1990s and later judge of the Constitutional Tribunal, stated that the Constitution of 1997 was written by constitutional practitioners, 'that is, people who, in their experience, have contact only with certain

[41] Bujak, *Konstytucja starsza niż myślisz*, 226.

[42] Ibid.

[43] Maria Kruk, 'Tryb przystąpienia Polski do Unii Europejskiej i konsekwencje członkostwa dla funkcjonowania organów państwowych', in Krzysztof Wójtowicz (ed.) *Otwarcie Konstytucji RP na prawo międzynarodowe i procesy integracyjne* (Wydawnictwo Sejmowe, 2006), 139.

cases of the operation of constitutional norms and who regulate in this act the situations they encountered'.[44] 'This whole constitutional debate proceeded as if there had not been actually one good book on constitutional law, the philosophy of the state, and the philosophy of law. It was all extremely pragmatic and related to the specifics or to the wording of provisions.'[45] And this – in his opinion – was one of the main reasons for the casuistic nature of the Constitution of 1997.[46] He criticised the Polish Constitution for the lack of a coherent theoretical vision and for being too detailed.[47] Considering the 'integration clause', this thesis may only be regarded as half the story. In this case, framers of the Constitution adopted the rule: the less is more. It can be assumed that one of the reasons for such a decision was simply Poland's lack of experience in the field of constitutional aspects of EU membership. Accession to the EU in 1997 was still quite distant in time and uncertain. Moreover, the trend of amending national constitutions to take fuller account of the country's membership in the EU was only just beginning (just as integration within the framework of the still relatively recently established EU was still developing). Therefore, both the substantive and procedural layer of Article 90 (1) is rather terse. Political compromises in the case of this clause took the form of 'constitutional silence' rather than casuistry. The tension between aspiration and fear of losing sovereignty is left unsaid. Article 90 does not contain the words 'Europe' or 'sovereignty'. This 'constitutional silence' may also be described as 'constitutional abeyance'. It does not arise because the issue has been overlooked,[48] but rather expresses the need 'to condone, and even cultivate, constitutional ambiguity as an acceptable strategy for resolving conflict'.[49]

The integration clause in the Polish Constitution is intentionally unfinished. 'What is explicit in the text rests on implicit understandings; what is stated rests on what is unstated.'[50] Article 90 'establishes a framework within which – and over which – further political deliberation takes place.'[51] This makes the interpretation of the constitution-makers' understatements all the more important. This part of the chapter focuses on the academic interpretation of the constitutional text. This type of interpretation – due to its epistemic authority – is often used to justify certain actions within the framework of constitutional practice (although constitutional practice – on the basis of synergy – also influences academic interpretation).

[44] Jerzy Ciemieniewski in conversation with Zbigniew Bujak, in Bujak, *Konstytucja starsza niż myślisz*, 292.

[45] Ibid., 284.

[46] Ibid.

[47] Ibid., 284–285.

[48] Martin Loughlin, 'The Silence of Constitutions' (2018) 16 *International Journal of Constitutional Law* 922, 926.

[49] Michael Foley, *The Silence of Constitutions: Gaps, 'Abeyances' and Political Temperament in the Maintenance of Government* (Routledge Revivals, 1989), 11.

[50] Loughlin, 'The Silence of Constitutions', 927.

[51] Ibid., 935.

Loughlin points out that constitutional text is often agonistic and contains the seeds of dissonance.[52] The tension between aspiration for Europe and fear of losing sovereignty is expressed again (after the completion of the constitution-making) in the academic interpretation of Article 90 of the Constitution. It shows the desire to establish a fragile balance between ideology and utopia. The ideology (fundamental symbolic structure) of the 'Integration clause' is the opening of the Constitution to Europe and the European system of values, while utopia is the Westphalian vision of sovereignty. On the one hand, it is pointed out that Article 90 plays the so-called role of legitimising (allowing) participation in integration processes. On the other hand, it is mentioned that it also functions as a safeguard of the Polish constitutional order and State sovereignty.[53] In its role as legitimiser, Article 90 is considered an expression of opening the Polish legal system to the power of international organisations. Legitimisation relates to two areas. First, the transfer of power to an international organisation. Secondly, the opening of the Polish legal order to the validity and application of legal norms created by other legal entities.[54]

The search for a balance between the roles of legitimisation and safeguard is visible in the academic search for an appropriate interpretation of the concept of the 'conferral of competences of State authorities'. The formulation that was eventually adopted was critically assessed by part of the legal doctrine.[55] It was pointed out that, in the act of conferring competences, 'the States only forego the exercise of relevant rights, although they remain [hereinafter] in their possession'.[56] The effects of 'conferral' are two-fold: first, Poland relinquishes the exclusivity of its authority in certain areas; secondly, it allows for the application of 'foreign sovereign acts, not originating from the Polish public authority' in these areas.[57]

In the discourse on the limits of conferring competences, it was emphasised that the constitution-makers did not use the 'politically delicate' term *sovereignty* in Article 90. C. Mik – a professor of European law – stated that in this decision one

[52] Loughlin, 'The Constitutional Imagination', 15.

[53] Maciej Szpunar, 'Art. 90', in Marek Safjan and Leszek Bosek (eds.), *Konstytucja RP. Komentarz, Tom II, Art. 87–243* (Duże Komentarze Becka, 2016), 125.

[54] Kustra, *Przepisy i normy integracyjne*, 319.

[55] Stanisław Biernat, 'Constitutional Aspects of Poland's Future Membership in the European Union' (1998) 36 *Archiv des Völkerrechts* 398, 406–408; Jan Galster, 'Konstytucyjnoprawne aspekty przystąpienia Polski do Unii Europejskiej', *Wejście w życie nowej Konstytucji Rzeczypospolitej Polskiej* (1998), 72; Cezary Mik, 'Przekazanie kompetencji przez Rzeczpospolitą Polską na rzecz Unii Europejskiej i jego następstwa prawne' in Cezary Mik (ed), *Konstytucja Rzeczypospolitej Polskiej z 1997 roku a członkostwo Polski w Unii Europejskie* (TNOiK, 1999), 150.

[56] Jan Galster, 'Konstytucyjnoprawne bariery przystąpienia Polski do Unii Europejskiej', in Cezary Mik (ed.) *Polska w Unii Europejskiej. Perspektywy, warunki, szanse i zagrożenia* (TNOiK, 1997), 28.

[57] Jan Barcz, 'Konstytucyjnoprawne problemy stosowania prawa Unii Europejskiej w Polsce w świetle dotychczasowych doświadczeń państw członkowskich', in Maria Kruk (ed.), *Prawo międzynarodowe i wspólnotowe w wewnętrznym porządku prawnym* (Wydawnictwo Sejmowe, 1997), 203.

can see the recognition of sovereignty as an inalienable property of the Polish state, a specific meta-competence (i.e., a general and primary competence), the competence to decide on the exercise of specific competences.[58] It was academic interpretation that filled with content the constitutional silence, especially with regard to the fear of losing sovereignty. The position expressed by K. Wojtyczek – a professor of constitutional law and author of a monograph on the conferral of competences – is representative in pointing out that

> State sovereignty now means not so much the exclusive jurisdiction of the State to decide on its affairs, but rather the presumption that the state has such competence and the right to decide to revoke this presumption to a certain extent. Sovereignty is now expressed primarily in the right to participate in international relations and various international organisations on an equal footing with all other states and in the participation in joint decision-making in the international arena.[59]

There is a noticeable departure from the Westphalian vision of sovereignty and inspiration from contemporary theory of law, which redefines this concept.[60]

Nevertheless, the academic interpretation of Article 90 – based largely on concepts developed in German legal doctrine[61] – also emphasises the function of the 'integration clause' as a safeguard of sovereignty. In addition to the protection of sovereignty as a fundamental constitutional category, constitutionalists also highlighted quantitative (the 'conferral of competences in *certain matters*'[62]) and qualitative limitations (the requirement to maintain the principle of a democratic state ruled by law and the requirement to respect fundamental rights and freedoms,[63] the

58 Cezary Mik, 'Przekazanie kompetencji przez Rzeczypospolitą Polską na rzecz Unii Europejskiej i jego następstwa prawne (uwagi na tle art. 90 ust. 1 Konstytucji)', in Cezary Mik (ed.), *Konstytucja Rzeczypospolitej Polskiej z 1997 roku a członkostwo Polski w Unii Europejskiej: IV Ogólnokrajowa Konferencja Prawnicza Toruń 19-20 listopada 1998 r.* (TNOiK, 1998), 150.

59 Krzysztof Wojtyczek, 'Polska w europejskim systemie konstytucyjnym', in Paweł Sarnecki (ed.), *Prawo Konstytucyjne Rzeczypospolitej Polskiej* (C. H. Beck, 2005), 14.

60 Neil Walker (ed.) *Sovereignty in Transition* (Bloomsbury, 2006); Neil Mc Cormick, *Questioning Sovereignty: Law, State, and Practical Reason* (Oxford University Press, 1999).

61 Krzysztof Wojtyczek, *Przekazywanie kompetencji państwa organizacjom międzynarodowym* (Wydawnictwo Uniwersytetu Jagiellońskiego, 2007), 183; Barcz, 'Konstytucyjnoprawne problemy', 203.

62 Kazimierz Działocha, 'Komentarz do Art. 90', in Leszek Garlicki (ed.), *Konstytucja rzeczpospolitej Polskiej. Komentarz* (Wydawnictwo Sejmowe, 1999), 3–4; Mik, 'Przekazanie kompetencji', 151; Krzysztof Wójtowicz, 'Konstytucja Rzeczypospolitej Polskiej a członkostwo w Unii Europejskiej', in Ewa Popławska (ed.), *Konstytucja dla rozszerzającej się Europy* (Instytut Spraw Publicznych, 2000), 161; Bartosz Pawłowski, 'Opinia w sprawie projektu Traktatu ustanawiającego Konstytucję dla Europy' (2003) (No 5) *Przegląd Sądowy* 85.

63 Działocha, 'Komentarz do Art. 90', 5; Mik, 'Przekazanie kompetencji', 154–155; Ryszard Mojak, 'Konstytucyjne podstawy integracji Polski z Unią Europejską', in Tadeusz Bojarski, Ewa Gdulewicz and Jan Szreniawski (eds.), *Konstytucyjny ustrój państwa: Księga jubileuszowa Profesora Wiesława Skrzydły* (Wydawnictwo UMCS, 2000), 174; Wójtowicz, 'Konstytucja Rzeczypospolitej Polskiej', 164; Jan Barcz, 'Członkostwo Polski w Unii Europejskiej a

requirement of axiological consistency[64]) resulting directly or indirectly from the content of Article 90. From the outset, the possibility of terminating an international agreement on the basis of which competences have been conferred was also accounted for, and the procedure under which this would be executed was considered. Despite the lack of an explicit reference to the EU in Article 90, academics narrowly interpreted the constitutional expression referring to 'an international organisation or body'. A. Wyrozumska – professor of international law – pointed out that the practice of applying Article 90 should be limited only to organisations that may be defined as supranational.[65] In turn, K. Wojtyczek emphasised that Article 90 *de lege lata* precludes the transfer of power to a future European federation.[66]

A distinct element of the academic interpretation of the 'integration clause' is its procedural dimension. Even long before Poland's accession to the EU, loopholes in this respect were revealed.[67] Although there were some shortcomings, as noted by M. Kruk – Professor of constitutional law and expert of the Constitutional Commission – any attempts to overly concretise the procedure for conferring power at the constitutional level would lead to an overextension of Article 90.[68] The main controversies concerned the national referendum for the ratification of an international agreement, which is the basis for the conferral of competences. Most constitutionalists criticised the reference in Article 90 to Article 125 of the Constitution, which regulates 'a referendum on matters of particular importance to the State'.[69] The basic problem was the requirement arising from Article 125 to obtain at least a 50 percent turnout for a referendum to be considered valid. The Constitution did not explicitly regulate (neither in Article 90 nor in Article 125) what would happen if this turnout was not reached. The academics unanimously adopted an interpretation according to which, in such a case, it would be necessary for the Sejm to choose again the manner of ratification: another referendum or the parliamentary avenue requiring the two-thirds majority in both chambers. It was

Konstytucja', in Jan Barcz (ed.), *Czy zmieniać konstytucję? Ustrojowo-konstytucyjne aspekty przystąpienia Polski do Unii Europejskiej* (Instytut Spraw Publicznych, 2002), 20; Wyrzykowski, 'Konstytucyjne aspekty referendum europejskiego', 54.

64 Działocha, 'Komentarz do Art. 90', 5; Anna Wyrozumska, 'Ratyfikacja traktatu akcesyjnego w drodze referendum', in Jan Barcz (ed.), *Czy zmieniać konstytucję? Ustrojowo-konstytucyjne aspekty przystąpienia Polski do Unii Europejskiej* (Instytut Spraw Publicznych, 2002), 89.

65 Anna Wyrozumska, 'Prawo międzynarodowe oraz prawo Unii Europejskiej a konstytucyjny system źródeł prawa', in Krzysztof Wójtowicz (ed.), *Otwarcie konstytucji RP na prawo międzynarodowe i procesy integracyjne* (Wydawnictwo Sejmowe, 2006), 76.

66 Wojtyczek, 'Polska w europejskim systemie konstytucyjnym', 16.

67 Jan Barcz, *Czy zmieniać konstytucję? Ustrojowo-konstytucyjne aspekty przystąpienia Polski do Unii Europejskiej* (Instytut Spraw Publicznych, 2002).

68 Maria Kruk, 'Tryb przystąpienia Polski', 142.

69 Kustra, *Przepisy i normy integracyjne*, 272.

argued that this was the only rational interpretation of Article 90.[70] It was postulated that, in this respect, it would be desirable to amend Article 90 but not necessary.[71] Prof. Wójtowicz emphasised that the constitutional 'loophole' may in this case be filled in with a statute.[72] And so it happened – the Constitution was made more precise by the act of 8 March 2003 on a national referendum. This act was challenged before the Constitutional Tribunal, which will be discussed in Section 7.4.

However, at this point it should be noted that the academic interpretation of the procedural dimension of Article 90 proves that constitutionalists sought to ensure the effectiveness of the 'integration clause'. Even before its first application in 2003, they tried to discourage its interpretation that might lead to a 'decisional impasse' in terms of conferring competences. Due to problems related to the approval of the Constitution in 1997, inter alia, they were aware of the dangers posed by a referendum procedure requiring at least a 50 per cent turnout. Thus, they avoided such an interpretation that could end up torpedoing the legitimising role of the Polish 'integration clause'. At the same time, they also searched for a way to accommodate the role of the integration clause as a safeguard of sovereignty. If the 50 per cent turnout in the referendum could not be obtained, it would be necessary to reach the two-thirds majority in both houses (i.e., the procedure would be more difficult than that for a constitutional amendment).

7.4 ACTION: CONSTITUTIONAL PRACTICE BEFORE AND AFTER 2015: TOWARDS UTOPIA AND AGAINST CONSTITUTIONAL COMPROMISE?

7.4.1 *The Application and Non-application of the 'Integration Clause'*

The third element of the constitutional imaginary (i.e., action/constitutional practice) is most often built gradually and with consideration of thought and interpretation. This does not always mean that all the elements are consistent. In the case of Article 90, until the illiberal turn in Poland, the constitutional practice reflected an attempt to establish a fragile balance between ideology and utopia. Until the victory of Law and Justice in the parliamentary elections in 2015, Article 90 was primarily interpreted and applied in constitutional practice as a provision enabling integration, and not hindering or restricting it. So, the function of legitimisation prevailed, whereas the meaning of Article 90 as a safeguard of sovereignty was discussed mainly in theory (e.g., in lengthy justifications of the decisions of the

[70] Barcz, 'Członkostwo Polski w Unii Europejskiej a Konstytucja', 18; Maria Kruk, 'Konstytucja narodowa a prawo europejskie: Czy Konstytucja Rzeczypospolitej Polskiej wymaga zmiany', in Ewa Popławska (ed.), *Konstytucja dla rozszerzającej się Europy* (Instytut Spraw Publicznych, 2000), 185; Wójtowicz, 'Konstytucja Rzeczypospolitej Polskiej', 167–168.

[71] Barcz, 'Członkostwo Polski w Unii Europejskiej a Konstytucja', 18–19 and 40.

[72] Wójtowicz, 'Konstytucja Rzeczypospolitej Polskiej', 167.

Constitutional Tribunal). The Eurosceptic politics of the executive authorities in recent years combined with the 'political capture of the Constitutional Tribunal' has made Europe in constitutional practice more of a concern than an aspiration.

This part of the chapter presents three components of constitutional practice in relation to Article 90 of the Constitution as an integration clause before the illiberal turn of 2015. The first component is the application of Article 90, and therefore the conferral of competences or political decisions not to confer, while opting for a default mode of ratifying an ordinary international agreement. The second component is the rulings by the Constitutional Tribunal involving interpretation of Article 90. The third component is related to the so far unsuccessful attempt to introduce a so-called European chapter to the Constitution, which would be an expression of a shift in the current perception of Europe in the Polish constitutional imaginary. Due to the importance of the illiberal turn for the shift in the perception of Europe within the Polish constitutional imaginary, analysis of constitutional practice post-2015 should be analysed separately, including cases of non-application of Article 90 and Eurosceptic rulings by the politically captured Constitutional Tribunal putting forward an illiberal reinterpretation of Europe.

The cases of application or decisions not to apply Article 90 of the Constitution are undoubtedly crucial for establishing constitutional practice with regard to where Europe stands within the Polish constitutional imaginary. To this day, Article 90 regarding the 'conferral of competences' has only been applied twice. The first case concerned the ratification of the Accession Treaty in 2003. The second case concerned the ratification of the Lisbon Treaty in 2009. In 2003, the Sejm decided to hold a ratification referendum for the Accession Treaty, whereas in 2008 the parliamentary procedure was chosen for the Lisbon Treaty. Meanwhile, the application of Article 90 was considered to ratify various international agreements (as well as other legal acts of international law) both related and unrelated to the EU but, ultimately, the ordinary procedure for ratifying international agreements was chosen, which proves the exceptional nature of Article 90.

With regard to the ratification of the Accession Treaty, it is worth noting that, at the beginning of 2002 (i.e., before completing the accession negotiations), a motion had already been submitted in the Sejm to hold an accession referendum. The motion implied that such a referendum would take place even before the signing of the Accession Treaty itself. After discussion, however, the Sejm rejected it as premature.[73] Although political arguments outweighed substantive arguments in the parliamentary discussion, the constitutionalists considered this decision as sound.[74] Finally, the Sejm passed a resolution to order a nationwide referendum

[73] Kustra, *Przepisy i normy integracyjne*, 270.
[74] Kruk, 'Tryb przystąpienia Polski', 147.

to approve the ratification of the Accession Treaty on 17 April 2003, and the referendum itself was held on 7–8 June 2003. At the very beginning of the public discussion related to the ratification procedure of the Accession Treaty, the prevailing position was that the public should be given the opportunity to express its view on Poland's membership in the EU and a referendum should be held in this regard. The greatest concerns involved the minimum turnout requirement but these concerns turned out unfounded as 58.8 per cent of those entitled to vote participated. Of the voters, 77.45 per cent were in favour of Poland's accession to the EU (significantly more than during the referendum on the Constitution), while 22.55 per cent were against.[75] The Accession Treaty was ratified by President Aleksander Kwaśniewski on 23 July 2003 and, on 1 May 2004, Poland became an EU Member State. The sovereign statement made in the 2003 referendum can be interpreted as the strongest confirmation so far in the constitutional practice of liberal ideology and the social desire for a 'return to Europe'. The accession referendum can also be seen as public support for the liberal elements of the constitutional imaginary.

As regards the Lisbon Treaty, the Sejm decided not to hold a referendum, opting for the procedure requiring the 2/3 majority in both houses. The politicians (not only Polish ones) were sceptical about the referendum, bearing in mind how France and the Netherlands rejected the Constitution for Europe. The case of Ireland (where a second referendum was required) showed that this scepticism was at least partially justified.

Apart from the above-mentioned two cases of applying Article 90, until 2015, the ratification of an international agreement in this procedure – implying the conferral of State authority competences – was considered at least several times in the public debate. In each case, arguments that the ratification of a given international agreement did not really entail the conferral of competences prevailed.

Chronologically, the first discussion on the application of Article 90 concerned the ratification of the Rome Statute of the International Criminal Court. The ratification of the Statute took place in 2001 – before Poland's accession to the EU. At that time, experts considered the possibility of applying Article 90 to ratify non-EU legal acts to an extent greater than following 2004. After Poland's accession to the EU, public debate on the possibility of applying Article 90 only concerned the ratification of acts forming part of the broadly understood EU legal order: the so-called Spanish Protocol (amending the Protocol on transitional provisions to the Treaty on European Union, the Treaty on the Functioning of the European Union and the Treaty establishing the European Atomic Energy Community); the treaty on the accession of Croatia to the EU, the European Stability Mechanism and the Treaty on Stability, Coordination and Governance in the Economic and Monetary Union (the so-called fiscal pact).[76]

75 Wyrzykowski, 'Konstytucyjne aspekty referendum europejskiego', 271.

76 Szpunar, 'Art. 90', 122–123.

7.4.2 *Constitutional Tribunal's Case-law*

The second component shaping constitutional practice in terms of how Europe is perceived in the Polish constitutional imaginary is the jurisprudence of the Constitutional Tribunal. Until 2015, the Constitutional Tribunal consistently enabled the effective application of EU law, while at the same time emphasising the constitutionally determined limits of European integration. This case law is therefore an attempt to find a balance between the ideology of returning to Europe, active participation in multi-level constitutionalism and the utopia of traditionally understood sovereignty. This is particularly well illustrated by the manoeuvring of the Constitutional Tribunal between classically defined supremacy of the constitution and its pro-European interpretation.

Before Poland's accession to the EU, the Constitutional Tribunal ruled on the act on national referendum, brought by two groups of Eurosceptic members of parliament.[77] The impugned provision stipulated that, in the absence of a 50 per cent turnout in a referendum concerning the ratification of an international agreement under Article 90, the Sejm may again adopt a resolution selecting the method of ratification. The Constitutional Tribunal rejected the allegation that this provision bypasses the negative outcome of the referendum and considered it to be a technical arrangement which does not constitute a normative novelty.[78] This adjudication was the first signal that the Constitutional Tribunal perceives the importance of the legitimisation role of Article 90 of the Constitution.

The fundamental principles concerning the constitutional and legal dimension of Poland's membership in the EU were formulated by the Constitutional Tribunal in the ruling concerning the Accession Treaty.[79] Three groups of Eurosceptic members of parliament submitted independent motions to the Constitutional Tribunal, in which they questioned many provisions of the European Treaties. The Constitutional Tribunal rejected the applicants' arguments concerning, inter alia, the allegation that Poland's sovereignty would be violated following accession to the EU, underlined the obligation arising from EU membership to interpret the Constitution in a manner that would be friendly to European law, while also pointing out the limits of this interpretation (no *contra legem* interpretation). This ruling is an excellent illustration of the ambiguity of Europe in constitutional practice. On the one hand, the Constitutional Tribunal specified the consequences of Poland's membership in the EU for the legal system and the interpretation of the Constitution (the need to ensure the effectiveness of EU law). On the other hand, it highlighted the classically defined supremacy of the Constitution. In case of an irresolvable contradiction between the Constitution and EU law, Poland would

[77] Constitutional Tribunal, Judgment of 27 May 2003, Case K 3/11.

[78] Wyrzykowski, 'Konstytucyjne aspekty referendum europejskiego', 59.

[79] Constitutional Tribunal, Judgment of 11 May 2005, Case K 18/04.

have to seek a change of EU law, amend the Constitution or, as an *ultima ratio*, leave the EU. Moreover, the ruling emphasised the role of Article 90 as a safeguard of sovereignty, pointing to the constitutional limits of transferring power to the EU. The Constitutional Tribunal stated that the concept of 'the conferral of competences in certain matters' should be understood as 'a prohibition of transferring all competences of a given body, transferring competences in all cases in a given field', and as a prohibition of transferring the 'hard-core' competences of a certain body ('competences as to the merits of a given matter, determining the prerogative of a given state authority body').[80]

The search for a balance between the aspiration to become an equal player in the multi-level constitutionalism of the EU and the protection of the supremacy of the Constitution is also visible in the ruling concerning the European Arrest Warrant.[81] An ordinary court made a reference asking whether the provision of the Polish Code of Criminal Procedure implementing the Framework Decision on the European Arrest Warrant complies with Article 55 of the Constitution, which at that time provided for the prohibition of extradition of Polish citizens without any exceptions. The Constitutional Tribunal ruled that the challenged provision was unconstitutional. Its argumentation was based on a statement that the European Arrest Warrant, despite its simplified procedure, is in fact a form of extradition, and the pro-European interpretation of Article 55 of the Constitution was not possible in that case. Yet, at the same time, the Constitutional Tribunal maintained the unconstitutional provision in force for the maximum period of 18 months and made clear that, during this time, Polish courts should still execute European Arrest Warrants. As a result of this ruling, Article 55 of the Constitution was amended before the 18-month period had elapsed.

Another important ruling concerned the Treaty of Lisbon. The case was initiated by two motions submitted by Eurosceptic parliamentarians (members of parliament and senators, respectively). The Constitutional Tribunal ruled that the Treaty of Lisbon complied with the Polish Constitution, but also once again spoke about the constitutional limits of European integration. Referring to the jurisprudence of the German *Bundesverfassungsgericht*, the Constitutional Tribunal stressed that constitutional identity marks the line that cannot be crossed when it comes to the transfer of power to the EU. Therefore, the ruling on the Treaty of Lisbon in its operative part expresses pro-European liberal ideology, while its justification reveals elements of the utopia of State sovereignty as traditionally understood, including the unconditional supremacy of the Constitution. Europe remains both an aspiration and a concern.

Much controversy was caused by the ruling concerning a constitutional complaint against Council Regulation 44/2001 on jurisdiction and the recognition and

80 Ibid., para. 4.1.
81 Constitutional Tribunal, Judgment of 27 April 2005, Case P 1/05.

enforcement of adjudications in civil and commercial matters, that is, an act of EU secondary law.[82] The Constitutional Tribunal decided to review the challenged regulation, referring to the need to ensure effective protection of constitutional rights and freedoms. On the merits, it did not agree with the plaintiff's arguments and upheld the constitutionality of the Council Regulation. It also stressed that constitutional complaints against EU secondary law would have to 'duly adduce that the challenged EU secondary law act significantly lowers the level of protection of rights and freedoms as compared to the one guaranteed by the Constitution'. This reservation resembles the 'Solange II' formula of the German *Bundesverfassugsgericht*, although the very decision to review the constitutionality of the EU regulation in terms of its compliance with constitutional rights refers to 'Solange I'. Although this ruling did not directly concern Article 90 State sovereignty, it yet again revealed the tension between opening up to the EU legal system and maintaining control over the observance of constitutional standards of protection of fundamental rights by acts of EU law, one of the tokens of State sovereignty and constitutional supremacy.

In the case concerning the ratification of European Council Decision 2011/199/ EU on the amendment of Article 136 of the Treaty on the Functioning of the European Union with regard to the stability mechanism for Member States whose currency is the euro, the key constitutional yardstick was indeed Article 90.[83] The allegations of the applicants (groups of members of parliament) concerned, inter alia, the way the decision was ratified. In their opinion, it should have been ratified pursuant to Article 90, implying the two-thirds majority in both houses or a national referendum, because this decision created grounds for conferring new State competences to the European Stability Mechanism. In the ruling of 26 June 2013, the Constitutional Tribunal rejected the arguments submitted by the applicants, referring to the CJEU ruling of 27 November 2012 in case C-370/12 (Thomas Pringle), indicating that the amendment to Article 136(3) of the TFEU does not confer any new competences to the European Union. Notably, five judges submitted dissenting opinions, arguing that the Constitutional Tribunal had adopted too narrow an interpretation of the concept of 'the conferral of competences', thus severely limiting the applicability of Article 90.[84] This ruling might be interpreted as one in which the Constitutional Tribunal narrowed down the applicability of Article 90 in order to not prevent the ratification in the political context in which the two-thirds majority would be unattainable. In that Parliament (with the majority formed by PO and PSL), PiS would not support the ratification probably.

To sum up, until 2015, constitutional practice regarding the perception of Europe in the jurisprudence of the Constitutional Tribunal was consistent with the layer of

[82] Constitutional Tribunal, Judgment of 16 November 2011, Case SK 45/09.

[83] Constitutional Tribunal, Judgment of 26 June 2013, Case K 33/12.

[84] Dissenting opinions were presented by judges: Zbigniew Cieślak, Mirosław Granat, Marek Kotlinowski, Teresa Liszcz and Marek Zubik.

thoughts and interpretations of the Polish constitutional imaginary regarding this issue. It was characterised by a sometimes rather precarious balancing between multi-level constitutionalism and traditionally understood constitutional supremacy and sovereignty. Despite the visible elements of the utopia of sovereignty in the jurisprudence of the Constitutional Tribunal, the ideology of (cautious) friendliness towards EU law prevailed until 2015. The Constitutional Tribunal ensured the effectiveness of EU law even in decisions that emphasised Article 90's function of a safeguard rather than a legitimisation tool.

7.4.3 *The European Chapter*

Difficulties in finding a balance between the ideology of returning to Europe and the utopia of classically Westphalian sovereignty brought to the surface of public debate the issue of extending the constitutional regulations concerning Poland's membership in the EU and adding a new 'European chapter' to the Constitution. In 2009, Bronisław Komorowski (then Marshall of Sejm) appointed a team of experts, who a year later prepared a draft of the 'European chapter'. It was brought to Sejm as a presidential draft, due to the fact that in 2010 Komorowski became the President of Poland. PiS presented its own draft as well. Both drafts were based on the notion of 'concentrating' constitutional regulations relating to European integration within one chapter (the new Chapter Xa), but each of them presented a different vision of Europe in the Polish constitutional imaginary. The presidential draft ossified the relative balance between the ideology of returning to Europe and the utopia of Westphalian sovereignty, which had been created so far in constitutional practice. On the other hand, the draft proposed by PiS was the first harbinger of the Eurosceptic shift that took place after 2015. Those opposing visions of Europe are most clearly demonstrated by the different regulation of the potential Polexit (mainly in response to Article 50 TEU). Whereas the presidential draft adopted the concept of *actus contrarius*, the draft of PiS MPs, in turn, envisaged that decision on the withdrawal of the Republic of Poland from the organisation international, to which Poland has transferred competences, requires consent in an statute law passed by a simple majority of votes.[85] However, the draft of PiS MPs *de facto* copied and pasted the wording of the binding 'integration clause', whereas the presidential bill had, on the one hand, 'Europeanised' the constitution by introducing the name of the EU into the 'integration clause' while, on the other hand, it also contained some elements that could potentially be abused by Eurosceptics

[85] It was an attempt to rectify a mistake made in 2010. At that time, when adopting the so-called Cooperation Act (regulating the cooperation between the government and parliament in matters related to EU membership) the Act on international agreements of 2000 was also amended. Then Article 22a was added, which provides in paragraph 2 that 'The submission of a draft decision to withdraw from the European Union to the President of the Republic of Poland shall be made after obtaining the consent expressed in the statute law.'

(such as the final part the proposed new 'integrational clause' in which it was stipulated that the EU 'ensures the protection of rights human being comparable to the protection of these rights in the Constitution').[86] Although none of the drafts were successfully passed, they constitute an important component of constitutional practice.

7.4.4 *The Constitutional Imaginary Post-2015*

Constitutional practice regarding the perception of Europe in the Polish constitutional imaginary began to undergo a fundamental change in 2015 when, for the first time since 2005, PiS won the parliamentary elections. From that moment on, the ruling coalition composed of right-wing parties has consistently tried to rebuild the systemic framework created by the Constitution and undermine the contested 'constitutional compromise'. Contrary to Orban's Fidesz party, Law and Justice, despite two parliamentary elections won in 2015 and 2019, does not have the necessary majority to amend the Constitution. Therefore, the adopted political strategy was to introduce changes to the system by means of ordinary acts, inconsistent with current constitutional practice. These acts are inconsistent with the rule of law and lead de facto to informal amendments to the Constitution. Academic conceptualisations reveal the multifaceted nature of this phenomenon, which is defined by various terms such as rule of law crisis,[87] constitutional crisis,[88] constitutional breakdown,[89] democratic backsliding,[90] statutory anticonstitutionalism[91] or even illiberal constitutionalism.[92]

The Eurosceptic turn in constitutional practice and the change in how Europe is perceived in the Polish constitutional imaginary are a reaction to the supranational dimension of rule of law crisis focused on the 'reform' of the judiciary. The current

86 This passage has been criticized by experts, further on this issue see: Aleksandra Kustra, '"Euronowelizacja" w projektach ustaw o zmianie Konstytucji RP. Próba oceny' (2011) *Przegląd Sejmowy* 31, 41.

87 Among many: Marcin Matczak, 'The Clash of Powers in Poland's Rule of Law Crisis: Tools of Attack and Self-Defense' (2020) 12 *Hague Journal on the Rule of Law* 421; Aleksandra Kustra-Rogatka, 'Country Report. Poland Rule of Law Overview', https://democracy-reporting.org/en/office/EU/publications/country-report-the-rule-of-law-in-poland.

88 Among many, Marcin Matczak, 'Poland: From Paradigm to Pariah? Polish Constitutional Crisis – Interpretations'; https://ruleoflaw.pl/poland-from-paradigm-to-pariah-polish-constitutional-crisis-facts-and-interpretations/; Aleksandra Kustra, 'Poland's Constitutional Crisis, from Court-packing Agenda to Denial of Constitutional Court's Judgments' (2016) 12 *Toruńskie Studia Polsko-Włoskie* 343.

89 Wojciech Sadurski, *Poland's Constitutional Breakdown* (Oxford University Press, 2019).

90 Among many: Wojciech Przybylski, 'Explaining Eastern Europe: Can Poland's Backsliding Be Stopped' (2018) 29 *Journal of Democracy* 52.

91 Maciej Bernatt and Michał Ziółkowski, 'Statutory Anti-Constitutionalism' (2019) 28 *Washington International Law Journal* 487.

92 Timea Drinóczi and Agnieszka Bień-Kacała, *Illiberal Constitutionalism in Poland and Hungary: The Deterioration of Democracy, Misuse of Human Rights and Abuse of the Rule of Law* (Routledge, 2022).

fragile balance between the ideology of returning to Europe and the fear of losing sovereignty has been shattered. Moreover, Europe is now not only becoming a matter of concern regarding loss of sovereignty, but also an obstacle to the realisation of illiberal democracy. However, it should be noted that, first of all, the Eurosceptic shift in how the EU is perceived did not happen overnight. Instead, it was a process of gradually rejecting the legitimising aspect of Article 90 and focusing on a fetishised Westphalian sovereignty. Secondly, there is an asymmetry in the two components of this constitutional practice (i.e., the decision on the application or non-application of Article 90 of the Constitution and the jurisprudence of the Constitutional Tribunal).

The superficial layer of decisions not to apply Article 90 following 2015 does not constitute a breakthrough in relation to current constitutional practice in this regard. The shift is visible in the political rhetoric of the government, which is beginning to approach Europe from a purely instrumental perspective. The EU is becoming a mere source of potential financial resources rather than a community of values. This thesis can be formulated on the basis of an analysis of the public debate regarding the mode of ratification of the Council Decision (EU, Euratom) 2020/2053 of 14 December 2020 on the system of the European Union's own resources (Reconstruction Fund). In this case, Law and Justice attempted to ratify the Reconstruction Fund in an ordinary procedure without relying on Article 90, not so much considering current constitutional practice, but rather working along the lines of political pragmatism. Within the ruling coalition itself, the most Eurosceptic party 'Solidarna Polska' (led by Zbigniew Ziobro) was against the ratification of the Reconstruction Fund. The main goal was to minimise the need to seek the votes of the opposition (pro-European, but critical of the National Reconstruction Plan prepared by the government).

On the other hand, the jurisprudence of the Constitutional Tribunal on European integration is gradually shifting in tandem with the completion of the political capture of this institution. Therefore, it is difficult to treat 2015 as a threshold year in this case. The first symptoms of the Eurosceptic turn in jurisprudence are noticeable in 2019 when, with the end of the so-called old judges' term of office, the majority of judges chosen by the current parliamentary coalition began to form. It was then that, after a fairly long period of paralysis in the case of the judiciary (2017–2018), the politically captured Constitutional Tribunal began to rule again in cases with a strong political context.[93]

The Eurosceptic narrative has been interwoven with justifications for decisions formally concerning domestic law, nevertheless directly related to the supranational

[93] Aleskandra Kustra-Rogatka, 'An Illiberal Turn or a Cunter-constitutional Revolution? About the Polish Constitutional Tribunal before and after 2015', in M. Belov (ed.), *Courts and Judicial Activism under Crisis Conditions: Policy Making in a Time of Illiberalism and Emergency Constitutionalism* (Routledge, 2022), 117.

dimension of the crisis of the rule of law. This concerns the rulings aimed to block the enforcement of the CJEU ruling of 19 November 2019 in the case of *AK vs Poland* (C-585/18, C-624/18 and C-625/18). The Constitutional Tribunal declared that a resolution of the joint chambers of the Supreme Court implementing the *AK* ruling was unconstitutional as it supposedly constituted an instance of law-making. The Constitutional Tribunal also resolved, at least formally, two 'jurisdiction disputes': one between the Sejm and the Supreme Court and the other between the President and the Supreme Court regarding the judicial review of judicial appointments. The latter decisions were in breach with the existing and rather restrained case law regarding how 'jurisdiction disputes' are to be understood. In practice, all these rulings were intended to delegitimise the resolution of the joint chambers of the Supreme Court, and indirectly also the judgment of the CJEU in the *AK vs Poland* case.[94]

The next stage of the Eurosceptic (or even anti-European) shift in the jurisprudence of the Constitutional Tribunal was formed by decisions directly related to EU law. These decisions are a manifestation of the negation of the previous jurisprudence of the Constitutional Tribunal in matters related to Poland's membership in the EU and the change of the current status of Article 90 in the Polish constitutional imaginary. In both rulings, the Constitutional Tribunal found that the norms of primary EU law were inconsistent with the Constitution insofar as they contained specific legal requirements as specified by the CJEU.

In the first case, the new Disciplinary Chamber of the Supreme Court asked the Constitutional Tribunal if the CJEU interim orders with regards to the judiciary in Poland are compatible with the Constitution. The Disciplinary Chamber *de facto* asked a question in its own case as the CJEU interim orders concerned a freeze of this specific Chamber for its potential lack of independence.[95] The Constitutional Tribunal stated that the second sentence of Article 4(3) of the TEU in conjunction with Article 279 of the TFEU 'to the extent that the Court of Justice of the European Union imposes *ultra vires* obligations on the Republic of Poland as a Member State of the European Union, issuing interim measures relating to the system and jurisdiction of Polish courts and the procedure before Polish courts' is inconsistent with several provisions of the Polish Constitution, including Article 90(1). The Constitutional Tribunal simply took the view that competencies regarding the organisation of the judiciary in Poland were not transferred to the EU, despite the now well-established interpretation of Article 19(1) TEU by the CJEU.

The second case was initiated by the Prime Minister, who sought for the CT to find that some of the core elements of the principle of primacy of EU standards of judicial independence – including the ordinary judges' competence to disregard a

[94] Ibid., 119–121.

[95] Jakub Jaraczewski, 'Polexit or Judicial Dialogue?: CJEU and Polish Constitutional Tribunal in July 2021', *Verfassungsblog*, 19 July 2021, https://verfassungsblog.de/polexit-or-judicial-dialogue/.

domestic law that is not compatible with EU law and to use a prior domestic law that raises no such concerns in this regard – are incompatible with the Polish Constitution.[96] The Constitutional Tribunal, using the extensive formula 'insofar as', implying that a specific part of impugned provision is declared unconstitutional (referring, inter alia, to the ultra vires of the CJEU and the loss of sovereignty by Poland) ruled that Article 1 (in connection with Article 4(3) of the TEU, Article 2 of the TFEU and Article 19(1)(2) of the TFEU) is incompatible with various provisions of the Constitution, including Article 90(1). In the press release published after the final hearing, the CT also referred to the concept of constitutional identity and claimed that interpretation of the challenged Treaty provisions presented in the CJEU case law, directly relate to the Polish judiciary system 'which does not constitute competence subject to transfer under Article 90(1) of the Constitution and belongs to the Polish constitutional identity.[97] Moreover, the CT emphasised that also Article 2 TEU, which formulates a catalogue of values on which the EU is based, cannot constitute the source of the CJEU's competence to adjudicate on Polish judiciary system, as domestic judiciary systems do not belong to the common constitutional identity of the Member States, which use different methods of appointing judges.[98]

Both rulings indicate that, in constitutional practice, Europe is losing its previous ambivalence. The dominant element is polemicism towards the axiology of the EU legal system, which turns out to be an obstacle in the implementation of illiberal democracy. Nevertheless, this shift in the constitutional imaginary is revolutionary. It is inconsistent with the layer of thought, text and constitutional practice that was shaped until 2015. It can be interpreted as a return to the contestation of the 'constitutional compromise' of 1997. The fragile balance between the ideology of returning to Europe and the utopia of the Westphalian vision of sovereignty has been shattered. The Eurosceptic turn in the case law of the politically captured Constitutional Tribunal is an element of the strategy towards building an illiberal democracy.

7.5 CONCLUSIONS

Europe as an element of the Polish constitutional imaginary was perceived from the very beginning as both an aspiration and a subject of concern. Hence, Article 90 of the Constitution is characterised by tension between two unspoken ideas: European integration and sovereignty. The reconstruction of thought (i.e., the first dimension of the constitutional imaginary) affords a thesis that this ambiguity was already

[96] Ibid.

[97] Point 17 of the press release, https://trybunal.gov.pl/postepowanie-i-orzeczenia/komunikaty-prasowe/komunikaty-po/art/11664-ocena-zgodnosci-z-konstytucja-rp-wybranych-przepisow-traktatu-o-unii-europejskiej.

[98] Ibid., point 19.

highlighted while the Constitution was being drafted. Article 90 is a compromise between the ideology of returning to Europe and the utopia of the Westphalian vision of sovereignty. Contestation of the 'constitutional compromise' by the non-parliamentary opposition meant that, at the final stage of work on the constitution, overt articulation of 'openness' to integration with the EU was avoided and the possibility of 'conferring competences' was abandoned as one of the fundamental principles of the system. Article 90 was intended by the authors of the Constitution to be, on the one hand, a provision 'facilitating' opening to Europe, and, on the other hand, an 'exceptional' provision, applicable only when jurisdiction was to be transferred to a supranational entity so, in practice, only the EU. The dimension of the text, reconstructed not only on the basis of the rather laconic wording of Article 90, but also its academic interpretation, is illustrated, in turn, by the interesting phenomenon of the academic filling in of the deliberate loopholes left by the authors of the Constitution. It demonstrates an attempt to establish a balance between the legitimising and safeguarding roles of Article 90. This applies both to the concept of the 'conferral of competences of State authority' and the procedural layer of the Polish 'integration clause'. With regard to the former, the academic interpretation was the first to fill the silence of the constitutional text with regard to fears of sovereignty loss. Commentators on Article 90, inspired by modern concepts of sovereign power, interpreted this constitutional abeyance in a post-Westwal spirit, while at the same time highlighting the qualitative and quantitative limitations of the transfer of competences to an international entity. On the other hand, with regard to the procedural aspect of the Polish 'integration clause', academic commentators avoided interpretations that could lead to a deadlock and torpedo the legitimising role of Article 90. The third element of the constitutional imaginary (i.e., action, identified with constitutional practice) indicates a turning point in the perception of Europe after the parliamentary elections were won by PiS in 2015. Until then, Article 90 had been interpreted and applied in constitutional practice primarily as a provision enabling Poland's membership in the EU, rather than limiting or hindering it. So, the legitimisation function prevailed, while the guarantee function was considered primarily in a theoretical dimension. This thesis is confirmed by an analysis of three components of constitutional practice until 2015: cases of application (as well as non-application) of Article 90, the interpretation of this provision in the jurisprudence of the Constitutional Tribunal concerning Poland's membership of the EU and in the drafts of the finally not adopted amendment to the Constitution providing for a separate chapter devoted to constitutional aspects of EU membership. What is noticeable in terms of the first of these components is the unique nature of Article 90 arising from the restrictive interpretation of the 'conferral of competences'. This provision has so far been applied only twice: the ratification of the Accession Treaty and the Treaty of Lisbon. The second component (i.e., the jurisprudence of the Constitutional Tribunal) has been characterised by a balancing act between multi-level constitutionalism and traditionally understood constitutional supremacy. Despite visible aspects of the utopia of Westphalian sovereignty, until 2015 an ideology of (cautious) friendliness towards EU law prevailed in the jurisprudence of the Constitutional Tribunal. The binding factor of the third component of constitutional practice until 2015 (i.e., draft amendments to the Constitution) was the concept of 'concentrating' constitutional regulations regulating participation in integration processes into one chapter (the new Chapter Xa). Nevertheless, the two submitted drafts presented a very different vision of Europe in the Polish constitutional imaginary. While the presidential bill ossified the relative balance created so far in constitutional practice between the ideology of returning to Europe and the utopia of Westphalian sovereignty, the Law and Justice bill was the first harbinger of the Eurosceptic turn that took place after 2015. This should be seen in a wider context of legal and political shifts taking place in recent years in Poland. Law and Justice has consistently tried to rebuild the systemic framework created by the Constitution and undermine the contested 'constitutional compromise'. Systemic changes are made by means of ordinary laws, which in fact lead to informal changes to the Constitution. The Eurosceptic turn is a reaction to the supranational dimension of the crisis of the rule of law centred on the 'reform' of the judiciary. Existing constitutional ideas about Europe have been swept away. There has been a gradual rejection of the legitimisation aspect of Article 90, focusing instead on a fetishised Westphalian sovereignty. First and foremost, Europe is starting to be an obstacle in the realisation of illiberal democracy. Nevertheless. there has been some asymmetry in the two components of constitutional practice after 2015. With regard to the decision not to apply Article 90 after 2015, the change is noticeable only in the political rhetoric of the government, which is starting to approach Europe in a purely instrumental fashion. On the other hand, the jurisprudence of the Constitutional Tribunal on European integration is gradually shifting in tandem with the completion of the political capture of the Constitutional Tribunal. The first symptoms of a Eurosceptic turn were decisions formally concerning the norms of domestic law, but in practice directed against the effective enforcement of the CJEU ruling that was unfavourable for the Polish government. Current constitutional practice (as well as the dimension of thought and text) has been fully negated in the recent adjudication made by the Constitutional Tribunal directly concerning the conformity of the EU primary law with the Constitution. In these unprecedented rulings, using the formula 'insofar as', the Constitutional Tribunal found several fundamental provisions of the TFEU and TEU to be unlawful, including Article 90(1) of the Constitution. The Eurosceptic turn in the case law of the politically captured Constitutional Tribunal is an element of the strategy of building an illiberal democracy. The dominant element is becoming polemical to the axiology of the EU legal system. Nevertheless, this phrase is inconsistent with the layer of thought, text, as well as constitutional practice shaped until 2015.

8

The Constitutionalised Image of Enemy in the Hungarian Fundamental Law

Attila Antal

8.1 INTRODUCTION

The Hungarian political system after the regime change has become extremely polarised and deep political fault lines have developed between the domestic political communities, so much so that these relations can be described in most cases in terms of hate. Reinhart Koselleck[1] speaks of so-called asymmetric counter concepts, that is, those cases in which the politically different from us is named and its identity is constructed, but the identity thus created is not necessarily in line with reality or with the self-definition of the person (the 'political otherness'). The two most important components of the political identity are the aforementioned self-definition and the definition by others (i.e., what others, especially political opponents, think of it). In my view, hatred and the resulting violence (verbal and non-verbal) and its post-2010 constitutional representation have become one of the main structuring factors of the domestic political and social space in such a way that asymmetric counter-concepts have become dominant in the identification war between opposing political sides: this means that almost all possibilities for dialogue between opposing positions have been lost, because the definition and domination of the identity of the other has become the main aspect. Similar processes of attribution and identification have been taking place in the refugee crisis since 2015, and this time the hatred has been directed towards the 'political other', only to return to the domestic political scene and further deepen the dichotomies that have become familiar since the regime change. The post-2010 constitution-making process elevated this hostility to the level of the Fundamental

[1] Reinhart Koselleck, *Futures Past on the Semantics of Historical Time* (MIT Press, 1985).

Law, which entered into force in 2012, and created a system of *Constitutionalised Image of Enemy* (CIE).[2]

The defining characteristic of the Hungarian Fundamental Law is its strong constitutional identity: the political identity of the supermajority has become constitutionalised. This identity image has a number of *positive* elements (i.e., elements that have been defined as desirable, a kind of fundamental characteristic of the public law system). These include Christianity, active memory politics, national cohesion and various aspects of sustainability. In this chapter, I argue that, in addition to the explicitly strong positive constitutional identity elements, the constitutional power intended that *negative* identity elements should be at least as strong as the positive ones (in many ways even stronger and more important in the daily political struggles relying constitutional identity). These are the pillars of constitutional identity that separate us from others in the political theoretical assumption of Gramsci, Koselleck and Schmitt and define boundaries and political fault lines.

The other main claim of this chapter is that the negative constitutional identity has been presented in the original constitutional conception, which started to unfold in 2010, but also since 2015 (embedded in the amendments to the Fundamental Law) the constitutional enemy formation pervades public law and political debates. Three basic strands of Constitutionalised Image of Enemy (CIE) have emerged (and this reflects the constitution-power's view of history and the past): (1) anti-Communism framed in actual political framework; (2) anti-immigration; (3) anti-gender as the opposition to non-heterosexual forms of coexistence. I propose that anti-Communism as CIE can be found in the following sections of the Fundamental Law: the 'Communist Constitution of 1949' and its declared invalidity; the responsibility of 'political organisations that gained legal recognition during the democratic transition as legal successors of the Hungarian Socialist Workers' Party'. The various aspects of anti-immigration as CIE have been raised to constitutional level (police involvement in preventing illegal immigration; the terrorist threat; the amendment of the constitutional clause on accession to the EU with regard to the inalienable right of disposal of the territorial unit, population, form of government and organisation of the state). The definition of marriage and the constitutionalising of the biological sex of the mother and father represent the anti-gender CIE. I will argue that the mentioned sections are suitable to define the various enemy images for the political community with public law force, and therefore they can be considered as CIE.

The main focus of this chapter is on how the public enemy formation of the mentioned CIEs predominates in Hungarian society, the main political and moral

[2] In this chapter, I will call Constitutionalised Image of Enemy (CIE) those constitutional rules and sections that define the various enemy images for the political community with public law force, so that their main purpose is to contribute to the cohesion of the political community by defining enemy images with feelings rather than positive values.

effects and how these may have an impact on the constitutional identity itself, as enshrined in the Fundamental Law.

8.2 ENEMY AND IDENTITY CONSTRUCTION AND THE ORBÁN REGIME

8.2.1 *Autonomy of the Political Sphere: Friend and Foe Relations*

The need to construct the political enemy and the political enemy itself have always been part of politics, with varying degrees of intensity. However, this process intensified with the emergence of modern politics and really began to sprout in the twentieth century. The political sphere became autonomous and emancipated from the state in several ways: the individualist approach of liberalism and the continuing rise of civil rights; the development of capitalism and its globalisation; the transformation of political representation by political parties; and, finally, with the spread of universal suffrage, the emergence of mass politics and mass media. In other words, everything points in the direction of society becoming increasingly detached from the state and, through various forms of regimes (civil rights, consumption, suffrage), essentially becoming the dominant sphere in which political structures can evolve. This process can also be understood as a move away from the elite structures (institutions of public power, rulers, aristocracy) and towards socialisation. It was to describe this new order that Carl Schmitt introduced the concept of the Political (*das Politische*), reflecting the fact that it is not possible to draw a clear line between the political and the non-political. Schmitt's concept of the political, however, seeks to provide points of orientation in this new world and sees the essence of the political in the systematic and consistent distinction between friend and foe, which determines political actions and motives. As Schmitt argues:

> The political enemy need not be morally evil or aesthetically ugly; he need not appear as an economic competitor, and it may even be advantageous to engage with him in business transactions. But he is, nevertheless, the other, the stranger; and it is sufficient for his nature that he is, in an especially intense way, existentially something different and alien, so that in the extreme case conflicts with him are possible. These can neither be decided by a previously determined general norm nor by the judgment of a disinterested and therefore neutral third party.[3]

He adds to this: '. . . the morally evil, aesthetically ugly or economically damaging need not necessarily be the enemy; the morally good, aesthetically beautiful, and economically profitable need not necessarily become the friend in the specifically political sense of the word'.[4] According to Schmitt,

[3] Carl Schmitt, *The Concept of the Political* (University of Chicago Press, 2007), 27.

[4] Ibid., 27.

the enemy is so basic a category of politics that it is not a metaphor or symbol, but an existential category. In the case of the enemy, a sharp line must be drawn between the private enemy (foe) and the public enemy (enemy): The enemy is solely the public enemy, because everything that has a relationship to such a collectivity of men, particularly to a whole nation, becomes public by virtue of such a relationship.[5]

8.2.2 *The Schmittian Concept of Repoliticisation*[6]

Carl Schmitt elaborated the dangers of depoliticisation,[7] the concept of which had a significant impact on the Orbán regime after 2010.[8] From Schmitt's perspective, modern politics has become such a complex system that we cannot easily decide what is political and what is non-political. Schmitt aimed to create a very clear boundary to explain what is political and introduced the mentioned category of *the Political* (*das Politische*), which is based on separating friends from enemies. Schmitt, summarised by Bellamy and Baehr, 'blamed the failure of liberalism to appreciate or resist the challenge posed by democracy on its lack of an adequate conception of the political and hence of the state'.[9] Schmitt's approach,[10] elaborated in *The Concept of Political*, has fundamentally influenced the political advisers around the Orbán's governments.[11] According to Schmitt, liberalism is about taking normative decisions and making consensus but, from Schmitt's approach, there is no consensus in the political sphere or at least it is undesirable. He is convinced that dangers and disputes concerning the political could only be settled through political decision – liberalism denies the relevance of the political. In my point of view this is one of the core elements of current authoritarian populism. After the Hungarian regime change in 1989, the 'really existing' liberal democracy has actually shown this anti-political attitude: the political elites and the institutions of liberal democracy weren't able to build the social and popular base of democracy, moreover no cohesive political community has been created in the decades since the regime change. The liberal democracy established in Hungary has not created and satisfied these popular demands. Orbán promised, on the basis of Schmitt's perception of politics, to repair this situation, which is why Orbán calls his regime 'National Cooperation'.[12]

5 Ibid., 27.

6 This analysis is based on Attila Antal, *The Rise of Hungarian Populism: State Autocracy and the Orbán Regime* (Emerald Publishing, 2019).

7 Schmitt, *Concept of the Political.*

8 Antal, *Rise of Hungarian Populism*, 78–81.

9 Richard Bellamy and Peter Baehr, 'Carl Schmitt and the Contradictions of Liberal Democracy' (1993) 23 *European Journal of Political Research* 163.

10 Schmitt, *Concept of the Political.*

11 Aron Buzogány and Mihai Varga, 'The Ideational Foundations of the Illiberal Backlash in Central and Eastern Europe: The Case of Hungary' (2018) 25 *Review of International Political Economy* 811.

12 Hungarian Government, 'The Program of National Cooperation' (Hungarian Government, 22 May 2010), www.parlament.hu/irom39/00047/00047.pdf.

Moreover, as Schmitt stated, liberalism denies the concept of enemy, which is the core element of Schmitt's theory. This is the reason why liberal democracies hesitate to act as political situations and crises require. According to Schmitt: 'Liberalism ... existed ... in that short interim period in which it was possible to answer the question "Christ or Barabbas?" with a proposal to adjourn or appoint a commission of investigation.'[13] From this point of view, it can be stressed that liberalism tries to depoliticise and neutralise all the political conflicts and turn political battles towards legal and economical fields. Schmitt denied the liberal rationalist's faith in the ultimate ethical harmony of the world.

> Good consequences do not always follow from good acts, or evil from evil ones; similarly, truth, beauty and goodness are not necessarily linked. Most importantly he recognized that we are often faced with difficult or tragic choices between conflicting but equally valuable ends – for no social world can avoid excluding certain fundamental values. In this situation, as Weber insisted, we cannot escape the responsibility of choosing which gods we shall serve and by implication deciding what are to count as demons.[14]

In fact, Weber can be seen in terms of the critique of liberal constitutionalism as a forerunner of Schmitt, even more precisely Weber's political theory has a significant impact on Schmitt. The main difference between the two is that Weber occupies a position which seeks to incorporate Machiavellian power-politics within a constitutional democratic framework.[15] For Schmitt, the dilemmas of politics can be solved politically, through political decisions, which take place in the state. Liberalism has no positive and adequate theory concerning the state and that is why liberalism cannot handle pluralism, which is the main source of political conflicts. Schmitt and Max Weber both argued that morals and politics are distinct and problems based on this fact can only be handled in a political way, through political debates and decision, and not from a liberal perspective (metaphysically and through rational discussion).

Schmitt is convinced that the locus of the mentioned political decisions is the sovereign state. The sovereignty of the state is a matter of politics and lies outside of the law. The sovereignty of the state is crucial in understanding why the 'sovereign is he who decides on the exception'.[16] The state of exception shows the real nature of politics: 'The existence of the state is undoubted proof of its superiority over the validity of the legal norm. The decision frees itself from all normative ties and

[13] Carl Schmitt, *Political Theology: Four Chapters on the Concept of Sovereignty* (University of Chicago Press, 2005), 62.

[14] Bellamy and Baehr, 'Carl Schmitt', 174.

[15] Rune Slagstad, 'Liberal Constitutionalism and Its Critics: Carl Schmitt and Max Weber', in Jon Elster and Rune Slagstad (eds.), *Constitutionalism and Democracy* (Cambridge University Press, 1988).

[16] Schmitt, *Concept of the Political*, 5.

becomes in the true sense absolute'.[17] According to Schmitt, the legal-based approach of liberalism overlooks that the legal instruments and the rule of law are products of political struggles.[18] Liberalism is so dangerous for Schmitt because it attempts to deny the need for a sovereign (state) and with this the political basis of law has become questionable.

8.2.3 *The Construction of Identities and the Asymmetric Counter Concepts*

Koselleck uses historical analysis to shed light on the basic contours of the construction of the identity of the enemy and of one's own group, since these two processes must take place simultaneously in order to be confronted with politically effective action:

> The efficacy of mutual classifications is historically intensified as soon as they are applied to groups. The simple use of 'we' and 'you' establishes a boundary and is in this respect a condition of possibility determining a capacity to act. But a 'we' group can become a politically effective and active unity only through concepts which are more than just simple names or typifications. A political or social agency is first constituted through concepts by means of which it circumscribes itself and hence excludes others; and therefore, by means of which it defines itself.[19]

The construction of identities is, therefore, a very fierce and intense political contest, since self-identification is the very process through which a political community is created. At the same time, the construction of a positive identity of oneself necessarily implies the construction of a perceived identity of the opponent and even more so of the political enemy.

On the basis of all this, we can also say that an integral part of one's own identity is the definition, and in some cases the domination, of the identity of the opponent/enemy. This is therefore a contest of identity construction, where the identity of the opponent/enemy could of course be defined – by means of counter concepts – in such a way that it fits the self-identification of the given party (symmetry), but the very essence of the contest is to be able to dominate the identity of political opponents/enemies. Analysing the examples of asymmetric counter-concepts across historical periods (Hellenes and Barbarian, Christians and Heathens, Mensch and Unmensch, Ubermensch and Untermensch), Koselleck argues:

> . . . a given group makes an exclusive claim to generality, applying a linguistically universal concept to itself alone and rejecting all comparison. This kind of self-definition provokes counter concepts which discriminate against those who have been defined as the 'other'. The non-Catholic becomes heathen or traitor; to leave

[17] Ibid., 12.
[18] Bellamy and Baehr, 'Carl Schmitt', 173.
[19] Koselleck, *Futures Past*, 159–160.

> the Communist party does not mean to change party allegiance, but is rather 'like leaving life, leaving mankind'... not to mention the negative terms that European nations have used for each other in times of conflict and which were transferred from one nation to another according to the changing balance of power.[20]

According to Koselleck, this exclusionary, discriminatory mechanism is realised by means of asymmetrical counter-concepts, since the self-definition of the opponent/enemy certainly does not correspond to the identity elements attributed to him/her:

> Thus there are a great number of concepts recorded which function to deny the reciprocity of mutual recognition. From the concept of the one party follows the definition of the alien other, which definition can appear to the latter as a linguistic deprivation, in actuality verging on theft. This involves asymmetrically opposed concepts. The opposite is not equally antithetical. The linguistic usage of politics, like that of everyday life, is permanently based on this fundamental figure of asymmetric opposition.[21]

So, the political enemy is a constructed, created phenomenon – as is self-identity. The most obvious ways of creating the identity of the enemy are to personalise (and through this, character assassination) and criminalise it.

8.3 THE ORBÁN REGIME AND THE CONSTITUTIONALISED IMAGE OF ENEMY

In this section, the theoretical framework of the Orbán regime, which has been institutionalised since 2010, will be used to illustrate the tendencies of the Constitutionalised Image of Enemy (CIE). First, the antecedents of the post-2010 CIE-regime and the basic elements of the right-wing's enemy-constituting identity have been analysed. Reflecting on the 2010 turnaround, the directions in which the Orbán regime has shaped CIEs by the adoption of the new Fundamental Law will be investigated: the constitutional framework of anti-Communism, anti-immigration and anti-gender.

8.3.1 *The Roots of Constitutional Enemy Creation before 2010*

Among the forces of the political right after the Hungarian regime change, the identity of Fidesz, constructed mainly since the early 2000s, is centred on the previously analysed Carl Schmitt's conception of politics, moreover it is based on the rehabilitation of the Political (*repoliticisation*) and unrelenting opposition to liberalism and inferiority complex in relation to liberal (or perceived) academic and political structures. This was accompanied by Koselleck's thinking in terms of

[20] Ibid., 160.
[21] Ibid., 160–161.

asymmetrical counter-concepts, the main aim of which is the hegemony of one's own identity and the presentation of the political opponent as an enemy, and in this context the domination of the enemy's self-identification.

Fidesz has proved to be quite successful in the political identity construction struggle, fuelled by the fact that it has a 'missionary' political identity and believes that it is the only party that can and will truly represent national interests. Two things follow from this. Firstly, this has predestined the party, which has been in government again since 2010, to derive its antithesis, the image of the Hungarian left and liberal opposition, from its very strong self-identification. On the other hand, the Fidesz's linked its self-definition to the question of national identity, and in this way any political identity against Fidesz can be interpreted against the Fidesz-dominated national identity (which is in fact a policy of exclusion from the nation). Another important peculiarity of the identity construction struggle between left and right is that the Fidesz-led right is not only better able to articulate its own identity, but in fact it is itself defining the identity of its opponents at many points.

The emerging Fidesz has linked its identity with the nation, creating an asymmetrical situation in which the left and the liberals can only be identified with the 'non-national' character. The right's thematisation of the national problem dates back to the pre-reform era, and in the case of Fidesz it became a coherent identity element with the beginning of the debates on the settlement of the situation of ethnic Hungarians living in neighbouring countries in 2001. The left criticised the tendency towards 'national unification', which from then on was at the centre of the right's political perception. All this culminated first in the 2002 election campaign and then in the 2004 referendum on the preferential access of the Hungarian citizenship for Hungarians living abroad, where the left and the liberals were seen by the right as having 'eradicated' itself from the nation. Gábor Egry aptly describes the technique used by Fidesz:

> ... a process of self-definition in which the right – In line with its position at the time of regime change – labels itself as anti-communist and labels everyone else as communist, whether they are or not. It is necessarily static, does not allow for nuances and tries to classify everyone and keep everyone in the category it has assigned to them, even if it has nothing to do with the actual situation.[22]

Fidesz has thus begun to define and dominate the communication over the identity of its political opponents.

In essence, Fidesz was able to build on the identity elements and solutions developed here during the 2002–2010 opposition period:

> Through symbolic politics and the unity of nation–party–governance, Fidesz tried to get society to accept a new type of cultural nation concept between 1998 and

[22] Egry Gábor, *Otthonosság és idegenség: Identitáspolitika és nemzetfelfogás Magyarországon a rendszerváltás óta [Homeliness and Strangeness: Identity Politics and the Concept of Nationhood in Hungary since the Regime Change]* (Napvilág Publishing, 2010).

> 2002. The downfall of the first Orbán government was also a sign of the forcefulness and majority rejection of this attempt. During its years in opposition, Fidesz successfully developed and established techniques to almost exclusively own the thematization of identity content issues in opposition to the left, liberals and greens. Despite the fact that the debates over the meaningfulness of certain canons and symbols could not be settled in 2002, the Fidesz was able to exploit their positional advantage stemming from the lack of performance of their party political rivals.[23]

After the defeat in 2002, Fidesz interpreted the national aspect of its own identity more and more broadly: this is expressed by the transformation into an alliance and the slogan 'one camp, one flag'. In other words, it was thinking in terms of a broad identity system that went beyond the previous political camp of the right. The 2006 Fidesz election defeat and the street riots were in fact a dress rehearsal for this identity politics, but they also introduced a new element, namely moral politicisation. According to Márton Szabó, Fidesz then 'defines the political community as a moral community, i.e., a democratic community whose members are bound together by commonly held moral principles, or at least expelled from the political community by any person or organisation that does not abide by these norms'.[24]

8.3.2 *The Emerging Hegemony of the Orbán Regime*

The turning point of the right-wing breakthrough in Hungary was believed to have happened in the year 2010, although in reality the process had begun much earlier. Indeed, the Hungarian right spent over a decade (the 2000s) to create a right-wing hegemonic structure in a Gramscian sense. The politics and tactics of Fidesz, the leading right-wing party since 1998, can be analysed from a Gramscian perspective. Fidesz began as a party in government (between 1998 and 2002), and then became the main opposition party (between 2002 and 2010) after a fierce struggle on political, economic and cultural fronts. The party managed to build a complex political and economic network as a historical bloc, which it has used to create a national popular movement ('civil circles'), thus politicising masses. The right claimed that the successive social-democrat governments (first from 1994 to 1998, then from 2002 to 2010) caused an organic crisis, also in a Gramscian sense, as it was framed within an economic and social crisis, which turned into a crisis of hegemony. This overlapping crisis culminated successively in 2006 (when the right-wing blew out rough street movements because of the moral crisis caused by the scandal surrounding the lies of the incumbent socialist prime minister), in 2009 (when the left-liberal governing coalition collapsed) and in 2010 (when Fidesz reached two-

[23] Policy Solutions and Friedrich Ebert Stiftung Büro Budapest, 'Nemzeti identitás – egység vagy sokszínűség? – Politikai Megbékélés Beszélgetéssorozat II', May 2013, www.policysolutions.hu/userfiles/elemzes/18/nemzeti_identitas_egyseg_vagy_sokszinuseg.pdf, 19.

[24] Márton Szabó, 'Ellenfél és ellenség a politikában' [Adversaries and Enemies in Politics] (2007) 1 *Politikatudományi Szemle* 16.

thirds in the parliament for the first time). The left-liberals lost their grip on the superstructures, while the authoritarian right put forward innovative ideas, perspectives and practices. Although the hegemonic project of the right has its roots in nationalism, antagonising rhetoric and xenophobia, it also reflects a Gramscian way of thinking. Fidesz can be seen as a counter-hegemonic project against the left-liberals. This is also true for Jobbik, which is the former leading extreme right-wing opposition party of Hungary.

8.3.3 *The Era of Constitutionalised Image of Enemy*

After the change of government in 2010, this national and moral identity of the Fidesz was intertwined into a whole and gained public relevance in the Fundamental Law. Fidesz experienced 2010 (hence the winning of the election has been named as a 'revolution') as a triumph over the left in both national and moral terms. From 2010, the 'what is Hungarian' thinking takes a new turn and aims to create a consistent national identity. The national–moral creed of Fidesz is represented by the much-debated Fundamental Law and its preamble, the National Avowal. The Orbán regime created the asymmetrical counter-concepts based on the identity politics it developed in the opposition period and began to build its own governmental–national identity with a constitutional majority. The Orbán regime's approach, however, went far beyond the classic Schmittian friend–enemy dichotomy, as the asymmetric counter-concepts developed by the government were incorporated into the Fundamental Law. In this chapter, I therefore refer to the phenomenon of the political identity of the post-2010 Hungarian Orbán regime unfolding within the framework of asymmetric counter-concepts with constitutional binding force as the *Constitutionalised Image of Enemy* (CIE). The constitutional identity construction of the Orbán regime can thus be considered unprecedented in the history of Hungarian politics after the regime change and at the same time in the history of constitutional identity constructions in that it elevated Koselleckian asymmetrical counter-concepts composed of negative identities excluding others to a constitutional level (Table 8.1). In this section, I will describe the three main nodes of this CIE system: anti-Communism, anti-immigration and anti-gender.

8.3.3.1 Anti-Communism after Twenty Years of the Regime Change

As can be seen on the basis of the above-mentioned parts of the Hungarian Fundamental Law, 2010 brought a new level of enemy thematisation: the category of public enemy. The Fundamental Law's National Avowal implied an anti-Communist identity, since it declared the 1949 Communist constitution invalid and declared that it denied 'any statute of limitations for the inhuman crimes committed against the Hungarian nation and its citizens under the national socialist and the Communist dictatorship'.

TABLE 8.1 *Constitutionalised Image of Enemy in the Hungarian Fundamental Law*

CIEs	Location in the Fundamental Law	Provisions
(1) Anti-Communism in actual political framework	National Avowal	'We do not recognise the suspension of our historic constitution due to foreign occupations. We deny any statute of limitations for the inhuman crimes committed against the Hungarian nation and its citizens under the national socialist and the communist dictatorship. **We do not recognise the communist constitution of 1949, since it was the basis for tyrannical rule; we therefore proclaim it to be invalid.** We agree with the Members of the first free National Assembly, which proclaimed as its first decision that our current liberty was born of our 1956 Revolution. We date the restoration of our country's self-determination, lost on the nineteenth day of March 1944, from the second day of May 1990, when the first freely elected organ of popular representation was formed. We shall consider this date to be the beginning of our country's new democracy and constitutional order.'
	Article U	'(1) The state structure based on the rule of law, established in accordance with the will of the nation through the first free elections held in 1990, and the previous communist dictatorship are incompatible. **The Hungarian Socialist Workers' Party and its legal predecessors and the other political organisations established to serve them in the spirit of communist ideology were criminal organisations and their leaders shall have responsibility without statute of limitations for**: (a) maintaining and directing an oppressive regime, violating the law and betraying the nation; (b) thwarting with Soviet military assistance the democratic attempt built on a multi-party system in the years after World War II; (c) establishing a legal order built on the exclusive exercise of power and unlawfulness; (d) putting an end to the economy based on the freedom of property and indebting the country; (e) subordinating Hungary's economy, national defence, diplomacy and human resources to foreign interests; (f) systematically devastating the traditional values of European civilisation; (g) depriving citizens and certain groups of citizens of their fundamental human rights or seriously restricting such rights, in particular for murdering people, delivering them to a foreign power, unlawfully imprisoning them, deporting them to forced labour camps, torturing them and subjecting them to inhuman

(*continued*)

TABLE 8.1 (*continued*)

CIEs	Location in the Fundamental Law	Provisions
		treatment; arbitrarily depriving citizens of their assets, restricting their rights to property; totally depriving citizens of their liberties, subordinating the expression of political opinion and will to coercion by the State; discriminating against people on the grounds of origin, worldview or political belief, impeding their advancement and success based on knowledge, diligence and talent; setting up and operating a secret police to unlawfully observe and influence the private lives of people; (h) suppressing with bloodshed, in cooperation with Soviet occupying forces, the Revolution and War of Independence which broke out on 23 October 1956, the ensuing reign of terror and retaliation, and the forced flight of two hundred thousand Hungarian people from their native country; (i) all ordinary criminal offences committed for political motives and left unprosecuted by the justice system for political motives. **Political organisations that gained legal recognition during the democratic transition as legal successors of the Hungarian Socialist Workers' Party continue to share the responsibility of their predecessors as beneficiaries of their unlawfully accumulated assets.'**
(2) Anti-immigration	Article E	'(2) With a view to participating in the European Union as a Member State and on the basis of an international treaty, Hungary may, to the extent necessary to exercise the rights and fulfil the obligations deriving from the Founding Treaties, exercise some of its competences arising from the Fundamental Law jointly with other Member States, through the institutions of the European Union. **Exercise of competences under this paragraph shall comply with the fundamental rights and freedoms provided for in the Fundamental Law and shall not limit the inalienable right of Hungary to determine its territorial unity, population, form of government and state structure.'**
	Article XIV	'(1) **No foreign population shall be settled in Hungary. A foreign national, not including persons who have the right to free movement and residence, may only live in the territory of Hungary under an application individually examined by the Hungarian authorities.** The basic rules on the requirements for the submission and assessment of such applications shall be laid down in a cardinal Act.'

CIEs	Location in the Fundamental Law	Provisions
	Article 51/A	'(1) In the event of a significant and direct **threat of a terrorist attack or in the event of a terrorist attack**, the National Assembly shall, at the initiative of the Government, declare a state of terrorist threat for a fixed period of time, and shall simultaneously authorise the Government to introduce extraordinary measures laid down in a cardinal Act. The period of the state of terrorist threat may be extended.'
(3) Anti-gender	Article L)	'(1) Hungary shall protect **the institution of marriage as the union of one man and one woman** established by voluntary decision, and the family as the basis of the survival of the nation. Family ties shall be based on marriage or the relationship between parents and children. **The mother shall be a woman, the father shall be a man**.'
	Article XVI	'(1) Every child shall have the right to the protection and care necessary for his or her proper physical, mental and moral development. **Hungary shall protect the right of children to a self-identity corresponding to their sex at birth, and shall ensure an upbringing for them that is in accordance with the values based on the constitutional identity and Christian culture of our country**.'

Source: The Hungarian Fundamental Law and the Classification of the Author.

This was further developed by the Fourth Amendment to the Fundamental Law of 15 March 2013, which introduced into the Fundamental Law Article U Section (1), which declares that the Hungarian Socialist Workers' Party (HSWP) and its predecessors and other political organisations established to serve Communist ideology were criminal organisations and lists the crimes for which their leaders are liable. This in itself can be regarded as a public element of identity politics, since the Fundamental Law is attempting to do historical justice and provide a kind of constitutional interpretation of historical issues. The real problem, however, is that the responsibility for these crimes is also imposed on the legal successor of the HSWP: 'Political organisations that gained legal recognition during the democratic transition as legal successors of the Hungarian Socialist Workers' Party continue to share the responsibility of their predecessors as beneficiaries of their unlawfully accumulated assets.' Thus, there is a new trend of enemy formation: when the negative identity is embedded of the political enemy in the Fundamental Law, although (in principle) the situation is that '[w]hen state authorities consider someone an enemy, it is a classic external or internal war situation or action.

Moreover, the state organs of democracy tend to refrain from making a hateful enemy out of their weak, small, and abnormal citizens . . .'.[25] From this point of view, one could even argue that from now on a kind of internal public war between the left and the right could break out, but this does not happen because the left has not been able to react in any meaningful way to the intervention of public power in its identity. From then on, the CIE has become a permanent tool of the Orbán regime to supposedly solve acute political disputes.

8.3.3.2 Anti-Immigration: The Refugees as the New Enemies

Hungary was hit by the refugee crisis in 2015 (390,000 people crossed the Serbian–Hungarian or Croatian–Hungarian border that year, of whom 177,000 were registered as asylum seekers). One of the main elements of the anti-refugee and anti-immigration campaign that unfolded from the beginning of the year was the presentation of a constructed enemy image. The government has demoralised the Hungarian society by stepping up the hate campaign. Society was almost 'prepared' for the 'enemy' to appear: between 1 and 5 September 2015, thousands of refugees queued up at Budapest's Keleti railway station. From the very beginning, the government not only argued at the political level but also involved and reprogrammed the entire Hungarian state apparatus for the war against refugees and immigrants.

By doing so, the Hungarian government took the next step in the domestic identity politics struggle and included the wave of migration triggered by civil wars and humanitarian disasters. Until 2015, Fidesz understood the left within the wider Hungarian political community, even if it excluded it from the nation. This exclusion can certainly be understood in the sense that the left was excluded from the political nation institutionalised by the Fundamental Law and the voting rights of Hungarians living abroad and should still be included in the nation of the state, which functions as a purely technical category. All this would be logical because Fidesz needs a political enemy or, more precisely, it needs to draw the outline of the enemy over and over again. In his speech at the XXVI Bálványos Summer Free University and Student Camp on 25 July 2015, Viktor Orbán stated that the left is interested in the radical loosening of the national framework and that is why immigration is in its interest, and he attributed this to the 'reasons' that emerged during the exclusion from the nation, moreover he argued that the left is suspicious of national identity and it incites against Hungarians abroad. As Orbán argued: 'The European left, dear friends, sees the problem of immigration not as a source of danger but as an opportunity. The left has always been suspicious of nations and national identity . . . These people, these politicians, simply do not like Hungarians,

[25] Szabó, 'Ellenfél és ellenség a politikában', 13.

and they don't like them because they are Hungarians.'[26] Viktor Orbán's speech at the launch of the 'Signs of the Times' discussion paper on 30 October 2015 went even further: he named the left as the force behind migration trends.[27]

The Orbán regime has also elevated its anti-immigration approach to a constitutional level. The *Sixth Amendment* to the Fundamental Law (14 June 2016), openly linking immigration and terrorism, declared by the votes of Fidesz-KDNP and the radical right Jobbik authorisation of the National Assembly that the initiative of the government was a 'state of terrorist threat'. This new form of state of exception means that, in the event of a significant and direct threat of a terrorist attack or in the event of a terrorist attack, the National Assembly shall, at the initiative of the government, declare a state of terrorist threat for a fixed period of time and shall simultaneously authorise the government to introduce extraordinary measures laid down in a two-thirds act. During this state of exception, the government may, by means of decrees, introduce measures derogating from the acts concerning the organisation, the operation and the performance of activities of public administration, the Hungarian Defence Forces, the law enforcement organs and the national security services, as well as those laid down in a two-thirds act.

The Orbán government adopted the *Seventh Amendment* to the Fundamental Law during the discussions with the EU on refugee resettlement quotas. The Jobbik supported the Seventh Amendment (28 June 2018) as well, and it can be seen as a new chapter of the CIE against migration and refugees. The Fundamental Law declares that no 'foreign population' shall be settled in Hungary. The protection of the constitutional identity and Christian culture of Hungary shall be an obligation of every organ of the state. By this constitutional revision, the following declaration has been added by the Orbán regime to the constitutional accession clause to the EU: 'Exercise of competences under this paragraph shall comply with the fundamental rights and freedoms provided for in the Fundamental Law and shall not limit the inalienable right of Hungary to determine its territorial unity, population, form of government and state structure' (Article E).

Since 2015, a new trend of CIEs has been unfolding: the governing right-wing parties identify the left with a political alien, the refugees (who are consistently called migrants in right-wing communication), not independently of the hate campaign that has been unfolding since 2015, and essentially begins to reposition it as an internal enemy, which, because of its political 'alienation', is ultimately a proliferator and servant of foreign interests, that is, the category of 'hostile internal alien' is only one step away from external enemies.

[26] Orbán Viktor, 'Lecture by Viktor Orbán at the XXVI Bálványos Summer Free University and Student Camp', 27 June 2015, https://2010-2015.miniszterelnok.hu/beszed/orban_viktor_eloadasa_a_xxvi._balvanyosi_nyari_szabadegyetem_es_diaktaborban.

[27] Orbán Viktor,'Speech by Viktor Orbán at the Launch of the "Signs of the Times" Discussion Paper', 30 October 2015, https://2010-2015.miniszterelnok.hu/beszed/orban_viktor_beszede_az_idok_jelei_vitairat_bemutatasakor.

8.3.3.3 Anti-Gender: Sexual Discrimination by Constitutional Framework

The third CIE used by the Orbán regime was the constitutionalising anti-gender agenda. In 2018, the Orbán regime cancelled the gender studies degree programme at Eötvös Loránd University,[28] systematically blocked Hungary's accession to the Istanbul Convention on action against violence against women and domestic violence and, in doing so, essentially declared a cultural war on Hungarian LGBTQ communities and all gender issues.[29] There is a demonstrable link between CIE in anti-refugee politics and anti-gender campaigns:

> In 2015, Orbán's government started a new communication campaign in order to strengthen the 'family-friendly thinking', to promote pro-family world views and to provide 'information about the positive results of family politics'. As the refugee crisis deepened, the campaign was postponed, but based on the experience of the anti-refugee campaign over the spring and summer 2015 as well as prior to the government-initiated referendum about refugee quotas in October 2016, we assume that this 'family-friendly' campaign could become another territory to mobilize afresh the vision of the enemy.[30]

The Ninth Amendment to the Fundamental Law represents an unprecedented intervention into the lives of LGBTQ communities by effectively declaring any gender issues openly. It states unquestionably that 'the mother shall be a woman, the father shall be a man', moreover it declares that 'Hungary shall protect the right of children to a self-identity corresponding to their sex at birth'.

The Hungarian anti-gender tendencies are embedded into the international framework of politicisation of anti-gender, as Pető and Kovács argue: '… these movements are rooted in a broader crisis phenomenon and the scale is much larger than specific local or national government or Church interests'.[31] At the same time, the Hungarian situation can be considered a tipping point in the international anti-gender discourse, as the Hungarian constitution power (i.e. the Hungarian parliament influenced by the executive power) is trying to make the social and family model being considered desirable rather than mandatory through constitutional means, and the constitution-maker has been able to continuously shape the constitutional directions of anti-gender ideology through constitutional amendments, responding to the tensions accumulating in society. The other main threat of this

[28] Keno Verseck,'Hungary's University Ban on Gender Studies Heats up Culture War', *Deutsche Welle*, 18 October 2019, www.dw.com/en/hungarys-university-ban-on-gender-studies-heats-up-culture-war/a-45944422.

[29] Éva Fodor, *The Gender Regime of Anti-Liberal Hungary* (Palgrave Macmillan, 2022).

[30] Pető Andrea and Eszter Kováts, 'Anti-Gender Movements in Hungary: A Discourse without a Movemet?, in Roman Kuhar and David Paternotte (eds.), *Anti-Gender Campaign in Europe* (Rowman & Littlefield, 2017), 126.

[31] Ibid., 118.

CIE is the improvement and constitutional legitimisation of the anti-gender movement claimed by Pető and Kovács: 'In the context of (Central and Eastern) European countries Hungary remains a unique case with a rather long history of anti-gender discourse, but without any palpable anti-gender movement. This, however, can easily change, should the Orbán's government or the NGOs near the government build up the new enemy "gender".'[32]

8.4 CONCLUSIONS: CONSTITUTIONAL IDENTITY BASED ON CIES

We conclude that Hungarian politics has been defined by Constitutionalised Images of Enemy, the Constitutional Court and the Orbán regime have increasingly invoked the concept of *constitutional identity*. In its decision 22/2016 (XII. 5.) AB,[33] the Constitutional Court explained that 'constitutional identity equals with the constitutional (self-) identity of Hungary'. As Gábor Halmai pointed out: 'The Court holds that the constitutional (self-)identity of Hungary is a fundamental value that has not been created but only recognized by the Fundamental Law and, therefore, it cannot be renounced by an international treaty. The defence of the constitutional (self-)identity of Hungary is the task of the Constitutional Court as long as Hungary has sovereignty.'[34]

At the heart of Hungarian constitutional identity, the Schmittian friend–enemy dichotomy was integrated in the framework of asymmetrical counter-concepts (anti-Communism, anti-immigration, anti-gender) and the significant social impact of which unleashed considerable anger and hatred. The situation is tragic because on the other side of the asymmetrical counter-concepts there are not Communists, not supporters of illegal immigration and not the sexual abusers of children as propagated by the government, but the political opposition, the people who are about to give humanitarian aid to refugees and the supporters of the LGBTQ communities. Relying on the CIEs, the Orbán regime has thus fundamentally reshaped Hungarian political attitudes after the regime change and, to an unprecedented extent, it has intensified the divisive attitudes that had already divided Hungarian society, which was already prone to a significant degree of isolation.

The transformation of the hate-political space indicated here has had a very serious negative impact on an already fragmented Hungarian society, prone to xenophobia and suffering from numerous social, cultural and health problems. Various sociological surveys and public opinion polls confirm that Hungarian society is one of the most closed societies in Europe, and one of the most intolerant

32 Ibid, 127.

33 www.kozlonyok.hu/kozlonyok/Kozlonyok/1/PDF/2016/28.pdf.

34 Halmai Gábor, 'The Hungarian Constitutional Court and Constitutional Identity', *Verfassungblog*, 10 June 2017, https://verfassungsblog.de/the-hungarian-constitutional-court-and-constitutional-identity/.

towards foreigners. According to the European Social Survey,[35] among the EU countries, Hungary and the Czech Republic were the countries where people least thought that migration would make their country a better place. The ESS data were collected in 2002 and 2014, and Hungary was massively and consistently ranked as one of the most vulnerable countries in both cases, before and a decade after EU accession. Moreover, it is notable from the ESS data that, when it comes to migration, it is primarily those people who we perceive as closer to our own culture or civilisational approach that we tolerate more: anyone else who is outside our civilisational preferences we want to keep outside our borders. Perhaps it is not surprising that older and less educated people have a higher proportion of people who reject migration from outside Europe. What is more interesting is that, in a European comparison, the gap between the anti-migration attitudes of the elderly/uneducated and the pro-migration attitudes of the young/educated is the smallest: we are facing a systemic problem, since even young people, for whom Europe as a cultural and economic area is open, have reservations about coming from outside Europe.

All these data are supported by Eurobarometer's research on EU member states for the period 2014–2018.[36] In 2014, 39 per cent of Hungarians surveyed said that migration from outside the EU was a rather negative phenomenon, while 28 per cent said it was very negative – both figures are roughly in line with the EU average. By 2018, however, 30 per cent of Hungarians surveyed said that migration from outside the EU was a rather negative phenomenon, while 51 per cent said it was very negative. The divergence from the European trend is striking at EU level, only 18 per cent of respondents were very negative. The timing of the trend reversal clearly confirms the above findings on hate politics: in the May 2015 Eurobarometer,[37] 21 per cent of Hungarian respondents thought migration from outside the EU was very negative, rising to 51 per cent by November 2015. Research published in September 2016 by the Pew Research Center (based on data collected in the Spring 2016 Pew Global Attitude Survey)[38] confirmed these multi-year, decade-long trends. Hungarians think highly above the European average of refugees as a burden, saying they take away jobs and welfare services, and that their

[35] European Social Survey, 'Attitudes towards Immigration and their Antecedents: Topline Results from Round 7 of the European Social Survey' (ESS Topline Results Series, 2016), www.europeansocialsurvey.org/docs/findings/ESS7_toplines_issue_7_immigration.pdf.

[36] Barna Ildikó and Júlia Koltai, 'Attitude Changes towards Immigrants in the Turblent Years of the "Migrant Crisis" and Anti-Immigrant Campaign in Hungary' (2019) 5 *East European Journal of Society and Politics* 48.

[37] European Commission, 'Standard Eurobarometer 83' (July 2015), https://europa.eu/eurobarometer/surveys/detail/2099.

[38] Dorothy Manevich, 'Hungarians share Europe's Embrace of Democratic Principles but are Less Tolerant of Refugees, Minorities' (Pew Research Center, 30 September 2016), www.pewresearch.org/fact-tank/2016/09/30/hungarians-share-europes-embrace-of-democratic-principles-but-are-less-tolerant-of-refugees-minorities/.

presence poses a higher risk of terrorism. Hungarian respondents also think highly above the European average of Jews, Roma, and above all Muslims.

The Orbán regime uses and mixes constitutionally codified asymmetrical counter-concepts as CIEs in parallel and inter-related ways. Éva Fodor points to very similar phenomena:

> Instead, 'gender' was most prominently used during these three years to weave a story about migration and Hungary's struggle against the European Union's migration quota… In 2018 43.6%, in 2019 41.4% and in 2020 47.1% of all articles which contained the term 'gender' also mentioned migrations and migrants. For example, Magyar Nemzet expresses concern about what it sees as 'the aggressive propaganda about gender and migration' … threatening the integrity of the Hungarian nation in one of its articles during the Christmas period. In a similar vein, an article two weeks later assures the public that 'Hungary … resists the integration of masses of migrants and the gender craze' … emanating from the West.[39]

The Hungarian Fundamental Law and its continuous amendments represent such a discursive strategy which has at its core a racist regime of asymmetrical counter-concepts that form a system of inter-related enemies.

[39] Fodor, *Gender Regime*, 18–19.

PART II

Bringing Back the Past (to Serve or Understand the Present?)

9

Political Integration through Constitutional Memory?

Historical Constitution and Community Building in Hungary

Kálmán Pócza

9.1 INTRODUCTION

'[C]an we build a community of states and peoples with a liberal-legalist constitutional imaginary?' – this is the question Jan Komárek puts in his essay on Joseph Weiler's masterpiece *The Transformation of Europe*.[1] Although, the fundamental *problematique* of Komárek's study concerns community building by various forms of constitutional imagination at the European level, it is of utmost importance to investigate the same question on a national level since it might have several implications concerning building a European community of states and peoples. Beyond the liberal–legalist way of community building, there are at least two other approaches to how this goal could be achieved. While both are moving away from the highly rationalistic strategy of legal constitutionalism, they differ on what the society's fundament should be: one finds material solidarity (i.e., class solidarity), the other one spiritual solidarity (i.e., national solidarity) as a crucial starting point for any community building project. While challenging the 'liberal-legalist constitutional imaginary' from the point of view of this spiritual solidarity shows several similarities with the challenge inspired by the idea of a social Europe, there are, of course, several points where the spiritual project diverges from the solidarity project.

Notwithstanding, it should be stressed that the present undertaking is a rather cautious one: it won't argue that it is advised *under any circumstances* to build a community on *emotional ties* connected to the idea of nation. This chapter is going to weigh arguments and counter-arguments and does not unambiguously defend one position. It will rather consider the dilemmas whether it is *useful* and *desirable* to reach back to the idea of the historical constitution and national emotions to create a sense of community. This chapter clearly goes against the 'liberal-legalist

[1] Jan Komárek, 'Why Read *The Transformation of Europe* Today? On the Limits of a Liberal Constitutional Imaginary', in Jan Komárek (ed.), *European Constitutional Imaginaries: Between Ideology and Utopia* (Oxford University Press, 2023), 131.

constitutional imaginary' and builds on the assumption that constitutional references to the historical constitution can contribute to the community building process in Hungary. While this assumption itself might be contended, this chapter puts aside the question of whether the Hungarian historical constitution could be revived in legal terms or whether it could have legally binding force in any way. Instead, it will approach the question from a non-legalistic point of view and consider the dilemmas whether references to the Hungarian historical constitution might be *useful* and *desirable* from the perspective of community building. To put it briefly: this chapter contends that it might be useful and desirable *but* only under certain circumstances. Unfortunately, whether these conditions prevail can only be established retrospectively.[2]

In what follows, this chapter starts with a brief literature overview on the role and functions of history and historical narratives in the constitutions. Next, it highlights the ahistorical character of constitutionalism in Hungary after the democratic transformation process in 1989/1990 to continue with outlining the historical turn in constitutional thinking after 2010. Afterwards, it presents the main argument of the chapter, contending that references to the historical constitution in the new Fundamental Law of Hungary *might* be useful and desirable from the perspective of community building. Nevertheless, the conclusion stresses that evaluation of the usefulness of the references to the historical constitution remains a task for future generations.

9.2 CONSTITUTIONAL MEMORIES AND HISTORICAL CONSTITUTION

Studying constitutional memory is an emerging research field with a growing theoretical and empirical literature which should be clearly distinguished from constitutional history. While the latter is a more or less linear narrative of the constitutional developments of a political community, the former refers to the manifestations of historical narratives and references to historical facts and symbols in present-day constitutional documents with a special focus on their implications for the current political communities. Surely, its subjects are mainly legal documents, but research on constitutional memories is less legalistic and takes inspirations mainly from the humanities and social sciences. While constitutionalized memory laws might have direct implications on how a society deals with its past, and regulations of transitional justice on the constitutional level have legally binding force, most of the constitutional manifestations of the past contribute rather to a (usually highly controversial) interpretation of the common past of the political community without having a direct legal effect on the everyday life of its citizens.[3]

[2] Martin Loughlin, 'The Constitutional Imagination' (2015) 78 *Modern Law Review* 1, 16.

[3] Uladzislau Belavusau and Aleksandra Gliszczyńska-Grabias (eds.), *Law and Memory: Towards Legal Governance of History* (Cambridge University Press, 2017); Uladzislau Belavusau and Aleksandra Gliszczyńska–Grabias, 'The Remarkable Rise of "Law and Historical Memory" in Europe: Theorizing Trends and Prospects in the Recent Literature' (2020) 47 *Journal of Law*

Nevertheless, the constitutionalized past might have a legitimacy function, an ideological function or an imaginary incitement function, which are clearly beyond its legal-regulatory function.[4]

This chapter contributes to this literature, by exploring whether the references to the Hungarian historical constitution in the new Fundamental Law of Hungary might be *useful* and *desirable* in the community building processes. It should be stressed that the chapter does not analyse the use of history in constitutional documents *in general*. While constitutional documents might contain explicit and implicit historical narratives, and, consequently, constitutional memory is a complex phenomenon, this chapter deliberately narrows down its focus only on one element of a complex phenomenon. To be more precise, it abandons to analyse the grand historical narratives as manifested mainly in the preamble (National Avowal) of the new Fundamental Law of Hungary and disregards explicit and implicit references to historical events and symbols abounding in the new constitution adopted in 2011.[5] This is an inevitable and necessary limitation, since references to the history of the political community in constitutional documents might take various forms: they might include (a) explicit historical narratives which determine a rather unambiguous interpretation of historical facts and events (constitutional master narratives); (b) implicit references to historical events without clearly determining the master narrative of the national history (open-ended constitutional narratives); (c) explicit references to national symbols embedded in national history with an unambiguously determined semantic field (predefined historical references)[6]; and (d) references to

and Society 325; Grażyna Baranowska and León Castellanos-Jankiewicz, 'Historical Memory in Post-communist Europe and the Rule of Law' (2020) 5 *European Papers* 95.

4 Martin Belov, 'Constitutional Memories: How do Constitutions Cope with Constitutional Past', in Martin Belov and Antoni Abat (eds.), *Revolution, Transition, Memory, and Oblivion. Reflections on Constitutional Change* (Edward Elgar, 2020), 115.

5 For a more general assessments of the constitutionalized past in Hungary, see Miklós Könczöl, 'Dealing with the Past in and around the Fundamental Law of Hungary', in Uladzislau Belavusau and Aleksandra Gliszczyńska-Grabias (eds.), *Law and Memory* (Cambridge University Press, 2017), 246–262; Uladzislau Belavusau, 'Mnemonic Constitutionalism and Rule of Law in Hungary and Russia' (2020) 1 *Interdisciplinary Journal of Populism* 1, 16; Heino Nyyssönen and Jussi Metsälä, 'Highlights of National History? Constitutional Memory and the Preambles of Post-communist Constitutions' (2019) 31 *European Politics and Society* 323; Katalin Miklóssy and Heino Nyyssönen, 'Defining the New Polity: Constitutional Memory in Hungary and Beyond' (2018) 26 *Journal of Contemporary European Studies* 322; Marina Bán, 'The Governance of History via Law: An Overview' (2023) 63 *Hungarian Journal of Legal Studies* 315; Anna Gera and Boldizsár Szentgáli-Tóth, 'The Parliamentary Margin of Movement for Strengthening the Role of Historical Dimensions in Interpretation and Law-making: The Case of Hungary' (2023) 63 *Hungarian Journal of Legal Studies* 329; Mónika Ganczer, 'The Impact of Historical Traditions on the Regulation and Practice of the Preferential Naturalization of Hungarians Living Outside the Borders' 63 *Hungarian Journal of Legal Studies* 352.

6 See the reference to the Holy Crown in the Fundamental Law with a rather exact semantic field: '… we honour the Holy Crown, which embodies the constitutional continuity of Hungary's statehood and the unity of the nation'.

phenomena and objects without a clearly defined semantic field (open-ended historical references). References to the historical constitution, if approached from a non-legalistic point of view, belong to this latter group.

The vagueness of the term 'historical constitution' triggered heavy debates in legal terms, mainly concentrating on the questions of formal and material indeterminacy of the term historical constitution or, alternatively, on the practical impossibility of the revival of the historical constitution in a legally binding way due to the incompatibility of its provisions with modern societies' circumstances or due to the disrupted constitutional traditions caused by the Soviet occupation of Hungary. While the theoretical and practical questions of the revival of the historical constitution in a legally binding form are intellectually highly appealing, here we are focusing only on the utility and desirability of the references to the Hungarian historical constitution from the extra-legal perspective of a community building process.

9.3 BACKGROUND: AHISTORICAL AND LEGAL CONSTITUTIONALISM IN HUNGARY, 1990–2010

History is a pervasive element of the Hungarian constitutional culture. Culture wars inspired by diverging and contradicting historical narratives were being waged as soon as in the early 1990s, that is, directly after the democratic transformation process. Debates on the state symbols or the potential re-emergence or re-establishment of the semi-authoritarian political system of the interwar period, restitution of property relations to post-WWII conditions and other questions of transitional justice were major topics of political and constitutional struggles in the 1990s.

Nevertheless, the past found no way into the emerging body of the new Hungarian constitution. Obviously, missing consensus on how to interpret Hungarian constitutional history (a quite long and rich one) and time pressure were major factors why, at the end of the day, no historical references have been included into the amended 1949 Communist constitution – which has been considered as a provisional constitution until a new one will be enacted. Members of the democratic opposition parties were firmly convinced that a completely new constitution should be adopted *after* the first democratic elections, since the new parliament will have a clear democratic mandate to shape the new political system. The only way history manifested itself in this provisional document is a negative one: it is a clear demarcation from the not-so-distant Communist past.

While Western liberal constitutional theory (based mainly on Dworkin's ideas) along with some innovation (like the theory of invisible constitution) became a dominant pattern of constitutional interpretation on the benches of the HCC (and even beyond that),[7] the quite long history of Hungarian constitutional thinking and

[7] Gábor Halmai, 'Silence of Transitional Constitutions: The "Invisible Constitution" Concept of the Hungarian Constitutional Court' (2018) 16 *International Journal of Constitutional Law* 969.

practice was simply neglected or even declared as reactionary, feudal and outdated.[8] Undoubtedly, one can find reactionary, feudal and outdated elements in the writings and speeches of the protagonists of the Hungarian constitutional tradition – as in constitutional traditions of all other countries. The question is rather whether such references should prevent any linkage with the past and the constitutional history of the country and whether it is *useful* and *desirable* to bring back historical references into the constitutional thinking in order to promote community building.

This ahistorical and liberal approach to constitutionalism dominated the Hungarian constitutional imagination for approximately 20 years.[9] In the early 1990s, what is now termed 'legal constitutionalism' became the dominant view in the Hungarian legal scholarship, which almost unanimously supported the activist approach of the Hungarian Constitutional Court (HCC) concerning the first generation of fundamental rights.[10] The 'crown jewel' of legal constitutionalism emerged surprisingly rapidly as a key institution of the new Hungarian democracy: there was no public debate on the adequate role of constitutional courts in a young democracy and on questions like who should have the final word in political and social debates.[11] Politicians have never challenged its legitimacy, not even in situations when the HCC declared some parts of the austerity measures of the left-wing-liberal constitutional majority unconstitutional in the mid-1990s.[12] This fact is even more striking since empirically oriented normative democratic theories rarely prefer an institution separated from popular involvement. Democratic theories which stress the consensual, deliberative, egalitarian, participatory or the majoritarian dimension

8 On the Hungarian constitutional history and the tradition of constitutional thinking, see: László Péter, *Hungary's Long Nineteenth Century. Constitutional and Democratic Traditions in a European Perspective* (Brill, 2012); Ferenc Hörcher and Thomas Lorman (eds.), *A History of the Hungarian Constitution: Law, Government and Political Culture in Central Europe* (Bloomsbury Publishing, 2018).

9 The legal scholarship has been reserved if not hostile to the idea of the historical constitution after the 1990 democratic transition. On that, see: László Péter, 'The Holy Crown of Hungary, Visible and Invisible', in L. Péter (ed.), *Hungary's Long Nineteenth Century: Constitutional and Democratic Traditions in a European Perspective* (Brill, 2012), 109.

10 Gábor Halmai, 'The Hungarian Approach to Constitutional Review: The End of Activism? The First Decade of the Hungarian Constitutional Court', in Wojciech Sadurski (ed.), *Constitutional Justice, East and West: Democratic Legitimacy and Constitutional Courts in Post-Communist Europe in a Comparative Perspective* (Kluwer Law Interntional, 2002); András Sajó and Renáta Uitz, *The Constitution of Freedom: An Introduction to Legal Constitutionalism* (Oxford University Press, 2017).

11 Kálmán Pócza, 'Judicial Review and Politics in Hungary 1990–2018', in Astrid Lorenz and Ellen Bos (eds.), *Politics and Society in Hungary: (De-)Democratization, Orbán and the EU* (Springer, 2023).

12 Although the HCC has never become the bulwark of social rights, it focused on the first generation of fundamental rights or settling disputes among state organs. Either way, the HCC performed as a poster-child of liberal constitutionalists. See: Kim Lane Scheppele, 'Constitutional Negotiations: Political Contexts of Judicial Activism in Post-Soviet Europe' (2003) 18 *International Sociology* 219. Kim Lane Scheppele, 'A Realpolitik Defense of Social Rights' (2004) 82 *Texas Law Review* 1921.

of democracy are rather hostile to the liberal democratic theory, which is based on the idea of judicial supremacy.[13] In Hungary, as in other Central and Eastern European countries, this lack of debates on what kind of democracy we really want implied that any challenge to the legal constitutionalist imagination has been identified as a danger to the democracy itself. Legal constitutionalism (identified with the concept of democracy) became the only game in the town.[14]

Given the controversial character of the Hungarian constitutional history and historical references to the past, along with the normative bias of the dominant perception of constitutionalism and the HCC's explicit adherence to the Dworkinian type of constitutional adjudication, no surprise that historical rhetoric and historical references were completely absent from Hungarian constitutionalism after 1990. But history (along with heavy controversies on how to interpret the Hungarian constitutional history and historical constitution) came back after the landslide victory of the Fidesz party in 2010. Viktor Orbán indicated during the election campaign in 2010 that if his party obtained a landslide victory it would enact a new constitution. This constitution would, he asserted, complete the unfinished task of the regime change which had begun in 1989 and help solve the economic and social problems that afflicted the country.[15] During the election campaign, however, no drafts of a new constitution were circulated, and the constitution-making process did not produce a new constitutional text until 2011, when it was adopted by the two-thirds right-wing majority of the parliament. The legitimacy of the new constitution was, however, challenged by the opposition parties which refused to participate in the drafting process and encouraged popular demonstrations against the new Fundamental Law.[16] One of the major objections of the left-wing and liberal parties against the Fundamental Law concerned the references to the historical constitution of Hungary, which was denounced as an anachronistic

[13] Kálmán Pócza, 'Democratic Theory and Constitutional Adjudication' (2015) 56 *Acta Juridica Hungarica* 199.

[14] Paul Blokker, *New Democracies in Crisis? A Comparative Constitutional Study of the Czech Republic, Hungary, Poland, Romania and Slovakia* (Routledge, 2014), 45–79.

[15] Viktor Orbán, '*Nem lesz árnyékkormány!, Beszéd a Magyar Polgári Együttműködés Egyesület Új államépítés, új irány, új feladatok című konferenciáján Kecskeméten*' 2009. november 8-án (There Won't be Shadow Cabinet! Speech at the Conference *New State-building, New Direction, New Tasks* organized by the Hungarian Civil Cooperation Association on 8 November 2009), http://2010-2015.miniszterelnok.hu/beszed/nem_lesz_arnyekkormany; furthermore: Viktor Orbán, Újjá kell építeni Magyarországot, évértékelő beszéd, 2010. február 5. (We Should Rebuild Hungary! Speech on State of Hungary on 5 February 2010), http://2010-2015.miniszterelnok.hu/beszed/ujja_kell_epiteni_magyarorszagot.

[16] The secession of two left-wing parties from the constitution-making process was implicated by the amendments of the 'old' 1989 constitution by the right-wing constitutional majority in the summer of 2010. This amendment cut the competences of the Constitutional Court. To the process, see Pál Sonnevend, Andras Jakab and Lóránt Csink, 'The Constitution as an Instrument of Everyday Politics: The Basic Law of Hungary', in Armin von Bogdany and Pál Sonnevend (eds.), *Constitutional Crisis in the European Constitutional Area: Theory, Law and Politics in Hungary and Romania* (Bloomsbury Publishing, 2015), 44.

reference to an ancient undemocratic tradition and which had legitimized and empowered a semi-authoritarian regime in the interwar period and paved the way for the horrors which afflicted Hungary in WWII.[17]

9.4 THE HISTORICAL TURN AND THE FUNDAMENTAL LAW AFTER 2010

Although the concept of the historical constitution was heavily criticized in the public sphere at the time of the adoption of the Fundamental Law, legal scholarship has shown rather moderate interest in it. Among those few studies engaging with the phenomenon of the historical constitution, one might equally find highly critical comments, analyses completely neglecting the references to the historical constitution and some endorsing the revival of the historical constitution.[18] Debates in the

[17] See, for example, the opinion of the Hungarian Socialist Party on the draft constitution from 21 March 2011, http://mszp.hu/nyomtatas/312.

[18] As for highly critical comments, see: Imre Vörös, 'A történeti alkotmány az Alkotmánybíróság gyakorlatában' (2016) 9 *Közjogi Szemle* 44; Zoltán Szente, 'A 2011. évi Alaptörvény és a történeti alkotmány összekapcsolásának mítosza' (2019) 12 *Közjogi Szemle* 1; Zoltán Szente, 'A historizáló alkotmányozás problémái – a történeti alkotmány és a Szent Korona az új Alaptörvényben' (2011) 3 *Közjogi Szemle* 1; Ivett Császár and Balázs Majtényi, 'Hungary: The Historic Constitution as the Place of Memory', in Markku Suksi, Kalliope Agapiou-Josephides, Jean-Paul Lehners and Manfred Nowak (eds.), *First Fundamental Rights Documents in Europe* (Cambridge University Press, 2015); Zoltán Szente, 'How Not to Use History in Constitutional Interpretation: The Aborted Resurrection of the Historical Constitution in Hungary', in Francesco Biagi, Justin O. Frosini and Jason Mazzone (eds.), *Comparative Constitutional History: Uses of History in Constitutional Adjudication* (Brill, 2022). Studies endorsing the revival of the historical constitution: Ádám Rixer, A *vívmány-teszt* (Ludovika University Press, 2018); Ádám Rixer, 'A történeti alkotmány lehetséges jelentéstartalmai' (2011) 3 *Jogelméleti Szemle* 1; Szakály Zsuzsa, 'A történeti alkotmány és az alkotmányos identitás az Alaptörvény tükrében' (2015) 3 *Pro Publico Bono* 24; Lóránt Csink and Johanna Fröhlich, 'Történeti alkotmány és kontinuitás az új Alaptörvényben' (2012) 5 *Közjogi Szemle* 9; Attila Horváth, 'A magyar történeti alkotmány tradíciói' (2011) *Alkotmánybírósági Szemle* 23; Attila Horváth, 'Tiszteletben tartjuk történeti alkotmányunk vívmányait és a Szent Koronát, amely megtestesíti Magyarország alkotmányos állami folytonosságát és a nemzet egységét', in András Patyi (ed.), *Rendhagyó kommentár egy rendhagyó preambulumról* (Dialóg Campus, 2019); Attila Horváth, 'A történeti alkotmány, a Szent Korona-tan mint a szuverenitás biztosítéka', in András Karácsony (ed.), *Szuverenitáskérdések. Elméletek* (Gondolat Kiadó, 2020); István Szabó, 'Az ősi alkotmány: Történeti előzmények', in Lóránt Csink, Balázs Schanda and András Varga Zs (eds.), *A magyar közjog alapintézményei* (Pázmány Press, 2020); Anna Gera, 'Történeti alkotmányunk vívmányai az Alaptörvény speciális alkotmányos rendszerében' (2021) *MTA Law Working Papers* 6, 1–32; József Szalma and Cservák Csaba, 'A történelmi/történeti alkotmány és értelmezési kérdései az új Magyar Alaptörvény fényében' (2017) 2 *Létünk* 47, 9–33; Jenő Szmodis, 'Az alkotmányos történelmi vívmányok szerepéről a normakontrollban: Széljegyzetek Vörös Imre akadémiai székfoglaló előadásához' (2016) 4 *Jogelméleti Szemle* 176; András Milánkovich and Boldizsár Szentgáli-Tóth, 'Díszítő elem, vagy új értelmezési távlatok? A magyar közjog történeti dimenziói az Alaptörvény tükrében' (2014) 1 *Közjogi Szemle* 7, 65–74; Zsolt Zétényi (ed.), A *történeti alkotmány: Magyarország ősi alkotmánya* (Magyarországért Kulturális Egyesület, 2010); András Varga Zs, 'Történeti alkotmányunk vívmányai az Alaptörvény kógens rendelkezésében' (2016) 12 *Iustum Aequum Salutare* 83. Rather pragmatic

legal scholarship focused mainly on questions of formal and material indeterminacy of the term 'historical constitution' or, alternatively, on the practical impossibility of the revival of the historical constitution with a legally binding force (due to incompatibility with modern society's circumstances or disruption of the constitutional traditions). In contrast to these studies, this essay does not reflect on the feasibility of reviving the historical constitution from a legal-dogmatic point of view but rather from the perspective of the humanities and social sciences by focusing on the *utility* and *desirability* of the references to the historical constitution in the community building process.

The term 'historical constitution' appears four times in the Fundamental Law: three times in the preamble (National Avowal), and once in the core text of the constitution:

> We honour the achievements of our *historic constitution* and we honour the Holy Crown, which embodies the constitutional continuity of Hungary's statehood and the unity of the nation. (National Avowal)
>
> We hold that the protection of our identity rooted in our *historic constitution* is a fundamental obligation of the State. (National Avowal)[19]
>
> We do not recognise the suspension of our *historic constitution* due to foreign occupations. We deny any statute of limitations for the inhuman crimes committed against the Hungarian nation and its citizens under the national socialist and the communist dictatorship. (National Avowal)
>
> The provisions of the Fundamental Law shall be interpreted in accordance with their purposes, the National Avowal contained therein and the achievements of our *historic constitution*. (Article R, para 3)

In the legal scholarship, these references have been heavily criticized and/or considered as irrelevant for constitutional interpretation. Several renowned legal scholars have proposed that they should be simply ignored and that the focus should be solely on the written text of the Fundamental Law.[20] By contrast, a significantly

approaches: Jakab András: Az új Alaptörvény keletkezése és gyakorlati következményei. Budapest, HVG-ORAC, 'Wiener György: Jogfolytonosság és megszakítottság a történeti alkotmányosság rendjében' (2017) 10 *Közjogi Szemle* 22; István Stipta, *A magyar történeti alkotmány és a hazai közjogi-közigazgatási jogvédelem* (Gondolat Kiadó, 2020); Ferenc Hörcher Balázs Fekete, 'Péter László öröksége: a történeti alkotmány rekonstrukciója' (2015) 8 *Közjogi Szemle* 11.

19 This was added to the National Avowal by the seventh amendment to the Constitution (28 June 2018).

20 Miklós Bánkuti, Gábor Halmai and Kim Lane Scheppele, 'Hungary's Illiberal Turn: Disabling the Constitution' (2012) 23 *Journal of Democracy* 138; Sándor Radnóti, 'A Sacred Symbol in a Secular Country: The Holy Crown', in Gábor Attila Tóth, *Constitution for a Disunited Nation. On Hungary's 2011 Fundamental Law* (CEU Press, 2012); Kim Lane Scheppele, 'The Unconstitutional Constitution' *The New York Times*, 2 January 2012; Gábor Halmai, 'The Hungarian Constitutional Court and Constitutional Identity', *Verfassungsblog*, 10 January

smaller group of scholars evaluated these references more positively.[21] Since there is no general agreement on the question which parliamentary acts and/or unwritten constitutional norms should be considered as part of the historical constitution, the majority of legal scholars rejected the idea of the revival of the historical constitution.

Nevertheless, these references exhibit their utmost relevance not from the perspective of their legalistic-dogmatic interpretation, but rather as part of a certainly vague and undetermined historical narrative. Surely, Article R, paragraph 3 gives an unambiguous command for the Hungarian Constitutional Court on how to interpret the Fundamental Law, and it has a legally binding force concerning constitutional interpretation. Nevertheless, the practice of constitutional adjudication of the HCC shows that this command has been neglected most of the time.[22] Apart from this instruction, which, at the end of the day, has been almost systematically disregarded by the HCC, all other references are included into the preamble of the constitution, which has typically extra-legal, non-binding or declarative character, thus it usually serves the aim to put the constitution into context and create a master narrative of the political community.[23] Besides the location of these references in the preamble, the wording of the text is also telling: terms like we 'honour', 'hold' or 'recognize' indicate the disposition of the community towards the historical constitution however it may be defined. Such dispositional expressions are intended to create a sense of attachment to the constitutional past of the political community and imply that the symbolic-integrative function of these references prevail over their legal character. Given that references to the historical constitution functions as a leeway for community building, the question arises as to whether it is a useful and desirable tool for promoting social integration.

2017, In Hungarian: Zoltán Szente, 'A historizáló alkotmányozás problémái'; Zoltán Szente, 'Az Alaptörvény és az alkotmányos változások szakmai és tudományos reflexiói 2010 után' (2015) 19 *Fundamentum* 62; Imre Vörös, 'A történeti alkotmány az Alkotmánybíróság gyakorlatában'.

[21] Ferenc Hörcher, 'The National Avowal', in Lóránt Csink, Balázs Schanda and András Zs. Varga (eds.), *The Basic Law of Hungary: A First Commentary* (Clarus Press – National Institute of Public Administration, 2012); Ferenc Hörcher, 'Communal Values in the New Hungarian Fundamental Law: The Habermas-Ratzinger Debate and the Use of the Humanities in Constitutional Interpretation', in Ellen Bos and Kálmán Pócza (eds.), *Verfassunggebung in konsolidierten Demokratien: Neubeginn oder Verfall eines politischen Systems?* (Nomos, 2014), 346–365; Ádám Rixer, A *történeti alkotmány helye mai jogunkban* (KRE ÁJK, 2012); Péter Smuk, 'Nemzetfogalom és történeti narratíva az Alaptörvényben', in Kecskés Gábor (ed.), *Doktori Műhelytanulmányok. Győr* (Széchenyi University Press, 2013).

[22] Anna Gera, 'Történeti alkotmányunk vívmányai az Alaptörvény speciális alkotmányos rendszerében', *MTA Law Working Papers* (2021), 6.1–32.

[23] Balázs Fekete, 'The National Avowal: More than a Conventional Preamble to a Constitution', in Zoltán Szente, Fanni Mandák and Zsuzsanna Fejes (eds.), *Challenges and Pitfalls in the Recent Hungarian Constitutional Development* (L'Harmattan, 2015), 11–24; Liav Orgad, 'The Preamble in Constitutional Interpretation' (2010) 8 *International Journal of Constitutional Law* 714.

9.5 COMMUNITY BUILDING BY REFERENCES TO THE HISTORICAL CONSTITUTION

Setting aside the question of whether the 'historical' narrative will prevail or simply disappear from the Hungarian political arena, one might be interested in to what extent such a project would be *useful* for both the Hungarian and the European political community. Furthermore, even if the project seems to be *useful*, it is less than obvious why such a project would be *desirable*. Therefore, we must consider the *normative* arguments which underpin or delegitimize the desirability of the community building by references to the Hungarian historical constitution.

The dominant view in the legal scholarship is that the most important functions of a constitution are to constitute, legitimate and limit state power, defend the rights of the citizens and secure the rule of law (including legal certainty and calculability).[24] Nevertheless, this dominant view has been challenged by several scholars. Other functions, like expressing fundamental values of the political community or being a symbolic focal point of debates on divergent visions of political and social order, might also be crucial functions. Constitutions might reflect the power struggle and power relations of the daily politics during the constitution-making process. In more fortunate cases they can also express the fundamental values of the political community. But they are even more than that since they also possess a symbolic dimension. They serve as a focal point for various social and political practices, interpretations, constitutional myths, memorial days and political debates over the correct form of social order.[25]

Thus, they are *symbolic* expressions of divergent visions of political and social order. They can serve as symbolic tools for *social integration*, as the example of the US constitution or the constitution of the German Federal Republic after WWII demonstrate.[26] Constitutions may acquire a totemic or symbolic importance and therefore contribute to social cohesion. It should be admitted that this integrative function might be performed by different means. In France, for example, it is not the constitution which serves as a dew point of the integration process but the idea of the nation. In Germany, for many years following the Bismarck-era, it was the

[24] Denis J. Galligan and Mila Versteeg, 'Theoretical Perspectives on the Social and Political Foundations of Constitutions', in D. J. Galligan and M. Versteeg (eds.), *Social and Political Foundations of Constitutions* (Cambridge University Pressm 2013), 3–50.

[25] Dieter Grimm, *Constitutionalism. Past, Present, and Future* (Oxford University Press, 2016), 131; András Jakab, 'The Two Functions of a Constitution', in Ellen Bos and Kálmán Pócza (eds.), *Verfassunggebung in konsolidierten Demokratien Neubeginn oder Verfall eines politischen Systems?* (Nomos Verlag, 2014), 78–104.

[26] For the thesis that constitutions have a highly important symbolic dimension and have, consequently, an integrative function, see: Hans Vorländer, 'Constitutions as Symbolic Orders', in Paul Blokker and Chris Thornhill (eds.), *Sociological Constitutionalism* (Cambridge University Press, 2017), 209–240; Dieter Grimm, 'Integration by Constitution', in Dieter Grimm (ed.), *Constitutionalism: Past, Present, and Future* (Oxford University Press, 2016).

abstract concept of the state which served as a focal point of social integration.[27] With some reservations, we could also argue that, in Hungary, the idea of the historical constitution and the ever changing *idea* of the Holy Crown were the central *loci* of this imaginative process.[28]

A constitutional practice based on this extended meaning of the term '*constitution*' generates emotional ties that promote the process of social integration, even if the concepts of political order symbolized by constitutions vary heavily over time and/or within one and the same political community in a given period.[29] Constitutions necessarily contain highly general and often stylistically elevated abstract terms and phrases, and, as a consequence, they cannot help but to induce different interpretations or visions of political order.[30] Surely, silence or explicit unanimity on constitutional issues produces social cohesion, but social cohesion will rarely be created by judicial interpretation. Social cohesion and community building need more emotion and less rigid logic and rationality.[31] Here politics is once again at the forefront: a political community cannot be governed in the long run without constructing a sense of community that appeals to the *emotional* dispositions of its members. And, for this reason, the most important functions of the constitutions do not exhaust in constituting or constraining political power and maintaining legal certainty. It seems inevitable that modern constitutions stand at the focal point of *social integration* processes that presuppose some kind of *emotional* engagement. Whether constitutions can fulfil this function in an appropriate manner might be evaluated on an individual basis, and, unfortunately, only retrospectively. Whether the new Fundamental Law of Hungary and its references to the historical constitution will achieve these goals at any time in the future remains an open question to be answered in the decades to come. But it is undeniable that constitutions, including the Fundamental Law of Hungary, play a highly important role in social integration that extends well beyond the formal functions of the constitutions.

Given the fact that fostering social integration seems to be a crucial function of constitutions, the question emerges how can constitutions best serve this purpose? How can they establish social integration? Here constitutional imagination might

27 Hans Vorländer, 'Integration durch Verfassung? Die symbolische Bedeutung der Verfassung im politischen Integrationsprozess', in Hans Vorländer (ed.), *Integration durch Verfassung* (Wiesbaden, 2002), 24.

28 Certainly, the idea and the meanings of the term 'Holy Crown' have changed over time, nevertheless, with varying and frequently contested connotations, the Holy Crown has served for several hundred years as the focal point of Hungarian political discourse. For the various meanings of the concept of the Holy Crown in Hungary see: László Péter, 'The Holy Crown of Hungary, Visible and Invisible', in László Péter (ed.), *Hungary's Long Nineteenth Century: Constitutional and Democratic Traditions in a European Perspective* (Brill, 2012), 15–113.

29 André Brodocz, *Die symbolische Dimension der Verfassung* (Wiesbaden, 2003), 228.

30 Loughlin, 'The Constitutional Imagination', 13.

31 Chris Thornhill, *A Sociology of Constitutions* (Cambridge University Press, 2011), 1–20.

have a decisive role. As Martin Loughlin argues, constitutional imagination is an important element of the collective self-representation of a political community created by a fruitful tension between ideology and utopia. While ideology is a technique of social integration which conceals the gap in legitimacy claims, utopian thought exposes this gap. Both have positive and negative attributes.

> The positive role of ideology is to achieve social and *political integration* through constitutional ordering, while for utopian thought the positive role seeks to elaborate and promote ideals that are implicit within a constitutional text. But on the negative side, ideology can operate primarily to mask the various forms of domination within constitutional arrangements, and, in striving for constitutional perfection, utopianism might simply amount to a flight from political reality.[32]

Furthermore, constitutional imagination can 'harness the power of narrative, symbol, ritual and myth to project an account of political existence in ways that shape – and re-shape – political reality. The phrase draws our attention to the capacity of constitutions to offer alternative perceptions of reality, revealing new ways of conceiving the boundaries of practical political action.'[33] Komárek adds that constitutional imaginaries are 'necessary fictions' of nationhood, common identity or shared history which integrate individual subjects and their beliefs into a common whole.[34]

By accepting these assessments and putting aside the question of utopian thinking for another study, we are focusing here deliberately on the ideological side of constitutional imaginaries and argue that constitutions are capable to produce social cohesion by *historical references*. Historical master narratives and open-ended historical references excite emotional reactions which can be transformed into a powerful tool of building social cohesion. Common narrative and shared history are certainly the most important elements of community building. They can create emotional commitments. Most recently even legal scholars begun to argue that emotions could not be neglected in constitutionalism, community building and establishing social integration. Contemporary constitutional systems are typically presented as if they were operating according to rationality. It is believed that this is achieved by successfully exiling emotions. But, in Sajó's view, 'emotions are the heroes of constitutional institution building'.[35] To be sure, these studies argue that enthusiastic commitment to human rights has its origin in a desperate resistance against the tyrants in seventeenth century Britain, late eighteenth century American colonies and in France. Emotional engagement for liberating the individuals from the

[32] Loughlin, 'The Constitutional Imagination', 13 (emphasis added).

[33] Ibid.

[34] Jan Komárek, 'European Constitutional Imaginaries: Utopias, Ideologies, and the Other' in Jan Komárek (ed.), *European Constitutional Imaginaries: Between Ideology and Utopia* (Oxford University Press, 2023), 1–17, 3.

[35] András Sajó, 'Emotions in Constitutional Design' (2010) 8 *International Journal of Constitutional Law* 354, 357.

tyranny should be considered as a crucial factor in the success story of human rights regimes as we know them today.[36]

The lesson we can learn from these studies is that emotional ties shaped by constitutional references to crucial historical moments are necessary factors of successful community building processes. Thus, we can rightly argue that historical master narratives and open-ended historical references on the constitutional level may strengthen the emotional ties among the members of the political community. Nevertheless, it should be admitted that they can also have the opposite effect. Historical narratives might divide society, strengthen polarization and, consequently, impede social integration. In the Hungarian context, László Péter argued that:

> The Holy Crown tradition is conducive to social and national cohesion. It undoubtedly has been for many people; at the same time, however, it has been culturally divisive, too. As we have seen, the doctrine creates social conflict as well as healing it.[37]

To be more concrete and give an example of how historical narratives and historical references might divide but, at the end of the day, even strengthen the emotional ties among the members of the political community, let's briefly summarize the story of the Holy Crown after the democratic transformation process of 1989/1990. After a highly adventurous journey from Budapest to Mattsee, the Holy Crown has been seized by the US Army in 1945 and the US government has preserved it at Fort Knox for two decades. As part of his new foreign policy of appeasement, Jimmy Carter decided that the masterpiece should be transferred back to Hungary. In 1978 the Holy Crown returned to Hungary and it has been exhibited as an artefact and as a historical object in the National Museum in Budapest. Nevertheless, the return of the Holy Crown generated wider public resonance and inspired even authors of the highly popular rock-opera *Stephen, the King* (*István, a király*) which became part of the cultural DNA of all Hungarians as early as in the early 1980s (i.e., well before the fall of Communism).[38]

The Holy Crown got once again into the forefront of political debates directly after the democratic transformation process of 1989/1990. Lengthy and passionate parliamentary and public debates on whether the Holy Crown should be included into the coat of arms of the new democratic state showed that the Holy Crown could still stimulate political emotions. Left-wing and liberal MPs and public intellectuals argued that the Hungarian coat of arms should not depict the Holy Crown because it

36 András Sajó, *Constitutional Sentiments* (Yale University Press, 2011).

37 László Péter, 'The Holy Crown of Hungary, Visible and Invisible', in L. Péter (ed.), *Hungary's Long Nineteenth Century: Constitutional and Democratic Traditions in a European Perspective* (Brill, 2012), 109.

38 László Péter, 'The Holy Crown of Hungary, Visible and Invisible' (2003) 81 *The Slavonic and East European Review* 421.

belonged to the feudal era of the Hungarian history – they opted rather for the so-called *Kossuth-címer*, a coat with clear allusions to the short-lived republican past of Hungary. Nevertheless, the right-wing parliamentary majority decided to adopt a law which made the coat of arms with the Holy Crown official. Even though the left-wing and liberal parties won the next parliamentary elections in 1994 with a two-thirds (constitutional) majority, they haven't changed the official coat of arms of Hungary. The issue was settled, and the new government did not open the file again.[39]

The next episode of the story started in 2000 as the first Orbán-government decided to transfer the Holy Crown from the National Museum to the Parliament as a symbolic event of the thousand years old foundation of the Hungarian state by King Saint Stephen in 1000 AD. Once again, heavy debates dominated the political life because left-wing and liberal parties opposed the idea to move the Holy Crown, a symbol of feudal monarchy in their view, to the Parliament which, in turn, has been generally considered as the temple of the republican idea. Nevertheless, the right-wing government transferred the Holy Crown to the Parliament in 2001 even though the issue seemed to increase political polarization. But, once again, after the left-wing and liberal parties came into power in 2002 there was no initiative to transfer the Holy Crown back to the National Museum, which has been regarded by the left-wing and liberal politicians and intellectuals as the most appropriate place for preserving a historically important but currently irrelevant artefact.[40] Nowadays, thousands of Hungarians are visiting the Holy Crown by guided tours all year round and especially on 20 August, the day when the Parliament opens its door during the national holiday commemorating the state foundation of Hungary in 1000 AD.

Once highly divisive and polarizing, the Holy Crown now attracts thousands of visitors in the Parliament and there is no debate or initiative to transfer it back to the National Museum. In that sense, the story of the Holy Crown might be an instructive example as far as the central question of this chapter is concerned: whether it is useful to rely on constitutional memory and historical references in the constitution while trying to promote social integration of the political community. Surely, the Holy Crown is only one example and there might be several differences between the Holy Crown and the references to the historical constitution in the Fundamental Law. Nevertheless, it shows that it is not *unconceivable* that historical narratives really promote social cohesion even if they were once highly divisive issues.

[39] József Zoltán Tóth, *Magyar közjogi hagyományok és nemzeti öntudat a 19. Század végétől napjainkig. Adalékok a Szent Korona-eszme történetéhez* (Szent István Társulat, 2008), 166.

[40] László Péter, 'The Holy Crown of Hungary, Visible and Invisible' in L. László Péter (ed.), *Hungary's Long Nineteenth Century: Constitutional and Democratic Traditions in a European Perspective* (Brill, 2012), 105.

9.6 CONCLUSIONS

This chapter considered the dilemmas of whether it is useful and desirable to reach back to the idea of the historical constitution and national emotions to create a sense of community. It approached the question from a non-legalistic point of view and contended that it might be useful and desirable *but* only under certain circumstances. It also stressed that whether these conditions prevail can only be established *retrospectively*. Since 2010, several right-wing voters have supported the historicization of politics and politically less committed voters have become aware of the importance of the history of the political community, but several opponents of the government have considered (and are still considering) the references to the historical constitution as an anachronistic effort which turns the attention towards the (less glorious) past instead of the future.

Thus, historical reminiscences, including the references to the historical constitution, might serve the cause of peaceful community building – but they can easily be focal points of intensive social conflicts as well. Counter-narratives which challenge the historical narrative of the new Fundamental Law or the usefulness of any historical narratives on a constitutional level in community building are flourishing in Hungary.[41] Consequently, as for now, we can't estimate whether community building by historical narratives and by references to the historical constitution will be a successful attempt. Even if social integration based on historical references has been launched on a rocky way, its polarizing effect might be chilled and transformed into an integrative power. Time will tell us whether constitutional references to the historical constitution will be successful in promoting social cohesion or it will fail due to the insurmountable gap existing between the two camps of the political community.

[41] Gabor Halmai, 'The Hungarian Constitutional Court and Constitutional Identity', *Verfassungsblog*, 20 January 2017, http://verfassungsblog.de/the-hungarian-constitutional-court-and-constitutional-identity/; Zoltán Szente, 'A historizáló alkotmányozás problémái' (2011), 1–13; Zoltán Szente, 'A 2011. évi Alaptörvény és a történeti alkotmány összekapcsolásának mítosza', *Közjogi Szemle*, 12 January 2019, 1–8.

10

The Constitutional Concept of the Historical Constitution and Illiberalism

The Case of Hungary

Tímea Drinóczi

10.1 INTRODUCTION

Starting from the last part of the nineteenth century but especially after the coming into force of the Fundamental Law (2012, FL),[1] various scholarly definitions have emerged about what the historical constitution of Hungary means, what its importance in the life of the nation is and how it had been able to change over time. The historical constitution was always a concept used in many different and conflicting ways[2] and it has retained this quality in recent years.

Hungary did not have a long-lasting written constitution until the adoption of the communist constitution in 1949, which ended the era of the millennium-old uncodified Hungarian historical constitution that governed the eras of the kingdom until 1918[3] and monarchy without a monarch (1920–1945). Hungary's post-communist (liberal) Constitution (Act XX of 1949 on the Constitution of the Republic of Hungary, hereinafter: Constitution)[4] did not contain any reference to the historical constitution, nor did the jurisprudence of the Constitutional Court (CC). The text, however, included specific provisions about the principle of democracy and the rule of law and had a chapter on fundamental rights. These provisions, and the entire substantially amended Constitution (1989–1990), along

I am grateful for the comments of Imre Vörös, Gábor Schweitzer, Marina Bán and Noémi Nagy on the first draft of this chapter.

[1] The FL is the new constitution of Hungary, adopted in 2011, by the new constitutional majority of the parliament elected in 2010, without any meaningful involvement of the public or opposition parties.

[2] A. Cieger, 'Alkotmányosság és nemzeti identitás – a magyar történelem kontextusában. Vázlat', http://atelier.org.hu/upload/category/mta_elte_atelier/kotoerok1.3_cieger_andras.pdf, 56.

[3] An independent kingdom, later as a part of the Habsburg Monarchy and Austrian Empire, and between 1867 and 1918, part of the Austrian–Hungarian Monarchy (dualism).

[4] This Constitution, even though still having the numbering of the original document from 1949, was substantially amended during the democratic transition process in 1989 and 1990 and became a democratic constitution respecting the rule of law and human rights.

with membership of the CoE, NATO and the EU, set Hungary on a special, Western-oriented path instead of the former Eastern one (with the Warsaw Pact, the Council for Mutual Economic Assistance and socialist ideology on society, state and law). Since 2012, the historical constitution has become a constitutional concept after decades of justified abandonment. It appeared in the Fundamental Law of Hungary (FL), the illiberal constitution replacing the post-communist one, and the jurisprudence of the CC – both link it to the concept of constitutional identity. The FL requires that the constitution must be interpreted in accordance with the achievements of the historical constitution and that the constitutional identity of Hungary rooted in the historical constitution must be protected.

Against this background, this chapter claims that the narrative of the Hungarian historical constitution as a constitutional concept that has been becoming predominant in legal texts and scholarly works is conducive to illiberalism.[5] It is so because, instead of leaving it in the domain of historical studies, it has been used by political and constitutional actors to oppose liberal values. Two arguments are presented to justify this claim.

First, the contemporary narratives on the two most important constitutive components of the historical constitution, that is, continuity and rights expansion, are contrasted with legal measures introduced in the second part of the nineteenth and the first half of the twentieth centuries. The documented history of Hungarian suffrage, minority rights protection under the realm of the Austro-Hungarian Monarchy and the changes in the form of state after WWI support the view that contemporary claims on rights expansion and continuity cannot be verified. It is suggested that the situation would be contrary: legal changes of that time rather imply exclusion and rights restriction and support the view of the discontinuity of the historical constitution. Second, the relevant jurisprudence of the Hungarian Constitutional Court suggests that the finality of introducing the historical constitution into the constitutional text, and their subsequent linking to the concept of constitutional identity, was to secure the traditional Westphalian understanding of ethnic-national sovereignty, mainly against the rule of law, that is, EU obligations and globalization.

In this light, the chapter is structured as follows: Section 10.2 gives a brief overview of how the term historical constitution has appeared in the constitutional text and the Hungarian literature. Section 10.3 will contrast views emerging in the literature about the two components of historical constitution, that is, rights expansion and continuity, and the legal and social reality of that era when the related reforms were introduced. Section 10.4 analyses the CC's relevant jurisprudence to show how judges got inspired by the scholarly narratives of the historical constitution and includes concluding remarks.

5 For the purpose of this chapter, illiberalism is viewed as a thin ideology challenging different dimensions of liberalism, such as political and cultural. More on this, see Marlene Laruelle, 'Illiberalism: A Conceptual Introduction' (2022) 38 *East European Politics* 303.

10.2 APPEARANCE OF THE TERM 'HISTORICAL CONSTITUTION'

After the adoption of the FL, which is a complete opposite of the post-communist Constitution in terms of *expressis verbis* value statements and historical references,[6] scholars immediately started to analyse the original version and, later on, its amendments. The term 'historical constitution' has been used, again, for different purposes, which is traceable not only in scholarly works but in the case law of the CC, due to the vagueness of the term and the fact that the constitutional text uses a concept that implies the lack of a codified constitution. It brings about a sense of anachronism instead of a forward-looking perspective and attempts to justify the Hungarian illiberalism, from both a scholarly and legal perspective.

10.2.1 *Constitutional Text*

The preamble to the FL, called National Avowal, not only gives a narrative of Hungarian history, the Hungarian people, and constitutional development, but it also formulates an aspiration for the future – paradoxically by using the reference to the historical constitution, which belongs to the past. It also provides a narrative of the identity of Hungarians, which is rooted in the historical constitution and, jointly reading it with other provisions of the FL, links the individual identity with that of the state. The National Avowal is of utmost importance in the constitutional interpretation as, since 2012, the FL in its Article R) prescribes that its provisions must be interpreted in accordance with their purposes, the National Avowal, and the achievements of our historic constitution.

In the context of history, the National Avowal portrays victory and half-truth. It mentions the first king, St. Stephen, building the state 1,000 years ago; it is proud that 'we fought for the survival, freedom and independence of our country' and that 'our nation has over the centuries defended Europe in a series of struggles', and it proclaims that Christianity preserves nationhood. About the twentieth century, it expresses that 'our nation's intellectual and spiritual unity was torn apart in the storms of the last century', not mentioning the roles Hungary played in the World Wars. It also states that Hungary did not have national self-determination between 19 March 1944 (Nazi Germany invaded Hungary, an ally state) and 2 May 1990 (the formation of the first democratically elected parliament after the transition). This narrative originates 'our current liberty' in the 1956 Revolution, not mentioning the declaration of the Republic in 1989, which not only happened symbolically on the same day when the anti-Soviet revolution of 1956 erupted but was adopted as a result of the Round Table negotiation, and thus with the involvement of the former

[6] See, e.g., András László Pap, *Democratic Decay in Hungary* (Routledge, 2017); Tímea Drinóczi and Agnieszka Bień-Kacała, *Illiberal Constitutionalism in Poland and Hungary: The Deterioration of Democracy, Misuse of Human Rights and Abuse of the Rule of Law* (Routledge, 2022).

Hungarian Socialist Workers Party. This party and officeholders of the socialist system became the first constitutionalized 'enemy' created by the Orbán regime, which was followed by others: homeless people (2013), non-traditional families (2013), migrants (2018) and LGBTQ people (2019). This process is based on populist rhetoric and emotional politics, resulting in exclusion and the waning of individual liberty (i.e., illiberalism).

The narrative of the National Avowal on the Hungarian people contains the following: fighters, defenders, victims and persons that have outstanding intellectual achievements, talents and diligence, but the 'decades of the twentieth century led to a state of moral decay', which now ends with the new era of national cooperation established by the FL.

The historical constitution appears in the following formulation (in the originally adopted text of the FL): 'we honour the achievements of our historic constitution and we honour the Holy Crown, which embodies the constitutional continuity of Hungary's statehood and the unity of the nation'. It is added that 'our historic constitution was suspended due to foreign occupations', which refers to the Nazi occupation and Communist rule in the twentieth century (without referencing the collaboration with the Third Reich).

Aspiration for the future implies that Hungary will be made great again and that, because of the state of moral decay, Hungarians need spiritual and intellectual renewal. Also, 'our nation's intellectual and spiritual unity needs to be preserved'. It implies that, also because of Article R), the FL needs to be interpreted in a way that does not allow division and fragmentation.

The National Avowal gives a narrative of the identity of Hungarians since the Seventh Amendment to the FL (2018). While with this sentence '[t]he protection of the constitutional identity and Christian culture of Hungary shall be an obligation of every organ of the State', the text of the FL[7] talks about the constitutional identity of Hungary, the National Avowal declares that of Hungarians: 'our identity is rooted in our historic constitution' and 'the protection of our identity is a fundamental obligation of the State'. The Ninth Amendment finally linked the individual identity with that of the state: 'Hungary shall protect the right of children to a self-identity corresponding to their sex at birth and shall ensure an upbringing for them that is in accordance with the values based on the constitutional identity and Christian culture of our country.'[8]

10.2.2 *Scholarly Works*

After 2010, as the constitutional provisions involving the terms of historical constitution and its achievements increased, the interest in their meaning has also increased among scholars, becoming an intersectional field of study between public law and constitutional history.

7 Article R(4) FL.
8 Article XVI(1) FL.

As early as 2012, some scholars criticized the National Avowal, claiming that it was too political and did not necessarily genuinely reflect the entirety of Hungarian history,[9] while others interpreted it as a new narrative of a sovereign Hungarian nation and the extract of Hungarian history.[10] While applauding the content, others asked whether the FL could provide a new value catalogue with which the polity would identify.[11] Constitutional law scholars conceptualized these provisions (on the historical constitution and its achievements) as a mere aide to constitutional interpretation, that is, emphasizing the historical approach,[12] and they expected that the CC would interpret the meaning and conceptual framework of these concepts.

There are three main challenges in determining what historical constitution and its challenges mean. One of the issues with defining these concepts, in both scholarly works and legal procedures, is that the historical constitution is a constitution of many centuries shaped by various laws, declarations, customary law and complemented by extra-legal components, such as the spirit of Hungarians/identity of Hungarians (*néplélek*) and the national genius.[13] These latter extra-legal categories used by scholars in the early twentieth century make it difficult – if not impossible – to define the historical constitution from a legal perspective.[14] This difficulty is overlooked by others who have made considerable effort to prove the raison d'étre of the term in the contemporary constitutional law as something more than an aide for constitutional interpretation – as scholarly support of the illiberal turn.[15] In this context, the historical constitution is viewed as a concept characterized by its perpetuance, which manifests in legal continuity[16] and has revolved around three components. The first is the maintenance of the feudal division of power, as 'nobles

9 Nóra Chronowski, Tímea Drinóczi and Miklós Kocsis, 'What Questions of Interpretation May be Raised by the New Hungarian Constitution?' (2012) 6 *ICL Journal* 41.

10 Péter Smuk, 'Nemzetfogalom és történeit narratíva az Alaptörvényben' (2013) *Doktori Műhelytanulmányok* 259, 292.

11 Ferenc Horkay-Hörcher, 'A nemzeti hitvallásról', in András Jakab and András Körösényi (eds.), *Alkotmányozás Magyarországon és máshol* (MTA TK Politikatudományi Intézet - Új Mandátum Kiadó, 2012), 288.

12 András Jakab, *Az Alaptörvény keletkezése és gyakorlati következményei [Genesis and practical consequences of the Fundamental Law]* (HVG-ORAC, 2011), 198.

13 See Gábor Schweitzer, A *Magyar Királyi Köztársaságtól a Magyar Köztársaságig: Közjog és tudománytörténeti tanulmányok* (Publikon Kiadó, 2017), 146, 147. He has used the works of the most distingushed professors, such as Kálmán Molnár (1881–1961) professor of public law and Andor Csizmadia (1910–1985) professor of legal history.

14 Schweitzer, A *Magyar Királyi Köztársaságtól a Magyar Köztársaságig*, 146 and 147.

15 See, e.g., István Szabó, 'Az ősi alkotmány: Történeti előzmények', in Lóránt Csink, Balázs Schanda and Zs. András Varga (eds.), A *magyar közjog alapintézményei* (Pázmány Press, 2020), Zsolt Zétényi, 'Bevezető tanulmány', in Zs Zétény (ed.), A *történeti alkotmány: Magyarország ősi alkotmánya* (Magyarországért Kulturális Egyesület, 2010).

16 An opposing view can be found in the work of the constitutional law scholar Szente. For example, Zoltán Szente, 'A historizáló alkotmányozás problémái – a történeti alkotmány és a Szent Korona az új Alaptörvényben' [Challenges of Historicizing Constitution-making: The Historical Constitution and the Holy Crown in the New Fundamental Law]' 1–3 *Közjogi Szemle* (2011) 1–13.

waived willingly of the power' and the 'former feudal representation was replaced by popular representation'.[17] The second element is the lack of rupture with the past whenever a new beginning came as opposed to what usually happened in Europe, with revolutions and new constitutions. The third component is the extension of rights, as 'no rights were withdrawn but extended to those who had not enjoyed them'.[18]

The other difficulty is connected to the appearance of the Holy Crown in the text of the FL: it 'embodies the constitutional continuity of Hungary's statehood and the unity of the nation'. Nevertheless, the doctrine of the Holy Crown, closely connected to the era of the historical constitution, held that it embodies the king, the territory of Hungary and the nobles, as described by Werbőzy in his Tripartitum.[19] In other words, the crown, usually (and in Hungary too, historically speaking) relates to monarchy as a form of state. Nevertheless, the doctrine of the Holy Crown and the idea of the historical constitution has been maintained even under different constitutional and political settings. So, historical changes after the dissolution of the Austrian–Hungarian Monarchy challenged the tenability of the doctrine of the Holy Crown and the idea of the historical constitution in situations in which there was no monarch, but the form of state was officially monarchy (1920–1945)[20] and when there was no monarchy (1946–1949)[21] and in which Hungary adopted codified constitutions, such as the communist one (1949), the liberal (substantially amended 1949 Constitution in 1989 and 1990) and the illiberal one (2011). Some constitutional scholars believe that the doctrine of the Holy Crown is simply incompatible with the European constitutional development after the transition of 1989/1990.[22] Others opine that, even if this doctrine cannot legitimate any CC decision, it could support arguments.[23]

The third challenge of interpreting the history-related FL texts is that the 'achievements' of the historical constitution must also be construed. Constitutional lawyers have been sceptical about the rationality of the provision. As the historical constitution contains many components that are nonsense (attached to the feudal state) or unacceptable (restriction of rights), the only rationale for using the term 'achievements' (of the historical constitution) could be to filter out these elements. Nevertheless, in this way, only those components will remain to be considered in

[17] Szabó, 'Az ősi alkotmány', 47 and 100.

[18] Ibid., 109.

[19] It is a collection of Hungarian customary law completed in 1514 by István Werbőczy and published in 1517. More on this in Martyn Rady, *Customary Law in Hungary: Courts, Texts, and the Tripartitum* (Oxford University Press, 2015).

[20] Between 1920 and 1945, the governor (head of state) was Miklós Horthy. It is also called the Horthy regime.

[21] The form of state of Hungary was a republic between 1946 and 1949.

[22] See e.g., Szente, 'A historizáló alkotmányozás problémái', Chronowski et al., 'What Questions of Interpretation?', 2.

[23] Lóránt Csink and Johanna Fröchlich, *Egy alkotmány margójára* (Gondolat, 2012), 131.

the constitutional interpretation, which are already compatible with modern constitutionalism and are part of the Hungarian legal system.[24] Others, however, claim that the achievements of the historical constitution embody its fundamental values, which transcend the written sources of law and can be found in customary law and, as such, are subject to interpretation. Three principles are identified: the division of power (horizontal and vertical as developed throughout the centuries), the protection of the constitution and the nation-unification role of the Holy Crown. As for the first two principles, these have been part of the constitutional text and constitutional jurisprudence since the transition – which supports the view of constitutional laws scholars. The actualization of this latter is found in that, after Trianon, the national 'togetherness' has become even more important and, after the EU accession, it helps preserve the national identity[25] – a view that explicitly appears in the jurisprudence of the CC.

10.3 THE CONTRAST

10.3.1 *Rights Expansion*

One of the results of the Hungarian revolution and the war of independence of 1848–1849 was the reform of voting rights, which also meant the expansion of the 'membership' in the Holy Crown (the manifestation of the source of power and subject to national sovereignty). Before 1848, every nobleman was part of the Holy Crown (i.e., part of the national sovereignty) and, after 1848, as reminded in the literature on the historical constitution in 2010, all citizens.[26] Both the literature and the FL, and its constitutional interpretation,[27] mention the protection of minorities, that is, nationalities, ethnicities (hereinafter nationalities), which is considered the noblest tradition of the Hungarian nation and an example of the rights expansion. This section contrasts the narrative on the expansion of rights in the field of the right to vote and protection of nationalities with the then prevailing legal, social and political circumstances and highlights that the historical constitution was not necessarily about rights expansion.

In the feudal parliament, noblemen, leaders of churches and representatives of the 'free royal cities' had the right to vote. Act V of 1848 extended the subjects of this political right according to the following criteria: male of 20/24 years old (active/passive right to vote, respectively), ownership of certain property, knowledge of the Hungarian language (for passive right to vote). This reform meant that 7.2 per cent of the population had the right to vote, which, at that time, was progress. Act XXXIII of 1874 introduced some more restrictions. The first was the ability to pay taxes

[24] E.g., Jakab, *Az Alaptörvény keletkezése és gyakorlati következményei*, 199.

[25] Szabó, 'Az ősi alkotmány', 113–116.

[26] Zétényi, 'Bevezető tanulmány', 55.

[27] National Avowal, Arts XXIX and 2 FL, 22/2016 (XII. 5) decision of the CC [65].

(those who were behind with the payment could not vote), and then it was that voting must be done verbally (until 1938). This resulted in a situation in which less than 6 per cent of the population had the right to vote, which was 5.3 per cent in 1899. Comparatively, it was very low as, in Europe, at that time, the average was 20–30 per cent. Struggles for suffrage for all started in the 1890s and the result was the Act of the People I of 1918 (during the short period of the democratic revolution after WWI). It established the right to vote for male voters of 21 years old and women of 24 years old who could read and write. The secrecy of voting was planned to be introduced and it would have meant that 50 per cent of the population had the right to vote, but this rule was never applied. Decree 5985 of 1919 of the new regime changed the law of 1918 and increased the age limit for male voters to 24 years, making, thus, 40 per cent of the population entitled to vote. Decree 2200 of 1922 and Act XXVI of 1925 increased the property and knowledge-based criteria and the age limit of women to 30 years. The percentage of the people that had the right to vote decreased to 29 per cent. Act XIX of 1938 further increased the age limit for men (to 26 years), maintained the age limit for women (30 years) and introduced certain property and knowledge-based criteria.[28]

Hungary's Act on the Equality of Nationality Rights (hereinafter: Nationalities Act) of 1868 is said to be very advanced[29] in the multinational Austro–Hungarian Monarchy at the time when the focus was the sovereign nation-state. The preamble of the Act (1868) guaranteed that all citizens of the Kingdom of Hungary (as part of the Austro–Hungarian Monarchy), regardless of their nationality, constituted politically a single nation, that is, the indivisible, unitary Hungarian nation under the constitution. It also declared that there should be no differentiation between the members of the united nation save for the official usage of the current languages and insofar as necessitated by practical considerations. The Hungarian governments did not necessarily respect this Act and, while nationalities tried to fight for their independence and rights, Hungarian politics was featured by Magyarization, which, as researches show, did not include repression or violent conflicts.[30] Nevertheless, despite the law, the use of minority languages was banished almost entirely from administration and even justice, Hungarian names for settlements were introduced and Hungarian language

[28] See e.g., Simándi Irén, *Küzdelem a nők parlamenti választójogáért Magyarországon 1848–1938* (Gondolat Kiadó, 2009).

[29] Noémi Nagy, 'Linguistic Legislation in Hungary during the Era of Dualism in Wakounig', in Marija Wakounig and Ferdinand Kühnel (eds.), *Central Europe (Re-)visited: A Multi-Perspective Approach to a Region* (LIT Verlag, 2015); Dóra Frey, 'Az Osztrák-Magyar Monarchia és a nemzetiségek – különös tekintettel a Birodalmi Tanácsban képviselt országokra' (2019) 9 *Acta Universitatis Szegediensis: forum: acta juridica et politica* 27, chrome-extension://efaidnbmnnnibpcajpcglclefindmkaj/viewer.html?pdfurl = http%3A%2F%2Facta.bibl.u-szeged.hu%2F70635%2F1%2Fjuridpol_forum_009_001_027–044.pdf&clen = 226357&chunk = true, 28-44. An overview: Szentgáli-Tóth Boldizsár and Gerő Anna, 'Az 1868-as nemzetiségi törvény és a politikai nemzet koncepciójának utólagos értékelése' (2020) 2 *Erdélyi Jogélet* 84.

[30] Frey, 'Az Osztrák-Magyar Monarchia és a nemzetiségek'.

and historical narratives dominated at schools.[31] This administrative Magyarization was slow, uneven across domains and contingent on local power dynamics,[32] but existed and was challenged.[33] Over the years, the ethnic antagonisms worsened, and there was no rising social class strong enough that could have changed the system, breaking through the fixed pattern of class, religion and regions.[34]

The 1868 Nationalities Act was discussed in the lower house of the Parliament for six days, and the opinion of the majority, that is, that there is a united Hungarian political nation and no other nationality is considered to be a nation, was adopted out of the three submitted draft laws. In the parliamentary debate,[35] both the majority and the minority opinion relied on the argument of the historical constitution to support their own claims. Several arguments supported the concept of a united nation. They referred to the principles of the historical constitution, the lack of fight of nationalities, the claim that it has always been like this, a united country was guarded by the ancestors and the sentiment that Hungarians deserve this type of nationhood. It was also reminded that a united nation was also necessary due to the national administrative law and that Hungary is a historically created unity that cannot be dissolved. They also argued that the draft law submitted by the minorities intended to dissolve this unity. Indeed, the arguments of the nationalities consisted of their sentiments and the demands of the new era. These demands required a distance from the old terms and laws and a way of thinking based on the spirit of the new age. They also used the argument of the historical constitution when highlighting that laws dating back to Saint Stephan recognized them as 'nation', these nationalities had de facto existed in the Hungarian territory until 1848, there was no political nation and the county system evidenced that Hungary had not been a country demanding a unified state.[36]

Nevertheless, the result of the debate was the mentioned Act, signalling that the liberal Hungarian elite at that time insisted on the status quo and adopted the concept of the French-type nation-state. Despite the provided rights and autonomies, the Act was not properly implemented. The unresolved minority issue is viewed as one of the main causes for the collapse of dualist Hungary.[37] Just as the history of the right to vote, it did not represent any inclusive attitude but focused on

[31] See e.g., László Marácz, 'Multilingualism in the Transleithanian part of the Austro-Hungarian Empire (1867–1918): Policy and Practice' (2012) 13 *Jezikoslovlje* 287.

[32] Ágoston Berecz, 'Top-down and Bottom-up Magyarization in Multiethnic Banat Towns under Dualist Hungary 1867–1914' (2021) 28 *European Review of History: Revue européenne d'histoire* 422.

[33] See, for instance, the Transylvanian Memorandum, which was sent to Emperor-King Franz Joseph in 1892. Leaders of the Romanians of Transylvania asked for equal ethnic rights with the Hungarians and demanded an end to persecutions and Magyarization attempts. The Memorandum met with refusal.

[34] Marácz, 'Multilingualism', 295.

[35] Based on the presentation of Noémi Nagy at the conference 'Történelem, alkotmány és identitás Magyarországon' on 18 November 2021, Budapest.

[36] A nemzetiségi törvény képiselőházi vitája, 1868. november 24–29. *Képviselőházi napló*, 1865. XI. kötet. 5-185.

[37] Marácz, 'Multilingualism', 295.

the status quo and an exclusive understanding of sovereignty, which certainly was one of the legitimate options for the decision-makers.

These examples illustrate that the expansion of rights, an important component of the historical constitution in the narratives of some contemporary authors, was, contrary to their narratives, not consistent and free from retrogression at all. There seem to be more arguments against the continuity of the historical constitution in a republican era than supporting it. Section 10.3.2 discusses the relevant jurisprudence of the CC. The CC also gives its own narrative on the historical constitution in its interpretation of the relevant provisions of the FL. This review might seem to break the previous logic of presenting continuity and rights expansion because the CC interprets and applies what is in the constitutional text, based on the content and request of the petition it receives. Nevertheless, by discussing the CC's concept of the historical constitution, along with that of the term 'constitutional identity', this section could provide important impetus for supporting the argument of this chapter, that is, constitutional narrative based on the historical constitution of Hungary is conducive to illiberalism (i.e., exclusion and inequality).

10.3.2 *Continuity*

Beyond the text of the FL, some in the literature also claims that both the historical constitution and the Holy Crown constitute legal continuity and represent the 1,000 years old history in which the FL fits.[38] A review of the documented legal change, however, proves otherwise.

The question of continuity emerged in the interwar period, during which Hungary was a monarchy without a monarch governed by the regime of the historical constitution and implied by the doctrine of the Holy Crown. After the publication of Act I of 1946 on the republican form of government, scholars agreed on the existence of continuity and considered Act I of 1946 as a written constitution,[39] which established a republic and that the new institutions of the interwar period, that is, the provisional legal order (the new parliament and the government instead of the monarch and the former parliament) were placed provisionally and beside the historical constitution.[40] It was also argued that the Holy Crown did not represent the monarchy but, from the fourteenth century, the state.[41]

[38] Szabó, 'Az ősi alkotmány'.

[39] Beér János in 1946 and Csekey István in 1947.

[40] Molnár Kálmán, 'Alkotmányos jogrendünk és a közjogi provizórium', *Pécs, Dunántúl Rt. Egyetemi Nyomda*, 1926, 9–26, referred to by Gábor Schweitzer, 'Közjogi provizórium, jogfolytonosság, új közjogi irány Az 1919/1920–1944 közötti magyarországi alkotmányjog-tudomány vázlata' [The public law provisorium, legal continuity, new directions of public law. Sketch of the Hungarian constitutional law scholarship between 1919/1920 and 1944] 1 *Közjogi Szemle* 8.

[41] Ferencz Eckhart, A *Szentkorona-eszme története* (Magyar Tudományos Akadémia, 1941) referred to by Iván Halász and Gábor Schweitzer: 'Nemzeti jelképek', in András Jakab,

Nevertheless, the Holy Crown was not included in the national symbols in 1849 and 1918 and between 1946 and 1949 – which could be viewed as a rupture with the past and looking into the future based on the new constitutional system without the Holy Crown.[42] It was obviously not mentioned in the communist constitution adopted in 1949, nor in its major amendment in 1972, the preamble of which, on the other hand, referred to the 1,000 years old history of Hungary. Beyond using the coat of arms displaying the Holy Crown in 1990 as a heraldic ornament, it was only in 2000 when the Holy Crown was brought back into the realm of law with some kind of public law function. Act I of 2000 defined it as a 'relic representing the continuity of the Hungarian statehood and independence', which 'lives in the consciousness of the nation and the traditions of Hungarian public law'.[43]

This formulation from the year 2000 seems to decide the debate on the nature of the Holy Crown by emphasizing traditions and continuity and considering it a symbol of the Hungarian statehood. It also expressively refers to the consciousness of the nation in which the Holy Crown lives. It did not consider the fact that the Holy Crown had not been used in the Hungarian public law in the past 50 years when declaring that it lives in its traditions.

These two elements (statehood and nation) also appear in the National Avowal of the FL: the Holy Crown represents the continuity of the constitutional Hungarian statehood and national unity. Nevertheless, there is no evidence about whether or not the people embraced the Holy Crown during the era of the unwritten constitution. However, what can be known is that the awareness of the population about the (communist) constitution was not high in the 1960s and 1980s. In the 1960s, the legal knowledge of the population was uncertain, especially in the field of constitutional law,[44] while in the 1980s, the content of the constitution was not really known.[45] After the transition, there have been no studies specifically surveying the awareness of the population in the field of the historical constitution or the Holy Crown.[46] This brings us to the issue of whether or not the Holy Crown represents

Miklós Könczöl, Attila Menyhárd and Gábor Sulyok (eds.), *Internetes Jogtudományi Enciklopédia (Alkotmányjog rovat)* (2020), http://ijoten.hu/szocikk/nemzeti-jelkepek, 9.

42 In the spring and summer of 1849, when Lajos Kossuth was the governor, and during the Aster Revolution (October 1918), which resulted in the first Hungarian People's Republic (1918–1919), then the Hungarian Soviet Republic (1919).

43 Act I of 2000 on the Memory of the founding of the state by Saint Stephen and the Holy Crown.

44 András Cieger, 'Alkotmányosság és hazafiság' 18 (No 11–12) *Magyar Szemle* 43.

45 Ibid.

46 Gajduschek explains why the Hungarian awareness studies have become less relevant and what methodological challenges the existing research results face and also summarizes these results. György Gajduschek, 'Empirirkus jogtudat-kutatás Magyarországon 1990 után' (2017) 13 *Iustum Aequum Salutare* 55. Similarly see István H. Szilágyi, 'Jogtudat-kutatások a magyar jogszociológiában a rendszerváltást követően I' (2021) 17 *Iustum Aequum Salutare* 41. There are controversial results as well. In a survey on the awareness of the content of the constitution among young people (18–19 years old), this awareness is quite low (12 per cent in 1998).

statehood and independence to the extent that the FL creates a constitutional institution (historical constitution) and a basis in which our identity is rooted. In the efforts of finding some clarity in this regard, it is worth referring to the explanatory memorandum of Act I of 1920. The Act is about restoring constitutionalism and the provisional arrangement of the state sovereignty, and, as explained in its preamble, it was adopted by the new parliament as the sole legal representative of the national sovereignty (Article 2). The preamble recalls that the exercise of the power of the monarch had ceased to exist on 13 November 1918 and that the parliament elected in 1910 also ceased to function on the very same day. Therefore, the exercise of state sovereignty became impossible within the ordinary framework of the (historical) constitution. As opposed to this observation of the preamble, the Act itself refers to the constitution, based on which the new parliament is entitled to determine the other ways of exercise of the state power (Articles 1 and 9). The Act created the position of a popularly elected governor (Article 12), the sole representative of the executive power until the question of the head of state would finally be decided. The governor has the same power as the monarch did with certain restrictions (Article 13).

The explanatory memorandum explains that, throughout Hungarian history, whenever necessary, the provisional exercise of power was generally vested in one person, starting from the thirteenth century, due to the many governors who had held power. This practice was followed by Act LVII of 1921 on the dethronement of IV Charles[47] and Act XIX of 1937 on the expansion of the governor's power and its election.[48]

These rules do not contradict the existence of the doctrine of the Holy Crown, as a symbol of a monarchy and the historical constitution in the interwar period. The form of state of this time was 'monarchy without a monarch', where the role of the monarch was substituted by a governor, as earlier, when it had been necessary. Nevertheless, it can also be argued that Governor Miklós Horthy substituted the king only until the adoption of the Act on dethronement (1921) and, after that, he governed the country in its own right. Notwithstanding the difference in opinions, the authors place the end of the historical constitution and the applicability of the doctrine of the Holy Crown in a period where Hungary did not have a written constitution and an explicit republican form of government. Act I of 1946 established a republic, without mentioning the interwar period. Its preamble focuses on the end

In another study, from 1998, on the same subject matter, the awareness is around 70 per cent (there were more questions), and yet, H. Szilágyi highlights that the awareness about the rules of the constitution was low. H. Szilágyi, ibid., 48, 52–53.

47 It maintained the monarchy, postponed the decision on the person of the following monarch and ordered the ministry to make recommendations in this regard at an appropriate time.

48 It reiterated the provisional character of Act I of 1920 and acknowledged that the past experiences since 1920 and the international situation warned that maintaining the position of the governor for an undetermined time might have been necessary.

of the monarchy in 1918 and the popular sovereignty, which belonged to the people that decided on the republican form of state in 1946. All of these seem to support the argument claiming that the doctrine of the Holy Crown is linked to the monarchy as a form of state and, along with the historical constitution, was dismissed by the subsequent power holders, that is, the subject of popular sovereignty in 1946, at the latest.[49] It was also rejected by the first written and communist constitution, which advocated for the understanding of law and society from the perspective of the Soviet Union. The Holy Crown as a symbol was resurrected as a part of the coat of arms in 1990, and in 2000 it was given more symbolic importance – even public law relevance. The controversy emerged when it was inserted into the National Avowal of the FL, which, due to Article R), became an applicable constitutional provision. It seems that the Holy Crown is intrinsically interlinked to the era of the unwritten, historical constitution, which represents backward-looking constitutionalism.

10.3.3 *The Jurisprudence of the CC*

The CC started applying and interpreting the history-related FL provisions since 2012.[50] It did so partly and mostly at the beginning of the 2010s, as constitutional law scholars have predicted, as suggested by advocates of the legal tenability of the concept of historical constitution. It has also coincided with the amendments to the FL. Accordingly, two phases of the jurisprudence of the CC on the historical constitution can be identified. The first phase features controversies that emerged within the body concerning the conceptualization of the term of the 'achievements of the historical constitution' and the interpretation of Article R). The second phase brought about the connection of the constitutional identity and the historical constitution emphasizing it 'nation-uniting power'.

The identification of what 'achievements' are have been surrounded by debates within the CC and the application of Article R) as an interpretation rule has been considered underdeveloped by judges in their concurring and dissenting opinions.[51] Nevertheless, during the period of 2012–2020, the CC identified, for instance, the

[49] I have used 'at the latest' as there are diverging opinions on the end of the period of the historical constitution. From one perspective, it could have ended by Act I of 1920 because it declared the parliament as a subject of sovereignty, which in itself contradicts the doctrine of the Holy Crown, which is postulated as a source of power and the subject of national sovereignty. In this context, the historical constitution and the Holy Crown can only be interpreted within the period of the Hungarian monarchy, particularly during the feudal years. I am grateful to Gábor Schweitzer for drawing my attention to this.

[50] The term of 'achievements of the historical constitution', which 'We respect' (National Avowal), Article R), which requires that the FL be interpreted according to these achievements and the provision of 'identity rooted in the historical constitution', after they appeared in the text.

[51] These critics and controversies appear in concurring and dissenting opinions. See e.g., Imre Juhász, dissenting opinion to 13/2013 (VI. 17) decision of the CC; Béla Pokol, concurring opinion to 28/2013 (X. 9) decision of the CC; Imre Juhász, dissenting opinion to 28/2013 (X. 9)

following achievements of the historical constitution:[52] judicial independence, separation of the judiciary and administration, administrative judiciary and justice, freedom of media, historical antecedents of disciplinary accountability of judges, freedom of religion and autonomy of churches, the law-making power of local governments.[53] Reviewing the jurisprudence of the CC on the topic, it was concluded in both 2016 and 2020[54] that the CC identifies laws that are in harmony with the FL as achievements of the historical constitution and simply does not refer to Article R) when something would not be in harmony with the FL. In this context, however, Article R), as an interpretation rule, is useless.[55] The CC does not interpret the FL in the light of/in accordance with the 'achievements of the historical constitution', as would be required by Article R), but select the (ineffective) rules of the historical constitution in order to establish that its rule is in harmony with the FL.[56] The vague text of the FL in this respect and the uncertainty of the constitutional terms do not serve legal certainty and the rule of law but provide an opportunity for arbitrary interpretation and abusive informal constitutional amendment.

Besides continuing this practice,[57] in the second phase, after it introduced the term of constitutional identity into the Hungarian constitutional jurisprudence in its first identity decision in 2016, the CC linked the term 'historical constitution' with history, identity and sovereignty that could be abusively[58] used against the collective entity to which Hungary belongs (i.e., the EU).

Nevertheless, the CC has not activated the concept of constitutional identity against any EU measures but used it to stall some politically sensitive constitutional reviews.[59] The concept of the historical constitution, however, has been

decision of the CC, collected by Imre Vörös, 'A történeti alkotmány az Alkotmánybíróság gyakorlatában' (2016) 4 *Közjogi Szemle* 44, 45.

[52] Until 2016: Vörös, 'A történeti alkotmány', 44–46.

[53] 33/2012 (VII.7), 2/2016 (II.8), 17/2015 (VI.5), 34/2017 (XII.17), 6/2013 (III.1), 29/2015 (X.2) decision of the CC, respectively. Some other issues that could hardly be connected to the historical constitution were also identified as its achievement, such as e.g., unfairness of the consumer loan agreements, in 3089/2016. (V.12) decision of the CC. Vörös, 'A történeti alkotmány', 46.

[54] Vörös, 'A történeti alkotmány'; and Anna Gera, 'Történeti alkotmányunk vívmányai az Alaptörvény speciális alkotmányos rendszerében', 6 *MTA Law Working Papers* (2021), https://jog.tk.hu/mtalwp/torteneti-alkotmanyunk-vivmanyai-az-alaptorveny-specialis-alkotmanyos-rendszereben, 21.

[55] It has been predicted by, e.g., Jakab, *Az Alaptörvény keletkezése és gyakorlati következményei*, 199.

[56] Vörös, 'A történeti alkotmány', 55.

[57] Gera, 'Történeti alkotmányunk', 21.

[58] Tímea Drinóczi and Pietro Faraguna, 'The European Constitutional Identity of the EU as a Counterbalance for Unconstitutional Constitutional Identities of the Member States'. In J. de Poorter, G. van der Schyff, M. Stremler, M. De Visser, I. Leitjen and C. van Oirsouw (eds.), *European Yearbook of Constitutional Law 2022* (T. M. C. Asser Press, 2023); Julian Scholtes, 'Abusive Constitutional Identity' (2021) 22 *German Law Journal* 534.

[59] Tímea Drinóczi, 'Illiberal Constitutional Courts and the Danger They Pose' (2022) (No 8) *Państwo i Prawo* 3, 4–5.

continuously employed. In 2019, a dissenting opinion of Béla Pokol to CC decision 22/2019 (VII. 05) emphasized the difference between the Western and the Hungarian constitutional developments of the eighteenth century. It explained that the Western model used the idea of constitutionalism against the status quo. As opposed to this, the emergence of the idea of historical constitutionalism in the 1850s in Hungary was not meant to be in opposition to the status quo but against integration into the Habsburg Empire. National independence and the defence of the country's own statehood were at the centre of the reference to the historical constitution. Therefore, goes the argument of the judge of the CC, the achievements of the historical constitution should not be used as 'historical anecdotes justifying the interpretation of the constitutional rules based on the contemporary democracy' but in the sense mentioned: against integration into an empire.

This message has not gone unnoticed. It resurfaced in CC decision 32/2021 (XII. 20), which was initiated on behalf of the Government seeking an explicit ruling on the possibility of (non-)application of certain EU measures. It wanted a similar decision to that of the Polish Constitutional Tribunal challenging the primacy of EU law and its interpretation by the CJEU,[60] which it welcomed in its governmental decision 1712/2021 (X. 9). This decision is entitled 'on the Hungarian opinion be represented in connection to the ruling of the Constitutional Tribunal of the Polish Republic on the relationship between national law and the EU law' and established the following: First, that the referred decision of the Polish Constitutional Tribunal 'was triggered by the bad practice of the European Union institutions, which does not take into account the principle of the delegation of powers, and by the stealthy expansion of powers without amending the basic treaties of the European Union, tries to take away powers from the Member States that the Member States never transferred to the European Union'. Second, that 'the primacy of EU law can only exist in those areas where the European Union has competence, the framework of which is laid down in the basic treaties of the European Union'. Third, that EU institutions 'are obliged to respect the national identity of the member states, which is an inseparable part of their basic political and constitutional system', while, also 'the law-enforcement bodies of the Member States – especially the constitutional courts and courts – are also entitled to examine the scope and limits of the European Union powers'.

In this case of the CC in 2021, interpretation of the FL was sought because, in the view of the petitioner, the implementation of a judgment of the CJEU,[61] because of

[60] Blog symposium on the Polish Constitutional Tribunal decision from October 2021 on the relationship between national and EU law, www.iconnectblog.com/tag/poland/

[61] CJEU, Judgment of 17 December 2020, Case C-808/18, *Commission v Hungary*, ECLI:EU:C:2020:1029. The CJEU found that Hungary's legislation on the rules and practices in the transit zones situated at the Serbian–Hungarian border was contrary to EU law; and identified breaches of provisions of the Asylum Procedures Directive (2013/32/EU), the Reception Conditions Directive (2013/33/EU) and the Return Directive (2008/115/EC).

the ineffective EU measures, might lead to a foreign national illegally staying in Hungary for an indefinite period of time and thus becoming part of the Hungarian population. This would violate Hungary's sovereignty and identity, which are based on its historical constitution. The CC interpreted the FL as follows: where the joint exercise of competences is incomplete, Hungary, due to the presumption of reserved sovereignty, can legislate until the EU institutions take measures necessary to ensure the effectiveness of the joint exercise of competences.

To achieve this result, the CC, among others, conducted the 'fundamental rights review' and the 'identity review'. The CC argued that an incomplete joint exercise of competences could result in an infringement of the right of the identity of people living in Hungary. Therefore, the state must protect this right. Reading the decision, it becomes clear that the 'self-identity of people' is a newly created constitutional right. It finds its origin in a determinism approach that denies individualism and autonomy and individual and social/cultural change, and yet the CC links it to the right to human dignity. The CC stated that a man is born into a given social environment, which can be defined as the traditional social environment, especially through its ethnic, linguistic, cultural and religious determinants. These circumstances create natural ties, determined by birth, which shape the identity of community members and these circumstances cannot or hardly can be changed by the individual, and form an integral part of the human quality that stems from human dignity.[62]

Under the identity review, the CC, while recalling the text of the FL and Hungarian history, noted that Hungary has a European identity (National Avowal) and realized that the terms constitutional identity of Hungary and national (state) sovereignty intertwine. It explained, first, that constitutional identity manifests itself primarily through a sovereign act, adopting the constitution.[63] Second, it clarified that taking into account Hungary's historical struggles, the aspiration to safeguard the country's sovereign decision-making powers is itself part of the country's national identity and, through its recognition by the FL, of its constitutional identity as well.[64] It also highlighted that the main features of State sovereignty recognized in international law are closely linked to Hungary's constitutional identity due to the historical characteristics of our country.[65] Against this background, the CC stated that the inalienable right of Hungary to determine its territorial unity, population, the form of government and state structure (Article E(2)) forms part of its constitutional identity.

The political intentions of the Hungarian Government and the case-law of the CC are deeply interconnected in this case, providing the bases for one another and, thus, challenging political liberalism in its sense of constraints and respect for the

[62] CC decision 32/2021 (XII. 20), [34].
[63] CC decision 32/2021 (XII. 20), [99].
[64] Ibid.
[65] Ibid.

rule of law. The CC's 2021 decision did not directly confront the mainstream approach of national constitutional courts and was quite restrained if compared, for instance, to the jurisprudence of the Polish and the Romanian constitutional courts,[66] which challenged the constitutionality of some EU measures, including CJEU rulings. On the other hand, first, this stance also allowed the Government to declare that the CC accepted its position.[67] Second, the CC not only gave a blanket authorization to the Executive but also implemented what the Government already laid down in its abovementioned decision 1712/2021 (X. 9), only two months before the delivery of the CC's ruling. This decision of the Government was published on 9 October 2021, while the CC's judgment was delivered on 20 December 2021.

10.4 CONCLUSION

This chapter claims that the narrative of the Hungarian historical constitution as a constitutional concept is conducive to illiberalism. It relies on, first, the contemporary narratives of continuity and rights expansion, which are the two most important constitutive components of the historical constitution. These narratives then have been contrasted with legal measures introduced in the second part of the nineteenth and the first half of the twentieth centuries and the changes in the form of government until 1949. Second, it considers the jurisprudence of the CC on linking two newly emerged concepts of the Hungarian constitutional law: the historical constitution and constitutional identity.

In connection to the narrative on the expansion of the right, as explored through the examples of the right to vote and the right of nationalities, it was found that neither of them represented any inclusive attitude. However, their regulation and, thus, the will of the political decision-maker, focused on maintaining the status quo and expressed an exclusive understanding of sovereignty. It should be noted that this understanding, not including the right to vote issues, certainly was one of the legitimate options open for them at that time.

It could be seen that continuity refers to the permanence of the historical constitution and implicitly its fundamental constituent element, the Holy Crown. The idea of the historical constitution, including the doctrine of the Holy Crown, was disrupted already in 1946. The lawmaker of the interwar period considered the governor as a substitute for the king; the form of state was a monarchy without a monarch. Even if statehood has continuously existed, it does not necessarily mean that its historical symbol, as a public law institution (the Holy Crown), needs to exist as well. In fact, it was not present in the public law arena after the end of WWII for decades. Therefore, no continuity can be claimed in which the FL could fit.

66 www.ccr.ro/wp-content/uploads/2021/07/Decizie_390_2021_EN.pdf.

67 Noémi Mrav, 'Orbán: az Alkotmánybíróság szerint a magyaroknak joguk van saját hazájukhoz', *Euronews*, https://hu.euronews.com/2021/12/20/orban-az-alkotmanybirosag-szerint-a-magyaroknak-joguk-van-sajat-hazajukhoz.

In relation to the jurisprudence of the CC, two main points deserve to be made. The first is that the CC cannot really and meaningfully apply the relevant historical constitution-related provisions of the FL. As research shows, it mostly selects the (ineffective) rules of the historical constitution to establish that this rule is in harmony with the FL but does not make any genuine interpretation in this regard.

The second is that, when it does apply it (more 'meaningfully'), due to the text of the FL, the CC necessarily links the term historical constitution with history, constitutional identity and sovereignty. This interpretation then could potentially be used against the collective entity to which Hungary belongs (i.e., the EU). Finally, it seems now that the overall finality of introducing the historical constitution and its achievements into the FL, and its subsequent linking to the concept of constitutional identity, was to use it for securing the traditional Westfalian understanding of ethnic-national sovereignty, mainly against EU obligations. It does not seem to offer, neither in the practice nor in the text of the CC rulings, anything that resembles inclusion, protection of rights, unity in diversity, constitutional dialogue and collaboration or a liberal approach towards constitutionalism and democracy. Moreover, it seems to be relying on one of the narratives of the concept of the 'historical constitution', which asserts that its main focus has always been the defence of statehood against 'empires'.

Thus, the historical constitution has been used by political and constitutional actors to jointly oppose liberal values making this constitutional concept conducive to illiberalism.

11

Estonians' European Imaginaries

The Soviet and Pre-Soviet Legacy

Epp Annus

11.1 INTRODUCTION: FROM THE WEST OF THE EAST, TO THE EAST OF THE WEST

On 12 June 1992, Edgar Savisaar, by then already the former head of Estonia's 1990–1992 transitional government,[1] gave a speech entitled *Eesti – Euroopa – maailm: geopoliitiline etüüd* [*Estonia – Europe – The World: A Geopolitical étude*].[2] Savisaar opens his talk by posing Estonia's integration to Europe as an 'inescapable imperative'. 'Our geopolitical situation over the last year has changed substantially', explains Savisaar.

> We used to be the Western part of the East-European zone of influence ('sovetskii zapad'), now we are the Eastern part of the West-European zone of influence. Until 1991, in the Soviet Union, the Baltics were the generators of ideas, the explorers of new paths, leaders at the fore. . . . Now we are obliged to accommodate ourselves to our new position as ones who are lagging behind.[3]

This research was supported by the grant 'Memory and Environment: The Intersection of Fast and Slow Violence in Transnational European Literature' of the Estonian Ministry of Education and Research (PRG2592).

1 Edgar Savisaar was in power until January 1992, when he was forced to step down due to popular dissatisfaction with his government's decision to declare a state of emergency and to give government special rights for fighting the devastating economic situation. His political career began in 1987, when he, Siim Kallas, Tiit Made and Mikk Titma came up with a proposal for Estonia's economic self-management, an initiative that became one of the major political and economic movements during the Perestroika era. Savisaar remained among Estonia's leading politicians for another thirty years.

2 The text of this speech, presented at the third meeting of the *Tuleviku Eesti Kongress* [The Congress of Future Estonia], was published in the November issue of the leading cultural journal *Vikerkaar.*

3 Edgar Savisaar, 'Eesti – Euroopa – maailm: geopoliitiline etüüd' (1992) *Vikerkaar* 53. Savisaar names Arno Köörna, Kalev Kukk, Kersten Saar and Erik Terk as participating in working out the ideas and hypotheses provided in the speech – in an academic sense, functioning as co-authors.

It is hardly surprising that economists and politicians of the 'times of transition' thought of Estonia's new geopolitical position and Estonia's aims and possibilities in relation to the recent past of the Soviet era. Savisaar's juxtaposition between Soviet Estonia ('a generator of ideas') and the newly independent Estonia (which is 'lagging behind') is greatly simplifying,[4] yet it is hard to disagree with his basic observation of Estonia's substantially changed geopolitical position – from the West of the Soviet Union to the East of Europe. Like many others before and since, Savisaar links 'the East' with passivity and 'the West' with leadership, as if this combination was a geopolitical inevitability rather than a cultural construct.

This chapter is interested in the ways that Estonia's self-perception has changed in relation to Estonians' European imaginaries. More specifically, the focus is on co-articulating the 'Soviet question' in relation to the 'European question': in what ways did the decades of Soviet rule impact the understanding of Europe and Europeanness in Estonian national imaginaries? In such an analysis, different factors have to be taken into account: the understanding of Europeanness before the Soviet era; the matter of the Soviet colonial matrix of power; changes within the USSR over the decades in question; the long-rooted orientalization of Eastern Europe in West-European imaginaries; and the role of Soviet state-promoted ideologies on local cultural imaginaries. The 'Soviet question', as this exploration will show, was never solely a question about the Soviet impact, but rather about how the intertwining of Soviet era sociopolitical realities with pre-Soviet value-systems produced complex and to some extent competing geographies of belonging.

In order to address this complex set of problems, it is useful to proceed from a *multi-scalar understanding of social phenomena*. From this perspective, Estonia's geopolitical 'relocation' from the Soviet West to the European East, occasioned by the re-establishment of the Estonian republic, can be articulated as a shift in the geopolitical scale-system. In more general terms, attention to scale as a 'tool for bounding space at different geographical resolutions'[5] enables us to perceive historical conditions as complexly multiscalar. A multiscalar approach reveals how meaning-making unfolds through interaction across different scales of sociopolitical

4 Politicians often have little incentive to consider more than a short-term perspective on historical developments. The relative passivity of Estonia in relation to 'old Europe' must indeed have felt like a substantial change compared to Estonia's position in the perestroika-era Soviet Union. In the late 1940s and early 1950s, however, the language of 'lagging behind' was used in describing the relationship of the Baltic states to the 'older' parts of the Soviet Union and especially to Russia; throughout the Soviet decades, the Russians assigned themselves the title of the leading nation. In the perestroika-era discussions in the Baltics, it was precisely the inability to make local decisions locally that was often foregrounded as a major problem that needed reform. For details, see Epp Annus, 'The Colonizer's Day Off: Colonial Subjectivities in the Soviet-Era Baltics', in Monika Albrecht (ed.), *Postcolonialism Cross-Examined: Multidirectional Perspectives on Imperial and Colonial Pasts and Neocolonial Present* (Routledge, 2020).

5 Andrew Herod and Melissa W. Wright, 'Placing Scale: An Introduction', in Andrew Herod and Melissa W. Wright (eds.), *Geographies of Power: Placing Scale* (Blackwell, 2002), 6.

realities and imaginaries, and how in the Soviet-era Estonian SSR, local, regional and global scales formed complex and dynamic systems of inter-dependency.

The collapse of the Soviet Union and the re-establishment of the Estonian Republic brought about substantial changes at all levels of social and political existence. During the decades of the Estonian SSR, the general category of 'the West' (not 'Europe') had provided a cultural counterpoint to 'Sovietness', and the scale of Europeanness was significantly deactivated. At the same time, analysis does reveal the hazy category of a tacit, internalized Europeanness, something perceivable mostly in contrast with certain imaginaries of Russianness. This tacit Europeanness included class and cultural competency and knowledge of European cultural traditions, yet it was only weakly (if at all) connected to then-current cultural developments in Europe. It lacked a dialogical dimension. In the early post-Soviet years, the newly rescaled relationship to Europe relied on longstanding imaginaries, yet it also – as Edgar Savisaar's 1992 speech attests – went through the shock of Estonia 'becoming the East'. The new situation (re)activated the concept of Europe as an imperative category and a point of reference for both political and cultural frameworks.

This chapter will first articulate the theoretical framework of cultural imaginaries and multiscalar thinking and then proceed to analyse the scalar cultural logic of the Soviet era, with a focus on the 'question of Europe'. The last section will summarize the consequences following from the re-establishment of Estonian independence. The complexities of the Soviet decades are, of course, considerable; the present essay will concentrate on the late Soviet period, from the 1960s to the mid-1980s. The chapter will focus on the Estonian-speaking cultural zone: while such a choice is necessitated by the scarcity of data concerning European imaginaries among other population groups in Soviet and early post-Soviet Estonia, it also conveys the logic of the present project. By the 2020s, Russophone populations have become to a significant extent integrated within Estonia's political and cultural sphere, yet, during the early post-Soviet period, when Estonia's policies of integration with Europe were formulated, Russophone populations participated in this process only marginally.

11.2 THEORETICAL FRAMEWORK: CULTURAL IMAGINARIES AND THEIR ROLE IN IDENTITY-PRODUCTION

To understand sociocultural processes during periods of (semi-)authoritarian rule, the *distinction between state policies and cultural imaginaries* helps to avoid simplifying arguments about mass-level 'ideological brain-washing' or an organized state-production of certain kinds of personality-types, leading to uncritical categorizations such as *homo sovieticus*.[6] State ideology and state policies are one factor, but not the

[6] For a critique of the label '*homo sovieticus*', see Gulnaz Sharafutdinova, 'Was There a "Simple Soviet" Person? Debating the Politics and Sociology of "Homo Sovieticus"' (2019) 78 *Slavic Review* 173.

only factor, contributing to people's views and behaviours – while this premise is taken for granted in analyses of democratic societies, it is too often overlooked in writings about the former Socialist bloc. Soviet rule was firmly established in the Baltics only at the end of the 1940s[7] and its heyday lasted barely forty years. During these decades, people's thoughts and value-systems continued to include ideas, values and beliefs from the pre-Soviet era. These became mixed with state-imposed ideologies and were additionally impacted by a large variety of images and narratives from cultural zones beyond the Soviet sphere – existentialist writings by Albert Camus were widely read, popular North-American TV serials (*Dallas*, for example) were available in northern Estonia by way of Finnish broadcasting and Eastern religious thought and global environmental discussions made their mark. The notion of 'cultural imaginaries' is useful in keeping a distinction between the ideological networks of institutionalized power and the popular circulation of ideas. This distinction is, of course, partial, as both are hazy and shifting categories which necessarily also influence each other. Nevertheless, identifiable kernels remain: a canonical speech by Lenin and the textbook of the Communist Party share little in common with Beatles' songs, Disney comics, nineteenth-century Estonian patriotic poetry and a grandmother's stories about life in the times of an independent Estonia – but they all circulated and comingled together in the Estonian cultural space.

I use the term 'cultural imaginaries' to designate diverse, multiscalar, hazy, ever-changing sets of images, ideas, and values that are accepted by the general population in any given period and thus form a tacit self-knowledge of that society. In this field, communal identity is produced metonymically, foregrounding certain parts at the expense of others – not everyone's voice is heard at every moment.[8] Us–them figurations function as important formal categories that condition cultural imaginaries – thus one of the questions in this investigation is whether and under what conditions Europe was considered as 'us'. Imaginaries form thematic clusters, which occasionally get condensed into core images that attain symbolic value and start to function metaphorically. Such core images become kernels for the signification of national identity – in Estonia, these have included the pillars of Tartu University,

7 In the Estonian SSR, the first post-war years are considered the 'post-Estonian period'. The mass deportations of 1949 and the eighth plenum of the Central Committee of the Estonian C (b)P in 1950 designate the end of the 'post-Estonian period' and the firm establishment of Soviet rule. Tiiu Kreegipuu, 'Eesti kultuurielu sovetiseerimine: Nõukogude kultuuripoliitika eesmärgid ja institutsionaalne raamistik aastatel 1944–1954' in Tõnu Tannberg (ed.), *Eesti NSV aastatel 1940–1953: sovetiseerimise mehhanismid ja tagajärjed Nõukogude Liidu ja Ida-Euroopa arengute kontekstis. Eesti Ajalooarhiivi Toimetised* 15 (22) (Eesti Ajalooarhiiv, 2007), 356–358. Notably, after Stalin died in March 1953, the system started to ease its grip. While the late 1960s saw a new tightening of regime control, from 1986 (in Estonia, from 1987) the Soviet regime once again started to loosen its grip – and never recovered it again before the collapse of the whole system.

8 Epp Annus, 'A Post-Soviet Eco-Digital Nation? Metonymic Processes of Nation-Building and Estonia's High-Tech Dreams in the 2010s' (2022) 36 *East European Politics and Societies* 399.

the medieval towers of Tallinn, junipers on the island of Saaremaa, Haapsalu castle, imagery from nineteenth-century romantic poetry and much more. Notably, these core images have historic depth – they carry the sense of 'having been there' for centuries, if not for thousands of years. Presentist imaginaries about social existence in any given era are bound together with a pre-existing fabric of interconnected values, ideas and images.

The concept of cultural imaginaries is related to Charles Taylor's concept of the 'social imaginary', which Taylor articulated as 'the ways people imagine their social existence, how they fit together with others, how things go on between them and their fellows, the expectations that are normally met, and the deeper normative notions and images that underlie these expectations'.[9] Cultural and social imaginaries are to a significant extent overlapping concepts and the 'political imaginary' – including 'constitutional imaginary' – belongs to the same set. For Taylor, 'social imaginary' describes the common ground of a particular moment in the existence of a society; as Jiří Přibáň notes, this concept puts an emphasis on 'the symbolic system of images and normative self-descriptions of society as the moral and meaningful unit'.[10] My own use of 'cultural imaginaries' includes *both* the present-era social and political imaginaries in a given culture *and* an emphasis on cultural continuity; this term also allows scholars to take account of the role of cultural artefacts – in architecture, visual arts, literature, film – in shaping and preserving shared imaginaries. I have elsewhere articulated the threefold temporality of cultural imaginaries: 'Cultural imaginaries consist of the shared images and narratives of the past, patterns of behavior for the present, and visions for the national future that together shape the self-conception of the community.'[11] In historical terms, the logic of shared imaginaries reflects larger global processes of growing diversification: over the last decades, the role of nationally shared imaginaries has shrunk substantially yet in the Soviet era, and during the first post-Soviet decade, their role was considerable.

Accessing something that is not fixed and not even fully articulated in a given culture will, of course, pose a challenge for scholars. Cultural imaginaries can be traced in life stories, diaries, memoirs and through performing interviews – all of which raise questions about the unreliability of memory, selective remembering techniques and narrative strategies. The lack of 'eventness' of the shared cultural common ground poses additional problems: the common cultural elements might be taken for granted to such an extent that they are not thematized in life stories. Media, fiction and film thus become valuable gateways to era-specific imaginaries, partly due to the sheer volume of such sources, which makes it possible to detect repeating patterns. However, reliable research into era-specific imaginaries is

9 Charles Taylor, *Modern Social Imaginaries* (Duke University Press, 2004), 23.

10 Jiří Přibáň, 'Constitutional Imaginaries and Legitimation: On Potentia, Potestas, and Auctoritas in Societal Constitutionalism' (2018) 45 *Journal of Law and Society* S30, S37.

11 Epp Annus, *Soviet Postcolonial Studies: A View from the Western Borderlands* (Routledge, 2018), 173.

perhaps best achieved through comparative methods which combine and compare the aforementioned sources.

Cultural imaginaries – like any other cultural phenomenon – can be analysed at different levels of generalization and focus. Imaginaries can be analysed across *different scales* – we might talk of imaginaries with a transnational spread or focus on national imaginaries, imaginaries that can typically be found within a nation-state. *National imaginaries* may well internalize transcultural ideas and practices – and reimagine them as specific to a given national culture.

In analysing the constitution of shared imaginaries, a pluriscalar approach allows us to observe the multiplicity of processes involved in meaning-making. Section 11.3 will offer a short introduction to scalar analysis and then delineate the basic outline of this threefold cultural logic, in order to then locate the European imaginaries within this network of constitutive power-relations.

11.3 PLURISCALARITY IN THE SOCIOPOLITICAL CONTEXT OF THE SOVIET UNION AS THE GROUND FOR EUROPEAN IMAGINARIES

In principle, there are countless ways to scale reality: in world-systems theory, the global world functions as the dominant scale; in phenomenological approaches, the human body and its experience provides the primary access to the world. Political geographers have held debates about the ontological status of scales, asking if scale is 'a material thing' or else an arbitrary, socially produced 'mental device which allows us to make sense of our existence'.[12] Scale-systems have been envisioned in different ways, as forming nested systems, or concentric ones, or ladder-type hierarchies or, following Bruno Latour, as networks without clear structure and subordinations.[13] A 'trilogy of geographical scales' is often used: a three-scale analysis distinguishes between international or global, national or state-scale and intra-national scales.[14]

In sociohistorical analyses, the nation-state or a particular region is often taken as the central focus, leading to classification of scales as 'interior' and 'exterior' with respect to the nation-state.[15] For a nation-state, the state-level forms the 'here and now' of the world, with other layers forming hierarchical constellations and standing in relation to this primary ground. Edgar Savisaar's 1992 speech, introduced at the start of this chapter,

[12] Herod and Wright, 'Placing Scale: An Introduction', 5.

[13] Andrew Herod, *Scale* (Routledge, 2010) 15, 48–52.

[14] Colin Flint and Peter J. Taylor, *Political Geography: World-Economy, Nation-State and Locality* (Routledge, 2018), 35.

[15] Lauristin and Vihalemm explain such an agenda: 'When speaking of "external factors", we mean those influences emanating from the presence of international, intersocietal and intercultural forces in a given society, whereas "internal factors" refers to the mutual interrelations of values and social structure (social classes, ethnic groups, generations, gender groups, etc.) as they are institutionalized in a given society.' Marju Lauristin and Peeter Vihalemm, 'The Political Agenda during Different Periods of Estonian Transformation: External and Internal Factors' (2009) 40 *Journal of Baltic Studies* 1, 2.

chose an international relations approach, in which three basic scales – Estonia, Europe and the world – were used to analyse smaller national and regional units, including different European countries, the Baltic states, Russia, China and more.

For the present purposes it is necessary to distinguish between cultural imaginaries and sociopolitical conditions. While scalar hierarchies tend to be dominated by sociopolitical facts (such as belonging to a union of states of being a part of an empire), cultural imaginaries question and complicate such sociopolitical realities and create alternative geographies of belonging. Our questions include: to what extent were European imaginaries in the Soviet era tied to pre-existing culture-specific imaginaries and to what extent did they reflect specific sociopolitical conditions? Which scales become foregrounded and which ones recede? How do scalar hierarchies organize the cultural distribution of meanings and values? Even when one limits the main focus to just a single scale – the nation-scale and its European imaginaries in the present case – this scale assumes its full meaning only in the context of the other scalar hierarchies of the era.

11.3.1 *Tensions and Autonomies: The All-USSR Scale versus the SSR Scale*

In the Soviet Union, tensions frequently arose between the interests of the central governing bodies and those of non-Russian republics. The *all-Union (the USSR-level) scale* foregrounded the USSR as a whole, but also singled out the capital city Moscow and the city of Leningrad as of privileged importance, as these housed major institutional headquarters and other ideologically crucial centres, and also fulfilled the function of showcasing Soviet life. From an all-Soviet perspective, non-Russian republic-levels[16] and lower-level scales (regional units) served to implement all-Soviet aims and to accommodate all-Union enterprises. In a centrally regulated economy, all localities fed into the all-Union economic system.[17] The all-Union scale as such consisted of a paradox: if it existed only as a sum of all republics, yet did not represent the interests of the republics, then what interests did it represent? What looks like the paradox of an empty signifier was in actuality a colonial-style system of power occasionally tempered by a socialist reticence with respect to extreme forms of exploitation.[18]

[16] The all-Union scale was in an ambiguous relation to the Russian SFSR: in some respects, the two scales merged, as the capital of the Russian SFSR was also the capital of the USSR, a separate Communist Party did not exist in the RSFSR until 1990, and the Russian nation was undoubtedly the ideological leader in the USSR. Even though in terms of geopolitical scalarity the RSFSR was a separate entity *within* the USSR, among Russians, the imaginary of the Soviet Union as one great homeland was widely internalized – a view that has led Russia to its present-day 'imperial hangover' and to new military annexations in the years after the collapse of the USSR.

[17] Some shorter periods, however, allowed for greater economic autonomy.

[18] Concerning the colonial matrix of power within the Soviet Union, see Annus, Soviet Postcolonial Studies; Epp Annus (ed.), *Coloniality, Nationality, Modernity: A Postcolonial View on Baltic Cultures under Soviet Rule* (Routledge, 2018).

At the *scale of the Estonian SSR*, local leadership would make an effort to foreground republic-level interests over the Union-scale, but local leaders were under Union-level supervision and had to constantly check their decision-making against the written and unwritten expectations of the centre.[19] Moreover, in economic terms, within the territory of the republics, one had to deal with all-Union and mixed union-republic level industries, where in both cases the republic-level leaders had little sway.[20] This created a typical colonial situation, where locals suffered the ecological consequences of industries over which they had little or no control. Similarly, the republics quartered all-Union military units and border guards, which, again, were beyond the jurisdiction of local decision-making. Thus, the republic scale *was not quite republic level* – rather, it was overwritten by the all-Union matrix of power. Notably, there were whole towns that belonged to the Union-level and were closed to visitors without special permission – Sillamäe (with its uranium-processing plant) and Paldiski (a military town), for example, were effectively non-Estonian sites within Estonia. At both the SSR-level and the USSR-level scaled systems, a clear internal–external division was missing: from the republic-level perspective, the SSR- and USSR-levels were thoroughly entwined and, for the Union-level, the Eastern bloc further functioned as its logical extension.

While in economic and sociopolitical terms the Estonian SSR was strongly dependent on all-USSR decision-making, Estonians' cultural imaginaries sustained some autonomy from sociopolitical realities. In cultural imaginaries, tradition, cultural memory, and one's personal, affective relationship to concrete surroundings all play a role, while the political dissatisfactions of any present situation can be partially compensated by cultural memory. The result is a 'messy scalarity', a hazy and flexible network of images, ideas and values. As we will see in Section 11.4, both 'Europe' and 'the West' had a role to play there.

11.4 THE CHANGING LOCATION OF EUROPE

In the all-Soviet scale of the post-war era, *Europe as a relatively coherent entity disappeared*; instead, Europe was split into the Soviet zone of influence and capitalist Western Europe. Eastern Europe, subject to guidance from Moscow,

[19] For the republic-level Central Committee of the Communist Party, the main decision-making organ, the first secretary (that is, the leader of the party and of the republic) would be chosen under strict supervision from Moscow; the second secretary was always non-local and directly appointed by Moscow. In case of the Estonian SSR, the first secretaries Johannes Käbin (1950–1978) and Karl Vaino (1978–1988) had both grown up in Russia and were sent to Estonia on the orders of the all-Union Communist Party.

[20] There were three classifications for Soviet-era industrial enterprises: 'All-Union' (under the direct control of Moscow), 'Union-Republic' (in which Moscow played the dominant role) and those under 'Republic' control. The role of local administration differed during different periods of the Soviet era; after the heavily centralized Stalininst era, more power devolved to the republics; with the end of the Khrushchev Thaw, a new wave of centralization took place.

functioned as an extension of the Soviet sphere, while Western Europe became inaccessible to the general Soviet citizenry.

It is worth noting that the early Soviet Union had been significantly better connected to Europe: figures like Vladimir Mayakovsky could spend extended periods in Paris, Ilya Ehrenburg would actively contribute to Soviet press while living in Paris, Soviet scientists published in Western journals and interacted with Western colleagues. Germany, of course, was an important partner for the USSR in the interwar period, with many major German companies maintaining some presence there.[21] This sustained connectedness was partially due to weaknesses in the state of the USSR in its early history; it was only later on that scientific and military collaboration with the Germans and with the rest of the world came to be regarded with great suspicion by Stalin, inspiring trials and persecutions.

In the Khrushchev era, networks of interaction were developed anew – delegations of architects, for example, travelled to Scandinavia and to Western Europe, to learn about mass-scale urban planning in line with new factory-assembled construction methods.[22] Yet westward travel from the Socialist bloc remained open only for a limited number of political, cultural and scientific or economic elites and was a complex undertaking with onerous limitations.

11.4.1 *From Sociopolitics to Cultural Imaginaries*

In the popular imagination, too, Europe as a functional category weakened as the 'iron curtain' split Europe in two. Imaginary 'Europeanness' could function only as a *relative category*, not as an entity with determinate boundaries – places could be more or less European. Europeanness in this context tended to be associated with *urban culture*: Bulgaria and Poland were considered somewhat less European than Prague, Budapest or Dresden, and unattainable Paris and London crowned the popular hierarchy.[23]

If Soviet-era Eastern Europe was not regarded as fully European, Western Europe as a category failed in its own way to secure a clearly defined identity. In lieu of 'Europe', the 'West' was the signifier of choice for the imaginary better world beyond the confines of the Soviet borders. Marju Lauristin has suggested that the categories of West and Europe were 'virtually synonymous',[24] yet both popular

[21] Ian Ona Johnson, *Faustian Bargain: The Soviet–German Partnership and the Origins of the Second World War* (Oxford University Press, 2021).

[22] Marija Drėmaitė, *Baltic Modernism: Architecture and Housing in Soviet Lithuania* (DOM Publishers, 2017).

[23] Even as personal correspondences with the 'outside world' became possible once again in the late Soviet era, without a support of the socio-political level, these epistolary encounters of (semi-)intimate scale did not become generalized into ideas of Europe. One would not say, for example, I received a package from Europe – no, the package came from my aunt or from Sweden.

[24] Marju Lauristin, 'The European Public Sphere and the Social Imaginary of the "New Europe"' (2007) 22 *European Journal of Communication* 397, 398.

culture and the general Cold War framework suggest otherwise. The late Soviet-era category of 'the West' also included American culture – indeed arguably the United States was regarded as the pre-eminent constituent of 'the West'.[25] Europe as a category was thus *doubly dispersed*: it was subsumed within the larger category of the West under American dominance and it was zoned into sites that were either more or less European.[26]

11.5 THE LOCATION OF EUROPE FROM THE ESTONIAN PERSPECTIVE: SOCIOPOLITICAL REALITIES

For Estonians, Soviet-era sociopolitical realities differed vastly from those in pre-Soviet times. The pre-war Estonian Republic had been situated in what retrospectively looked like a clearly defined system of nested sociopolitical scalarity: Estonia – Europe – the world. This system was interwoven by various political, economic and cultural networks.

The Soviet colonial matrix of power dismantled historical ties that had organized the Baltic sea region and had linked Estonia with other European countries. Colonial-style centre–periphery relations made it nearly impossible for the Soviet borderlands (including the Estonian SSR) to sustain or develop direct connections with institutions or businesses outside the USSR. Prior to the Soviet annexation, geographical and linguistic proximity with Finland had facilitated close, even intimate relations between Estonians and Finns – connections included business and politics, of course, but also ties of love and friendship.[27] With the new era, political, economic and cultural interactions with the world outside the USSR had to be routed through Moscow; in such instances, republic-level interests were secondary and personal connections unsustainable. This was a particularly suggestive example of the colonial matrix of control exerted by the USSR, as regards the Estonian SSR: the disruption and rerouting of former economic and cultural ties that had formerly bound Estonia closely with Finland and other European countries.[28] As a result, not only did Estonia cease to be a political and economic entity which could interact with the rest of the world in pursuit of its own interests, the whole sociocultural sphere was permeated with such limitations: only on rare occasions could Estonian musicians participate in major international competitions

[25] Examples include a widespread fascination with the TV serial *Dallas*, the popularity of Micky-Mouse and Donald Duck comic books and American popular music.

[26] Mapping of Europeanness also privileged cities over countries: Prague would thus be associated with stronger Europeanness than Czechoslovakia.

[27] The late nineteenth-century and the early twentieth-century history of Estonian culture is the story of a deep connectedness with Finland. Friedebert Tuglas, a classic Estonian author, hid in Finland from Tsarist authorities; Marie Under, perhaps the most celebrated Estonian poet of all time, loved to vacation in Finland; Aino Kallas, the most celebrated pre-war Finnish female writer, married an Estonian and lived mostly in Estonia until its Soviet annexation.

[28] Annus, *Soviet Postcolonial Studies*.

outside the Soviet Union[29] and foreign films reached Estonian audiences only after being selected, cut, censored and dubbed in Russia, with Estonian subtitles composed according to the Russian dubbing, and without access to the original.[30] Cultural exchanges of the late Soviet years, such as Estonian theatre performances in Finland and Finnish theatre troupes' visits to Estonia could not bypass Moscow.[31] Soviet tourist groups did occasionally include members of the Estonian Soviet elite, but the company as a whole would in such cases be identified as Soviet.[32] The 'iron curtain' hid the borderlands more profoundly than it hid the Soviet centre: for most of the rest of the world, the Soviet Union became equated with Russia.

Given the structural hindrance suffered by Estonian scientists and artists seeking contact with the outside world, it was, paradoxically, Leningrad and (to a lesser extent) Moscow that started to function as *access points to Europe* – these were the cities one could visit to gain access to information, knowledge and high art.[33] In the Russian centres, a certain limited openness was restored after the period of Stalinist excess and research budgets were by far more generous than those disbursed in the borderlands. Leading Russian academic centres could order scientific journals published in the West and thus open up access to global knowledge production. Estonian scholars and intellectuals would visit libraries in Leningrad and Moscow to browse through Western scholarly and cultural journals that were indispensable for their work: the library at the Hermitage, for example, included exhibition catalogues and art journals that never reached Estonian libraries.[34] International artists would more likely visit Moscow and Leningrad than Tallinn; similarly, the occasional exhibitions of Western art (such as the Picasso exhibition in 1956) were shown in

[29] Anu Kõlar, 'Interpretatsioonikunst ja kontserdielu sulaperioodil', in Tooman Siitan (ed.), *Eesti Muusikaajalugu II* (Estonian Academy of Music and Theatre, forthcoming).

[30] For film clubs, however, circulation might work differently. Once Helsinki–Tallinn ferry traffic was opened in the 1960s, it became one of the channels through which film clubs could acquire films. These were shown with synchronous translation, in Tallinn Polytechnic Institute, with two professional translators covering ten languages; in Tartu, students were also used. Tiina Hoffmann, *La Traduction cinématographique en Estonie soviétique: Contextes, pratiques et acteurs* (University of Tartu, 2021).

[31] Luule Epner, 'Soome dramaturgia Nõukogude Eesti teatrilaval' (2019) 62 *Keel ja Kirjandus* 849, 852–853.

[32] Soviet elites did indeed travel around. When, in 1979, a group of twenty-two Estonians toured Canada and the United States, for the writer Aadu Hint it was already his fourth visit to Canada. Ene Maremäe, 'Kolm nädalat Ameerika mandril', *Sirp ja Vasar* 31 December 1976, 4 and 12.

[33] The role of Leningrad and Moscow is well documented in life-writing: sources include diaries by the writer Vaino Vahing, several interviews with the artist Tõnis Vint, published recollections by the art historian Krista Kodres, life stories in the volumes of *Eesti elulood*, memoirs by the composer Veljo Tormis and more. Literary examples include Aili Paju's novel *Merkuuri tütar*; Mats Traat's novel *Inger* and short stories by Maimu Berg.

[34] Krista Kodres, 'The Soviet West? Shifting Bounderies of Estonian Culturescape', in Natalya Zlydneva (ed.), *At the Crossroads of the East and the West: The Problems of Borderzone in Russian and Central European Cultures* (Institut Slavovedeniya, Rossiiskaya Akademiya Nauk, 2021), 438.

Moscow and Leningrad and nowhere else.[35] The Sixth World Festival of Youth and Students in Moscow 1957, which included many Western participants, gave many visiting Estonians inspiring encounters with the contemporary Western cultural sphere.[36] There were historical roots to this phenomenon: St Petersburg, historically Estonia's closest major European city, had long functioned for Estonians as an access point to Europe. During the late Tsarist era, this city functioned for many cultural figures (Johann Köler, Miina Härma) as a place to acquire (typically German-style) education or to find fulfilling employment.[37]

The Europeanness of Russia more broadly, however, had also been repeatedly contested over different periods by Russian cultural elites themselves – most famously by Pyotr Chaadayev in his *First Philosophical Letter* (1829): the author argued that Russians had 'bestowed not even a single idea upon the fund of human ideas, contributed nothing to the progress of the human spirit'.[38] Madina Tlostanova has used the notion of the 'quasi-Western subaltern Russian Empire' (Tlostanova)[39] to describe Russia's historical struggle with its subalternity or its feeling of secondariness with regard to other major European powers.[40] For visiting Estonians, similarly, the experience of visiting Leningrad and Moscow often included a high degree of ambivalence.

11.6 THE AESTHETICS OF EUROPEANNESS: CONTINUITIES IN CULTURAL IMAGINARIES ACROSS POLITICAL REGIME CHANGES

The double dispersal of Europe – its split into two and its subsumption within the larger category of the 'West' – could not erase Europe from Estonian cultural imaginaries. The slowness, inertia and multiplicity of cultural processes guarantees the preservation of traces of 'what used to be' throughout periods increasingly dominated by new sets of values and ideas. An annexation or a revolution can change the sociopolitical order of a state or a territory within a period of a few years, yet the process of changing collectively shared cultural understandings might well take decades and may only ever be partially successful. At a personal and regional

35 Maria Dmitreva, 'The Riddle of Modernism in the Art Historical Discourse of the Thaw', in Krista Kodres, Kristina Jõekalda and Michaela Marek (eds.), *A Socialist Realist History: Writing Art History in the Postwar Decades* (Böhlau, 2019).

36 Kädi Talvoja has documented the impact of the festival for emerging Estonian avant-garde movements in the visual arts. Kädi Talvoja, *Karm stiil Eesti kunstiajalookirjutuse kontekstis: Severe Style in the Context of Estonian Art History Writing: Dissertationes Academiae Artium Estoniae* 27 (Eesti Kunstiakadeemia, 2019).

37 Annus, *Soviet Postcolonial Studies*, 132; Jaan Ross, 'Eestlaste Kultuurielu Peterburis', *Sirp* 19 November 2021.

38 English translation is from Nicholas V. Riasanovsky, *The Image of Peter the Great in Russian History and Thought* (Oxford University Press, 1992), 99.

39 Madina Tlostanova, *Gender Epistemologies and Eurasian Borderlands* (Palgrave Macmillan, 2010), 64.

40 Annus, *Soviet Postcolonial Studies*, 129.

level, continuity is also sustained by material culture and by natural environment: the same physical items, similar architectural structures and kindred topographical features support the sense of continuity or permanence.

After the Soviet takeover, the new regime contended against earlier cultural traditions and values and created new hybrid imaginaries, yet supposedly displaced images and values and tropes persisted. Key cultural works and events of various kind, notably those attached to school curricula, continued to function as resources for cultural continuity.[41] The Soviet state could not impose a wholesale rejection of major cultural developments before the Soviet era, so much of the pre-Soviet Estonian cultural canon was appropriated into the Soviet ideological framework and continued its cultural circulation. During the Soviet era, Estonian school curricula included nineteenth-century patriotic songs and poems, but also classic twentieth-century novels that had defined a pre-Soviet national consciousness.[42] For the imaginaries about Estonia's situatedness vis-à-vis Europe, the early twentieth-century Noor-Eesti (Young Estonia) movement played a special role.

The Noor-Eesti movement, founded in 1905, earned its place in the Estonian cultural canon for its Nietzschean programme of radical cultural innovation.[43] Its young members decisively rejected the German and Russian influences that had been dominant in nineteenth-century Estonian culture, instead they valorised Scandinavian and Romance cultures.[44] Such nuances became lost in popular imaginaries, however, and Noor-Eesti became synonymous with the aspiration towards Europeanness in general. In its 1905 manifesto *Noorte püüded* [*The Strivings of Young People*], the movement declared that its mission was 'to seek those aims and forms, to which we are guided, from one direction, by the spirit of our nation and the natural capacities and requirements of our nation, and, from the other direction, by European culture'.[45] The same text also supplied the slogan 'Let's be Estonians, but let's also become Europeans!' and the short catch-phrase

[41] As the Soviet Union made no effort to encourage new settlers to become acquainted with the local cultural sphere, in the Estonian SSR there remained strong contrasts between ethnic Estonians and Russophone Soviet-era settlers – contrasts that diminished somewhat over the Soviet decades, due to similar everyday material circumstances. Research from the 1990s reveals clear differences in the self-identities of ethnic Estonian and Soviet-era settlers and their children – a difference that started to diminish over the course of the 1990s.

[42] The Soviet era rhetoric presented nineteenth-century nation-building as resistance to Baltic German landlords and thus established linkages with Soviet discourse of its arch-enemy, the Germans – in Soviet parlance as 'exploiters of the toiling masses'.

[43] Epp Annus, 'Noorte püüded ja rõõmus ajalugu: Gustav Suits ja Friedrich Nietzsche' (2005) *Keel ja Kirjandus* 526.

[44] Virve Sarapik, 'Young Estonia and the Early Twentieth-Century Cultural Utopias' (2014) 45 *Journal of Baltic Studies* 207, 208.

[45] Gustav Suits ['Noor Eesti' toim], 'Noorte püüded. Üksikud mõtted meie oleviku kohta', *Noor-Eesti I* (Kirjanduse Sõprade kirjastus, 1905), 19.

'More culture! More European-style culture!'[46] The formulaic structure of these proclamations made their dissemination all the easier.

The Noor-Eesti movement was treated critically during the period of high Stalinism,[47] but the Khrushchev era re-established its cultural importance. Somewhat paradoxically, the Noor-Eesti slogan found its way into Soviet school curricula: it was helpful that Noor-Eesti leaders had been excited about the 1905 revolution, since this positioned them on the 'right' side of history.[48] Voldemar Miller wrote in the weekly *Sirp ja Vasar*, in 1970: 'The Noor-Eesti movement developed under the direct impact of the 1905–1906 revolution, their slogan was "Let's be Estonians, but let's also become Europeans!" The Noor-Eesti movement turned into an important landmark (verstapost) in the development of the aesthetic view of Estonians, in their Europeanization.'[49] And Mai Levin, in 1979, stressed in the same weekly newspaper the role of Noor-Eesti in the context of its era, while pointing to the combination of the European and the national: 'at this stage of the development of national culture, a deeper investment in European culture was both unavoidable and necessary, much as the demand for a national subject matter in art was objectively conditioned'.[50]

For Noor-Eesti, *Europeanness was an aesthetic, not a political category* – this was an important precondition for the adoption of their slogan in the Soviet era. In cultural circulation, the Noor-Eesti declaration acquired a life of its own, however, partly independent of its original historical context. A colourful example is provided in Herbert Vainu's vulgar-Soviet lampoon of a typical member of Soviet Estonia's economic elite:

> Kui tal koolipõlves muud 'Noor-Eestist' pole meelde jäänud, siis vähemalt kujundlik loosung 'Olgem eestlased, aga saagem ka eurooplasteks!' Ja ta tõestab, et ta on see ja teine – omainimene Rannamõisa 'Rannapiigas', ei jää tolaks Helsinki ravintola's ega Place Pigalle'il ja kultuuriinimesena käib ka Grand Opera's ära.
>
> [If he hasn't remembered anything else from 'Noor-Eesti' in his school years, then at least he remembers the figurative slogan 'Let's be Estonians, but let's also become Europeans!' And he proves that he is both – welcome in Rannamõisa's 'Rannapiiga',[51] but not a gaping fool at a restaurant in Helsinki or on Place Pigalle – and, as a cultured person, he will also go to the Grand Opera.][52]

[46] Ibid., 17. This short version, now part of Estonian imaginaries, redacts an intervening sentence. The original reads: 'And our call is: More culture! This is the first condition of all aspirations and efforts for liberation. More European-style culture!' Ibid., 17.

[47] The historian Ea Jansen records that, in 1950, the Stalinist functionary Max Laosson called Noor-Eesti 'a marriage between a syphilitic French lady and an Estonian peasant'. Marika Mikli and Ea Jansen, 'Vestlus Ea Janseniga' (1995) *Vikerkaar* 153, 155.

[48] Sarapik, 'Young Estonia', 208.

[49] Voldemar Miller, 'Raamat Eesti Kultuuriloos' (1970) *Sirp ja Vasar* (18 September 1970) 4, 6.

[50] Mai Levin, 'Aleksander Promet', *Sirp ja Vasar* (19 October 1979), 8.

[51] A popular modern restaurant on the outskirts of Tallinn.

[52] Herbert Vainu, 'Renessansist Maarjamaal' (1976) *Sirp ja Vasar* 3, 10.

Such an easy appropriation suggests that, by the late Soviet era, the Noor-Eesti dictum had become a commonplace in Estonia's cultural self-identification. It had engraved itself as a cultural imaginary with historic depth, one of those core ideas with a special symbolic value that play a significant role in building and sustaining national identity. Notably, this imaginary figured the future of Estonian culture as securely bound together with that of Europe.

Yet, even as Noor-Eesti foregrounded the necessity of close relations with Scandinavian and Romance cultural spheres, its central statement is directed elsewhere: it is the acknowledgement of a lack. For Noor-Eesti, Estonian Europeanness was not a given, but rather an aim and a direction. Noor-Eesti's leading voices coupled their European aspirations with criticism of the 'overly Germanic' Estonian culture of their era. In its original context, the slogan hardly offered an easy positive identification with Europe, yet, in the Soviet context, it nevertheless served to affirm Estonia's imaginary affiliation with Europe – Noor-Eesti members had, after all, freely travelled all over Europe. The temporal distance from Noor-Eesti times was necessary for their call to crystallize into a symbolic gesture and the historic distance was further accentuated by the cultural rupture of the Soviet annexation. I have elsewhere described such a situation through the double dialectics of nostalgia and colonial rupture: 'first, the colonial split initiated a discourse of national nostalgia; and second, the nostalgic lens further intensified the colonial conflict'.[53] The mere fact of the Soviet annexation guaranteed the Noor-Eesti slogan a special place in national imaginaries.

11.7 BINARISMS IN EVERYDAY CULTURAL IMAGINARIES: EUROPE AND RUSSIA

In addition to the persistence and deepening of various pre-Soviet cultural aspirations, era-specific factors – especially those linked to the Soviet-era colonial conflict – also contributed to the cultural imaginary of Estonia's Europeanness. The 'Soviet gaze' classed the *Pribaltika* as the 'Soviet West' and thus supported local self-understandings as being more Western than the rest of the USSR. Examples abound: Elena Zubkova even opens her monograph *Pribaltika i Kreml'* (*The Baltics and the Kremlin*) with a recollection of the *Soviet Pribaltika* enjoying a special significance for those living in the USSR.[54] Art curator Alla Rosenfeld remembers: 'I traveled to Tallinn to see art exhibitions, which seemed so Western-like and avant-garde for us in Leningrad, where it was almost impossible to exhibit openly what they were showing in Estonia'.[55] While the common rhetoric labelled

[53] Annus, *Soviet Postcolonial Studies*, 10.

[54] Elena Zubkova, *Pribaltika i Kreml*, 1940–1953 (Rosspen, 2008), 3.

[55] Alla Rosenfeld, 'Preface', in Alla Rosenfeld and Norton D. Dodge (eds.), *Art of the Baltics: The Struggle for Freedom of Artistic Expression Under the Soviets, 1945–1991* (Rutgers University Press and The Jane Voorhees Zimmerli Art Museum, 2002), ix.

the Balts as 'Western', in this context, the semantic difference between 'Europe' and 'the West' was irrelevant: Estonia as 'Western' could only signify Western in European terms.

Estonians, for their part, shored up their national pride together with their European difference by juxtaposing themselves against the new Soviet-era settlers, whom they homogenized into a coherent entity they referred to as 'Russians'. Estonian manners and habits were deemed superior, starting from the everyday basics: eating sunflower seeds and spitting the shells carelessly about was held in disdain, the use of low-quality, strongly smelling cooking oil (as compared to relatively odourless margarine) was considered an inferior cultural practice. 'Tuck your shirt in, son – you are not some kind of a Russian', a man interviewed in 1993 remembers his grandmother saying. 'At home it was always important to behave like a proper Estonian and not to shame oneself with behaving like a Russian', this informant added.[56] Such everyday oppositions functioned as a decolonial reaction, a strategy for supporting communal self-respect.

Even during the era of Soviet censorship, oppositional motifs found their way into fiction, often through passing remarks or marginal characters. Characters such as Georgi Nikanorov in Teet Kallas's *Eiseni tänav* (*Eisen Street*, 1979) or Bobrin in Mats Traat's *Rippsild* (*Suspension Bridge*, 1980) are presented as simpletons compared to Estonians with their complex inner dilemmas. Bobrin gives a young Estonian couple an embarrassingly banal speech about the importance of making children: 'Down with the pants and skirts, off with the bras and undershirts, out with the fake modesty – and then go at it!'[57] Nikanorov, the father of five children, encourages his former colleague Rein to follow a similar path: to beget children in order to get a new apartment with all the modern comforts in a Soviet suburb. Both Bobrin and Nikanorov are loud, robust and simpleminded, not to be taken seriously. In *Rippsild* there is also a passing reference to an open conflict between different nationalities: when Kaida, a young Estonian woman, starts a relationship with a Russian-speaking man from Ukraine, Kaida's mother refuses to acknowledge their marriage and takes her daughter's child away to live with herself.

In Lilli Promet's novel *Primavera* (1971), the Estonian–Russian juxtaposition is developed in considerable detail. The main character, Saskia, an actress, provides a lengthy description of her everyday circumstances:

> Pärast päevatööd tõid täiskiilutud trammid meid koju, naistel käe otsas rasked kandevõrgud, enamasti ikka õli, sibulad, leib ja kapsad. Nädalalõpp algas rõõmsate pidudega, aga esmaspäeval taoti lõhutud akna- või ukseklaaside asemele vineertahvlid ette. Sõitsin selle mittepaigalise rahvaga iga päev ainult trammis koos või seisin poejärjekorras, teatrisse nad ei tulnud. (15)

56 Jaak Rakfeldt and Helle Rakfeldt-Leetmaa, 'Rahvusliku identiteedi säilitamine okupeeritud Eestis' (1996) *Akadeemia* 1571, 1580.

57 Mats Traat, *Rippsild* (Eesti Raamat, 1979), 10.

[After a day's work, the crowded trams brought us home, women carrying heavy carrying shopping bags, filled with cooking oil, onions, bread and cabbage. The weekend started with joyous parties, but by Monday, plywood boards were fixed over broken windows and door panes. I rode the tram with these non-local people every day or stood in line at the store – they didn't come to the theatre.]

Greasy food, onions, cabbage, noisy parties sliding into destructive behaviour, non-participation in cultural life, primitive modes of gender relations – one finds here a suggestive list of era-specific attributions externalized onto the image of the cultural Other: the unwanted, unwelcome new settler, whose growing presence was a continual marker of the colonial-style disregard for local interests.[58]

Promet's *Primavera* offers a nearly perfect setting for considering the Europeanness of Estonians: the novel accompanies an Estonian actress on a Soviet tourist trip to Italy, where Saskia shares a hotel room with Fevronia, a woman from Russia.[59] Slender Saskia enjoys the trip fully, orients herself easily in art museums, drinks wine in local cafes, attracts the interest of several male companions and is mistaken for a German. Full-figured Fevronia, in contrast to Saskia, is clearly out of place in Italy: she displays ignorance and chauvinistic attitudes and is demanding and pretentious. Like the Italians, Saskia relies on strong coffee for energy, whereas Fevronia is upset when tea is unavailable. While Saskia and her attentive male companions enjoy Italian street life until late in the night, Fevronia gets lost because she is unable to read the Latin alphabet. In short, the novel emphasizes the Europeanness of the Estonian woman through her contrast with her markedly 'less cultured' Russian roommate. The contrast between Saskia and Fevronia is so extreme that the Finnish reviewer Pekka Lilja had to cautiously admit, in his review of the Finnish translation in 1977, that Fevronia's character is presented in a such a grotesque light that it could 'almost be considered racist'.[60]

Pekka Lilja proposed that Promet's novel escaped serious imputation of racism by introducing another Russian, Konstantin, an intelligent and knowledgeable Russian professor, a researcher of classical culture.[61] Saskia's new Russian-speaking friends –

58 Prior to the Soviet takeover, Estonia had been a relatively homogeneous nation-state, with the eponymous ethnicity making up 88.1 per cent of the population in 1934 and 97.3 per cent in 1945, after Hitler's *Umsiedlung* of the Baltic German population. By 1989, Estonian-speakers were reduced to 61.5 per cent of the total, while in some regions Estonians had become a minority – a situation that for a nation of about one million caused anxieties of total assimilation. This data comes from Kalev Katus and Allan Puur, 'Rahvastikuteadus ja Eesti rahvastikuarengu pöördepunktid' (2006) *Akadeemia* 491, 500; Annus, *Soviet Postcolonial Studies*, 45.

59 Lilli Promet and her husband Ralf Parve, writers loyal to the Soviet regime, travelled extensively and published several travelogues. *Primavera* is a fictionalized travelogue.

60 Pekka Lilja, 'Lilli Prometi Itaalia-reis', in *Koos lahus: Uurimusi ja kriitikat eesti ja soome kirjandusest* (Tartu Ülikooli Kirjastus, 2017), 228.

61 In the Russian reception of the novel, the character of Konstantin did not neutralize the shocking presence of Fevronia. Promet's novel was translated and published in Russia, where it caused a considerable scandal. Johanna Ross, *Aira Kaalust Mari Saadini: Nõukogude Eesti naisarenguromaan ja selle lugemisviisid* (Tartu Ülikooli Kirjastus, 2018), 132.

a Jewish writer and the Russian professor – also accommodate themselves to the Italian setting with easy elegance and they share Saskia's irritation with plump, ignorant Fevronia. In short, these two men, coming from Russia, are as European as Saskia is. Europeanness thus turns out to be correlated to categories of class and education: a Russian intellectual turns out to be no less European than his Estonian counterpart. The motif appears similarly in the novel *Rippsild*, where Dr Levin, whom an Estonian couple visits for treatment in Leningrad, is presented as both knowledgeable and desirable.

In a way, this corresponds to the Noor-Eesti mode of thinking: one becomes European by attuning oneself to European culture, through study and research, through choosing certain modes of creative self-expression. Europeanness is here understood as a category of aesthetics and knowledge. At the same time, the novel pokes fun of Fevronia's diligent note-taking – the assumption is that the necessary knowledge should *always already* have been acquired and acquired somehow effortlessly and playfully. According to this formula, being European implies lightness, pleasure and enjoyment, instead of a wrong-spirited scribbling of a guide's already oversimplified explanations – being European is characterized by a certain aesthetics of being, which the novel elaborates as an ontological positioning towards the surrounding world.

Promet's novel *Primavera* follows characters in exceptional circumstances – only very few from Soviet Estonia could enjoy leisure trips to Italy. The actress Saskia, likewise, has an exceptional profile: how many in the Estonian SSR would have displayed similar ease in recognizing and appreciating classical works of art? Yet thousands read Promet's novel, laughed at Fevronia and enjoyed the admiration that Saskia attracted on her fictional travels. The passive, non-dialogic Europeanness of a reader of fiction who faces not actual people in Italian streets and cafes, but instead follows words on the printed page and travels in an imaginary Europe from his or her cosy armchair – such armchair-Europeanness was secure from threats of Orientalization and excluded the least hint of cultural discomfort. The novel's ambition, however, met with some indignities in its Finnish translation: the editor was obliged to correct many mistakes about Italy and its classical heritage.[62] But, since rumours of Finnish editorial corrections would hardly reach Soviet Estonian audiences, Saskia's European success could be enjoyed domestically without critical disturbance.

In one of the 1976 issues of the cultural weekly *Sirp ja Vasar*, a group of Estonian elites shared their travel impressions after the trip to Canada and the United States. Among other general commentaries, the writer Enn Vetemaa observed casually: 'For the European, Canada feels homier, both in terms of architecture and even in interpersonal relations. The United States feels inadvertently more foreign.'[63] In the context of North America, Vetemaa easily identified with Europe. Even as the scale of

62 Lilja, 'Lilli Prometi Itaalia-reis', 227.
63 Maremäe, 'Kolm nädalat Ameerika mandril', 4.

Europe was in Soviet era significantly deactivated, the identification with Europe clearly survived in national imaginaries as embedded within the category of Estonianness.

11.8 FROM SOVIET TO POST-SOVIET: CHANGES AND CONTINUITIES

The armchair-Europeanness that had been part of the Estonian self-image in the Soviet era was shaken up in the early 1990s, when the collapse of the Soviet Union brought about a rescaling of geopolitical realities and accompanying imaginaries. Transition-era political rhetoric foregrounded the vocabulary of a return: the emphasis was on the *re-establishment* of the independent state and *re-connecting* Estonia politically and economically with the rest of Europe and the world.[64] The discourse of restoration also implied a return to the nested scalar system 'Estonia – Europe – the world' or, in the more detailed version, 'Estonia – the Baltic sea region – Europe – the world'. Yet, in the 1990s, the dream of such safely nested belongingness could be realized only partially: the Soviet Union, albeit now dissolved, continued to loom over the new era with its continuing presence in global political imaginaries. What used to be the Soviet Union was now commonly referred to as 'the former Soviet sphere' and what used to be the Socialist bloc or the Soviet sphere of influence now became the so-called post-socialist countries.

From the late 1980s onward, Estonians and other non-Russian nationalities of the USSR had to struggle against the cultural erasure that had taken place during the past half century, when one geopolitical label – the Soviet Union – had obscured the great diversity within its imperial borders. Notes taken at the European Student Forum 1989 in Bologna are telling. Jüri Luik, who later made a name for himself as a distinguished politician, was then one of the two participating Estonian students and commented on how Estonians had to contend with the perspective of the students from the EEC countries:

> Meie struktureerime maailma poliitilist kaarti nii, et loeme ennast Euroopa osaks. Sealtpoolt vaadates on Euroopa kõik see, mis lõpeb Saksa Liitvabariigi idapiiril. … Sealt paistame me Venemaa provintsina, mässava provintsina, kes võitleb mingi mõistetamatu iseseisvuse eest …
>
> On muidugi detaile, millega võid rabada. Et sul on viisakas ülikond, et sa oskad korralikult Euroopa kultuurkeeli. Selleks, et olla võrdne, pead olema veidike parem. (45)
>
> [We structure the political map of the world to reflect ourselves as part of Europe. But looking from their vantage point, Europe ends on the eastern border of the

[64] Different varieties of such rhetoric were typical of this era also in other post-Socialist countries. Mikko Lagerspetz offers a comparative perspective in Mikko Lagerspetz, 'Postsocialism as a Return: Notes on a Discursive Strategy' (1999) 13 *East European Politics and Societies* 377.

> Federal Republic of Germany. . . . From there we look like a province of Russia, a rebellious province that fights for some incomprehensible independence . . .
>
> Of course, there are details that can impress. That you have a smart suit, that you have mastered the main European languages. In order to be equal, you have to be a little bit better.][65]

As Luik observes, the renewal of actual, two-way encounters led to the realization that there was a clear and uncomfortable mismatch between the Estonians' sense of Europeanness and the EEC-countries' more exclusive vision of Europe. Such a mismatch continued to be produced by way of labels such as 'post-Soviet' or 'post-socialist' – both implying a significant difference from 'real Europe'. The post-Soviet-era geographical imagination, like its Cold War predecessor, reinforced the historical orientalization of eastern Europe – the division of Europe into East and West – and judging the West as superior to the East[66] – but this was now newly strengthened by the dire need for Western investment in these societies undergoing transition.[67] While the rarity of direct interaction with countries outside the state-socialist bloc had neutralized the relevance of orientalising visions during the Soviet Era, now new encounters with the orientalising gaze of the 'West' threatened Estonians' internalized sense of Europeanness and created existential discomfort. The humiliating poverty of the years of transition exacerbated this unhappy situation.[68]

For Estonia and other 'post-Soviet' countries, the two simultaneous imaginary geographies – the aspirational 'nested Europe' and the orientalising binary judgement 'post-Soviet East versus more advanced West' – clashed and intermingled in disconcerting ways. The imaginary of Europe, now again very concretely tied to geopolitical realities, also became divided into different institutional entities – in political terms, it was generally not 'Europe', but NATO, the Schengen area, the EEC and later the EU that was the locus of Estonia's aspirational belonging. In the Soviet era, Europeanness had survived as a *cultural* marker of imaginary

65 Jüri Luik, 'Ühinevas Euroopas' (1989) *Vikerkaar* 37, 45.

66 Edward Said deployed the term 'Orientalism' to characterize the West's strategies of encountering the Middle East. This concept has been likewise used to describe the West's regard towards Eastern Europe. In this context, it is necessary to acknowledge the different conceptual coverage of the concepts 'orientalism' and 'colonialism': while both terms indicate the relationship of subordination and othering, 'colonialism' also involves the establishment of a specific sociopolitical system of subordination. Both involve a clearly hierarchical structure of scalarity, which is tied to questions of worth and value. Annus, 'A Post-Soviet Eco-Digital Nation?' (n 8). See also Annus, *Soviet Postcolonial Studies*, 186.

67 According to Larry Wolff, Orientalist associations with regards to Eastern Europe emerged in the Enlightenment era, when 'the east of Europe' – in French *l'orient de l'Europe* – could easily be read as 'the Orient of Europe'. Larry Wolff, *Inventing Eastern Europe: The Map of Civilization on the Mind of the Enlightenment* (Stanford University Press, 1994), 6.

68 Jüri Luik's review of the 1989 European Student Forum also refers to the embarrassments in Bologna, when the invited Estonian students could not even afford to buy a cup of coffee. Luik, 'Ühinevas Euroopas', 49.

belongingness – now, for Estonian political elites, Europeanness became understood in terms of *economy*, *politics* and, importantly, *national security*. Marju Lauristin and Peeter Vihalemm summarize the priorities set at the beginning of Estonian transition as 'economic competitiveness coupled with national security' – a combination that Lauristin and Vihalemm attested to be still in place in 2009, regardless of the deepening global economic crisis.[69] Thus, the former Soviet empire continued its presence in political imaginaries as a reminder of military threat, lending special urgency to Estonia's ambition to join European institutional and security frameworks.[70]

In cultural imaginaries of the transition period, regained independence raised new questions about belonging – exactly how European are we? Actual encounters with the world outside the former Eastern bloc diminished the role played by Russia and Estonia's Russophone populations as cultural others – the role that formerly gave impetus to Estonians' imaginary sense of Europeanness during the Soviet era. The Noor-Eesti slogan 'Let's be Estonians, but let's also become Europeans!' continued to be taught in schools, but, in a strongly future-oriented cultural era, its cultural relevance diminished. While in the Soviet-era the slogan had significant performative power, it now became part of national pedagogy, outside the active repertoire of cultural imagery.

The most widely discussed literary work of the 1990s period, the novel *Piiririik* (*The Border State*, 1993) by Emil Tode (a pen name for Tõnu Õnnepalu) was strongly marked by a sense of East-European Otherness. The main character of the novel, a gay man in Paris, feels both attraction and revulsion towards his new surroundings, with their Western consumer culture and sterile functionability. The main character's sense of non-belonging in Paris and yet his unwillingness to return lead him to an indefinable, liminal, border-state existence and also to the realization that it is impossible to shake off one's past: past moods, colours and landscapes continue to re-emerge in his thoughts regardless of geographic distance. While *Piiririik* was able to capture something important about its era, the 1990s cultural ferment escapes simple delineation – this era was characterized by great multiplicity, by a variety of hopes and aspirations, as a well as by bitter disappointments.

In Estonia, the economic crisis of the transition period was relatively short-lived: the national currency was successfully introduced in June 1992 and the economic situation started to improve in early 1993. By September 1993, the president of the Estonian Bank judged the crisis to be over.[71] In Lauristin's and Vihalemm's report,

69 Lauristin and Vihalemm, 'The Political Agenda', 22.

70 Russian troops left Estonia only in August 1994, and especially during the period from 1992 to 1996, Russia was considered a direct threat to Estonia's security. According to the analysis provided by Erik Männik, by 1997, the Russian threat was regarded by Estonia as of secondary importance. Erik Männik, 'Small States: Invited to NATO – Able to Contribute?' (2004) 20 *Defense & Security Analysis* 21, 27.

71 Sulev Vahtre (ed.), *Eesti ajalugu VI: Vabadussõjast taasiseseisvumiseni* (Ilmamaa, 2005), 403.

'[a]ccording to World Bank analysis, Estonia in 1994 belonged to a group of countries that had ... reached high levels of political freedom and economic stabilization'.[72] Yet the restoration of national self-esteem and the feeling of collective agency vis-à-vis newly scaled geopolitical structures of the world required more time to develop. As with other former Eastern bloc countries, the judgemental, orientalising 'Western gaze' complicated this process.

In time, Estonia's early 1990s crisis of collective agency developed into a story of collective success. By the 2010s, what had been an unstable post-colonial identity, defined by its struggle to come to terms with its Soviet heritage, had become overwritten by a new narrative gradually emerging: that of Estonia as the *eco-digital nation*,[73] a country and culture that cherishes and cares for its well-preserved natural habitats, while also moving at the forefront in digital technology.[74] Importantly, the ecodigital national narrative replaced the transition-era mismatch between the country's self-image as European and the orientalising gaze of the old imperial centres of the European West: the new narrative promoted the local sense of being, in certain respects, among the most successful in Europe and being appreciated as such. The culminating point in the new national narrative might be considered the 2017 EU digital summit in Tallinn, when, according to the *The New Yorker*, a speech by the President of Estonia Kersti Kaljulaid earned praise from the German chancellor, Angela Merkel: 'You're so much further than we are'.[75]

In the 2010s, being European had become a basic condition of life, the normal paradigm for being an Estonian. The formula for achieving this had already been articulated by Jüri Luik in 1989: 'In order to be equal, you have to be a little bit better'.

11.9 CONCLUSION

As we have seen, Europeanness is a relational category, its role and its function in Estonian imaginaries are dependent on other identificatory categories active at the same period. 'Europe' as an imaginary and as part of era-specific sociopolitical scalarity plays a different role in different eras: each era creates its own scalar logics, while activating certain geopolitical scales at the expense of others; in each era,

[72] Marju Lauristin and Peeter Vihalemm, 'The Political Agenda during Different Periods of Estonian Transformation: External and Internal Factors' (2009) 40 *Journal of Baltic Studies* 1, 9.

[73] The eco-digital Estonia narrative is based on Estonia's actual success in the IT-sector by the 2010s, both in terms of public services and in terms of providing a flourishing start-up environment. According to the European Commission Country Report Estonia, 2019, 'The country is a frontrunner as regards the digital provision of public services and has the highest proportion (96%) of e-Government users in Europe.' European Commission, *Country Report Estonia 2019* (Brussels, 2019), 43.

[74] Annus, 'A Post-Soviet Eco-Digital Nation?'. Note that this article also points to the selective or metonymic nature of such identity-formation.

[75] Nathan Heller, 'Estonia: The Digital Republic' *The New Yorker* (11 December 2017).

cultural imaginaries rewrite geopolitical parameters through the lens of prior cultural experiences, thus forming competing imaginary geographies. These processes are accompanied by normative value-judgements which unavoidably enforce scalar hierarchies of higher and lower standings; secondary effects variously include feelings of superiority or otherness and processes of orientalization.

In the Soviet-era Estonia, the Soviet colonial matrix of power disabled nation-level political agency and severed economic agency. However, while the Soviet leadership was able, within a period of a few years, to reorganize Estonian governmental structures, economy and trade networks, the conservatism or inertia of processes of cultural identification made it impossible to switch the country into a full 'Soviet' mode of cultural self-identification. The pre-Soviet decades of cultural development, including the Noor-Eesti, call 'Let's be Estonians, but let's also become Europeans!' continued to support Estonians' sense of Europeanness. The rather insubstantial imaginary construction of such a mental framework could, however, find support in the continuing and visible presence of pre-Soviet material culture, architecture, natural environments, specific forms of cultural self-expression and more. Continuing European standing on the cultural scale, however, gave some compensation for the enforced separation from Europe on the socioeconomic scale. Even as the Soviet colonial matrix of power worked to deactivate and downgrade the sociopolitical category of Europe, Europe continued its existence as an imagined, implicit quality Estonians could claim for themselves. The rarity of direct encounters neutralized the typically orientalising gaze of Western Europeans towards East-Europeans; instead, Estonia's position as 'the Soviet West' within the USSR affirmed its imaginary belonging with Europe. As Savisaar's speech suggested, the intense generation of new ideas in the perestroika era heightened the local sense of agency – and to such an extent that Estonians could during this period self-identify as the avant-garde of the USSR.

Estonia emerged from the USSR with a strong sense of national agency and with a determined commitment to Europe. This strong, unquestioned sense of belonging to Europe, together with the continuing threat that Russia posed to national security, inspired the political leadership of the 1990s to prioritize an agenda of joining 'all possible clubs':[76] NATO, the Schengen area, the EEC and later the EU – an agenda that operated under the 'logic of securitization'[77] to proceed with radical reforms that led to growing levels of inequality within the state, but that indeed found success in providing both security guarantees and a flourishing economic climate. The imaginary of Europe itself had changed substantially during this process and changed from a predominantly aesthetic category to a predominantly geopolitical one.

[76] Mikko Lagerspetz and Henri Vogt, 'Estonia', in Sten Berglund, Joakim Ekman, Kevin Deegan-Krause and Terje Knutsen (eds.), *The Handbook of Political Change in Eastern Europe*, 3rd ed. (Edward Elgar, 2014), 55.

[77] Ibid., 67.

In his 1992 speech *Estonia – Europe – the World*, Edgar Savisaar reflected on global future scenarios – among others, on the possibility of a Europe that has integrated Russia to become a global entity that stretched 'from Gibraltar to the Urals' – a scenario that in the early 1990s did not sound utterly implausible.[78] Thirty years later, Russia's new wave of imperial warfare has effaced such visions from Estonian imaginaries, and Estonia's belongingness to Europe has emerged as an existential imperative, not simply one imaginary among others.

78 Savisaar, 'Eesti – Euroopa – maailm', 54.

12

Czechoslovakia

Remembering and Forgetting the Failures of a State

Mary Heimann

Czechoslovakia, a state which first came into being on 28 October 1918 and ceased to exist at midnight on 31 December 1992, lasted less long than an average human lifespan. During these years, the newly imagined polity underwent a bewildering number of constitutional changes. Not only was it federalized, centralized, dissolved, reconstituted, re-centralized and re-federalized; it also went through a wide variety of political regimes, from military dictatorship to parliamentary democracy; from authoritarian democracy to Nazi colony; from people's democracy to Soviet satellite; and from Communist dictatorship and command economy to democracy and the free market.

It was because the case of Czechoslovakia offers, as it were, a compressed history of twentieth-century Europe, of many ways that the modern state has been imagined, that it first captured my interest. It is not often that one is privileged, as a historian, to see the entire history of a state, from its planned creation to its premeditated extinction. Themes familiar to those of us who grew up in the West during the Cold War – the failures of democracy and rise of authoritarianism in the 1930s, the horrors of Nazism and the Holocaust in the 1940s, the spread of Stalinist terror in the 1950s, the height of Cold War anxiety in the 1960s, détente in the 1970s, the reform and eventual overthrow of Communism in the 1980s – seemed neatly pre-packaged, as if into so many teaching segments, in the compact history of this modern European state.

To live in Prague, in that first decade after the overthrow of the Communist regime was, unsurprisingly, to discover that Czechoslovak history was remembered, packaged and imagined differently there. Czech historiography, Czech documentaries, Czech museums, Czech monuments, Czech films, Czech exhibitions, Czech newspapers, in those years of what was termed post-Communist 'transition', were as striking to a Westerner for their unspoken assumptions – especially about the salience of nationality – as for what they said explicitly. There were patterns which at first seemed curious to an outsider: the 'othering' of Communists, for example, who were invariably described as 'they' despite the proportion of local Communist Party members having been proportionately larger, per head of population, than that of any other political party at any time anywhere in the world.[1] Or the ubiquitous characterization of Czechoslovakia as a 'small' European nation, despite being of average size in both land mass and population. And there were the absences and silences: the repurposed synagogues and formerly Jewish quarters in provincial towns; the abandoned German businesses and neglected cemeteries in the Bohemian and Moravian borderlands; the invisibility of Roma and Vietnamese in official narratives; the way that the suffering of some groups was downplayed or ignored, while that of others was heightened. As throughout the rest of Central Europe, both official and popular memory emphasized the antiquity of the dominant 'nation' and its repeated martyrdoms, betrayals and victimhood at the hands of foreigners. Whereas, in the West, nations competed as to which was supposed to be the greatest, in Central Europe the competition seemed to turn on which had suffered the most.

My aim in researching and writing a new history of Czechoslovakia was to try to understand, in as objective a way as possible, how a state which ceased to exist in 1993 had been imagined, created and reimagined as it went through a succession of political incarnations before finally being dissolved. I wanted to provide what it seemed impossible at the time to find in libraries and bookshops: a clear, accessible account of the whole history of the state which did not present the story from the perspective of one nationality at the expense of all the rest, which did not ignore alternative readings and counter-narratives, and which looked at people as having agency and individual responsibility. The first step to enable me to try to do this – learning Czech – took three years of formal university study followed by two years of immersion. The second step was to use the grant which I won from the Leverhulme Trust to travel throughout the whole of the former Czechoslovak state and to read as wide a range of primary source materials (both published and manuscript) as time would permit. Since it is not possible to do everything, I tried to focus particular attention on under-researched times and places: to sample security files from the years which fell between the landmark years 1918 (independence), 1938 (Munich Crisis), 1968 (Prague Spring) and 1989 (Velvet Revolution), for example; or to look closely at the experiences of a city like Užgorod (Uzhhorod, Ungvár, Ужгород), to see how things might look from that lesser-known perspective.

The fact that Czechoslovakia was a multinational state whose history could be examined right from birth to death, so to speak, made it a fascinating object of study to me. I had no previous association with Czechoslovakia, no Czechoslovak ancestry, no skin in the game. When I began researching the topic, I had no idea what the overall thesis of the book would turn out to be. I went where the evidence took me. My work included extensive research, over a period of eight months, in the Czechoslovak Ministry of Interior (StB/ŠtB, the state security or secret police)

[1] Gordon Wightman and Archibald H. Brown 'Changes in the Levels of Membership and Social Composition of the Communist Party of Czechoslovakia, 1945–73' (1975) 27 *Soviet Studies* 396.

archives; several months spent in the Czech National Library, where I read the entire *Sbírka zákonů* (Collection of Laws and Ordinances) from 1918 to 1992; months looking at materials from the German-controlled Protectorate of Bohemia-Moravia and the Communist Central Archives; further weeks in the collections of Czechoslovak presidents Beneš and Masaryk's private papers; and time spent in the Slovak National Library, as well as a number of regional archives. I tried, wherever possible, to favour primary sources over secondary works. Apart from the manuscript sources to be found in the archives, I also read through hundreds of published primary sources, published mainly in Czech, Slovak, English and French. Sometimes, as with Ukrainian and Hungarian sources, I needed to rely on the help of professional translators.

The themes which began to emerge from my developing understanding of Czechoslovak history were not those which I had been led to expect from such heroic characterizations as the 'land of an unconquerable ideal'[2] which had been publicised from the 1920s, but with particular vigour after the Munich Crisis in 1938 and again after Czechoslovakia was invaded by Soviet-led Warsaw Pact troops in 1968. The state which was so often characterized, especially in the English-language literature, as humane and tolerant, and whose propaganda made much of it being a naturally democratic island set in an authoritarian sea, turned out (unsurprisingly) to be much more like its Central European neighbours than its Western Allies in its ways of perceiving the world. (The Western Allies, of course, had their own distortions and self-illusions; the point is that they were different ones). Again, like its neighbours, the Czechoslovak state, too, was sometimes responsible for the persecution of ethno-linguistic, racial and religious minorities. The importance of what I was beginning to uncover about the experiences of the non-Czech minorities in the state – from the moves taken against Jews *before* the establishment of the German Protectorate (1939–1945) and Tiso's fascistic Slovak Republic (1939–1945) to the fine detail of the post-war treatment of Germans and forcible 'Slovakization' of Hungarians; and from the treatment of Czech Roma during the post-Munich, pre-War Second Czecho-Slovak Republic (1938–1939) to the workings of the Tiso regime in Slovakia, both when it was autonomous (1938–1939) and independent (1939–1944), for example, made me feel that it was important to write the book for as wide a potential readership as would be consistent with intellectual and scholarly integrity. It seemed to me then, and it seems to me now, that we ignore the ugly, xenophobic side of nationalism in Europe at our peril: that Europe will be a safer, more humane and tolerant place only after its nations and states recognize their own part as sometimes perpetrators, as well as sometimes victims, of extreme intolerance. I wanted, in short, to write for the General Reader.

[2] The phrase is taken from the title of a characteristic introduction to the new Czechoslovak state from the mid-1920s. This was Jessie Mothersole, *Czechoslovakia: The Land of an Unconquerable Ideal* (John Lane, 1926).

The risk was always that the resulting book would fall between two stools: too populist for academics and too scholarly for non-specialists.

The book, which was originally to be called *The Czechoslovak Experiment* (a title which turned out to have been used before), was first published with Yale University Press in 2009 as *Czechoslovakia: The State that Failed*. The title, which followed the cadence of a well-known short story by Saki,[3] and whose inclusion of the word 'failed' was provocative, was intended to signal three different things at once. First, the use of the terms 'Czechoslovakia' and 'state' was supposed to make clear that the book's subject matter was a state, a polity, rather than a people or peoples: what was being offered was a history of Czechoslovakia, not the Czech and Slovak nations. Second, the subtitle 'The State that Failed' signalled that the book was not going to be structured as a simple chronology of selected political events but had an overarching argument or thesis. Finally, the use of the term 'failed' warned the reader that the book's interpretation of the Czechoslovak state was not going to be the Czech-centred narrative of Czechoslovak exceptionalism with which the world was already familiar, but instead a sharply revisionist critique of that consensus.

The inclusion of the word 'failed' in the book's title was risky. In English, the word 'failed' has a number of associations which make it difficult to translate into Czech without making the word sound either too gentle (*neúspěl*) or too harsh (*selhal*). The eminent Czech translator Zdeněk Hron's choice of '*zklamal*' in the Czech version of the book which was eventually brought out by Petrkov publishers in 2020, is probably the best compromise: but inevitably, as is the case with any translation, some associations are lost. In a very obvious and literal way, the Czechoslovak state 'failed', did not succeed, in that it ceased to exist (*propadl*), not just once, but twice, in the space of just 74 years. The primary sense in which I meant to suggest that the state 'failed', however, was in the sense of a scientific experiment which does not result in the intended or expected outcome. Czechoslovakia was a 'failed experiment' (*neúspěšný experiment*) in this fundamental sense: the Czechoslovak state was explicitly set up to be a multinational, liberal and democratic state, 'a sort of Switzerland', as Foreign Minister Edvard Beneš promised at Versailles, in which Germans and other minorities would benefit from something like the Swiss canton system; Slovaks would be treated as equals; and Subcarpathian Ruthenia would be fully autonomous. These promises were either broken – as in the case of Subcarpathian Ruthenia, whose formal autonomy was not implemented but eventually seized in 1938, following the Munich disaster – or else not felt to be honoured, as in the case of both Slovakia and the German, Hungarian and Polish minorities.

The second way in which the state did not succeed was in its intended geopolitical function. Czechoslovakia's creation at the end of WWI, as a predominantly Slav

[3] Hector Hugh Munro, 'Filboid Studge, The Story of a Mouse that Helped', in *Saki: The Complete Short Stories* (Penguin Modern Classics, 2011).

multinational state in the midst of majority German-speaking territory, was commended to the peacemakers at Paris, and to all who dreamed of a 'New Europe', as a means of promoting stability and keeping the balance of power in Central Europe by containing Germany, protecting France, and preventing the possibility of another European war to follow the Great War. Although it was of course Germany which was most responsible for destabilizing Europe, and then launching the unspeakably brutal WWII, Czechoslovak foreign and domestic policy in the 1920s and early 1930s did itself few favours. By promoting the interests of Czechs over other nationalities within the state, speaking on behalf of peoples it had little or no mandate to represent, running roughshod over the sensibilities of most of the state's minorities and treating its easternmost province like a virtual colony, by the mid-1930s Czechoslovakia had lost the support of most of its domestic non-Czech populations at the same time that its foreign policy was alienating nearly all of its neighbours. This put the state in an exceptionally vulnerable position, especially once it became apparent that the largest threat to its liberty came from Germany, by then under Nazi control, rather than – as had been expected initially – from a revanchist Hungary or Austria. None of this is to downplay the aggressive nationalism and intolerance towards minorities which was shown by Czechoslovakia's neighbours – above all, Germany – but rather to suggest that Czechoslovakia was not, as is usually claimed, an exception which fit better into a Western than a Central European model. Rather, Czechoslovakia offered variations on common contemporary themes of nationalist, ethnic, religious and racial intolerance which were at the time a striking part of the European, and especially Central European, *zeitgeist*.

Czechoslovakia's failures to remain a liberal, democratic and stabilizing force in Central Europe came about because of a complex series of interactions between external pressures, which are well known, and internal decisions, which are not. The ultimate results, as the book details, were that Czechoslovakia ceased to be liberal, with regard to its non-Czech citizens, during the First Czechoslovak Republic of 1918–1938; ceased to be democratic, in all but name, during the Second Czecho-Slovak Republic of 1938–1939; and, over the course of WWII (1939–1945) and the Third Czechoslovak Republic (1945–1948), lost most of its claim to be either multinational or tolerant of minorities. After a further forty-one years of Communist Party rule, followed by three years of rapid reorientation towards democracy and the free market, Czechoslovakia divided into Czech and Slovak halves, ceasing to be a unitary Czechoslovak state at all. None of this made the Czechoslovak state out to be worse than any other: but it returned the notion of agency and individual responsibility to a country which was too often presented as a passive victim, the plaything of Great Powers, a stalwart nation which had the misfortune to be stuck between Russia and Germany, and to whom political misfortunes fell like so many natural disasters.

The Czechoslovak state may have failed, but the Czech and Slovak nations succeeded, and spectacularly, in creating separate, seemingly durable, largely homogenous nation-states by the end of the twentieth century. It is easy to overlook how remarkable these Czech and Slovak successes were. That the old Bohemian Crown Lands, today's Czech Republic or Czechia, and the old Hungarian highlands, today's Slovak Republic or Slovakia, exist as separate European Union partners and NATO members could not have been confidently predicted even as recently as a generation ago. At the beginning of the twentieth century, Czech (as opposed to Bohemian) and Slovak independence were equally unthinkable. The very scale and improbability of this success makes it sometimes difficult for Czechs and Slovaks to comprehend that the multinational Czechoslovak state, for all its initial support from France, Britain and the United States, and for all its subsequent economic, industrial, literary, cultural, artistic and other successes, contained within itself the seeds of its own failure.

In making these arguments, a number of which had not been heard before, and comprehensively challenging the narrative that had dominated both Czechoslovak exile and Western Cold War propaganda, back in 2009 the book sharply divided opinion. Today, over a century after the Czechoslovak state was brought into being, thirty years since the collapse of the Communist regime and after a generation of further scholarship, the book's arguments are no longer new, and no longer threatening, in the way that they seemed to many at the time. Czechoslovak historiography, once so uniform in its interpretations, has become an infinitely more varied and complex field, one characterized by orthodoxies, reinterpretations and properly historical debates. Old nationalist and state-serving narratives die hard, however, and one can still see the familiar lines of the old Czech-centred view implicit in what is included, and what is left out, of *Kroniky*, *Dějiny v datech*, museum guidebooks, tour guide examinations, school textbooks, government websites, plaques, memorials, television programmes, radio documentaries, block-buster films, public commemorations and much else besides. The book may, therefore, still serve a purpose in offering a corrective, or at least an alternative, to what remains the popular version of Czech, and by extension Czechoslovak, history in these and other places.

While it was clear to my generation of American and British historians that the story we had grown up with about Central Europe was ripe for revision, the newly independent Czech and Slovak republics were naturally more sensitive about their public image. When, on 28 October 2009, *Czechoslovakia: The State That Failed* was first published, in English, by Yale University Press, the book was immediately denounced in a public speech by the Czech Consul-General in Los Angeles, as a 'step away' from a 'crime against humanity'.[4] At the same time, the book was effusively welcomed by *Literární noviny*, albeit with a warning that it held up a

4 'Czech Consul General Condemns "Anti-Czechoslovak" Book' (29 October 2009) https://legacy.blisty.cz/art/49625.html.

'shocking mirror' in which Czech society might not recognize itself.[5] The current affairs magazine *Respekt* included on its glossy front cover the news item: 'female historian from the USA provokes the Czechs' (*Historička z USA provokuje Čechy*).[6] *Lidové noviny*'s Saturday Arts supplement took a more humorous angle, reproducing the image of David Černý's St Wenceslas riding an upside-down horse with the caption: 'Mary Heimann turns twentieth-century Czech history on its head' (*Mary Heimannová staví české dějiny 20. století na hlavu*).[7] The editor of *The Prague Post* reported that 'Central European history did a somersault' with the release of a book that 'upended almost every conventional view of the country' and 'shattered the traditional perception of Czechoslovakia as a victim'.[8] The *Times Literary Supplement* welcomed the book as 'truly a history of Czechoslovakia not just Czechs and Slovaks' which did well to remind readers that 'this vanished country was home to Germans, Hungarians, Ruthenes, Roma and Poles, to Lutherans, Uniates and Jews as well as Roman Catholics and atheists'. The book, it judged, was 'astonishing not so much for revealing new facts' although it had 'done its share of archival sleuthing', but for 'bringing into relief a narrative that was hiding in plain sight during the Cold War', one of 'Czech ruthlessness' with regard to minorities and non-Czech nationalities in the now defunct Czechoslovak state.[9]

People who grew up in the former Czechoslovakia reacted strongly to the book: they loved it or hated it. For some, the book's title was enough. The Czech philosopher Erazim Kohák attacked the book at length in *Literární noviny* while at the same time frankly admitting that he had not actually read it.[10] Madeleine Albright, who was known as the daughter of Czechoslovak diplomat, politician and historian Josef Korbel long before she became US Secretary of State, told me that her advisor had warned her not to read the book because she 'wouldn't like it'. A retired civil servant, intrigued by the debate, began collecting press cuttings from around the world, marking with an asterisk those reviews in which the reviewer acknowledged that he or she had not actually read the book. This turned out to be 50 per cent. 'Good for you for stirring things up!' wrote a Balkans journalist who told me that his editor had been angrily instructed by the Czech ambassador not to publish a favourable review of the book. 'Are they sending you death threats?' he asked. *The Economist*, which featured the book on its Books and Arts (Culture) page, praised the 'archival research and attention to detail' as 'exemplary' but considered its tone 'vinegary' and 'spiteful'.[11] The 'venom of many of the reviewers', countered

[5] 'Jsme to my v tom šokujícím zrcadle?', *Literární noviny* 26 October 2009; http://literarky.cz/civilizace/89-civilizace/1522-jsme-to-my-v-tom-okujicim-zrcadle.

[6] *Respekt* (10–17 January 2010), cover.

[7] 'Orientace/kritika', *Lidové noviny* (23 January 2010), 1.

[8] 'The Dark Side: A New History of Czechoslovakia Casts a Troubling Shadow', *The Prague Post* (24–30 March 2010).

[9] 'Beyond Prague', *Times Literary Supplement* (26 March 2010).

[10] 'Všechno je jinak', *Literární noviny* (2 November 2009).

[11] 'Czechoslovakia: A Chequered History', *The Economist* (21 November 2009), 100.

an elderly Austrian scholar who spoke Czech, Slovak, German, Hungarian, French and English, 'just confirms your thesis about Czech *nesnášenlivost* and *šovinismus*' (intolerance and chauvinism).

Emails, letters and phone calls from journalists followed. The most surprising private communications included a congratulatory letter from a former head of a Western intelligence service who had served in Prague during the Cold War; purportedly leaked documents from the Czech Foreign Ministry; and a request for help from a displaced Bohemian princess seeking restitution of her family's property. Some correspondents were hurt or angry, stung by what they saw as attacks on their national identity. Others were grateful to have their own sense of injustice or hurt acknowledged. Perhaps the most humbling letter I received was from a circle of Czech engineers in Prague who explained that, because they had grown up under Communism and knew only the official version of Czechoslovak history, they had been meeting, week by week, to discuss each chapter of the book through a series of informal seminars. Further surprises – including being asked to take part in a debate with the former Czech Prime Minister Petr Pithart in the Czech Senate as part of the Prague Writers' Festival in 2013, to make policy recommendations to a NATO Partnership for Peace workshop held in Kyiv in 2015 and to spend an evening discussing the book with members of the Prague Business Club in 2019 – followed.

Apart from the controversy that took place in public, in full view, there was also another story which went on in the background. This was in itself an education. I knew that journalists, critics and reviewers could hype up or undermine a book; but I had not previously realized that academic publishers, in a free country, would go so far as to break legally binding contracts – in effect to censor themselves – in response to real or imagined political pressure. In 1945, the English writer George Orwell wrote an essay, intended to serve as a preface to his forthcoming novel *Animal Farm*, entitled 'The Freedom of the Press'. In this little-known piece, which was not published during his lifetime, Orwell set out the difficulty he had had in finding a publisher for the book for which, along with the dystopian novel *Nineteen Eighty-Four*, he was ultimately to be best remembered. When publisher after publisher refused to bring out *Animal Farm*, Orwell slowly came to realize that he was being censored: not overtly, since post-war Britain was, after all, a free country; but unofficially, indirectly and voluntarily.

The publishers who rejected Orwell's manuscript did not do so because they found his political allegory poorly written, dull to read or unlikely to sell well: on the contrary, the new manuscript's clarity and popular appeal were immediately apparent. The problem with Orwell's short allegorical novel was not that it was a bad book but that it implicitly criticized Stalin and the Soviet Union; and this at a time when the Soviet Union was Britain's ally, Socialism seemed to many to represent the future and Stalin's achievements were widely admired, including in British literary, governmental and intellectual circles. Only one of the publishers who rejected Orwell's *Animal Farm* did so for overtly party-political reasons. The others had no clear political stance and one publisher, as Orwell tells us, 'actually started by accepting the book', even 'making preliminary arrangements to bring it out' only to change his mind after consulting the Ministry of Information who 'warned him, or at any rate strongly advised him, against publishing it'. As the editor of the publishing house explained to Orwell in a letter, the 'reaction' he had had 'from an important official in the Ministry of Information' led him to see that Orwell's political fable 'might be regarded as something which it was highly ill-advised to publish at the present time', given that it 'so completely [followed] the progress of the Russian Soviets and their two dictators' and especially given the offensive 'choice of pigs as the ruling caste' since this would 'no doubt give offence to many people, and particularly to anyone who is a bit touchy, as undoubtedly the Russians are'.

Orwell's *Animal Farm*, in short, was repeatedly refused publication, not because it was thought to be substandard; or unlikely to sell; or even libellous; but rather because it was critical of the contemporary Soviet system in general, and of Stalin in particular, at a time when influential people did not wish Stalin or the Soviet Union to be criticized. What disturbed Orwell most about the widespread ignoring or downplaying of inconvenient facts about the Soviet Union under Stalin was that the conspiracy of silence was largely self-imposed and voluntary. 'Unpopular ideas', as Orwell pointed out, 'can be silenced, and inconvenient facts kept dark, without the need for any official ban'. At any given moment, Orwell went on,

> there is an orthodoxy, a body of ideas, which it is assumed that all right-thinking people will accept without question. It is not exactly forbidden to say this, that or the other, but it is 'not done' to say it ... Anyone who challenges the prevailing orthodoxy finds himself silenced with surprising effectiveness. A genuinely unfashionable opinion is almost never given a fair hearing, either in the popular press or in the highbrow periodicals.

Although George Orwell was describing the situation that existed in post-war Great Britain, not the Czech Republic in the first decades after Communism, the phenomenon of the voluntary censorship that he described soon became all-too recognizable to me. In those days in the Czech Republic, of course, it was not Stalin's atrocities that were ignored or downplayed (quite the reverse) but rather such sensitive topics as the post-war treatment of ethnic Germans, the degree of Czech collaboration in the Protectorate of Bohemia-Moravia, the degree of local responsibility for Fascist and Communist authoritarian regimes, the place of the Roma in Czech society and the extent to which Slovak and Rusyn nationalism were suppressed. Other topics were not so much ignored as genuinely forgotten: the role of the Prague government in bringing about the March 1939 crisis which led to Slovak independence and to the establishment of the Protectorate, for example; the initial welcome being prepared for the Warsaw Pact armies by both *Rudé právo* and the Slovak branch of the Communist Party in the first, confused hours on 21 August 1968; the extent to which authoritarianism, fascism and antisemitism characterized all parts of the Second Czecho-Slovak Republic of 1938–1939; the extent to which the Czechoslovak Communist Party was involved in what turned into the 1989 anti-regime revolution, and other such episodes which suggest a more complex picture than the traditional division into villains and heroes, victims and perpetrators, and which have since been scrutinized in more depth by Jan Tesář, Michal Pullmann, Muriel Blaive, David Green and various other scholars.

Czechoslovakia: The State that Failed, which evidently transgressed against the unwritten rules as to how it was permissible to evaluate the Czechoslovak state's political record, went through precisely the same kind of voluntary censorship that Orwell described in his essay on the freedom of the press (an essay which itself remained unpublished until after his death).[12] Within weeks of the book first appearing in English, five separate Czech publishers approached me with offers to bring out a Czech translation. I decided to go with the most prestigious of the academic publishers which had approached me; the book underwent the usual anonymous peer-review process and a contract was signed for an initial print run of 1,500–3,000 copies, publication within 18 months, and 8 per cent of the retail price, which the publisher estimated at 350 kč, suggesting that the book was expected to sell. The book was contracted, the translator chosen, my university informed and the information that the book was to be published included on some public websites.

All continued as normal, with the usual number of emails back and forth, until suddenly everything went mysteriously quiet from the publisher's end, when an innocuous query about some aspect or other of the book went unanswered; and remained unanswered after a first reminder; then a second; then a third. After several weeks of this unexplained silence, which came at the height of a negative campaign in the Czech press, I eventually emailed to ask directly whether everything was still all right with the contract or whether there was some problem. Floods of reassurances followed: yes, of course, everything was fine; there were no problems, everything was still working to schedule and the translated version of the book would be ready and published on time. Then, just days after receiving these reassurances, came an agonised email from my editor, attaching a copy of an anonymous letter from someone – not a peer reviewer and not, judging by the tone and wording of the letter, an academic – asserting his or her view that the book ought not to be published. It seemed clear from the wording of the letter that the motives were political: my guess is that it came from whichever Ministry is the modern Czech equivalent of George Orwell's Ministry for Propaganda. Whoever wrote it must have had a good deal of clout, because even a university publisher with standing was evidently so anxious to please, or so afraid to offend, that it was willing to break its own rules – indeed, to break the law – and go back on its own decision and contractual obligation to publish.

[12] www.orwellfoundation.com/the-orwell-foundation/orwell/essays-and-other-works/the-freedom-of-the-press/.

Unsure what to do, I phoned Yale University Press to ask for their assessment of what had just happened. My editor at Yale, after discussion with the press's lawyer, explained that the Czech academic publisher was in clear breach of contract; that I would be within my rights to sue them; and that Yale would 'back me all the way' if I decided to take this route. The notion of *forcing* a publisher to honour its contractual agreement seemed a very distasteful proposition to me: presuming that the court case won, which Yale seemed to feel confident that it would, what would it be like to work with a publisher against its will?

I did not go public with what had happened at the time, partly because I did not want to put my editor, who was already stressed, under yet more pressure; and partly because I was finding the whole affair exhausting. I confined myself to writing a private letter to the head of the university press. It was only when, a couple of years later, I was invited to speak at the twenty-third Prague Writers' Festival and the organizers wanted to get hold of the Czech version of my book, that I had to explain why my book had not yet appeared in Czech. To my surprise, the organizer of the Prague Writers' Festival went public with the news by mentioning it in his introduction to a live discussion about the book that took place in the Czech Senate, on 18 April 2013, between myself, former Prime Minister Petr Pithart and the Czech historian Jan Rychlík. Towards the end of the discussion, which was filmed and livestreamed, Petr Pithart mentioned his hope that the book, which he judged important and necessary, though painful, would appear in Czech soon.[13]

Within a few days of the Prague Writers' Festival on 'The Birth of Nations' at which there was a panel presentation about my book in the Czech Senate, another reputable publisher, this time a private one, expressed their wish to publish a Czech translation of the book. 'We would be very honoured to have the opportunity to be your Czech publisher', wrote the editor. 'The book would suit our publishing profile very well and we would dedicate all our resources to promote it.[14] This second contract with a Czech publisher, and third publishing contract for the book, was agreed and signed by both parties and dated 15 April 2013 though not in fact sent until June 2013. The publisher paid an advance, agreed to a relatively large initial print run of 2,000 copies, and, after some discussion, to 8 per cent royalties. At my request, my previous experience having made me a little cautious, it was required by the terms of the publishing contract that the book be published within 18 months, by the end of the year 2014, or else the rights would revert to the author.

Once again, everything seemed to be proceeding normally at first: terms were agreed, two copies of the contract signed. A translator was selected and, at least according to what I was told by the publishers, got to work on the manuscript straightaway. It was only when, nearly a year after signing the contract, and the translator still had no questions for me, that I began to wonder. When I asked my

[13] www.ceskatelevize.cz/porady/10000000101-festival-spisovatelu-praha-2013/.

[14] Email to Mary Heimann (11 May 2015).

editor, the same editor who had been answering emails immediately, whether everything was still OK with the contract – exactly as had happened before with the academic publisher – there was a sudden, inexplicable silence. When I pressed, I got the same flood of reassurances: of course there was no problem, my dear Mrs Heimann; the translator was very busy working on the manuscript and it would be ready by April 2014 at the earliest. As for the translator's email address, should I wish to contact him directly? Unfortunately, I was told, the translator does not use email, the only way to contact him would be via the publishers, via the editor himself. I felt a sickening sense of recognition when the junior editor I had been dealing with, and who had always been so straightforward and helpful, suddenly began to show the same signs of stress the junior editor at the first academic publisher had shown. This time, presumably because this particular junior editor was too honest to play along with a charade, I received an email to explain that the junior editor 'frankly, no longer knew what was happening' with my book, and suggested that I speak directly to the director of the publishing house.

Just as the deadline of 18 months was coming up, and under pressure to answer, the director of the publishing company emailed me to state baldly that he had decided not to publish the book. No explanation, not even the pretence that there was a legitimate reason to suddenly pull the plug, just as we were coming to the end of the 18-month period specified in the contract and despite having sent me a cash advance. Either this commercial publisher had, like the university publisher, begun with honest intentions and been suddenly warned by someone influential not to proceed to publish; or perhaps the cash advance had, all along, been intended not as an advance on sales but rather as the price for preventing the book from being made accessible to Czech readers for at least a further few years. Either way, it did not seem a very good sign for freedom of the press.

At the same time that Czech publishers were apparently being pressured not to bring out a Czech edition of my book, there were other indications of interference in the normal reviewing process for a new book. From the very first there had been some signs to suggest that the book was not going to be treated simply as a routine work of revisionist history. On the day of publication, as already mentioned, the book was denounced by a Czech diplomat in a public speech.[15] On 17 March 2010, a Senate committee of the Czech Parliament was apparently alerted to the displeasure felt by some émigrés about the book. After a 'lively discussion', according to the report, the Senators agreed to 'deal with' the book through the committee for Education and Culture. It was further noted that Czech world service (*Český rozhlas*) would make a programme about the book, which would also be discussed at a conference to take place in Tábor between 27 June and 3 July 2010.[16]

[15] 'Czech Consul in Los Angeles Criticizes "Anti-Czechoslovak" Book', http://w1.blisty.cz/art/49625.html.

[16] M. Krupička, 'Zasedala krajanská komise Senátu' (17 March 2010) *Krajene.net* (krajene.radio.cz). See also www.svu2000.org.

Meanwhile, in February 2010, a journalist who had just published a positive review of my book, and who I had never met, emailed to let me know that the Czech ambassador in his country had demanded a face-to-face meeting with his editor-in-chief at which he 'tried to extract some kind of apology'. 'He didn't get it', reported the journalist, 'but he did write to me, sending me a stack of hostile reviews of your book and suggesting I read them'.[17]

In September 2010, during the 'Ties that Bind' conference held at the Czech and Slovak embassies in London, to which I was invited by the then Czech Ambassador, and at which former US Secretary of State Madeleine Albright took a prominent part, a good five minutes were spent denouncing passages from my book, which were read aloud, before the ambassador moved on to denounce the work of historian Muriel Blaive, who was also in attendance and who was clearly shaken by the experience. Next came phone calls from journalists working for the Czech state, most of whom were especially interested in one thing: was I of Sudeten German ancestry? It was lucky for me that I wasn't. Otherwise the book – even though it had been researched and written by a professional historian, drawing on evidence – presumably would have been dismissed out of hand. The book sold, and was widely reviewed, but was still only available in English.

In 2015, I received an invitation to speak at the annual Czech journalism summer school run by Milan Pilař in Havlíčkův Brod. Trying to think of what, as an historian, I might usefully find to say to an audience of aspiring journalists, I decided to talk about the importance of acknowledging the dark passages in one's own national history and to examine the sometimes subtle ways in which censorship can operate. One of the examples I drew on, together with George Orwell's *Animal Farm* and Hannah Arendt's *Eichmann in Jerusalem*, involved explaining, since this was the case I knew best, why there was still no Czech-language edition of my own *Czechoslovakia* book.[18] The Czech journalism students at the Summer School gave my talk a sympathetic hearing, and Milan Pilař afterwards took up the cause of bringing out a Czech edition of the book as a matter of honour. It was thanks to his perseverance that an excellent new translator and publisher were found. Interested to know more, Luboš Drobík invited me to speak at the Prague Business Club in 2019.[19] After a welcoming evening of food, drink and discussion in Wenceslas Square, a majority of members of the Prague Business Club, themselves divided between those who hated and those who loved the book, decided to crowdfund the costs of translation and publication in order to bring out a Czech-language edition. Zdeněk Hron, the translator, and Petrkov, the publisher, took on the task and the book was translated, copy-edited and printed. The final version included generous

[17] Private email to Mary Heimann (16 February 2010).

[18] 'O zamlčování nepohodlných dějin', Letní žurnalistická škola, Havlíčkův Brod (22 August 2015), www.letnizurnalistickaskola.cz/.

[19] 'Diskusní večeře s americkou historičkou Mary Heimann', www.businessclub.cz/cs/udalosti/.

endorsements by the former dissident, and later Czech Prime Minister, Petr Pithart, who wrote both an introduction and a jacket blurb; by the former dissident and Charter 77 spokesman Jan Urban; and by the famous Slovak actress, diplomat and politician Magdaléna Vášáryová, whose career included being the first post-Communist Czechoslovak Ambassador to Austria; Slovak ambassador to Poland; and Secretary of State for Slovakia. The book launch, with speeches by Petr Pithart and Jan Urban and with HE the British Ambassador Nick Archer and other dignitaries in attendance, was again hosted by the Prague Business Club. I was lucky: within a few weeks, COVID-19 restrictions were imposed and travel between the United Kingdom and the Czech Republic would no longer have been possible.

The story, once might say, ended well in that it is now possible for Czech readers, should they so wish, to read a book which presents Czechoslovak history in a very different light from the version which has long been officially favoured and promoted. The fact that it took ten years for this to happen and that it was evidently deemed necessary by some to seek to prevent, delay or discredit a book which was critical of Czech and Slovak nationalism, should nevertheless cause us to reflect a little on the role of history and its troubled relationship with nationalism, not just in the former Czechoslovakia but throughout Europe, including the United Kingdom. It is not difficult to understand why a book which is sharply critical of the dangers inherent in nationalism, in this case principally Czech and Slovak nationalism, should have received some hurt, angry or indignant responses. My motives were not, however, anti-Czech or anti-Slovak; nor was the book written out of spite or vinegar. My purpose in showing the darker side of nationalism was not to single out Czechoslovakia as better or worse than other states, still less to discredit Czechs, among whom I count many friends and (through marriage) family, as a people. Rather, it was to illustrate for the general reader – of whatever ethnic, linguistic, national or religious background – the inherent danger in perpetuating nationalist myths in which one's own side is presented as the righteous victim and the injury done to others ignored or downplayed.

It is one thing to disapprove of or dislike a book and quite another to seek to prevent others from being able to read it. I can only assume from the actions of those who sought to prevent the book from being read, from being reviewed impartially or from being translated into Czech, that those who sought to silence it knew themselves that the content of the book is true. This is not to say that there are no mistakes in the book (of course there are, as with any published book: some 14 errors were brought to my attention for correction in the second edition; as it happens, this is an unusually low number of typos and other minor errors for a 400-page book). But, just to state the obvious for a moment: if the book were fundamentally unsound, laughable, riddled with mistakes and based on poor research, as a concerted effort by internet trolls sought to persuade the world, it would hardly have been contracted even by one serious university press, let alone two. It would not have passed the scrutiny of six expert peer-reviewers (two apiece for each of the academic presses, including Yale University Press, which sent the unpublished manuscript out for anonymous assessment, and two for the commercial press). Nor would it have been viewed as worth silencing. As Orwell pointed out: one does not feel the need to prevent the publication of a bad book.

My generation grew up steeped in knowledge about the horrors perpetrated by Nazi Germany. Far less well known was the extent to which the persecution of minorities came to be justified in the name of nationalism and codified in legal statutes, right across Central Europe. It seemed to me especially important, a decade after the 'end' of the Cold War, to advertise the fact that this could happen *even* in a democratic country, *even* in one which held up France, Britain and the United States as political models, *even* in one which suffered at the hands of Nazi Germany, *even* in a state which was widely described as humane, tolerant and progressive. If we in the so-called democratic West were to avoid repeating the injustices and cruelties which characterized Central Europe in the twentieth century, it seemed to me that we needed to face the dark parts of that past squarely. Everyone already knew about the evil of Hitler's Germany. The lesson of the Czechoslovak state's seventy-four-year history, as I saw it, was the extent to which people like *us* were culpable, through intolerance of other minority, ethnic and national groups, of bringing about precisely the sorts of injustices to which we object when practised by others. It is perfectly possible for a nation to be both a victim and a perpetrator. To divide the world mentally into 'good' and 'bad' nations is not only misleading; it is also potentially dangerous.

The warning which I sounded in 2009 – about the limits and fragility of democracy and liberalism and the dangers of ethnic stereotyping and generalization – may have seemed far-fetched in those far-off days before Orbán, Trump, Johnson, Brexit, Erdoğan, Zeman and the many promoters of hate and scapegoating who have been crowding the international political stage more recently. In today's political climate across Europe, so reminiscent of the 1930s, in which populist xenophobia and protectionism are back, anti-Semitism, Islamophobia and other forms of racial hatred actively exploited by political leaders, a war which may well prove to be a Third World War being waged by Russia against Ukraine and refugees (including children) once again dehumanized, locked up, turned away or threatened with forcible relocation to Africa, the example of how the Czechoslovak state – a country which prided itself on its decency – descended from liberal democracy into authoritarianism and various iterations of police state is more politically salient than ever. Today, it is Britain's increasingly questionable attitude to human rights which worry me far more than those of the Czech or Slovak Republics. But this could change again: the point is precisely that no country, no people, is immune from such dangers.

As historians, it is our job to struggle as best we can against the assumptions and prejudices of our times, our outlook, our century, our nationality: to swim against the current, to refuse to accept the fashionable view of the moment. It is most emphatically not, in my opinion, the historian's job to begin with any established, fixed set of beliefs – whether that Communism was evil or the Germans warmongers or the Czechs innately democratic – and then 'select' those facts that seem to support that belief (or prejudice). And here I think that the Central European *penchant* for the *Kronika* – selected events to promote particular political outlooks and/or to support any particular regime – needs to be questioned.

History can challenge our own assumptions and prejudices and teach us to empathize with others and to understand the complexity – moral and otherwise – of the real world. One reviewer claimed that my *Czechoslovakia: The State That Failed* 'changed forever' the historiography of Czechoslovak history. Another, writing for the Communist Party's *The Morning Star*, predicted (no doubt accurately) that Julius Fučík's *Notes from the Gallows* will 'remain evergreen long after this book is consigned to the university bookshops' bargain bins'. My hope was, and remains, that presenting the history of Czechoslovakia from a fresh, non-nationalist, perspective will encourage some – whether Czech, Slovak, British, American, Hungarian, whatever – to consider the arbitrariness of nationality, the often unconscious chauvinism to which groups of human beings are prone and the degree to which each of us contributes, for good or for ill, to the regimes under which we live.

13

A Constitution without Qualities?

Three Narratives about Austrian Constitutional Law

Ulrich Wagrandl

13.1 INTRODUCTION

Every constitution is accompanied by imaginaries: ideas about how and why it emerged and what it is for.[1] Constitutional imaginaries are supported by narratives: stories that help to make sense of the text and the reality of a given constitutional order. Some of these stories are part of a country's national identity, as the American Founding Fathers' drafting of the Constitution in Philadelphia, or the French Revolutionaries' Declaration of the Rights of Man and of the Citizen. Other such narratives are confined to the ranks of constitutional lawyers. But they, too, need a set of background stories to guide their work.

This chapter seeks to explore and to contextualise three of these background stories of Austrian constitutional law. Those basic narratives are:

1. The Austrian constitution is in ruins.
2. The Austrian constitution is value-neutral and formalist.
3. The Austrian constitution is a role model for European integration and it gave the world judicial review.

These three narratives are deliberately arranged in reverse chronological order. The 'ruins' metaphor has its origin in the flood of legislation after 1945. It was coined to denote the poor state of constitutional law after a myriad of amendments allegedly made its text an incomprehensible mess. The narrative of value neutrality and formalism can be traced back to Austria's constitutional founding in 1920. Buttressed by Hans Kelsen's pure theory of law and his procedural theory of democracy, it is supposed to capture the constitution's essence as being a historical compromise between hostile political forces, which is, because of that, devoid of any

[1] See Jan Komárek, 'European Constitutional Imaginaries: Utopias, Ideologies and the Other', in Jan Komárek (ed.), *European Constitutional Imaginaries: Between Ideology and Utopia* (Oxford University Press, 2023), 2; Martin Loughlin, 'The Constitutional Imagination' (2015) 78 *Modern Law Review* 1.

substantial values. Both these narratives have made it hard to promote something like constitutional patriotism or at least surround the constitution with an aura of respect. The third narrative, however, compensates for this, as it showcases the achievements of the rule of law, constitutional adjudication and a unique openness towards European integration, which have their roots in 1867 and the Austro-Hungarian monarchy. The years of 1867, 1920 and 1945 mark the three defining constitutional moments in recent Austrian history. Each symbolises a moment of defeat that was only later reinterpreted as a new beginning. Like all such narratives, each contains some truth but glosses over the details.

Each one of the Austrian constitutional stories seems to be in flux. The 'ruins' narrative has recently been challenged by Austria's president, who admiringly spoke of the constitution's 'elegance and beauty'. The neutrality narrative begins to crumble as human rights and value-laden constitutional amendments demand a more purposive interpretive approach. The 'model for Europe' narrative is the youngest and is more and more promoted. Its future looks bright. Taken together, these three narratives about Austrian constitutional law provide insight into the ways that Austrian lawyers think. But they also have something to offer for the project of European integration; they can act as a warning or present a path worth emulating. They may have their basis in various constitutional provisions but, more than anything, they are *stories.*[2] Stories are important. No constitutional project has ever been successful without one.

13.2 NARRATIVE 1: RUINS AND BEAUTY

13.2.1 *Constitutional Aesthetics*

Studying law in Austria, one sooner or later comes across a famous quote by former Minister of Justice and professor of constitutional law, Hans Klecatsky, who declared the Austrian Constitution to be in ruins.[3] He continued his critique for years to come and in the starkest terms – 'work of destruction'[4] – and almost all constitutional scholars agreed.[5] It is difficult to evaluate if Klecatsky only expressed a widely held sentiment or if he managed to single-handedly create a new narrative. At any rate, the 'ruins' dictum became influential and has shaped the thinking of generations of Austrian constitutional lawyers. While there are a number of

[2] See, e.g., Jack Balkin, *Constitutional Redemption: Political Faith in an Unjust World* (Harvard University Press, 2011), 17ff.

[3] Hans Klecatsky, *Das österreichische Bundesverfassungsrecht*, 2nd ed. (Manz, 1973), V.

[4] See Hans Klecatsky, 'Bundes-Verfassungsgesetz und Bundesverfassungsrecht', in Herbert Schambeck (ed.), *Das österreichische Bundes-Verfassungsgesetz und seine Entwicklung* (Duncker & Humblot, 1980), 97, where he also quotes everyone who agreed with him over time.

[5] See Ewald Wiederin, 'Verfassungsbild', in Harald Eberhard, Michael Holoubek, Thomas Kröll, Georg Lienbacher and Stefan Storr (eds.), *100 Jahre Republik Österreich: Kontinuität – Brüche – Kompromisse* (Verlag Österreich, 2021), 62.

somewhat less scathing metaphors for the Austrian Constitution, none of them express great respect for it. For example, former President of the Constitutional Court, Karl Korinek, likened Austrian constitutional law to suburban sprawl;[6] professor of constitutional law, Ewald Wiederin, to a village of larger and smaller houses, some of them with ugly backyards.[7] Another Minister of Justice, Supreme Administrative Court President and professor of constitutional law, Clemens Jabloner, felt the need to warn against constitutional cynicism.[8]

How is it possible that so many ministers, court presidents, professors – in short, the top of the Austrian legal world – could talk in such a way about the constitution? They were not populists intent on overthrowing the old order. They have devoted their life to studying the constitution and defending it. How do we make sense of their attitude? To be fair, these critiques were directed more at the legislature rather than the constitution itself.[9] The main point of contention has been and still is the constitution's impenetrable fragmentation and complexity, which are not the result of centuries of precedent, custom and statute but caused by the fact that the constitution is easily amendable and that constitutional provisions can be put in many places. Provisions do not need to be enacted within the core document but can be put into separate constitutional acts or even in regular statutes. Decades of governments with the parliamentary two-thirds majority required to amend the constitution have simply written into the constitution what would otherwise have been unconstitutional, aided by over-zealous constitutional scholars who saw unconstitutionalities everywhere.[10] This procedure has mostly been used to circumvent the constitution's cumbersome division of powers between the federal and the state level, but it has also been abused for whatever political compromise was the order of the day (written into the constitution, subsequent governments have a harder time undoing it). Today, there are more than 500 constitutional provisions outside the core document. Tellingly, no one knows the exact number. The core document – the *Bundes-Verfassungsgesetz* (Federal Constitutional Act) – had its centennial in 2020. It is itself a mere trunk, a torso,[11] to quote another unkind characterisation, because it does not include a list of fundamental rights. These and other contentious issues were left out

[6] Karl Korinek, 'Einleitungsstatement', in Bernd Wieser and Armin Stolz (eds.), *Verfassungsrecht und Verfassungsgerichtsbarkeit an der Schwelle zum 21 Jahrhundert* (Verlag Österreich, 2000), 126.

[7] Ewald Wiederin, in a radio interview with Austrian public broadcaster radio Ö1, 13 June 2019.

[8] Clemens Jabloner, 'Verfassungsentwicklung und Verfassungsvoraussetzungen', in Harald Eberhard, Michael Holoubek, Thomas Kröll, Georg Lienbacher and Stefan Storr (eds.), *100 Jahre Republik Österreich: Kontinuität – Brüche – Kompromisse* (Verlag Österreich, 2021), 1, 11ff.

[9] Ewald Wiederin, 'Über Ruinen und Verfassungen' (2003) 15 *juridikum* 192.

[10] See also Theo Öhlinger, 'Braucht Österreich eine Verfassung?' (2000) 12 *juridikum* 4. Öhlinger poignantly asks whether Austria, faced with all this debris, would need an actual constitution.

[11] Former Constitutional Court President Ludwig Adamovich in a speech reported by Wiener Zeitung, 2 October 2000.

in order to secure approval in 1920 and have since been addressed (again, outside the core document).

It should be mentioned, however, that the unkind metaphors and comparisons of which the constitution has been the target are mostly concerned with its outer appearance. It is a question of constitutional aesthetics: We would like a booklet that we can carry around in our breast pockets. Scholars may lament the constitution's length and confusing structure, its needless attention to detail, its silence on the topic of fundamental rights, its politically motivated declarations and promises devoid of any enforceable meaning. But, apart from the occasional debates and reforms, it stands unchallenged as the (all-in-all well-functioning) basis of democracy, the rule of law and federalism in Austria. Even as the constitution was scheduled for a major overhaul and clean-up in the early 2000s (which did not happen),[12] the scholars and politicians involved in this project did not question its basic mechanisms, its institutions, its division of powers and the structure of administrative authorities it prescribes. Many of the ideas developed during this reform project were gradually introduced into the constitution later and without much fanfare.[13] The problem that the constitution allows for the creation of constitutional law outside the core document has not been remedied; it remains a point of contention and a technique sometimes used excessively. Apart from the fact that it is practically impossible for Austrian citizens to find and read their constitution in its entirety, it works well. The fact that so many scholars have taken part in its disparagement actually indicates a widespread concern for what has proven to be a time-tested, reliable document.

One might wonder, however, if the issue of constitutional orderliness would not have been better served if the constitution had been praised more often than maligned. While the critique of the lawgivers' excesses is justified, it seems that it missed its target and hit the constitution instead of those who made it. One can be forgiven for losing any sense of attachment to a constitution that looks so misshapen, has such a bad name and has been treated so badly by the legistlature.[14] It remains to inquire, though, why constitutional scholars, professionals and the interested public have let it come that far and why they have been complicit in treating the constitution like any other technical statute, to be amended at will. It seems that the state of being in 'ruins' is both cause and consequence of that widespread constitutional cynicism or, to put it more mildly, indifference. After all, a document revered and respected would not have been tampered with in the way the Austrian constitution has been. Obviously, once a disparaging narrative about the constitution takes hold,

[12] The so-called Österreich-Konvent, see Walter Schwartz, 'Structure, Objectives and Results of the Austrian Constitutional Convention, or: How Not to Change a Constitution' (2006) 12 *European Public Law* 167.

[13] Walter Schwartz and Irene Mayer, 'New Broom Sweeps Clean? An Attempt to Gradually Change the Austrian Constitution' (2009) 15 *European Public Law* 151.

[14] See Theo Öhlinger, 'Braucht Österreich eine neue Verfassung?' (2002) *Journal für Rechtspolitik* 1.

the constitution will be treated carelessly, which in turn reinforces the idea that it is just a haphazard accumulation of ideas and provisions that do not belong in it in the first place. That, in turn, makes it hard to promote it.[15] The constitution is not part of Austrian national identity.[16]

13.2.2 *Constitutional Pride*

The Austrian constitution and attitudes towards it unfavourably contrast with how the German constitution is seen in Germany (with whom we Austrians always like to compare ourselves). Without delving into the sometime grandiose rhetoric of German constitutionalism, one can agree that the German Basic Law and the case law of the Federal Constitutional Court (FCC) have given the German constitution a much greater importance than merely being an instrument of government. It is, as is well known, a 'value-based order' (Wertordnung),[17] a 'total constitution'[18] founded upon human dignity and able, in principle, to provide answers to all social and political questions. That has not always been the case. It was the FCC's seminal *Lüth* judgment that set the tone for German constitutionalism.[19] As we now know, the Court wanted the Basic Law to be the embodiment of a historical breaking point. As Germany had to reinvent itself after Nazism, its constitution had to be built from a completely new foundation.[20] The Basic Law is, as the FCC once said, the counter-project to National Socialism and designed to prevent the possibility of fascism ever rising again.[21] The Basic Law is a new beginning that followed a decade of horror and devastation; a confession of guilt and a solemn promise never to be guilty again. What could be more inspiring? And, aesthetically, it is a concise booklet that can be carried around in one's pocket.

Like Germany's, Austria's 'constitutional moments'[22] mostly came at times of defeat: In 1867, when Austria received its first democratic and rule-of-law-based

15 See also Herbert Schambeck, 'Gedanken über einen Verfassungspatriotismus in Österreich' in Franz Matscher, Peter Pernthaler and Andreas Raffeiner (eds.), *Ein Leben für Recht und Gerechtigkeit: Festschrift für Hans R. Klecatsky zum 90. Geburtstag* (WUV, 2010), 657, 659.

16 See Oliver Rathkolb, *The Paradoxical Republic: Austria 1945–2020*, 2nd ed. (Berghahn, 2021), 52. He rehearses the argument that the Constitution is needlessly complex and confusing.

17 See Michaela Hailbronner, 'Rethinking the Rise of the German Constitutional Court: From Anti-Nazism to Value Formalism' (2014) 12 *International Journal of Constitutional Law* 626.

18 Mattias Kumm, 'Who's Afraid of the Total Constitution? Constitutional Rights as Principles and the Constitutionalization of Private Law' (2006) 7 *German Law Journal* 341.

19 Federal Constitutional Court, decision of 15 January 1958, nr 1 BvR 400/51, *Lüth*, collected under nr BVerfGE 7, 198.

20 See, e.g., Inga Markovits, 'Constitution Making after National Catastrophes: Germany in 1949 and 1990' (2008) 49 *William & Mary Law Review* 1307.

21 Federal Constitutional Court, decision of 4 November 2009, nr 1 BvR 2150/08, *Wunsiedel*, collected under nr BVerfGE 124, 300.

22 After Bruce Ackerman, *We the People, vol I: Foundations* (Harvard University Press, 1991), 22, 40–41.

constitution, it had lost a war against Prussia and had to make concessions to Hungary (the so-called compromise). In 1920, when the current constitution was first adopted, Austria was the 'state that no one wanted',[23] the 'rest, as French president Georges Clemenceau is reported to have said,[24] that had started and lost WWI. Then 1945, when the 1920 constitution was readopted, saw the even more crushing total collapse after WWII. But, unlike Germany, Austria missed its opportunity to reinvent itself. After Nazi Germany was defeated in 1945, Austria saw itself as Hitler's first victim.[25] It consequently did not see the need for a new beginning and a new constitution. It seemed logical to turn the time back to before the *Anschluss* and to reactivate the constitution of 1920. Austria's own participation in Nazism was something not to be mentioned; its own home-made variety of fascism in the years before the *Anschluss* was to be forgotten. Apart from these myths, which have begun to crumble only since the 1990s, there were legitimate strategic reasons for returning to the old constitution instead of creating something new. As Austria was occupied by the victorious Allied Powers, politicians sought to avoid a partitioning of the country like the one Germany would suffer. In the days after the end of WWII, the Austrian provisional government had to demonstrate that it was capable of governing the entire country. It needed an unquestionable basis for holding power. Taking up the former constitution, then, was an almost obvious choice. It had been agreed upon only twenty-five years prior by the same political parties that now ran the provisional government. Any lengthy constitutional debate would have weakened its stance and stalled its efforts.[26] Thus, the opportunity to initiate a new beginning and to shape a new society was not simply missed, it was actively prevented to secure the country's undivided independence.

Based on these two very different origin stories, it is understandable that Germany might see something called constitutional patriotism, whereas the idea has never really taken hold in Austria. Constitutional patriotism does not mean an uncritical reverence for a founding document. But it consists, as its progenitor Dolf Sternberger thought, in replacing nationalist love of a country with open-minded attachment to the constitution as the embodiment of a people's common values:[27] democracy, human rights, the rule of law and all the mechanisms and institutions they entail. As a consequence, the German Basic Law enjoys overwhelming support in the general public and its defence is to be conducted in the form of militant

[23] After the popular title by Hellmut Andics, *Der Staat, den keiner wollte* (Herder, 1962).

[24] This quote is probably a myth; see Manfred Zollinger, '"L'Autriche, c'est moi"? Georges Clemenceau, das neue Österreich und das Werden eines Mythos', in Lorenz Mikoletzky and Stefan Karner (eds.), *Österreich – 90 Jahre Republik* (Studienverlag, 2008), 621.

[25] See Rathkolb, *The Paradoxical Republic*, 23, 257ff.

[26] See ibid., 49ff

[27] Dolf Sternberger, 'Verfassungspatriotismus', in *Frankfurter Allgemeine Zeitung*, 23 May 1979.

democracy.[28] Jürgen Habermas developed this idea further and emphasised that collective identities, including those anchored in patriotism, should be shaped by discursive processes of rational reflection, for which a state based on a constitution that guarantees democracy and the rule of law is the best environment.[29] Attachment to the constitution is not a mere *ersatz* for nationalism. Rather, allegiance to the constitution is generated by debate and conflict about what it means.[30] This theory seems to be backed up by the facts: the Basic Law entered public conscience in the 1970s at a time when social issues began to be negotiated in legal language, that is, in terms of the constitution and human rights. Since then, and regardless of Habermas' conception, which may be faulted for being somewhat too intellectual and sophisticated, the German public has professed a high degree of respect for the Basic Law.[31] Jan-Werner Müller has taken constitutional patriotism to the European level, where it could serve as a vehicle of European integration.[32]

13.2.3 *Constitutional Identity*

The flip side of this pride in a state's constitution may be said to be constitutional identity. The concept surely can be used to hide darker, nationalist motives directed against the alleged overreach of supranational bodies. As such, it has already been taken up by various actors intent on countering European integration.[33] Seen more benignly, it makes sense to hold on to a constitution that has become the focal point of collective identity, even more so if that constitution is highly developed and offers robust protections for human rights and the rule of law. No wonder, then, that constitutional identity is, originally, a German thing. It is no coincidence that the seminal *Solange I* judgment takes issue with the protection of fundamental rights on the European level because, as the Court declared, fundamental rights as enshrined in the Basic Law are part of Germany's identity.[34] A collective identity shaped by the adherence to and protection of human rights is nothing but constitutional patriotism. As patriotism in general, constitutional patriotism can become

28 This synopsis is based on Jan-Werner Müller, *Constitutional Patriotism* (Princeton University Press, 2007), 23.

29 E.g., Jürgen Habermas, 'Struggles for Recognition in the Democratic Constitutional State', in Amy Gutmann (ed.), *Multiculturalism: Examining the Politics of Recognition* (Princeton University Press, 1994), 107.

30 See Müller, *Constitutional Patriotism*, 28ff.

31 Hans Vorländer, 'Die Deutschen und ihre Verfassung' (2009) 18/19 *Aus Politik und Zeitgeschichte* 8.

32 Müller, *Constitutional Patriotism*, 93ff.

33 Federico Fabbrini and András Sajó, 'The Dangers of Constitutional Identity' (2019) 25 *European Law Journal* 457.

34 Federal Constitutional Court, decision of 29 May 1974, nr BvL 52/71, *Solange I*, collected under nr BVerfGE 37, 271.

exaggerated, and the German Court's subsequent judgments on constitutional identity and ultra-vires[35] have been highly criticised in this respect.[36]

Where the constitution is not such a big factor in the collective self-image, the notion of constitutional identity does not have the same persuasiveness. It is then either abused for ulterior motives[37] or applied to technical details that may move some lawyers but do not affect what a state's citizens think about its constitution. This is the case in Austria. There are three judgments concerning matters of constitutional identity; only one may be said to have any bearing on identity, and it is a judgment by the ECJ, not a national court:[38] the *Sayn-Wittgenstein* decision, in which the court held that the prohibition of titles of nobility is justified in light of Austria's radical abolition of the monarchy and the constitutional status of that prohibition.[39] The other two concern the organisation of the executive branch. In one, the Constitutional Court declared that, if Article 6 of the European Convention on Human Rights really required broad access to courts against administrative decisions, it would be incompatible with the constitutionally mandated, democratic responsibility of the executive.[40] In the other, the Court alluded that the EU-induced proliferation of independent administrative agencies (which are not under the control of the executive) could, at some point, go beyond what Austria had agreed to when it had joined the EU, again because there is a constitutional principle that the executive branch must be responsible for administration.[41] Organisational details of the executive branch do not easily inspire constitutional patriotism.

Based on this tradition of constitutional thinking, it should come as no surprise that the Austrian constitution is not disseminated, celebrated or invoked outside of professional circles. There is no official holiday dedicated to it (although the Constitutional Court holds an annual event, which is – tellingly – not open to the general public), there are no free copies distributed in schools, there are no famous quotations taken from it and printed on t-shirts. At least there are some commemorative stamps. Its framers are mostly forgotten, with the one exception of Hans Kelsen. In this climate – a non-tradition of constitutional patriotism, a

35 Federal Constitutional Court, decision of 30 June 2009, nr 2 be 2/08 et al, *Lissabon*, collected under nr BVerfGE 123, 267; Federal Constitutional Court, decision of 5/5/2020, nr 2 BvR 859/15 et al, *PSPP*, collected under nr BVerfGE 154, 17.

36 See, e.g., Mattias Wendel, 'Paradoxes of Ultra-Vires Review: A Critical Review of the PSPP Decision and Its Initial Reception' (2020) 21 *German Law Journal* 979.

37 Julian Scholtes, 'Abusing Constitutional Identity' (2021) 22 *German Law Journal* 534.

38 Thomas Kröll, 'The European Court of Justice, a Guardian (Hüter) of the Republican Principle of the Austrian Federal Constitution – Case Note on C-208/09, Sayn-Wittgenstein' (2012) *Vienna Journal on International Constitutional Law* 110.

39 European Court of Justice, judgment of 22 December 2010, Case C-208/09, *Sayn-Wittgenstein*, ECLI:EU:C:2010:806.

40 Constitutional Court, judgment of 14 October 1987, nr B 267/86, *Miltner*, collected under nr VfSlg 11.500/1987.

41 Constitutional Court, judgment of 16 December 2021, nr G 390/2020, *AQ Austria*, collected under nr VfSlg 20.522/2021.

somewhat technical constitutional identity, a constitution said to be in ruins – it needed a non-lawyer to remind constitutional scholars of the appeal that the Austrian constitution can and should have.

13.2.4 *Constitutional Surprises*

In 2019, Austria was shocked by the so-called Ibiza scandal. A secretly recorded video showed the person who would later – but before the recordings emerged – become vice chancellor, Heinz-Christian Strache, in a villa in Ibiza, talking openly to a presumed Russian oligarch about how he would take money for getting laws passed, how he would try to get Austrian newspapers under his control, which campaign donations should be solicited and other such details. He resigned after the video was leaked to the press. Then chancellor Sebastian Kurz was faced with the first successful parliamentary vote of no confidence in Austria. He and his government had to step down. The president, Alexander van der Bellen, appointed a cabinet of experts to govern until an election was held and a new government could be formed. It was the first time Austria had seen any of this happening.[42]

Something else that was unusual happened during these days: the Austrian president praised the 'elegance' and 'beauty' of the constitution. It was elegant and beautiful, he said, because it contained all the necessary precautions and procedures for what to do in these uncertain times.[43] It was an interesting thing to say. On the one hand, the constitution simply contains what constitutions are supposed to contain: provisions for the appointment and dismissal of governments. This may surprise someone who has never read the document but not constitutional scholars. On the other hand, it was quite surprising indeed to hear the constitution being praised rather than ridiculed. The president's remarks did not fail to impress the general public. A myriad of newspaper articles was devoted to that great unknown: the constitution. In hindsight, it proved the perfect prequel to its centennial in 2020, when another round of newspaper articles, speeches, interviews and exhibitions followed. One might suspect that it would not have been celebrated quite as much if van der Bellen had not brought the constitution to public attention. One can dispute whether 'elegant' and 'beautiful' are meaningful adjectives to describe a legal instrument (I think they are). The president chose these words because of their positive connotations. What he probably intended to express with them is that the constitution contains sensible

[42] Konrad Lachmayer and Lukas Wieser, 'Entering into New Constitutional Territory in Austria: From a Conservative Minority Government to a Transitional Expert Government' (3 June 2019) *Verfassungsblog*, https://verfassungsblog.de/entering-into-new-constitutional-territory-in-austria/.

[43] Speech by President of Austria Alexander van der Bellen on 21 May 2019; see www.bundespraesident.at/aktuelles/detail/gespraech-mit-bundeskanzler-sebastian-kurz. He later called it 'the Magna Charta of our country', see Alexander van der Bellen, 'Über die Schönheit unserer Bundesverfassung' (2020) *Anwaltsblatt* 537.

arrangements, ingenious solutions and exemplary innovations and that it is, therefore, beautiful in the sense of well-crafted.[44] The president did not comment on its outer appearance, at which so much derision had been directed and which remains poor. He chose to emphasise what was good about it and, thus, gave Austrian constitutional discourse an entirely new spin. Finally, we scholars are allowed to actually like the document we spend so much time exploring.

Yet, old habits die hard. There is still no constitutional patriotism in Austria, and public engagement with the constitution remains weak. But it seems that something is growing. For its centennial celebration, the Constitutional Court arranged for the constitution to be illustrated and printed in the form of a magazine (not the whole, sprawling text but the main documents). It further organised an exhibition devoted to the constitution and the court, which travelled around the country, and it instituted a cooperation scheme with schools. In a historical first, the candidates running for president in the October 2022 election were subjected to an exam on constitutional law by the national broadcaster on live television.[45] It was (to my knowledge) the first time that the constitution got so much attention in political reporting. Ironically, Alexander van der Bellen, whose public praise had won the constitution this newfound interest, did not participate in the TV debate. He was re-elected.

A critical stance towards one's own constitution is not entirely bad. Yes, the way the Austrian constitution is talked about – ruins, torso, sprawl – has its drawbacks. People are not brought to meaningfully identify with 'their' constitution if constitutional lawyers themselves talk about it in such a way. Still, this attitude keeps us from putting the constitution onto a pedestal and from expecting too much of it. To quote Jabloner: what Austria seems to have is a kind of constitutional pragmatism.[46] The constitution is respected and upheld even if it is not admired and celebrated. Constitutional scholars identify with it even if they do not talk fondly about it. However, as we will see in Section 13.4, sometimes, they cannot hide a certain pride in the achievements of the Austrian – 'their' – constitution. After all, someone must believe in the constitution if it is to be successful.[47]

13.3 NARRATIVE 2: FORM AND SUBSTANCE

13.3.1 *Constitutional Bleakness*

The 'ruins' metaphor is often accompanied by another narrative that is well-entrenched in academia as well as in the interested public. It is the trope that

44 Benjamin Kneihs, 'Die Schönheit der Verfassung' (2020) 75 *Zeitschrift für öffentliches Recht* 209; Christoph Hofstätter, 'Die Regierungskrise 2019 oder zur Eleganz und Schönheit der österreichischen Bundesverfassung', in Gerhard Baumgartner (ed.), *Jahrbuch Öffentliches Recht* 2020 (NWV, 2020), 27.

45 See Österreichischer Rundfunk (17 September 2022), https://orf.at/stories/3284783/.

46 Jabloner, 'Verfassungsentwicklung und Verfassungsvoraussetzungen', 11.

47 See Balkin, *Constitutional Redemption*, 2.

Austria's is a 'value-neutral constitution of rules of the game' (*wertneutrale Spielregelverfassung*). With this goes the assumption that Austrian constitutional law is purely formal. Since the constitution is said to be neutral regarding political ends, its provisions are to be understood as formal procedural rules rather than material guiding principles. Although this idea has never been entirely correct and is even less true today, it continues to shape how Austrian lawyers think about the constitution, even if it is mostly agreed nowadays that a purely formal approach does not fit most constitutional issues. The idea of the constitution as a purely formal set of rules to be interpreted 'formally' is deeply connected with Hans Kelsen, whose influence on Austrian constitutional thinking as a legal theorist, drafter of the constitution and judge at the Constitutional Court is unmatched. The formality narrative has three main roots: the minimalist compromise arising from the political climate surrounding the adoption of the 1920 constitution, Kelsen's procedural theory of democracy and Kelsen's pure theory of law. If ruins are not a fertile ground for the development of constitutional patriotism, neither is a supposedly neutral and formal constitution. These two underlying understandings of Austrian constitutional law may therefore well go hand in hand. Like the 'ruins' metaphor, to talk of a neutral and formal constitution can be a sign of contempt: Carl Schmitt famously argued that a purely neutral political system was bound to self-destruct.[48] Again, there is a core of truth here: the Austrian constitution, at least in its unadulterated 1920 version, exhibits much less rhetorical pomp and grandeur than others. But, unlike ruins, neutrality and formality are something of which Austrian constitutional scholars have been proud, especially because it sets us apart from many other constitutional traditions. Ruins can be beautiful. But when the Austrian president talked about the beauty and elegance of the constitution, what he had in mind were its transparent procedures and precise rules – in short, its formality.

The starting point of Austria's neutrality narrative is also the starting point of its constitution, namely that it begins without a preamble. The preamble question marks the convergence of two historical strands that mutually reinforced each other and the narrative that sprung from it: a climate of political tension that led to minimalist compromise and Hans Kelsen's well-known aversion to constitutional ornament.[49] He was even opposed to including what would become the constitution's first article: 'Austria is a democratic republic. Its law emanates from the people.' In his view, this superfluously stated the obvious. It was then Chancellor Karl Renner who overruled Kelsen in stating that a constitution needed to begin with something beautiful. He was proven correct. Nowadays, Article 1 of the Constitution graces the Constitutional Court's courtroom wall, while Kelsen's bust

[48] Carl Schmitt, *Legality and Legitimacy* (Duke University Press, 2004 [1932]), 45ff.

[49] A preamble can be much more than that; see Liav Orgad, 'The Preamble in Constitutional Interpretation' (2010) 8 *International Journal of Constitutional Law* 714.

stands in the hallway.[50] Yet, Kelsen shaped the narrative for years to come and managed to downplay one of the few uplifting passages the constitution contains:

> Article 1 has no relevant legal content. Whether the constitution really represents a democratic republic follows from its formal and substantial provisions.[51]

To be fair, in the years from 1918 to 1920, when the constitution was negotiated, drafted and adopted, there probably was a widespread feeling of constitutional disillusionment. As Kelsen notes, the preamble was omitted because not everyone was convinced of the viability of the new Austrian state.[52] In addition to famine, destruction, millions dead or displaced and massive unemployment, Austria had to come to terms with the fact that, after more than 600 years, the Habsburgs – and the power and glory that had come with them – were gone. Austria was reduced from an empire of almost 60 million to a tiny landlocked country of about 6 million people, many of whom did not consider themselves Austrians but Germans. Unsurprisingly, the provisional constitution of 1918 declared so-called German-Austria to be part of Germany. Both the name[53] and the unification[54] would be prohibited by the treaties of Versailles and St. Germain in 1920.

13.3.2 *Constitutional Beginnings*

In 1920, Austria needed a definitive constitution. The political spectrum was divided between the Social Democrats, who were socialist in orientation and favoured annexation by Germany because of the strong socialist movement there; the German Nationalists, more classically liberal, fiercely anti-Semitic and equally in favour of joining Germany; and the Christian Social Party, conservative, clerical, monarchist and the only party favouring Austrian independence. As the government consisted of a coalition between the Social Democrats and the Christian Social Party, constitutional negotiations were primarily conducted between these two parties, whose stark ideological differences did not make the task easier. Parliament appointed a Constitutional Committee and a Subcommittee; whose reports and drafts are an indispensable resource for constitutional interpretation

50 Which is still a pretty good spot, since Kelsen's is the only bust on display at the Court.

51 See Hans Kelsen, Georg Froehlich and Adolf Merkl, *Die Verfassungsgesetze der Republik Österreich, vol V: Die Bundesverfassung vom 1. Oktober 1920* (Franz Deuticke, 1922), 65 (author translation).

52 Ibid., 62.

53 See Michael Ioannidis, 'Naming a State: Disputing over Symbols of Statehood at the Example of Macedonia' (2010) 14 *Max Planck Yearbook of United Nations Law* 507 (see 538ff about the name 'German-Austria').

54 See Detlef Merten, 'Siegermacht und Selbstbestimmungsrecht der Völker. "Deutschösterreich": Vereinigungsverbot zweier jahrhundertelang verbundener Staaten' (2020) 75 *Zeitschrift für öffentliches Recht* 317.

today. The chief expert consulted during these talks was, of course, Hans Kelsen, who also contributed several drafts.

Whereas the Social Democrats saw democracy as the best way for the working class to seize power and to bring about socialism, the conservative Christian Social Party saw it as the best way to prevent a proletarian dictatorship. Both parties agreed, in a sense, that a democratic constitution was instrumental for political survival but was not an end in itself. Both parties had radically different visions of the state and society, but neither was strong enough to marginalise the other. Otto Bauer, leader of the Social Democratic Party and Marxist thinker, even came up with the concept of 'class balance' to justify why his party would compromise with the bourgeoisie:[55] its domination was over, but it was still large enough for proletarian dictatorship to not be feasible.[56] When the Social Democrats sought to introduce a constitutional article declaring that all power rests with the people, the Christian Social Party leader Ignaz Seipel, an ordained priest, objected on the grounds that the question of supreme power was a theological issue. The article was omitted.[57] Taking up John Rawls, one might say that the Austrian constitution was not an 'overlapping consensus' but a 'mere modus vivendi' born out of necessity.[58] The fragile political accord represented by the constitution broke apart in 1933 when the Christian Social government exploited an error in parliamentary proceedings to suspend Parliament for good, to ban the Social Democratic Party and to promulgate a fascist constitution a year later.[59] As Adolf Merkl, a disciple of Kelsen and himself a leading Austrian scholar of constitutional law, remarked after this authoritarian turn: 'Today, we know that democracy was but a legal platform from which the big political groups thought to best avert the others' dictatorship.'[60] Apart from the great ideological struggles, there were two basic points of contention between the Social Democratic and Christian Social parties: fundamental rights and federalism. The Social Democrats wanted only weak protections for property but strong rights to work, leisure and welfare. They favoured central government, especially as their only power base was Vienna. The Christian Social Party, in turn, felt the need to protect the propertied classes, opposed social rights, feared Social Democratic secularism, especially in such issues as civil marriage, divorce and cremation (none of which was allowed), and wanted Austria to become a federal state, as this would give

[55] Otto Bauer, *Die Österreichische Revolution* (Wiener Volksbuchhandlung, 1923), 96, 245.

[56] See also Jan-Werner Müller, *Contesting Democracy: Political Ideas in 20th Century Europe* (Yale University Press, 2011), 58.

[57] See Ignaz Seipel in the transcript of the ninth session of the Subcommittee of the Constitutional Committee on 23 August 1920; reprinted in Felix Ermacora, *Quellen zum österreichischen Verfassungsrecht 1920* (Berger und Söhne, 1967), 336.

[58] See John Rawls, 'The Idea of an Overlapping Consensus' (1987) 7 *Oxford Journal of Legal Studies* 1.

[59] See Steven Beller, *A Concise History of Austria* (Cambridge University Press, 2014), 221ff.

[60] Adolf Merkl, *Die ständisch-autoritäre Verfassung Österreichs: Ein kritisch-systematischer Grundriss* (Springer, 1935), 2 (author translation).

the conservative-controlled rural regions an advantage. As Jabloner suggests, these differences persist. They lie dormant as long as the current constitution is in place but would return with full force the moment a new constitution was discussed.[61]

The Constitutional Committee dealt with these differences by way of omission, which inspired the constitution's reputation for being a trunk or a torso: even to its framers, the constitution looked incomplete without a set of rights.[62] As Ignaz Seipel freely admitted, the party negotiators did not manage to find common ground and decided to eliminate the chapter on fundamental rights in the spirit of mutual sacrifice.[63] But, as the constitution needed fundamental rights after all, it was decided to simply carry over the 1867 Bill of Rights (*Staatsgrundgesetz über die allgemeinen Rechte der Staatsbürger*), which had served well during the monarchy and was the basis for fundamental rights review by the Imperial Court of Justice (which I shall discuss in Section 13.4). This episode is at the root of the idea that Austria's is a constitution of compromise, which is neutral in substantial political matters because the big opposing parties could not agree with one another. As history shows, however, this narrative has always been ambivalent, if not false. The rights catalogue of 1867 was not politically neutral; it was an ideological win the liberal bourgeoisie managed to wrestle from a weakened monarch,[64] and it embodies the basic tenets of nineteenth century liberalism. As such, it could not be further away from what the Social Democrats had hoped to achieve, especially in matters of property law and economic planning. As was said out loud much later but was equally true back then, the constitution, via the rights to property, to freedom of movement and to private enterprise, has always enshrined a capitalist market economy.[65] Still, the *Staatsgrundgesetz* already had a venerable tradition, which probably made its acceptance easier. The fact that it was a separate constitutional act surely helped to cement the narrative that the core document remained 'neutral'. This situation interestingly echoes Carl Schmitt's distinction between a constitution's 'political' and 'legal' parts.[66] In Austria, these two parts even form two separate documents.

The thorny question of federalism was resolved in an equally ambivalent compromise, which, for once, seemed to favour the Social Democrats. With the 1920 constitution, Austria became a federal union divided into nine states. While this may look like another win for the conservative agenda, the federal government retained

[61] Jabloner, 'Verfassungsentwicklung und Verfassungsvoraussetzungen', 10.

[62] See Kelsen et al., *Die Verfassungsgesetze der Republik Österreich*, 62.

[63] Ignaz Seipel, *Der Kampf um die österreichische Verfassung* (Braumüller, Wien, 1930), 96–97.

[64] See Pieter M. Judson, 'The Lost Heroes of Austria's Fundamental Laws', in Franz Merli, Magdalena Pöschl and Ewald Wiederin (eds.), *150 Jahre Staatsgrundgesetz über die allgemeinen Rechte der Staatsbürger* (Manz, 2018), 1.

[65] See the influential article by Karl Korinek, 'Das Grundrecht der Freiheit der Erwerbsbetätigung als Schranke für die Wirtschaftslenkung', in Karl Korinek (ed.), *Beiträge zum Wirtschaftsrecht. Festschrift für Karl Wenger zum 60. Geburtstag* (Orac, 1983), 243.

[66] Carl Schmitt, *Constitutional Theory* (Duke University Press, 2008 [1928]), 93.

all important powers. These had to be enumerated expressly, which makes the division of competences between the federal and state legislatures the longest and most complex in the world.[67] This is why the constitution revels in details such as the responsibility for 'log driving' or 'air pollution control without prejudice to the states' jurisdiction over heating installations' (Article 10, para 1, nr 10 and 12). In a fatal reversal of fortunes, the Social Democrats were ousted from government just after the ratification of the constitution. As their only real power base was the state of Vienna, they henceforth took a federalist position in order to be left alone, whereas the Christian Social Party pushed for centralism so as to rein in 'Red Vienna'. Fundamental rights did not represent much of a political factor in the interwar years, but the division of powers did: two major constitutional conflicts arose around cremation and divorce. The issue was not framed in a fundamental-rights discourse but in terms of who had the power to decide (the federal or the state government?).[68] The division of power was the main reason for which the Constitutional Court was vested with the power to invalidate laws: the federal and the state governments feared mutual unlawful encroachment, and this fear was exacerbated by the different political alignments.

To recapitulate: 1920 saw Austria torn between irreconcilable political alternatives represented by hostile parties. The parties agreed on a minimalist constitution that laid down the institutions and procedures of government. As they could not agree on what the constitution should be about in the first place, a preamble was left out. They could not find agreement with regards to fundamental rights (too ideological) and federalism (too important), so they struck a deal to carry over the existing Bill of Rights, creating a nominally federal system with a massive central government. The constitution of 1920 was indeed a formal document. It laid out the rules of the political process and provided the basis for constitutional justice and the rule of law. It did not contain any material guidelines for politics, such as fundamental values to be upheld, goals or objectives to be achieved or national interest to be furthered.

13.3.3 *Constitutional Theory*

It is unsurprising, then, that it was during the interwar years in Austria in which Hans Kelsen developed his value-neutral conception of democracy and his formalist style of legal reasoning. There probably is an ambivalent relationship between Kelsen's theoretical positions and his practical experiences. His theory of democracy seems clearly influenced by the formalist compromise that was Austria's

[67] Greg Taylor, *Characterisation in Federations: Six Countries Compared* (Springer, 2006), 95ff.

[68] The question was, strikingly, resolved by a judgment by Hans Kelsen as a member of the Constitutional Court; see Clemens Jabloner, 'Kelsen and his Circle: The Viennese Years' (1998) 9 *European Journal of International Law* 368, 374–375; Tamara Ehs, 'Felix Frankfurter, Hans Kelsen, and the Practice of Judicial Review' (2013) 73 *Zeitschrift für ausländisches öffentliches Recht und Völkerrecht* 451, 464–465.

constitution. In turn, his reflections on democracy have shaped Austrians' common understanding of our constitutional system.[69] Kelsen thought of democracy as a mere method for creating the legal order, a method that was, by definition, content-neutral.[70] Anything could be decided by a majority vote as long as the required formalities were met, because democracy is tacit about what constitutes a good state and a good society. It rests on parliamentary representation and, importantly, on the protection of political minorities: for there is no majority without a minority, and any minority must have the chance to become a majority one day. From the majority–minority dialectic, Kelsen inferred that political reality in a democracy is marked by compromise, because the majority is not all-powerful and the minority is not disenfranchised.[71] His praise of democracy being indifferent to the ends pursued and of compromise being democracy's true actualisation conveniently coincided with political reality in Austria. With his theory, Kelsen perhaps even sought to legitimise the new constitution. Democracy presupposes, as Kelsen famously argued, a relativistic worldview.[72] There are good reasons for doubting this,[73] and one can wonder if Kelsen himself really was a relativist.[74] But his theory provides a good explanation of a certain democratic mindset without which parliamentary debate, freedom of speech and recurrent elections lose their meaning:[75]

> He who views absolute truth and absolute values as inaccessible to the human understanding cognition must deem not only his own, but also the opinion of others at least as feasible. The idea of democracy thus presupposes relativism as its worldview. Democracy values everyone's political will equally, just as it gives equal regard to each political belief and opinion . . .[76]

69 See Péter Techet, '"Historical turn" in der Hans-Kelsen-Forschung? Wechselwirkungen zwischen Rechtstheorie und Rechtsgeschichte' (2021) 76 *Zeitschrift für öffentliches Recht* 1329.

70 Hans Kelsen, *The Essence and Value of Democracy* (Rowman & Littlefield, 2013, 2nd ed. 1929), 94ff, 101.

71 Ibid., 67ff.

72 For an account of Kelsenian relativism relating to democracy, see Carlo Invernizzi Accetti, *Relativism and Religion: Why Democratic Societies Do Not Need Moral Absolutes* (Columbia University Press, 2015), 163ff.

73 The theory of 'militant democracy' presumes that democracy is built upon certain fundamental values that must be defended, sometimes, even against democratic movements. See the influential Karl Loewenstein, 'Militant Democracy and Fundamental Rights' (1937) 31 *American Political Science Review*, part I: 417, part II: 638; for a critique in Kelsenian spirit, see Carlo Invernizzi Accetti and Ian Zuckerman, 'What's Wrong with Militant Democracy?' (2017) 65 *Political Studies* 182; for an application of militant democracy to an allegedly value-neutral constitution, see Ulrich Wagrandl, 'Militant Democracy in Austria' (2018) 2 *Vienna Law Review* 95 and Ulrich Wagrandl, *Wehrhafte Demokratie in Österreich* (Verlag Österreich, 2019).

74 Ulrich Wagrandl, 'Kelsen was no Relativist: Reading Hans Kelsen in the Light of Isaiah Berlin's Value Pluralism', in Matthias Jestaedt, Ralf Poscher and Jörg Kammerhofer (eds.), *Die Reine Rechtslehre auf dem Prüfstand / Hans Kelsen's Pure Theory of Law: Conceptions and Misconceptions* (Steiner, 2020), 373.

75 As Carl Schmitt claimed they already had, see Carl Schmitt, *The Crisis of Parliamentary Democracy* (MIT Press, 1988 [2nd ed. 1926]), 49.

76 Kelsen, *The Essence and Value of Democracy*, 103.

We can now see that the formality and neutrality narrative about Austria's constitution is amalgamated from different sources and that it encompasses the idea of compromise and the conception of relativism. In a parallel development but on another plane, Kelsen also provided a legal theory that by its very name seems well-suited to guiding the understanding of a value-neutral and formal order: the pure theory of law. As so often, it is difficult to establish a chain of causality here. We know that Kelsen laid the basis of his thinking well before the inception of Austria's 1920 constitution,[77] but it only came to fruition well after the constitution had been drafted.[78] It seems that his work as a legal adviser influenced Kelsen's theory as much as his constitutional drafts were an outcome of his theoretical work.[79] Kelsen's legal theory is famous for many reasons, such as the radical is–ought distinction, the basic norm, the identification of law and state and – especially relevant for constitutional interpretation – the *Stufenbau* theorem (the hierarchy or pyramid of norms, which was actually Adolf Merkl's idea). The latter represents the notion that the whole legal order forms a hierarchical structure of different levels, so that norms of a lower order gain their validity insofar as their creation is determined by laws of a higher order. The *Stufenbau* idea emphasises the law's perpetual changing as it brings the process of law-making (that is, the creation and abolition of norms) to the centre of attention. The constitution, as the highest norm, regulates the creation of all other norms within the system (that is, it defines the institutions, procedures and responsibilities of lawgiving), but the dialectic of norm creation and norm application recurs at every level of the legal order.[80] The *Stufenbau* doctrine is completed by the so-called *Fehlerkalkül* (reckoning with errors). As errors will inevitably be made when legislating, and every error – as a deviation from the norm empowering the lawgiver – would lead to absolute nullity, the legal system needs rules for dealing with these errors. The *Fehlerkalkül* theory posits that, as long as there is a legal remedy against erroneous and thus unlawful norms, these norms are not null and void but valid and applicable until revoked.[81]

77 Hans Kelsen, *Hauptprobleme der Staatsrechtslehre entwickelt aus der Lehre vom Rechtssatze* (Mohr, 1911).

78 Hans Kelsen, *Introduction to the Problems of Legal Theory* (Clarendon Press, 1997 [1st ed. 1934]); Hans Kelsen, *Pure Theory of Law* (Clarendon Press, 1967 [2nd ed. 1960]).

79 See Clemens Jabloner, 'Kelsen comme technicien constitutionnel', in Eleonora Bottini, Bernard Harcourt, Pasquale Pasquino and Otto Pfersmann (eds.), *Nouveaux regards sur des modèles classiques de démocratie constitutionelle: Etats-Unis, Europe* (mare&martin, 2018), 157; Clemens Jabloner, *Zum Nachhall verfassungsrechtlicher Probleme der Monarchie in Rechtstheorie und Verfassungsrecht / Some Specifically Austrian Aspects of the Pure Theory of Law: Problems of Constitutional Law of the Austro-Hungarian Monarchy and Their Repercussions on the Theory of Law and Constitutional Legislation* (Verlag Österreich, 2021).

80 See Kelsen, *Pure Theory of Law*, 221ff and, e.g., Stanley L. Paulson, 'How Merkl's Stufenbaulehre Informs Kelsen's Concept of Law' (2013) 21 *Revus* 29.

81 See Kelsen, *Pure Theory of Law*, 276–277 and e.g., Christoph Kletzer, 'Kelsen's Development of the Fehlerkalkül-Theory' (2005) 18 *Ratio Juris* 46.

No theory has had a bigger impact on Austrian constitutional law than Kelsen's. One of the classic Austrian constitutional law textbooks opens with a long theoretical disquisition about the nature of norms and their hierarchy. In this seminal work, the constitution is not characterized via its content, historical importance or philosophical foundation but as the 'norm of norm creation'.[82] Even those who have always taken another approach have to acknowledge that this formal view about the nature of the constitution has had a huge influence on constitutional thinking and on constitutional adjudication,[83] just as it is acknowledged that the 'rules of the game' metaphor is true to the constitution's roots but does not fully capture today's constitutional law.[84] Kelsen's relativistic account of democracy is approvingly repeated even by non-Kelsenians.[85]

13.3.4 *Constitutional Interpretation*

How do the historical background of the constitution and Kelsen's theories translate into actual constitutional interpretation? In a widely read article, Ewald Wiederin posited the *modus austriacus* of constitutional law scholarship,[86] which takes the law, not the state as its starting point for constructing the constitution. As Kelsen's pure theory dispenses with extra-legal, metaphysical entities, the notion of the state had to be dropped from constitutional thinking.[87] What remains is the law. The law, in turn, is structured via the *Stufenbau*, which broadens the viewpoint. The law not only consists of the constitution and statutes, but also of 'individual norms' such as administrative decisions and judicial opinions. As the *Stufenbau* doctrine makes no qualitative distinctions between these different levels of the legal order, the constitution looks like any other norm. Consequently, there is no specialised method of constitutional interpretation.[88] The constitutional sprawl, as discussed in Section 13.2, may have furthered this attitude among scholars, who, in a sense, only

82 Robert Walter, *Österreichisches Bundesverfassungsrecht* (Manz, 1972), 1ff. This tradition is continued by Walter's intellectual heirs, Heinz Mayer, Gabriele Kucsko-Stadlmayer and Karl Stöger, *Grundriss des österreichischen Bundesverfassungsrechts*, 11th ed. (Manz, 2015), 2ff.

83 See the other great classic, Theo Öhlinger and Harald Eberhard, *Verfassungsrecht*, 13th ed. (facultas, 2022), 36–37.

84 See the third classic, Walter Berka, *Verfassungsrecht: Grundzüge des österreichischen Verfassungsrechts für das juristische Studium*, 8th ed. (Verlag Österreich, 2021), 25.

85 See, e.g., Ludwig Adamovich, *Handbuch des österreichischen Verfassungsrechts*, 6th ed. (Springer, 1971), 82.

86 Ewald Wiederin, 'Denken vom Recht her: Über den modus austriacus in der Staatsrechtslehre', in Helmuth Schulze-Fielitz (ed.), *Staatsrechtslehre als Wissenschaft* (Die Verwaltung Beiheft 7, Duncker & Humblot, 2007), 293.

87 See Andras Jakab, 'Two Opposing Paradigms of Continental European Constitutional Thinking: Austria and Germany' (2009) 58 *International Comparative Law Quarterly* 933, 935ff.

88 See Alexander Somek, § 33. Wissenschaft vom Verfassungsrecht: Österreich', in Armin von Bogdandy and Peter M. Huber (eds.), *Ius Publicum Europaeum*, vol II (C. F. Müller, 2008), nr 12.

replicated the lawmakers' own indifferent views of constitutional law. If the constitution is nothing but a statute, the only difference being that its adoption requires a supermajority, it is going to be treated like a statute. This attitude gave rise to the formalist style of constitutional interpretation; a term that was once used as proud self-identification[89] but has since taken on a pejorative connotation.[90] Formalism, here, means allegedly restricting oneself to plain textual meaning, thus rejecting purposive (teleological) arguments, relying on historical research to see what the lawgiver 'really' meant[91] and avoiding balancing competing interests and values.[92] It has somewhat lost its decisive influence on constitutional issues,[93] but the narrative it shaped persists. The fate of the formalist style can be illustrated by two examples.

Austria's complex federalism, combined with a strictly formal interpretive approach, gave rise to the so-called petrification theory.[94] This applies when delineating the federal and the state powers, to which the constitution devotes much attention. The constitution's minuteness and the interpretation's rigidity are at the core of the ruins or sprawl problem. Since the division of powers is needlessly complex and often prevents reasonable solutions, the federal government has had to resort to constitutional amendments again and again to allot itself the legislative powers needed. According to the petrification theory, then, when interpreting a provision regarding the federal division of powers, one must assume that the constitution employs its vocabulary according to the meaning it had when the constitution was enacted. In this, it is comparable to American originalism.[95] This meaning, however, must first be gleaned from the statutes in force at the time that regulated the subject matter in question – this meaning is then 'petrified'. For example, the protection of monuments falls within federal power. At the time the constitution was enacted, the law on the protection of monuments only concerned human-made objects. Historical parks and gardens, being products of nature, even if shaped by human activity, did not count as monuments. Consequently, the federal

89 See then Constitutional Court President, Ludwig Adamovich, 'Probleme der Verfassungsgerichtsbarkeit' (1950) 72 *Juristische Blätter* 73, who writes that the constitution is 'strictly formal' law.

90 See Öhlinger and Eberhard, *Verfassungsrecht*, 37.

91 See also Ewald Wiederin, 'Verfassungsinterpretation in Österreich', in Georg Lienbacher (ed.), *Verfassungsinterpretation in Europa: Heinz Schäffer-Gedächtnissymposion* (Sramek, 2011), 84ff.

92 Somek, 'Wissenschaft vom Verfassungsrecht', nr 11.

93 Wiederin, 'Denken vom Recht her', 307ff; Jakab, 'Two Opposing Paradigms', 943ff; Somek, 'Wissenschaft vom Verfassungsrecht', nr 24ff.

94 See, generally, Taylor, *Characterisation in Federations*, 95ff; Anna Gamper, 'Judge Made Federalism? The Role of the Constitutional Court in Austria', in Hans-Peter Schneider, Jutta Kramer and Beniamino Caravita di Toritto (eds.), *Judge made Federalism? The Role of Courts in Federal Systems* (Nomos, 2009), 205ff; Jakab, 'Two Opposing Paradigms', 944ff.

95 Although it is not clear whether petrification is 'original intent' or 'original public meaning' originalism; see Keith E. Whittington, 'Originalism: A Critical Introduction' (2013) 82 *Fordham Law Review* 375.

government had no authority to extend the protection of monuments to parks and gardens, a matter which therefore fell under state jurisdiction.[96] In the tradition of constitutional sprawl, the federal government amended the Monuments Protection Act and inserted a constitutional provision containing fifty-six named parks which, from then on, counted as monuments.[97]

Human-rights legislation provides the second example. Austrian constitutional scholarship came late to the widespread human-rights euphoria of the post-war era.[98] Again, Hans Kelsen's position forms the backdrop against which scholarship had to evolve. His view was somewhat contradictory. Kelsen viewed fundamental rights as leading to dangerous judicial activism;[99] at the same time, he considered them meaningless if they contained limitation clauses and thus could be restricted by law.[100] Constitutional rights are not precepts of justice or nature but simply content-defined negative conditions of norm creation (in that they prohibit norms with a certain content).[101] In his democratic theory, Kelsen briefly but approvingly mentions rights regarding the protection of minorities.[102] His work as a Constitutional Court judge is reported not to have been encumbered by his theoretical positions.[103] At any rate, the Constitutional Court's case law was marked by a decidedly formalist approach, to the effect that hardly any statute was ever unconstitutional because of a fundamental-rights violation. As almost all fundamental rights provided for limitations enacted by law, the Constitutional Court granted an immense amount of discretion, constrained only by the rather theoretical limit that no fundamental right was allowed to be 'effectively eliminated'[104] or 'hollowed out'.[105] Legislation hardly ever came close to this. Unlike the petrification theory, which enjoys overwhelming support and is still adhered to, the formalist approach to fundamental rights has always been met by severe criticism. It is in this arena that the neutrality and formality narrative was most contested and eventually began to crumble.[106] Beginning in the 1980s, the Court could not help but be influenced by German *Grundrechtsdogmatik*, the European Court of Human Rights and the scholarship of those 'rebels'[107] who demanded that

96 See Constitutional Court of 19 March 1964, nr K II 4/63, collected under nr VfSlg 4680/1964.

97 Protection of Monuments Act, Sec 1 para 12 (Denkmalschutzgesetz), published in Federal Law Gazette Nr 533/1923 as amended.

98 See Samuel Moyn, *The Last Utopia: Human Rights in History* (Harvard University Press, 2010).

99 Hans Kelsen, *The Nature and Development of Constitutional Adjudication* (Cambridge University Press, 2015 [1929], ed. and trans. Lars Vinx), 60f.

100 Ibid., 29.

101 Kelsen, *Pure Theory of Law*, 223–234.

102 Kelsen, *The Essence and Value of Democracy*, 67–68.

103 See Ehs, 'Felix Frankfurter', 451.

104 Constitutional Court, judgment of 8 December 1956, nr G 16/56, collected under nr VfSlg 3118/1956.

105 Constitutional Court, judgment of 17 March 1976, nr B 165/75, collected under nr VfSlg 7770/1976.

106 See Jakab, 'Two Opposing Paradigms', 944–945.

107 See Somek, 'Wissenschaft vom Verfassungsrecht', nr 33–34.

fundamental rights be taken seriously. They have since become the majority.[108] In a seminal judgment of 4 October 1984 concerning the regulation of scrap-metal markets, the Constitutional Court introduced the principle of proportionality into Austrian fundamental rights law[109], where it has remained. Judicial activism has, expectably, increased.

All in all, the narrative around neutrality and formality, compromise and relativism has seen better days. It was not completely true in the first place and its excesses are met with less and less tolerance. The constitution has changed as well. Its 1920 version is very lean compared to its current state after more than 100 years of service and more than 120 amendments (more than one per year, on average!). Nowadays, the constitution contains a host of 'material' principles, such as a commitment to fighting discrimination based on gender and disability, a long list of values that public schools are required to teach and a separate constitutional act dedicated entirely to another long list of commitments of dubious enforceability, such as commitments to sustainability, the protection of animals, the environment, the natural water supply, the provision of healthy, locally produced food and the funding of research.[110] Newer textbooks tell students that the constitution embodies a social consensus on certain fundamental values that is not neutral but based on liberty, equality and solidarity.[111] The last thirty years have seen an ever denser development of the constitution's 'basic order', which is immune to constitutional amendment but requires a referendum to change.[112] It took a German law professor teaching in Austria to tell the truth: The 'value-neutral constitution of rules of the game' is gone.[113]

13.4 NARRATIVE 3: EMPIRE AND EUROPE

13.4.1 *Constitutional Comparisons*

The third narrative to be presented here is the most recent, although it refers back to the oldest developments in Austrian constitutional law and is generally presented

[108] Jakab, 'Two Opposing Paradigms', 944–945; Somek, 'Wissenschaft vom Verfassungsrecht', nr 33; and Stephan Kirste, 'Das B-VG als Werteordnung – Zum Abschied vom Mythos einer wertneutralen Spielregelverfassung' (2020) 75 *Zeitschrift für Öffentliches Recht* 173, 178ff, refer to Ludwig Adamovich junior, Walter Berka, Bernd-Christian Funk, Karl Korinek, Theo Öhlinger, Peter Pernthaler and Günther Winkler.

[109] Constitutional Court, decision of 4 October 1984, nr G 70/84, *Schrottlenkung*, collected under nr VfSlg 10.179/1984.

[110] Federal Constitutional Act on Sustainability, the Protection of Animals, the Comprehensive Protection of the Environment, the Safeguard of Water and Food Supply, and Research, published in Federal Law Gazette I Nr 111/2013.

[111] Berka, *Verfassungsrecht*, 25; Christoph Grabenwarter and Michael Holoubek, *Verfassungsrecht – Allgemeines Verwaltungsrecht*, 5th ed. (facultas, 2022), nr 21.

[112] See Wiederin, 'Verfassungsbild', 64–65. I have participated in this endeavour; see Wagrandl, 'Militant Democracy in Austria'.

[113] Kirste, 'Das B-VG als Werteordnung', 173.

with unabashed pride. Forget that the constitution is (allegedly) in ruins and that it (allegedly) only contains formal rules. Austria is the inventor of modern constitutional adjudication and a champion of European integration. What is there not to love? At last, the ubiquitous Austrian nostalgia for all things imperial[114] has found its way into constitutional thinking. It is justified, as, for once, Austria proved to be on the right side of history.[115] As has been alluded to before, the current Austrian constitution carries over many institutions and ideas of the old monarchy (such as its judiciary and system of administration, the division into states, etc.) and Hans Kelsen's thinking was shaped by his pondering over constitutional issues of the Empire. This story shall not be retold here.[116] Rather, I will explore how the old monarchy is represented as a model for Europe and the world and how Austrian constitutional law and practice relate to that. It is not a purely Austrian narrative but a 'World-Austrian'[117] one. No part of the Austrian constitution has given rise to more international, English-language literature than the so-called Austrian or Kelsenian model of constitutional adjudication. The Austro-Hungarian monarchy, once derided as a 'dungeon of peoples' (*Völkerkerker*), is increasingly seen as an early model of peaceful coexistence of nations under a common supranational roof and, hence, as a model for Europe.[118]

As always, the present narrative has more than one root. Kelsen himself drew a connection between his pure theory of law and the constitutional situation of the Austro-Hungarian empire. Kelsen, of Galician-Jewish origin, grew up in Prague but

[114] Promoted by such authors as Stefan Zweig, Robert Musil and Joseph Roth and visible on any stroll through the streets of Vienna. See, e.g., Katy Heady, 'Self-Ridiculing Nostalgia: Joseph Roth's Die Kapuzinergruft' (2018) 54 *Seminar: A Journal of Germanic Studies* 23.

[115] See Franz-Stefan Gady, 'Habsburg Nostalgia: Europe's Most Embarrassing Anachronism? Paradise Saved?' (10 June 2014) *Huffington Post*, www.huffpost.com/entry/habsburg-nostalgia-europe-austria_b_5473374.

[116] See Ewald Wiederin, '§ 7: Grundlagen und Gundzüge staatlichen Verfassungsrechts: Österreich', in Armin von Bogdandy and Peter M. Huber (eds.), *Ius Publicum Europaeum*, vol I (C. F. Müller, 2007), nr 1ff: 'the monarchy's long shadow'; Somek, 'Wissenschaft vom Verfassungsrecht', nr 1ff: 'the imperial heritage'; Jabloner, *Zum Nachhall.*

[117] To quote Christoph Bezemek and Alexander Somek, 'Die Wiederentdeckung Weltösterreichs: Eine Denkschrift' (2018) 57 *Der Staat* 135.

[118] See, e.g., Caroline de Gruyter, *Das Habsburgerreich: Inspiration für Europa?* (Böhlau, 2022); Philippe Gréciano and Martial Mathieu (eds.), *L'Autriche, un modèle pour l'Europe?* (Institut Francophone pour la Justice et la Démocratie, 2021); Jana Osterkamp, *Vielfalt ordnen: Das föderale Europa der Habsburgermonarchie (Vormärz bis 1918)* (Vandenhoeck & Ruprecht, 2020), 413ff; Helmut Rumpler, 'Introduction: The Habsburg Monarchy as a Portent for the New Europe of the Future', in Helmut Rumpler and Ulrike Harmat (eds.), *Die Habsburgermonarchie 1848–1919, vol XII: Bewältigte Vergangenheit? Die nationale und internationale Historiographie zum Untergang der Habsburgermonarchie als ideelle Grundlage für die Neuordnung Europas* (Verlag der Österreichischen Akademie der Wissenschaften, 2018); Johannes Feichtinger and Heidemarie Uhl (eds.), *Habsburg neu denken: Vielfalt und Ambivalenz in Zentraleuropa* (Böhlau, 2016); Solomon Wank, 'Some Reflections on the Habsburg Empire and Its Legacy in the Nationalities Question' (1997) 28 *Austrian History Yearbook* 131.

spoke German and completed his studies in Vienna. His life and career are a typical example of trajectories in this period (including forced emigration and death in exile).[119] He identified state and law and shed the traditional, metaphysical notion of the state because, as he claimed:

> the state closest to me, the one I knew best from personal experience, the Austrian state, obviously was a mere union of law. Faced with the Austrian state, which was composed of so many different groups defined by race, language, religion and history, such theories that sought to found the state's unity on whatever social-psychological or social-biological connection between the people legally belonging to it were revealed as obvious fictions.[120]

It is not a big step to apply Kelsen's reasoning to European integration, which has been famously conceptualised as 'integration through law'.[121] The European Union itself is referred to as a 'community based on the rule of law',[122] which carries even more meaning in the German *Rechtsgemeinschaft* – a community of law. It has become fashionable to compare Austria-Hungary and the European Union,[123] with such comparisons often focusing on broad characteristics rather than technical details.[124] The similarities are striking enough. The Austrian half of the Austro-Hungarian so-called double monarchy was, at the beginning of the twentieth century, inhabited by approximately 29 million people of eight different language communities:[125] German, Czech, Polish, Ukrainian, Romanian, Slovenian, Italian and Croatian-Serbian (nine if one also counts Yiddish). As the Austrian half of the monarchy had no official language, anyone could address the authorities in their respective mother tongue.[126] Of the 516 representatives in the Austrian Parliament, only a (sizeable) minority, 233, spoke German. A complicated electoral system

[119] For a monumental biographical work, see Thomas Olechowski, *Hans Kelsen. Biographie eines Rechtswissenschaftlers* (Mohr Siebeck, 2020).

[120] Hans Kelsen, *Autobiographie* (1947), reprinted in Matthias Jestaedt (ed.), *Hans Kelsen Werke, vol I: Veröffentlichte Schriften 1905–1910 und Selbstzeugnisse* (Mohr Siebeck, 2007), 29 (60; author translation).

[121] See Mauro Cappelletti, Monica Seccombe and Joseph Weiler (eds.), *Integration through Law, vol I: Methods, Tools and Institutions, book 1: A Political, Legal and Economic Overview* (de Gruyter, 1986).

[122] European Court of Justice, Judgment of 23 April 1986, Case C-294/83, *Les Verts*, para 23.

[123] See, e.g., David Lawday, 'The Return of the Habsburgs' (18 November 1995) 337/7941, *The Economist*; Robert Cooper, 'The European Union and the Habsburg Monarchy' (2012), *Transit online*, www.iwm.at/transit-online/the-european-union-and-the-habsburg-monarchy; Caroline De Gruyter, 'Habsburg Lessons for an embattled EU' (23 September 2016), https://carnegieendowment.org/2016/09/23/habsburg-lessons-for-embattled-eu-pub-64658.

[124] See, e.g., Anthony M. Stevens-Arroyo, 'Austria-Hungary 1914: Nationalisms in Multi-National Nation-State' (2015) 75 *Comparative Civilizations Review* 99.

[125] For an excellent recently published history, see Pieter M. Judson, *The Habsburg Empire* (Harvard University Press, 2016).

[126] See Rosita Rindler-Schjerve and Eva Vetter, 'Linguistic Diversity in Habsburg Austria as a Model for Modern European Language Policy', in Jan D. ten Thije and Ludger Zeevaert (eds.), *Receptive Multiculturalism* (John Benjamins Publishing, 2007).

ensured that everyone could vote for a representative who shared their language. The 1867 Bill of Rights guaranteed the right of every national group to protection and development of its culture and language, especially the right to the required state-funded schools, and it allowed everyone to choose to which national group they belonged. As Austria was a single country, there was, of course, free movement of persons, goods and services as well as shared Austrian citizenship in those parts of Europe that are now Austria, the Czech Republic, Slovenia and Bosnia as well as in parts of Poland, Croatia, Ukraine and Romania (Austrian citizenship did not apply to Hungary and the realms attached to it). To complete the picture, Austria-Hungary was also a customs[127] and a monetary[128] union. Its scientific and artistic zenith, captured by the 'fin-de-siècle Vienna' imaginary, barely needs any mention.[129] As nostalgic narratives go, all of this is a rosy image,[130] but it is not false.

13.4.2 *Constitutional Adoptions*

How does this tale of a benevolent, multicultural, supranational polity shape the Austrian constitution of today? In my view, the empire's legacy is best seen in a specific openness towards international law and, specifically, European integration. As mentioned in Section 13.2, no strong constitutional identity has ever developed that could be levelled against European demands. Here, the 'ruins' metaphor and the constitution's fraught origin story have prevented any sort of exaggerated pride. The Constitutional Court, for instance, never shied away from requesting preliminary rulings from the European Court of Justice. There have been four such requests, the first of which came in 1999, only four years after Austria's accession to the EU.[131] Incidentally, it was the first national Constitutional Court ever to issue such a request. The German Federal Constitutional Court only asked its first question in 2014,[132] despite having had the opportunity to do so for more than fifty years. Deep down, Austrian thinking about the constitution seems used to the fact that there is always one more level above it.

However, the Habsburg past and Kelsen's musings do not fully explain why there is no fear of contact between national and supranational law in Austrian legal

[127] Georges de Ménil and Mathilde Maurel, 'Breaking Up a Customs Union: The Case of the Austro-Hungarian Empire in 1919' (1994) 130 *Weltwirtschaftliches Archiv* 553.

[128] See Marc Flandreau, 'The Logic of Compromise: Monetary Bargaining in Austria–Hungary, 1867–1913' (2006) 10 *European Review of Economic History* 3.

[129] Carl E. Schorske, *Fin-de-siècle Vienna: Politics and Culture* (Knopf, 1979).

[130] For a critical account, see Helen Thompson, 'The Habsburg Myth and the European Union', in Francesco Duina and Frédéric Merand (eds.), *Europe's Malaise: The Long View* (Emerald, 2020).

[131] Constitutional Court, decision of 10 March 1999, nr B 2251/97; see the Judgment of the European Court of Justice of 8 November 2001, nr C-143/99, *Adria Wien Pipeline*.

[132] Federal Constitutional Court, decision of 14 January 2014, nr 2 BvR 2728/13 et al.; see the Judgment of the European Court of Justice of 16 June 2015, Case C-62/14, *Gauweiler*.

practice. The real reason is the immense impact of the European Convention on Human Rights. Austria is one of the very few countries in which the Convention enjoys direct constitutional status.[133] When the Convention was ratified in the late 1950s, Austria's only source of human rights was the above-mentioned Bill of Rights of 1867 along with scattered provisions in various other places. To close the gap before a new, complete list of rights would be formulated, the Convention was retroactively declared a constitutional act in 1964.[134] A new Austrian Bill of Rights never materialised. It did not need to. Because its provisions enjoyed constitutional status and could be invoked before the courts, the Convention radically transformed Austrian constitutional law. Innovations in the field of human rights from now on came from Strasbourg, and the Constitutional Court learnt to acquiesce. Nowadays, it cites case law from the European Court of Human Rights frequently and extensively, without making any difference between the domestic and international level.[135] In a seminal judgment, the Constitutional Court even arrogated to itself the power to review conformity with the European Charter of Fundamental Rights,[136] which had been thought to be outside the Court's purview because it is not part of the constitution.[137] The establishment of administrative tribunals in 2014 can be seen as the ultimate concession to Strasbourg.[138] The ECHR's extensive case law on Article 6 regarding the right to a fair trial always posed a problem for Austria as there was no comprehensive judicial review of administrative acts.[139] A centuries-old tradition of review within the administrative branch itself was upended because

[133] See David Harris, Michael O'Boyle, Ed Bates and Carla Buckley, *Law of the European Convention on Human Rights*, 4th ed. (Oxford University Press, 2018), 28.

[134] See H. Petzold, 'The European Convention on Human Rights in the Austrian Constitutional Court' (1972–1973) 46 *British Yearbook of International Law* 401.

[135] See, e.g., Anna Gamper, 'Foreign Precedents in Austrian Constitutional Litigation' (2015) *Vienna Journal on International Constitutional Law* 9 27; Anna Gamper and Francesco Palermo, 'The Constitutional Court of Austria: Modern Profiles of an Archetype of Constitutional Review' (2008) 3 *Journal of Comparative Law* 64, 66, 75.

[136] Constitutional Court, decision of 14 March 2012, nr B U 466/11, collected under nr VfSlg 19.632/2012.

[137] See, e.g., Andreas Orator, 'The Decision of the Austrian Verfassungsgerichtshof on the EU Charter of Fundamental Rights: An Instrument of Leverage or Rearguard Action?' (2015) 16 *German Law Journal* 1429; Reinhard Klaushofer and Rainer Palmstorfer, 'Austrian Constitutional Court Uses Charter of Fundamental Rights of the European Union as Standard of Review: Effects on Union Law' (2013) 19 *European Public Law* 1; Stefan Kieber and Reinhard Klaushofer, 'The Austrian Constitutional Court Post Case-Law after the Landmark Decision on Charter of Fundamental Rights of the European Union' (2017) 23 *European Public Law* 221; Heinz Verdino, 'The Charter of Fundamental Rights of the European Union as Review Standard in Proceedings before the Constitutional Court' (2013) 7 *Vienna Journal on International Constitutional Law* 93.

[138] See, generally, Stefan Storr, 'Administrative Procedure and Judicial Review in Austria', in Giacinto della Cananea and Mauro Bussani (eds.), *Judicial Review of Administration in Europe* (Oxford University Press, 2021), 37.

[139] The above-mentioned *Miltner* case (n 40) illustrates the Constitutional Court's reluctance to accept Strasbourg's view; in the end, it had no choice.

the Convention required it.[140] The change happened remarkably smoothly, but took a few decades. The Austrian constitution is used to Europe.

13.4.3 *Constitutional Innovations*

A second strand of the Empire-to-Europe narrative concerns the institution and radiance of the Austrian model of constitutional adjudication. It is even more self-congratulatory, depicting Austria as the nation that gave the world judicial review. As always, there is some truth and a lot more embellishment. The establishment of the Imperial Court of Justice (*Reichsgericht*) in 1867, which was entrusted with protecting the 1867 Bill of Rights, indeed marks a historical turning point. It was the world's first specialised court whose only task was fundamental-rights review; it could not, however, examine the constitutionality of laws.[141] After having exhausted all other remedies, persons who saw their fundamental rights violated by administrative acts could sue before the Imperial Court of Justice. In the almost fifty years of its existence, it developed a refined case law and enforced the promise that all nations of the empire had equal rights opportunities. There are countless examples in which the Court took the side of a national, religious or linguistic minority, be it the apportionment of school funds or the fight against antisemitism.[142]

Hans Kelsen's 1920 design for the Constitutional Court draws heavily on this already existing and well-respected institution. The new Constitutional Court inherited its judges, staff and procedure from the old Imperial Court of Justice. What Kelsen and the 1920 constitution essentially did was to give an additional function to an institution that had already worked well. It received the full power of judicial review, that is, the power to quash laws that it found to be unconstitutional.[143]

[140] See Friederike Bundschuh-Rieseneder and Alexander Balthasar, 'Administrative Justice in Austria in the Stage of Transition: From Administrative Appeals to Administrative Courts or the Final Stage of "Tribunalization" of Administrative Disputes', in Dacian Dragos and Bogdana Neamtu (eds.), *Alternative Dispute Resolution in European Administrative Law* (Springer, 2014), 209.

[141] See Christoph Grabenwarter, 'The Austrian Constitutional Court', in Armin von Bogdandy, Peter M. Huber and Christoph Grabenwarter (eds.), *The Max Planck Handbooks in European Public Law vol III: Constitutional Adjudication: Institutions* (Oxford University Press, 2020), 21–26.

[142] See Ewald Wiederin, 'Die Rechtsprechung zum Staatsgrundgesetz', in Franz Merli, Magdalena Pöschl and Ewald Wiederin (eds.), 150 *Jahre Staatsgrundgesetz über die allgemeinen Rechte der Staatsbürger* (Manz, 2018), 71; Gerald Stourzh, *Wege zur Grundrechtsdemokra tie* (Böhlau, 1989).

[143] See Grabenwarter, 'The Austrian Constitutional Court', 19; Christoph Bezemek, 'A Kelsenian Model of Constitutional Adjudication' (2012) 67 *Zeitschrift für öffentliches Recht* 115; Konrad Lachmayer, 'Austria: Constitutional Courts as Positive Legislators', in Allan R. Brewer-Carías (ed.), *Constitutional Courts as Positive Legislators. A Comparative Study* (Cambridge University Press, 2011), 251; Gamper and Palermo, 'The Constitutional Court of Austria', 64; Ronald Faber, 'The Austrian Constitutional Court: An Overview' (2008) 1 *Vienna Online Journal on International Constitutional Law* 49.

Hans Kelsen is often credited with having developed the idea of a centralised, specialised court with the monopoly on judicial review of legislation.[144] More recent research has shown that he did not invent the full structure from scratch but worked on the basis of existing institutions and conceptions.[145] Rather than having born the idea of judicial review out of nowhere, Kelsen's genius manifests itself in his clever combining of and improving upon what he was given to work with. The idea of judicial review of legislation had been known at least since *Marbury v Madison*,[146] and the discussion around it had reached Germany and Austria in the mid-nineteenth century. The revolutionary constitutions of 1848/49 all provided for a court vested with the power of judicial review, but none of them lived long enough for such a court to be established.[147] Some Latin-American states had already copied US-style judicial review in the nineteenth century but had concentrated it in their respective apex courts.[148] The discussion around judicial review in Austria was revived by famous scholar of constitutional law Walter Jellinek in 1885, when he posited that only a specialised court could adjudicate on matters of (quasi-)federal division of competence between the empire and its provinces.[149] Only recently, a long forgotten draft from 1916 resurfaced, which devised a special court tasked with reviewing the legality of administrative regulations.[150] Kelsen drew on all these inspirations. His achievement was to give constitutional justice its final shape within a specialised, separate court outside the judiciary and with a monopoly on repealing

[144] See Alec Stone Sweet, 'Constitutional Courts', in Michel Rosenfeld and András Sajó (eds.), *The Oxford Handbook of Comparative Constitutional Law* (Oxford University Press, 2012), 816; Mark Tushnet, 'Comparative Constitutional Law', in Mathias Reimann and Reinhard Zimmermann (eds.), *The Oxford Handbook of Comparative Law*, 2nd ed. (Oxford University Press, 2019), 1193, 1208ff; Ewald Wiederin, 'Der österreichische Verfassungsgerichtshof als Schöpfung Hans Kelsens und sein Modellcharakter als eigenständiges Verfassungsgericht', in Thomas Simon and Johannes Kalwoda (eds.), *Schutz der Verfassung: Normen, Institutionen, Höchst- und Verfassungsgerichte* (Duncker & Humblot, 2014), 283; Sara Lagi, 'Hans Kelsen and the Austrian Constitutional Court (1918–1929)' (2012) 9 *Co-herencia* 273.

[145] See, most recently, Ewald Wiederin, *Vergessene Wurzeln der konzentrierten Normenkontrolle in Österreich / Forgotten Roots of Concentrated Judicial Review in Austria* (Verlag Österreich, 2021); Ewald Wiederin, 'From the Federalist Papers to Hans Kelsen's "Dearest Child": The Genesis of the Austrian Constitutional Court' (2021) 76 *Zeitschrift für Öffentliches Recht* 313.

[146] See *Marbury v Madison*, 5 U.S. 137 (1803) and Stanley Paulson, 'Constitutional Review in the United States and Austria: Notes on the Beginnings' (2003) 16 *Ratio Juris* 223.

[147] See, e.g., Wolfgang Hoffmann-Riem, 'Two Hundred Years of Marbury v. Madison: The Struggle for Judicial Review of Constitutional Questions in the United States and Europe' (2004) 5 *German Law Journal* 687, 693ff; Helmut Steinberger, 'Historic Influences of American Constitutionalism upon German Constitutional Development: Federalism and Judicial Review' (1998) 36 *Columbia Journal of Transnational Law* 189, 199ff; Christoph Gusy, *Richterliches Prüfungsrecht: Eine verfassungsgeschichtliche Untersuchung* (Duncker & Humblot, 1985); Werner Frotscher, 'Die ersten Auseinandersetzungen um die richterliche Normenkontrolle in Deutschland' (1971) 10 *Der Staat* 383.

[148] Keith S. Rosenn, 'Judicial Review in Latin America' (1974) 35 *Ohio State Law Journal* 785; Phanor J. Eder, 'Judicial Review in Latin America' (1960) 21 *Ohio State Law Journal* 570.

[149] Georg Jellinek, *Ein Verfassungsgerichtshof für Österreich* (Hölder, 1885).

[150] See Wiederin, 'From the Federalist Papers to Hans Kelsen's "Dearest Child"'.

unconstitutional laws – which is now state of the art in constitution-making. Federalism, not human rights, would prove to be the decisive factor for establishing the Constitutional Court in 1920.[151] As the political parties fiercely fought about the centralism–federalism issue and only reached a fragile and complicated compromise, they did not trust each other to keep the peace. In this climate, erecting a Constitutional Court as a neutral arbiter was seen as a viable solution.[152] The protection of fundamental rights was inherited from the Imperial Court of Justice because it had a long tradition, not because it was the most pressing concern. It was not in Austria, however, that Kelsen's ideas would be implemented first. The Constitutional Court of Czechoslovakia was established a few months earlier than the one in Austria. Nowadays, it is the German Federal Constitutional Court that is most often depicted as the archetype of European judicial review, and judicial review itself is strongly associated with the protection of fundamental rights, not so much with questions of jurisdiction. The Austrian narrative ('We invented it!') must, therefore, be taken with a grain of salt. But, faced with rather unkind narratives about our constitutional law, the Constitutional Court provides a rare source of unquestioned pride.

13.5 CONCLUSION

What is there to learn from these constitutional narratives? The 'ruins' dictum and its belated refutation teach us that Austrian constitutional law scholars should be more careful with the words they use. They self-identify as guardians of the constitution. As such, they have a responsibility to show the constitution its due respect. Because, why should the public if even constitutional lawyers do not? Apart from that, it is true that accessible and easily comprehensible constitutions are important. Constitutional aesthetics should be upheld in the face of ever growing legislative and regulatory activity. Constitutions should not be abused to entrench whatever the current government wants in order to tie the hands of future governments. Democracy needs room for manoeuvre and meaningful choices. German constitutional court justice and professor, Dieter Grimm, has famously argued that the European Union is over-constitutionalised. Its treaties contain too many policy decisions that should be left to the political process.[153] This is not to say that the European Constitution is in ruins, no more so than the Austrian one. But they share a common trait that should not be the basis of pride in either case: they seem

[151] As is true for all older constitutional courts; see Tom Ginsburg and Mila Versteeg, 'Why Do Countries Adopt Constitutional Review?' (2014) 30 *Journal of Law, Economics and Organization* 587.

[152] Many constitutional courts were established based on the same rationale; see Tom Ginsburg, 'Economic Analysis and the Design of Constitutional Courts' (2002) 3 *Theoretical Inquiries in Law* 49; Francisco Ramos Romeu, 'The Establishment of Constitutional Courts: A Study of 128 Constitutions' (2006) 2 *Review of Law and Economics* 103.

[153] Dieter Grimm, *Europa ja – aber welches?* (Beck, 2016), 95. For an English translation, see Dieter Grimm, *The Constitution of European Democracy* (Oxford University Press, 2017).

bloated. However, derision, even if directed at obvious flaws, is not the way to go. It can easily miss its target and hit the innocent. A European constitutional patriotism, extravagant as this concept might be,[154] needs a constitution that is appreciated by the people closest to it: judges, public officials, constitutional scholars and their students.

This does not mean that we need a more formal, neutral style in European treaty making, at least if formality and neutrality are taken as ends in themselves. As shown, imagining the constitution as a purely formal set of rules of the game has never captured what a constitution is all about. A formalist approach to constitutional interpretation makes sense when delineating competences, jurisdictions and powers. These constitutional contents normally do not inspire great devotion. But every constitution is built on certain assumptions and certain values. If democracy, human rights and the rule of law are to be Europe's treasured principles, they require us to presuppose a certain notion of freedom and equality that must be defended when necessary, such as via militant democracy or in regard to Russia's invasion of Ukraine. The Austrian approach can teach us, though, that a constitution need not be treated as an article of faith in order to flourish.

Loyalty towards institutions, such as constitutional courts, requires a reason and motivation for it that everyone can grasp. In other words, it needs a persuasive story. In Austria, the Constitutional Court is perceived as a uniquely Austrian invention by constitutional superhero Hans Kelsen. That makes for a good foundation. The idea of judicial review remains unchallenged. I would suggest that, out of all the different constitutional features, it is the one most easily recalled by the public. The Constitutional Court's judgements are publicly discussed and often widely celebrated, in particular when they are seen as dealing a blow to the government. Not every court can tell such tales; not every court is as self-confident; not every court is as widely acclaimed. Founding stories cannot be generated out of a void. But they can be told more or less convincingly; they can be spun strategically; they can be directed at the public or at the experts.

The constitutional narratives presented here do not form an exhaustive list of the many ways the Austrian constitution has been thought of. I endeavoured to showcase three main currents of Austrian constitutional law scholarship. Some convey a feeling of malaise, such as the 'ruins' metaphor. Others are based on historical origin stories and theoretical reflection, such as the myth of the value-neutral constitution. Others still are told in retrospect because they are about something that has become seen as a great achievement, such as the 'invention' of constitutional adjudication. As the Austrian constitution embarks on its 105th year, some narratives will fade and others will arise. Old stories will be forgotten and new stories will be told. A constitution without narratives about it would be like a constitution without qualities: a curious object of study, but not fit for use.

154 But see Müller, *Constitutional Patriotism*, 93ff.

PART III

The Varieties of Liberalism in Europe

14

Rule of What Law?

Authoritarian Pasts, Liberal Politics and Constitutional Imagination in Early Post-Communist East Central Europe

Michal Kopeček

The rise of illiberal populist regimes in the Eastern flank of the EU is deeply rooted in the ambivalence of the post-1989 liberal transition project. At the core of the liberal vision for the post-communist era was a belief in the democratic *Rechtsstaat* and the concomitant loyalty to the politics of liberal constitutionalism. Reimagining the relationship between state and citizen, embodied through law reform at all levels, was a springboard from which the entire post-communist transformation was launched, from the separation of powers to democratic elections to the policy of wide-ranging privatization to the constitutional enshrinement of the principles of the inviolability of human rights and their supremacy over the legal system guaranteed by the state.

Today's illiberal backlash is most evident in its assault on the salient features of the post-1989 constitutional architecture. Much of the social science literature to date has sought to locate the causes of the illiberal backlash in various aspects of neoliberal transformation's social costs and to uncover the fatal cleavages within the liberal consensus of the 1990s. Constitutional scholarship is understandably devoted to trying to grasp the flaws or one-sidedness of liberal constitutionalism and the roots and reasons for the emergence of counter-constitutionalism or illiberal constitutionalism. This chapter is a historian's attempt to look at the post-communist constitutional imagination from the point of view of the rule of law concept and its political context.[1] Unlike, for example, the economic policy of shock therapy, the rule of law was an unquestioned and shared principle across the emerging political spectrum. What were the political, cultural and historical drivers of this overall

This chapter was prepared with the support of the research grant project 'Towards Illiberal Constitutionalism in East Central Europe: Historical Analysis in Comparative and Transnational Perspectives', sponsored by the Volkswagen Foundation for the period 2022–2025.

[1] For the concept of 'constitutional imagination', its historical background and methodological implications, see Marin Loughlin, 'The Constitutional Imagination' (2015) 78 *The Modern Law Review* 1. Compared to Loughlin, my approach comes more from the perspective of the history of political thought rather than constitutional theory.

political compromise based on the rule of law? How did it develop over time? Were kernels of its future breakdown palpable from the start?

The project of constitutional democracy and the rule of law concept served as a powerful unifying platform for political compromise in the transition era. Although rule of law was originally an idea primarily associated with liberalism in European history, by the end of the twentieth century, the demand for rule of law by no means required liberal Weltanschauung. Socialists and social democrats, radical democrats, conservatives, and republican-oriented democrats in East Central Europe were all in favour of the rule of law. The legal sphere and legal-political ideas played a vital role in the liberal democratic transformation following communist rule. Today's challenge to the liberal rule of law calls for a re-evaluation of our understanding of that period and its deeper historical contextualization.

In an effort to provide such a historicizing perspective and to look beneath the surface of the post-communist *political compromise through the rule of law,* this chapter offers a tentative historical typology of the various rule of law understandings of the period of 'liberal consensus'. I proceed in three steps. First, I briefly outline the historical roots of the 1989 democratic and constitutional revolutions in East Central Europe (ECE), pointing out their several major sources, namely the import of Western constitutional theory, dissident human rights activism and the mostly neglected yet important authoritarian socialist constitutionalism. Second, I look at the nature of the politics of liberal constitutionalism in the 1990s – almost the only game in town then. However, I emphasize its internal diversity in terms of the variety of political and thus also constitutional imagination depending on the different political ideas and ideologies proliferating at that time. This will set the stage for the third and final step, where I explore the different conceptions of the widely invoked rule of law, namely neoliberal, substantive, positivist and non-liberal. Although this chapter takes a transnational view of the entire ECE region, in Section 14.3, for the sake of concision and clarity, I focus primarily on the Czech context. On this basis, I offer a preliminary historical typology of the various conceptions of the rule of law that we encounter on the broad platform of liberal constitutionalism at the time. Albeit significantly diverging these conceptions coexisted within the 'liberal consensus' of the period. Yet this diversity contained within itself the seeds of a future schism.

14.1 EXPOSITION: TOWARDS THE CONSTITUTIONAL REVOLUTIONS OF 1989

The constitutional imagination in the post-communist era was pre-determined by the fact that the democratic revolutions of 1989 in ECE represented an apogee of the struggle for a *Rechtsstaat* in the previous decades.[2] The legalist character of the

[2] On the constitutional and legalistic character of the 1989 revolutions in east central Europe, see, e.g., Jiří Přibáň, *Dissidents of Law: On the 1989 Velvet Revolutions, Legitimations, Fictions*

1989 revolutions was a result of the power encounter of socialist legalism with its evolving project of socialist authoritarian *Rechtsstaat* and its dissident challengers. Liberal constitutionalism that dominated the constitutional imagination and legal practice in the region after 1989 has long been interpreted as the offspring of a dissident struggle for human rights whose godmother was the legal-political experience of post-war Western Europe and its institutional framework. In reality, however, the other unacknowledged parent was socialist constitutionalism, which underwent quite dynamic transformations in the late communist period.

Let us take a brief look at both of these parents. Legalism was a key element of the dissident political strategy for the public renegotiation of rights, particularly human and civil rights. The human rights origins and the legalist character of dissidence are sometimes difficult to distinguish. Yet human rights discourse and dissident legalism are two different things: the first was an ideological and philosophical foundation for dissidence, while the second was primarily a strategy of resistance in the authoritarian regime. The international circumstances, such as a new phase of détente and the new international human rights politics following the Helsinki Accords in 1975, created favourable conditions for the rise of the new democratic opposition in communist countries. However, as I have shown in another study, to work on the ground, the human rights doctrine appropriated by dissidents had to be transformed into a concrete and efficient strategy of legal resistance or legal defence, that is, *dissident legalism*. The newly internationalized human rights doctrine was an inevitable precondition for the rise and sustainability of dissidence and its international visibility. Yet, without dissident legalism on the ground, the human rights doctrine would hardly have become an efficient mechanism.[3]

The dissident legalistic struggle, however, was not a struggle against lawless totalitarianism, as often portrayed by dissidents themselves as well as Western observers. It was civic activism and a strategy of legal resistance in a state governed largely by an authoritarian and often repressive socialist legality. Dissident legalism became a regular part of the opposition's tactical repertoire only because the late socialist regimes adhered more emphatically than ever before to law as a crucial instrument of governance.

The role of law in state socialist dictatorships changed significantly between the 1950s and 1980s. The Soviet Stalinist system was characterized by a combination of

of Legality and Contemporary Version of the Social Contract (Ashgate, 2002); Jiří Přibáň and Wojciech Sadurski, 'The Role of Political Rights in the Democratization of Central and Eastern Europe', in W. Sadurski (ed.), *Political Rights under Stress in 21st Century Europe* (Oxford University Press, 2006).

3 Michal Kopeček, 'Dissident Legalism. Human Rights, Socialist Legality, and the Birth of Legal Resistance in the 1970s Democratic Opposition in Czechoslovakia and Poland' in Celia Donert, Ana Kladnik and Martin Sabrow (eds.), *Making Sense of Dictatorship: Domination and Everyday Life in East Central Europe after 1945* (Central European University Press, 2022). See also Benjamin Nathans, 'The Dictatorship of Reason: Aleksandr Vol'pin and the Idea of Rights under "Developed Socialism"' (2007) 66 *Slavic Review* 630.

the *prerogative state*, whose use of force was quasi-regulated through a system of norms, and the *normative state*.[4] In such a system, there was a tendency to make abrupt changes in legal rules or their application in the interest of maximizing the power of the state or party over the individual. Yet, the expansion of the normative state and development of state socialist 'legal culture' received major impetus under Stalinism.[5] The growth of the normative state during Stalinism and its extensive legislation was not created to invest the authorities with any political legitimacy. The Communist Party of the Soviet Union was strong and, therefore, law was not important as a legitimating factor. However, it was still a crucial tool of governance. An instrumental legality par excellence, the Stalinist legal doctrine formulated by Vyshinsky saw the law as a pure instrument of social management, not as a self-standing social formation.[6]

The instrumentality of law characterized communist legal and constitutional doctrine throughout the existence of communist rule in Eastern Europe. However, in practice, the recurrent reformist attempts to give law as a whole a greater degree of autonomy in the functioning of a real socialist society have been extremely important. In East Central Europe, there was a significant change in socialist jurisprudence in the late 1950s and 1960s as a reaction to 'Stalinist dogmatism' and its 'voluntaristic understanding' of socialist law. In legal thinking, it involved a reinterpretation of the Stalinist concept of socialist legality and further consolidation of the normative state. These changes did not mean that the prerogative state disappeared. Still, in the reformist understanding, law and the concept of socialist legality started to be understood as a major check against the future possible misuse of power, as occurred under Stalinism, and simultaneously as an important source of legitimacy for both the socialist state and the reform communist movement. The reformists understood the law as a general civilizational instrument. As such, socialist societies, once the revolutionary changes had been implemented, should have been governed primarily by law, not by direct political interventions.

The legal reformist trend was reversed again to some extent in the consolidation regimes of the 1970s and during the first half of the 1980s. Unlike the revolutionary Stalinist regimes during the first decade after WWII, the late communist

4 The application of Ernst Fraenkel's concept of 'dual state' to Soviet and East European communism has many pitfalls. It has produced considerable discussion among scholars, see, e.g., Stefan Plaggenborg, *Experiment Moderne: Der sowjetische Weg* (Campus Verlag, 2006), 201–220; Joachim von Puttkamer, 'Sozialistische Staatlichkeit: Eine historische Annäherung', in Jana Osterkamp and Joachim von Puttkamer (eds.), *Sozialistische Staatlichkeit* (Oldenbourg Verlag, 2012).

5 Robert Sharlet, 'Stalinism and Soviet Legal Culture', in Robert C. Tucker (ed.), *Stalinism: Essays in Historical Interpretation* (W. W. Norton & Comp, 1977).

6 The most outspoken claim about the centrality of law as a governance tool and practice and not just a smokescreen of prerogative power in the Soviet system from the very beginnings is Scott Newton, *Law and the Making of the Soviet World: The Red Demiurge* (Oxford University Press, 2015).

dictatorships did not use political terror and revolutionary zeal as the central tools of their rule. While they certainly did not cease to be repressive, open state violence started to recede from the public eye as early as the late 1950s and 1960s and remained so, in most cases, until 1989.[7] From a doctrinal perspective, the period was characterized by a compromise. The legal systems of the late communist dictatorships kept most of the 1960s 'liberalization' institutional forms; however, legal theory and assertion were again there predominantly to serve the political and ideological needs of communist governance and, importantly, the socialist state.

Far from being the proverbial 'golden age of stagnation', as the Brezhnev era has been seen for decades, this period witnessed dynamic changes in governance techniques, with law at the forefront.[8] The concept of the state retained its primary definition as an organization of class dominance but was transformed into a theoretically inclusive concept of an 'all-people's state'; thus, the dictatorship of the proletariat was no longer emphasized.[9] The technocratic project of 'developed socialism' should have been characterized not by the revolutionary charisma of the party but by the 'scientific management of society'. In such a system, law was to play an enormously important role. The concept of *socialist legality* was once more interpreted as a means of implementing the political domination of the party. Binding the state administration to the existing legal order and the question of the guarantee of legality – the main concern in the reformist age – became of secondary importance behind the ruling qualities of law and the legal system. Yet, the binding nature of socialist legality did not disappear altogether, for it was a part of the general processes of 'normalization of rule' in state socialist societies, which, after all, had already been in existence for decades.[10] Hence, importantly, the gap between reality and statutory law effectively diminished. Not only technocratic governance but also political repression and terror, such as that in Poland after the establishment of martial law in 1981, were realized through legal regulation.[11]

The increasing importance of legal regulations for the late communist dictatorship prepared new ground for the dissident challengers of the regime and, along

7 Generally, to the consolidation regimes in East Central Europe, see Grzegorz Ekiert, *The State against Society: Political Crises and Their Aftermath in East Central Europe* (Princeton University Press, 1996).

8 For revaluation of the Brezhnev period in current historical literature, see, e.g., Boris Belge and Martin Deuerlein (eds.), *Goldenes Zeitalter der Stagnation? Perspektiven auf die sowjetische Ordnung der Brežnev-Ära* (Mohr Siebeck, 2014); S. Schattenberg, *Leonid Breschnew: Staatsmann und Schauspieler im Schatten Stalins: Eine Biographie* (Böhlau, 2017); Edwin Bacon and Mark Sandle (eds.), *Brezhnev Reconsidered* (Palgrave Macmillan, 2002).

9 Mark Sandle, 'Brezhnev and Developed Socialism: The Ideology of Zastoj?', in Edwin Bacon and Mark Sandle (eds.), *Brezhnev Reconsidered* (Palgrave, 2002).

10 See Mary Fulbrook (ed.), *Power and Society in the GDR 1961–1979: The Normalisation of Rule?* (Berghahn Books, 2009).

11 Cf. e.g., Andrzej Swidlicki, *Political Trials in Poland 1981–1986* (Croom Helm, 1988); Antoni Dudek (ed.), *Stan wojenny w Polsce 1981–1983* (IPN, 2003); Antoni Dudek and Krzysztof Madej (eds.), *Świadectwa stanu wojennego* (IPN, 2001).

with the new international human rights mechanisms, improved their chances to sustain their activities. It marked the playing field between the repressive regime and the so-called democratic opposition or dissent. Violations of human rights, as well as violations of the constitution and applicable laws by the repressive forces and the state administration, were the subject of the main critical arguments of dissident legalism. There was a little doctrinal controversy between dissidents and the communist regime about the human rights interpretation. The socialist constitutions, after all, contained all the basic civil and political rights and diction on par with the constitutions of liberal regimes. The major issue was the question of their constitutional protection and legal accountability of the state organs and, thereby, indirectly, of the Party organs.

Since the birth of the human rights opposition in ECE in the second half of the 1970s, law and legality, the regime's rule by law and the dissident-envisioned rule of law were a matter of regime-opposition interaction, communication and semantic struggle. The field of contest marked out by existing positive legal norms, but also expanding through the accepted international human rights conventions, predetermined the possibilities for the communist authorities that still tried hard to use their political prerogatives in a one-party dominated dictatorship but ultimately became increasingly bound by their normative state.

This tendency was ever more strengthened in the second half of the 1980s, the time of *perestroika* and *glasnost* in the Soviet Union and elsewhere, with efforts to introduce an authoritarian socialist *Rechtsstaat* all across the region.[12] The most exemplary case of the gradual 'constitutionalization' of the dictatorship was Poland, due to the specific situation during and after Solidarity and the authoritarian turn in December 1981. A relatively strong stream of Polish reform communist lawyers within state and party organizations managed to pass legislative projects establishing several institutions meant to strengthen the Polish normative state and, thus, also, the social support of the population through the image of the rule of law. As early as 1980, the Highest Administrative Court, the first in communist-ruled Eastern Europe, was established. It was followed in 1982 (the year of martial law) by the Tribunal of the State. In 1985, the Constitutional Tribunal came into being and, finally, in 1988, the office of the Ombudsman, the public spokesperson of civic rights and watchdog on the state authorities and their dealings with citizens, was created. The tendency towards a socialist *Rechtsstaat* in Poland is quite visible and represents an important pre-condition for the negotiated regime change in 1989.[13]

[12] Michal Kopeček, 'Was There a Socialist *Rechtsstaat* in Late Communist East Central Europe? The Czechoslovak Case in a Regional Context' (2020) 18 *Journal of Modern European History* 281.

[13] Paweł Kowal, *Koniec systemu władzy: Polityka ekipy gen. Wojciecha Jaruzelskiego w latach 1986–1989* (Trio, 2012), 119–125.

The constitutional court system was introduced as a part of the 'socialist renewal' strategy by which Jaruzelski's regime tried to increase its legitimacy. An example of 'liberalization without democratization', rule of law was offered to the population as a surrogate for the democratization demanded by Solidarity and a promise for law and order. It is not by chance or through the clumsiness of the Polish communist leadership that some of the major steps in creating the socialist *Rechtsstaat*, such as the creation of the Tribunal of State and the Constitutional Tribunal, were undertaken during the martial law period.[14] It certainly did not create a satisfying system of checks and balances for ensuring that administrative organs adhered to existing law and it left a big enough space for both the party and state apparatus to exercise their prerogative powers. Nevertheless, it contributed considerably to strengthening the legal-constitutional elements of the authoritarian system.[15]

While Poland serves as the most institutionally elaborate example of this process, rudiments of the socialist *Rechtsstaat* started to emerge all over the region during the late 1980s. The legislative reforms initiated by the regimes were not intended as methods of democratization but as constitutional reforms to reshuffle the balance of the communist dual state in favour of the normative state and stabilize the power system and the 'leading role' of the party.

From a longer-term historical perspective, the 1980s socialist *Rechtsstaat* is a specific and historically located subset of the notion of an authoritarian *Rechsstaat*, which had many historical predecessors and institutional forms in Central and Eastern Europe. Democratic deficits, strong authoritarian states as modernizing agents, an emphasis on formal legality and fewer safeguards of civic rights and freedoms traditionally characterized this region. The different genealogies of the law-governed state also produced different interpretations of the central notion of *Rechtsstaat*, which developed over time.[16] In the German or Russian tradition up until 1918, the *Rechtsstaat* mainly represented the legality of administrative acts and checks on the discretion of government officials. Its main thrust – to save authoritarian law and order – stands in contrast to the evolution of the rule of law in contemporary England and Scotland, which was accompanied by the rise of democratic representation. 'In this formally rational understanding, *Rechtsstaat*

[14] Jakub Szumski, 'The State Tribunal and the Paradoxes of Socialist Legality in 1980s Poland' (2020) 18 *Journal of Modern European History* 297.

[15] Lech Mażewski, *Posttotalitarny Autorytaryzm PRL 1956–1989: Analiza Ustrojowopolityczna* (Biała Podlaska, 2010), 115–121.

[16] The experience with and the development of the *Rechtsstaat* notion differs substantially in the different empires in the region depending, among others, on the strength and fortunes of the liberal movement. See, e.g., Gerald Stourzh, *Wege zur Grundrechtsdemokratie: Studien zur Begriffs- und Institutionengeschichte des liberalen Verfassungsstaates* (Vienna, 1989); Ernst-Wolfgang Böckenförde, 'The Origin and Development of the Concept of the Rechtsstaat', in *State, Society and Liberty: Studies in Political Theory and Constitutional Law* (New York, 1991); Andrey N. Medushevsky, *Russian Constitutionalism: Historical and Contemporary Development* (London, 2006).

was about procedures, not about rights' and served mainly to maintain the authoritarian system of government.[17] As opposed to the German development, however, in the Austro-Hungarian Empire, due to its composite nature and the rising political importance of nationalist movements, rights played a more important role in the political struggle and thus also in constitutional design.[18]

Thus, we need to differentiate between two contrasting *Rechtsstaat* notions. First, a rights-based democratic *Rechtsstaat* emphasizing substantive justice, whose most influential form in Europe nowadays is represented by the German Basic Law as a response to the obvious abuse of the democratizing 'Prussian' *Rechtsstaat* by the Nazis. Second, a notion of the authoritarian *Rechtsstaat* based on procedural rather than substantive justice, which can help us better understand the legal and constitutional changes in authoritarian societies. The project of the authoritarian *Rechtsstaat* and that of the democratic *Rechtsstaat* always coexisted in the modern history of Central and Eastern Europe, with the former representing the historically more weighty tradition in the region. From this perspective, the notion of a socialist *Rechtsstaat* is a specific and historically located subset of the notion of an authoritarian *Rechsstaat*, which had many historical forms in the region evolving throughout time.

As the doctrine and practice of socialist constitutionalism dynamically developed in the 1980s, the dissident constitutional vision, too, began to consolidate. Dissidents continued challenging the repressive legality of the system and pointing out the internal contradictions of the evolving vision of the authoritarian socialist *Rechtsstaat*. They started offering their own evolving vision of a democratic *Rechsstaat* based on human rights observance.[19] Hence, from this point of view, the 1980s were a decade of an increasing confrontation between two semiotic and ideological systems, two mutually encountering, evolving constitutional imaginations: socialist legalism, with the socialist *Rechtsstaat* as the leading motif in the second half of the 1980s, and dissident legalism, with the vision of the democratic *Rechtsstaat* as, progressively, its main vantage point.

[17] Jens Meierhenrich, *The Remnants of the Rechtsstaat: An Ethnography of Nazi Law* (Oxford University Press, 2018), 81. For detailed development of the German public law see Michael Stolleis, *Public Law in Germany, 1800–1914* (Berghan Books, 2001); Michael Stolleis, *Public Law in Germany: A Historical Introduction from the 16th to the 21st Century* (Oxford University Press, 2017).

[18] See, e.g., Gerland Stourzh, *Die Gleichberechtigung der Nationalitäten in der Verfassung und Verwaltung Österreichs 1848–1918* (Verlag der Österreichischen Akademie der Wissenschaften, 1985); Pieter Judson, *Exclusive Revolutionaries: Liberal Politics, Social Experience, and National Identity in the Austrian Empire, 1848–1914* (Ann Arbor, 1996), 117–272.

[19] See, e.g., František Šamalík, *Právní stát kontra stalinismus* (NLN, 1991); Zdeněk Jičínský, *Charta 77 a právní stat* (Doplněk, 1995), 94–149; Ferenc Fehér and Agnes Heller, 'From Totalitarian Dictatorship through "Rechtsstaat" to Democracy: Legal-Constitutional Changes in Soviet-Type-Societies' (1990) 26 *Thesis Eleven* 7; Jacek Kurczewski and Barry Sullivan, 'The Bill of Rights and the Emerging Democracies' (2002) 65 *Law and Contemporary Problems* 251.

14.2 POST-COMMUNIST LIBERALISMS AND THE LEGACIES OF THE PAST

After the 1989 revolutions in East Central Europe, liberal constitutionalism and the rule of law were to have a crucial role in securing the transition to liberal democracy and market economy. The motivations for supporting liberal constitutionalist policies varied significantly among political actors. The non-violent revolutions of 1989 in East Central Europe are sometimes called legalist or constitutional – and for good reason. They happened in the foreground of 'pre-constitutional' round-table negotiations and represent an apogee of the struggle for the character of the *Rechtsstaat* in the previous decade.

After 1989, Western and global influence was of great importance in the spread of liberal constitutionalism in the region. Most constitutions in the region that were either new or amended shortly after 1989 feature institutions 'borrowed' from established Western democracies.[20] The post-1989 democratic transition in post-communist Europe ushered in an era of 'new constitutionalism', which was supposed to be qualitatively different from the 'old' one and the classic liberal idea of the rule of law. With the human rights revolution of the last decade of the twentieth century, the constitutionalist tradition entered a new global stage, which was marked by the massive adoption of bills of rights and constitutional courts as the quintessential institutions of the new constitutionalism.[21] Liberal constitutional institutions symbolized by new or amended constitutions, bills of rights, and constitutional courts became an entrenched and influential factor in the political life of post-communist countries.[22]

Liberal constitutionalism theoretically had alternatives. Some scholars, such as Paul Blokker, detected 'rudiments' of alternative democratic constitutionalist visions in the late 1980s, coming from dissident democratic activism that stressed participatory and self-organizing elements.[23] Yet a few of these visions translated into constitutional politics after 1989. The partial exception was Poland, where 'civic constitutionalism' became a synonym for the post-Solidarity democratic right's struggle against the Western-inspired liberal constitutionalism promoted by liberal

20 Anneli Albi and Samo Bardutzky (eds.), *National Constitutions in European and Global Governance: Democracy, Rights, the Rule of Law: National Reports* (Asser-Springer, 2019), 687–1177.

21 Saïd Amir Arjomand, 'Law, Political Reconstruction and Constitutional Politics' (2003) 18 *International Sociology* 7.

22 See, e.g., Radoslav Procházka, *Mission Accomplished: On Founding Constitutional Adjudication in Central Europe* (Central European University Press, 2002); Wojciech Sadurski, 'Judicial Review in Central and Eastern Europe: Rationales or Rationalizations?' (2009) 40 *Israel Law Review* 500.

23 Paul Blokker, *New Democracies in Crisis? A Comparative Constitutional Study of the Czech Republic, Hungary, Poland, Slovakia and Romania* (Routledge, 2014), 79–98; Paul Blokker, *Multiple Democracies in Europe: Political Culture in New Member States* (Routledge, 2010).

parties and the post-communist left.[24] As such, what was envisaged as 'civic constitutionalism' became part of the party-political struggle and thus a political elite matter, contributing very little to citizens' direct participation in the constitution-making processes.[25]

In retrospect, it often seems that the Western influence was overwhelming, for better or worse. Yet, the cultural, political and ideological pre-conditions for liberal constitutionalism to thrive must not be neglected. Local legal culture and political traditions mattered, as did the political constellations and struggles. In general, the politics of liberal constitutionalism were a true triumph in East Central Europe in the 1990s. However, behind the triumph was a rather heterogeneous coalition of interests and forces with diverging constitutional imaginations standing for very different understandings of what a constitution is and how the relations between the state, the rule of law, society, and the market should be organized. Liberal or legal constitutionalism of that period must, therefore, be understood as a composite notion. This chapter aims to unpack it by looking at the political and ideological currents behind its historical success.

Liberalism in post-communist East Central Europe was a broad and variegated ideological stream with a diverse genealogy. There are different ways of categorizing it ideologically, culturally and historically.[26] For this chapter, I propose to speak schematically about two major liberal streams behind the visions of the democratic, parliamentary *Rechtsstaat* in the given period. The first one, *human rights liberalism*, stands for a broad and initially only vaguely defined political stream coming partly from a post-dissident environment and building the vision of constitutional democracy on the principle of the salience of human rights in political life and state organization. The second, *neoliberalism*, stresses the economic foundations of the transformation from communist etatism to a free society based on the market principle, where the rule of law was to play a central role. To understand the

[24] Emilia T. Kowalewska, 'Between Civic and Legal Constitutionalism: Dynamics of Poland's Constitution-making Projects of the 1990s' (2020) 10 *Oñati Socio-Legal Series* 903. Available at: https://opo.iisj.net/index.php/osls/article/view/1245.

[25] Ewa Poplawska, 'Constitution-making in Poland: Some Reflections on Popular Involvement' (2008) 45 *Zbornik radova Pravnog fakulteta u Splitu* 279; more broadly to the displacement of social rights, fundamental for Solidarity, in Polish constitutional discourse after 1989, see Michał Krajewski, 'The Constitutional Quandary of Social Rights: Questions in Times of the Polish Illiberal Turn' (2023) 21 *International Journal of Constitutional Law* 156.

[26] See, e.g., Balazs Trencsényi et al., *A History of Modern Political Thought in East Central Europe: Volume II, Negotiating Modernity in the "Short Twentieth Century" and Beyond: Part II, 1968–2018* (Oxford University Press, 2018), 181–213; Michal Kopeček and Piotr Wciślik (eds.), *Thinking through Transition: Liberal Democracy, Authoritarian Pasts, and Intellectual History in East Central Europe after 1989* (Central European University Press, 2015); Jerzy Szacki, *Liberalism after Communism* (Central European University Press, 1995); Miłowit Kuninski, 'Liberalism in Poland: What Is Left?'(1997) 49 *Studies in East European Thought*, 241; Ervin Csizmadia, *Két liberalizmus Magyarországon* (Századvég Kiadó, 1999); Milan Znoj, *České spory o liberalismus: Masaryk a Havel* (Karolinum, 2024).

ideal-typical character of these categories is essential. They are designed exclusively to analyse the various liberal conceptions of the rule of law and their ideological anchorage. If we were interested in another aspect of post-communist liberalism and liberal transformation, such as the liberal understanding of civil society or the role of social rights, the categories would look different.

Given the historical development in East Central Europe after 1989, with the economic transformation towards market capitalism playing a central part, neoliberalism is considered the more influential form of liberalism in this period. Yet, in terms of both historical memory and the legal and constitutional anchoring of the emerging democracy, *human rights liberalism*, with its distinct post-dissident character, played a decisive role.[27] The dissident experience of the struggle for civic and human rights against the repressive, illiberal dictatorship was not only compatible with the current West European liberal constitutional doctrine, especially its post-fascist branch, it also imbued it with a compelling historical justification.

Human rights liberalism in post-1989 East Central Europe was a broad political and cultural-political stream that continued to carry significant features of its dissident origin. As such, it was broader and vaguer than, for instance, the Rawlsian-style Western political liberalism of the time, which elaborated a project of a society based on legal equality and social justice. More than Rawlsian political liberalism, post-dissident human rights liberalism is reminiscent of the broad current of thought and politics, sometimes referred to as 'Cold War liberalism'.[28]

The post-dissident liberal camp – in contrast to the neoliberals – defined itself as liberal only reluctantly, sometimes to the point of being resentful about the label. Its representatives among former dissidents were not only icons of dissident cultural liberalism, such as Václav Havel, György Konrád or Adam Michnik, but also conservatives, such as Tadeusz Mazowiecki, Petr Pithart or Gaspár Miklós Tamás, and radical democrats and leftists, such as Jacek Kuroń, Miklós Haraszti, Petr Uhl or Miroslav Kusý. Many of these 'liberals' understood their liberalism – if they ever accepted the designation – as a commitment to basic liberal-democratic institutional structures such as the rule of law, which they then combined with a plethora of conservative, socialist or radical democratic sensibilities. They often had wildly divergent political visions and understandings of democracy. Yet, in terms of historical consciousness and vague constitutional imagination, they had much in common due to their shared past.

27 For discussions in recent human rights historiography about the mutual conditioning of human rights and neoliberalism, see Samuel Moyn, *Not Enough: Human Rights in an Unequal World* (Harvard University Press, 2018); Jessica Whyte, *The Morals of the Market: Human Rights and the Rise of Neoliberalism* (Verso, 2019).

28 It is represented by such a diverse group of thinkers as Raymond Aron, Isaiah Berlin, Arthur Schlessinger Jr., Karl R. Popper, Michael Oakeshott, Ralf Dahrendorf, Norberto Bobbio or Judith Shklar. Jan-Werner Müller (ed.), *Isaiah Berlin's Cold War Liberalism* (Palgrave Pivot, 2019); Terry Nardin (ed.), *Michael Oakeshott's Cold War Liberalism* (Palgrave Macmillan, 2015).

As a broad political, intellectual and cultural stream, *human rights liberalism* should not be conflated with liberal constitutionalism. However, the two phenomena are closely inter-related. Liberal constitutionalism as an expertise in constitutional matters provided human rights liberalism with a constitutional imagination that defined, to a great extent, their constitutional agenda. Human rights liberalism, in contrast, supplied liberal constitutionalism with historical legitimacy. The dissident genealogy was probably not an element *sine qua non*. Liberal constitutionalism would appear after 1989, even without the former dissidents' moral and political support. However, the fact remains that former dissidents, representatives of human rights liberalism, gave liberal constitutionalism in East Central Europe moral standing and a mark of authenticity.[29]

The struggle against the repressive authoritarian dictatorship was the defining experience of former dissidents. The rule of law was supposed to be a major means of eliminating the possible 'totalitarian comeback' and taming possible authoritarian intentions of the new political movements and their leaders. Such concerns, widely spread in post-dissident politics and media, were linked to the programmatic idea, generated by dissident strategists from their opposition experiences, about a 'self-limiting revolution'.[30] During Solidarity's upheaval or in the democratization movements on the eve of the 1989 democratic revolutions, conscious self-limitation was supposed to prevent radicalization on both sides of the power conflict and, thus, the potential for violent conflict. The newly built democratic system was likewise meant to incorporate self-limiting mechanisms and a strong system of checks and balances against any claim to a usurpation of power or the temptation to settle scores violently.

Human rights liberalism and its anti-authoritarian and anti-populist motivation were not the only factors behind robust constitutional politics. There was also the widespread belief of the liberal reformers of the early 1990s – post-dissident or not – that speedy economic reforms would facilitate political and cultural democratic change. Many were convinced that learning lessons from the past and safeguarding against its repetition were important. However, it was equally essential to set the right course for a free society, which presupposed, above all, the creation of functioning market structures. Only a few of the liberal reformers were dogmatic neoliberals. Rather, their projects tended to be based on the current neoclassical mainstream of economics, which already contained a mixture of distinct neoliberal elements. This approach was referred to at the time and later in literature as the so-called Washington consensus.[31] Part and parcel of it was the conviction that fundamental economic reforms should not be the subject of democratic politics and political negotiation, at least not at the beginning.

29 Přibáň, *Dissidents of Law*.

30 Jadwiga Staniszkis, *Poland's Self-Limiting Revolution* (Princeton University Press, 1984).

31 Béla Greskovits, *Political Economy of Protest and Patience: East European and Latin American Transformations Compared* (Central European University Press, 1998); Paul Dragos Aligica and Anthony J. Evans, *The Neoliberal Revolution in Eastern Europe: Economic Ideas in the Transition from Communism* (Edward Elgar, 2009).

The latter idea was firmly rooted in both the global neoliberal doctrine as well as the practice of economic reformers in the region. The long-term goal of all different types of neoliberalism in the twentieth century was to separate the nation state's powers and the rules governing economic life. In other words, to foster an 'economic constitution' that could exist outside the nation state and democratic parliamentary sovereignty. Based on their historical observation and analysis, neoliberals have long assumed that democratic participation often obstructs desirable economic change.[32] This concern was the driver of the ordoliberal plan, formulated by Wilhelm Röpke with the help of Carl Schmitt's conceptual frame, to provide a double government comprising a strained balance between the world of politics and nations (*imperium*) and the world of economics (*dominium*). Such an arrangement observed by the guardians of economic constitutions would keep economic governance safe from mass democratic demands for social justice and redistributive equality. Transposed into the globalizing condition, such ordoliberal tenets translated into a design of international economic rules that would constrain sovereign nation states so that they could not endanger the international economic order.[33]

Often criticized predominantly as 'market fundamentalism,' from the perspective of contemporary legal and historical literature, neoliberalism now increasingly appears as a distinct legal or juridical project whose main aim is not simply to liberate markets but to redesign state and other institutions to protect markets. Some authors attempt to define 'neoliberal constitutionalism' both as a theoretical concept and a particular political practice in countries such as Chile, the 'first laboratory of neoliberalism', or the United States, where neoliberal principles permeate fundamental constitutional structures.[34] So far, however, 'neoliberal constitutionalism' remains a theoretical project rather than a widely accepted analytical tool. One reason for this is the fact that a great part of Western constitutional theory tends to be oriented prevalently towards a 'negative' understanding of the field, emphasizing how constitutions constrain power, limit government and prevent majoritarian tyranny.[35] In that respect, the supposed 'neoliberal constitutionalism' would be very much a part of the constitutionalist mainstream – wary of all possible democratic excesses – rather than a separate entity.[36]

32 Thomas Biebricher, *The Political Theory of Neoliberalism* (Stanford University Press, 2018), 79–108.

33 Quinn Slobodian, *The Globalists: The End of Empire and the Birth of Neoliberalism* (Harvard University Press, 2018).

34 Benjamin Alemparte, 'Towards a Theory of Neoliberal Constitutionalism: Addressing Chile's First Constitution-making Laboratory' (2022) *Global Constitutionalism* 11, 83–109; Jedediah Purdy, 'Neoliberal Constitutionalism: Lochnerism for a New Economy' (2014) 77 *Law and Contemporary Problems* 195.

35 Some authors therefore distinguish rather between negative and positive constitutionalism; Nicholas William Barber, *The Principles of Constitutionalism* (Oxford University Press, 2018).

36 Jeremy Waldron, 'Constitutionalism: A Skeptical View', in T. Christiano and T. Christman (eds.), *Contemporary Debates in Political Philosophy* (Harvard University Press, 2009), 267–282; see also Mark Tushnet 'The Globalization of Constitutional Law as a Weakly Neo-liberal Project' (2019) 8 *Global Constitutionalism* 29.

Neoliberal ideas were close to many liberal reformers in Central and Eastern Europe. Not because they were devout followers of Hayek or Buchanan but because these ideas offered the imminent promise of a proper tool for the gigantic task of economic transformation. Moreover, to a large extent, neoliberal ideas also corresponded to their own historical experience. In late socialism, the economic experts, technocrats and reformists were used to bureaucratic-technocratic governance. As advisors of communist rulers, they did not have political power nor did they have to be accountable to any constituency. Their historical experience taught them that the desired change towards a functional economy was not easy to achieve in uneven negotiation with the power centre. At the same time, any such change in the past was prepared in the front rooms of political power, far from direct democratic control.

In Poland, another piece of accumulated historical knowledge directly related to the post-communist economic reform was the experience with the first Solidarity in 1980–1981. With its socialist egalitarian economic program and tendencies towards worker's self-management and economic democracy, it was unanimously read by both reform communists as well as Polish liberals as a negative example of the chaos that an unleashed and unfettered democracy can bring to the economy and to reform plans.[37] So, it was better to leave the re-establishment of the functioning market economy to the experts and technocratic decision-makers without much political debate.[38]

Neoliberalism and its constitutional imagination had certain intellectual and socio-cultural roots in East Central Europe during the last decades of state socialism. Less so among the democratic opposition, even though some neoliberals, such as the Gdańsk group around Donald Tusk, had a dissident past.[39] These roots were more present among various semi-independent circles critical of the communist regime and the anti-communist opposition, such as the Cracow neoliberals and neoconservative circles around Mirosław Dzielski.[40] But the most consequential environment from where leading neoliberal reformers such as Leszek Balcerowicz, Václav Klaus or Lajos Bokros emerged were expert circles and epistemic communities at official academic, administrative and advisory institutions. Since the early 1980s, these milieus and 'grey zone' expert circles, far from consisting of neoliberal zealots, increasingly emphasized the importance of the economic sphere, the need for its thorough reform and its primacy over politics.[41]

37 Szacki, *Liberalism after Communism*, 119–134.

38 Tadeusz Kowalik, www.polskatransformacja.pl (Muza 2009).

39 Piotr Biegasiewicz, 'The Gdańsk Liberals: An Exemplification of Polish Pragmatic Liberalism', *CSIE Working Papers*, No. 6 (2017), 19–34.

40 Dorothee Bohle and Gisela Neunhöffer, 'Why Is There No Third Way? The Role of Neoliberal Ideology, Networks and Think Tanks in Combating Market Socialism and Shaping Transformation in Poland', in Dieter Plehwe, Bernhard Walpen and Gisela Neunhöffer (eds.), *Neoliberal Hegemony: A Global Critique* (Routledge, 2006); Szacki, *Liberalism after Communism*, 119–170.

41 Greskovits, *Political Economy of Protest and Patience*; Sean Hanley, *The New Right in the New Europe: Czech Transformation and Right-Wing Politics 1989–2006* (Routledge, 2008), 40–65.

The final issue to tackle in relation to the constitutional imagination in the transition period is the conscious historical burden of post-communist liberalism.[42] All variants of liberalism at the time were a mixture between the party of memory (the past) and the party of hope (the future). *Human rights liberalism* and *neoliberalism* were both oriented towards achieving the transition – that is, getting rid of the burden of the past to produce a desired liberal democratic future. *Human rights liberalism* defined the burden of the past in cultural terms, stressing the memory of totalitarianism to foster civility. *Neoliberalism* defined it in economic terms, stressing the hubris of the planning state to foster the market society. Both sought to constitutionally enshrine fear of repeating the past as a mechanism of prevention. Both also dealt with the *homo sovieticus* problem, in other words, the supposed immaturity of the citizenry in a free society, for which both designed a sort of liberal pedagogy to deal with that problem.[43]

The politics of liberal constitutionalism after 1989 was the practical realization of liberal post-communist historical sensitivities. Its main aims were to keep people away from the populist temptation, to overhaul the economic foundations of society, and to prevent future misuse of power. As a result, independent and robust juridical institutions, with the constitutional courts at the helm, and the liberal checks and balances, were established. The purpose was not to hinder the development of democracy. Rather, it was supposed to be a democracy protected from itself, at least for some time. Solid constitutional safeguards were intended to help the young democracy develop under the protection of strict rule of law institutions. The intention was to limit the potential majoritarian and collectivist features of democracy in the interests of protecting individual and minority rights as well as the developing market economy. Liberal reforms took the lack of civility as a fundamental premise for their version of constrained democracy that institutionalized mistrust in the immature citizenry.[44] Later, these efforts to cultivate a democratic and liberal

[42] The historical consciousness of liberalism in post-communist times – of all possible kinds – has sometimes been encapsulated by the concept of liberalism of fear suggested by Judith Shklar in an influential essay from the eventful year of 1989. Judith Shklar, 'The Liberalism of Fear', in Nancy L. Rosenblum (ed.), *Liberalism and the Moral Life* (Harvard University Press, 1989); see, e.g., Marcin Król, *Liberalizm strachu czy liberalizm odwagi* (Znak, 1996).

[43] Metaphorically speaking, human rights liberalism based its pedagogy on civic education about the totalitarian past (*Vergangenheitsbewältigung*), neoliberalism on the pedagogy of the market whose symbol was the coupon privatization envisioning popular shareholder capitalism. Piotr Wciślik, 'Homo Sovieticus and the Neoliberal Legacy of Polish Dissent' (2024) 38 *East European Politics and Societies* 931–958; Marta Bucholc, 'Law and liberal pedagogy in a post-socialist society: The case of Poland' (2020) 18 *Journal of Modern European History* 324; Václav Rameš, *Trh bez přívlastků, nebo ekonomickou demokracii? Spory o podobu vlastnické transformace v porevolučním Československu* (ÚSD AV ČR 2021).

[44] In many ways, this is reminiscent of the fears of democrats of various stripes following the fall of fascism in Europe after WWII, see, e.g., Martin Conway, *Western Europe's Democratic Age: 1945–1968* (Princeton University Press, 2020); Jan-Werner Müller, *Contesting Democracy: Political Ideas in Twentieth-Century Europe* (Yale University Press, 2011), 125–170.

culture in a sort of greenhouse were criticized by both the left and right as undisguised liberal efforts to depoliticize democracy and gut the power of the political sovereign, the people.

14.3 THE RULE OF LAW IN THE POST-COMMUNIST CONSTITUTIONAL IMAGINATION

In this final section, we will look at how the substantive political profiling within and outside the liberal camp imprinted itself on the constitutional imagination of emerging democracies in ECE or, more specifically, on the notion of what the rule of law is and what it should do.[45] I can only attempt a preliminary typology here, as a detailed analysis requires more extensive research. I use the context of the Czech political and constitutional legal environment of the early 1990s as the main reservoir of examples. However, in an attempt to capture more general features of developments across the ECE region, I also refer to comparable concepts and key actors in other neighbouring countries as suitable examples.

Rule of law is a narrower concept than constitutionalism. Both deal with how the powers of government and authorities are to be limited. However, while constitutionalism works with a range of devices and procedures and assumes a more comprehensive political theory, the rule of law, understood in a narrower sense, 'is based on values which are inherent in the very notion of law itself'.[46] In theory, therefore, it is easier to find agreement on the requirement of the rule of law than on the broader concept of constitutionalism. And yet, rule of law is an essentially contested concept, which means that the interpretative struggle concerns the core, not just the borderlines of the idea. 'There are many different definitions of the rule of law, and none of them can claim to be canonical'.[47] Although they agreed on the priority of rule of law for the post-1989 transition policy, variants of the local liberal understanding of rule of law, advocated and elaborated by representatives of *human rights liberalism* and *neoliberalism*, had quite different motives and arguments. Theoretically, we could think of this as the difference between Dworkinian and Hayekian conceptions of the rule of law.

[45] From a constitutionalist perspective, the notion of the rule of law in the 'extraordinary' period of transition to democracy and a market economy was seen as in many ways paradoxical, R. Teitel, *Transitional Justice* (Oxford University Press, 2000); Adam Czarnota, Martin Krygier and Wojciech Sadurski (eds.), *Rethinking the Rule of Law after Communism* (Central European University Press, 2005).

[46] Chin Liew Ten, 'Constitutionalism and the Rule of Law', in Robert E. Goodin, Phillip Pettit and Thomas Pogge (eds.), *A Companion to Contemporary Political Philosophy* (Blackwell, 2017), 494.

[47] Jeremy Waldron, 'The Rule of Law as an Essentially Contested Concept', in Martin Loughlin and Jens Meierheinrich (eds.), *The Cambridge Companion to the Rule of Law* (Cambridge University Press, 2021), 121; Cf. Geranne Lautenbach, 'The Rule of Law Concept', in *The Concept of the Rule of Law and the European Court of Human Rights* (Oxford University Press, 2013), 18–69.

What was for a long time predominantly the domain of domestic legal politics, the rule of law internationalized as it became, in the second half of the twentieth century, an important tool in international development policy. In the first post–WWII decades, 'law and development' politics was based on the Keynesian paradigm of strong government and industrialization models. It was tested in the postcolonial world above all in Africa and Latin America. From the 1980s, however, a significant change occurred. The post–Cold War 'rule of law promotion' embraced by the World Bank, the International Monetary Fund (IMF) and other international financial institutions (IFIs), but also regional development banks emphasized 'opening' the developing states – thus also post-communist ones – towards export-led growth, foreign investment and global competition. This shift in the rule of law understanding meant placing serious constraints on the nation state's economic policies while enhancing legal structures (the rule of law institutions) guaranteeing the protection of foreign investment and international trade.[48]

International development policy played a crucial role in the post-communist transformation. It greatly enhanced the prestige of rule of law conceptions that leaned towards the neoliberal pole by making them compatible with the legal-economic discourse that prevailed in the IFIs and, increasingly, in the European Communities.[49] However, neoliberals in East Central Europe did not develop a self-standing constitutionalist doctrine after 1989. The fact that they relied on the existing liberal constitutionalist framework is quite consistent with what we know about the spread of neoliberal economic ideas in post-communist Europe. The 'neoliberal revolution' after 1989 did not prove to be an outburst of extremist neoliberal ideas promoted by 'market fundamentalists' but was instead a neoclassical synthesis leaning on the current mainstream of Western economic theory.[50] We can say the same about neoliberal constitutionalism. There was hardly an outburst of distinct neoliberal economic constitutionalism anywhere in the region. The Western liberal constitutionalist mainstream and its resourceful adaptation and elaboration were all that mattered in the constitutional debates and policies. Thus, it is within this mainstream and especially in its subset leaning more toward 'negative constitutionalism' that we have to look for the neoliberal premises taking root.

[48] Shane Chalmers and Sundhya Pahuja, '(Economic) Development and the Rule of Law', in Martin Loughlin and Jens Meierheinrich (eds.), *The Cambridge Companion to the Rule of Law* (Cambridge University Press, 2021), 377–405; Martin Loughlin, 'The Apotheosis of the Rule of Law' (2018) 89 *The Political Quarterly* 659; Bojan Bugaric, 'Law and Development in Central and Eastern Europe: Neoliberal Developmental State and Its Problems', 17 September 2012, https://ssrn.com/abstract=2163073.

[49] Jiří Přibáň, 'From "Which Rule of Law?" to "The Rule of Which Law?": Post-Communist Experiences of European Legal Integration' (2009) 1 *Hague Journal on the Rule of Law* 337.

[50] Aligica and Evans, *The Neoliberal Revolution in Eastern Europe*; Joahnna Bockman, *Markets in the Name of Socialism: The Left-Wing Origins of Neoliberalism* (Stanford University Press, 2011).

To date, we have no studies on what legal concepts played a primary role in the thought and practice of various neoliberal milieus before and especially after 1989 in the region. Generally, however, it seems safe to say that the greatest influence was the thinking of Friedrich A. Hayek, who devoted most of his later work to the interpretation of the role of law in securing liberty and prosperity, as well as the difference between law and legislation.[51] Hayek's influential and wide-ranging work has had a profound impact on political and social thought in the region since the collapse of the communist dictatorship, especially during the democratic transition. Here, we will limit ourselves to two aspects of his rule of law concept, namely its connection to political liberty and its moral dimension. In his 1943 *Road to Serfdom*, Hayek fleshed out the difference between a 'free country' where the government was bound by the rule of law and a 'country under arbitrary government'. In other words, politically determined rules needed to be relatively fixed and publicly known to create a stable and accountable framework in which individual planning and complex but non-coerced social coordination could flourish. In his later work, such as *The Constitution of Liberty*, Hayek elaborated on the social institutions crucial for attaining the goal of political liberty. The rule of law – where laws are prospective, equally enforced, abstractly stated, and stable – was a crucial mechanism for supporting institutions such as free markets and democratic polity, with a strong constitution protecting the private sphere and well-defined and enforced property rights, all of which permit individuals to pursue their vales and allow them to make the best use of their localized knowledge.

Although sometimes dismissed as a 'market fundamentalist' by his opponents, Hayek had a distinct moral dimension in his teachings. In his late work, he distinguished between 'spontaneous orders' and 'constructed orders' such as socialism. Many traditional social institutions such as language, money, the common law, the moral code, or trade were, historically, instances of spontaneous orders. Because they were not the product of human design but of myriads of individual actions and dispersed knowledge, they were able to adapt more readily in environments characterized by rapid change and widespread uncertainty. Constructed orders, in contrast, lacked such adaptability as state socialist planning perfectly exemplified.[52]

Taking after the great Austrian thinker, neoliberals in ECE understood the rule of law primarily as a precondition for the 'constitution of liberty' and the functioning market mechanism enabling socioeconomic prospects and, thus, societal peace and

[51] Friedrich August Hayek, *The Political Ideal of the Rule of Law* (National Bank of Egypt Printing Press, 1955), and Friedrich August Hayek, *The Constitution of Liberty* (University of Chicago Press, 1960).

[52] Christopher S. Martin and Nikolai G. Wenzel, 'Generality and Knowledge: Hayek's Constitutional Theory of the Liberal State' (2020) 31 *Constitutional Political Economy* 145; Rachel S. Turner, 'Neo-Liberal Constitutionalism: Ideology, Government and the Rule of Law' (2008) 1 *Journal of Politics and Law* 47; A. I. Ogus, 'Law and Spontaneous Order: Hayek's Contribution to Legal Theory' (1989) 16 *Journal of Law and Society* 393.

progress. But they put even more emphasis on the free market as potentially one of the most readily available spontaneous orders. Most of these were destroyed by the extreme 'constructivism' of communist revolutions in the region, but the free market promised to be the first to be re-established again. The Hayekian conception of the rule of law was not devoid of a moral dimension. However, its significance lay primarily in its instrumental function, serving chiefly to ensure the proper functioning of the key mechanism of social coordination—namely, the market. Furthermore, law was imagined and constructed as a form of pedagogy for constituting citizenry and as an institutional system for regulating and enforcing the new economic norms. In sum, the function of law in the understanding of post-communist neoliberals was to work primarily towards economic ends and the creation of *homo economicus*.

Hayek, in general, and his specific understanding of the rule of law was much more influential among non-lawyers, especially economists and politicians, who were often the central figures in the post-1989 market economic transformation. Hayek, the so-called Austrian School, and neoliberalism generally provided reformers with the most comprehensive model of the working capitalist system (modelled on Anglo-American capitalism), which – despite Hayek's prohibition of social constructivism – formulated capitalism as an ideological project and provided a graspable idea of the path from point A, the socialist planned economy, to point B, market capitalism.[53] Also, Hayek was one of the few liberal thinkers of the twentieth century who fundamentally addressed the issue of freedom and, of these, Hayek was the most systematic. Moreover, his theory of freedom was developed to counterbalance the temptations of totalitarianism from the right and the left, which was eminently suited to the needs of the fundamental transformation from a communist welfare dictatorship to a liberal democracy based on a market economy.[54]

We most often encounter Hayek, as a philosopher of freedom and theorist of a specific kind of liberal constitutionalism, in the contemporary journalism of the future fathers of economic reform, such as Leszek Balcerowicz in Poland and, even more so, the so-called Gdansk liberals such as Jan Szomburg, Jan Lewandowski and Donald Tusk.[55] In the Czech context, the most important expert and promoter of Hayek was the economist Tomáš Ježek, the Minister of Privatization in 1990 and advisor to Václav Klaus. In the 1980s, Ježek translated some of Hayek's most important works, such as *The Road to Serfdom* or *Law, Legislation and Liberty*, for the samizdat and promoted Hayek as the most important beacon of liberal order.[56]

[53] Szacki, *Liberalism after Communism*, 119–170.

[54] Joahanna Falk, *Freiheit als politisches Ziel: Grundmodelle liberalen Denkens bei Kant, Hayek und Böckenförde* (Campus, 2012), 82–146.

[55] Janusz Lewandowski, *Neoliberałowie wobec współczesności* (Gdynia, 1991); Ireneusz Krzemiński, 'Liberalny wybór', in Ireneusz Krzemiński (ed.), *Liberalizm polski*, I. (Sedno, 2015).

[56] Tomáš Ježek (ed.), *Zásady liberálního řádu* (Academia, 2001); also his memoirs Tomáš Ježek, *Zrození ze zkumavky: svědectví o české privatizaci 1990–1997* (Prostor 2007); J. Schwarz, 'Nebál se jít proti proudu' (2017) *Katolický týdeník* 49, 8.

In the 1990s, Klaus himself – although primarily coming to neoliberalism from monetarist positions and not a devoted Hayekian like Ježek – discovered Hayek for himself, often quoted him, and even more often used his political philosophy to defend his vision of economic transformation in Czechoslovakia, later Czechia.[57]

Conversely, Hayek was not a basic reference figure for most constitutional lawyers and legal philosophers. He was hardly a part of the standard constitutional legal curriculum during the second half of the twentieth century because, among other reasons, his thinking hardly fit into the post-war Western mainstream liberal constitutionalism based on a centralized constitutional review of legality and the growing importance of human rights. Yet, among the prominent figures of constitutional law in ECE, we find those on the 'negative side' of the liberal constitutional spectrum who claimed Hayek in one way or another in their writings and considered him indispensable for understanding the broader societal implications of the liberal constitutional project.[58]

In the Czech context, a good example is Vojtěch Cepl, a civil lawyer, university teacher and one of the prominent personalities of the first generation of the Czech Constitutional Court, active between 1993 and 2003 and figuring sometime under the nickname 'Havel's CC'. According to the testimony of his colleagues and pupils, he was mainly a rhetorician, not a writer, that is, he left behind only a meagre written legacy. Through his informal influence and quite a visible media presence, however, he was considered one of the most influential liberal-conservative lawyers of the early transition period.[59] A member of the neoliberal conservative ODA party, a junior partner to Klaus' transformation governments, he started his political engagement as a Vice-Chairman of the Legislative Group of the Ministry of Finance under Václav Klaus. Somewhat later, he also became a member of the drafting committee for the Czech Constitution adopted in December 1992 that has remained in force until today. Cepl, who frequently confessed his US inspirations,

57 The collection of Klaus' early 1990s essays most comprehensively shows the political philosophy and social theory behind his politics: Václav Klaus, *Mezi minulostí a budoucností: filozofické a humanologické úvahy* (Nadace Universitas Masarykiana, 1996); for his monetarism before 1989 see Adam Geršl, *Ekonomické myšlení Václava Klause do roku 1990* (Karolinum, 2006).

58 This applies, for example, to one of the most important liberal constitutional scholars in the region, András Sajó, who is certainly no dogmatic Hayekian but at the same time has always referred to Hayek, among others, in the basic idea that runs through Hayek's late work, namely that the rule of law is constitutive of, not merely instrumental to, political freedom. See, e.g., András Sajó, *Limiting Government: An Introduction to Constitutionalism* (Central European University Press, 1999) and its reworked version reacting to the illiberal challenges to liberal rule of law in the 2010s symptomatically referring directly to Hayek in its title: Renáta Uitz and András Sajó, *The Constitution of Freedom: An Introduction to Legal Constitutionalism* (Oxford University Press, 2017).

59 Tomáš Němeček and Vojtěch Cepl, *Život právníka ve 20. století* (Leges, 2010).

was one the the most influential members of the drafting committee.[60] In his views on the constitution and constitutional law, Cepl was hardly a radical neoliberal. He was able to defend the principles of constitutional parliamentary democracy as well as the work of the Constitutional Court against the radical economic reformers with Klaus on the top. Yet, in his public statements on the principles of the rule of law as the basis of a liberal free order and in his conception of the *Rechtsstaat* in its historical and moral dimensions, the distinctive influence of Hayek's thought is unmistakable.[61]

Quite a different legal and constitutional imagination was coming from post-communist *human rights liberalism.* Having a strong dissident imprint, the democratic *Rechtsstaat* or rule of law was seen by human rights liberals in a prevalently Kantian way, that is, as a morally based institutional framework for 'eternal peace', falling neatly within the tradition of the classical rule-of-law liberalism marked by the lineage of Locke, Kant and Tocqueville.[62] In this sense, *human rights liberalism* was fundamentally linked to the liberal-constitutional mainstream prevailing in Western democracies at that time, where the rule of law stood for an autonomous value corresponding to the idea of freedom on an individual level. The rule of law in this view is understood from a substantive position leaning on the classical liberal tradition, European humanism after the Renaissance and humanist anthropology, while also being enhanced by the rise of human rights ideas in the twentieth century.[63]

To subsume most post-communist *neoliberals* and their constitutional imagination under Hayek's conception of the rule of law seems historically justifiable. It is less justifiable to present Ronald Dworkin as the common denominator of post-communist *human rights liberals* and their constitutional imagination. If only because Hayek was read and admired by neoliberals, whereas Dworkin was hardly known in the region and was read by very few philosophers and legal theorists in the 1980s and 1990s. Moreover, Dworkin's understanding of the rule of law was derived primarily from the historical experience of the United States and common law countries (which is actually also the case for Hayek, despite his origins), thus making it more difficult to apply it to legal and political systems based on continental legal tradition. And yet, Dworkin's rights-based conception of the rule of law seems to be a perfectly fitting description of the type of thinking that dominated among many human rights liberals, with rights at the centre of their constitutional imagination and representing the so-called substantive or material conception of the rule of law.

60 Jan Brož and Jan Chmel, 'Pohled za oponu: studie o vzniku Ústavy České republiky a o kontextu její interpretace' (2016) *Život právníka* 78–79.

61 Eg Vojtěch Cepl, 'Bottlenecks in the Transformation of Eastern Europe' (2000) 4 *Washington University Journal of Law & Policy* 23, https://journals.library.wustl.edu/lawpolicy/article/id/1691/ and selected articles and interviews published as www.cepl.eu. For a direct Hayekian reference, see Vojtěch Cepl, 'The Road Out of Serfdom' (1992) 12 *Vera Lex* 4.

62 Falk, *Freiheit als politisches Ziel.*

63 Přibáň, 'From "Which Rule of Law?"', 338–346.

The concept of the rule of law *per se* was hardly a major preoccupation for Dworkin at any time of his prolific career. As observed by David Dyzenhaus, the twentieth-century philosophy of law paid relatively little attention to the rule of law because the major issue was 'what the law is that rules, after which there is little left to say about the rule of law'.[64] Not surprisingly liberal authors provided mostly accounts linking the rule of law concept with traditional liberal values aimed at protecting basic individual freedoms. The major difference, then, was what hierarchy of these values they imagined and how these values were to be written into the construction of the rule of law and the constitutional order.

Dworkin's approach to the rule of law stands for a paradigmatic example of the 'substantive view'. He developed his theory in a decades-long polemic with the liberal mainstream in legal philosophy, strife often described as a positional struggle between legal positivism and anti-positivism. Representing the latter, Dworkin distinguished between what he called the 'rulebook' conception of the rule of law, advocated by positivists such as H. A. L. Hart or Joseph Raz and the 'rights' conception that he elaborated on. In the positivist view, the power of the state should never be exercised against individual citizens unless it is 'in accordance with rules explicitly set out in a public rule book available to all'.[65]

So, these rules pre-determine the behaviour of citizens and government officials. But they could be changed by the lawmakers and replaced by other rules. Such an idea of the rule of law is, therefore, rather narrow and non-substantive, yet not value-free. For liberal thinkers leaning towards positivism, such as Joseph Raz, the rule of law and constitutionalism have primarily negative values. They are designed to minimize harm to the freedom and dignity of individual citizens against whatever noble causes of government and other powers. Raz was far from merely negative and proceduralist; in his view, the rule of law is linked to various fundamental liberal values such as individual autonomy and respect for human dignity.

But Dworkin's substantive approach to the rule of law goes further, building on different ideas of the nature of law. If, as Dworkin argues in his oeuvre, there is a substantial connection between law and morality, the rule of law must be, to some extent, the rule of good law. The positivist rule of law, determining primarily rules of conduct, has nothing to do with substantive justice exercised by judges in courts. In contrast, Dworkin's 'rights conception' sees the rule of law and substantive justice as intrinsically connected. For him, the rule of law cannot be limited to certain formal criteria of a 'proper legal system', for individuals also have 'moral and political rights' that need to be regularly enforced upon demand of individual citizens through courts.[66]

64 David Dyzenhaus, 'The Rule of Law as the Rule of Liberal Principle', in Arthur Ripstein (ed.), *Ronald Dworkin* (Cambridge University Press, 2007), 57.

65 Ronald Dworkin, A *Matter of Principle* (Harvard University Press, 1985), 11.

66 Roberto Gargarella, 'Constitutionalism and the Rule of Law', in Jens Meierhenrich and Martin Loughlin (eds.), *Cambridge Companion to the Rule of Law* (Cambridge University Press, 2021), 426.

It is truer of Dworkin than 'of any other that his account of the rule of law is an account of the particular theory of liberal justice that he argues is embedded within the law'.[67]

Not all of the post-communist liberals that we categorized in our ideal-typical model under *human rights liberalism* were Dworkinians. In fact, only a very few of them were so consciously. The most obvious example, by any means, is János Kis, liberal philosopher and former leader of the Hungarian democratic opposition in the 1980s, who at best represents a direct connecting line between the dissident human rights activism prior to and the liberal order and constitutional democracy after 1989. Although remaining active as a public intellectual, Kis soon chose an academic career instead of politics. He became a creator, among others, of an original theory of constitutional democracy characterized by a striving for balance and mutual conditioning of principles of liberal equality and constitutional democracy, an approach highly valued by Dworkin himself.[68]

Although few of the active supporters of liberal constitutionalism in the post-communist ECE were as directly influenced by Dworkin and his theory of rights as Kis, many of them participated in the victorious march of a substantive conception of the rule of law, with an active constitutional court at its head, whose role was not only to protect constitutionalism but also to contribute substantially to the formation of a new, democratic and rights-based legal and political culture. Vladimír Klokočka, a legal scholar, political scientist, signatory of Charter 77 and another constitutional judge of the first constitutional court (CC), is a good example in the Czech context. A prominent representative of the value-based conception of the constitution and a defender of supra-positive law, he was widely seen as a promoter of the substantial conception of the rule of law in the early liberal democratic Czech public and legal-professional discourse, as well as in the jurisprudence of the first Czech CC.[69]

Already at the time of the democratizing Prague Spring between 1967 and 1969, Klokočka, as a reform communist and an expert on electoral systems in Western European democracies, prepared a proposal for a new electoral law for the Czech National Council (i.e., the Czech Parliament in the new socialist federation), which was not implemented due to the Warsaw Pact invasion and authoritarian consolidation. After signing Charter 77 and enduring subsequent police harassment, he emigrated from Czechoslovakia to West Germany. Although Klokočka did not belong to the Czech democratic opposition or active democratic exile, he found himself, after 1989, in the circle of President Havel. At the same time, he was one of

67 Dyzenhaus, 'The Rule of Law as the Rule of Liberal Principle', 57.

68 See Kis' most significant work in this respect: János Kis, *Constitutional Democracy* (Central European University Press, 2003); Dworkin's introduction in Ronald Dworkin (ed.), *From Liberal Values to Democratic Transition* (Central European University Press, 2004), 11–15.

69 Eliška Wagnerová, 'Koncept právního státu', in Ivo Pospíšil and Eliška Wagnerová (eds.), *Vladimír Klokočka liber amicorum: in memoriam emeritního soudce Ústavního soudu* (Linde, 2009), 235–250.

the prominent publicly-engaged liberal legal experts.[70] He returned permanently to Czechia as a newly elected judge of the Czech CC in 1993, where he was among the most outspoken and trustworthy – due to his exile experience – advocates of using the case law of the German Federal Constitutional Court as inspiration for post-communist constitutional courts.[71] Klokočka was, among other things, the author of the first-ever plenary ruling of the Czech CC that assessed the constitutionality of the law on the illegality of the communist regime and resistance to it. In this ruling, he subscribed to the value-based conception of the Constitution, and it is generally considered to be a ground-breaking decision in its substantive argumentative structure.[72]

But the rights-based rule of law conception, along with the idea of substantive justice and judicial democratic activism, aptly describes not only liberal but also many conservative constitutionalists of that period. Sometimes, as in the case of László Sólyom, they even became the foreground figures symbolizing the liberal constitutionalist hegemony of the period. Sólyom was the most dominant jurist in post-1989 liberal democratic Hungary and one of the most visible personalities in the constitutional realm in the whole region. He was the first Hungarian Constitutional Court's Chief Justice from 1990 to 1998 and the main symbol of its extraordinary powers in Hungarian politics, epitomized by the doctrine of the 'invisible constitution'.[73]

In Czechia, there was no one in the liberal-conservative camp of similar stature and influence as Sólyom. Still, there are similar figures in constitutional law and practice with regard to their Christian Democratic ideological and Catholic religious background, such as Vladimír Čermák. Yet another in the bright line of 'Havel's Constitutional Court' judges, a lawyer and philosopher, liberal-conservative thinker and a devout Catholic, he too was an outspoken advocate of the substantive rule of law conception in the post-communist constitutional imagination. His

[70] From among his most influential legal-political writings of that period, see, e.g., Vladimír Klokočka, *Politické reprezentace a volby v demokratických systémech* (Aleco, 1991), Vladimír Klokočka, *Ústavní systémy evropských států* (Linde, 1996).

[71] The FRG served as a successful example of coping with the totalitarian past with the substantial help of constitutional law and the active role of the CC, an inspiration widely spread throughout the ECE, not only in Czechia. In the first Czech CC, besides Klokočka, the leading representative of this tendency was Pavel Holländer, an admirer of Gustav Radbruch. See, e.g., Tomáš Němeček and Pavel Holländer, 'Vím, že ty běsy tady pořád jsou', https://jinepravo.blogspot.com/2008/07/vm-e-ty-bsy-tady-pod-jsou.html, download 23 March 2024; Pavel Holländer, *Verfassungsrechtliche Argumentation - zwischen dem Optimismus und der Skepsis* (Duncker & Humblot 2007).

[72] Přibáň, 'From "Which Rule of Law?"', 344–346.

[73] Gábor Attila Tóth, 'Chief Justice Sólyom and the Paradox of "Revolution under the Rule of Law"', in Rehan Abeyratne and Iddo Porat (eds.), *Towering Judges: A Comparative Study of Constitutional Judges* (Cambridge University Press, 2021); Kim Lane Scheppele, 'Guardians of the Constitution: Constitutional Court Presidents and the Struggle for the Rule of Law in Post-Soviet Europe' (2006) 154 *University of Pennsylvania Law Review* 1757.

personal history is quite different from most of his fellow constitutional judges since he was not a member of the legal or political establishment until he joined the institution. With a connection to the so-called underground Catholic Church, he was affiliated with the vibrant cultural milieu in Brno towards the late 1980s. His main scholarly work, which places him in the field of philosophy and general sociology rather than law, is his five-volume oeuvre 'The Question of Democracy', published successively between 1992 and 1999 and comprising more than 1,200 printed pages. The work was written in seclusion between 1975 and 1988, while Čermák worked as a corporate lawyer after being dismissed from the judiciary at his own request in 1975. It is a comprehensive, systematic reflection on the question of democracy as both a political principle and a way of life, in which the author consciously draws on Masaryk. It is quite the paradox that a trained lawyer and judge devoted only marginal space of his extensive and systematic work on democracy and its preconditions to the topic of the rule of law and the lawful state – a mere passage about the role of the judiciary in modern political regimes.[74]

Čermák, however, together with Klokočka, was one of the most prominent personalities of the first CC, contributing to its proverbial activist democratic ethos, which was reflected in the Court's jurisprudence. As shown by some of the CC's opinions and as he himself later reflected in some interviews, he was trying to bring the values of a substantive democratic rule of law to the interpretation of law both at the constitutional and general judiciary levels. Along with Klokočka and some others, he stood for a distinctly supra-positivist conception of law and justice since, as he repeatedly emphasized on various occasions, 'law is more than law'. In this view, law must be framed in the general social context and democratic principles in order to be understood and accepted by citizens as a legitimate exercise of justice.[75]

However, we also find many post-communist liberals who did not share these presumptions about the rule of law presupposing the rule of the good law. Most legal practitioners and jurisprudence scholars came not from the dissent or democratic exile but rather from the official institutions supported by the communist state and from the so-called grey zone, that is, the broad layer of experts that was critical of the late communist state but was not willing to go into direct conflict with it, as the dissidents did. Many of these people on the liberal side of the political spectrum shared a constitutional imagination closer to the rule-book conception of positivists such as Hart or Raz (i.e., the opponents of Dworkin in the liberal camp). They recognized the increasing role of human rights in domestic and international politics. However, in their conception, law and the rule of law were linked to human rights only ideologically or symbolically, not substantively.

74 Vladimír Čermák, *Otázka demokracie* (CDK, 2017), 443–448.

75 Petr Fiala and František Mikš, *Rozhovory s Vladimírem Čermákem. O filosofii, politice a právu* (CDK, 2000), 108. Cf. Jiří Baroš (ed.), *Vladimír Čermák. Člověk – filozof – soudce* (Masarykova univerzita, 2009).

There is a lively debate today in legal philosophy about the nature and variety of legal positivism in domestic and international systems of law. The Central European tradition plays a significant role in these discussions, with the influence of Hans Kelsen looming large.[76] Much less is known, however, about the multi-layered life of the legal positivist tradition in Central Europe itself, esp. the non-German speaking part. One of the areas where the issue has been debated is the question of the lingering influence of socialist law in the constitutional legal imagination after 1989. This includes discussions about institutional legacies, the fundamental differences between socialist and Western liberal constitutionalism, socialist values embodied in one way or another in post-socialist constitutional orders and also positivist or formalist practices and behavioural models among legal practitioners.[77]

Here, we are interested solely in one aspect, namely how late socialist lawyers, judges and jurisprudence scholars negotiated their position during the triumph of liberal constitutionalism in post-communist ECE and how they related to the liberal rule of law concept. As much of the literature claims, after abandoning the original Marxist revolutionary dreams about abolishing the state and law in a classless society, the communist state engendered positivism in legal thought and practice. This development found fertile ground in ECE, where strong traditions of legal positivism had survived since the interwar period. In the Czech context specifically, the so-called Brno normative school of František Weyr, contemporary and friend of Hans Kelsen, was considered the most significant Czech pre-communist legal tradition. This tradition found its communist metamorphosis in the thinking and practice of legal experts and practitioners of the late socialist period. As argued, for instance, by Zdeněk Kühn, legal positivism in a communist garb served as a counter-reaction to politicized Stalinist legal practice and its turn, in practice, to textual positivism or legal formalism represented a standard in the legal professions, especially the judiciary, since the 1960s.[78]

Legal positivism was a suitable thinking tool and attitude of legal theorists and practitioners in the consolidation period of the communist dictatorship. After the ethos of social and political revolution had disappeared from the public sphere or was limited to ideological proclamations and the law was becoming an increasingly important means of governance, the positivist approach enabled them to achieve an

[76] Somewhat misleadingly is the Central European tradition often subsumed in the English-speaking field of research under the title of 'German law', Torben Spaak and Patricia Mindus (eds.), *The Cambridge Companion to Legal Positivism* (Cambridge University Press, 2021); Luca Siliquini-Cinelli (ed.), *Legal Positivism in a Global and Transnational Age* (Springer, 2019).

[77] See, e.g., Zdeněk Kühn, *The Judiciary in Central and Eastern Europe* (Brill, 2011); Jan Komárek, 'The Struggle for Legal Reform after Communism' (2014) *LSE Law, Society and Economy Working Papers*, https://eprints.lse.ac.uk/60568/1/WPS2014-10_Komarek.pdf; Sergei Belov, William Partlett and Alexandra Troitskaya, 'Socialist Constitutional Legacies' (2021) 9 *Russian Law Journal* 8.

[78] Kühn, *The Judiciary in Central and Eastern Europe*, 65–161.

acceptable degree of apoliticality (insofar as this is possible in law) and to devote themselves to their profession in good conscience. Positivists usually hold that law is the command of a sovereign, that law is the product of explicit or tacit legislation or, in other words, that all law is positive law. It is, therefore, a matter for the political sovereign and the legislator what law and on what principles will be enacted. But it will always be law. This position also opens up a considerable range of possibilities for political worldviews. Legal positivism writ large can be associated with a variety of political ideologies and attitudes. A legal positivist can be a Marxist or communist but also liberal, social democrat or national conservative. In other words, from this point of view, political allegiance and legal expertise are theoretically easily separable.

Late communist legal positivist lawyers were well prepared, both in theory and practice, for the relatively easy adoption of liberal constitutionalism after 1989. This applies not only to judges, lawyers and prosecutors but even to jurisprudence scholars who, more than others, were compelled to explicitly express their loyalty and ideological commitment to the cause of communism. Prominent socialist constitutional lawyers and legal theorists such as Josef Blahož, Jiří Grospič and the somewhat younger Aleš Gerloch fairly effortlessly shifted to a position in favour of the democratic rule of law after 1989. In the period before 1989, they had no qualms about respecting the system of communist dictatorship and the constitutionally undefined but comprehensive political sovereignty of the communist party.[79] After the democratic revolution, they accepted the fact that the one-party dictatorship had been replaced by a politically pluralist liberal-democratic state, whose basic construction and fundamental values were substantially different. However, this difference did not necessarily apply to the principles of the functioning of law in society. As legal positivists, they cultivated an approach to understanding the operation of law in society, which functions similarly in highly modern societies, regardless of the political principles on which they are based.[80]

Referring to the Czech example, we can see that communist legal thinkers and practitioners could have developed in different directions over time, depending on the overall political changes and their individual situation. Those who were associated with the reform process of the Prague Spring in the 1960s and later became part of the human rights opposition in dissent or exile, including the aforementioned V. Klokočka (but also Z. Jičínský, F. Šamalík, P. Pithart, P. Rychetský, and many others), often

[79] See, e.g., the representative writings of the prominent regime human rights lawyer Josef Blahož (ed.), *Kritika buržoazních a revizionistických koncepcí demokracie* (Academia, 1983); Josef Blahož (ed.), *Občan a jeho práva a povinnosti v současném světě* (Academia, 1987).

[80] E.g., Josef Blahož, 'Human Rights, Their Guarantees and the Constitutional Judiciary in the CSFR' (1992) 43 *Austrian Journal of Public and International Law* 31; Josef Blahož, *Soudní kontrola ústavnosti, Srovnávací pohled* (Aspi Publ, 2001); Josef Blahož, *Sjednocující se Evropa a lidská a občanská práva* (Aspi Publ, 2005); Aleš Gerloch, 'Právní stát v minulosti a v současnosti', in Jiří Kunc and Zdeněk Pinc (eds.), *Demokracie a ústavnost* (Karolinum, 1996), 40–53; Aleš Gerloch (ed.), *Základy teorie práva a právního státu* (Policejní akademie ČR, 1997).

figured, after 1989, as leading representatives of pro-Western liberal constitutionalism of the Dworkinian type. The rule of law became the major pillar of the new democratic regime, and it was supposed to be the rule of good or, at least, not evil law. Often, those who were reformists in the 1960s but who linked their fate and careers with the Husák consolidation regime in the two following decades, such as the aforementioned Jozef Blahož or Aleš Gerloch, did not become the main spokespersons of liberal constitutionalism but adopted it unreservedly nevertheless. Their approach, however, was siding much more closely with the positivist rule-book conception of the rule of law, where the nature of law was not systematically addressed.

We should keep in mind that what is presented here is only a preliminary typology using two opposite poles. Most individual representatives of liberal constitutionalism would probably find themselves somewhere between the two poles.[81] A case in point is the youngest generation, who grew up professionally in the era of late state socialism but often received a part of their postgraduate or postdoctoral education at Western universities in the late 1980s and early 1990s. More or less radically oriented reform-minded lawyers in the 1980s, they were strongly influenced by Marxist and post-Marxist critical sociology of law. It is from this generation that many of the greatest figures of liberal constitutionalist theory in post-communist ECE were recruited, such as András Sajó in Hungary, Wojciech Sadurski in Poland and Pavel Holländer in Czechia. As a rule, their attitude to liberal constitutionalism, while generally supportive, is highly critical if not sceptical: liberal or legal constitutionalism is the best of what is available, but it does not mean it will work in every society.

Finally, to complete the typology, there were some on the margins of the 'liberal constitutionalist consensus' who did not accept the mainstream liberal constitutionalist doctrine and remained in mild opposition. A good Czech example is Viktor Knapp (1913–1996),[82] one of the greatest but also most controversial Czech jurists of modern times and an outstanding Marxist civil law scholar serving the Czechoslovak communist regime in all its phases.[83] After 1989, Knapp remained a leading figure in legal studies, mildly critical of the post-communist developments. He distanced

[81] A good example in the Czech context is the discussion from the end of the 2000s on the issue of law and the good in a constitutional democracy; Jiří Přibáň and Pavel Holländer (eds.), *Právo a dobro v ústavní demokracii: Polemické a kritické úvahy* (Slon, 2011).

[82] Among the Marxist legal experts in ECE countries, we can find more figures like Knapp, who, after 1989, integrated into the new system but kept their distance. One example is Béla Pokol in Hungary, who, while profiling himself as a theorist of the liberal democratic constitutional system, was among the first critics of the alleged juristocracy in post-communist Hungary and later found a prominent role in the illiberal constitutional project of Orbán's Hungary, among others as a Constitutional Court justice.

[83] Zdena Žáčková, *Viktor Knapp v Československé akademii věd. Kariéra českého právního vědce* (Praha, 2015); see also my study on the Czechoslovak communist legal expertise related to governance practices where Knapp plays a prominent role, Michal Kopeček, 'Vládnout právem. Česká právní věda od ‚represivní legality' kprávnímu státu, 1969–1994', in Michal Kopeček (ed.), *Architekti dlouhé změny: expertní kořeny postsocialismu v Československu* (Argo-ÚSD AV ČR, 2019), 41–101.

himself from the new political paradigm of liberal constitutionalism in various principal ways. Even in the 1990s, for instance, in accordance with socialist constitutionalism, he maintained his lifelong view of state power as unified, separated only in terms of its different functions, not in terms of checks and balances.[84] He also treated the prevailing natural law theory espoused by the great majority of liberal lawyers and politicians with the benevolent indulgence of a seasoned doyen. 'Nobody really knows anyway what natural law is, so what point would there be in arguing over it?'[85] For Knapp, law was always a product of society and its power structure, not a codification of higher philosophical principles or moral rules.

As a respected teacher of a large part of the post-communist legal elite, as a leading expert on civil law, but also as a prominent figure in a number of legal subfields such as comparative law, legal cybernetics and so on, Knapp enjoyed considerable respect in the 1990s, which was reflected in his numerous academic positions. He once more became the director of the Institute of State and Law, and a member of the Board of the Czechoslovak Academy of Sciences and, somewhat later, a member of the government's legislative council. At the same time, Knapp was in no sense at the centre of the newly emerging liberal democratic legal culture. He could have remained outside the 'liberal consensus' of the time, but his distanced and sometimes ironic views did not threaten the core of it, which was the liberal-conservative compromise over the rule of law. Knapp was neither a liberal lawyer nor an outspoken illiberal.

Knapp himself was not particularly interested in the rule of law. In a short essay on the rule of law concept, Knapp doubted that it could be precisely defined in terms of legal analysis because 'it often tends to be understood intuitively or as a political postulate or political slogan, rather than scholarly'. While keeping his distance, however, he more or less subscribed to the liberal, positivist rule-book conception of the rule of law, stating that the rule of law is when a state 'not only strictly observes legality as one of the defining hallmarks of the rule of law, but also sets limits on itself when using law as a means of governing a society'. He further elaborated that 'Under the rule of law, the legal regulation of citizens' behaviour is based on the principle that citizens are fundamentally free, and legal norms limit their fundamental freedom to the extent that is socially necessary'.[86]

14.4 CONCLUSION: RULE OF LAW RULED THEM ALL

The political and constitutional status of the rule of law seemed incontestable during the liberal democratic transformation of ECE in the 1990s. The concept of the rule of law played an important role in shaping the political compromise of the

[84] Viktor Knapp, 'Zákonodárná moc ústavního soudu' (1993) 132 *Právník* 101.
[85] Viktor Knapp, 'Člověk, občan a právo' (1992) 131 *Právník* 8.
[86] Ibid., 9–10.

time, namely as one of the platforms on which that compromise could be built.[87] However, political compromise based on the notion of the rule of law is not the same as agreement on what the rule of law means. As we saw in Section 14.3, there was a striking variety of ideas and understandings of the rule of law within the jurisprudence and constitutional practice of the time. Whereas the constitutional mainstream symbolized by the evolving constitutional doctrine of the new CC stood for the so-called substantial or material concept of the rule of law based on the primacy of human rights and their constitutional adjudication, a significant number of legal experts leaned instead towards a positivist, non-substantial conception of the rule of law, where human rights play a more symbolic supporting role. In the 'liberal consensus' period, however, we also find thinkers and practitioners closer to the neoliberal constitutional imagination with their concept of the rule of law inspired by Hayek's legal thought, as well as representatives of the illiberal constitutional doctrine, who remained on the edge or outside the spectrum of the broad field of liberal constitutionalism, though not questioning the liberal concept of the rule of law in any fundamental way.

This diversity in itself is not surprising, and we can find similarities in many other countries and cultural regions. However, the striking degree of political consensus on the rule of law was due to specific historical conditions as well as the political situation during the early liberal transition period. In this chapter, I have attempted to link the constitutional imagination of the liberal era to this historical and political context in an effort to better understand the uniqueness but also the fragility of post-communist *compromise on the rule of law.*

The unique position of the notion of the rule of law as both a political ideal and a constitutional legal tool emerged historically as a result of the years-long political struggle between the late communist dictatorship and the human rights movement in the region. The ideological, political and semantic struggle between the evolving socialist constitutional project of authoritarian socialist *Rechsstaat*, or rule-by-law dictatorship, and its dissident opponents and their increasingly prominent vision of a democratic *Rechtsstaat* based on respect for human rights culminated in the 'constitutional revolutions' of 1989, where the rule of law played the role of the central unifying bolt. From a longer-term perspective, this historical constellation was yet another phase in the competition between different notions of the *Rechtsstaat*, namely democratic and authoritarian, a centuries-old tradition in the region.

Post-communist liberalism was the main political vehicle for the liberal democratic transformation in the ECE region. However, this aggregate notion contains considerable heterogeneity. For the purpose of this chapter focusing on

[87] For a perspective on the liberal-conservative compromise preceding the culture wars in ECE, see Pavel Barša, Zora Hesová and Ondřej Slačálek (eds.), *Central Europe Culture Wars: Beyond Post-Communism and Populism* (Faculty of Arts, Charles University, 2021), open access version available online https://dspace.cuni.cz/bitstream/handle/20.500.11956/170756/H-15_Central_European_culture_wars_web.pdf.

constitutional imagination, we characterized the post-communist liberal spectrum as bound by two ideal-typical poles, the post-dissident *human rights liberalism* and *neoliberalism*, both with symbolic ties, ideological roots and inspirations in domestic as well as international contexts. The two strands of liberalism shared historical concerns regarding the need to overcome the communist legacy, yet they diverged in their interpretations of the communist experience and in their visions of the principal tasks required to achieve a future free and democratic society. Both were grounded in the core instruments of liberal constitutionalism, which emerged as the dominant constitutional doctrine in post-communist East Central Europe. However, as evidenced by the varying interpretations of the rule of law, liberal constitutionalism itself is a composite concept, encompassing a range of distinct constitutional imaginations.

The striking differences in the rule-of-law understanding did not matter much in the 1990s for, in most instances, these ideas and constitutional imaginations worked well in the liberal hegemony, contributing to the 'liberal consensus' of the time. In this sense, the historical situation was quite unique, for in different historical settings, the diverging understanding of the rule of law could have important, if not fatal, political consequences. It is, namely, of great significance whether the rule of law is understood as an autonomous value and thus an indispensable part of democratic order and societal peace, whether it is intrinsically connected to substantive justice exercise based on rights adjudication. Or whether it could be, in certain circumstances, replaced by an authoritarian *Rechtsstaat* (which has a rich historical tradition in the region) that would provide its supposedly most important function, that is the structural regulation of the market or legal field of political agency based on majoritarian democratic principles or some other way of choosing a political sovereign.

Yet these diverging understandings of what the rule of law is and what could be expected from it in the longer run were not thematized in the early transition years. There were other issues related to the rule of law, animating the political discussions of the time. For instance, whether there can be a rule of law without transitional justice and, in particular, whether the nascent rule of law can rest on the corrupt judges of the old regime.[88] Conflicts over concrete implications of the rule of law in the political and social life of post-communist societies notwithstanding, the value of the rule of law remained unquestioned. What united all liberals and was shared by most other political streams – liberal conservatives, socialists or even a small number of radical democrats – was the importance of the rule of law and constitutionalism in the newly established democratic order. Most of the actors also endorsed, albeit for

[88] This political debate played an important role in culture wars in the post-communist ECE and has only recently received more attention in legal scholarship in connection with illiberal court-packing, Katarina Šipulová and David Kosař, 'Purging the Judiciary after a Transition: Between a Rock and a Hard Place' (2024) *Hague Journal on the Rule of Law* 1.

different reasons, the de-politicization function of the rule-of-law institutional mechanisms. Some due to fear of populism and misuse of political power, others with concern for the economic reforms and their possible disruption by democratic politicking. The political *compromise in the rule of law* might have been only superficial. Yet, it was highly productive in creating the liberal democratic political hegemony of the 1990s. And this is also why, after the dissolution of the hegemony, it became the main bone of contention.

15

From the Façade to Solid Foundation?

The Evolution of the Polish Constitutional Law Discourse in 1944–1989

Wojciech Zomerski

15.1 INTRODUCTION

In the contemporary Polish constitutional law discourse, the beginnings of modern constitutionalism in the Third Polish Republic (from 1989) are usually associated with the last decade of the Polish People's Republic (1944–1989) (*Polska Rzeczpospolita Ludowa – PRL*). In this widely accepted narrative, modern constitutional thought emerged as a response to the painful experience of socialist authoritarian rule. On the contrary, the constitutional law thought developed in PRL is treated as non-existent or, at best, as invaluable and useless. It is simply assumed that the socialist constitutional theory – due to the absence of PRL's sovereignty and this regime's authoritarian character – was radically ideologized and subordinated to the realm of politics. Thus, the traditions and roots of genuine constitutionalism are traced back to the Second Polish Republic (1918–1939),[1] the Napoleonic Duchy of Warsaw (1807–1815)[2] or the First Polish Republic (1569–1795).[3] The European constitutional discourse goes even

I would like to express my gratitude to the participants of the seminar 'European Constitutional Imaginaries', organized by the IMAGINE Project in Warsaw on 10 December 2021, and the participants of CLEST Seminar, Faculty of Law, Administration and Economics of the University of Wroclaw, 22 December 2021, for the opportunity to present my working paper and discuss it in a genuine scientific atmosphere. Special thanks shall be directed to Michał Krajewski for encouraging me to elaborate on the subject of this chapter.

[1] See for example, Tomasz Stawecki, 'Wykładnia konstytucjijako przedmiot analiz teoretycznych, porównawczych oraz badań empirycznych' in Tomasz Stawecki and Jan Winczorek (eds.), *Wykładnia konstytucji: Inspiracje, teorie, argumenty* (Wolters Kluwer Polska, 2015), 20; Paweł Sarnecki, 'Stan nauki prawa konstytucyjnego w Polsce' (2010) (No 7) *Państwo i Prawo* 5, 6, 10.

[2] See, Sarnecki, 'Stan nauki prawa konstytucyjnego w Polsce', 5.

[3] See for instance, Mark Brzezinski, *The Struggle for Constitutionalism in Poland* (reprint, Palgrave MacMillian, 2000), 1, where the author described the Polish Constitution of 1952 as 'imposition from abroad, a socio-political anachronism, and alien to Polish constitutional heritage' and contrasted it with 'rich, indigenous constitutional heritage' of the First Polish Republic (1569–1795) that was reflected in the enactment of the 1791 Constitution, which made Poland the second country in the world history to adopt a written constitution.

further in this regard. According to a quite popular narrative, the aspiration for a constitutional rule in Central Eastern Europe (CEE) had not emerged until the 1990s, and its emergence was stimulated and structured, above all, by the process of EU accession.[4]

Both narratives are problematic. A one-sided and negative assessment of the Polish constitutional law thought of 1944–1989 overlooks its important features.[5] First of all, the authors expressing this assessment treat the entire period of PRL as consistent and uniform,[6] disregarding that post-1956, after the failed attempt to install Stalinism, the Polish academia began to enjoy at least some autonomy to pursue scientifically valuable discussions. Secondly, they overlook that any constitutional discourse is entangled with political ideology, which does not render it invalid. Thirdly, they reject the entire constitutional law thought of that period, without considering whether some parts of it could be potentially valuable and, as such, worth preserving. Not only does the European constitutional law discourse overlook the pre-1989 struggle for constitutional rule in the CEE countries, but it also ignores the pre-1944 constitutional traditions of these countries.

In this chapter, I argue that the role of constitutional law discourse in PRL was more complex and ambiguous than it is usually assumed and that the assessment of this discourse should give justice to its complexity and ambiguity. The way the Polish constitutional law discourse went through in the period of real socialism might be characterised as a path from a façade to the foundation for constitutional democracy.[7]

4 This is the common reading of Paul Blokker, *New Democracies in Crisis? A Comparative Constitutional Study of the Czech Republic, Hungary, Poland, Romania and Slovakia* (Routledge, 2015). This reading is attractive as it explains the emergence of the rule-of-law crisis as resulting from the unsuccessful transplant of 'Western' constitutionalism. However, Blokker's argument is more complex. The author – despite not including in his analysis the pre-1944 constitutional traditions of the region – acknowledges that the aspirations in the Central Eastern Europe for a constitutional rule emerged prior to 1989 and that they were an important part of the dissident movements across the region (ibid., 56–74, 81–98). His claim is that the specific *type* of constitutionalism that emerged in the 1990s in the region ('legal constitutionalism') was determined by the external factors (a 'legal-constitutionalist bias of the EU') against alleged local aspirations of dissidents for something that might be described as 'civic constitutionalism'. In other words, according to Blokker, it was the specific subtype of constitutionalism, not the very idea of a constitutional rule, that was imposed on the Central Eastern Europe. See ibid., 165.

5 Note, however, that speaking of 'constitutional law' in the context of PRL is an ahistorical simplification. In fact, until the 1970s, it was common to speak of 'State law' rather than 'constitutional law'. See, Mirosław Granat, *Prawo konstytucyjne: Pytania i odpowiedzi*, 10th ed. (Wolters Kluwer, 2021), 26–27. For the sake of simplicity, however, hereinafter I use the notion of 'constitutional law' to denote the whole discipline as it evolved over the years.

6 See Brzezinski, *The Struggle for Constitutionalism in Poland*, passim, where the author described the entire reality of PRL as 'totalitarian', not differentiating between the truly totalitarian Stalinist period (1944–1956) and post-Stalinist authoritarianism (from 1956 onwards).

7 Alternatively, one may argue that it was a path from 'State law' to 'constitutional law', as the very idea of 'constitutional law' displays the aspiration of law to a greater autonomy and reflects the idea that a State in its operations, including legislative ones, is not absolutely sovereign but

Legal academia, by developing a doctrine of constitutional review from the late 1960s, enabled the subsequent transformation towards constitutional democracy. It prompted domestic political elites – remaining under internal and external pressure – to become the precursor of institutional changes in the CEE. The most essential element of these changes, the Constitutional Tribunal (*Trybunał Konstytucyjny – TK*), made Poland the only country in the Warsaw Pact with constitutional review. Despite the original intention of making the TK just another façade, it in fact played a crucial role in the constitutional transformation. From this perspective, the reforms of the 1980s should not be considered a rejection but, rather, an institutionalisation of the Polish constitutional law theory as it evolved over the previous decades. Consequently, the contemporary negative assessment of the constitutional legal thought from this period is oversimplified and unjustified.

15.2 CONSTITUTIONAL LAW THOUGHT IN THE POLISH PEOPLE'S REPUBLIC

15.2.1 *Introduction*

Considering the negative assessment of the PRL's constitutional scholarship, one would expect that constitutional law theory of that time was theoretically flawed and incompatible with modern constitutional law thought. Considering the likely influence of Soviet constitutional theory (as founded originally by Lenin and later developed by prominent lawyers of the regime – Evgeny Pashukanis and Andrey Vyshinski),[8] one would especially expect some reflections of the Marxist idea of the withering away of law or the primacy of politics over law.[9] This tendency would particularly concern the Stalinist period of 1944–1956, perceived as totalitarian in

subjected to external standards. Thus, the very shift from 'State' to 'constitutional' law in the self-identification of the discipline, which could be observed in the 1970s, sheds some light on the evolution of the constitutional law in PRL.

8 See, for example, Andryi Vyshinsky, *The Law of the Soviet State* (Macmillan, 1948), 339–340, who claimed that in capitalist states constitutional review 'is broadly used by monopolist cliques of exploiters to obtain a declaration of "unconstitutionality" as to laws running counter to their interests'. On the Soviet constitutional theory in general, see, Alec Nove, 'Some Aspects of Soviet Constitutional Theory' (1949) 12 *The Modern Law Review* 12.

9 The relation between Marxism and post-war Polish legal science is a topic itself worth to investigate. Elsewhere, I have argued that the relation between Marxism – as either a philosophical tradition or ideology (Marxism-Leninism) – was of complex nature. In the Stalinist period (1944–1956) it was a leading tradition, structuring the content of theoretical programs developed in legal science. After October 1956 most legal scholars shifted towards more positivist approaches, meanwhile they were still trying to appear as they were inspired by Marxist tradition. In the post-1968 era, Marxism practically disappeared as a methodological orientation in legal science, remaining – if at all – just an ornament to purely positivistic considerations. I try to explain it briefly below (see point 2.4.1). For more see, Wojciech Zomerski, W *kierunku demokratycznej nauki prawa? Dogmatyka, edukacja, postanalityczność* (Wydawnictwo Naukowe Scholar, 2023).

contrast to the post-1956 authoritarian rule in the region. However, these intuitions do not withstand close scrutiny. Although the primacy of politics over law, especially in the Stalinist period, was a social fact, the constitutional law discourse from the very beginning put much effort into portraying itself as committed to the ideals of legalism. I argue that its aim was to legitimise rather than describe or reform the surrounding reality. In this sense, it had a purely façade character. As we would see, however, this character of constitutional law discourse was slowly changing, along with the advent of a new generation of constitutional scholars who, starting from the late 1960s, attempted to take constitutional theory seriously and actively advocated for bridging the gap between the theory of the regime's political system and its practice.

To grasp the evolution of the constitutional law discourse over 1944–1989, I confront it with relevant socio-political events. I will examine this evolution in four conventional periods:

a. The Stalinist period (1944–1956) – a totalitarian period between the installation of the regime in 1944 and the October Thaw of 1956, in which the basis of socialist constitutionalism was formed.
b. The stabilisation period (1956–1968) – a period in which the regime stabilised, socialist constitutionalism emerged in its mature form and the first critique of the socialist constitutionalism was raised; the end date of this period is March 1968, when the regime started to lose its support among the intellectuals.
c. The correction period (1968–1979) – a period in which, due to institutional reforms that took place in other socialist countries in the 1960s and the heated internal atmosphere following the events of 1968 and 1970, the constitutional law discourse started to treat its doctrine seriously and openly demanded changes, which resulted in institutional reforms of the 1970s concerning especially the introduction of constitutional review.
d. The decline period (1979–1989) – a period in which the hitherto purely academic demands for the institutionalisation of the fully-fledged constitutional judicial review became a political demand widely-spread among social actors, including political and social movements, which ultimately resulted in setting up the Constitutional Tribunal.

15.2.2 *The Stalinist Period (1944–1956): Laying Down the Foundations of Façade Constitutionalism*

After the communist government came to power in July 1944, one of its first decisions was to invalidate the pre-war 1935 Constitution and to act temporarily on the basis of the 1921 Constitution, the latter being based on the idea of parliamentary supremacy. The main aim was to adopt a new constitution that would institutionalise and stabilise the newly established regime.[10] On 17 February 1947, the Polish parliament (the *Sejm*) adopted a transitional 'Small Constitution' (*Mała Konstytucja*), based on the 1921 Constitution and providing at least formally for the separation of powers and a parliamentary system. After the adoption of the Small Constitution, some limited discussions concerning the shape of the future constitution flared up. Seemingly, the biggest controversy concerned the problem of constitutional review, the institutionalisation of which began at that time in West Europe.[11] But the Small Constitution of 1947 continued the pre-war traditions of the II Republic of Poland,[12] explicitly prohibiting constitutional judicial review. This prohibition was justified with a principle of parliamentary supremacy. Consequently, its decisions could not be challenged by the courts. Controversies surrounded the question of whether the future constitution of the Polish People's Republic would reproduce this prohibition or – to the contrary – whether it would provide for some form of constitutional review.

Earlier, before the enactment of the Small Constitution, the establishment of a constitutional court that would examine the conformity of laws with the constitution was backed by the First Congress of the Democratic Alliance in 1946 (*Stronnictwo Demokratyczne – SD*; a satellite, non-Marxist ally of the communist Polish United Workers' Party).[13] This idea also found some limited support in legal academia. Makowski, a professor of international law (Jagiellonian University), drawing from Kelsen's works, argued that constitutional review, either in its centralised or diffuse version, was a necessary component of a State governed by the rule of law, as it allowed to secure the effectiveness and sustainability of constitutional norms.[14]

10 The aspiration of the socialist government for the constitutional rule was in line with the post-war trends on both sides of the Iron Curtain and with the pre-war constitutional traditions of Poland, which, in the interwar period, had two constitutions and its first constitution was adopted as early as in 1791.

11 In the interwar period, constitutional courts were operating only in Austria and Czechoslovakia. In the post-war period, the first constitutional court was established in 1947 in Italy and the Federal Republic of Germany, later in Greece (1975), Spain (1978) and Portugal (1982). For this reason, the post-war emergence of constitutional courts, as a reflection of a general rejection of the concept of parliamentary supremacy, is explained with the experience of fascism or – to put it more universally – authoritarianism. In this regard see, for instance, Mauro Cappelletti, 'Repudiating Montesquieu? The Expansion and Legitimacy of "Constitutional Justice"' (1985) 35 *Catholic University Law Review* 1, 16–17.

12 Both pre-war Polish constitutions ruled out judicial constitutional review. This was in line with the constitutional tendencies at that time as the pre-war European constitutionalism was in general dominated by the French concept of parliamentary supremacy, which precluded constitutional judicial review.

13 One of the peculiarities of the Polish real socialism was a limited political pluralism, which the multi-party system was a most visible reflection of. Interestingly, the SD managed to sustain its non-Marxist orientation, being one of a few non-Marxist parties in the Eastern Bloc.

14 Julian Makowski, 'Materiały do projektu przyszłej konstytucji' (1947) (No 11) *Państwo i Prawo* 32, 42–43.

Makowski saw constitutional judicial review as indispensable in the reality of people's democracy[15].

This idea was challenged by another prominent jurist of the newly established regime, a professor of constitutional law, Rozmaryn (University of Warsaw).[16] Rozmaryn justified the rejection of judicial constitutional review in socialist constitutionalism with the concept of parliamentary supremacy. As he argued, from the perspective of socialist legal thought, the idea of a constitutional court is a restriction motivated by a distrust of people's representation. As such, it is a distinctive feature of the capitalist states. It restrains the representation of the people through instruments lacking democratic legitimacy.[17] Interestingly, the rejection of constitutional review did not prevent Rozmaryn from declaring commitment to the doctrine of constitutional supremacy.[18] He saw the Sejm as the supreme authority of the people and, consequently, the only body competent to ensure the conformity of laws with the constitution.[19] In this view, the prohibition of judicial review was not a contradiction but the institutional consequence of the idea of people's democracy.[20]

Considering the subordination of the post-war regime to the Soviet Union, as well as the fact that Rozmaryn was the president of the committee preparing the draft of the constitution, his ideas unsurprisingly prevailed over those expressed by Makowski. The Constitution of the Polish People's Republic adopted on the 22 July 1952, based on the socialist principle of the unity of State power, provided for the supremacy of the Sejm and did not provide any basis for judicial review.[21]

This discussion was not particularly elaborate due to the historical moment in which it occurred. In the totalitarian pre-1956 period, there was no atmosphere for

[15] Interestingly, Makowski saw the absence of constitutional review in the tradition of European constitutionalism as a remnant of the monarchic ideas. In this perspective, constitutional review was seen as a democratic 'development' against the post-monarchic traditions of the Second Republic of Poland (1918–1939). Note, however, that Makowski, as a pre-war professor educated in Antwerp, Paris and other pre-war Polish universities, was himself a 'remnant' of a non-socialist legal tradition.

[16] See Stefan Rozmaryn, 'Kontrola konstytucyjności ustaw' (1948) (No 11) *Państwo i Prawo* 36 (part 1) and Stefan Rozmaryn, 'Kontrola konstytucyjności ustaw' (1948) (No 12) *Państwo i Prawo* 3 (part 2).

[17] See, Rozmaryn, 'Kontrola konstytucyjności ustaw' (part 2), 20: 'The constitutional control of statutes by extra-parliamentary bodies, particularly judicial and quasi-judicial, is a reactionary institution and because of that, there is no room for it either in a socialist State or in a State of people's democracy, which trusts the people's justice and the will of the people'.

[18] Stefan Rozmaryn, *Polskie prawo państwowe*, 2nd ed. (Książka i Wiedza, 1951), 301.

[19] Ibid., 301–302.

[20] Ibid., 302, note 42.

[21] At the same time, the Constitution of 1952, in contrast to the previous Polish constitutions, did not include an explicit prohibition of constitutional judicial review, which made room for the further discussions in this regard. As we will see, the discussions on the admissibility of constitutional review under the Constitution of 1952 were continued almost through the entire period of PRL and ceased only in the 1980s, when the constitutional court was eventually established.

public discussions on the legal and political matters and any opposite claims in this regard were made only for propaganda purposes.[22] However, that discussion defined the character of constitutional law theory for the two post-war decades (i.e. that of 'façade constitutionalism'). On the one hand, it offered legalistic views in constitutional theory (such as the supremacy of the constitution). On the other hand, it affirmed the institutional arrangements that undermined the purported legalism in practice (such as the thesis on the inadmissibility of judicial review). In order to see it more clearly, it is worth moving now to 1956 and subsequent years.

15.2.3 *The Stabilisation Period (1956–1968): The Façade Constitutionalism and Its Twilight*

15.2.3.1 The Polish October 1956 and Its Consequences

The end of the totalitarian period in Poland is usually associated with the events that took place in 1953–1956, first in the Soviet Union (the Khrushchev Thaw) and then in Poland (the Polish October 1956). The Khrushchev Thaw was prompted by the death of Stalin and the subsequent condemnation of the Stalinist rule by the new Soviet leader – Nikita Khrushchev. The Polish United Workers' Party (*Polska Zjednoczona Partia Robotnicza – PZPR*) allowed for the circulation among the society of the Khrushchev's so-called Secret Speech, critical of the Stalinist regime, which was an exception in the Eastern Bloc. This decision led to social unrest, only strengthened by the death of the Polish communist leader, Bierut, in March 1956. This unrest culminated in the workers' protests of June 1956 that demanded liberalisation and a more nation-centred and independent rule from the Soviet Union.

The new communist leader, Gomułka, addressed some of these demands. He was a reformist. At least initially, he wished to pursue a more independent path, known as 'the Polish way to socialism'. The changes in the socio-political realm stirred up discussions about the functioning of the State, which were part of a broader phenomenon known as a 'period of dealing with the mistakes and deviations' of the pre-1956 period. An editorial in *Państwo i Prawo* – the most important legal journal of that time – openly acknowledged that constitutional principles had often been violated during the Stalinist period,[23] signalling an official consent for limited criticism. In the subsequent volumes of *Państwo i Prawo*, legal scholars

[22] It is commonly said that the draft of the Constitution of 1952 – despite the alleged subjection to the public discussion – was created by the narrow group of lawyers that were under strong influence of the Party. The final draft was allegedly prepared by Joseph Stalin himself, who introduced fifty amendments on the project prepared by the committee led by Rozmaryn. See Andrzej Garlicki, 'O mój Rozmarynie' (2014) *Polityka*, www.polityka.pl/pomocnikhistoryczny/1527195,1,o-moj-rozmarynie-czyli-konstytucja-prl.read.

[23] See, Editorial, 'Niektóre zagadnienia polityczno-prawne w świetle III Plenum KC PZPR' (1955) (No 10) *Państwo i Prawo* 361, 369.

acknowledged that, in the pre-1956 period, there were abuses in the exercise of power and advocated for changes in this regard.

The very idea behind the concept of 'mistakes and deviations' implied that the unlawful character and brutality of the regime were not the consequences of socialist theory, but solely a matter of practice that, for various reasons, deviated from the theory. Undoubtedly, however, the very fact that academic discourse could challenge social reality signalled deeper changes in the socio-political system in the post-1956 period, in which the academia would enjoy at least some autonomy. The legal literature from that period started to resemble – in contrast to pre-1956 ideological writings – a classic positivistic discourse. This change was clearly visible in legal theory and constitutional law. In particular, the latter emphasised the significance of the rule of law for the proper functioning of people's democracy. However, the constitutional law discourse remained a façade, as evidenced in the remainder of this section.

15.2.3.2 Dispute over Judicial Review

Inspired by demands to subject people's democracy to the rule of law, Biskupski, a constitutional law professor, called for introducing the constitutional review of parliamentary statutes by courts.[24] Although this call found some support from political actors,[25] it was again rejected by the legal academia, just like in 1946, and abandoned for another decade. The idea of judicial review and a constitutional court was denounced by Grzybowski (a professor of history of law from Jagiellonian University) as a bourgeois one.[26] One should be careful – as he argued – not to replace the diktat of administrative bureaucracy (with which the abuses of power in the pre-1956 era were explained) with the diktat of the judiciary that would place itself above the Sejm.[27]

Other authors reflected on the idea of judicial review on the margins of their reflection on the restoration of the rule of law in the post-1956 era. The idea of the rule of law, understood through the lenses of the sovereignty of the people, was – according to these authors – not compatible with the concept of constitutional judicial review of legislative acts. In this vein, a professor of international law, Izdebski (Lodz University), argued that, in a socialist State the classic concept of the separation of powers is rejected and replaced with the principle of unity of State power exercised by the parliament designed as the 'supreme organ of State

[24] Kazimierz Biskupski, 'Niektóre problemy socjalistycznego parlamentaryzmu' (1956) (No 10) *Państwo i Prawo* 545, 547.

[25] Note that the call for the institutionalisation of constitutional judicial review was expressed again in the resolution of the Central Committee of SD from 10 October 1956.

[26] Konstanty Grzybowski, 'Stalinizm w socjalistycznym prawie konstytucyjnym' (1957) (No 6) *Państwo i Prawo* 1053, 1063.

[27] Ibid.

authority'.[28] As a consequence, in a socialist State, the legislature should have control over the remaining branches of power, in particular, the executive power. The supreme position of the parliament could justify the idea of administrative courts (that would be empowered to invalidate individual administrative decisions issued by administrative authorities) and the judicial review of executive acts for compliance with legislative statutes,[29] but, at the same time, it ruled out the judicial review of legislative acts. This position was expressed in even more explicit terms by a prominent philosopher of law of that time, Ehrlich (University of Warsaw), who rejected the constitutional judicial review of statutes, but advocated for the judicial review of executive and administrative acts.[30] Underlying the calls for the rule of law of 1956 was, at best, the intention to eliminate abuses of the executive branch and to revindicate the constitutional position of the Sejm as the supreme State authority, rather than providing for complex institutional changes in the realm of rule-of-law safeguards.

The gap between the theory and practice of the political regime of that time was so striking, however, that one may doubt whether the quoted authors really aimed at a change or, perhaps, their sole aim was to legitimise the status quo. The arguments concerning the alleged supremacy of the Sejm should be assessed against the political practice in which the Sejm was not a real place of making political decisions, either in the pre-1956 or in the post-1956 period.[31] The real power was in the hands of the Party leadership, not necessarily holding any official posts.[32] The judicial review of administrative decisions and executive acts – which could be justified by the supreme position of the Sejm – remained fiction until the late 1980s, when the Supreme Administrative Court and the Constitutional Tribunal began to operate. The political elites were effectively ruling by means of executive acts that in practice enjoyed primacy over statutes, as the former frequently determined the latter's practical meaning.[33] Most importantly, however, the weak position of the Sejm resulted from constitutional arrangements. The Constitution required the Sejm to convene only twice a year, without specifying the duration of each session. This arrangement might be contrasted with the setup of the Council of State (*Rada Państwa*), the permanent executive organ of the Sejm, which was equipped with substantial legislative, executive and judicial powers. As Brzezinski noted, as typically the officially recorded votes of the Sejm were unanimous, 'the Sejm, the traditional cornerstone of popular government, was transformed into a rubber stamp

[28] See, Zygmunt Izdebski, 'Rewizja teorii podziału władz' (1957) (No 11) *Państwo i Prawo* 787.
[29] Ibid., 799–800.
[30] Stanisław Ehrlich, 'Uwagi o praworządności socjalistycznej' (1958) (No 8–9) *Państwo i Prawo* 233, 244–246.
[31] Brzezinski, *The Struggle for Constitutionalism in Poland*, 67.
[32] See ibid., 135.
[33] See ibid., 68–69.

for Party policies as promulgated by the Council of State'.[34] Thus, the Council of State, in theory subordinated to the Sejm, in practice replaced the Sejm as the supreme organ of State authority.[35] This did not change until the fall of real socialism in Poland. One may therefore argue that the Sejm was not even meant to be the place in which the political decisions were to be taken.

One could expect that the reality that contradicts the theory to such an extent would trigger either a reformulation of the theory or an open critique of the reality. Nothing like that occurred. By the late 1960s, the above-discussed gap between the theory and practice had not been acknowledged in the legal scholarship. The normative theory was perceived as a description of reality. However, its only function was to legitimise the status quo.[36] The Sejm and any argumentation built on its allegedly supreme position had a façade character. The practical consequence of façade constitutionalism was political (declarative) rather than legal (normative) character of the constitution.

15.2.3.3 Towards the Complex Theory of Socialist Constitutionalism

Constitutional debates that emerged in 1956 concerned specific issues, such as the admissibility of constitutional review in a socialist regime. At the same time, a complex theory of socialist constitutionalism was offered in 1961 in Rozmaryn's *Constitution as the basic law of PRL*.[37] Its content and wide reception in the constitutional law discourse reflected the stabilisation of the post-war socio-political formation. It was also a reflection of deeper changes in the academia. Although Rozmaryn clearly remained under the strong influence of socialist thought, he justified his theoretical assertions in a purely positivistic manner, namely by reference to the content of the written constitution. Interestingly, not only the manner of justification but also the content of Rozmaryn's theory in principle did not deviate much from modern legal constitutionalism. The author advocated for recognising: (1) the supremacy of the constitution, (2) the fully binding character of the entire constitution, (3) a universal – not particular – model of the interpretation of the constitution,[38] (4) the direct application of the constitution by the ordinary judiciary,

[34] Ibid., 67.

[35] Ibid., 68. See, Nove, 'Some Aspects of Soviet Constitutional Theory', 12, who in the context of constitutionalism of the Soviet Union argued that it is a common failing of both 'friends and enemies of the USSR', to mistake the avowed purpose of constitutional institutions with its actual functioning.

[36] On the legitimizing rather than normative character of socialist constitutions see, Harold G. Skilling, *The Governments of Communist East Europe* (Crowell, 1966), 50.

[37] Stefan Rozmaryn, *Konstytucja jako ustawa zasadnicza PRL*, 1st ed. (Państwowe Wydawnictwo Naukowe, 1961).

[38] In the Polish constitutional law theory, the distinction between 'universal' and 'particular' models of the interpretation refers to the controversy, whether the constitution should be interpreted as any other piece of legislation or in a specific manner different from the interpretation of ordinary laws. Meanwhile, the 'universal' theory of constitutional

and (5) the co-application of the constitution and pro-constitutional interpretation of legislative and other legal acts.[39] Regardless of how revolutionary these calls might sound at that time, Rozmaryn remained a zealous opponent of constitutional judicial review, explaining that, in the case of an unconstitutional provision, the court should limit itself to declare this unconstitutionality, but it should consider itself bound by the provision in question. It was the exclusive role of the Sejm to eliminate this provision from the system of law.[40]

Rozmaryn put much effort into showing that his position was not normative but descriptive.[41] Although the Constitution of 1952 did not explicitly prohibit constitutional judicial review, it made the Sejm the supreme organ of State authority, remaining beyond the control of any other authorities.[42] Therefore, for Rozmaryn, an explicit prohibition of constitutional review in the constitution was simply redundant. Also, according to the Constitution, the judges in adjudication were to be subject only to parliamentary statutes. Moreover, to Rozmaryn, there was 'absolutely nothing' in the Constitution that would have been subject to a nationwide discussion and that would reflect the intent to depart from the rejection of constitutional judicial review, typical for the tradition of Polish constitutionalism. In view of this tradition, the adoption of constitutional judicial review would have needed an explicit constitutional basis.[43]

Anticipating the allegation of the 'façade' character of his constitutional theory, Rozmaryn openly argued that the Constitution – despite the rejection of constitutional judicial review – provides for various safeguards of economic[44] and legal character. In particular, the proper fulfilment of Sejm's tasks and the conformity of Sejm's acts with the Constitution is secured with the constitutional subordination of the elected members of the Sejm to the will of voters[45]. Eventually, however, the author – exceptionally and meaningfully departing from his positivist outlook – admitted that the safeguard of the highest resort is the politics of the Party 'that holds the view that without strict observance of the laws of the Polish People's Republic one may not speak of the rule of law'.[46]

interpretation seems to go hand in hand with legal constitutionalism, the 'particular' theory of constitutional interpretation might be associated with its political counterpart.

39 See Rozmaryn, *Konstytucja jako ustawa zasadnicza PRL*, passim.

40 Ibid., 268–269.

41 Ibid., 185–186.

42 Ibid., 183–184.

43 Ibid., 186–187.

44 According to Rozmaryn, the distinctive feature of socialist constitutionalism is the institutionalisation of material (economic) safeguards of the rule of law. According to him, such safeguards are necessary if one wants to ensure the effectiveness of constitutional rights and freedoms. Ibid.

45 Ibid., 193. By the subordination of parliamentary members to the will of the voters, Rozmaryn understood the constitutionally enshrined imperative mandate that obliged MPs to pursue policies that agreed with the voters and provided for the right to recall MPs that failed to act in such manner.

46 Ibid., 213.

Rozmaryn's reflection on the alleged constitutional safeguards appears somewhat shallow and not entirely consistent. On the one hand, he argued that the socialist constitution is effective thanks to the subordination of the Sejm to the voters (which was not executed in practice at all). On the other hand, he explicitly stated that the real and only guarantee of the Constitution's social importance is the Party and its politics (admitting explicitly that the Party has the last word on the constitutionality of its own actions).

15.2.3.4 The Twilight of Façade Constitutionalism?

As for 1961, the façade character of socialist constitutionalism was beyond any discussion. However, that the constitutional theory did not correspond to the reality did not render it entirely meaningless. Crucially, the Polish doctrine of constitutional law declared a firm commitment to legalistic ideals. The theory was not flawed, but it could not be materialised because of existing institutional arrangements and authoritarian politics. Therefore, the evolution of PRL towards constitutional democracy did not require a rejection or replacement of the existing constitutional law doctrine but, above all, changes within the institutional framework that could be reconciled with this doctrine. Interestingly, this part of sociopolitical reality later became the subject-matter of the main constitutional debates, culminating in the reforms of the 1970s and 1980s, including the setting up of the Constitutional Tribunal and other essential constitutional institutions.

The first voices challenging the theoretical rejection of constitutional review were expressed in the very year of Rozmaryn's book publication.[47] At the annual meeting of the constitutional lawyers of 1961, Sobolewski, a professor of constitutional law from Jagiellonian University, while commenting on a paper regarding the alleged inadmissibility of constitutional judicial review in a socialist State, argued that the paper 'provides much material for the hypothesis that constitutional judicial review, might be eventually, after its thorough transformation, usefully applied also in a

[47] Simultaneously, one may observe in this period the emergence of scholarship that supported the inadmissibility thesis. Particularly active in this regard was Janina Zakrzewska, who, discussing the function of the constitutional court in the Western countries, denounced it as an instrument of class violence. See, Janina Zakrzewska, 'Kontrola Konstytucyjności ustaw w powojennej Francji' (1961) (No 12) *Państwo i Prawo* 922; Zakrzewska, 'Trybunał Konstytucyjny a zabezpieczenie zgodności ustaw z Konstytucją we Włoszech' (1963) (No 11) *Państwo i Prawo* 705; Janina Zakrzewska, *Kontrola konstytucyjności ustaw (we współczesnym państwie burżuazyjnym* (Wydawnictwo Prawnicze, 1964), 167; Janina Zakrzewska and Marek Sobolewski, 'Instytucja kontroli konstytucyjności ustaw w współczesnych państwach Europy Zachodniej' (1965) (No 1) *Ruch Prawniczy, Ekonomiczny i Socjologiczny* 1. Interestingly, in the 1980s, Zakrzewska joined the opposition to become eventually, in 1989, a judge of the Constitutional Tribunal. In this regard, see also note 123.

socialist state'.[48] This view has been expressed also by other constitutional law professors reviewing Rozmaryn's book.[49]

Further discussions were stimulated by institutional developments in other socialist countries. In 1963, Yugoslavia – as the first socialist country – decided to establish the Federal Constitutional Court, as well as constitutional courts at the level of each republic. Five years later, in 1968, Czechoslovakia changed its constitution that, along with the implementation of a federal structure of the state, provided a framework for the institutionalisation of the federal constitutional court. Although the Czechoslovak constitutional court never began to operate, this turn of events provided arguments for the supporters of constitutional review and posed a challenge to their opponents. Until that moment, the opponents justified their stance by pointing out that constitutional courts characterise capitalist states and, as such, it cannot be reconciled with the foundation of people's democracy, e.g. the principle of the people's sovereignty.

Following these events, other constitutional law academics started to argue in favour of some sort of the constitutional review of legislative acts: Siemieński (Adam Mickiewicz University),[50] and a prominent professor Burda (Maria Curie-Skłodowska University), who argued that judicial review of the constitutionality of statutes can be 'introduced in a socialist State without belittling the role and authority of parliamentary representation'.[51] Eventually, even Rozmaryn shifted away from the strict inadmissibility thesis.[52] As we would later see, the perspective of a fully-fledged constitutional court was still distant. Moreover, constitutional review at that time was justified in the Kelsenian manner as an instrument to secure

48 Jan Ziembiński, 'Sesja naukowa katedr prawa konstytucyjnego' (1961) (No 12) *Państwo i Prawo* 1051, 1053–1054.

49 Karol M. Pospieszalski, 'Recenzja: S. Rozmaryn Konstytucja jako ustawa zasadnicza PRL, Warszawa 1961' (1962) (No 1) *Ruch Prawniczy, Ekonomiczny i Socjologiczny* 305, 309. The author, in order to challenge the main Rozmaryn's argument referring to the position of Sejm as the supreme State authority, argued that if, according to the Constitution each authority, including Sejm, shall strictly observe the law, the notion of 'supreme authority' cannot be interpreted in such manner that would result in the exemption of Sejm from the force of system, created by the former. The supreme is not the authority itself – argued Pospieszalski – but the constitution adopted by such authority.

50 Feliks Siemieński, *Organy przedstawicielskie w systemie organów państwa socjalistycznego* (UMCS, 1964), 265–271.

51 Andrzej Burda, 'Janina Zakrzewska: Kontrola konstytucyjności ustaw (we współczesnym państwie burżuazyjnym), Warszawa 1964, Wyd. Prawnicze' (1956) *Państwo i Prawo* 865, 867. See also in this regard: Andrzej Burda, *Praworządność w systemie demokracji socjalistycznej* (Instytut Nauk prawnych IPN, 1967), 112.

52 In the second edition of his book, published in 1967, he admitted that under the Constitution of 1952 some limited form of constitutional review is admissible (exercised either by a special committee of the Sejm or by the Supreme Court, provided that the opinions or rulings of these bodies would not be binding upon the Sejm). He even suggested that the introduction of a fully-fledged constitutional court would have been theoretically possible, provided that the Constitution had been amended accordingly. See, Stefan Rozmaryn, *Konstytucja jako ustawa zasadnicza PRL*, 2nd ed. (Państwowe Wydawnictwo Naukowe, 1967), 215.

the separation of powers and hierarchy of law rather than the guardian of individual rights. In any case, the shifts that might be observed in the Polish legal discourse at that time[53] were a clear sign that the theoretical dispute over the admissibility of constitutional review was open and its outcome was not yet sealed.

15.2.4 *The Correction Period (1968–1979): Taking Constitutional Law Theory Seriously*

15.2.4.1 March 1968 and Its Consequences

In the mid-1960s the situation in Poland was gloomy. The disparity between the expectations raised by the Polish October and the reality of life in the post-1956 era was striking.[54] The political elites were faced with domestic and international economic problems. To unload the growing disappointment within the society, the Party – following the conflict of the Soviet Union with Israel in June 1967 – decided to launch an anti-Jewish campaign. Not only were the Jews used as scapegoats for the disappointments of the post-1956 period but they also served the Polish communist leader, Gomułka, as an excuse to combat revisionism among the intelligentsia and the political establishment.

These developments were followed by the series of protests among students and intellectuals, culminating in the events known as March 1968. The protests were brutally quelled and student strikes suppressed. Thousands of Poles of Jewish origin – including, above all, academics, professionals and party officials – had to leave Poland. Paradoxically, however, as one author noted, these events were tantamount to the end of Marxism as a living theoretical and philosophical phenomenon.[55] On the one hand, it was the simple consequence of the expulsion of Marxists thinkers. On the other hand, the very fact of launching the anti-Jewish campaign undermined and compromised the ideological underpinnings of the socialist regime, which had built its legitimacy on the alleged ethical superiority over fascism and Nazism.

Following trends present in other social sciences,[56] Marxism practically disappeared as a methodological orientation in legal science. The alleged commitment to Marxism, if made at all, was merely a formal declaration. Its sole purpose was to facilitate the given work to pass the censorship but it had no consequences for the

[53] According to Janusz Trzciński, *Funkcja prawna konstytucji socjalistycznej* (Wydawnictwo Uniwersytetu Wrocławskiego, 1978), 128–129, Poland was one of the only countries, along with Yugoslavia and Czechoslovakia, where constitutional judicial review became a subject of broader academic discussions.

[54] Dariusz Stola, *Kampania antysyjonistyczna w Polsce 1967–1968* (Instytut Studiów Politycznych PAN, 2000), 13–27.

[55] Marek J. Siemek, 'Filozofia i społeczeństwo w powojennej Polsce', in Marek J. Siemek (ed.), *Wolność, rozum, intersubiektywność* (Oficyna naukowa, 2002), 320.

[56] Ibid.

merits. This development is clearly visible in the Polish theory of law but also in the constitutional law discourse of that time, which was additionally challenged by the institutional developments in the Eastern bloc that undermined the basic principles of the socialist constitutional doctrine, such as the emergence of constitutional courts. Initially, the authors who had been sceptical about constitutional judicial review modified the inadmissibility thesis. They argued that constitutional review was inadmissible under the socialist constitution as a matter of principle, but with an important exemption of the federal states.[57] Eventually, even this assertion did not fully correspond to reality.[58] Thus, the inadmissibility thesis became more and more difficult to defend.

15.2.4.2 The Revival of the Constitutional Law Discourse in the Late 1960s and Early 1970s

At that time, one may speak of a revival of the constitutional law discourse.[59] Discussions from that period concerned, among other things, the possibility of changing the character of the socialist constitution from the 'constitution of state' to the 'constitution of and for the society'.[60] They also concerned increasing the significance of the rule of law principle and its institutional safeguards in the post-1956 period.[61] Some authors had openly criticised the reality of real socialism as failing to realise the ideal of rule of law.[62] Above all, the main interest of the constitutional law theory shifted towards the ways to ensure the conformity of laws with the constitution.[63] This shift was openly explained by the disparity between the doctrine of constitutional supremacy and the practice of State authorities.[64] It was also noted that, in socialist constitutionalism, there was a visible trend of institutionalising some form of constitutional review, which was explained by the tendency to

57 See Brzezinski, *The Struggle for Constitutionalism in Poland*, 23, who noted that 'the establishment of the Constitutional Court was a radical departure from the theory of unity of State power, and the Soviet regime legitimised this development by maintaining that Yugoslavia, as a federal system, required a limited form of judicial review to settle disputes between republics'.

58 On this, see note 77.

59 See Blokker, *New Democracies in Crisis?*, 65, who argued that 'from the 1970s onwards, a heightened interest in constitutionalism and constitutionality could be noticed in communist Poland'.

60 This change was understood as an ongoing process of constitutionalisation of the social sphere, meanwhile the traditional 'constitution of state' was associated with solely legal and political realm. See, Jerzy Stembrowicz, 'Konstytucja a ustrój państwowy i społeczny' (1971) *Państwo i Prawo* 231; Witold Zakrzewski, 'Konstytucja państwa a konstytucja społeczeństwa' (1969) (No 11) *Państwo i Prawo* 778; see also: Kazimierz Działocha, 'Konstytucja PRL po nowelizacji z 10 II 1976 (Uwagi o zmianie koncepcji konstytucji)' (1977) (No 2) *Państwo i Prawo* 5, 7.

61 Andrzej Burda, 'Instytucjonalne gwarancje praworządności i ich rola w państwie socjalistycznym' (1971) (No 8–9) *Państwo i Prawo* 215, 215.

62 Ibid., 227, as well as Andrzej Gwiżdż, 'Główne kierunki rozwoju współczesnego konstytucjonalizmu socjalistycznego' (1971) (No 8–9) *Państwo i Prawo* 244, 248.

63 Burda, 'Instytucjonalne gwarancje praworządności', 227–228.

64 Gwiżdż, 'Główne kierunki rozwoju', 248.

strengthen the constitution as a legislative rather than a purely political act.[65] Further discussions in this regard were stimulated by political actors. In December 1971, the Sixth General Assembly of the PZPR announced preparations for an amendment of the Constitution. This event provoked constitutional law theoreticians to discuss the desired direction of this change. They put particular emphasis on ensuring the conformity of laws with the constitution.[66]

The most important contribution was published by Siemieński, who openly challenged the inadmissibility thesis.[67] He started from an observation that the problem of conformity of laws with the constitution arises only in those legal systems that differentiate between ordinary legislative acts (statutes) and acts enjoying a superior status (the constitution, basic law). In this sense, the problem of constitutional review is inherently associated with those legal systems that have written constitutions and in which there is a basis for differentiating between the constitution-maker (i.e. the State authority that adopts the constitution, such as the constituent assembly) and the ordinary law-maker (e.g. a state authority that adopts ordinary statutes, such as the parliament).[68] Siemieński argued that, as a consequence, the problem of constitutional review arises in all socialist states as all of them bear such features, regardless of whether they are of a federal or unitary structure.[69]

This observation allowed the author to challenge the main argument of the opponents of constitutional review in socialist states, namely its alleged incompatibility with the character of the Sejm as the supreme organ of state authority. The parliament – argued Siemieński – cannot be equated with the Sovereign.[70] No constitution defines the parliament as a Sovereign. In modern constitutionalism the Sovereign is 'the nation', 'the people' or 'the monarch'. This is accurate also when it comes to socialist constitutions, including the Constitution of 1952, according to which the 'working people' are the holder of the supreme power. If so, the constitution-maker, while empowering the legislature to adopt legislative acts, might simultaneously set up an authority that would evaluate the conformity of legislative acts with the constitution. If it would have been otherwise, one could not claim that the constitution-maker is in its actions 'sovereign'.[71]

Having argued that a constitutional court by no means limits the supremacy of the Sejm, Siemieński also challenged the idea that the absence of provisions allowing

[65] Ibid.

[66] See Zbigniew Witkowski, 'Rada Państwa jako organ czuwający nad zgodnością Prawa z Konstytucją' (1977) *Państwo i Prawo* 37, 37. See also: Bogusia Puchalska, *Limits to Democratic Constitutionalism in Central and Eastern Europe* (Ashgate, 2011) 42, who spoke of a 'fundamental turn in constitutional thinking by the main political powers' that were happening at that time.

[67] Feliks Siemieński, 'Problem kontroli konstytucyjności ustaw w państwie socjalistycznym' (1972) (No 4) *Ruch Prawniczy, Ekonomiczny i Socjologiczny* 1.

[68] Ibid., 1–4.

[69] Ibid., 25.

[70] Ibid., 18.

[71] Ibid., 20.

explicitly for judicial review in the constitution excludes the admissibility of such a mechanism. The author referred in this regard to the case of the United States[72], where judicial review was established by the means of constitutional interpretation.[73] Thus, according to Siemieński, what mattered was that the constitution did not rule out judicial review explicitly. The main argument in favour of the constitutional court was the very existence of the legally binding constitution. If such a document was to impact reality, institutional safeguards for its observance needed to be established.[74]

As the constitutional law theory became pluralistic at that time, Siemieński did not become such an influential figure as Rozmaryn in the 1950s and 1960s. Nevertheless, it is clear that his distinction between the superior constitution-maker and the 'ordinary' law-maker challenged the main theoretical argument underpinning the inadmissibility thesis. Thus, he offered a theoretical justification for institutional changes that began in the region in the 1960s and that were to happen also in Poland in the 1970s and 1980s.

15.2.4.3 Institutional Reforms of the 1970s

The shifts in constitutional theory were followed by institutional reforms that aimed to meet growing demands for limited constitutional review. In March 1972, the Parliamentary Legislative Work Committee (*Sejmowa Komisja Prac Ustawodawczych*) was established. Its main task was to evaluate the drafts of statutes for compliance with the principles of legislative technique and the binding legal provisions. Its establishment was positively received by constitutional law scholars, who saw it as the institutionalisation of the intra-parliamentary model of the constitutional review of draft laws. Due to its non-binding character, this model was deemed compatible with the principle of the sovereignty of the people.[75] As one may guess, however, the establishment of the Committee was of marginal significance as a safeguard of the rule of law.[76] To provide for the legal rather than only the declarative supremacy of the Constitution, further institutional reforms were needed. On the 10 February 1976, four years after the Sixth General Assembly of PZPR announced that a constitutional amendment was being prepared, the Constitution was eventually amended. The February Amendment, co-drafted by constitutional law professors, empowered the State Council (the principal executive authority of the Sejm) to 'supervise the compliance of law with the Constitution'. Assigning such a competence to the State Council, as an authority subordinated to

[72] This fact alone demonstrates how the constitutional law discourse evolved over the years. Back in Rozmaryn's era, the case of the USA was only cited to depict the flaws of the Western bourgeois constitutionalism. See for example: Rozmaryn, *Polskie prawo państwowe*, 301–302 or Rozmaryn, 'Kontrola konstytucyjności ustaw' (part 1), 52–60.

[73] Siemieński, 'Problem kontroli konstytucyjności ustaw', 12.

[74] Ibid., 26.

[75] Witkowski, 'Rada Państwa jako organ czuwający', 40.

[76] See Leszek Garlicki, 'Reforma wymiaru sprawiedliwości a kontrola konstytucyjności ustaw' (1982) (No 1–2) *Państwo i Prawo* 34, 36.

the Sejm, was in line with the tendencies in other socialist countries[77] and, as such, it was generally positively received in the constitutional law discourse.[78]

At the same time, the amendment led to controversies, thereby reviving the Polish constitutional law discourse. The constitutional law academics generally assessed the new constitutional provision as too general and, as such, causing interpretative problems. It was argued that the law-maker should adopt a statute that would allow the State Council to exercise its new competence. The main controversy concerned the scope of this competence, in particular, whether the State Council was entitled to control the compliance of legislative acts with the constitution. Opponents of such an interpretation of the amendment argued that the amendment's authors 'unluckily' used a too broad notion of 'law'. To them, it was clear that the State Council, as a body subordinated to the Sejm, lacked the competence to control the compliance of legislative acts with the constitution. Rather, the new competence was to cover only the legal acts issued by the other state authorities, excluding the Sejm.[79] In contrast, the proponents of the 'full' constitutional review relied on the linguistic meaning of the amendment and argued that the extension of the competence of the State Council to all normative acts did not undermine the supreme position of the Sejm.[80]

The concretisation of the State Council's competence took place three years later, through the adoption of the resolution of 14 July 1979.[81] The resolution was well received in the legal scholarship.[82] However, the State Council's new competence, similarly to that of the Parliamentary Legislative Work Committee, had no practical significance for safeguarding the rule of law.[83] Nevertheless, it was an important step towards the fully-fledged constitutional judicial review.[84]

77 Earlier, similar developments took place in Romania (1965) and Hungary (1972). In GDR the State Council was entitled to review the constitutionality of laws under the Constitution of 1949 in its original content.

78 See Andrzej Gwiżdż, 'Trybunał Konstytucyjny' (1983) (No 1–2) *Państwo i Prawo* 3, 7–8, who praised the amendment as the reflection of the rule that 'there can be no law but that which is consistent with the constitution'.

79 See, Witkowski, 'Rada Państwa jako organ czuwający', 42 and Stembrowicz, 'Konstytucja a ustrój państwowy i społeczny', 63.

80 See Stanisław Gebert, 'Czuwanie przez Radę Państwa nad zgodnością prawa z Konstytucją' (1980) *Państwo i Prawo* 26, 28 and 34; Andrzej N. Wróblewski, 'Kontrola konstytucyjności prawa w państwach socjalistycznych' (1978) *Państwo i Prawo* 47, 52.

81 The resolution provided for the very limited model of constitutional review, as regards its scope (non-parliamentary acts, international agreements and draft of statutes) as well as its legal consequences (the state organ that issued the act that was later found as violating a statute or the constitution, was only obliged to inform the State Council about the steps that it undertook to eliminate 'irregularities' found by the State Council). Not surprisingly, the State Council had never exercised its competence in this regard.

82 See for instance: Gebert, 'Czuwanie przez Radę Państwa', 41.

83 See Garlicki, 'Reforma wymiaru sprawiedliwości', 36; Tadeusz Ereciński, 'Aktualne problemy ustroju sądownictwa' (1981) *Państwo i Prawo* 18, 30; Wróblewski, 'Kontrola konstytucyjności', 60.

84 See Działocha, 'Konstytucja PRL po nowelizacji', 14; Wróblewski, 'Kontrola konstytucyjności', 56.

15.2.5 *Decline Period (1979–1989): Towards Fully-Fledged Constitutional Review?*

15.2.5.1 From the Emergence of Civil Society to the Institutional Reforms of the Early 1980s

In the late 1970s, civil society began to emerge in Poland. The Amendment of 1976 also brought other constitutional changes. The one that attracted the greatest public interest emphasised Poland's 'fraternal ties with the Soviet Union' and enshrined the leading role of the Party. Although similar amendments were introduced in other countries of the Warsaw Pact at that time, in the case of Poland, the amendment – exceptionally and surprisingly – caused vigorous protests, coming from the intelligentsia and the Church.[85] The amendment was seen as undermining the very sovereignty of the country and as something that could be used in the future as an excuse for military intervention in Poland.[86]

Simultaneously, the regime suffered from serious and structural economic problems. As the government presented a plan for a sudden increase in the price of many basic commodities, a series of protests and demonstrations took place, known in the history of PRL as June 1976. The protests were quelled again. However, they turned out to be successful to some extent. The plan for the price increase was shelved and the Prime Minister dismissed. In the aftermath, intelligentsia founded an opposition organisation, the Workers' Defence Committee (*Komitet Obrony Robotników – KOR*), whose aim was to provide legal and financial support to the workers persecuted after June 1976. The emergence of KOR is usually considered as the beginning of civil society in Poland, which made space for further developments in this regard, particularly the emergence of Solidarity in the 1980s.

Subsequently, in the attempt to accommodate further demands for the safeguards of the legality of the state apparatus, the regime considered the introduction of the judicial review of individual administrative decisions and executive regulations,[87] as was already the case in other socialist countries.[88] On 31 January 1980, the Sejm amended the code of administrative procedure and established the Supreme Administrative Court (*Naczelny Sąd Administracyjny* – NSA). The NSA has been empowered to apply a limited form of judicial review as regards the executive regulations and individual administrative decisions. As it has been noted, despite

[85] See Garlicki, 'O mój Rozmarynie'. The regime realised that 'some part of the society treats the constitution seriously'. See also Brzezinski, *The Struggle for Constitutionalism in Poland*, 74, who underlined the exceptional character and importance of the criticism of this amendment. In his view, this 'criticism … represented the first time that the totalitarian foundation of the regime, rather than its individual policies, were openly attacked'.

[86] Brzezinski, *The Struggle for Constitutionalism in Poland*, 73.

[87] Note that the call for the introduction of judicial review of administrative decisions, as it was noted earlier, was expressed in the constitutional law doctrine as the aftermath of October 1956.

[88] Earlier, the administrative judiciary was successfully implemented in Yugoslavia (1952), Hungary (1957), Romania (1967) and Bulgaria (1970).

the limitation of its jurisdiction, 'the NSA quickly assumed an active role in protecting individual rights against arbitrary administrative actions'.[89]

Although the establishment of the NSA played a crucial role in the increase of the legality of administrative actions, it could not remedy to the PRL's economic problems. These problems led to massive workers' protests in the Lenin Shipyard in Gdańsk in August 1980. The protests ended on 31 August 1980 with the conclusion of the Gdańsk Agreement between the Solidarity trade union and the government. The Gdańsk Agreement secured a right to strike and officially recognised the Solidarity as an independent trade union, the first in the whole Eastern Bloc. The Solidarity – not only a trade union but a broad social movement – represented at some point one-third of the country's working-age population. It played a key role in the reforms of the 1980s that heralded the end of the real socialism in the region and prompted a liberalisation of the regime, which, however, only lasted until December 1981, when the regime introduced the Martial Law.[90]

In this period, the institutionalisation of constitutional judicial review became a matter of broad consensus within legal academia,[91] including leading constitutional law scholars, such as the already mentioned Burda, Siemieński[92] and Leszek Garlicki,[93] later to be joined by Andrzej Gwiżdż[94] and others.[95] The arguments supporting the inadmissibility thesis of constitutional judicial review, as one author

[89] See Brzezinski, *The Struggle for Constitutionalism in Poland*, 139–140, where the author noted that 'NSA was directly relying on Constitution to support its rulings, and were dealing with many constitutional problems, particularly concerning the constitutional parameters of executive branch law-making'. 'In this way' – argued Brzezinski – 'the NSA acted as a custodian of Constitution and created an atmosphere favourable to the further development of mechanisms of constitutional protection'.

[90] In view of further developments, it seems justified to claim that Martial Law only constrained but did not destroy the public demand for the democratisation of the regime. On the role of the Gdansk agreement, as well as the importance of the discourse of rights in the Solidarity's struggle for the constitutional rule, see Jarosław Kuisz, *Charakter prawny porozumień sierpniowych 1980–1981* (Warszawa, 2009), 469–478.

[91] Garlicki, 'Reforma wymiaru sprawiedliwości', 35, who argued that, although the call for institu tionalisation of constitutional judicial review in the Polish socialist doctrine was present from the late 1960s, it was the 'August breakthrough' that allowed for the rearticulation of this call and made space for its potential realisation.

[92] From that time, see, Feliks Siemieński, 'Pozycja ustrojowa i właściwość Trybunału Konstytucyjnego' (1985) 4 *Ruch Prawniczy Ekonomiczny i Socjologiczny* 7.

[93] It is worth noting, however, that Garlicki supported the idea of empowering the Supreme Court with the judicial review of conformity of laws with the constitution, rather than the setting up of a separate specialised constitutional court. See Garlicki, 'Reforma wymiaru sprawiedliwości', 35.

[94] Gwiżdż, 'Trybunał Konstytucyjny', 9.

[95] See Trzciński, *Funkcja prawna konstytucji socjalistycznej*, 127–139; Hanna Suchocka, *Konstytucyjne gwarancje praworządności w europejskich państwach socjalistycznych* (Wydawnictwo Naukowe UAM, 1979), 35; Michał Domagała, *Kontrola zgodności prawa z konstytucją w europejskich państwach socjalistycznych* (Wydawnictwo prawnicze, 1986), 4; Jerzy Bafia, *Praworządność* (Książka i Wiedza, 1985), 102–105.

argued, were at that moment deemed to be 'based either on a misunderstanding or on legal sophistry'.[96]

Most importantly, the support for the establishment of a constitutional court at that time went way beyond academic circles and was shared by prominent social and political actors. This idea was initially proposed by the National Congress of the Bar (*Ogólnopolski Zjazd Adwokatury*) in January 1981.[97] Two months later, in March 1981, the Twelfth Congress of SD, expressed its support for deep institutional reforms, advocating for the establishment of the Tribunal of the State, the Ombudsman, the Senate and the constitutional court, also providing an outline for the institutional arrangement of these new bodies. Surprisingly, this time the SD was backed by the PZPR. The Ninth Extraordinary Assembly of PZPR obliged the PZPR's parliamentary club to consider either the establishment of a constitutional court or to empower the Supreme Court to examine the compliance of laws with the Constitution. Eventually, the idea of a constitutional court was also supported by the Solidarity on its First National Congress that took place in October 1981.[98] Thus, this idea united the opposing political and social actors, such as the legal academia, legal practitioners, the socialist government and the democratic opposition.

Whether at that time we can speak of any significant change as regards the justification of the constitutional review is not clear. On the one hand, as early as in the mid-1970s. there were some political and legal developments that were indicating the future emergence of a language of rights in the region.[99] This was followed with the emergence of civil society, including Solidarity, that certainly picked up the language of rights, but at the same time continued to think of a constitutional court as above all the guarantor of formally understood legality and compliance of ordinary laws with constitution.[100] In any case, the shift towards right-based justification of constitutional review was not reflected in the constitutional law discourse, and more importantly in the practice of the Constitutional Tribunal, that, as discussed in the reaminder of this section, in its first years of operation secured the

96 Jerzy Kowalski, 'Problemy reformy systemu politycznego Polskiej Rzeczypospolitej Ludowej' (1981) *Państwo i Prawo* 3, 6.

97 Resolution of the Ogólnopolski Zjazd Adwokatury from 4 January 1981 (1981) 3–4 *Palestra* 198. On the role of the bar in the institutionalisation of the constitutional court, see Zdzisław Czeszejko-Sochacki, 'Trybunał Konstytucyjny a adwokatura' (1986) (No 2) *Palestra* 1.

98 See *Resolution of the First National Congress of Solidarity no. 28/81*, especially the thesis no. 23, available at www.solidarnosc.org.pl/ws/wp-content/uploads/2010/10/1-KZD-I-tura-Gda%C5%84sk-1981.pdf.

99 In 1975, Helsinki Final Act was signed by PRL and other socialist countries. Subsequently, on 3 March 1977 UN International Covenants on Human Rights were ratified. On the importance of the latter for the changes in the Polish legal system, see Ereciński, 'Aktualne problemy ustroju sądownictwa', 19.

100 See Resolution no. 28/81 (n 98), thesis no. 23, where the need for higher protection of the individual rights and freedoms was stressed, and institutionalisation of the constitutional court was in fact deemed as one of the means to achieve this aim, but, on the other hand, in the excerpt devoted to the constitutional court itself, its role was explained in a purely Kelsenian manner.

constitutional role of the Sejm rather than protected rights of individuals. In this sense, one may claim that, despite some developments in this regard, eventually the right-based justification of the constitutional review was not reflected in the constitutional law discourse, that till the end of communist regime remained under classic Kelsenian imaginary in this regard.

15.2.5.2 The Establishment of the Constitutional Tribunal and Other Institutional Reforms

Following this broad and exceptional consensus, in November 1981, the Sejm appointed the Committee of Experts consisting of constitutional law professors from the leading law faculties that would examine the possibility of setting up a constitutional court in a socialist State.[101] The Committee carried on its task despite the announcement of Martial Law in December 1981, which aimed to combat and curb the growing democratic opposition centred around Solidarity. In January 1982, the idea of a constitutional court was confirmed by the new communist leader, Jaruzelski.[102] Eventually, a draft constitutional amendment was submitted to the Sejm in February 1982 and adopted in March 1982. The March Amendment provided for the creation of the Constitutional Tribunal and the State Tribunal.[103] Interestingly, the amendment was negatively received in other socialist countries, and there were voices that the Party should 'delay' the setting up of the Constitutional Tribunal, like in Czechoslovakia.[104]

Ordinary legislation was needed to operationalise the constitutional amendment, leading again to discussions in the constitutional law doctrine.[105] The Committee of Experts prepared a dozen drafts in three years. The main theoretical challenge for the Committee was to reconcile the concept of constitutional judicial review with the basic principles of socialist constitutionalism, such as the idea of the parliamentary supremacy and the unity of State power. The main practical challenge was to reconcile the idea of a constitutional court with the lack of political will to implement a judicial mechanism that would effectively examine the constitutionality of governmental actions.[106]

The statute creating the Constitutional Tribunal was eventually adopted on 29 April 1985. Unsurprisingly, the constitutional review was to be limited in scope

[101] The Committee consisted of professors from leading Polish law faculties elected by: PZPR (A. Burda from Maria Curie-Skłodowska University and L. Kubicki from Polish Academy of Sciences), SD (J. Jodłowski from University of Warsaw and A. Gubiński from University of Warsaw) and Zjednoczone Stronnictwo Ludowe (H. Groszyk and J. Ziembińskim, both from Maria Curie-Skłodowska University), to be joined by non-partisan A. Gwiżdż (University of Warsaw).

[102] Gwiżdż, 'Trybunał Konstytucyjny', 4.

[103] The State Tribunal (*Trybunał Stanu*) was an impeachment court deciding on the criminal liability for constitutional and statutory infringements by high State officials. These officials were to become accountable for abuses committed while in office for the first time.

[104] See Zdzisław Czeszejko-Sochacki, *Trybunał Konstytucyjny PRL* (Książka i Wiedza, 1986), 46–49.

[105] See for example: Gwiżdż, 'Trybunał Konstytucyjny'.

[106] On this see notes 123–125.

and as regards the access to the TK. The TK was entitled to review laws and statutes that came into power only after the adoption of the 1982 Amendment, and it generally could not review international agreements.[107] Its rulings were final only with regard to executive regulations, whereas its decisions regarding the constitutionality of statutes could be rejected by the Sejm. Moreover, the statute ruled out *actio popularis* (the individual right of petition), providing that constitutional review might be only initiated by official State authorities, which meant that the democratic opposition centred around the Solidarity could not benefit from the new institution.

This limited constitutional review received mixed reactions. In the legal scholarship, it was mainly praised, first and foremost, for its due regard to the principles of socialist constitutionalism.[108] Such a position was taken surprisingly even by Siemieński, seemingly a zealous supporter of the idea of a fully-fledged constitutional court.[109] It was also shared by one of the members of the Committee (Gwiżdż), who praised the Polish lawmakers for solving the problem of constitutional review in a socialist State in the 'correct and only possible manner'.[110] However, in an interview published in a nation-wide newspaper, the other members of the Committee (Ziembiński) admitted that, as drafters, they were not fully satisfied with the final outcome of their cooperation with the parliament. Ziembiński stated that, although the TK might be considered a 'child' of professors Gwiżdż, Groszyk and Ziembiński, the final draft of the statute only partially reflected their propositions.[111] The main flaws of the TK, according to the quoted author, were the already mentioned limited scope of review, the limited access to it and the only partially binding character of its rulings in the case of statutes.[112] This led Ziembiński to a somewhat bitter conclusion that the statute on the TK, as drafted by the Sejm, was a 'compromise between the needs and possibilities', which would

[107] In view of the ratification of international human rights treaties in the late 1970s (see, n 99) it was a clear sign that the Tribunal was not designed to become a guardian of individual rights.

[108] See Domagała, *Kontrola zgodności prawa*, 102–110, who affirmatively discussed the institutional set-up of the TK as the reflection of the supremacy of parliament over the Tribunal. Interestingly, the subordination of the Tribunal towards the Sejm also had a symbolic character, as its initial seat was located in the basement of the Sejm.

[109] See Siemieński, 'Pozycja ustrojowa i właściwość Trybunału Konstytucyjnego', 12, where the author affirmatively discussed the supremacy of the Sejm over the Tribunal and ibid., 34–35, where the author in the conclusion described the institutional set-up of the Tribunal as 'optimal'.

[110] Gwiżdż, 'Trybunał Konstytucyjny', 10–11.

[111] Stanisław Jadczak, 'Dobrze, że będzie' – interview from 20 January 1985 with Jan Ziembiński, professor of law from Marie Skłodowska-Curie University (1985) 29 Polityka, https://trybunal.gov.pl/fileadmin/content/dokumenty/pierwsza-rozprawa/Dobrze_ze_bedzie_wywiad_z_Janem_Ziembinskim.pdf.

[112] See ibid., where Ziembiński described this feature of the adopted model of constitutional review as its 'shortcoming' and stated that 'it is the most courteous solution in the contemporary law, as the parliament would decide whether the statute, adopted by this parliament, is in compliance with the Constitution or not'. This feature of the TK was also negatively assessed by Leszek Garlicki, *Ewolucja polskiego prawa państwowego w latach 1980–1982* (IOZiDK, 1983), 38, who argued that, in the view of this limitation, the Tribunal 'is not a constitutional court in the appropriate meaning of this notion'.

result in the 'original Polish model of the Constitutional Tribunal', of which the biggest advantage was that 'it would exist', and which was truly needed in a country in which the legality of State actions was often a fiction.[113]

15.2.5.3 The Functioning of the Constitutional Tribunal: Between Dependency and Independency?

Despite the mixed assessment of the newly created body in the legal scholarship, it should be stressed that, with its establishment in 1985, PRL became the only country in the Warsaw Pact with a constitutional court. The Tribunal was filled mainly with legal academics.[114] That was a clear sign that the Tribunal – addressing in this regard normative claims present in legal scholarship[115] – was going to build its epistemic authority on the idea of scientificity as the guarantee of objectivity and the apoliticality of the constitutional adjudication.[116] As I have tried to show elsewhere, this legitimation strategy was strictly related to the general legitimation strategy characteristic for Polish jurisprudence, which is based on the ideas of scientificity, objectiveness and apoliticality.[117]

The TK began to operate on 1 January 1986. Its very first ruling of 28 May 1986 (U 1/86), just as most of its further cases from the period 1986–1989,[118] concerned the conformity of executive regulations to parliamentary legislation.[119] Although the case itself was of little political importance, the TK managed to make out of it a case of constitutional significance, using it to curb the scope of the law-making powers of the executive authorities. The TK underlined that, under the Constitution of 1952, the executive authority must exercise its rule-making powers in strict compliance with the statutory delegation clause. This meant that the law could no longer be created by executive authorities to the detriment of the Sejm's prerogatives. Therefore, 28 May 1986 might be treated as a symbolic end date of the façade

[113] Jadczak, 'Dobrze, że będzie'.

[114] Out of the original twelve judges of the Tribunal, nine were professors closely related to the academia (including former deans and rectors) and the remaining three had a more judicial background. The field of expertise of the 'academic' judges varied from criminal law (K. Buchała, S. Pawela), through administrative (A. Kabat) and financial law (N. Gajl), to international (A. Klafkowski, H. de Fiumel, L. Łukaszuk) and constitutional law (K. Działocha), as well as the theory of State and law (H. Groszyk).

[115] The postulate that the TK should be an expert, apolitical and scientific body has been present in the doctrine of constitutional review from its emergence. In this regard see, above all, Siemieński, 'Problem kontroli konstytucyjności ustaw', 22–24.

[116] On this topic see, Hanna Dębska, 'Trybunał Konstytucyjny w poszukiwaniu legitymizacji. Szkic z socjologii prawa' (2015) 4 *Studia prawnicze* 23.

[117] Zomerski, *W kierunku demokratycznej nauki prawa?*

[118] See Brzezinski, *The Struggle for Constitutionalism in Poland*, 158, who noted that in the years 1986–1989, of the 33 cases reviewed in this period, only three involved parliamentary statutes, of which only one statute has been found 'partially inconsistent' with the Constitution of 1952.

[119] On this judgement and its constitutional significance, see Leszek Garlicki, 'Pierwsze orzeczenie Trybunału Konstytucyjnego (Refleksje w 15 lat później)', in Adam Jankiewicz and Ferdynand Rymarz (eds.), *Trybunał Konstytucyjny: Księga XV-lecia* (Biuro Trybunału Konstytucyjnego, 2001).

constitutionalism: the theoretical principle of the alleged supremacy of the parliament over the executive power, repeated like a mantra in the constitutional law doctrine from 1944 onwards, eventually became a normative standard that the state authorities needed to observe. That meant that the biggest beneficiary of constitutional review, as it was expected in the legal scholarship,[120] became the Sejm, as the TK in its first years of operation assumed a role of a guardian of the parliamentary prerogatives rather than a guardian of the constitution and rights of individuals.[121] This changed in 1989, when the TK assumed a more active role in the shift towards a fully-fledged constitutional democracy.[122]

The TK did not subdue to the intents of its authors who tried to make it a weak and façade body. This surprising development led commentators in the 1990s to describe it as an 'unwanted child of the previous regime' that was only forced on political authorities.[123] According to this narrative, the reforms of the 1980s, including the establishment of the TK, the State Tribunal, and the Ombudsman in 1987, were made only to legitimise the regime in the eyes of foreign countries rather than truly rebuilding the structure of State power.[124] As such, they were never considered as being able to change the very essence of the political system: the leading role of the Party.[125] But the regime lost control over the course of events. The institutions introduced to strengthen the legitimacy of the regime in decline, acting as checks against the most striking abuses of power by State authorities, managed to reform it from the inside and push towards further changes that eventually ended the socialist authoritarian rule. Although the analysis of factors that allowed TK for such a reform from the inside goes beyond this chapter, it seems that the efficiency of this process confirms the above-mentioned autonomy of academia in PRL and, at the same

120 See Gwiżdż, 'Trybunał Konstytucyjny', 15, who in the conclusion stated that in the view of the institutional set up of the Tribunal 'it would be to the lesser extent the organ of judiciary control over the activities of the parliament, but rather the organ of the parliamentary control over the activities of the administration'.

121 Brzezinski, *The Struggle for Constitutionalism in Poland*, 159.

122 About this shift, see ibid., 161–165.

123 See Janina Zakrzewska, 'Trybunał Konstytucyjny – konstytucja – państwo prawa' (1992) (No 1) *Państwo i Prawo* 3, 6–7, who, discussing the context of the establishment of the TK, claimed that in 1982 the authorities were 'under tremendous popular pressure' to increase the accountability of the regime, which was only constrained but not destroyed by Martial Law. At the same time, however, the regime did not want to resign from its monopoly of power and the lack of accountability. In consequence, the regime agreed to address 'certain popular demands' in form rather than in substance. By doing so, the regime hoped that it would satisfy the society's democratic ambitions, meanwhile the structure of power would remain unchanged.

124 Such a view was expressed among others by a professor of legal history – Zygmnut Izdebski, as quoted by Brzezinski, *The Struggle for Constitutionalism in Poland*, 141. According to Izdebski, the regime introducing changes for the 'foreign consumption only' initially hoped to repeat Czechoslovakia's 'creation' of a constitutional court in 1968, that had never started to operate.

125 Kazimierz Działocha, 'Państwo prawne w warunkach zmian zasadniczych systemu prawa' (1992) (No 1) *Państwo i Prawo* 13, 27. See also: Jacek Kurczewski, *The Resurrection of Rights in Poland* (Clarendon Press, 1993) 18, who argued that the introduction of all these bodies was deemed to be unsatisfactory, as the public knew by experience that 'the invisible "leading role" of the Party is of decisive character'.

time, it proves that building epistemic authority of TK on the scientificity, apoliticallness and objectivity, occurred to be, at least in the period of transition, an effective legitimisation strategy.

15.3 CONCLUSION

In this chapter, I argued that the domestic constitutional law theory, as it evolved in 1944–1989, played an essential role in pushing Poland towards the direction of constitutional democracy which it eventually became in the post-1989 era. Is it naïve to assume that, in the authoritarian reality of PRL, the academia had any social agency? After all, one may claim, all the decisions were made by political elites that did not have to take into consideration the views present within the society. The political elites themselves were not even independent in their actions, as they had remained under a strong influence of the Soviet Union, were they? Perhaps, one may add, the changes in Poland were only a reflection of the greater changes in the whole Eastern Bloc that, starting from the 1980s, was in decline, caused mainly by economic problems.

It is important to stress, first and foremost, that the interplay between the events in the socio-political realm and the development of domestic constitutional law thought is beyond any doubt. Most important events in the history of PRL (October 1956, March 1968, December 1970, June 1976, August 1980), which all together gave birth to the civil society centred in the 1980s around the Solidarity, were accompanied and followed by the shifts in the constitutional law doctrine. The intellectual evolution was also possible thanks to the emergence of the new generation of constitutional law professors. Despite the initially façade character of the constitutional law doctrine, they had taken its substance seriously, namely not only as a legitimising tool of the socio-political and legal regime, but as a normative ideal that should be observed by State authorities. What facilitated this shift conceptually was the inclusion in the constitutional law theory from the first decades after the WWII theoretical claims compatible with the modern constitutionalism, such as the supremacy of constitution, its fully justiciable and binding character and its direct applicability. For all these reasons, tracing the evolution of the post-war Polish constitutional law theory, we speak of shifts and the evolution rather than raptures and the revolution.[126]

The conceptual easiness of this shift should not obscure its exceptional character. Poland – apart from Yugoslavia, that remained independent from the Soviet Union – was the only socialist country with an operating constitutional court in the

[126] See Blokker, *New Democracies in Crisis?*, 50, where the author claimed that the guiding principle of the Polish transformation was 'legal continuity' or ibid., 64, where he argued that in the Polish case it is more justifiable to speak of 'creeping constitutionalization' rather than 'constitutional revolution', as the main steps towards enhancing a constitutional dimension to the Polish political regime were already taken from the 1970s onwards.

region. Its establishment did not necessarily engender positive reactions in other socialist states. Thus, it is not possible to explain the emergence of the TK as a reflection of a broader tendency in the socialist bloc, as there was simply no such tendency. Or, to put it differently, in the absence of external factors that would explain the emergence of a constitutional court in socialist Poland, it is hard to downplay the role of internal factors. As I have demonstrated, the crucial role in this regard was played legal academia, which, starting from the late 1960s, developed a doctrine of constitutional review which eventually led to the establishment of a constitutional court – thanks to the emergence and efforts of the civil society in the 1980s.

Certainly, the decision to establish the TK was taken by the political elites rather than by professors of law. The representatives of legal academia, however, made this decision possible, as they delivered theoretical foundations for this decision. They also actively participated in setting up the Constitutional Tribunal. Subsequently, academics assumed the role of constitutional judges. As it has been noted in the literature, the epistemic authority of academia played a considerable role in building the authority of the TK as an objective and apolitical arbiter of State actions, which allowed the TK to push for the changes of the regime from within. These dynamics allowed for the transformation towards constitutional democracy, in which the TK played a crucial role. Thus, the constitutional law theory, which emerged in the 1950s as a façade legitimising the authoritarian rule, eventually became a solid foundation for the democratisation of the PRL. The role of constitutional law doctrine in PRL was more complex and ambiguous than it is usually admitted nowadays. Post-1989 constitutionalism did not appear out of nowhere, but – as in the case of many other European countries – from the internal demand to curb the authoritarian rulers.[127] This development was possible thanks to the pre-war constitutional traditions of the region,[128] as well as

[127] Consider that, in the context of many European countries, the institutionalisation of constitutional review was a reaction to the authoritarian past and was thought of as a vehicle from authoritarian rule to constitutional democracy or at least the safeguard of the latter. This observation seems to be accurate in the case of post-Nazi or post-fascist Western Germany and Italy (that institutionalised their constitutional courts in 1947), as well as post-authoritarian Greece (1975), Spain (1978) and Portugal (1982). Similarities between these countries do not stop here. They do concern not only the starting point (authoritarian past) but also the ending point: return to the family of European democracies. In this regard, note that the creation of a constitutional court in each of the said countries preceded the accession to the European structures (Italy and Western Germany – 1957, Greece – 1981, Spain and Portugal – 1986).

[128] Note that Poland, along with other countries from the region, such as Czechoslovakia, Hungary and Yugoslavia, had pre-1944 constitutional traditions. As examples of these traditions might serve pre-war constitutions of each of these countries (dating back in case of Poland to the Constitution of 1791, being the first such document in the European history) and Czechoslovakian constitutional court (being along with its Austrian counterpart the only such body in the pre-war period in Europe).

the survival of the non-socialist legal thought in the local constitutional imaginary.[129]

The argument presented here nuances the widely accepted narrative of the peculiarity and novelty of the emergence of constitutional rule in early 1990s in Central Eastern Europe. There are more similarities than differences between the countries of Western and Eastern Europe that wished to reject their authoritarian past through constitutionalism at different points in time. The similarities concern the aim of the reforms (a transition from authoritarianism to constitutional democracy seen as 'the return to Europe'), but also their theoretical foundations (the non-socialist legal thought, namely Kelsenism) as well as the institutional means implemented to achieve this aim (the constitutionally entrenched rule of law implemented and guarded by the specialised constitutional court). This observation, on the one hand, sheds some light on the normative value of the post-1989 Central Eastern European constitutionalism[130] but, on the other, it might imply that the emergence of the rule of law crisis in the region demands further explanations than those explaining it in terms of the alleged unsuccessful transplant surgery.[131] As addressing this issue in detail goes beyond the scope of this chapter, further discussions in this regard, especially investigating specific regional socio-political and economics factors, are needed.[132]

[129] It seems that there was nothing 'socialist' in the socialist constitutional law theory as it evolved in the 1970s and 1980s, even if authors put much effort to appear as they were deriving their theoretical views from the socialist legal tradition. Although it is hard to trace it with the scientific precision, as the scholars writing at that time were not explicitly referring to non-socialist authors, usually – due to the historical bounds of the region with Austria – it is assumed that it was Kelsenism that remained a tradition structuring regional legal minds. The internal logic of this tradition naturally led to the question of the conformity of higher laws with lower laws, which eventually brought about the institutionalisation of constitutional review.

[130] Note that the post-2015 subordination of the TK to ruling political elites was justified by domestic political actors as necessary due to the alleged post-communist and post-authoritarian origin of this body. See for example: Jarosław Kaczyński, 'Wykład na Uniwersytecie Jagiellońskim' (2010) 24 *Pressje* 222, 227, where the leader of Law and Justice party, holding a PhD degree in law, explained the emergence of TK, NSA as well as Ombudsman as the reflection of far-reaching phenomenon of 'juridification' of the socialist regime that allegedly allowed socialist elites to remain in power despite the breakdown of the socialist regime.

[131] Such a conclusion does not exclude that there was something peculiar in the emergence of constitutionalism in the region that would explain its further fatigue. Such a thesis should, however, be proved rather than simply assumed. One possible line of argument would be that the experience of fascism and Nazism – regarded as 'own', in contrast to socialism, which was imposed or at least perceived as such – had different implications for the constitutional sphere and the European integration project. See: Signe Rehling Larsen, 'Varieties of Constitutionalism in the European Union' (2021) 84(3) *Modern Law Review* 477.

[132] Luckily, such discussions are already taking place. See, for instance, Adam Czarnota, Martin Krygier and Wojciech Sadurski (eds.), *Anti-constitutional Populism* (Cambridge University Press, 2022), especially part 3, on the socio-political and economical roots of the crisis of rule of law in Poland and Hungary, including the chapters of Gabor Halmai, Paul Blokker and Michał Stambulski. See also: Wojciech Zomerski, 'Populism: What, Where and Why?' (2023) 175(1) *Thesis Eleven* 126.

16

Nordic Democratic Exceptionality after the End of History

A Neoliberalized Constitutional Imaginary?

Johan Strang

16.1 INTRODUCTION: NEOLIBERALIZATION OF NORDIC DEMOCRACY?

The Nordic countries have a long history of being celebrated, by themselves as well as by others, as 'models of democracy' and, to a certain extent, they continue to be so today. The starting point of this chapter is the observation that the nature and characteristics of the 'democracy' championed by the Nordics has changed. No longer distinctively connected to national and popular sovereignty, public participation, social or economic equality, or civil society and labour market arrangements, Nordic democratic exemplarity is today increasingly associated with rule of law, individual and human rights as well as economic freedom. No longer a social democratic alternative, the Nordic countries are today excelling as exemplars of the universal principles of (neo-)liberal democracy that became dominant after 'the end of history'.

There are always good reasons to be suspicious of claims to Nordic exceptionality. Nonetheless, this chapter proceeds from the idea that the Nordics shared a distinctive interpretation of the democratic ideals during the short twentieth century, the time that in Scandinavia itself has been labelled the Age of Social Democracy, the Labour Party State and the Golden Epoch of the Nordic Welfare State.[1] This distinctiveness was not so much a matter of different constitutional arrangements, but rather of the ideas, beliefs and values that determined the boundaries of the political discussions, that is, the constitutional imaginary of the Nordic post-war welfare states.[2] The Scandinavian anomaly becomes especially evident when one considers the recent literature on European post-war democracy. To be sure, like elsewhere in Western Europe, the democratic regime that emerged in Scandinavia

[1] Francis Sejersted, *The Age of Social Democracy: Norway and Sweden in the Twentieth Century* (Princeton University Press, 2011); Rune Slagstad, *De nasjonale strateger* (Pax forlag, 1998).

[2] Jan Komarek (ed.), *European Constitutional Imaginaries: Between Ideology and Utopia* (Oxford University Press, 2023).

after WWII was largely anti-ideological, corporatist, bureaucratic, mundane and male,[3] but it is less easy to see how the Nordic countries fit into post-war narratives of a 'Christian Democratic moment' or a 'centre-right political hegemony'.[4] Above all, it is very hard to force Scandinavia into Jan-Werner Müller's idea of a 'constrained democracy'.[5] According to Müller, the lesson from the interwar period, the totalitarian experience and WWII was that popular sovereignty was perilous and that democracy had to be protected from being its own wrong. The solutions included rigid constitutions guarding the rights of the citizens on the one hand, and an international framework of treaties and courts that kept the national government in line on the other hand. Contributing to all of this was also a threat from domestic as well as Soviet communism. As such, it has been argued that post-war constitutionalism and the Western European engagement in human rights emerged primarily with the conservative aim of restricting the power of the national governments or even as a romantic quest for a lost Christian civilisation.[6]

The Scandinavian constitutional imaginary of the post-war era was built on very different premises. The prevailing interpretation was that it had been the solid democratic traditions on the one hand and the progressive policies of the Social Democratic governments on the other hand, that had saved the Nordics from totalitarianism. 'Constraining' democracy was not on the agenda, as that would endanger rather than protect democracy. It would alienate citizens from the state and make it more difficult for the governments to pursue the progressive policies needed to protect democracy in the first place. In contrast to Müller's idea of a 'European post-war democratic settlement', historians have therefore proposed a 'Scandinavian post-war democratic settlement' that could be understood in terms of a special 'social democratic constitutionalism' or a 'popular constitutionalism built on a folkish heritage'.[7]

Among the key elements of this constitutional imaginary was the idea that popular sovereignty was firmly in the hands of the national parliaments, while the judiciary was comparatively weak. Indeed, according to the Scandinavian legal realists, who

3 Martin Conway, *Western Europe's Democratic Age 1945–1968* (Princeton University Press, 2020).

4 Martin Conway, 'The Rise and Fall of Europe's Democratic Age' (2004) 13 *Contemporary European History* 67; Marco Duranti, *The Conservative Human Rights Revolution: European Identity, Transnational Politics and the Origins of the European Convention* (Oxford University Press, 2017).

5 Jan-Werner Müller, *Contesting Democracy: Political Ideas in Twentieth Century Europe* (Yale University Press, 2011).

6 Duranti, *The Conservative Human Rights Revolution*; Samuel Moyn, *Christian Human Rights* (University of Pennsylvania Press, 2015).

7 Jeppe Nevers and Jesper Lundsby Skov, 'The *Folkish* Heritage in Nordic Democracy: Examples from Denmark and Norway' (2019) 17 *Journal of Modern European History* 432; Anine Kierulf, *Judicial Review in Norway: A Bicentennial Debate* (Cambridge University Press, 2018); Johan Strang, 'The Other Europe? Scandinavian Intellectuals and the Fragility of Democracy in the Wake of World War II' (2019) 17 *Journal of Modern European History* 500.

dominated the theoretical discussions on the relation between law and politics in the region, the task of the judiciary was to assist rather than constrain the popular will, to serve as 'rational technicians' at the service of the elected politicians.[8] This firm belief in the primacy of politics over law was combined with the ambition to spread democracy across society, building on the traditionally strong position of the local assemblies in Nordic governance, but focusing as well on engaging citizens in a highly active and influential associational life. These so-called people's movements (*folkrörelser*) did not form an alternative to the state, but served to connect the citizens to the state in an intricate form of 'democratic' corporatism.[9] Adding to this, there was also a strong egalitarian ambition connected to the Nordic concept of democracy, associated with the redistributive social welfare state.

The degree to which this imaginary differed from (continental) European ones is of course debatable but, more often than not, the idea of a distinctive Nordic version of democracy also built upon an explicit or implicit rejection of Europe, its political solutions and historical traditions.[10] Nordic democratic distinctiveness was legitimized by embracing national narratives of peasant freedom and Lutheran legacies, which were given much weight and specific and sometimes quite tendentious interpretations during the social democratic age.[11]

This chapter is motivated by the observation that many of these elements of Nordic democratic distinctiveness have been challenged or abandoned during the past decades, but also by the lack of not only empirical studies but also of theoretical tools by which this transformation can be understood in its specific political and transnational context. The notion of a constitutional imaginary can provide one such tool. To be sure, the constitutional imaginary of a society is per definition hegemonic, but it can change as a result of political crises, the establishment of a new constitutional settlement or a shift in political dominance.[12]

There is certainly no shortage of literature on the transforming nature of Western democracy. During recent years there has been a virtual boom of books on the 'crisis

[8] Alf Ross, *Om ret og retfærdighed: En indførelse i den analytiske retsfilosofi* (Nyt Nordisk Forlag, 1953), 472.

[9] Risto Alapuro and Henrik Stenius (eds.), *Nordic Associations in a European Perspective* (Nomos, 2010).

[10] Lene Hansen and Ole Wæver (eds.), *European Integration and National Identity: The Challenge of the Nordic States* (Routledge, 2002); Bo Stråth, *Folkhemmet mot Europa: Ett historiskt perspektiv på 90-talet* (Tidens förlag, 1993); Johan Strang, 'The Rhetoric of Nordic Cooperation: From the Other Europe to the Better Europe', in Jani Marjanen, Johan Strang and Mary Hilson (eds.), *Contesting Nordicness: From Scandinavism to the Nordic Brand* (De Gruyter, 2021).

[11] Erik Bengtsson, *Världens jämlikaste land* (Arkiv förlag, 2020); Jussi Kurunmäki and Johan Strang (eds.), *Rhetorics of Nordic Democracy* (SKS, 2010); Åsa Linderborg, *Socialdemokraterna skriver historia: Historieskrivning som ideologisk maktresurs 1892–2000* (Altlas förlag, 2001); Øystein Sørensen and Bo Stråth (eds.), *The Cultural Construction of Norden* (Scandinavian University Press, 1997).

[12] See Chapter 1.

of democracy', its 'hollowing out' due to the incapability of the traditional parties to connect with the citizens, the challenge from right-wing populism, or the democratic deficit of the EU.[13] Without diminishing the significance of this literature, this chapter will draw particularly on the bourgeoning literature on neoliberalism. One important reason for this is that neoliberalism in many ways represents an antipode to what the Nordic countries by virtue of their social democratic dominance and extensive welfare states have traditionally been understood as representing. Thus, to the extent that the Nordic democracies have been neoliberalized, it has been a paradigmatic shift in Nordic political culture. Another reason for focusing on the neoliberalism-literature is that it has arguably come the furthest in forging a *historical* perspective on the transformations of global politics and society at the end of the twentieth century. In a certain respect, this literature has even succeeded in bracketing 'a neoliberal age' starting at the end of the Keynesian post-war period and (perhaps) ending with the 2008 financial crisis.[14]

The literature on neoliberalism and democracy is also quite large and growing rapidly. Thomas Biebricher distinguishes between analyses that point at a *restriction* of democracy under neoliberalism and accounts that focus on a *replacement* of democratic procedures with market logics.[15] The first category includes studies of how economic policy and the market have become insulated from democratic pressures through, for example, an increased autonomy of central banks,[16] commitments to various international treaties protecting trade interests[17] or a juridification of democracy that commits and restricts legislators to pre-existing rules.[18] Studies in the second category point at the pervasiveness of neoliberal reason and value systems,[19] at the institutionalization of competition at all

[13] Peter Mair, *Ruling the Void: The Hollowing Out of Western Democracy* (Verso, 2013); Yascha Mounck, *The People vs. Democracy: Why Our Freedom Is in Danger and How to Save It* (Harvard University Press, 2018); Jan-Werner Müller, *What Is Populism?* (University of Pennsylvania Press, 2016).

[14] Aled Davies, Ben Jackson and Florence Sutcliffe-Braithwaite (eds.), *The Neoliberal Age? Britain since the 1970s* (UCL Press, 2021).

[15] Thomas Biebricher, 'Neoliberalism and Democracy' (2015) 22 *Constellations* 255.

[16] Thomas Piketty, *Capital and Ideology* (Harvard University Press, 2020); Wolfgang Streeck, *Buying Time: The Delayed Crisis of Democratic Capitalism* (Verso, 2014); Adam Tooze, *Crashed: How a Decade of Financial Crises Changed the World* (Allen Lane, 2018).

[17] Stephen Gill & A. Claire Cutler, *New Constitutionalism and World Order* (Cambridge University Press, 2014); Quinn Slobodian, *Globalists: The End of Empire and the Birth of Neoliberalism* (Harvard University Press, 2018).

[18] Ran Hirschl, 'The Judicalization of Mega-Politics and the Rise of Political Courts' (2008) 11 *Annual Review of Political Science* 93; Danny Nicol, *The Constitutional Protection of Capitalism* (Hart, 2010).

[19] Wendy Brown, *Undoing the Demos: Neoliberalism's Stealth Revolution* (MIT Press, 2015); Luc Boltanski and Éve Chiapello, *The New Spirit of Capitalism* (Verso, 2005).

levels of society,[20] and at the empowerment of the consumer on behalf of the citizen.[21]

While tremendously inspirational, much of this literature is hampered by a rather one-dimensional normative ambition to criticise neoliberalism on the one hand, and by an ill-placed urge to forge rigid definitions of both neoliberalism and democracy on the other. At times, the concepts appear as universal ideas with a stable and unchangeable meaning, as ideal types whose realization in everyday politics always ends up as somewhat incomplete. The approach in this chapter is historical and constructivist. The aim is to deconstruct and operationalize neoliberalism as a historical process – neoliberalization – that has taken different forms in different political contexts. Transnational connections and influences were important but need to be studied as appropriations and adaptions to various local contexts and traditions.[22] Neoliberal ideas and policies were introduced with different intentions, purposes and challenges in the Nordic region, than in, for example, the Anglo-American world or in Eastern Europe. Moreover, 'neoliberalism' and 'democracy' are political key concepts – *Grundbegriffe* in the terminology of Koselleckians – that have been subject to continuous political controversy and struggle that cannot be separated from the history of these phenomena themselves.[23] Indeed, studying conceptual change is a way of studying political transformation. As such, the main question in this chapter is not so much how neoliberalism is *replacing* or *restricting* democracy, but rather how the term 'democracy' itself has been redefined. Such a conceptual perspective is necessary in order to understand why and how neoliberals were able to present their ideas as a call for a *democratization* of the Nordic societies. It is only by acknowledging the arguments of neoliberal actors themselves that we can understand how and why the transformation of the Nordic constitutional imaginary took place.

All of the above-mentioned perspectives on the tensions between neoliberalism and democracy would merit examination also from a Nordic perspective and the literature is growing rapidly.[24] This chapter, however, will focus on the key elements of the Scandinavian post-war democratic settlement and, as such, the principal hypothesis is that 'democracy' during the past decades has become defined less in terms of participation, interest articulation, negotiation, compromise and equality,

[20] Ove Kaj Petersen, *Konkurrencestaten* (Hans Reitzels Forlag, 2011).

[21] Niklas Olsen, *The Sovereign Consumer: A New Intellectual History of Neoliberalism* (Palgrave, 2018).

[22] Cornel Ban, *Ruling Ideas: How Global Neoliberalism Goes Local* (Oxford University Press, 2016).

[23] Reinhart Koselleck, 'Einleitung', in Otto Brunner, Werner Conze and Reinhart Koselleck (ed.), *Geschichtliche Grundbegriffe: Historisches Lexikon zur politisch-sozialen Sprache in Deutschland*, vol I (Klett-Cotta, 1972).

[24] Ilkka Kärrylä, *Democracy and the Economy in Finland and Sweden since 1960: A Nordic Perspective on Neoliberalism* (Palgrave, 2021); Olsen, *The Sovereign Consumer*; Jesper Vestermark Køber, *Et Spørsmål om nærhed* (Københavns universitet, 2017).

and more as a set of fixed rules regulating the rights and freedoms of the individual. The argument is not that this transformation is unique to the Nordic region: similar developments have occurred across Europe and beyond. However, the Nordic countries form a particularly interesting case due to their continuous assertion of democratic exceptionality.

16.2 REDEFINING THE RELATIONSHIP BETWEEN POLITICS AND LAW

The judicialization of politics – and of the concept of democracy – has become a central topic of discussion both in the Western world in general and in the Nordic region.[25] The shift from politics to law is related to many processes such as globalization, European integration, as well as an increased attention to minorities and identity politics. Identifying the key actors is a difficult task, but during 'the long 1990s', there was, in the Nordic region, a growing confrontation with the idea of Nordic democratic exceptionality. The criticism came mainly from the opponents of the Social Democratic hegemony, but there was a wide sense among intellectuals, historians, political and legal scholars that something was happening with the concept of democracy. At some point, however, the idea of Nordic democratic exceptionality returned in a more juridified and constitutionalized form and was furnished with historical roots as legitimation.

The confrontation took place particularly after the end of the Cold War, when the Nordic model lost its legitimacy as a 'middle way' between capitalism and communism. Even more importantly, the accelerating European integration meant that the idea of Norden as 'the other Europe' lost currency, provoking a re-evaluation of Nordic democratic traditions. To be sure, there had always been a conservative critique of the Social Democratic hegemony and of the legal realist instrumentalization of law[26] but, starting in the 1980s, a number of liberal intellectuals managed to get more attention to their ideas than previously. In Denmark, Henning Fonsmark's *Historien om den danske utopi* (*The History of the Danish Utopia*) challenged the Danish left-wing's cultural radical monopolization of the concept of democracy, calling for a liberal alternative.[27] In Norway, the historian Rune Slagstad bracketed the Labour Party state as a particular historical period in Norwegian political history, focusing on its statist ambitions and on its troublesome

[25] Hirschl, 'The Judicalization of Mega-Politics'; Neal C. Tate and Torbjörn Vallinder, *The Global Expansion of Judicial Power* (New York University Press, 1997); Malcolm Feeley and Malcolm Langford, *The Limits of the Legal Complex: Nordic Lawyers and Political Liberalism* (Oxford University Press, 2021).

[26] Strang, 'The Rhetoric of Nordic Cooperation'.

[27] Henning Fonsmark, *Historien om den danske utopi: Et idépolitisk essay om danskernes velfærdsdemokrati* (Gyldendal, 1990).

conception of the relation between law and politics.[28] In Finland, the Social Democratic hegemony had always been weaker than in the other Nordic countries, but the young IR-scholar Risto E. J. Penttilä made a name for himself as a liberal intellectual by criticising Finnish statist traditions and by his attempt at re-establishing the liberal Young Finns Party.[29] In Sweden, the reorientation was most closely connected to a criticism of the paternalistic and oppressive features of the welfare state. Professional as well as amateur historians delved into the atrocities committed by the Scandinavian welfare states, such as the forced sterilizations.[30] Especially active was the market friendly think tank *Timbro*.[31]

Across the Nordic region, the state was increasingly becoming viewed as a threat to the individual. Among legal and political scientists, there was a rising concern about the lack of judicial review, and the weak protection of individual rights in the Nordic countries, arguments that were inspired by and connected to the processes of Europeanization. More often than not, the proposed remedy was to cast doubts about democratic traditions and call for a Europeanization of Nordic law. The Swedish legal scholar Joakim Nergelius called for a stronger role for both domestic and international courts in the political system, welcoming it as a turn towards common liberal principles of a division of powers, whereas the Danish political scientist Marlene Wind criticised Denmark as a democratic anomaly where the parliament has exceptional powers.[32]

That something was happening to Nordic democracy did not go unnoticed by the contemporaries. In the late 1900s, all three Scandinavian parliaments commissioned large-scale public inquiries into the state of power and democracy in their nations.[33] The internationalization of the legal system following the globalization of the economy in general and European integration in particular were central themes,

[28] Rune Slagstad, *Rett og politikk: et liberalt tema med variasjoner* (Pax forlag, 1987), Slagstad, *De nasjonale strateger*.

[29] Risto E. J. Penttilä, Jaakko Tapaninen and Janne Jutila, *Utlimatum isänmaalle: Nuorsuomalainen näkemys Suomen mahdollisuuksista* (Otava, 1994).

[30] Gunnar Broberg and Mattias Tydén, *Oönskade i folkhemmet: rashygien och sterilisering i Sverige* (Gidlunds, 1991); Macej Zaremba, *Minken i folkhemmet* (Timbro, 1992).

[31] Johan Strang, 'Rights against the Welfare State: Timbro and the Neoliberal Mobilization of Legalist Constitutionalism in Sweden 1980–2000', in Jenny Andersson and Chris Howell (eds.), *Nordic Neoliberalisms. Perspectives on Economic, Social and Cultural Change in the Nordics after 1970* (Routledge, 2025), 55–74.

[32] Joakim Nergelius, *Konstitutionellt rättighetsskydd: svensk rätt i ett komparativt perspektiv* (Fritze, 1996); Joakim Nergelius, Aleksander Peczenik and Ola Wiklund, *Löser juridiken demokratins problem? Demokratiutredningens skrift nr 23* (SOU, 1999), 58; Marlene Wind, 'When Parliament Comes First: The Danish Concept of Democracy Meets the European Union' (2001) 27 *Nordisk tidsskrift for menneskerettigheter* 272.

[33] Demokratiutredningen, *En uthållig demokrati! Politik för folkstyrelse på 2000-talet* (Fritze, 2000); Makt-og demokratiutredningen, *Makt og demokrati: Sluttrapport fra Makt-og demokra tiutredningen* (Statens Forvaltningstjeneste, 2003), 19; Lise Togeby, Jørgen Houl Andersen, Peter Munk Christiansen, Torben Beck Jørgensen and Signild Vallgårda, *Magt og demokrati i Danmark: Hovedresultater fra Magtudredningen* (Aarhus universitetsforlag, 2003).

but the degree to which this was seen as a threat to democracy was different in the three investigations. Whereas the Swedish and particularly the Danish investigations were more positive, the Norwegian one was quite concerned that popular rule was 'cutting its wings' with the shift of power from the domestic political representatives to the international institutions and their rules.

Now, it is certainly presumptuous to interpret the redescription of democracy as a sign of neoliberalization alone. At the same time, there is no denying that the idea of rigid legal constitutionalism, of justified limitation of parliamentary power, the appeal to inviolable individual rights to bind temporary majorities, are key elements of neoliberal classics like Hayek's *The Constitution of Liberty* (1960).[34] More recently, it has become part and parcel of the critical literature to point at neoliberalism's preference for the judicial and executive rather than the parliamentary powers or even to propose that law has become 'the code of capital'.[35] Constitutionalism is a handy vehicle for forces that want to shield the market from democratic politics. In neoliberal experimental grounds like South America in the 1970s and 1980s or Eastern Europe in the 1990s, 'rule of law' became synonymous to a constitutional protection of individual and property rights.[36] The globalization perspective is also important. As shown by Quinn Slobodian, cementing the rules of the global market in various international treaties and courts, thus protecting them from national legislators, has been part of the neoliberal agenda since the 1930s.[37] Similarly, Honor Branbazon has argued that market principles and economic freedoms have, during the last decades, developed into *Grundnorms* of the global order.[38]

In particular, there is something to gain from connecting the Nordic countries to the growing literature on the uneasy relation between neoliberalism and human rights. Most famous is arguably Samuel Moyn's contention that human rights, in focusing on sufficiency rather than equality, have served as a powerless companion, or even as a *Doppelgänger*, to neoliberalism.[39] Jessica Whyte, in turn, has forcefully argued that 'neoliberals', including both the key intellectuals (Röpke, Hayek, Friedman) and key institutions (WTO, EU), have used human rights not merely in order to protect the rights and freedoms of individuals but the rules of the market

[34] Friedrich Hayek, *The Constitution of Liberty* (University of Chicago Press, 1960).

[35] David Harvey, *A Brief History of Neoliberalism* (Oxford University Press, 2005); Katarina Pistor, *The Code of Capital: How the Law Creates Wealth and Inequality* (Princeton University Press, 2019).

[36] David Singh Grewal, 'Introduction: Law and Neoliberalism' (2014) 77 *Law and Contemporary Problems* 1.

[37] Slobodian, *Globalists*.

[38] Honor Branbazon (ed.), *Neoliberal Legality: Understanding the Role of Law in the Neoliberal Project* (Routledge, 2017).

[39] Samuel Moyn, 'A Powerless Companion: Human Rights in the Age of Neoliberalism' (2015) 77 *Law and Contemporary Problems* 147; Samuel Moyn, *Not Enough: Human Rights in an Unequal World* (Belknap, 2018).

economy as such.[40] From this perspective, social democracy was as totalitarian as communism and (perhaps even more totalitarian than) fascism as it threatened the central values of liberal market economy. From a British perspective, Danny Nicol has even more explicitly made the case that human rights legislation in general and the ECHR in particular serve as a 'constitutional protection of capitalism'.[41] Not only does he follow Whyte in arguing that human rights give neoliberalism a human face, he also suggests that human rights dethrone politics by suggesting that there is a law superior to, and beyond the reach of, politics. In practise, human rights serve as a rhetorical tool to justify the supremacy of international law over national legislation, which, according to Nicol, is at odds with the traditional model of British constitutionalism, which sees the parliament as supremely sovereign.

To be sure, these are uneasy arguments in times of Brexit-nationalism and populist rhetoric of 'taking back control' (not to speak of Orban's calls for an illiberal democracy). At the same time, it is certainly the case that the idea of popular and parliamentary sovereignty as the core of the very concept of democracy has been an important part of British as well as Scandinavian reluctance towards European integration throughout the post–WWII-period.[42] Indeed, the first successful ECHR-case against a Nordic country was the *Sporrong-Lönnroth* case, which concerned property rights and targeted the 'illegal' expropriation of real estate. By conservatives this was celebrated as a victory over the legal realist tradition, which, according to some notable critics, had been in 'secret marriage' with Social Democracy throughout the twentieth century, and become acutely dangerous when Olof Palme's government set out to 'introduce socialism' in the 1970s.[43] At the same time, it would be wrong to interpret the *Sporrong-Lönnroth*-case parochially as the point in time when the European human rights regime finally arrived in Sweden. The case also figures prominently as a turning point in international literature, for example, in Danny Nicol's account of how the ECHR has contributed to constitutionalizing neoliberal capitalism across Europe.[44] The juridification of politics relates to the development of global capitalism and cannot be seen as a development peculiar to the Nordic countries, but it is certainly the case that the recent developments clash dramatically with the post-war constitutional

40 Jessica Whyte, *The Morals of the Market: Human Rights and the Rise of Neoliberalism* (Verso, 2019).

41 Nicol, *The Constitutional Protection of Capitalism*.

42 Mikael af Malmborg, *Den ståndaktiga nationalstaten: Sverige och den västeuropeiska integrationen 1945–1959* (Lund University Press, 1994); Alan Milward, *The European Rescue of the Nation State* (Routledge, 1992).

43 Jacob Sundberg, *fr. Eddan till Ekelöf: repetorium om rättskällor i Norden* (Akademiskt förlag 1978); Jacob Sundberg, *Sporrong-Lönnroth: en handbok* (Institutet för offentlig och internationell rätt, no 63, 1985); Jacob Sundberg, 'Human Rights in Sweden: The Breakthrough of an Idea' (1986) 47 *Ohio State Law Journal* 951; see also Johan Strang, 'Scandinavian Legal Realism and Human Rights' (2018) 35 *Nordic Journal of Human Rights* 202.

44 Nicol, *The Constitutional Protection of Capitalism*, 138–140.

imaginary in Scandinavia and with how democracy was conceptualized in the region in the mid-twentieth century.

The human rights perspective is crucial in order to understand how the critics of traditional Nordic democracy during 'the long 1990s' thought they were arguing for a *democratization* of Nordic political culture. For them, the idea of Nordic democratic exceptionality was built on forged premises and perhaps also on a misconception of democratic principles. As such, they called for an adjustment of Nordic political culture to the European mainstream. The human rights-perspective is also important in order to understand how and why the political left co-opted this idea of individual rights as a fundamental aspect of the notion of democracy. Human rights thrived as 'the last utopia' and as an attempt to resurrect politics on a moral basis after 1968.[45] Rights-rhetoric was used by the left wing as a criticism of the technocratic and oppressive social democratic welfare state. Individual and human rights became an important part of not only the political rhetoric, but also of the political practise as domestic and international courts became sites where the interests of vulnerable minorities could be defended. Increasingly, and arguably more so in Finland and Norway than in Denmark and Sweden, the left tends to refer to 'the constitution' and to 'individual rights' in order to further their political aims. One explanation for this is simply that the left has embraced economic liberalism and scaled back on their ambition to replace capitalism with economic planning and public ownership, aiming instead to tame and manage it through legislation. Another explanation might be that the increasing awareness of the cultural heterogeneity of the Nordic societies (and the increasing *de facto* heterogeneity) calls for a more judicial and rights-based approach to democracy. The progressive and political welfare state was perhaps only possible in the comparatively (or blindly) homogeneous societies of post–WWII and at the cost of somewhat oppressive homogenizing policies. A final hypothesis for the left-wing embrace of a rights-based constitutional language is perhaps that it serves the conservative (!) aim of defending the welfare state in a period when it has been under prolonged relentless neoliberal fire. Indeed, there are significant signs of a corresponding anti-constitutional turn in the political right. In Finland, representatives of both the neoliberal and the populist right have denounced the left-wing opposition, as well as Human Rights lawyers like Martin Scheinin, as 'constitution-Talibans' that make political change impossible.[46] Be that as it may, Nordic democracy is no longer, as it was during the 1960s and 1970s, associated with popular sovereignty but rather with a more constitutionalized notion of democracy, based on the notion of a strong protection of individual rights.

45 Samuel Moyn, *The Last Utopia: Human Rights in History* (Belknap, 2010); Moyn, 'A Powerless Companion'; Moyn, *Not Enough*.

46 Björn Wahlroos, *Hiljainen vallankuomous: tekikö uusi perustuslaki Suomen hallitsemisen mahdottomaksi?* (EVA, 2017); www.hbl.fi/artikel/jussi-niinisto-i-nytt-hart-angrepp-mot-twittrande-professor/.

Individual and human rights have become key parts of what we today consider the Nordic democratic tradition or the Scandinavian constitutional imaginary.

16.3 TRANSFORMING THE NORDIC CORPORATISM

It is often argued that associational life provides the best perspective for studying Nordic conceptions of democracy.[47] Civil society scholars talk about a special Nordic 'popular mass movement model' characterized by high membership figures but by passive membership. The logic was *representation* rather that participation and, as such, the members trusted the association looked after the interested of its members in negotiation with the state. The aim of the voluntary organizations was never to challenge or overthrow the state but to connect citizens to the state, to channel interests and contribute to the progress of society as a whole. The relationship between the state and the organisations was intimate, to the degree that it was sometimes difficult to discern the boundaries between state and civil society actors.

This Nordic corporatist notion of democracy was also criticised in the 1990s. Critics argued that it was undemocratic that an individual could increase his vote or influence by joining these powerful associations and that the close relationship between the associations and the state was a system that was liable for corruption. Some even claimed that the Nordic statist societies lacked a conception of an independent 'civil society', pointing to the fact that, in the Nordic languages, state and society are often used interchangeably – a discussion that either was blind to or aimed at undermining Nordic corporative traditions.[48] There were, of course, many reasons for the re-evaluation of Nordic corporatist traditions and for the transformations that it has undergone during the past decades – globalization, digitalization, social media, and so on. It is, however, also easy to connect this debate to the neoliberalism literature. Scholars like Wendy Brown or Laura Morales have argued that neoliberal rationality compels people to make individual choices like consumers on the market, rather than to promote their interests through collective mobilization.[49] Of particular importance are, of course, the labour market arrangements. Scholars point at a diminished role of labour market associations following from the slow but steady decline in trade union membership, while the employer's seem to turn their organizations into think tanks and lobbying organizations rather than as parties in a negotiation. Indeed, the traditional tripartite negotiation system, central to Nordic democracy since the 1930s, has in all Nordic countries been questioned and modified towards more decentralized forms of wage bargaining. Scholarship point at flexibilization, deregulation, decollectivization and

[47] Alapuro and Stenius, *Nordic Associations in a European Perspective*.

[48] Lars Trägårdh, *Civilt samhälle kontra offentlig sektor* (SNS förlag, 1995).

[49] Brown, *Undoing the Demos*; Laura Morales, *Joining Political Organisations: Institutions, Mobilisation and Participation in Western Democracies* (Rowman & Littlefield, 2009).

decentralization as key features of neoliberalization on the labour market and that this has also been the case in the Nordic countries.[50]

At the same time, the neoliberalization of Nordic democracy has not led to a more decentralized notion of democracy, but rather to a strengthening of the state on behalf of the associations. The associations are no longer trusted to represent interests and to solve issues among themselves. Their autonomy has decreased. The state can ask them to carry out state functions, for example in the welfare sector but, in that case, they tend to be treated as corporations or social enterprises, not as grass-root movements with a democratic responsibility. When it comes to influencing key decisions on a national level, the associations are today more and more seen as lobby organizations, whose power consists in their direct contacts to leading politicians, not in the fact that they represent a constituency of citizens.[51] Democracy is no longer understood to be something that should take place across society, but rather in Schumpeterian terms as an issue for professional political elites.[52]

There are also good reasons to claim that the Scandinavian countries have largely abandoned the third and final feature of the Scandinavian post-war democratic settlement, the idea of democracy being closely associated with economic equality. The literature on the shift from welfare states to competition states is extensive and points at declining redistribute ambitions across the Nordic region.[53] During the mid-twentieth century, many social democrats nursed the idea that their task was to develop the *political* democracy they inherited to a *social* and onwards to an *economic* democracy. With economic democracy, the idea was that the workers should not only be able to participate in decision-making in the industries but also, through the notorious wage earner funds, to gain ownership of the companies themselves. This idea was vehemently criticised and abandoned during the late 1970s and early 1980s.[54] In many ways, the notion of economic equality has been disassociated from democracy during the past decades.

[50] Lucio Baccaro and Chris Howell, 'A Common Neoliberal Trajectory: The Transformation of Industrial Relations in Advanced Capitalism' (2011) 39 *Politics & Society* 521; Maiju Wuokko, 'The Curious Compatibility of Consensus, Corporatism, and Neoliberalism: The Finnish Business Community and the Retasking of a Corporatist Welfare State' (2019) 63 *Business History* 668; Aaro Sahari, Elina Kuorelahti, Henrik Tala, Maiju Wuokko and Niklas Jensen-Eriksen, *Loputtomat kihlajaiset: Yritykset ja kolmikantakorporatismi Suomessa 1940–2020* (Siltala, 2020).

[51] Alapuro and Stenius, *Nordic Associations in a European Perspective*.

[52] Vestermark Køber, *Et Spørsmål om nærhed*.

[53] Jenny Andersson, *Between Growth and Security: Swedish Social Democracy from a Strong Society to a Third Way* (Manchester University Press, 2006); Johannes Kananen, *The Nordic Welfare State in Three Eras: From Emancipation to Discipline* (Routledge, 2014); Pauli Kettunen and Klaus Petersen (eds.), *Beyond Welfare State Models: Transnational Historical Perspectives on Social Policy* (Edward Elgar, 2011), Petersen, *Konkurrencestaten*.

[54] Kärrylä, *Democracy and the Economy*; Bengt Furåker, 'The Swedish Wage-earner Funds and Economic Democracy: Is There Anything to be Learned from Them?' (2016) 22 *Transfer: The European Review of Labour and Research* 121.

16.4 DISCUSSION: NORDIC DEMOCRACY AFTER THE END OF HISTORY?

The aim of this chapter has been to discuss changes in the constitutional imaginary in the Scandinavian countries through a discussion of the notion of democracy. Using neoliberalization as a perspective, the chapter has argued that the democracy championed by the Nordics is no longer primarily connected to national or popular sovereignty, public participation or civil society and labour market arrangements, but rather to rule of law, human rights and political and economic freedom. To be sure, as emphasized above, this is a global development and as such not *peculiar* to the Nordic countries. Arguably, however, the transformation is of a more profound significance in the Nordic political culture, which traditionally (albeit to different degrees in the different countries) has prioritized popular sovereignty, associational life and equality over individual rights and economic freedom.

Moreover, while the focus here has been on conceptions of democracy *within* the Nordic states, I think that the general hypothesis also finds support in previous and ongoing scholarship on Nordic foreign relations. Studies on Nordic development aid, for example, suggest that there has been a shift in the way that the governments have understood the criteria of 'democracy-promotion'.[55] If democracy-promotion during the 1960s and 1970s was understood in terms of supporting national consolidation, popular sovereignty, corporatist structures and economic equality, Nordic development policies and projects have since the 1990s become a matter of requiring that the countries adhere to a pre-defined set of principles of human rights and rules for international trade.

How are we to make sense of this transformation? At a more general level, one could perhaps relate the redefinition of Nordic democracy to Francis Fukuyama's infamous notion of an End of History.[56] The idea that a particular notion of western liberal democracy in 1989 emerged, not merely as victorious, but also as a kind of pinnacle and end-point of humankind's ideological development. To borrow from the French intellectual historian François Hartog: we reached the age of *presentism* where it was no longer possible to imagine a society radically better than the liberal

[55] Liisa Laakso, 'Promoting a Special Brand of Democracy: Denmark, Finland, Norway and Sweden', in Peter J. Schraeder (ed.), *Exporting Democracy: Rhetoric vs Reality* (Lynnie Rienner, 2002); Johan Karlsson Schaffer, 'How Democracy Promotion became a Key Aim of Swedish Development Aid Policy', in Antoine de Bengy Bjørkdahl and Kristian Puyvallé (eds.), *Do-Gooders at the End of Aid* (Cambridge University Press, 2021). See Johan Strang, 'Nordic Peace since the End of History: Exceptionality without Distinction', in Christopher S. Browning, Marko Lehti and Johan Strang (eds.), *Nordic Peace in Question: A Region of and for Peace* (Routledge, 2025), 98–210.

[56] Francis Fukuyama, 'The End of History' (1989) 16 *The National Interest* 3; Francis Fukuyama, *The End of History and the Last Man* (The Free Press, 1992).

democracies of the western world.[57] Whereas the great ideologies of the modern period (1789–1989) were characterized by the utopian promise of a radically better future, human rights and the more constitutionalized form of democracy served more as a critique of these utopian visions, portraying the future more in terms of threats to the present. At such a point, it became important to cement the principles of the universal good in constitutions in order to protect them from future revisions.[58]

It is easy for an intellectual historian to overplay the significance of the ideational. More materialistically inclined historians would probably pursue the transformation of Nordic democracy in terms of an *Europeanization* of the legal and political frameworks in the Nordic countries since the 1990s, a *globalization* of the economy that has narrowed down the variety of capitalist systems or the dawn of a country ranking industry that has served to streamline national political horizons.[59] There is, however, something to be said for the contention that the Nordic countries no longer purport to represent a *different* form of democracy; instead, they have become the countries with the *best implementation* of the universal principles of liberal democracy, the western post-Cold War *doxa* that emerged in the wake of the End of History. The Nordic embrace of human rights as a leading principle in domestic politics was part of this transition from Nordic democratic exceptionality as *difference* (and superiority) to exceptionality as *superiority*.[60] Indeed, in 2011 Fukuyama himself suggested that 'getting to Denmark' was the ultimate aim for countries around the world.[61]

Paradoxically, at the same time as western conceptualizations of 'democracy' were narrowed down to a particular form of liberal democracy, there was also a cultural turn and return of the *Sonderweg*-narrative in Nordic historical scholarship on the welfare state. If ideas of Nordic peasant freedom and Lutheran legacies in the mid-twentieth century had been used by Social Democrats to fend off totalitarianism and to legitimize social reforms,[62] they were now turned against Social Democracy and operationalized as part of an argument that depoliticized the welfare state and turned the Nordic model into a question of DNA. The cultural turn was operationalized to dismantle 'the social interpretation of the welfare state'.[63] *The Nordic Way*

57 François Hartog, *Regimes of Historicity: Presentism and the Experiences of Time* (Columbia University Press, 2015).

58 Stefan-Ludwig Hoffmann, 'Human Rights in History' (2016) 232 *Past and Present* 279.

59 Tori Kirkebø, Malcolm Langford and Haldor Byrkjeflot, 'Creating Gender Exceptionalism: The Role of Global Indexes', in Eirinn Larsen, Sigrun Marie Moss and Inger Skjelsbæk (eds.), *Gender Equality and Nation Branding in the Nordic Region* (Routledge, 2021).

60 Strang, 'The Rhetoric of Nordic Cooperation'.

61 Francis Fukuyama, *The Origins of Political Order: From Prehuman Times to the French Revolution* (Farrar, Straus & Giroux, 2011).

62 Kurunmäki and Strang, *Rhetorics of Nordic Democracy*; Sørensen and Stråth, *The Cultural Construction of Norden*.

63 Peter Baldwin, 'The Scandinavian Origins of the Social Interpretation of the Welfare State' (1989) 31 *Comparative Studies in Society and History* 3.

was no longer a result of partisan Social Democratic policies, but the outcome of longer historical trajectories and socio-cultural features inherent in the Nordic societies and, as such, it became possible to neoliberalize the welfare state in the name of the Nordic model.[64]

Finally, the normative lesson from associating human rights or constitutionalism with neoliberalism is usually to dethrone law and human rights as the ultimate manifestation of 'the good' by pointing at the economic and social inequalities it contributes to or is incapable of fighting.[65] This has also been the purpose of this chapter. But the converse must also be considered: does the association with individual and human rights bring neoliberalism into a more positive light from a historical perspective? The time is probably ripe for intellectual historians to take the prospect seriously. There were undoubtedly some good sides to neoliberalism as well, also and perhaps particularly in the Nordic countries. The political message of individual freedom, the juridification of democracy and the rise of human rights have provided vulnerable minorities and individuals with strong political arguments and sometimes even constitutional guarantees and, thus, neoliberalism has contributed to the downfall of at least some of the abusive paternalism associated with the social democratic welfare state. Studying the transformation of the constitutional imaginary of the Nordic region, we should avoid falling into the trap of a nostaligizing a perfect Nordic democracy that never was.

64 Henrik Berggren and Lars Trägårdh, 'Social Trust and Radical Individualism: The Paradox at the Heart of Nordic Capitalism', in *The Nordic Way: Shared Norms for the New Reality* (World Economic Forum, 2011); Henrik Berggren and Lars Trägårdh, *Är svensken människa? Gemenskap och oberoende i det moderna Sverige* (Norstedts, 2015).

65 Moyn, *Not Enough*; Whyte, *The Morals of the Market*.

17

Fifty Years of Democratic Constitutionalism in Portugal

Between Constitutional Aspirations and the European Path

Mariana Canotilho

17.1 INTRODUCTION

Approved in the aftermath of the democratic revolution of 1974, the Portuguese Constitution of 1976 (PC) was a solid success, both from political and constitutional points of view. With it, the basic pillars of a solid democratic political regime were established, as well as a broad catalogue of fundamental rights and institutional guarantees that have proved themselves to be essential elements of a new, transformed country. Both the post-revolutionary and pre-constitutional period and the first decades of democratic constitutionalism were marked by the public expression of very different ideologies and worldviews, as well as social, economic and political projects for the country that were deeply distinct. The content of the PC, in its various versions (it was amended seven times between 1982 and 2005), is the result of arduous political negotiations and broad social consensus.

The development of democratic constitutionalism in Portugal in the last (almost) fifty years has been marked by some important debates, which still influence different views and interpretations of the Constitution. I would like to highlight two of them: first, a discussion of the nature and limits of the 'constitutional project' enshrined in the CP, the normative strength of the constitution, and the margin of appreciation given to the democratic legislator. Second, the debate about constitutional openness, European integration, and the constitutional consequences of the overwhelmingly desired 'European path' of the country, which evolved more recently to be a reflection on the contradictions between such a path and national constitutional characteristics, especially during and after the euro crisis. The objective of this work will be to reflect on the *constitutional imaginary* of democratic Portugal, in particular on the discrepancies between national constitutional aspirations and European integration, which are particularly acute in what regards the so-called social question (i.e., the social project, including social rights as limits to the

The views in this chapter are my own, and do not, in any way, reflect an institutional stand.

legislator, and views of the political economy that are strikingly different at the national and EU levels).

17.2 CONSTITUTIONAL CONSENSUS

To understand Portuguese constitutionalism, one has to know a bit of national history and the idiosyncrasies of the country. The Portuguese Constitution entered into force on 25 April 1976, two exact years after the military coup d'état of 1974, which opened the path for a democratic revolution that brought deep structural transformations, not only at the political and constitutional levels, but also in the economic and social spheres.

Until 1974, and since 1926, Portugal lived under an authoritarian regime. Its concrete features are debated, varying between its classification as a parafascist State and a 'Portuguese form of fascism', without a fascist movement; nevertheless, it was certainly a dictatorship with corporatist and fascist characteristics.[1] However, a distinct element must be immediately pinpointed, as it is especially important for constitutional history and to understand its specific imaginary: the national dictator, the man who designed the *Estado Novo* (the 'New State') regime and ruled the country as 'president of the council of ministers' for decades, was a professor of law. The Portuguese dictatorship was, in many ways, *a dictatorship of law professors* who were protagonists – and not mere ideologues or side helpers – of the definition and implementation of the regime.[2] The main consequence of this fact is that almost

[1] Manuel Lucena and Manuela Pena Gomes, 'Reflexões sobre a queda do regime salazarista e o que se lhe seguiu' (2002) 37 *Análise Social* 7; Roger Griffin, *Modernism and Fascism: The Sense of a Beginning under Mussolini and Hitler* (Palgrave Macmillan, 2007); Jorge Pais de Sousa, *O Fascismo Catedrático de Salazar* (Imprensa da Universidade de Coimbra, 2011); António Costa Pinto (ed.), *Corporatism and Fascism: The Corporatist Wave in Europe* (Routledge, 2017); Cláudia Ninhos, 'The Estado Novo and Portuguese–German Relations in the Age of Fascism', in Arnd Bauerkamper and Grzegorz Rossolinski-Liebe (eds.), *Fascism without Borders: Transnational Connections and Cooperation between Movements and Regimes in Europe from 1918 to 1945* (Berghahn Books, 2017), 142–167. Rita Almeida de Carvalho, 'Ideology and Architecture in the Portuguese 'Estado Novo': Cultural Innovation within a Para-Fascist State (1932–1945)' (2018) 7 *Fascism* 141.

[2] The main protagonist of the regime was António Oliveira Salazar (1889–1970), full professor of Political Economy and Finance at the Faculty of Law of the University of Coimbra, and head of Estado Novo for several decades. Nevertheless, others are worth mentioning: Marcello Caetano (1906–1980) was the successor of Salazar as head of government and full professor of administrative law at the Faculty of Law of the University of Lisbon; João Pinto da Costa Leite (Lumbrales) (1905–1975), full professor of Political Economy at the Faculty of Law of the University of Lisbon, was a minister, with different positions, for many years, and president of the Central Board of the Portuguese Legion and of the *National Union* (the only political party); Afonso Queiró (1914–1995), full professor of administrative law at the Faculty of Law of the University of Coimbra, was one of the regime's strongmen and a member of the Corporate Chamber, from 1945 to 1974. A significant number of other famous law professors held prominent positions during Estado Novo, fifteen of whom were removed from their offices at the university after the 1974 democratic revolution.

half a century of authoritarianism was anchored on an 'illusion of legality', a sort of civilisational *patine* quite different from typical fascist military dictatorships, with which the authorities tried to disguise or justify the existence of censorship, political police and political prisoners, torture, colonialism, and an overall lack of pluralism and of democratic institutions. The 'New State' held a plebiscite to approve a constitution, in 1933, which stayed in force until the democratic revolution, in 1974. It was an interesting and eclectic legal document, with a list of fundamental rights (mainly civil and political rights, whose exercise depended on legal or administrative regulations and should not 'hurt society or disrespect moral principles'[3]), a strong corporatist trend and a clear illiberal identity.

The similarities and differences between the 1933 constitution and the democratic constitution of 1976 conditioned the early constitutional debates in the recently implanted Portuguese democracy. Both the constitutional imaginary and democratic constitutional settings were characterized at the time by utopian elements (what the democratic regime should aim at), very pragmatic agreements on constitutional design (how the new democratic institutions should work), but also by a clear rejection of the 'constitutionalism' of dictatorship (what the new regime should not do, or tolerate in any circumstance).

The approval of the Portuguese Constitution of 1976, following a *revolutionary* two-year period (1974–1976), was the culmination of a difficult path, which entailed serious political conflict and a long negotiating process. I believe this is one of the reasons why the PC has proved to be quite resilient during the last decades: the fact that it was born out of true conflict and not of fake consensus. The divergences between the participants in the constituent process were clear (and quite considerable) and the final text was a good mixture between different elements and distinct political affiliations and traditions, from the catholic social doctrine and Christian democracy to the more prevailing socialist and social-democratic views. Although the very idea of *constitutional consensus* was disputed by some,[4] who stated that the 1976 PC was transitory in nature or necessarily contradictory, the dominant opinion today is that the constitution embodied a political compromise, combining the pluralist and representative political democracy, typical of liberal western thinking, with an economic, social and cultural democracy of socialist tradition. Furthermore, the consolidation and the persistence of the PC (that is about to celebrate its forty-eighth anniversary) was accomplished through complex political agreements, which went beyond the time of the constituent assembly and had important manifestations in the constitutional amendments of 1982 and 1989.[5]

[3] Mariana Canotilho, 'A Constituição Portuguesa de 1933', in António Simões do Paço (ed.), *Os Anos de Salazar, vol 2: A Constituição do Estado Novo* (Planeta d'Agostini, 2008).

[4] Francisco Lucas Pires, *Teoria da Constituição de 1976: a Transição Dualista* (Universidade de Coimbra, 1988).

[5] Jorge Miranda, *A Constituição de 1976: Formação, estrutura, princípios fundamentais* (Petrony, 1978); Jorge Miranda, 'A constituição e a democracia portuguesa', in *Revista do Ministério*

17.2.1 A *Normative Constitution*

The main elements of the PC confirm this idea of compromise and a common political project embodied in the constitution.[6]

First and foremost, the PC was conceived as a *normative constitution* in pure German terms. As such, it is considered, in line with the teachings of K. Hesse, to be the general objective order of the complex relations of life, the fundamental act of the polity. The Constitution not only regulates the division of power (establishing who can do what, when, and how) but also imposes concrete tasks.[7] Having normative primacy over the entire legal order, it conforms the actions of the state, creating legal limits to political choices.

It is important to bear in mind that many of the members of the constituent assembly (1975–1976) and other key political actors were lawyers and legal academics, heavily influenced by German legal tradition, which was very strong in Portuguese academia at the time. The idea of constitutional supremacy enshrined in the PC echoes not only the known teachings of H. Kelsen, but also the works of H. Heller and K. Hesse.[8] The normative strength of the constitution conferred legitimacy on the state's powers, but also directed and limited their action. An intricate system of constitutional justice, which combined European centralized abstract review with the common law judicial review of constitutionality (allowing every single judge to refuse to apply any norm that they deemed in contradiction with constitutional rules and principles), was set in place; initially, the final decision in the process of abstract review of constitutionality belonged to a military organ (the Council of the Revolution), whereas, after the first amendment of the constitution, in 1982, such powers were conferred upon the Constitutional Court, created after the extinction of said Council.

The PC encapsulated a vision of social transformation through law, akin to a Weimar Constitutional Moment.[9] The constitutional norms aimed at liberating Portuguese society from the previous decades of political suppression and economic destitution, relying on the establishment of new public institutions and strong legal

Público. Rio de Janeiro: MPRJ 31 (2009); Jorge Miranda, *Manual de Direito Constitucional, tomo I. Preliminares: O Estado e os Sistemas Constitucionais*, 10th ed. (CoimbraEditora, 2014); José Joaquim Gomes Canotilho, *Direito Constitucional e Teoria da Constituição*, 7th ed. (Almedina, 2003).

6 For a different view on the main features of the Portuguese Constitution, see also Catarina Santos Botelho, 'The Presentist Portuguese Constitution', in Richard Albert (ed.), *The Architecture of Constitutional Amendments: History, Law, Politics* (Hart Publishing, 2023).

7 Konrad Hesse, *Die normative Kraft der Verfassung* (Mohr Siebeck, 1959).

8 Hermann Heller, *Staatslehre* (Sijthoff, 1934); Konrad Hesse, *Die normative Kraft der Verfassung* (Mohr Siebeck, 1959).

9 Teresa Violante, 'Portugal: From Transformative to Open Constitutionalism', in Marco Dani, Marco Goldoni and Agustín Menéndez (eds.), *The Legitimacy of European Constitutional Orders* (Edward Elgar, 2023).

frameworks, which were supposed to organize, condition and direct the actions of State's organs. The discussion about the *normative strength of* the constitution therefore encompasses the debate about the so-called margin of appreciation or scope for action of the democratic legislator and the limits imposed on everyday political decisions by the text and the constitutional project.

17.2.2 *Centrality of Fundamental Rights*

The second important feature of the PC is the *centrality of fundamental rights*: it has one of the largest catalogues of fundamental rights, spread over fifty-six articles. It includes civil and political rights (called *rights*, *freedoms* and *guarantees*) and economic, social and cultural rights. There are different legal rules regulating the application of both sets of rights, with more stringent constitutional norms regarding the first one, which has allowed for their more effective judicial protection. Still, economic, social and cultural rights are conceived as true, subjective, fundamental rights that may be used to justify claims against the State and not only principles according to which public policies should be designed. It should also be noted that the completeness and detail of fundamental rights provisions are much larger than in most similar constitutional texts, including issues such as the right to data protection, a general prohibition of interference in *telecommunications*, or the right to an ecologically balanced environment (and the duty to defend it) decades before they were main political and constitutional concerns. This is, of course, generally useful, but it can also prove troublesome in the context of multilevel fundamental rights protection. General correspondences are easily made between international human rights and national fundamental rights catalogues; however, as often happens, *the devil is in the details*. Therefore, the comprehensive provisions of the PC sometimes make the contradictions emerging between the content or meaning of a given right at the national and international spheres particularly evident. Now, this is not a very difficult problem to solve if international human rights standards are regarded as *minimum* levels of protection, to be guaranteed in a given constitutional space, with the States being able to confer a higher level of protection. It may, however, prove a lot more complicated when the quest for a uniform application of EU law is interpreted in such a way as to prevent the strengthening of the guarantees afforded to a certain right at the national level (situation in which it is conceivable that a demand imposed by EU law is contrary to the PC).

17.2.3 *Openness*

Another distinctive element of the PC is its *openness*, also said to be a manifestation of *legal internationalism*. There are several examples of this: the constitutional consecration of a general principle of equal treatment of foreigners (who enjoy the same fundamental rights as Portuguese citizens, with a few exceptions); the duty to interpret fundamental rights' norms according to the Universal Declaration of Human Rights and to apply internationally recognized rights in the national legal order; the principle of respect for human rights in international relations and a general integration of international and EU law into the Portuguese legal order.

Also, in the realm of international relations, the PC has consistently embraced a remarkably open approach, evident, for example, in the prevision of an automatic incorporation of general and conventional international law into the domestic legal order. The emancipatory and optimistic narrative of the Constitution is apparent in its vision for Portugal's integration in the European Union and the global community, outlined since the first version of the constitutional text. Over subsequent constitutional amendments, these principles were either maintained or reinforced; this is especially noticeable in the 1992 amendment, whereby an addition to Article 7 of a provision allowing agreements with other Member States for the joint exercise of powers necessary for EU construction was approved. Additionally, Article 8(4), introduced in the 2004 constitutional amendment, underscores the openness of the national constitutional order to the EU legal framework, subject to conditions defined by the EU itself. The constituent legislator acknowledged the imperative to adapt the PC to the evolving reality of 'inter-constitutionality' or 'multi-level constitutionalism'[10] and did so with enthusiasm and under a large consensus.

17.2.4 *Political Pluralism and Democratic Governance*

The constitution also designed a political regime firmly based on democratic decision-making and *political pluralism*. This is a distinctive feature of the Portuguese constitutional project, in slightly different terms than compared to similar legal orders, as the constitution goes much further than the establishment of a democratic form of government, with a hybrid semi-parliamentarian regime, a directly elected Head of State, with relevant powers, a government with broad legislative competences and independent courts.

The idea of *democratic governance* and pluralism goes way beyond that, with a significant number of constitutional provisions regarding *self-government* and *participation* in many spheres of public life. Examples of this are, of course, the institution of free political parties and a general freedom of association, but also the right to broadcasting time conferred to both political parties *and unions*; the fundamental right of workers' commissions to participate in the drafting of labour legislation and to oversee companies' management; the principle of decentralized and participated management of the national health service; the right to take part in the drafting of urban planning instruments; or the right of students and teachers to take part in the democratic governance of schools. The idea of an effective,

[10] Mariana Canotilho, '40/30 – 40 years of Constitution, 30 years of European Integration: Between Past and Present, Openness and Belonging' (2017) 3 *UNIO–EU Law Journal* 38.

decentralized, popular and prevailing *democracy* is displayed throughout the constitutional text, with a much deeper meaning and scope than mere representative democracy, although representative institutions are the basis of the democratic regime.

This particular concept of self-government is, therefore, both an important part of national constitutional imagination, deriving from an *anti-oligarchic narrative*[11] shared by a large majority during the period of democratic consolidation. Therefore, throughout the Portuguese Constitution – from the catalogue of fundamental rights and respective institutional guarantees, to the legal provisions on the form of government, including the economic constitution – there is an implicit ideal of popular participation and democratic legitimization of the management of public affairs and of political decision-making. This is a relevant feature, not only because it falls within the scope of national constitutional imagination, but also because, if taken seriously, it constitutes an important limit regarding the design of institutions and public policies under the responsibility of the democratic legislator.

17.2.5 *Regulation of Economic Infrastructure and Public Policies*

Lastly, I would like to notice one important feature of the PC, largely ignored in the last few decades: the detailed regulation of the economic infrastructure and policies. The PC has general rules regarding economic government and planning, with emphasis on the subordination of the economic organization to democratic political power; the public, private and cooperative property of production resources; public/common goods; and industrial, commercial and agricultural policies. Also, the PC establishes the right to property as a fundamental social and economic right (and not a civic right) and affords the private sector a central position in the economic process, but gives the State very relevant powers in terms of guidance and control of economic activities and income (re-)distribution.

Some of the provisions of the *economic constitution* have been overtaken by contemporary reality and especially by European integration and policies. This is one of the problematic dissonances between the national constitutional order (the national constitutional imaginary?) and the EU. Whereas EU constitutional law, particularly the Treaties, intend to design and protect an economic system of neoliberal features, the PC presupposes a strong degree of State intervention in the economy and a very strong subordination of economic policies to the fulfilment of constitutionally defined State's fundamental objectives and fundamental rights. This is combined with the central role of *work* and *workers* in the PC, which is also problematic in some areas of European integration and a possible source of tension (the constitutional right to strike, for example, clearly affords a higher standard of protection to workers and unions in the national legal order than what results from

[11] Violante, 'Portugal'.

the ECJ jurisprudence, and there is a constitutional express prohibition of lock-down).[12]

The constitution was amended seven times between 1982 and 2005. The current text is strikingly different from the original one in a few symbolic aspects, namely the fundamental aim of the Republic, stated in Article 1, which changed from 'the transformation into a classless society' to 'the construction of a free, just and solidary society'. Still, it has been able to maintain its most relevant and unique elements, and I think one may say that the PC remains the same, although it has changed significantly.

17.3 CONSTITUTIONAL DEBATES

The constitution was a key element of the political stabilization of the country, and it allowed Portugal to affirm itself as a consolidated democracy and to begin the path towards European integration. Nevertheless, the initial consensus quickly gave way to fierce debates about certain constitutional questions, which were, in reality, the legal side of broader political divergence.

17.3.1 *Social Transformation through Constitutional Law*

The first dogmatic and ideological confrontation over constitutional interpretation that I would like to signal occurred mainly in the 1980s, just before, and after, the significant – and politically divisive – constitutional reform of 1982. It was a debate about the role of the constitution in conforming the action of the State, around the concept of *directive constitution* ('Constituição Dirigente'). It was also, truly, a discussion about the very nature of a constitution, what it is, what it does and how it works and, therefore, a conversation about constitutional imaginaries and traditions and about constitutional utopia.

Extensively grounded in German doctrine and scholarship (especially in the works of K. Hesse) and the object of significant revision over the years, even by its main proponents, the idea of a *directive constitution* is based on an understanding of the constitution as much more than an instrument of government; it is conceived as the container of a shared political, economic and social project that is, in its origin, primarily counter-factual, but aims at being progressively accomplished and institutionalized. Therefore, the purpose of a *directive constitution* is to achieve deep social change through law, engaging all State's organs in that task.

However, insofar as these objectives are intensely political, its primary actors should also be political ones – the directive constitutionalism's main subject is *the*

[12] On the broad constitutional definition of the right to strike, see the resume by Catarina Santos Botelho, 'Some Distinctive Traits of the Portuguese Constitutionalism', in *Liber Amicorum Benedita Mac Crorie* (UMinho Editora, 2022).

legislator, and not the courts, unlike its later evolution towards *transformative constitutionalism*, particularly in the Global South. The idea of achieving transformation through constitutional law presupposes the legal effectiveness of the so-called *programmatic norms*, otherwise often understood (and consequently interpreted and applied) as mere political declarations. The theory also presupposes a *theory of the State* and a theory of *sovereignty*, because the existence of a sovereign State is both an unsurpassable precondition and an essential tool of directive constitutionalism.

The long, deep and fierce debate about this issue still resonates today and it had significant consequences in constitutional jurisprudence that I will briefly analyse later. It was also exported to Brazil (and Latin America in general) through the active participation of Portuguese leading academics in the country's constituent process in 1988 and other academic ties. It is, however, in essence, the *Latin version* of a German debate. The main proponents of the interpretation of the PC as a *directive constitution* were professors of the University of Coimbra[13] under the influence of K. Hesse[14] and also of the work by P. Lerche[15] on the binding of the legislature by constitutional principles and the teachings of W. Abendroth[16] about the Social State. Their intention was to use legal tools and the usual dogmatic instruments to interpret and apply constitutional norms regarding the *social* dimension of the social and democratic State in a way to allow them to be as effective as other kinds of legal provisions. Still, more than a conflict over the so-called programmatic norms, there was a serious disagreement on whether or not the legislator was completely free to pursue any goals, independently of their constitutional conformity, or if the constitutional rules and principles about State's aims and duties had a binding effect.

Some of the adversaries of the *directive constitution* were influenced by the work of E. Forsthoff,[17] and favoured the idea of a broad power of command of the State, with a very wide margin of discretion of the legislator regarding not only the means, but also the ends of the norms it enacted. Also, almost all the opponent authors shared a notable preference by the notion of *Rechtsstaat*, or rule of law, opposed to the more socialist leaning *Sozialstaat*, or welfare state; they stood for limited judicial constraints over the democratic legislator, even if grounded on the constitution, and

[13] For a better explanation of the debate, see Violante, 'Portugal'. Also, the two main debaters, J. J. Gomes Canotilho, *Constituição dirigente e vinculação do legislador: Contributo para a compreensão das normas constitucionais programáticas* (Coimbra Editora, 1982) and Francisco Lucas Pires, *Teoria da Constituição de 1976: a Transição Dualista* (Universidade de Coimbra, 1988).

[14] Konrad Hesse, *Die normative Kraft der Verfassung* (Mohr Siebeck, 1959).

[15] Peter Lerche, *Übermass und Verfassungsrecht: zur Bindung des Gesetzgebers an die Grundsätze der Verhältnismässigkeit und der Erforderlichkeit*, 2nd ed. (Keip Verlag, 1999).

[16] Wolfgang Abendroth, 'Zum Begriff des demokratischen und sozialen Rechtsstaats im Grundgesetz der Bundesrepublik Deutschland', in Hans-Jürgen Urban, Michael Buckmiller and Frank Deppe (eds.), *Antagonistische Gesellschaft und politische Demokratie* (VSA, 1972).

[17] Ernst Forsthoff, *Der totale Staat* (Hanseatic Publishing Company, 1933); Ernst Forsthoff, *Verfassungsprobleme des Sozialstaates* (Aschendorff, 1954); Ernst Forsthoff, *Lehrbuch des Verwaltungsrechts: Bd. Allgemeiner Teil* (Beck, 1973).

debated the possibility of existence of unconstitutional constitutional norms, after O. Bachof's work.[18]

As I said before, the debate had important consequences not only in the academic world, but also in constitutional jurisprudence. The problem regarding the existence and extension of a *directive dimension of the constitution* was the framework under which a more specific and practical problem was discussed: to determine whether or not the PC enshrined a general principle of prohibition of social regression, implying that, once a certain level of development of social rights has been achieved, such standard becomes both an *institutional guarantee* and a *subjective fundamental right*, binding to the legislature. The recognition of said principle does not mean there can be no reversion or change of social policies according to the democratic will and the political context, but it does entail that legislation that completely reverses the standard of achievement of a social right or seriously threatens to do so, without providing alternatives or compensation, should be ruled unconstitutional. Early constitutional jurisprudence often mobilized this argument, although in a very limited and sensitive way: the prohibition of social regression should be applied only where there are clear and concrete constitutional injunctions for State's action (and not general principles of action or an enunciation of the objectives of public institutions), whenever the legislator annuls or totally reverses previous legislation that enacts it. This was the basis for the ruling of unconstitutionality of a law that abolished the National Health Service (see Judgement of the Portuguese Constitutional Court no. 39/1984) and an important element in various other decisions. Still, the principle was contested from the beginning, initially by a minority of constitutional judges, whose view grew more popular over time. In the decades of 1990 and early 2000, the Court seemed to abandon it completely, often expressly mentioning the idea of prohibition of social regression in order to refuse it, on the basis of the need to accommodate a large margin of appreciation of the legislator, who should be able to approve new norms and design public policies according to its democratically sanctioned views. Overall, the Court consciously acted as a weak counter-majoritarian organ, self-restraining its potential to influence or condition political actions and choices.

Still, the debate about the directive dimension of the constitution and the prohibition of social regression would soon return, under new robes: the general principle of the protection of legitimate expectations that would go on to be the constitutional parameter on which many rulings of unconstitutionality were grounded, in particular during the period of the so-called *crisis jurisprudence*. According to several constitutional decisions, some of which are prior to the economic crisis, such principles should operate when the reduction of the content of a certain social right affects its minimum core or when it entails an 'arbitrary or manifestly unreasonable' reversal (see, for example, Judgements of the Portuguese Constitutional Court

[18] Otto Bachof, *Verfassungswidrige Verfassungsnormen?* (Siebeck, 1951).

no. 509/2002 and 188/2009). Again and again, Portuguese constitutionalism and constitutional jurisprudence are confronted with the *meaning of the constitution*, its possibilities and limits and the consequences they entail to State's actions, democratic choices and fundamental rights. With a very rich and far-reaching constitutional text, this question – nowadays usually framed under the question of whether the State can undo what it previously did – remains central to the national constitutional imaginary.

17.3.2 *Constitutional Contradictions: Between Social-Democratic Origins and European Neoliberalization*

Portugal joined the EU in 1986, ten years after the approval of its Constitution, only four years after its first amendment, in 1982, in which the military were definitely removed from power.

For a long time, the potential problems arising from the dissonances between national and European constitutional law were largely ignored. The main argument was that the existence of a common constitutional tradition would help solve any difficulties, and that serious sources of stress regarding the relationship between the national and the European legal orders were not really foreseeable. There was some debate about this around the period of 2003–2008, when the process of approval of a constitution for Europe was taking place, and when the ECJ's Judgements in *Laval* and *Viking* came out, showing that the very different standards of protection of workers' rights at the EU and national level could perhaps cause some trouble. Still, European integration and its legal and constitutional consequences were generally welcomed.

The most important contradictions obviously regard the EU's and the Portuguese *economic constitution*. Whereas the former has a neoliberal nature, especially after the Maastricht Treaty, favouring market freedoms, limited States' intervention in the economy and tight budgetary and fiscal rules, the latter's main features (and, actually, the political and economic project underlying the whole PC) have a clear social-democratic inclination. As I said before, the economic chapter of the PC has been largely ignored during the last few decades, but the differences seem almost unsurmountable. Nevertheless, this did not seem to pose a serious hurdle, as the most problematic national constitutional norms regarding the economy are mostly principles and not rules and are not usually used in constitutional adjudication.

However, the economic chapter of the constitution and the catalogue of fundamental rights are not watertight compartments, especially when that catalogue is as large and detailed as the Portuguese. Some social and economic rights, such as the right to health and the right to education, are to be ensured, first and foremost, by public services (the National Health Service and the public-school system), very thoroughly regulated at the constitutional level. Although the PC recognizes the existence of private schools and private medicine, such goods are thought to be largely outside of the market, due to their fundamental status. Moreover, the idea of subordination of the economy to the democratic political powers, which prevails in the national constitution, may lead to very different outcomes regarding constitutional adjudication at national and EU level.

The country tragically realized this during the period of economic crisis, from 2010 to 2015, when the clash between the PC's social-democratic origins and the later European neoliberalization became evident. In 2011, a bailout programme was negotiated with the European Commission, the European Central Bank and the International Monetary Fund, which took the form of an agreement on a Financial and Economic Adjustment Programme in exchange for a financial loan of EUR 78 billion. Not all of the austerity measures adopted during that period were coming from pressure of the EU bodies but many of them indeed corresponded to demands made in the Memoranda, as acknowledged even by the Constitutional Court.[19]

The contradictions surrounding the main elements of the national constitutional imaginary posed difficult questions and raised a harsh debate: how could Portugal combine its European vocation – and fulfil the demands of the EU's budgetary rules – with its social-democratic political project? Did we have to accept social regression and a significantly lower standard of fundamental rights, in particular social rights (or even the absence thereof), in order to maintain the desired openness of our constitutional legal order? Did the national constitution still have clear normative strength? Suddenly, the country was facing its very own *Sophie's choice*: it could affirm the normative strength of its constitution and to uphold its social-democratic constitutional project or it could willingly abide by EU demands, under a very difficult financial and economic crisis; but it could not have *both*.

The role played by the Constitutional Court in this dilemma is well known. Called to adjudicate in several cases of abstract review of constitutionality of austerity measures – both by the President of the Republic, the Ombudsman, and parliamentary minorities, who made a conscious decision to constitutionalize the political conflict – the Court assumed a role of intervention and defence of fundamental rights, against the mentioned measures of austerity. Still, a more detailed analysis of the so-called *crisis jurisprudence* actually shows that the position of the Constitutional Court has been much more complex and nuanced; far from the judicial activism of which it has been accused, the Court has exercised a remarkable

[19] On the economic adjustment programme, see European Commission – Directorate-General for Economic and Financial Affairs, 'The Economic Adjustment Programme for Portugal' (2011) *European Economy: Occasional Papers* 79; on the impact of the measures adopted, see European Parliament, Directorate-General for Internal Policies of the Union and Mariana Rodrigues Canotilho, *The Impact of the Crisis on Fundamental Rights across Member States of the EU – Country Report on Portugal* (European Parliament, 2015), https://data.europa.eu/doi/10.2861/68362.

degree of self-restraint in its decisions about the measures taken by the government in response to the economic and financial crisis.[20]

In general, during the crisis period, the Constitutional Court was called on to assess the constitutionality of norms concerning three main types of measures: (i) legislation on the public employment sector, in particular provisions regarding pay-cuts and reducing the payment of overtime; (ii) legislation on social security benefits, especially pay-cuts and 'special contributions' imposed upon pensions, as well as changes to the legal regime of old age pensions; and (iii) lastly, legislation concerning taxes and the fiscal system. This was the very core of the *social state*: in a crisis, who pays for what? Which fundamental rights may be affected, which social benefits are to be cut and which are to be maintained, and what is the constitutional framework to do so?

Initially, in the first two judgments (see Judgements of the Portuguese Constitutional Court no. 399/2010 and 396/2011), the Court did not strike down any element of the recent austerity policy. On the contrary, it adopted a deferential stance towards the legislature, recalling its frequent argument regarding the margin of appreciation of the democratic parliament and the epistemic limitations to the exercise of constitutional adjudication in such cases. Furthermore, the Court relied on an evaluation of exceptionality and proportionality, claiming that the reviewed measures did not breach the principle of protection of legitimate expectations nor the prohibition of retroactive taxation. As time went by, however, the Constitutional Court's stance changed. Several judgments of unconstitutionality of State's budgetary laws and labour and social security reforms (see Judgements of the Portuguese Constitutional Court no. 353/2012, 187/2013, 474/2013, 862/2013, 413/2014, 572/2014, 574/2014 and 575/2014) were adopted and external political criticism of the Court's position grew stronger and more aggressive. Even though there was a clear division inside the Court itself – with some of its justices' dissenting opinions openly criticizing the majority for interfering with the political options, claiming epistemic insufficiency to review public policies' choices and arguing for a weak scrutiny and

[20] On this issue, see Mariana Canotilho, 'Constitutional Law and Crisis: The Portuguese Constitutional Court under Pressure?', in Zoltán Szente and Frusina Gárdos-Orosz (eds.), *Constitutional Law and Crisis* (Routledge, 2018); Mariana Canotilho, Teresa Violante and Rui Lanceiro, 'Austerity Measures under Judicial Scrutiny: The Portuguese Constitutional Case-Law' (2015) 11 *European Constitutional Law Review* 155. Ana Maria Guerra Martins, 'Constitutional Judge, Social Rights and Public Debt Crisis: The Portuguese Constitutional Case Law (2015) 22 *Maastricht Journal of European and Comparative Law* 678; Jorge Reis Novais, *Em Defesa do Tribunal Constitucional* (Almedina, 2014); Gonçalo de Almeida Ribeiro and Luís Pereira Coutinho (eds.), *O Tribunal Constitucional e a Crise – Ensaios Críticos* (Almedina, 2014); Roberto Cisotta and Daniele Gallo, 'The Portuguese Constitutional Court Case Law on Austerity Measures: A Reappraisal', in Claire Kilpatrick and Bruno De Witte (eds.), *Social Rights in Times of Crisis in the Eurozone: The Role of Fundamental Rights' Challenges*, EUI Working Papers Law 2014/05; Cristina Fasone, 'Constitutional Courts Facing the Euro Crisis: Italy, Portugal and Spain in a Comparative Perspective', EUI Working Paper MWP 2014/25.

for an interpretation of the constitution in light of the constitutional commitment to European integration – the building of a quite coherent body of case-law, based upon the principles of the protection of legitimate expectations, equality and proportionality went on, gaining huge popular support and reaffirming some of the key elements of the national constitutional imaginary: the primacy of fundamental rights, including social rights, enshrined in a normative constitution that, though opened to the European legal order, had not lost its central role in national political life. Political pluralism and democratic governance also proved relevant, as the intervention of the Constitutional Court was rendered possible by initiative of several key political actors, namely minority MPs.

17.4 MULTIPLE CONSTITUTIONAL PERSONALITIES OR THE SEARCH FOR CONSTITUTIONAL IDENTITY

The contemporary Portuguese constitutional imaginary faces a crossroads. Although it has overcome the financial crisis' period without a clear rupture between one or more of its main components, the truth is that it is becoming increasingly difficult to find a compromise. As the European integration process advances in an unbalanced way (or stalls) and new crises arise, one must question the opportunity and usefulness of the constitutional debates that fill the Portuguese imaginary.

Yet, interestingly enough, the contradictions that came about during the financial crisis' period were neither a crisis of the idea of *directive constitution* nor of the idea of social transformation through (constitutional) law. Such ideas emerged from that time *reinforced*, only not at the national level. What became evident during the years of economic disaster was the prevalence of the European political project and its own *directive constitutionalism*, imposing significative restraints on the legislator and other national bodies, upholding its own balances between fundamental rights and economic organization and promoting its own idea of systemic change and evolution. The paradoxes and contradictions resulting from this phenomenon, from a constitutional point of view, have more to do with the (at least partial) opposition between the national and European constitutional projects than with any other fact.

Therefore, the main problem seems to be the future of the social state, and of the idea of social, economic and cultural democracy, guaranteed through law, whose implementation and promotion is binding upon all State's powers. In other words: if the EU is intrinsically neoliberal, can we be social-democratic at the national level? Is it possible for our constitutional framework to remain opened but plural and democratic, normatively strong and constitutionally coherent, with a strong commitment towards *all* fundamental rights enshrined in the national constitution? Is there even a choice, after the Brexit experience? Abandoning the European integration project does not sound like a sensible answer nor would it have the support of the majority of the citizenship. On the other hand, it is doubtful that the same citizenship would endorse the clear and honest assumption of limits to the exercise of sovereignty and free democratic choice in non-harmonized matters or in the sphere of exclusive national competences.

Portuguese constitutionalism needs an honest discussion on what we want to keep, what we are willing to change and what we have already lost. However, that must be done within an environment of political honesty, where those who argue in favour of *openness* do not do so only because they prefer neoliberalism to social-democracy; and those who sustain the *normative strength of the constitution* and the use of law as an instrument of social transformation bear in mind that such transformation may or may not be the one that they would defend.

The years ahead, with new and more difficult crises looming on the horizon, promise to make the tension between the written constitution and its imaginary, on one hand, and the real constitution, on the other, much clearer. In other words, the strain between constitutional imagination and the effective application (or lack thereof) of constitutional norms in a context of inter-constitutional and inter-normative dialectic exchanges will probably become more evident.

The main problem seems to be the ability to determine whether this tension is simply the result of the limits of the normative strength of the Constitution, due to social and economic factors, or the manifestation of a new type of limit, not only economic, but also *institutional* and *systemic*, in the current EU context. In other words, rather than to a situation of economic and/or political fragility *per se*, are these tensions due to the resizing and complexification of the constitutional system in the European framework? If so, what methodological approach – if any – may be useful to preserve national constitutional consensus, while still fundamentally respecting the obligations of EU membership? Will the constraints dictated by the economic system be so strong that, in the long-term, and even within the framework of the European Union, they make it impossible to change or alter other elements of the system (social, political, legal and economic)?

Constitutional law is, at the same time, a limit to the exercise of power, and a socio-political project, a repository of the fundamental objectives of a social and political community. If it proves incapable of binding the sovereign bodies to its own hierarchy of values, which should preside over the design of any public norm or policy, and if it allows the deterioration of legal and institutional guarantees of fundamental rights – that is, the pillars of the constitution – very little remains.

Naturally, it will ultimately be up to citizens to decide which dimensions of the original constitutional project they want to rescue, which features are so fundamental that they still identify with them. There is a strong political dimension to the problems described above that is not something to be denied, nor is it to be solved solely through legal means. But the truth is that it is the task of constitutionalism to explain and propose conditions for guaranteeing the greatest possible effectiveness to the constitutional norms in force.

I believe that there are two fundamental methodological premises to achieve this objective. Reconciling them will not always be easy – perhaps not always even possible – but they constitute a starting point for a discussion that deserves to be deepened.

17.4.1 *Preserving Openness, with Feet on the Ground*

First of all, I think we would benefit from highlighting the possibilities allowed by the very idea of openness and the concrete constitutional provisions that support it – especially in what concerns the relationship with the EU's legal order – without losing sight of sovereignty, normativity and a tiny bit of constitutional utopia. Openness is a good feature more often than not and, in order to walk a shared path, one needs to listen and learn. Many fundamental rights provisions may not be read through a single national lens anymore and the search for meaning, the definition of limits to the actions of public powers in every level of the European constitutional space, as well as a balancing of parameters through comparative constitutional law seems a good way to go forward. Therefore, whenever that is necessary, the interpretation of constitutional parameters should take European standards of protection of fundamental rights into account, allowing the interpretation of national constitutional provisions to change and widen, in order to promote similarity and coherence regarding EU law. As an example, I would highlight the reasoning in the Judgments of the Portuguese Constitutional Court no. 268/2022 and 800/2023, on metadata retention, where the majority of judges upheld an interpretation of relevant national constitutional norms according to the standards drawn by the European Court of Justice on the same subject.

Still, there is a lot that is worth preserving from the specific national constitutional imaginary. First and foremost, the idea of a much deeper and significant meaning of democracy, one that is pursued across different levels of society, and goes beyond civil rights, encompassing demands of democratic governance of many public (and even private) institutions, and the guarantee of social conditions to do so. Any contradictions with EU law in this sphere should, therefore, be resolved, favouring democracy, as a more effective and decentralized democracy is probably a pathway to solve some of the European hurdles anyway. The greatest difficulty in applying this principle comes from the European Union itself, and from the idea apparently inherent in the discourse of its institutions, in particular the ECJ, according to which constitutional idiosyncrasies (sometimes even the institutional and organizational schemes on which national constitutions are grounded) must yield in all circumstances to guarantee the principle of the primacy and uniform application of Union law.

However, EU constitutionalism seems to remain today insufficient to provide any operative notion of *collective self-representation*, to be able to replace the national sphere as the *core of the constitutional imagination* of European peoples (the Portuguese certainly included).[21] In this sense, the preservation of *openness* at national level requires, at the very least, a fruitful dialectic with European institutions, and a set of mutual concessions without which, sooner than later, the conflict over the meaning of rights and the implications of dissonant political projects will arise.

In the specific realm of fundamental rights, it is important to notice that regarding rights *more* is often *better* and a good instrument of protection of political and cultural minorities. Therefore, we should not give up on either our own catalogue of fundamental rights nor on the national understanding of their practical meaning (which is an important part of our constitutional imagination), in order to maintain openness. Openness is not structurally incompatible with strong national fundamental rights' standards, not even with a political and socio-economic constitutional program of social democratic nature, in which social and economic rights have a strong stance. Also, openness allows for the reinforcement of rights regarding new issues, being especially useful with regard to complex and transnational problems, the solution of which requires international cooperation and even a joint exercise of sovereign powers.

Finally, the boundaries that limit the application of fundamental rights should preferably be defined at the national constitutional level or at least with its participation, unless very specific problems of EU law are at stake. Subsidiarity provides context, closeness and more thorough proportionality reviews and I believe it avoids many problems. In the motto 'united in diversity', promoting respect for diversity seems to be a sensitive way to go. The re-emergence of the individual States in every successive crisis actually shows it is even in part unavoidable. The search for a shared constitutional identity at EU level seems to give way to national interests and needs and to national democratic claims whenever there are serious problems. As such, the normative strength of both legal orders would be strengthened if both the scope of application of the principle of subsidiarity and the insurmountable borders of the common European project were more clearly and wisely defined.

17.4.2 *Preserving the Transformative Nature of the (National and European) Constitution*

The transformative nature of constitutionalism depends on its ability to promote agreed social changes and to resist setbacks. Such transformation is multidimensional, acting at the political-ideological, legal and social levels. Under the influence of a certain constitutional framework, it is possible to observe profound alterations in the sphere of individual rights, in the economic organization, in the system of legal sources, in the organic distribution of competences and in the institutional framework of a given community, in a given sovereign space and in a relatively short

[21] Martin Loughin, 'The constitutional imagination' (2015) 78 *The Modern Law Review* 1.

period of time. This is what happened in Portugal after the approval of the constitution in 1976, which was followed by a period of expansion of the fundamental rights effectively ensured, with the consequent improvement of a series of social indicators. The constitutional framework was thus an essential element in the impulse of social progress in the sense of the promotion of fundamental rights – both in the civil and political dimension, as well as in relation to economic, social and cultural rights.

The process of European integration is also an example of the transformative potential of constitutional law, since the adoption of European Union constitutional law changed in an equally profound way the countries that progressively joined the EU. In a short period of time, these states opened up to the outside world, accepting the free movement of workers, services and capital, recognized an additional status of citizenship conferring rights to non-nationals (European citizenship) and reorganized their economic system in the sense of opening up markets, guaranteeing respect for competition rules and strengthening the role of the private sector in the economy.

The clash between the two transformative impulses inevitably came about when, in an everchanging crisis scenario, it is becoming increasingly clear that the two transformational projects, enshrined in the different constitutional levels (national and European), are not always on a path of complementarity, as had long been advocated. The future reconciliation of the two tendencies, within the framework of a genuine European constitutional law, will therefore require the clear predominance of one of the two dimensions – the social or the market dimension – in the service of a true European constitutional law.

Thus, preserving the transformative potential of national constitutional law requires, in the Portuguese case, increased attention to the dimensions of EU constitutional law that reinforce it, to the detriment of those that contribute to its weakening. The idea of a socially committed Europe and the strengthening of the normative force of the provisions of the European Pillar of Social Rights and the European Social Charter could perhaps help. The problems of democratic legitimacy for the imposition of certain measures and the difficulties arising from contradictory claims to sovereignty, however, remain unresolved issues.[22]

[22] About the clash of decisions on social matters at national and European level as a conflict between competing ideas of sovereignty, see Luís Miguel Nogueira de Brito, 'A Comment on Miguel Poiares Maduro's "Crisis between Crises": The Portuguese Constitutional Court's Jurisprudence of Crisis between Autarchy and Sovereignty' (2017) 4 *e-Pública* 43.

18

Constitutional Drift

Exploring the Deeper Roots of Polish Constitutional Crisis

Karol Muszyński and Paweł Skuczyński

18.1 INTRODUCTION

The goal of this chapter is to show the deeper roots of the so-called Polish *constitutional* or *rule of law crisis*. The crisis may be characterised as a period of constant conflict between the legislative and executive authorities on the one hand and the judiciary on the other, as well as the increasingly extensive subordination of the judiciary to the former. The structural imbalance within the separation of powers has led to the weakening of the constitutional checks and balances through a series of formal measures (changes in the law, disciplinary proceedings against judges) and informal measures (pressure on judges, chilling effects, etc.).[1] Despite the risks associated with the direction of these changes, their political authors have been winning several successive parliamentary and presidential elections, pointing at least to indifference towards changes constituting the constitutional crisis.[2]

In this chapter we argue that, while the constitutional crisis itself started in 2015, processes similar to those happening to the judiciary had started much earlier. The introduction of the rule of law principles in Poland following a period of political transformation in 1989 was a gradual process rather than a result of a distinct

This chapter was created as part of the research project No. 2015/19/B/HS5/00132 entitled 'Legal Policy against the Professional Self-governments: Towards a Model of Reflexive Law Making', financed by the National Science Centre.

[1] Aleksandra Kustra, 'Poland's Constitutional Crisis: From Court-Packing Agenda to Denial of Constitutional Court's Judgments' (2016) 12 *Toruńskie Studia Polsko-Włoskie* 343; Anna Chmielarz-Grochal and Jarosław Sułkowski, 'Appointment of Judges to the Constitutional Tribunal in 2015 as the Trigger Point for a Deep Constitutional Crisis in Poland' (2018) (No 2) *Przegląd Konstytucyjny* 91.

[2] Jan Winczorek and Karol Muszyński, 'The Access to Justice Gap and the Rule of Law Crisis in Poland' (2022) 42 *Zeitschrift für Rechtssoziologie* 5; Grażyna Skąpska, 'Abuse of the Constitution as a Means of Political Change: Sociological Reflections on the Crisis of Constitutionalism in Poland' (2019) *Polish Sociological Review* 421.

constitutional moment.[3] The 1997 Constitution created highly flexible provisions allowing for multiple types of interpretations of the possible constitutional arrangement but guaranteed the involvement into governance and the policy-making process of social actors such as civil society, trade unions, religious organisations, local and professional self-governments and organisations. In sum, we argue that the 1997 Constitution created ground for the functioning of competitive constitutional imaginaries that fertilised constitutional discourse immediately after its adoption. However, after the adoption of the 1997 Constitution and until 2015, the constitutional provisions were subject to the process which we refer to as *constitutional drift*, which involved marginalisation of the societal imaginary underpinned by the Constitution. During this period, more dominant liberal and communitarian imaginaries created grounds for a new paradigm of governance which strengthened the executive at the expense of the parliament, social partners and other social actors in general. This period includes Poland's integration to the European Union, with the formal accession on 1 May 2004 and the gradual Europeanisation of the Polish legal order. In this period, processes fundamental for the emergence of the current *constitutional crisis,* which began in 2015, were started. Our perspective aims to provide deeper, institutional perspective on how and why the constitutional crisis was possible – related to the adverse direction which Polish constitutionalism took after the adoption of the 1997 Constitution.

This makes us question the existing literature, which suggests a few possible explanations for the constitutional crisis.[4] First, some scholars see it as being caused by the actions of populist politicians aiming to dismantle the limits of power,[5] attacking the liberal principles of the system and the institutions that embody these principles while seeking broad popular support[6] through social transfers and the accompanying anti-elitist and anti-pluralist rhetoric aimed at excluding various minorities.[7] The second and similar group of explanations are cultural, which point to the lack of alignment between formal constitutional provisions and cultural conditions.[8] This led to a disenchantment of citizens with the Constitution, related to the lack of identification with liberal values and preference towards different

[3] Michał Ziółkowski, 'Constitutional Moment and the Polish Constitutional Crisis 2015–2018 (a Few Critical Remarks)' (2019) (No 4) *Przegląd Konstytucyjny* 76.

[4] For an excellent review, see Maciej Pichlak, 'Sytuacja autorytarna i rządy prawa: Socjologiczno-prawne wyjaśnienia kryzysu konstytucyjnego' (2021) 43 (No 1) *Studia nad Autorytaryzmem i Totalitaryzmem* 173.

[5] Pablo Castillo-Ortiz, 'The Illiberal Abuse of Constitutional Courts in Europe' (2019) 15 *European Constitutional Law Review* 48; Martin Krygier, 'The Challenge of Institutionalisation: Post-Communist "Transitions", Populism, and the Rule of Law' (2019) 15 *European Constitutional Law Review* 544.

[6] Wojciech Sadurski, *Poland's Constitutional Breakdown* (Oxford University Press, 2019).

[7] Ibid., 8–9 and 19–25.

[8] Skąpska, 'Abuse of the Constitution as a Means of Political Change'; Marta Bucholc, 'Commemorative Lawmaking: Memory Frames of the Democratic Backsliding in Poland After 2015' (2019) 11 *The Hague Journal on the Rule of Law* 85.

model of community – a more ethnic one, often built on a sense of insecurity. Finally, antagonistic explanations claim that constitutional provisions were attacked because of its 'capture' by lawyers[9] or because, while they appeared neutral, they effectively secured neoliberal economic principles and interests of the narrow elite.[10]

Although these interpretations often start from the right premises, they do not capture the phenomena in question entirely and lead to erroneous generalisations. In our view, the approaches focusing on populism do not place it in the context of the existing constitutional practice. In particular, they fail to consider how the constitutional practices prior to 2015 reflected the existing constitutional model, while some scholars argue that the adherence to constitutional provisions was rather poor even before the crisis.[11] Focusing on populism can mostly demonstrate the rather obvious fact of its existence and describe the havoc it wreaks in the constitutional sphere but cannot show either its historical genesis or explain how such a vast constitutional space was created for its development.

Rejecting the thesis of purely populist sources of the crisis – without, however, denying the responsibility of the populists themselves and rejecting the thesis of the inability to overcome the errors of the transformation – we propose another way. It consists in noticing and highlighting the period of constitutional drift for shaping the constitutional practice. A series of processes took place in 1997–2015 that led to the rejection of an imaginary allowing interpretation of the Polish Constitution in the spirit of societal constitutionalism (which we call the 'societal imaginary'). At the same time, a new paradigm of governance favourable to the concentration of power was taking shape underpinned by different imaginaries. Noteworthy among these processes was the development of the ideology of strengthening the executive (i.e., the Prime Minister and the cabinet) at the expense of social actors and entrusting the former with the task of bringing about significant social changes, the technocratic Europeanisation of the legal order and the increasingly broader practical understanding of the Constitution as a carrier of values rather than a vehicle of social ontology.

The structure of the chapter will not be chronological. First, we will set the outset by discussing potential ways of interpreting the Polish 1997 Constitution in the context of competitive imaginaries which are present in it. Then, we will discuss the constitutional drift, that is, the institutional practice that contradicted the societal

9 Adam Czarnota, 'Constitutional Correction as a Third Democratic Revolutionary Moment in Central Eastern Europe' (2019) 11 *The Hague Journal on the Rule of Law* 397; Michał Stambulski, 'Constitutional Populism and the Rule of Law in Poland' in Martin Krygier, Adam Czarnota and Wojciech Sadurski (eds.), *Anti-Constitutional Populism* (Cambridge University Press, 2022).

10 Adam Sulikowski, 'Apolityczność w prawoznawstwie. Kryzys idei a zjawisko populizmu' (2018) (No 3) *Archiwum Filozofii Prawa i Filozofii Społecznej* 74.

11 Winczorek and Muszyński, 'The Access to Justice Gap'; Joanna Kusiak, 'Rule of Law and Rules-Lawyering: Legal Corruption and "Reprivatization Business" in Warsaw' (2019) 43 *International Journal of Urban and Regional Research* 589.

imaginary and led to a significant divergence with the potential of the functioning of a corporatist social model, showing how the executive strengthened itself at the cost of social partners, NGOs and professional self-government organisations citing democratic accountability and the necessity to integrate with the European Union. In Section 18.4, we discuss the transition from the constitutional drift to the constitutional crisis.

18.2 FORMING OF POLISH CONSTITUTIONAL MODEL AND COMPETITIVE IMAGINARIES OF THE POLISH CONSTITUTION

The debates over the enactment of the new constitution between 1989 and 1997 emphasised the need to avoid strongly political and ideological components and focus on its legal role. The 1997 Constitution was, therefore, a deliberate attempt to create a text which is juridical, focused on justiciable formal arrangements, the norms defining competences and rights. It was foreseen that the inclusion of various declarations on values could be a source of difficulties in the future constitutional practice[12] and would risk turning the text into a manifesto.[13]

Consequently, the systematic interpretation of the provisions of the Polish 1997 Constitution has been and still is a practical and theoretical challenge as it contains references to different sets of ideas and beliefs.[14] One can speak of a constant task to search for such a theoretical formula which, on the one hand, will not limit itself to stating that there are various conflicts of constitutional values which require balancing on the grounds of concrete cases and, on the other hand, will not reduce this task to the necessity to undertake unifying measures with regard to these values, achievable only at the cost of marginalising certain contents contained in the act in question. Such systematic interpretations can be understood as different as competitive constitutional imaginaries which function in the Polish constitutional discourse as alternative 'readings' of the constitution.[15] Such imaginaries refer to the fundamental principles or ideas contained in the given constitution, which explain their meaning in the context of a specific political philosophy or social theory. The role of an imaginary is to propose an understanding of the basic notions of a given constitution convergent with a given political philosophy or social theory while granting legitimacy to the particular rulemaking and governance processes on the grounds of that philosophy or theory. In other words, imaginaries

[12] Piotr Winczorek, 'Nowa Konstytucja Rzeczypospolitej Polskiej: Problem aksjologii' (1996) 4 (No 4) *Przegląd Sejmowy* 9.

[13] Piotr Winczorek, 'Konstytucja i Wartości', in Janusz Trzciński (ed.), *Charakter i struktura norm konstytucji* (Wydawnictwo Sejmowe, 1997), 55.

[14] Michał Stambulski and Adam Czarnota, 'The Janus Face of Constitutionalism' (2019) 11 (No 1) *Krytyka Prawa: Niezależne studia nad prawem* 18.

[15] Wojciech Ciszewski, 'Republikańskie odczytanie Konstytucji Rzeczypospolitej Polskiej' (2017) (No 4) *Przegląd Konstytucyjny* 4.

help to 'motivate and justify the practice of the government and collective self-rule'[16] underpinning this process by references to coherent sets of ideas and beliefs. Practically speaking, imaginaries allow us to structure constitutional norms and their mutual relations and solve legal and political problems associated with complexities and paradoxes of democratic governance.

The discussions about the nature of the Polish 1997 Constitution have been predominantly conducted between most dominant liberal and communitarian constitutional imaginaries. Liberal imaginary assumed that the function of constitutional architecture is to limit power to protect individual rights and freedom understood negatively. This way of reading the constitution in principle understands every form of interference, including legal interference, as a limitation of individual freedom. On the other side lies the principle of the sovereignty of the people, associated with democracy, by dint of which citizens can express their political will through law that can, among other things, limit individual freedom. Freedom and the sovereignty are thus described as being in conflict and are additionally counterbalanced by antagonistic principles, such as the rule of law, the separation of powers, the independence of the judiciary or constitutional review. The status of constitutional norms as conflicting principles which need to be balanced allows for synergistic effects – a kind of optimum between individual freedom and the sovereignty of the people. This perspective of looking at the constitution was particularly present in the Constitutional Tribunal's case law.[17]

Alternative imaginary contributing to the discussions about the nature of the Polish constitutional project was a communitarian (republican) one that understood constitutional values such as freedom in a positive way, that is, as increasing capability of action/choice.[18] This capability is determined not only by the restrictions set by political power but also by the operations of political power which may actually increase these capabilities. The sovereignty of the people as well as the rule of law and other principles such as the separation of powers serve this purpose. All of them are to be interpreted as reducing the arbitrariness of governments and preventing a group from gaining unlimited power. Because of the teleological subordination of these principles, there is no antagonism between the principle of freedom and the sovereignty of the people and both principles can be fully realised – not one at the expense of the other, as in the liberal view.[19]

While we do not question that both liberal and communitarian imaginaries provide a coherent and possible interpretation of the 1997 Constitution, we believe

[16] Jan Komárek, 'European Constitutional Imaginaries: Utopias, Ideologies, and the Other', in Jan Komárek (ed.), *European Constitutional Imaginaries: Between Ideology and Utopia* (Oxford University Press, 2023), 2.

[17] Adam Sulikowski, 'Trybunał Konstytucyjny a Polityczność. O Konsekwencjach Upadku Pewnego Mitu' (2016) 71 *Państwo i Prawo* 4; see also Chapter 15, by Wojciech Zomerski.

[18] Ciszewski, 'Republikańskie odczytanie Konstytucji Rzeczypospolitej Polskiej'.

[19] Ibid., 18–24.

that they have effectively contributed to the constitutional drift that we will discuss in Section 18.3. We will concentrate on highlighting the differences between our proposal of the societal reading of the constitution built upon the principles of societal constitutionalism rather than on the liberal and communitarian imaginaries. As a result, we suggest that 'societal' imaginary based upon societal constitutionalism is underpinned by the 1997 Constitution, played a role in the Polish constitutional discourse after 1997, and should be revitalised as a means of overcoming the constitutional crisis.

Societal constitutionalism, while not negating the status of freedom as a constitutional value, focuses on the safeguards of social diversity, the autonomy of existing social actors and the normative orders they produce, against the drift towards social authoritarianism and its transformation into political authoritarianism.[20]

The societal interpretation of the Polish Constitution that we put forward assumes that, on the grounds of liberal or communitarian imaginaries, the autonomy of social actors is too narrowly understood as threatening political expression. Societal constitutionalism highlights, however, that, in any social subsystem, individuals can be subject to dependencies limiting their freedom, whether it's the system of economy, health, the media or science. In any social subsystem, individuals can be coerced into theoretically voluntarily giving up their freedom and submitting to more or less formal social control measures. Notably, the mere safeguarding of political freedom with the increasing restriction of the individual's possibilities for social development will sooner or later[21] – due to the expansionism of social subsystems – lead to a restriction of the former.

We may recognise that the tension between individual rights and the people's sovereignty is a structural antagonism, as in the liberal imaginary. Also, we may see the possibility of resolving the conflict between the two, as in the communitarian imaginary. But there is a third element to this relationship, which transforms it into a triangle, and this element is a society and various forms of its self-organisation. Only in this way is it possible to constitutionally secure autonomy. Without securing autonomy of the society, only the following two scenarios are possible. First, political power's increasing influence on social life results in increased politicisation, bureaucratisation of society and communication overload.[22] Second, the extension of

[20] For a broader description of societal constitutionalism, see David Sciulli, *Theory of Societal Constitutionalism: Foundations of a Non-Marxist Critical Theory* (Cambridge University Press, 1992); Gunther Teubner, *Constitutional Fragments: Societal Constitutionalism and Globalization* (Oxford University Press, 2012); Chris Thornhill, 'The Citizen of Many Worlds: Societal Constitutionalism and the Antinomies of Democracy' (2018) 45 *Journal of Law and Society Journal of Law and Society* 73; Paweł Skuczyński and Karol Muszyński, *Rozwój i Kryzys Konstytucji Społecznej: Przypadek Samorządów Zawodowych* (Wydawnictwo CH Beck, 2020).

[21] Niklas Luhmann, 'Differentiation of Society' (1977) 2 *Canadian Journal of Sociology / Cahiers canadiens de sociologie* 29; Teubner, Constitutional Fragments.

[22] Niklas Luhmann, *Political Theory in the Welfare State* (De Gruyter, 1990).

individual rights into social relations (e.g. as part of their horizontal effect) increases the juridification of social life.[23] The attempt to secure social freedom by means familiar to traditional juridical or democratic constitutionalism and the subsystems linked within it must therefore aim at an expansion of either politics or law – and thus ultimately at a reduction of social differentiation due to the loss of autonomy.

Of course, the inclusion of societal autonomy in the relationship in question must find a basis in the constitutional text. Such a basis exists in the Polish 1997 Constitution, which mentions many institutionalised social actors and forms of self-government. The different interpretations of the Constitution differ in their visions of how these entities are to fulfil their roles.

Within the liberal imaginary, civil society is first and foremost supposed to control the political power, thereby contributing to its limitation. At the same time, the role of politics is supposed to secure a legal framework protecting individual rights. The political power and the civil society are thus mutually balanced. Such an approach pre-supposes competition between social actors and state bodies. By necessity, it must drive strategic action, bureaucratisation, and social control. Thus, if it even contributes to securing political freedom, it sacrifices the autonomy of social entities. Within the communitarian imaginary, the people's sovereignty, individual rights, and social actors all interact to maximise the same value of positive freedom. Politics is tasked with unifying social subsystems with a common goal. This reading ignores the societal fragmentation into different subsystems such as economics, health and science, that act in the name of different and sometimes conflicting values.

Within the societal imaginary, the political and legal systems must be open to socially produced normativity. Instead of leaving these processes and their effects in the private sphere, the Constitution should consider them in a genuinely democratic process of law-making. This can take various forms but, in essence, social actors should be able to influence public policies and law-making, create their own norms and self-regulate as broadly as possible.

The proposition of a societal imaginary is ultimately linked to a classic corporate social model characteristic for continental Europe, opposed primarily to the American pluralist one and focused on resolving social conflicts – mainly in the economic sphere, but not exclusively – through negotiations and compromises between social partners.[24] The premises for the functioning of a corporate social model are: (1) self-organisation of the society in various forms (from civil society organisations, through trade unions and employers' organisations to professional and territorial self-government), (2) consensual agreement-making modes (from informal dialogue mechanisms through bipartite and tripartite social dialogue to the co-

[23] Gunther Teubner (ed.), *Juridification of Social Spheres: A Comparative Analysis in the Areas of Labor, Corporate, Antitrust and Social Welfare Law* (De Gruyter, 2012).

[24] Georg Nolte, *European and US Constitutionalism* (Cambridge University Press, 2005).

governance by social partners) and (3) mechanisms of inclusion of social norms formed bottom-up (from effective forms of consultation and opinion-forming, through social participation in the creation of public policies, to self-regulatory regimes).

The societal imaginary of the Polish 1997 Constitution is underpinned legally, politically and historically by four arguments.

The first argument concerns the material scope of the Constitution. The Constitution provides regulations in several areas which do not need to (as rights and freedoms of citizens and to structure the operations of public administration) – but can – be regulated at the constitutional level.[25] Such 'possible but not necessary' norms provided in the Constitution protect and regulate various forms of self-organising such as: (1) self-government (local and professional), (2) civil society (foundations, association etc.), (3) social partnership (trade unions and employers' organisations) and (4) religious entities (churches and religious associations).

The second argument underpinning societal imaginary relates to the position of social actors in the act who are mentioned in the very first chapter which sets down rules for the functioning of the socio-political system. It is assumed that their inclusion in the first chapter implies a duty to ensure autonomy of their operations and that the constitutional regulation of social actors is declaratory rather than constitutive in nature, and that, as a rule, civil society subjects exist prior to their establishment in a legal sense.[26] The duties of the public authorities should here be understood not only as related to guaranteeing the freedom of association but also 'to increase and diversify the possibilities of their activity, opening the way for the growth of these possibilities'.[27] Thus, the point is to create pro-developmental conditions both in the sense of increasing the pluralism of social actors and their opportunities for action. The latter should also include increasing their influence on public policies. It is because civil society is a political actor and citizens become political agents also through institutions that self-organise and produce their own social orders.

The third argument under-pinning societal imaginary concerns the historical formation of the regulation of social actors and the constitutional identity. In the Polish constitutionalism, the autonomy of civil society is understood in a Hegelian tradition as being in opposition to the State, which heavily influenced the Polish constitutional discourse in the 1980s and 1990s.[28]

[25] Christopher J. Thornhill, *A Sociology of Constitutions: Constitutions and State Legitimacy in Historical-Sociological Perspective* (Cambridge University Press, 2013).

[26] Paweł Sarnecki, 'Organizacja Społeczeństwa Obywatelskiego', in M. Zubik (ed.), *Księga XX-lecia orzecznictwa Trybunału Konstytucyjnego* (Wydawnictwo Trybunału Konstytucyjnego, 2006).

[27] Ibid., 598.

[28] Jacek Kuron, *Kuron: [pisma polityczne]* (Wydawnictwo Krytyki Politycznej, 2009); Jacek Luszniewicz, *Solidarność, Samorząd Pracowniczy, Transformacja Systemu: O Programie*

The fourth and final argument underpinning societal imaginary refers to the historical process of drafting of the Constitution where principles linked to societal constitutionalism were explicitly included due to pressures from civil society.[29]

The above argumentation indicates that the Constitution aimed at the institution alisation of the social model and that the societal imaginary provides a coherent alternative to the liberal and communitarian one based on the constitutional text. In our view, it was only in the subsequent period that the range of potential interpretations was significantly narrowed down, whereas the corporatist-like social model was gradually excluded from the constitutional practice, the power was consolidated in the hands of the executive and a space for populism was created.

18.3 CONSTITUTIONAL DRIFT

We argue that the constitutional order has been subject to a phenomenon that could be described as constitutional drift which we understand as a process of marginalisation of the societal imaginary by the developments underpinned by liberal and communitarian imaginaries. Here, we refer to Sciulli's concept of drift resulting from the increase of competition among social actors in the context of rising societal differentiation.[30] Social actors, operating in different societal subsystems and unable to influence them to the extent that they would have envisaged, increasingly adopt strategic, bureaucratised methods of operation to increase the efficiency of their actions. These actions result in the rise of social authoritarianism – in our case, located in the political system – relying on various forms of social control which are not counteracted. Moreover, Sciulli points to the fact that instruments traditionally designed to prevent the rise of social authoritarianism further exacerbate the problem. For instance, replacing market forces with administrative governance creates a *de facto* parallel market utilising bureaucratic instead of market logic. A second example are social movements that naively aim at liberation from pervasive social control, which are very often so unstructured and spontaneous that they are vulnerable to various forms of strategic action by other players.

These conceptualisations are a good starting point for the analysis of the drift that took place after the adoption of the Polish 1997 Constitution. We track constitutional drift in three areas – social dialogue (relationships with trade unions and employers' organisations), civil society (relationships with NGOs) and professional self-government organisations (relationship with associations of professions of public

Gospodarczym Sieci Organizacji Zakładowych NSZZ 'Solidarność' Wiodących Zakładów Pracy, Rok 1981 (Szkoła Główna Handlowa w Warszawie, 2008).

29 Stanisław Gebethner, 'Rzeczpospolita w Świetle Postanowień Rozdziału Pierwszego Konstytucji z 1997 roku', in E. Zwierzchowski (ed.), *Podstawowe pojęcia pierwszego rozdziału Konstytucji RP* (Wydawnictwo Uniwersytetu Śląskiego, 2000), 13.

30 Sciulli, *Theory of Societal Constitutionalism.*

trust). The cooperation between social actors (i.e., trade unions and employers' organisations, NGOs, and professional self-government organisations) and policy-makers (including the executive and political parties) in the area of law- and policy-making has been tightening in the early years after 1989. However, due to overlooking of the possibilities stemming from societal interpretation of the Constitution, the relationships between the executive and society developed in a way contributing and accelerating the drift. While various policy actions, including reforms to the social dialogue explained in Section 18.3.1, have been undertaken to stop the process, the requirements of social coordination resulted in subordination of social actors to the bureaucratic expectations of the political power. On the level of constitutional discourse this was fuelled by the liberal and communitarian interpretations of the Constitution, aiming to construct a maximally functional architecture of public administration and the government, while voices from self-organising society were treated as undermining public interest.

A new political paradigm emerged transforming the practice of the constitutional framework. In this paradigm, interferences in the activities of social actors were justified with liberal (protection of individual rights, free market, etc.) or communitarian arguments (protection of the common good). Social actors were publicly accused of particularism. Consequently, the policies against their influence on public policies and law-making were carried out, which we describe in Sections 18.3.1–18.3.4. Ironically, these political developments accelerated and boosted particularistic orientation among social actors and contributed to the growing disenchantment with the institutional framework, which further accelerated the drift.

18.3.1 *Social Dialogue*

As we have described, social partners (trade unions and employers' organisations) have been given a particularly strong role in the Constitution. Trade unions have been traditionally involved in the political process after 1989 and have been even described as 'one of the pillars of Polish party politics'[31] due to their active involvement and intersections with political parties (both on the left and on the right side of the political spectrum). However, after the adoption of the 1997 Constitution, the ties between trade unions and political parties have been significantly loosened. This stemmed from various factors, including a serious political failure of the right-wing electoral coalition built by the Christian democratic trade union Solidarity that had previously won the 1997 election.

In the late 1990s, trade unions were slowly distancing themselves from party politics while focusing on building their own capacities rather than commodifying

[31] Bogusław Jagusiak, *OPZZ i NSZZ Solidarność w Systemie Politycznym Polski w Latach 1989–2001* (CEE, 2004).

various political opportunities.[32] This pathway was formalised around 2001–2002, when a new system of social dialogue was constructed which assumed an active role of social partners in economic governance, with developed, formalised and relatively wide consultation rights. However, over time and particularly since 2005, a gap between the executive and particularly trade unions has been widening. The executive had very little trust towards social partners, suspecting them of rent-seeking behaviours and, in fact, questioning their role as the legitimate representatives of workers. These actions were underpinned by liberal imaginary that intended to downgrade a 'special' channel of relationships with social partners to a typical liberal way of policy-making aimed at communication between the government and equally treated external actors, as well as communitarian imaginary which was sceptical towards supposedly rent-seeking behaviour by the social partners.

This system has evolved into what J. Gardawski called 'consultative etatism'[33] – with the role of social partners reduced to a function of 'expressing'[34] the interests of narrow groups of workers, given the low trade union and employers' organisation density. This development was particularly visible during the economic crisis of 2009, when social partners have made a substantial effort to sign a social pact suggesting a new, more solidaristic way of dealing with the crisis. This attempt was ignored by the executive convinced that it is the sole actor able to represent the public interest.[35] A similar situation happened in 2013, when the retirement age was prolonged despite the largest protests by the trade unions since 1989, as well as in 2017 when the education reform was implemented against a desperate opposition of the strongest trade union of teachers.

In all these circumstances, social partners were unable to win any concessions from the executive. Secondly, social partners, confronted with a low level of trust from the executive, have aligned themselves with party politics to at least partially regain power. This interaction increased competition and strategic cooperation between and across social partners and policy-makers, in fact forcing trade unions and employers' organisations into repeated alignment with political parties. This development has been visible from 2015 onwards, where Christian democratic trade union Solidarity expressed vocal support in both presidential and parliamentary elections for the right-wing party Law and Justice in exchange for reversal of some of the policies that had been introduced against its will under the previous liberal

[32] Juliusz Gardawski, *Dialog Społeczny w Polsce: Teoria, Historia, Praktyka* (Ministerstwo Pracy i Polityki Społecznej. Katedra Socjologii Ekonomicznej SGH, 2009).

[33] Ibid.

[34] Franz Traxler, 'Corporatism(s) and Pacts: Changing Functions and Structures under Rising Economic Liberalism and Declining Liberal Democracy' (2010), After the Euro and enlargement: social pacts in the EU, Brussels: European Trade Union Institute (ETUI) and Observatoire social européen (OSE).

[35] Karol Muszyński, *Polityka regulacji zatrudnienia w Polsce: kryzys ekonomiczny a destandaryzacja stosunków pracy* (Wydawnictwo Naukowe Scholar, 2019).

government.[36] In this way, the autonomy of social partners was further reduced as they were able to win an influence over the policy-making only by paying for it with political concessions.

18.3.2 *Civil Society*

The second example is provided by the developments in the sphere of relationships between the executive and the civil society. The policy-makers after 1989 assumed that the involvement of civil society in public sphere should not include economic interests and conversely focus on the neutral, non-partisan and particularly non-economic activities within the society.[37] This resulted in a discursive segmentation of civil society into 'real' NGOs and lobbying organisations.[38] While – from the side of policy-makers and politicians – the former represented the 'genuine' public interest and mostly focused on non-partisan activity directed at excluded and marginalised groups, the latter were perceived as fostering shady interests and thus treated suspiciously.[39]

At the same time, the organised part of the civil society was actively reshaped by the public governance paradigm underpinned by both liberal and communitarian imaginaries which resulted in an influx of funds directed at public services provision via NGOs, also in the context of an influx of EU funds. This development resulted in the bottom-up depoliticization of NGO sphere, since 'suspicious', interest-driven NGOs have been marginalised while 'non-partisan' NGOs have been increasingly reliant upon public funding,[40] which required them to become more professional, bureaucratic and similar to administrative agencies.[41] This can be summarised as a paradoxical development, where NGOs have been expected to abandon their own agenda and partisanship while becoming more dependent upon political power, particularly due to scarcity of private funds,[42] and started to increasingly perform functions in fact outsourced by the state while being supervised by public administration. Thus, the executive was strategically forcing civil society into a subordinate

36 Wiesława Kozek, NSZZ *'Solidarność' Wobec Nowych Wyzwań Od Roku* 1989 (Wydawnictwo Naukowe Scholar, 2020).

37 Joanna Dzwonczyk, 'The Barriers for the Development of Civic Society in Poland after 1989' (2003) 32 *Polish Poitical Science Yearbook* 117.

38 Piotr Gliński, *Style Działań Organizacji Pozarządowych w Polsce: Grupy Interesu Czy Pożytku Publicznego?* (Wydawnictwo IFiS PAN, 2006).

39 Kerstin Jacobsson and Elżbieta Korolczuk, 'Introduction: Rethinking Polish Civil Society', in Kerstin Jacobsson and Elżbieta Korolczuk (eds.), *Civil Society Revisted: Lessons from Poland* (Berghahn Books, 2017).

40 Stanisław Mazur and Agnieszka Pacut, *System Finansowania Organizacji Pozarządowych w Polsce* (Małopolska Szkoła Administracji Publicznej Uniwersytetu Ekonomicznego 2015).

41 Ewa Cierniak-Szóstak, 'Kultura Organizacyjna NGO Wobec Wymagań Funduszy Strukturalnych' (2011) *Ekonomia Społeczna* 41.

42 Grzegorz Makowski, 'Rozwój Sektora Organizacji Pozarządowych w Polsce Po 1989 r.' (2015) *Studia BAS* 57.

position, while civil society (namely: NGOs) have been adapting to this to pursue their own financial interests. As a result, Polish civil society has been characterised as largely 'made from above'.[43]

18.3.3 *Professional Self-Government Organisations*

The third and final example comes from the interactions between policy-makers and professional self-government organisations, that is, compulsory, corporatist-like associations of professions of public trust including legal (attorneys-at-law, legal advisors, bailiffs, etc.), healthcare (physicians, dentists, nurses, etc.) and engineering professionals (engineers, architects). As we have already discussed, professional self-government organisations have been given an important role in the Constitution and have been relatively widely used to consult and organise social subsystems directly after the adoption of the Constitution.[44] In our book,[45] we show that, while policy-makers have been becoming more hostile towards professional self-governments, the latter were increasingly using informal ways of influencing policy-making to circumvent this attitude. As a result, a self-propelling mechanism was created. The executive was slowly restricting the autonomy of the professional self-government organisations, reducing their competences to merely bureaucratic functions and crowding out autonomous competences with political control, citing the 'shady' involvement of self-government in lobbying for their supposedly particularistic interests. This development has been manifested by several changes adopted by the government to undermine and lower the autonomy of professional self-government organisations in the area of: the access to professions (right to regulate access to professions was severely restricted against their will and citing free market principles); the disciplinary proceedings (largely unified accordingly to political requirements to put professionals under political scrutiny citing democratic accountability); and the rules pertaining to the provision of their services (which narrowed and bureaucratised their competences in the name again of securing political control).

To pursue this agenda and in the context of formal competences of self-governments stipulated in the law and rooted in the Constitution, the executive has adopted three practices.[46] First, the executive engaged in 'sham' consultations giving self-governments a very short time to consult the drafts while the outcomes of these consultations were eventually ignored in the legislative process, draining these self-governments' resources and incentivising them to operate in self-interest.

[43] Jacobsson and Korolczuk, 'Introduction'.

[44] Karol Muszyński and Paweł Skuczyński, 'Changing Legal and Social Role of Professional Self-Governments during Systemic Transformation in Poland' (2020) 12 *Krytyka Prawa. Niezależne studia nad prawem* 149.

[45] Skuczyński and Muszyński, *Rozwój i Kryzys Konstytucji Społecznej*, 363.

[46] Ibid., 248–254.

Secondly, the executive used a 'bypass' strategy consisting of pushing legislative drafts created in fact by the executive through a less restrictive route of parliamentary initiatives. This route did not include obligatory consultations with self-governments, limiting their ability to formally influence the drafts. Thirdly, a strategy which we call 'ordo ab chao' involved maximally broad consultations, covering as many stakeholders as possible, with the intention to create an illusion of the absence of any consistent voice from the 'society'. This allowed the executive to unilaterally pursue the previously determined goals. All three strategies allowed in fact the circumvention not only of self-governments voices, but to implement drafts that were not significantly changed in the legislative process at all, treating all formally involved parties (the Sejm – the lower chamber of the Polish parliament; the Senate – the upper chamber; other consulted bodies such as Supreme Court and NGOs, etc.) as an element of the pipeline. All these strategies effectively restricted professional self-government organisations influence not only in the area of their vital interests, but also where they were pointing to the technical problems in the consulted drafts.

In the context of the government using informality or – conversely – excessive formality to limit professional self-governments' voice, the latter were seeking informal lobbying, unofficial contacts, and political protection among politicians and administration as a way of coping with pressure from the policy-makers, while increasingly focusing on the protection of its own interests instead of the common good. We describe these strategies in detail in our book,[47] but they involved attempts to influence the legislative drafts informally at an early stage (before they were formally announced), seeking political protection, trying to stimulate political conflicts within the government (between the policy-makers in the cabinet and between the executive and legislative branches of power) or acting outside the realm of politics in the wider metapolitical and public discourse. Again, these interactions resulted in the rise of strategic orientation of both professional self-government organisations and the policy-makers.

18.3.4 *Governance Structure and European Integration*

The aforementioned events need to be put into the context of wider political developments that effectively isolated the executive from most external influences. In the early 2000s, and particularly when J. Hausner was the vice-prime minister (2003–2005), a substantial attempt was made to create co-governance, corporatist-like structures expressing the ideas associated with societal imaginary. J. Hausner sought to strengthen the executive, while at the same time securing wide consultation and the co-governance rights of social actors, in particular trade unions, employers' organisations and professional self-government organisations. The latter

[47] Ibid., 262–279.

were also expected to bear the responsibility for the governing process which required social partners and professional self-governments to limit expectations, political actions and lobbying. Hausner's policy was somewhat effective, creating a short-lived period of more intensive involvement of social partners and professional self-government organisations in the governing structures.

From 2005, the paradigm of governance began to evolve as new political leaders, including Jarosław Kaczyński of the right-wing Law and Justice (chairman of the ruling party in years 2005–2007 and from 2015 onwards) and Donald Tusk of the liberal Civic Platform (chairman of the ruling party and the Prime Minister in years 2007–2014) decided to pursue a different political path, where social partners, NGOs and professional self-governments were put under more intense pressure due to allegedly fostering their own interest at the detriment of the public. On the one hand, the executive attempted to transform itself into a body representing the public, competing not only against obvious social actors such as social partners, NGOs, and professional self-government organisations, but also against political parties that formed the executive itself, as well as the parliament that formally elected it. This paradoxical development relied upon the fact that party leaders, Donald Tusk and Jarosław Kaczyński, were largely suspicious towards their own political parties and maintained a high level of control over them, contributing to the actual dominance of the executive over its political background. At the same time, new leaders were highly suspicious of parliamentary politics that was seen as particularistic, pluralist, chaotic and rather shady, which incentivised a reduction of the role of the parliament to a 'voting machine'.[48] These developments, which where back by liberal and communitarian imaginaries focusing on the dominant role of the executive, stressed the importance of a central body – the Council of Ministers – independently absorbing input from the outside in the form of consultations and expert analyses. Interest-driven actions of social actors were expected to be limited by the executive capable of imposing solutions fostering public interest. In fact, however, it effectively reduced the role of broader discussions and co-governance structures provided in the Constitution, creating a governance structure heavily centred and dominated by the executive, further alienating both the parliament and social actors, as exemplified by the cases of social partners, NGOs and professional self-government organisations.

Noteworthy, such tendencies were strengthened by the process of accession and integration with the EU. The governing structure was largely reorganised to increase the efficiency of absorbing European funds to build infrastructure, ignoring the possibilities to adopt a more corporatist social model assuming a strengthened role of social actors in co-governance. The corporatist social model embedded within societal imaginary was unattractive for two reasons. Firstly, it contradicted the

[48] Agnieszka Dudzińska, '"Voting Machine": Legitimization of Government Decisions as the Main Function Parliament' (2016) 20 *Białostockie Studia Prawnicze* 129.

objectives of the political movements described in Section 18.2, which aimed at weakening the participation of social actors citing their alleged particularism. Secondly, the co-governance was treated as an element of a problem related to the democratic deficit existing at the EU-level. The legal and communitarian imaginaries focused on the necessity of having a strong central executive deriving legitimacy directly from the 'people'. It made it possible to conclude that stronger executive mitigated problems associated with the EU democratic deficit.

Further, from the point of view of the law-making, the necessity to implement the European *acquis communautaire* and participate in the European project has become another argument for strengthening the top-down and instrumental approach to law-making as backed by liberal and communitarian imaginaries. The executive was seen as a vehicle for the modernisation of Polish law that had to reform the institutional framework and assure compliance with basic European standards.

Thus, putting restrictions on the executive in terms of law-making (e.g., in the form of elaborated and lengthy consultations) was seen as hindering the European integration process. The social partners, civil society and professional self-government organisations were treated as competitors wanting to foster their own interests threatening the integration with the EU.[49] This narrative was aligned with the political agenda of strengthening the executive shared by political parties across the political spectrum, legislators, policy-makers and experts. The requirement of the European integration was used on numerous occasions as an argument for strengthening the executive to assure that it can coordinate divergent interests in a way that would be compliant with the European law. Such arguments were given for instance in the discussions on the Hausner plan, and in the largely influential 2005 program put forward by Jan Rokita and Stefan Kawalec as a roadmap for the planned cabinet formed by Civic Platform and Law and Justice,[50] as well as in the discussions on the creation of Government Legislation Centre and the reform of the legislative process which centralised law-making in Poland and reduced the role of other social actors, citing the necessity for more coordination.[51]

The second problem revolved around transposition and compliance. Poland has one of the worst transposition rates in the whole EU. Quite interestingly, when Gerda Falkner and Oliver Treib published their influential book arguing that Central Europe is a 'land of dead letters', where European law was formally transposed but not observed, there was one exception in their data, which was Poland.[52] Poland was a country where not only European law was not properly implemented, but also where

[49] Radosław Zubek, *Core Executive and Europeanization in Central Europe* (Palgrave Macmillan, 2008).

[50] Jan Maria Rokita, Stefan Kawalec and Maciej Jankowski, *Państwo Dla Obywateli: Plan Rządzenia* 2005–2009 (Instytut Państwa i Administracji, 2005).

[51] Skuczyński and Muszyński, *Rozwój i Kryzys Konstytucji Społecznej*.

[52] Gerda Falkner and Oliver Treib, 'Three Worlds of Compliance or Four? The EU-15 Compared to New Member States' (2008) 46 *Journal of Common Market Studies* 293.

it was not observed when implemented. This problem is analysed in the literature on two levels: the transposition deficit referring to the percentage of directives which are not transposed at all in national framework, and compliance deficit which refers to the number of directives that are incorrectly transposed. Poland, next to Italy, is the biggest laggard in both categories in the entire EU. This issue became even more severe during the Civic Platform and Law and Justice governments (from 2005 onwards).[53]

Most importantly, it has been shown that EU law transposition in Poland suffers precisely because of the executive's actions, namely, formulating legislative propositions implementing EU directives in a way that does not give other stakeholders enough time to proceed on the draft.[54] In most cases, when there are transposition problems, the executive drafts a legislative proposal very late and then expects the parliament and social partners to accept it without significant changes, arguing that there is no time to review the draft. In the case of European law, the executive's actions are even more visible and detrimental to the parliament and social partners as there is a threat of infringement procedure by the Commission. It is necessary to stress that social dialogue is a fundamental component of the European social model. Among other things, the transposition of the directives should consider national context through the lenses of social actors that should be involved in decision-making and implementation of the EU law (151–156 TFEU). In fact, assuming such involvement of the social partners can be seen as a pathway to create a common European demos[55] and also intends to legitimise EU law. However, a formalistic and instrumental approach backed by the liberal and communitarian imaginaries assumed by the executive in fact reverses this effect, rather contributing to the alienation between the EU bodies and Polish citizens.

This gives to the executive an interesting yet dangerous tool, as it creates a self-fulfilling prophecy that can be used to play on the anti-EU sentiments. The government is a laggard in terms of EU law transposition and implementation, which hinders the European social model ideal of involvement of social actors in the co-governance structures assumed by the societal imaginary. This again means that social actors' role in the transposition process is rather limited, if at all present. In this way, the process that was meant to increase the agency of social actors in fact can contribute to their distrust towards EU law.

In the Polish case, the directives around green transition provide good examples.[56] While the directives were ambitious and set out many goals difficult

[53] European Commission, *Single Market Scoreboard*, available: https://single-market-scoreboard.ec.europa.eu/countries/poland_en.

[54] Jacek K. Sokołowski and Dariusz Stolicki, 'Przyczyny opóźnień w transpozycji dyrektyw europejskich do polskiego porządku prawnego w świetle analizy ilościowej krajowego procesu legislacyjnego' (2017) *Przegląd Politologiczny* 40.

[55] Sandra Kröger, 'Creating a European Demos? The Representativeness of European Umbrella Organisations' (2013) 35 *Journal of European Integration* 583.

[56] Renewable energy directive (2009/28/EC), Directive (EU) 2018/2001 of the European Parliament and of the Council of 11 December 2018 on the promotion of the use of energy from renewable sources.

to reach for Poland, they assumed an extensive cooperation between the executive and social partners in reaching these goals. However, the transposition of the directives was largely faulty and social partners were alienated and even ignored during the process. We see that, currently, Law and Justice government is using the green transition to build up distrust towards the EU institutions during its various battles with the EU, primarily on the judicial level.[57] Interestingly, this approach is intended to marginalise two competitors for power – both EU and social partners.

18.4 CONCLUSION: FROM CONSTITUTIONAL DRIFT TO CONSTITUTIONAL CRISIS

Marginalising societal imaginary widened the gap between the policy-makers, politicians and social actors. By interfering in their functioning, the policies towards social actors in 1997–2015 created grounds for the power creep and, eventually, the constitutional crisis. Common explanations claiming that the absence of an active resistance against this crisis from the civil society results from its disinterest in civil involvement are inaccurate. Social actors have become passive or rather channelled their activity through informal avenues as a result of many years of hostile public policies, constitutionally empowered by liberal or communitarian imaginaries. These actors had no choice but to develop various alternative and informal strategies to participate in the policy-making.

In this sense, the events that are described as Polish 'constitutional' or 'rule of law crisis', which come down to the limitation of judicial independence, do not come as a surprise. The same processes had already been occurring vis-à-vis trade unions and employers' organisations, NGOs and professional self-government organisations. The same narrative is currently employed by the executive against the judges, while the same liberal and communitarian arguments allegedly protecting the freedom of individuals or the public interest are now repeated and again contrasted with 'particularistic' rent-seeking by judges accused of attempting to build 'juristocracy'.[58]

The authoritarian tendencies also continue in the fields which we invoked to illustrate the constitutional drift. During the constitutional crisis, the social dialogue has been unprecedently politicised and marginalised.[59] The NGOs found themselves under even more pressure, with the Law and Justice cabinet centralising and taking control over their funding, making a distinction between 'genuine' and

[57] Sylwia Mrozowska, Jan A. Wendt and Krzysztof Tomaszewski, 'The Challenges of Poland's Energy Transition' (2021) 14 *Energies* 8165.

[58] Ramona Coman, 'Antagonistic Understandings of Sovereignty in the 2015 Polish Constitutional Crisis' (2022) 20 *Comparative European Politics* 275.

[59] Krzysztof Jasiecki, '"Conservative Modernization" and the Rise of Law and Justice in Poland', in Katharina Bluhm and Mihai Varga (eds.) *New Conservatives in Russia and East Central Europe* (Routlege, 2018), 130.

'insincere' civil society.[60] Finally, professional self-government organisations have been further marginalised and brought under political scrutiny.[61] This marks an effective 'loss' of the societal imaginary that does not find its effective defenders who abandoned previous attempts to build a corporatist social model and subordinated to the principles of liberal and communitarian imaginaries.

All these processes should be seen as a continuation of the 1997–2015 trends. They do not bring a substantial qualitative change but rather an acceleration. Moreover, they were rather propelled by formal liberal and communitarian constitutional imaginaries, whereas these interpretations are now presented as means to overcome the crisis.

Our understanding suggests a different route. The constitutional crisis should be seen as enabled precisely by the liberal and communitarian imaginaries against the societal imaginary that would underpin protection of the social model. Marginalising societal imaginary unleashed the possibility of power struggles contributing to the constitutional drift and the crisis in the relationships between the political power and society. Resolving such tension should thus involve revitalising societal imaginary where social actors might find a transparent and effective way of participating in public policy-making. Such a way of interpreting the 1997 Constitution would also promise a more solidaristic form of European integration that would actually involve the society in co-governance structure and not simply use transposition requirements to increase the power of the executive and/or spread distrust against the European institutions.

[60] Stanley Bill, 'Counter-Elite Populism and Civil Society in Poland: PiS's Strategies of Elite Replacement' (2022) 36 *East European Politics and Societies and Cultures* 118.

[61] Paweł Skuczyński, *Dialog Społeczny, Państwo Prawa i Polityczny Populizm: Porozumienie Samorządów Zawodowych i Stowarzyszeń Prawniczych–Doświadczenia i Perspektywy 2016–2017* (Palestra, 2017), 19–29.

19

On the French Constitutional Imaginary

The Erosion of the Long-standing Republican Tradition

François-Xavier Millet

19.1 INTRODUCTION

It is somewhat paradoxical nowadays to reflect on collective imaginaries at a time of individualism, post-nationalism and transnational governance. It is even more paradoxical to reflect on such imaginaries with a national key. Examining national imaginaries indeed entails looking at idiosyncrasies, that is those specific, unique, unparalleled features of a given national community that distinguish the latter from other national communities.

Such a type of idiosyncrasies, which often happen to be based on emotions, may understandably be perceived with suspicion in the context of European integration as both a unity-driven and reason-based political endeavour. They are the result of collective imaginaries that prominent scholars have called 'imagined communities', 'imagined structures of belief' or 'invented traditions'.[1] Where current times primarily value the present and, to some extent, the future, those imaginaries overlap with mental representations inherited from a certain mythical past that has often more to do with collective memory than scientific historicity.

Based on a supposedly pre-existing and mysterious 'We, the People', they create a sense of kinship, a feeling of national exceptionalism and a reason for pride for those sharing them that may ultimately turn into sheer nationalism and oppose political communities against one another. With their inherent dreamlike component, imaginaries bear a degree of irrationality and can therefore fuel potentially fateful passions when those passions are turned into political claims and ground nationalistic aspirations or populist claims.

[1] See, respectively, Benedict Anderson, *Imagined Communities: Reflections on the Origin and Spread of Nationalism* (Verso, 2016); Paul Kahn, *Political Theology: Four New Chapters on the Concept of Sovereignty*, (Columbia University Press, 2012); and Eric Hobsbawm and Terence Ranger, *The Invention of Tradition* (Cambridge University Press, 2012).

Researching on national collective imaginaries is thus arguably quite politically incorrect in a post-national Europe as it seems to be bound to be premised on an introspective and backward-looking interest into kinship, group psychology and self-perception and may foster divisive political claims leading to Europe's fragmentation. Now, however, can such research be redeemed if it mainly looks into collective imaginaries from a constitutional viewpoint? Is it that constitutional imaginaries mitigate the risks associated with collective imaginaries and render them more acceptable? Can they do so without undermining the virtues of collective imaginaries? All those questions require us to determine what a 'constitutional' imaginary is, what makes a collective imaginary constitutional and what that concretely entails.

There is an apparent tension within a simultaneously constitutional *and* collective imaginary. Its imaginary pole is potentially closed and gregarious and thus dangerous, while its constitutional one would appear open, more universal and individual-based. It is indeed often assumed in Europe – and more broadly in the Western world – that constitutionalism refers to universal, individual-based values (often under the banner of 'liberal constitutionalism' or 'liberal democracy') as opposed to community values defined along national lines.

The distinctive imaginary that France has forged over the centuries makes it a unique case-study to understand both the construction of national constitutional imaginaries in Europe together with the challenges that EU integration, with its own concepts, narratives and values, represent for those imaginaries. The self-perceived exceptionalism is indeed not confined to the United States. The French imaginary has generated its own political and social model. That feeling of uniqueness inherited from the French Revolution appears entrenched in the 'Great Nation'. Not only has it induced the widespread belief that France has something to say to the world but it also largely explains France's past as a colonial power yearning to share its model with other peoples as part of the 'civilising mission' of European states, often referred to in the English language as the 'white man's burden'.

The French constitutional imaginary is therefore worth examining as a domestic product but also as an export product that travelled, together with the political model underpinning it, to French ex-colonies but also to those former communist states in Europe where the French revolutionary ideals have inspired the Russian Revolution and thus shaped the own imaginary of those states. What is that imaginary? Has it changed over time and how? It is submitted in this chapter that the French 'constitutional' imaginary is the result of an enduring competition between two lines of political thoughts that rest on different concepts of liberty (positive and negative):[2] on the one hand, the dominant Republican thought as understood especially by Rousseau, and, on the other hand, the liberal thought as

[2] Isaiah Berlin, *Two Concepts of Liberty* (Oxford University Press, 1958).

understood especially by Locke and which, albeit not foreign to the French political tradition, was somewhat less significant during the Westphalian times.

(National) constitutional imaginaries are similar to tectonic plates. While they have a smooth co-existence when they stay apart, the disruption may be immense where certain factors lead them to collide. That is arguably the case on the fertile ground offered by European integration as the most successful regional experiment of globalisation that thrives on neoliberalism, the rule of law, fundamental rights and more broadly liberal constitutionalism as the contemporary dominant type of liberalism in Europe. It would appear that the deep divide within French society nowadays is – at least partly – the result of a struggle, within the French imaginary, between the Republican thought and the liberal one, whereby the grand old French Republican pillars are shaken by Anglo-American narratives vehicled by European Union law (hereinafter 'EU law') together with the system established by the European Convention on Human Rights (hereinafter 'the ECHR') and its individualistic tide.

Against that background, this chapter explores the evolution of the French constitutional imaginary in the mirror-inverted light of the liberal imaginary inherited from Locke in particular. It is on the basis of the findings in Section 19.2 regarding the available tools to determine the past and current content of the constitutional imaginary of a given community that Section 19.3 teases out, in contrast with the Anglo-American tradition premised on negative liberty, how the Republican conception of positive liberty has had a hegemonic role in France through Rousseau's influence in particular. That latter section looks at how Republicanism found its concrete expression in France in the nature of public power, the concept of the separation of powers, the relationship between state and society and also property. It also examines the embedded character of the Republican tradition by showing how difficult it has been for French liberal authors to impose themselves within the intellectual history of France and the influence that Republican ideas have had on their own views. Section 19.4 subsequently addresses the liberal shift prompted by globalisation and European integration from the 1970s onwards and how it altered public law. It shows how the French long-standing Republican tradition, deeply engrained within the collective psyche, is being eroded by the Anglo-American political culture conveyed by the European Union and more generally by globalisation and the correlative rise of individualism and human rights. Section 19.5 looks at various political moments that bring to light the resistance of the French Republican tradition towards (neo) liberal tremors. The conclusion in Section 19.6 recaps the main findings.

19.2 HOW CAN WE KNOW ABOUT CONSTITUTIONAL IMAGINARIES?

Delineating the content of any constitutional imaginary requires in the first place to understand what a constitutional imaginary is, what function it fulfils within a society and how it relates to power and the law.[3] Addressing those issues then makes it possible to come up with appropriate heuristic tools that allow us to grasp the content of specific imaginaries.

19.2.1 *Collective Imaginaries as Social Artefacts*

Constitutional imaginaries are a subcategory of collective imaginaries, which themselves are social artefacts. Collective imaginaries have little to do with scientific historicity. They have a lot to do instead with self-representation as a group. Because they are socially constructed, they primarily derive from (selective) memory, psychology or sociology. They consist in uniting myths whose function is to create a comforting feeling of kinship connecting the dead and the living. Truth does not matter as far as collective imaginaries are concerned. It does not matter indeed whether their subjective, memory-based content is in line with their objective, history-based substratum. Since they imply the idealisation and, often, the extrapolation of given community features, collective imaginaries are actually most likely to be erroneous or partial, without that being an issue in itself. What matters instead with collective imaginaries is that they manage to fulfil both their herding and dissociating functions: building a community feeling, a 'we', that is distinct from 'the others' and which may subsequently develop political aspirations to self-rule as 'We, the People'.

Nations are arguably one of the most – if not *the* most – successful and long-lasting collective imaginaries that have ever been conceived of by human mind. National imaginaries, often branded as 'national identity', are a made-up, subjective construct based on objective elements that have been sorted and ranked on the basis of their respective weights, those weights being themselves determined according to given criteria and preferences. In his influential lecture on the concept of the nation delivered at the Sorbonne in 1882,[4] French intellectual Ernest Renan explained that a nation was characterised by 'a rich legacy of memories' and by 'the desire to live together, the desire to continue to invest in the heritage that we have jointly received'. According to him, there would be no nation without 'forgetting' since 'the essence of a nation is that all individuals have many things in common and also that they have forgotten many things'. Nations and national identity, as any other collective imaginary, thus display a high degree of subjectiveness.

[3] On constitutional imaginaries (or imagination), see, e.g., Martin Loughlin, 'The Constitutional Imagination' (2015) 78 *Modern Law Review* 1, 1; Paul Blokker, 'Populism; Constituent Power and Constitutional Imagination', in Martin Belov (ed.), *Populist Constitutionalism and Illiberal Democracies: Between Constitutional Imagination, Normative Entrenchment and Political Reality* (Intersentia, 2021).

[4] Ernest Renan, *What Is a Nation? And Other Political Writings* (Columbia University Press, 2018), 247–263.

That subjectiveness raises in turn the issue of the authors of such social artefacts: *who* selects those specific community features that are to become the backbone of those imaginaries? As a social construct, imaginaries are arguably the creation of hegemonic elites who decide on the content of the legacy, what to keep and what to discard (or to forget, in Renan's parlance), what to insist on and what to set aside. Collective imaginaries are thus the result of an enterprise conducted by a happy few who pretend to speak on behalf of a given people in order to strengthen the ties within that community.

At the same time, however, collective imaginaries cannot be a sheer social construct devised by purely rational minds. Those elites are themselves influenced, at least unconsciously, by the groundswell constituted by those entrenched imaginaries inherited from the past. Although those elites shall certainly shape them and modify them, they also receive them as a given since those imaginaries are a part of their very autobiography. This bears a crucial consequence – addressed in Section 19.5 – regarding the possibility for an imaginary to be substituted by another: although an imaginary may certainly be redirected, it cannot arguably be entirely revamped. It is to be lasting.

19.2.2 *Constitutional Imaginaries as Collective Imaginaries*

As specifically regards *constitutional* imaginaries, this chapter adopts Jan Komárek's proposed definition:

> a set of ideas and beliefs that help to motivate and justify the practice of government and collective self-rule. Such imaginaries are as important as institutions and office holders formally embedded in constitutions. They provide political action (anchored in the constitution and getting expression through the medium of law) with an overarching sense and purpose recognized by those governed as legitimate.[5]

Two aspects within constitutional imaginaries appear salient in this proposed definition: the foundational dimension and the unconsciousness dimension. It is in the light of each of these aspects that heuristic tools can be devised in order to determine the content of a given imaginary.

First, as far as the *foundational* element underpinning constitutional imaginaries is concerned, those imaginaries are characterised by their axiological importance for the building up and continued existence of a given political community. They confer democratic legitimacy and popular support on their political institutions by virtue of the supposedly deep adherence of the people to that mobilising imaginary. This chapter shall look at those foundations through two main tools. First,

5 Jan Komárek, 'European Constitutional Imaginaries: Utopias, Ideologies and the Other', in Jan Komárek (ed.), *European Constitutional Imaginaries: Between Ideology and Utopia* (Oxford University Press, 2023), 2.

intellectual history – as contextualised political thought[6] – will allow us to find the various strands within the political thought and their respective weights in a given community, at a given time. It will especially allow us to unearth continuity and rupture within political thought. Second, constitutional law – and more generally public law – arguably reflects constitutional imaginaries. It is thus opportune to examine the grand narratives contained in particular in the preamble or first provisions of a constitution. A certain imaginary will also be reflected by the structure and content of a constitution, together with the constitutional arrangements provided for therein regarding the form of the state, the type of separation of powers, the balance of powers among political institutions, judicial review and the degree of commitment towards fundamental rights achieved by the constitution and by constitutional jurisprudence.[7]

Second, as regards the *unconsciousness* element, it appears somehow more problematic: how may that element be unearthed? Constitutional imaginaries are indeed most of the time invisible.[8] They are so deeply engrained in a given collective psyche that they, for those who partake in it, sound like self-evident truths that are certainly hard to challenge but, above all, hard to identify in the first place. While looking at the foundations through intellectual history and public law may help unveil the content of those imaginaries, political events or moments are another heuristic tool to bring the invisible to the fore. The meaning of those events involving the people is not always easy to grasp of course. They may, however, support the conclusions on the content of constitutional imaginaries that derive from intellectual history and public law. Let us call *epiphanies* those – rare – eruptive moments of 'apparition' where the main features of a constitutional imaginary emerge as a society's reaction to a countervailing movement. Epiphanies refer to those moments of collision between tectonic plates where the old meets the young. Epiphanies are like precipitates in chemistry where the addition of a new substance to the invisible old mix suddenly reveals the nature and content of the latter. Accordingly, epiphanies occur when the heart of national imaginaries surface as the result of a tension, of a strain between an entrenched political culture and competing ideologies or trends.

6 On the methods in intellectual history, see in particular Quentin Skinner, 'Meaning and Understanding in the History of Ideas' (1969) 8 *History and Theory* 3, 8.

7 In France, the contribution of constitutional scholarship to the study on constitutional imaginaries has been unfortunately somewhat limited because of the dominant positivistic tradition that has downplayed constitutional history and philosophy. There is little interest in the study of 'constitutional law in context' in France, apart from the notable exception of the Institut Michel Villey and its e-journal *Jus Politicum*. Even there, it is usually done with a retrospective, learned interest in past authors, with limited attention to the political and social context within which those authors developed their thoughts and to what could be, *mutatis mutandis*, their contribution for the present times. See, however, for a proposal to look at constitutions 'in their becoming', Denis Baranger, 'Le piège du droit constitutionnel' (2009) (No. 3) *Jus Politicum* 1, 13, http://juspoliticum.com/article/Le-piege-du-droit-constitutionnel-146.html.

8 See, e.g., Laurence H. Tribe, *The Invisible Constitution* (Oxford University Press, 2018).

19.3 THE FRENCH CONSTITUTIONAL IMAGINARY AS A REPUBLICAN IMAGINARY

19.3.1 *French Republicanism and Anglo-American Liberalism: A Tale of Two Different Liberal Traditions*

When looking at intellectual history, both liberalism and liberty appear to be multifaceted concepts. As Sir Larry Siedentop, an American-born British renowned specialist of French liberalism, explained in a famous essay first published in 1979,[9] there are – at least – two liberal traditions: the Anglo-American tradition and the French tradition. Despite their common commitment to liberty, those two traditions stand in stark contrast with one another. While the former is premised on Berlin's negative liberty as non-interference, the second one rests on positive, civic or political liberty. It follows that French liberalism would significantly differ from Anglo-American liberalism. For that reason, the terminology French Republicanism should arguably be preferred over that of French liberalism in order to avoid confusion.[10]

Within the Anglo-American scheme of thought, ever since John Locke at least, society prevails over the state and more generally over public authority. Accordingly, individuals enjoy rights that shall be enforced against the state. According to Locke, that entailed in the first place the absolute protection of the right to property as a condition for individual liberty. More generally, the Anglo-American liberal tradition acknowledges the importance of individual rights, ranging from the free exercise of religious beliefs up to the right to non-discrimination. Within that tradition, far from being an instrument the aim of which is to fulfil the goals of the state, law shall protect individual emancipation from undue state interferences (and the latter should themselves be limited since state intervention is itself curtailed in the Lockean type of liberalism). Law – and in particular constitutional law – thus serves as a limitation on state action in the name of the individual, of subjective rights, of liberal (or negative[11]) constitutionalism within a pluralistic society.

9 Larry Siedentop, 'Two Liberal Traditions', in Alan Ryan (ed.), *The Idea of Freedom: Essays in Honour of Isaiah Berlin* (Oxford University Press, 1979).

10 While this chapter adopts Siedentop's distinction, it is reckoned, first, that the two concepts of liberty are present in French and Anglo-American political cultures and, second, that there are potentially other concepts of liberty in those cultures, such as Skinner and Pettit's freedom as non-domination if it is admitted that the latter does not overlap with either positive or negative liberty (see Quentin Skinner, *Liberty before Liberalism* (Cambridge University Press, 2012); Philip Pettit, *Republicanism: A Theory of Freedom and Government* (Oxford University Press, 1999)). That said, on top of its pedagogical dimension, Siedentop's somewhat essentialising distinction presents the advantage to put to the fore the tradition dominant within idiosyncrasies defined along national lines.

11 See Loughlin, 'The Constitutional Imagination', 8.

The French Republican tradition is at odds with such an approach.[12] It primarily values political liberty. Where Anglo-American liberalism focuses on the individual as both a starting point and an end in itself, Republicanism focuses on the abstract citizen. Where Anglo-American liberalism is deprived of grand narratives, collective mobilising stories pushing for voluntaristic, political action flourish within the Republican ethos. According to the Republican approach, the state is to shape society since what primarily matters within that model is not individual liberty, but the political liberty of – and as – 'We the people'.

Under that voluntaristic tradition, the bottom line of the French political thought for centuries has indeed been the state (and more generally the public sphere), be it in economic, political, social or legal matters. From Louis the Fourteenth (*'l'Etat c'est moi'*) up to the present times, the state has played in France that mystical and mythical role as the sole source of legal authority entrusted with the noble mission of creating the French citizen. While the Anglo-American thought rests on a strict separation between public and private, that is between state and society, the French Republican tradition, under Rousseau's influence in particular, embraces a looser approach to that separation on the somewhat authoritarian premise that the state knows better what is good for society than society itself. The state does not therefore need in all circumstances the latter's consent to decide and implement policies.

In that respect, the concept at the heart of the Republican culture is that of the general will.[13] Far from being the sum of individual interests within a pluralistic society (in a Smithian way), the general interest is presented as a transcending interest (in a Rousseauian way) that ultimately – and conveniently – allows state rulers to mould society at will.[14] It logically follows that, within that pattern, individual rights cannot be the paramount consideration. They will often be superseded by general will, that is public interest.

It thus appears that the French and Anglo-American 'liberal' traditions are different in essence because they are themselves based on significantly different definitions of liberty. The French tradition is premised on collective liberty (positive, civic liberty) where the state is the main, if not only, vector for realising such liberty

[12] On French republicanism, see, e.g., Claude Nicolet, *L'idée républicaine en France. Essai d'histoire critique (1789–1924)* (Tel Gallimard, 1995); Jean-Fabien Spitz, 'On the Supposed Illiberalism of Republican Political Culture in France', in Stephen W. Sawyer and Ian Stewart (eds.), *In Search of the Liberal Moment: Democracy, Anti-totalitarianism and Intellectual Politics in France since 1950* (Palgrave, 2016), 111–129.

[13] See Patrick Riley, *The General Will before Rousseau: The Transformation of the Divine into the Civic* (Princeton University Press, 2016).

[14] On the prevailing Rousseauian philosophy in French legal thought, in particular with regard to Europe, see Justine Lacroix, *La pensée française à l'épreuve de l'Europe* (Grasset, 2008); Céline Spector, 'La "voie rousseauiste" et les impasses de la critique souverainiste de l'Union européenne', in Tristan Coignard and Céline Spector (ed.), *Europe philosophique, Europe politique: L'héritage des Lumières* (Classiques Garnier, 2022), 171–189.

by achieving the common good. Such a view, with Rousseau as the main protagonist, has arguably been the dominant political thought over centuries in France. Dating back to the Enlightenment and the French (Jacobine) Revolution, it is however possible, with some minor stretching, to hold that that Republican thinking was already present in a specific form during the Ancien Régime. As famously shown by Tocqueville,[15] there are indeed key elements of continuity between the Republican thinking and the Ancien Régime. In particular, the state has always had a key role in the construction of France and the French people as a nation; and the general interest is ultimately the secular avatar of the Ancien Régime's common good.

19.3.2 *Traces of the Republican Imaginary within French Public Law*

Now, what are the expressions of that dominant political culture in the law? Several traces of the Republican tradition may be identified in French constitutional law.

First of all, in France there has always been an unbridled passion for constitutions. Since 1791, France has had no fewer than fifteen constitutions, when the United States has notoriously had only one. While the constitution that is currently in force in France bears the longevity record (67 years old), it has however itself been revised on numerous occasions. One could assume that such constitutional frenzy suggests the adherence of the French people to Montesquieu's separation of powers, to his plea in favour of the English constitution and to the now widespread vision of constitutionalism as an individual-rights-based limit on state action (that is liberal or negative constitutionalism). Such a view is ill-conceived. The fact that the French appear so eager about constitutional change rather suggests adherence to a very different approach to constitutionalism that appears somewhat forgotten in learned discussions on constitutionalism nowadays, namely positive or political constitutionalism: the will to achieve the best political regime through constitutional arrangements.[16]

Such trust for constitutions as tools to establish an ideal regime is a noteworthy trait of the Republican thought. What matters is not the protection of the individual but the type of collective, political liberty and the most suitable balance between the executive power and the legislative power. The key question within the Republican model is therefore not how to best safeguard individual liberty against public encroachments, but what is the suitable balance of powers to ensure political liberty.

[15] See Alexis de Tocqueville, *The Ancien Regime and the Revolution* (Cambridge University Press, 2011).

[16] For notable exceptions, see Loughlin, 'The Constitutional Imagination'; Richard Bellamy, *Political Constitutionalism: A Republican Defence of the Constitutionality of Democracy* (Cambridge University Press, 2007); Nicholas W. Barber, *The Principles of Constitutionalism* (Oxford University Press, 2018).

In other words, the French seem to have been more generally concerned with maximising political liberty through political institutions rather than with constraining the latter in order to maximise individual freedoms. Accordingly, when it comes to constitutionalism, French political thinkers – Sieyès in the first place but also Mably – preferred the positive version thereof under which a constitution is the expression of the sovereign people's absolute *pouvoir constituant* (constitution-making power) as opposed to the negative version under which a constitution is primarily a means for individuals to be protected against the sovereign people.[17]

Second, the pervasiveness of Republicanism throughout French constitutions is shown by those grand narratives and principles that are usually mentioned in the preamble or the very first provisions of a constitution. Most French constitutions up to the present times have begun with the mention of France as 'one and indivisible'.[18] Such statements are certainly illustrative of the significance of the centralisation of power in Paris. They are also indicative of the indivisible character of sovereignty and of the general will in France: one people, one power, one state. It is what has precluded until now any evolution of France towards a federal form of the state or any recognition of another people within France but the French people.[19]

Third, in accordance with the conception under which the public interest (under the label 'general interest' or 'general will') is paramount in France, the French republican imaginary has not been primarily concerned with individual rights. The traditional precedence of the general interest over rights has taken different forms in French law, ranging from the lack, until relatively recent times, of an adequate judicial review mechanism designed to enforce individual rights against a parliament that could adopt any law in the name of the general will. Such priority granted to the general interest has also taken the form of a limited protection of certain individual rights on account of the sacrosanct general will. Within the Republican pattern, individuals are indeed still primarily seen as abstract citizens, not as individuals with their specific features. Individuals seem worth consideration only to the extent that they contribute to political liberty as active citizens.

It follows that, up to the present days, the right to non-discrimination for instance has been interpreted in a restrictive manner in France. Unlike in those jurisdictions where different situations must be treated differently, in France different situations may be treated in the same way if the general interest mandates it.[20] By the same token, the

[17] See, e.g., Martin Loughlin and Neil Walker (eds.), *The Paradox of Constitutionalism: Constituent Power and Constitutional Form* (Oxford University Press, 2008).

[18] See, for instance, the first sentence of Article 1 of the 1958 Constitution: 'France shall be an indivisible, secular, democratic and social Republic'.

[19] See decision n° 91-290 of the Conseil constitutionnel of 9 May 1991, that refused to admit the existence of the 'Corsica people'.

[20] See, for example, judgment of the French Conseil d'Etat of 29 March 1997, *Société Baxter*, case no 179049.

Republican model also finds its expression in the curtailed freedom of religion.[21] As is well-known, France is characterised by a strong commitment towards the hardly translatable term of *laïcité* and French courts have been adamant regarding in particular the wearing of the Islamic veil in schools or other public services.[22] Although that exception has until now been upheld by the European Court of Human Rights (ECtHR) under the margin of appreciation doctrine, it arguably constitutes a significant, perhaps even disproportionate, restriction to freedom of religion.

Likewise, and in stark contrast with Locke's view, private property has hardly been central within the Republican thought. During the French Revolution, Robespierre unambiguously expressed his doubts regarding private property and explained that it was supposed to yield to the right to exist and live as human beings.[23] Still nowadays, there is in France a significant fringe of the population and of political parties or trade unions that believe in collective property, demonise private property and defend public property of network industries. In such contexts, there is therefore little wonder why a significant body of legal rules (known as 'droit administratif des biens') aims at protecting public property in France.

That said, it would be of course erroneous to think that fundamental rights were not protected at all in France until recent times. Their status has long been somewhat ambiguous, ever since the famous 1789 Declaration of the Rights of Man and of the Citizen.[24] Most interestingly, the first fundamental rights that have been effectively safeguarded and enforced in France are not individual rights, but collective, public freedoms ('*libertés publiques*'), that is those rights (such as freedom of the press, freedom of reunion, freedom of association) that foster that very political liberty central to the Republican ethos. The modus operandi whereby those freedoms have been protected is equally interesting: they were laid down *by Parliament*, not by courts, which is again illustrative of the fact that it has been considered in France the task of political institutions (as opposed to judicial organs) to realise political liberty by putting forward such freedoms.

As a fourth and last illustration of the pervasiveness of the Republican imaginary in French law, it appears necessary to insist on that specific branch of public law that has emerged in the wake of the French revolution and which is either envied or looked at with suspicion, if not horror, by those who embrace the Anglo-American, negative approach to liberty and thus rather logically look at judicial review of administrative action from a subjective rights perspective.[25] Despite the French

[21] See Cécile Laborde, *Critical Republicanism: The Hijab Controversy and Political Philosophy* (Oxford University Press, 2012).

[22] See, for instance, judgment of the French Conseil d'Etat of 2 November 1992, *Kherouaa*, case no 130394.

[23] See Spitz, 'On the Supposed Illiberalism of Republican Political Culture in France', 114–117.

[24] See Stéphane Rials, *La Déclaration des droits de l'homme et du citoyen* (Hachette, 1988).

[25] See, e.g., Albert Venn Dicey, *Introduction to the Study of the Law of the Constitution* (Oxford University Press, 2013); Bernard Schwartz, 'French and Anglo-American Conceptions of

passion for constitutions and unlike in the United States or Great Britain, constitutional law is certainly not the most prestigious discipline within public law in France. The most noble branch is administrative law. The very existence in France of *ad hoc* administrative courts (for a long time the sole Conseil d'Etat) to adjudicate on disputes involving state organs and the gradual definition by that Conseil d'Etat of a corpus of special, derogatory rules favourable to the public interest is itself revealing. Together with the *summa divisio* within French academia between public law professors and private law professors, administrative law attests to the special status of public authorities that, at least in theory, are entrusted with the eminent task of implementing legislative choices made by Parliament in the name of Rousseau's general interest. In particular, in the wake of Léon Duguit, a famous administrative and constitutional lawyer from the early twentieth century, administrative law was meant to provide a framework for the state to deliver various public services with an explicit solidarity aim inspired by Emile Durkheim. The objective of ensuring social interdependence between individuals justified the derogatory character of those rules and the unilateral enforcement privilege enjoyed by executive organs of the state, with no need for the explicit consent of individual addressees of administrative measures.

19.3.3 *Are French Liberal Authors* Liberals?

Against that strong Republican background, France has often been criticised or mocked, for example by Hayek, for what appears to be an illiberal political culture when liberalism is defined in Anglo-American terms. The claim is that France could never convert to a liberal culture that would value the likes of private property, entrepreneurship and individual rights. That is perhaps true. However, it would be caricatural to claim that there have never been any liberal authors in France so that the individualist approach to liberalism would be entirely foreign to the French political thought.[26] Admittedly, purely liberal authors are scarce and little known or studied. Views like those of Frédéric Bastiat or Jacques Rueff, who believed first and foremost in individuals and entrepreneurship and wished to limit state interference within economics, politics and society, have always been marginal in France. Even someone like Raymond Aron,[27] despite all his intellectual prominence in the 1970s,

Administrative Law', 6 *University of Miami Law Review* 433 (1952); John Bell and François Lichère, *Contemporary French Administrative Law* (Cambridge University Press, 2022), 1–25.

[26] For a comprehensive approach on French liberals ever since the Enlightenment, see Raf Geenens and Helena Rosenblatt (eds.), *French Liberalism from Montesquieu to the Present Day* (Cambridge University Press, 2012). See especially the editors' introduction 'French Liberalism, an Overlooked Tradition?', 1–12.

[27] See, e.g., Aurelian Craiutu, 'Raymond Aron and the Tradition of Political Moderation in France', in Raf Geenens and Helena Rosenblatt (eds.), *French Liberalism from Montesquieu to the Present Day* (Cambridge University Press, 2012), 271–290.

seems to have been forgotten, as if his own liberal legacy did not matter much in Republican France.

There are, however, several names who are usually associated with an individualistic, Anglo-American approach to liberty: Montesquieu in the eighteenth century and Benjamin Constant, Alexis de Tocqueville or Guizot in the nineteenth century. All those thinkers have, however, developed a complex, non-conventional liberal approach that combines what has been described above as the two liberal traditions. Those authors have indeed endorsed a refined political thought that does not conform to Anglo-American liberalism but rather reaches a unique mix between political liberty and individual rights. Starting with early French liberals, Montesquieu developed more a theory of moderation than a liberal theory and his '*doux commerce*' theory is not as favourable to free trade and globalisation as one may think.[28] He was also primarily concerned with the separation of powers, that is ensuring that no political institution would abuse its own power at the expense of another institution. Montesquieu appeared less interested in how power could negatively affect individual rights. It is also well-known that he did not have high trust in courts of law and only saw in judges the mere 'mouths of the law'.

By the same token, even among those authors that have advocated in favour of individual rights, be it Constant or Tocqueville, neither of them has embraced a one-sided conception of freedom.[29] Their works displayed an equal insistence on political liberty. In particular, in the famous *Discours de l'Athénée*,[30] Constant expressly distinguished between *liberty of the Ancients* (in essence, the Republican freedom) and *liberty of the Moderns* (in essence, Anglo-American, liberal liberty), but considered that both were important and should therefore be valued. For its part, a statesman such as Guizot in 1830, who is usually presented as a liberal, did not hesitate to implement state-based policies. Guizot, thus, equally proved Republican in his approach to the extent that his economic liberalism appeared somewhat authoritarian, top-down and definitely state-friendly as opposed to being purely market-based.[31]

As far as more recent liberal authors are concerned, their commitment towards liberalism appears equally dubious and by all means contingent. As is well-known, France offered a vibrant intellectual scene in the 1970s. That time was not only

[28] See Céline Spector, 'Was Montesquieu Liberal? The Spirit of the Law in the History of Liberalism', in Raf Geenens and Helena Rosenblatt (eds.), *French Liberalism from Montesquieu to the Present Day* (Cambridge University Press, 2012), 57–72.

[29] Andrew Jainchill, 'The Importance of Republican Liberty in French Liberalism', in Raf Geenens and Helena Rosenblatt (eds.), *French Liberalism from Montesquieu to the Present Day* (Cambridge University Press, 2012), 73–89.

[30] Benjamin Constant, 'De la liberté des anciens comparée à celle des modernes' in *Ecrits politiques*, 2nd ed. (Gallimard, 1997), 618.

[31] See Lucien Jaume, 'The Unity, Diversity and Paradoxes of French Liberalism', in Raf Geenens and Helena Rosenblatt (eds.), *French Liberalism from Montesquieu to the Present Day* (Cambridge University Press, 2012), 36–54.

characterised by libertarian aspirations but also by the discovery of the crimes committed in the name of communism, especially in the wake of the publication of Solzhenitsyn's writings. Several authors who used to be at least sympathetic towards communism changed under what was usually called 'the liberal turn' of the 1970s,[32] when Constant and Tocqueville, in particular, who had fallen into oblivion, were rediscovered.[33] That is the case of François Furet but also of Claude Lefort or Marcel Gauchet, who started embracing the cause of individual rights protection.[34] However, before being liberal in the negative sense of liberty, the 'liberal turn' was actually anti-totalitarian or at least anti-fascist in the first place. Although philosophers such as Lefort and Gauchet started to embrace liberalism, it would be wrong to see in the evaluation of their political thought a conversion to Anglo-American liberalism, especially on the part of Lefort who actually had limited interest in subjective rights. Instead of coming up with a theory on the limitation of power (negative constitutionalism), Lefort came up with a theory of political regimes and democracy, illustrating yet again that French interest in the ideal type of political regime (positive constitutionalism). He developed on that occasion a theory of *political* rights which assumed the 'situatedness' of human beings as a legacy, in Lefort's case, of both Rousseau's Republicanism and Marxism. By the same token, Pierre Manent or Marcel Gauchet embraced Tocqueville and Aron while remaining deeply indebted to the Republican thought, as illustrated both by their strong critique of the 'human rights ideology' and by their attachment to the figure of the nation-state, outside of which they consider that democracy cannot be achieved.

Thus, it is highly debatable whether, *intellectually*, France went through a liberal turn in the 1970s. It seems almost impossible for French thinkers to embrace with resolve Anglo-American, negative liberalism precisely because of that entrenched Republican imaginary, especially when that latter was combined with a Marxist ideology. It is worth recalling that, back in the 1970s, it was considered more appropriate 'to be wrong with Sartre [the Marxist] than right with Aron [the liberal]'. French intellectual elites' affinity with Marxism was considered the ultimate

[32] On that liberal turn in French political thought, see especially Stephen W. Sawyer and Iain Stewart, 'Introduction: New Perspectives on France's "Liberal moment"', in Stephen W. Sawyer and Ian Stewart (eds.), *In Search of the Liberal Moment: Democracy, Anti-totalitarianism and Intellectual Politics in France since* 1950 (Palgrave, 2016).

[33] For a collection of the main articles dedicated to Tocqueville written by various authors in the 1970s or 1980s, see Laurence Guellec (ed.), *Tocqueville et l'esprit de la démocratie* (Presses de Sciences Po, 2005).

[34] See, e.g., Samuel Moyn, 'The Politics of Individual Rights: Marcel Gauchet and Claude Lefort', in Raf Geenens and Helena Rosenblatt (eds.), *French Liberalism from Montesquieu to the Present Day* (Cambridge University Press, 2012), 291–310; Noah Rosenblum, 'Rethinking the French Liberal Moment: Some Thoughts on the Heterogeneous Origins of Lefort and Gauchet's Social Philosophy' in Stephen W. Sawyer and Ian Stewart (eds.), *In Search of the Liberal Moment: Democracy, Anti-totalitarianism and Intellectual Politics in France since* 1950 (Palgrave, 2016), 61–83.

offspring of a type of Republicanism stretched to its outer limits. Today, the situation does not seem to have drastically changed. Robespierre and Sartre are still 'alive' while Raymond Aron is off radar. By the same token, the entrenched Republican imaginary in France seems to make it almost impossible to think of Europe in a 'non-French', that is in a 'non-Republican' way. As a consequence, not only is it hard to grasp an idea such as federalism, the latter being arguably not a part of the French hardware, but there is also a tendency to conceptualise the European Union as a bigger, centralised France, thus on the basis of French political concepts such as sovereignty,[35] the Republic[36] or the state. As regards the latter, it is striking, as Lacroix pointed out, that the issue of the nature of European integration is still discussed nowadays in French scholarship in institutional terms (is the EU a (federal) state or a mere international organisation?), as if it was simply impossible for a French mind to think of European integration outside an *institutional* framework.[37]

19.4 THE LIBERAL TURN IN FRENCH CONSTITUTIONAL LAW

French intellectual history thus appears out of tune with the specific developments that France has gone through since the 1970s. While the 'liberal turn' of the 1970s *within political thought* is ambiguous in its meaning and motivations, it remains that the French Republican imaginary has been specifically shaken up from the 1970s by major political and legal transformations largely induced by (Anglo-American) liberal tremors under the influence of external factors such as globalisation, the belonging to the EU and the ECHR system, the rise of rule of law considerations together with judicial protection of individual rights and the correlative distrust towards a transcendental approach to the general interest and what can be done in its name. Although those factors have not provoked a shift in the political thought (yet have triggered resistance and discussion among political philosophers), they have pushed or at least supported significant changes in the theory and practice of French law, especially public law.[38] That liberal turn in the law has materialised in at least two ways: first, those various factors have put to the test several key concepts that have been at the crossroads between French constitutional law and Republican political thought; second, they have fostered the Anglo-American, negative version of liberalism, economically through neoliberalism and politically through liberal constitutionalism.

35 See Emmanuel Macron's speech on Europe in September 2017 at the Sorbonne.

36 See, e.g., Philippe Crignon, 'De l'Europe républicaine à la République européenne', in Tristan Coignard and Céline Spector (ed.), *Europe philosophique, Europe politique* (Classiques Garnier, 2022).

37 See Lacroix, *La pensée française à l'épreuve de l'Europe*, 14.

38 See, on the impact of that transformation on scholarship, Wanda Mastor and Jean-Gabriel Sorbara (eds.), *La doctrine publiciste et le tournant des années 1970* (La Mémoire du Droit, 2024).

First, the demise (or at least transformation) of the traditional concepts of constitutional law can be witnessed. As explained by French professor of constitutional law Baranger, 'the key concepts of constitutional law are leaving the stage. That withdrawal takes the form of a gradual loss of meaning. The words are still used but one does no longer know what they mean'.[39] For instance, while the figure of the (abstract) citizen was central in the Republican ethos and notably found its specific legal expression in the case-law on equality, the concept of citizenship is often used nowadays as a mere vague adjective. Where it is used as a noun, like in EU law, it refers to citizens who enjoy substantive rights within a conception of freedom as individual emancipation, not as civic participation in the general interest of society. A similar transformation has affected the concept of constitution. That concept is increasingly replaced by that of constitutionalism understood as liberal or negative constitutionalism. Nowadays, constitutions are increasingly seen, including in France, as an instrument to limit public power, not mainly an instrument to devise the best and most suitable political regime. That explains the more and more frequent paradox whereby a constitution can be deemed unconstitutional.

By the same token, the concept of sovereignty, which has been salient in France since the emergence of the modern state, no longer appears intelligible or useful to understand state power while it used to be a defining element of the latter. The traditional meaning of sovereignty is at odds with liberal constitutionalism. Even when bestowed upon the people and not the king, it still refers to the idea of an absolute, unitary and indivisible power that is intrinsically incompatible with the idea of limitation of power underpinning liberal constitutionalism. Moreover, its meaning has become diluted because of the variety of its uses. Sometimes, (state) sovereignty is said to be pooled or shared (but is it still 'sovereignty' once the classic concept has been stripped of its constitutive element?). Sometimes, sovereignty is just discarded for its being no longer a fully operative concept to describe those nation states that have now become member states. It is then replaced by another discourse, that of 'constitutional identity', which appears to be a pale substitute of a bygone sovereignty. Sometimes again, if no longer used in relation to the states, the word sovereignty is simply used in relation to the European Union to suggest some kind of strategic autonomy vis-à-vis other regions of the world.

Second, the major transformation of constitutional law that has been prompted by the liberal turn from the 1970s onwards is the result of the constant rise of fundamental rights protection and rule of law considerations. In France, there used to be no review of legislation with regard to individual rights. Three reasons may explain that legal vacuum: the primary role initially assigned to the French constitutional court by the Constitution of 1958 currently in force was to enforce the separation of powers, not fundamental rights; the Constitution did not enumerate fundamental rights nor contained a bill of rights; parliamentary sovereignty (the so-called

[39] Baranger, 'Le piège du droit constitutionnel', 19.

légicentrisme, that is the intangible character of acts adopted by parliament) together with distrust towards courts have been material to the Republican tradition and have long precluded judicial review of legislation. It is in 1971 that liberal constitutionalism started to pervade French constitutional law in a seminal judgment of the Conseil constitutionnel (the French *Marbury v Madison* so to speak) whereby the constitutional court has for the first time struck down a parliamentary bill for a breach of a fundamental right (or rather 'public liberty' in French parlance), namely freedom of association. Despite that major change, the Conseil constitutionnel was still not entitled to review parliamentary acts after their enactment. Once in force, parliamentary acts could not be challenged on constitutionality grounds. It is only four decades later, from 2010, that France revised its constitution and provided for a constitutional adjudication procedure allowing the Conseil constitutionnel to carry out *ex post* review of acts of parliament (the now famous 'QPC', standing for *question prioritaire de constitutionnalité*).[40]

However, the rise of liberal constitutionalism in the 1970s and 1980s is primarily the result of external factors, namely EU integration and the ECHR. French ordinary courts have indeed gradually accepted to enforce international and above all European treaties and acts adopted on the basis of the latter against French acts of parliament.[41] Such Copernican revolution prompted from outside France significantly undermined the French Republican imaginary in at least two ways: first, that transformation empowered non-democratically-elected courts to the expense of democratically-elected institutions, Parliament in the first place; second, such transformation did not only entail that nation-states were not the only source of law and power but that legal norms created outside the state could prevail over state law. Accordingly, ever since the 1970s, the Republican imaginary has been constantly undermined through a phenomenon of legal acculturation to liberal constitutionalism.

19.5 EPIPHANIES OF THE REPUBLICAN TRADITION IN REACTION TO ANGLO-AMERICAN LIBERALISM

Should it be needed to further demonstrate the fact that the French imaginary is being insidiously shaken up by the rise of Anglo-American liberalism, it suffices to look at those political acts of resistance or contestation that highlight the tensions within French society itself, between the entrenched Republican tradition and the pervasiveness of Anglo-American liberalism. As previously explained, epiphanies are those moments full of dramatic intensity where various competing strands of

[40] See François-Xavier Millet, 'From messianic republicanism to global constitutionalism: the paradigmatic changes of French public law through European law', forthcoming in *European Law Open*, 2025.

[41] See Daniel Halberstam, 'How Europe Brought Judicial Review to France: A Response to Bruce Ackerman', in Richard Albert (ed.), *Revolutionary Constitutionalism: Law, Legitimacy, Power* (Hart Publishing, 2020), 239–264.

thought, *in casu* the Republican tradition and the liberal thought, frontally clash, thereby confirming the core Republican content of the French constitutional imaginary. Three epiphanies are well illustrative of the tectonic tension between the French and Anglo-American traditions diffused by European integration and globalisation: the referendum on the Maastricht Treaty in 1992, the referendum on the European Constitution in 2005 and the Yellow Vests movement. First, the referendum on the ratification of the Maastricht Treaty in 1992, which was narrowly won by the 'Yes' side, shed light on a split within French society between what French philosopher Régis Debray called the 'nationaux-républicains' and the 'libéraux-libertaires'.[42] That terminology is revealing in itself since it opposes, on the one hand, the Republican thought, which is attached to the nation-states and to the concepts of Republicanism and, on the other hand, the liberal thought that focuses on individual freedoms. Second, the referendum on the ratification of the European Constitution in 2005 opposed the two same groups. However, another divide along economic lines also appeared within French society between those in favour of a 'social Europe' and those in favour of a 'neoliberal Europe'. Although that second divide did not correspond to the earlier one but cut across it, it suggests that there is also another type of opposition prompted by EU integration, this time between neo-liberals and those that adhere to the solidarity component of the Republican ideal. Finally, although the Yellow Vests movement in 2018/2019 was not directly born from a public discussion on Europe, it largely overlapped with the pro-Maastricht and the anti-Maastricht divide, between those that make gains out of globalisation and those do not.

Interestingly, those moments have always concerned debates closely or remotely relating to Europe. That is not surprising inasmuch as the latter tests the very Republican concepts and political thought.[43] EU integration as a regional embodiment and experiment of globalisation has carried with it values different from those characteristic of the Republican thought. Not only does the EU's existence suggest that there can be legitimate law – and even constitutionalism – beyond nation-states, the EU itself was founded on neoliberal premises that praise the market and competition and limit state interferences in the economy. The EU has gradually also embarked on the liberal constitutionalism ship to such an extent that the Court of Justice has recently taken the view that the protection of individual rights and the rule of law are part and parcel of no less than the EU's own constitutional identity.[44] In all three events, the lurking Republican tradition thus abruptly erupted to the surface in the context of liberal perceived threats for its integrity. Although it is hard to know whether all three epiphanies show a persistently strong, albeit rather

[42] Régis Debray, *Le Code et le Glaive: Après l'Europe, la Nation?* (Albin Michel, 2016).

[43] See Lacroix, *La pensée française à l'épreuve de l'Europe*; Céline Spector, *No Demos? Souveraineté et démocratie à l'épreuve de l'Europe* (Seuil, 2021).

[44] CJEU, Case C-156/21, Judgment of 16 February 2021, *Hungary v European Parliament and Council*, ECLI:EU:C:2022:97, para. 232.

unconscious, adherence of the French people to the Republican thought as a whole or merely to certain of its dimensions (such as solidarity), they all highlight a rejection of Anglo-American liberalism by a significant portion of the population.

19.6 CONCLUSION

In order to unearth the content of the French constitutional imaginary, I have started with providing a method to that effect. I have proposed to examine the grand narratives and key concepts as they notably derive from French intellectual history and constitutional law. I have also suggested to look at epiphanies, that is salient political events in times of crisis, for a confirmation of the content of constitutional imaginaries, where tectonic tensions between opposing ideologies come to the fore within public discussion. Relying on that method, this chapter showed how republicanism differs from liberalism, primarily on account of the importance assigned to political liberty and to constitutions as instruments that allow to realise that type of liberty through the search of the ideal political regime. Rousseau's Republican thought permeates French constitutional law. It is what explains the latter's key concepts, the adherence to the political approach to constitutions and the French passion for constitutions to fulfil political liberty. Political liberty, the underlying vision of society and the role of political institutions in shaping society have indeed been the red thread that has been running through French political thought and legal practice for decades. The Republican imaginary appears so strong that a great deal of French authors who are usually portrayed as liberals, Montesquieu included, have in fact endorsed a conception of liberalism that differs from Anglo-American authors by combining political liberty and civil liberties.

The rise of Anglo-American liberalism in the Western world from the 1970s onwards has, however, created fertile ground for a destabilisation of the French Republican tradition. The latter is being shaken up by the vehicles of negative liberty, such as the European Union and the system established by the European Convention on Human Rights, which have promoted individualism and strengthened fundamental rights and rule of law considerations to the detriment of the general will. Those vehicles have triggered major, insidious changes in the law through the demise or semantic transformation of the grand Republican narratives and concepts and the emergence of new modus operandi and procedures.

Although legal practices have significantly changed over the past fifty years, French political philosophers and, *a fortiori*, the people themselves seem to remain attached to the Republican imaginary. The rise of Anglo-American liberalism in Europe has not translated yet into a new corpus of political thought (nor into a significantly 'new people') that would clearly privilege civil liberties. Intellectuals appear so much imbued with general-interest-based Republican thinking that it appears virtually impossible to fully embrace in France a different approach to liberty, as if intellectuals were captive of their own context, as if the Republican values were so deeply rooted in the collective psyche in France that it is impossible to significantly depart from it and embrace a new intellectual path. It is striking, from intellectuals who should precisely be totally insulated from their own autobiography so to speak, be it individual or collective, that few French philosophers have theorised liberalism until its ultimate boundaries without bouncing back to some Republican ideals. It is equally striking that 'non-Republicans', politically speaking (that is monarchists or Bonapartists), also embraced the view of an overriding general interest, which is so central in the Republican thought.[45] Of course, different contents are then assigned to the general interest by those 'non-Republicans'. Yet, what seems to unite them is the concept and function of an overhanging general will that justifies limits to individual action and empowers the state in shaping society: the 'Res Publica'.

Accordingly, there seems to be no proper escape from the Republican tradition in one form or another and that it is perhaps simply impossible to be 'properly' liberal in France. At best, the Republican tradition could adopt a slightly new shape under the sway of liberalism. This is probably what is already happening now.

[45] Spitz has shown that bonapartism is not far away from the Republican culture, nor from the Ancient Régime (Spitz, 'On the Supposed Illiberalism of Republican Political Culture in France', 113).

20

From Legal Impossibilism to the Rule of Law Crisis

Transitional Justice and Polish Counter-Constitutionalism

Michał Krotoszyński

20.1 INTRODUCTION

In contemporary liberal democracies, there is a tension between the democratic element, which demands that the sphere of political decision-making be as large as possible, and the liberal component, which sees some rights as inherent and some norms as inviolable and therefore not open to debate. The tension exists not only because the majority may use the democratic process in a way that infringes on the rights of an individual or a minority, but also because constitutional provisions designed to divide the power between the branches of government and to protect human rights regulate the political process and limit the scope and content of political decisions.[1] Thus, as Wiktor Osiatyński puts it, 'the more there is in the constitution, the less room there remains for democracy and for compromises within society and, consequently, the less power for parliament and more power for those courts in which constitutional claims are settled'.[2] However, one may also argue that this conflict exists not between constitutionalism and democracy but internally within constitutionalism itself. According to Paul Blokker, contemporary constitutionalism is informed by two conflicting imaginaries. A dominant modernist one sees constitutions as regulatory instruments which impose stability and order and are closely related to ideas such as state sovereignty, rational social engineering and universal norms and values. On the other hand, democratic imaginary is connected to notions such as self-government, autonomy, creativity and indeterminacy.[3] While the former vision serves as a base of legal constitutionalism, the latter imaginary is closely connected to its political counterpart.

[1] See, e.g., András Sajó, *Limiting Government: An Introduction to Constitutionalism* (Central European University Press, 1999), 49–68; Wiktor Osiatyński, *Human Rights and Their Limits* (Cambridge University Press, 2009), 72–81.

[2] Osiatyński, *Human Rights and Their Limits*, 79.

[3] Paul Blokker, 'The Imaginary Constitution of Constitutions' (2019) 3 *Social Imaginaries* 167.

According to some interpretations, Polish constitutional crisis can be seen as yet another example of the tensions between legal and political constitutionalism. Between 2015 and 2023, the Law and Justice government significantly altered the composition of the Polish Constitutional Court[4] (PCT), the Supreme Court (SC) and the National Council of Judiciary and expanded the power of the executive branch in relation to the courts. Even though many Polish legal scholars saw this period as a time of 'anti-constitutional populist backsliding'[5] during which the multidimensional assault on the rule of law caused Poland to become a constitutional pariah,[6] alternative interpretations were also present. Adam Czarnota claimed that the actions of the previous government could be seen as a 'necessary adjustment of the system implanted in this part of the world after 1989':[7] a change aimed at curbing 'an excess of legal constitutionalism which was definitely anti-democratic in its nature'.[8] Thus, for Czarnota the crisis had a 'democratic, emancipatory potential': it was a turn towards political constitutionalism and a search for an independent constitutional identity promoting the rule of 'a political nation' and 'dejuridization' of the public sphere.[9] Other authors, even if they also explained the crisis in terms of the clash between the liberal and the political component of a democratic system,[10] did not share this optimism. As Maciej Pichlak aptly observed, this so-called democratization was superficial in nature and boiled down to bolstering the role of the dominant political actor. The citizens remained excluded from the political process, as their role was restricted to legitimizing the government through the elections.[11]

4 As Wojciech Sadurski points out, in the case of the PCT, its takeover was conducted in two stages. In the first one, the government's goal was to 'paralyze' the Tribunal by measures such as court-packing, legislative amendments and the refusal to publish its judgments. Once this stage was completed by the end of 2016, in the second one the PCT was turned into an active, loyal partner of the executive. Wojciech Sadurski, *Poland's Constitutional Breakdown* (Oxford University Press, 2019), 58–95.

5 Sadurski, *Poland's Constitutional Breakdown*.

6 Marcin Matczak, 'Poland: From Paradigm to Pariah? Facts and Interpretations of Polish Constitutional Crisis', 12 March 2018, https://ssrn.com/abstract=3138541. For more on the crisis, see, e.g., Aleksandra Kustra, 'Poland's Constitutional Crisis: From Court-packing Agenda to Denial of Constitutional Court's Judgments' (2016) 12 *Toruńskie Studia Polsko-Włoskie* 343; Grażyna Skąpska, 'The Decline of Liberal Constitutionalism in East Central Europe', in Peeter Vihalemm, Anu Masso and Signe Opermann (eds.), *The Routledge International Handbook of European Social Transformations* (Routledge, 2018).

7 Adam Czarnota, 'Populist Constitutionalism or New Constitutionalism' (2019) 11 *Krytyka Prawa* 43, 44.

8 Ibid., 51.

9 Ibid., 54.

10 Adam Sulikowski, 'Trybunał Konstytucyjny a polityczność. O konsekwencjach upadku pewnego mitu' (2016) *Państwo i Prawo* 3.

11 Maciej Pichlak, 'Polskie spory między populistycznym a prawnym konstytucjonalizmem wobec refleksyjności konstytucji' (2022) (No. 1) *Archiwum Filozofii Prawa i Filozofii Społecznej* 63, 69–70. For a similar point, see Paul Blokker, 'Populism as a Constitutional Project' (2019) 17 *International Journal of Constitutional Law* 536.

A unique feature of the Polish constitutional crisis was that it also had a transitional justice dimension. According to Marcin Matczak, the previous government deeply mistrusted the 1997 Polish Constitution,[12] seeing it as an impunity instrument enacted in bad faith to protect the beneficiaries of communism from substantive justice using procedural justice as an excuse.[13] This mistrust had been even deeper with regards to the pre-2015 Polish Constitutional Court, which interpreted constitutional provisions as imposing certain limits on transitional justice measures. Because of the PCT case law in transitional justice cases, the Law and Justice leader Jarosław Kaczyński had dubbed the Court a bastion defending the post-transitional system in which the communist elite allegedly maintained power and privileges. His political group also coined the term 'legal impossibilism' which was generally used to refer to strict constitutional constraints supposedly stopping the parliamentary majority from introducing reforms necessary for the proper functioning of the state, including those that seek to overcome the legacy of the communist past.[14] The Supreme Court transitional justice rulings were subject to similar criticism. This critique was used by the Law and Justice government to justify the provisions reshaping the judicial branch, some of which were presented by their supporters as decommunization measures.[15] Regardless of whether these claims were rational or sincere, this rhetoric shows that the Polish rule of law crisis also had a strong transitional justice dimension.[16]

In 2023, the Law and Justice party lost parliamentary elections to the democratic opposition led by the Civic Platform. Nevertheless, until now the new government has been unable to reverse most of the changes in the judiciary introduced by their predecessors – and, with the President and the PCT loyal to their political affiliates, the crisis lingers on. What is more, a true challenge is to find an answer to the constitutional backsliding which will stand the test of time, including future political changes. Thus, studying the roots of the Polish crisis remains relevant both domestically and internationally, as it can help to provide such a long-term, sustainable solution to the problem of constitutional backsliding.

In this chapter, I further explore the relationship between the Polish constitutional crisis and transitional justice. I begin with the analysis of the normative

[12] The Constitution of the Republic of Poland of 2 April 1997 (OJ 1997, No. 78, item. 483).

[13] Matczak, 'Poland: From Paradigm to Pariah?', 9–12.

[14] For other uses of the term see Katarzyna Krzyżanowska, 'Legal Impossibilism versus the Rule of Law', *Review of Democracy* 29 June 2021, https://revdem.ceu.edu/2021/06/29/legal-impossibilism-versus-the-rule-of-law/.

[15] For example, the statement of purpose of the SC Act, which allowed for the removal of all SC judges, provided a list of eleven rulings deemed especially unfair: seven of them concerned transitional justice, including five regarding lustration. The bill was vetoed and did not go into force. For a description of the SC rulings, see Michał Krotoszyński, 'Transitional Justice and the Constitutional Crisis: The Case of Poland (2015–2019)' (2019) (No. 3) *Archiwum Filozofii Prawa i Filozofii Społecznej* 22, 32–33.

[16] Krotoszyński, 'Transitional Justice'.

transitional justice framework of Polish legal constitutionalism. This is a fact-checking enterprise, which aims to verify the claim that constitutional restrictions in this sphere were so strict that they amounted to legal impossibilism. Next, I identify possible inspirations which may have informed the transitional justice constitutional framework in order to assess whether, as some scholars state, Polish constitutionalism simply imitated Western ideas. Finally, in order to trace the origins of the Polish constitutional crisis, I examine the spectrum of alternative transitional justice responses, including the ones supported by the previous government. In the end I claim that the belief in legal impossibilism in the transitional justice domain is rooted in a specific understanding of the objectives of political transition. According to the Law and Justice government, such a transformation must involve a fundamental change in social hierarchy, including an exchange of elites. The belief that liberal constitutionalism prevented this change served as one of the pillars of Polish conservative counter-constitutionalism.

20.2 POLISH TRANSITIONAL JUSTICE FRAMEWORK AND LEGAL IMPOSSIBILISM

In Poland, constitutional provisions related to transitional justice are scarce. A 1989 amendment[17] to the 1952 Polish Constitution introduced the principle of democratic state governed by the rule of law and the principle of social justice to the legal system (this regulation was later repeated in the 1997 Polish Constitution). While the law also repealed provisions burdened with communist ideology, changed the name of the State and altered the national coat of arms, additional past-oriented provisions were not implemented until the new Polish Constitution was enacted in 1997. Its preamble refers to 1989 as a year when Poland regained 'the possibility of a sovereign and democratic determination of its fate' and recalls 'bitter experiences of the times when fundamental freedoms and human rights were violated' in Poland. The Constitution bans political parties and other organizations whose programmes are based upon totalitarian methods and practices of Nazism, fascism or communism (Article 13). It also includes the *nullum crimen sine lege* principle, but it states that this principle does not prohibit punishing acts which, while domestically legal, were crimes under international law (Article 42(1)). Finally, the Constitution stipulates that there is no statute of limitations for war crimes and crimes against humanity (Article 43) and that the period of limitation does not run when a crime committed by a public official in the performance of their duties is not prosecuted for political reasons (Article 44).

Due to the lack of more extensive constitutional regulations, it was down to the PCT to establish a normative framework with regards to dealing with the past. This

[17] Polish People's Republic Constitution Amendment Act of 29 December 1989 (OJ No. 75, item 444).

is not an exceptional case: in post-communist countries a normative shift towards liberal democracy was to a large extent carried out through constitutional court's rulings, and especially through their interpretation of the rule of law principle. This principle was incorporated into constitutions of almost all post-communist countries[18] but, due to its general character, its precise meaning in each of the states had to be determined through constitutional adjudication.[19]

That this meaning was in no way fixed is most evident in two well-known rulings of Eastern European constitutional courts, both related to laws lifting or prolonging statutes of limitation for criminal acts committed during the communist era and not prosecuted for political reasons. In 1992 the Hungarian Constitutional Court (HCC) declared such a provision unconstitutional.[20] Drawing on a somewhat paradoxical notion of 'the revolution of the rule of law', the HCC stated that: 'A State under the rule of law cannot be created by undermining the rule of law. The security of the law based on formal and objective principles is more important than the necessarily partial and subjective justice'.[21] According to the ruling, 'if the statute of limitations had run its course, the offender acquires the right as a legal subject not to be punished'[22] – and the rule of law demands that this trust in one's impunity be protected. Therefore, lifting or extending the statute of limitations violates the principle of legal certainty, a core part of the formal aspect of the rule of law which must be protected even in the unique historical circumstances of transition.[23]

On the other hand, a year later, the Czech Constitutional Court (CzCC) upheld a similar provision.[24] The CzCC relied on a more substantive understanding of the rule of law. According to the Court, even though the principle of legality is an important constitutional virtue, it should not be understood only formally: its interpretation and application should follow its purpose and respect democratic values. The rule of law cannot protect the impunity of communist perpetrators

[18] Theodor Schweisfurth and Ralf Alleweldt, 'New Constitutional Structures in Central and Eastern Europe' (1998) 24 *Review of Central and East European Law* 289, 307.

[19] For more on a role of constitutional courts in post-communist countries, see, e.g., Ruti Teitel, 'Post-Communist Constitutionalism: A Transitional Perspective' (1994) 26 *Columbia Human Rights Law Review* 167; Ruti Teitel, *Transitional Justice* (Oxford University Press, 2000), 191–211; Wojciech Sadurski, *Rights before Courts: A Study of Constitutional Courts in Postcommunist States of Central and Eastern Europe* (Springer, 2005).

[20] HCC, Judgment of 5 March 1992, No. 2086/A/1991/14. Available in English in Neil J. Kritz (ed.), *Transitional Justice: How Emerging Democracies Reckon with Former Regimes. Volume III: Laws, Rulings, and Reports* (United Stated Institute of Peace Press, 1995), 629–640.

[21] Ibid., 633.

[22] Ibid., 638.

[23] The HCC accepted the prosecution of crimes under international law, as these are not subject to the statute of limitations. See Sadurski, Rights before Courts, 253.

[24] CzCC, Judgment of 21 December 1993, Pl. ÚS 19/93. Available in English at www.usoud.cz/fileadmin/user_upload/ustavni_soud_www/Decisions/pdf/Pl%20US%2019-93.pdf.

against just demands for their prosecution, as such an immunity would threaten the legitimacy of a new political system.[25]

These two paradigmatic understandings of the rule of law can serve as a background against which the rulings of the PCT will be examined. This section concentrates on the PCT cases regarding the most salient areas of Polish transitional justice: lustration, the reduction of pensions and the prosecution of communist crimes. As I discuss in Sections 20.2.1–20.2.3, this analysis does not support the claim that legal impossibilism existed in the transitional justice sphere.[26]

20.2.1 *Lustration*

The first judgment in which the PCT dealt with lustration was related to the 1992 parliamentary resolution ordering the Minister of Internal Affairs to present a list of top government officials, including members of parliament, who between 1945 and 1990 collaborated with the communist secret service.[27] This unverified list, which included the names of sixty-six people, was leaked to the press. Its publication led to the downfall of the Jan Olszewski coalition government, part of which was Kaczyński's Centre Agreement Party. The resolution itself was invalidated by the PCT on both formal and substantive grounds.[28] On the formal level, the act was found to be unconstitutional due to violations of parliamentary procedure, the lack of statutory form and the vagueness of its provisions. This last flaw – together with the absence of procedural guarantees for the accused – was also found to violate the rule of law due to its impact on individual rights. According to the PCT, the above defects meant the resolution itself, regardless of the way it was applied, 'threatened to violate human dignity' by not protecting personal rights.[29] Thus, formal aspects of the rule of law were seen as guarantees of the more substantive ones. Still, the requirements introduced in the ruling were very basic and rather easy to fulfil by law-makers.

In 1997, Polish Lustration Law[30] was passed with the votes of the agrarian Polish People's Party, liberal Freedom Union and social-democratic Labour Union. In contrast to Czech or German regulations, which banned certain categories of people – such as top government officials, members of the communist party or those tied to communist secret police – from holding specific positions in democratic

[25] For more on these two rulings see Sadurski, Rights before Courts, 249–258.

[26] Sections 20.2.1–20.2.3 are partly based on Michał Krotoszyński, *Modele sprawiedliwości tranzycyjnej* (Wydawnictwo Naukowe UAM, 2017), 250–255.

[27] Resolution of Polish Sejm of 28 May 1992 (M.P. No. 16 item 116).

[28] PCT, Ruling of 19 June 1992, U 6/92 (OTK 1992 part I, item 13).

[29] Ibid., para. 44. Paragraph numbers are given after the PCT online judgments database (ipo.trybunal.gov.pl).

[30] Act of 11 April 1997 on Disclosing Work for, Service in, or Collaboration with State's Security Services between 1944 and 1990 by Persons Exercising Public Functions (consolidated text: OJ 1999 No. 42 item 428).

public life ('decommunization'), Polish lustration has been devised as a historical clarification mechanism. Those subject to lustration are, therefore, required to submit a statement on whether they were officers or employees of the communist secret service or knowingly and secretly collaborated with it. Only if this declaration proves to be false, the lustration liar is banned from holding certain public positions. Even though in 2006 the Law and Justice government enacted new, broader lustration law,[31] the vetting model remained virtually unchanged.[32]

In 1998 the PCT upheld the constitutionality of the 1997 Lustration Act, invalidating only two minor provisions.[33] The Court stated that lustration is generally consistent with both the rule of law and international standards, as long as its goal is to protect democracy and human rights and not to punish those with a communist past. However, in order to comply with the rule of law, lustration provisions must be precise and the procedure needs to protect the rights of an individual.[34] To ensure such protection, the Court formulated a binding definition of collaboration: it had to be, *inter alia*, secret, conscious and real.[35] Thus, merely signing a declaration of collaboration was not sufficient: there had to be proof of an actual cooperation, whether fruitful or not. This definition directly influenced the outcomes of many lustration cases. It protected those who, despite having been listed in the archives, had in fact never cooperated with the communist secret service. Yet, as many of the files had been destroyed in 1989, it also introduced an evidentiary threshold that may have been impossible to meet even in the case of some real collaborators.

In 2003, the PCT invalidated an amendment enacted by the government of the post-communist Democratic Left Alliance and the Labour Union which had altered the definition of collaboration in a way that it no longer covered, gathering or providing data as a part of intelligence, counterintelligence and border protection tasks. As the internal structure of the communist secret service was heavily complicated, it is notoriously difficult to distinguish those duties from the actions targeting democratic opposition. According to the PCT, this ambiguity violated the rule of law's formal requirements, as the vetted had no straightforward way to assess whether their actions had fallen within the scope of the statutory exception: from their point of view, the outcome of lustration proceedings could not be foreseen. Thus, the PCT yet again invalidated a provision due to the possible infringement of the rights

[31] Act of 18 October 2006 on the Disclosure of Information on Documents of State Security Agencies from Years 1944–1990 and the Content of These Documents (consolidated text: OJ 2021 item 1633).

[32] For an overview of the history of Polish lustration, see, e.g., Adam Czarnota, 'The Politics of the Lustration Law in Poland, 1989–2006', in Alexander Mayer-Rieckh and Pablo de Greiff (eds.), *Justice as Prevention: Vetting Public Employees in Transitional Societies* (Social Science Research Council, 2007), 222–258; Michał Krotoszyński, 'Polish Lustration and the Models of Transitional Justice' (2014) 3 *Adam Mickiewicz University Law Review* 199.

[33] PCT, Judgment of 10 November 1998, K 39/97 (OTK 1998 No. 6, item 99).

[34] Ibid., paras. 88–96, 103–104.

[35] Ibid., para. 107.

of the vetted; interestingly though, the ruling meant that the definition of collaboration expanded significantly.[36] Finally, in a manner similar to its Czech counterpart, the PCT claimed that the continuity of the Polish State after the democratic transition did not mean that the axiological basis of the State and its legal system remained unchanged. On the contrary, the 1989 constitutional amendment discussed above was direct proof of a clean break with the past on the axiological level.[37] Even if this part of the judgment seems rather detached from the rest of the arguments, it shows dedication to a more substantive understanding of the rule of law.

The PCT's judgment on the 2006 Lustration Act (enacted by the Law and Justice government) is by far the most thorough review of the Polish lustration regulations up to date. In 2007, the PCT invalidated a large part of the law. The Court reiterated that lustration can be consistent with the rule of law, as long as its goal is to protect democratization and human rights, the restriction of individual rights is proportional and the procedural guarantees are met.[38] However, many provisions were found to breach exactly these principles, while other infringed on equality or the right to informational self-determination.[39] According to the PCT, the act also violated formal aspects of the rule of law. Many provisions were invalidated because their imprecision or arbitrary nature infringed on the principle of proper legislation.[40] The principle was also violated by regulations which gave no discretion to disciplinary courts in choosing how to punish lustration liars and ordered their removal from legal professions: the PCT argued that, without such discretion, the power of a disciplinary court is merely a façade.[41] Finally, an amendment to the 1998 Act on the Institute of National Remembrance[42] (IPN) was found to have breached the requirement for a law to be public. Its provisions ordered the publication of a catalogue of communist secret service agents and collaborators, but their categories could not be properly understood without using secret instructions of communist security agencies, which cannot be treated as a source of law.[43] The PCT's extensive reasoning in this case became a core of Polish *acquis constitutionnel* with regards to lustration: while this framework was widely accepted among liberal and left-wing

36 Other reasons for invalidation included the violation of the equality principle and citizens' right to obtain information on persons in public functions. PCT, Judgment of 28 May 2003, K 44/02 (OTK ZU 2003, No. 5A, item 44), paras. 48–82.

37 Ibid., para. 46.

38 PCT, Judgment of 11 May 2007, K 2/07 (OTK-A 2007, No. 5, item 48), paras. 263–265, 281, 285.

39 Ibid., paras. 381–414, 432, 435–443, 472–473, 476–484.

40 Ibid., paras. 372–380, 407, 429. The principle of proper legislation was inferred by the PCT from the principle of democratic state governed by the rule of law. It requires legal provisions to be, *inter alia*, clear, precise and rational. See, e.g., PCT, Judgment of 30 October 2001, K 33/00 (OTK ZU 2001, No. 7, item 217), para. 45.

41 The provisions also violated the principle of proportionality. K 2/07 (n 38), paras. 442–443.

42 Act of 18/12/1998 on the Institute of National Remembrance – Commission for the Prosecution of Crimes Against the Polish Nation (consolidated text: OJ 2021 item 177).

43 K 2/07 (n 38), paras. 358–366, 371.

social actors, the ruling was heavily criticized by the Law and Justice politicians and their supporters. It was also after this judgment that the term 'legal impossibilism' started to be used in the public discourse by the political right. However, even though the PCT framework was indeed robust, lustration was still possible: for instance, although the Court restricted lustration to the public sphere, its scope was still broader compared to pre-2006 regulations.

Finally, in 2015 the PCT deemed the absence of a duty to waive judicial immunity before launching lustration proceedings unconstitutional. The Court claimed that the lustration of judges is an instrument of ensuring their high moral standards and judicial independence, both necessary for the rule of law and human rights protection. However, as launching lustration proceedings marks the vetted with a social stigma, judicial independence cannot be protected if these are instigated without due consideration – and the need to waive judicial immunity is a tool to ensure such restraint.[44]

The PCT case law shows an ongoing tension between the demands for lustration, understandable in a young democracy, and the need to ensure that this process is carried out in line with the rule of law. While the PCT stressed in each ruling that lustration is fully compatible with the rule of law, it also used its judgments to create an *acquis constitutionnel* in this regard. This framework was often based on formal aspects of the rule of law, due to their direct impact on the protection of individual rights. The PCT also sought to ensure that lustration did not restrict these rights in a disproportionate way. While the framework created by the Court was comprehensive and detailed, it did not render lustration impossible. In fact, this framework was even more permissive regarding other transitional justice measures, to which I now turn.

20.2.2 *Reduction of Pensions*

On 1 January 2010, a statute enacted by the Civic Platform and the Law and Justice Party lowered retirement pensions of former communist security service officers and members of the Military Council of National Salvation (WRON), a military junta which ruled the country during the 1981–1983 martial law. In the case of the former group, the pensions were reduced for each year of service in the communist security forces, while the pensions of WRON members were decreased for each year of army service starting from 8 May 1945.[45]

The reduction was challenged before the PCT, which in its 2010 judgment upheld the law, finding only one provision partly unconstitutional. According to

[44] PCT, Judgment of 2 April 2015, P 31/12 (OTK ZU 2015, No. 4A, item 44), paras. 123–152.

[45] Act of 23 January 2009 Amending the Act on the Retirement Pensions of Professional Soldiers and Their Families and the Act on the Retirement Pensions of the Officers of the Police, the Internal Security Agency, the Foreign Intelligence Agency, the Military Counterintelligence Service, the Military Intelligence Service, the Central Anti-Corruption Bureau, the Border Guard, the State Protection Service, the State Fire Service, the Prison Service and their Families (OJ 2009, No. 24 item 145).

the PCT, the actions of WRON and communist secret police were fundamentally inconsistent with current constitutional values and the lawmaker had a right to reduce unjust retirement privileges enjoyed by their former members.[46] As recalculated pensions were on average still higher than the average ordinary pension – and therefore (high) above the social minimum – the Court decided that the law was proportional and did not infringe on human dignity or the core of the right to social security.[47] The act did not impose collective responsibility either: it was not repressive, as it involved no sanctions, but merely revoked privileges.[48] It was also consistent with the equality principle, though with one exception: the PCT decided that the reduction of pensions of WRON members for the years of army service prior to the martial law was discriminatory and unconstitutional as, in those years, future junta members did not differ in any way from other professional Polish soldiers.[49]

Finally, the law did not violate the doctrine of acquired rights. According to the PCT, even if an officer of the communist secret service passed the 1990 vetting and subsequently served in a similar agency in post-transitional Poland, this fact did not guarantee that the pensions for their service between 1944 and 1990 would remain intact. The retirement privileges were acquired unjustly and were, therefore, not protected: as the Court noted 'guarantees of impunity and economic privileges granted by the dictatorship for service in institutions and bodies which used repressions cannot be treated as an element of justly acquired rights'.[50] Taking away those privileges did not violate the principle of legal certainty either: between 1989 and 2009 the parliament repeatedly condemned the crimes of martial law, the communist secret service and communism itself, and the 2010 reduction of pensions could hardly have been a surprise.[51] The constitutional principle of social justice warranted the reduction of pensions: the PCT stressed that, in a democratic state governed by the rule of law, service in pre-transitional state institutions which violated human rights cannot justify claims to maintain retirement privileges.[52] Therefore, according to the PCT, by reducing these unfairly acquired privileges in a proportionate manner, the lawgiver 'acted justly'.[53]

In contrast to the Hungarian Constitutional Court, which focused on the protection of legal certainty and acquired rights (regardless whether they were acquired justly), the PCT based its ruling on more substantive considerations, including a resort to justice itself, in a manner somewhat similar to its Czech counterpart.

46 PCT, Judgment of 24 February 2010, K 6/09 (OTK ZU 2010, No. 2A, item 15), para. 388–442, 486.
47 Ibid., para. 492–541.
48 Ibid., para. 603–615.
49 Ibid., para. 581–602.
50 Ibid., para. 561.
51 Ibid., para. 577.
52 Ibid., para. 574.
53 Ibid., para. 579.

20.2.3 *Prosecution of Communist Crimes*

Article 9(1) of the Transitional Provisions to the Polish Criminal Code[54] stated that the statute of limitations for intentional offences against life, health, liberty or the administration of justice, punishable by prison sentences exceeding three years, which had been committed by public officers in the performance of their duties between 1944 and 1989, had started to run anew on 1 January 1990. Article 9(2) of the same act stipulated that any amnesties or indemnity acts enacted before 7 December 1989 did not apply to the perpetrators of these crimes. The latter provision was challenged before the PCT. Much like the Czech and Hungarian courts in the cases discussed earlier in this section, it had to assess the extent to which a democratic state can use legislation to overcome obstacles to punishing the perpetrators of pre-transitional crimes.

In 1999, the PCT upheld the provision. According to the Court, the *lex retro non agit* principle did not prohibit from revoking an amnesty. The principle demanded that a person be punished only for an act which constituted an offence at the time it was committed; anything that happened after this point, including repealing an amnesty, was outside its scope. Therefore, the culprit had no right to remain unpunished.[55] However, even if such a right had existed, the contested regulation would have constituted 'a statutory provision necessary in a democratic state governed by the rule of law for the protection of its security, public order, and public morals, which demand ending the impunity of perpetrators of crimes protected by a totalitarian state'.[56] Just like its Czech counterpart, the PCT understood public morals as 'a trust of citizens towards the state: towards its officials and towards the law it enacts, [the law] which binds both the citizens, regardless of their positions, and the State itself'.[57] Moreover, making the punishment of such perpetrators possible satisfied the constitutional principle of social justice, as it removed systematic injustice from the criminal law.[58] On a personal level, repealing such an amnesty also served human dignity, which demands that all people were treated equally and impartially. In a rather mysterious passage, the PCT claimed that 'justice which is present while combating impunity should be free of biased interests and forms, and of random force; it should be a justice which punishes but does not avenge. In this sense, justice is stronger even than law'.[59]

Even though both Hungarian and Polish constitutional courts based their rulings on the *lex retro non agit* principle, their interpretation could not differ more. The

54 Act of 6 June 1997 – Transitional Provisions to the Criminal Code (OJ 1997 No. 88 item 554).

55 PCT, Judgment of 6 July 1999, P 2/99 (OTK ZU 1999 No. 5, item 103), para. 43–52.

56 According to the Court, repealing an amnesty is also justified by the need to protect individual rights, as it opens a possibility of seeking damages in civil lawsuits. Ibid., para. 59.

57 Ibid., para. 60.

58 Ibid., para. 63–66.

59 Ibid., para. 62.

PCT rejected the wide understanding of the principle rooted in the struggle for legal certainty. Even though it did stress the importance of non-retroactivity of criminal law, the Court interpreted the principle in a narrow way. This allowed the PCT to refer directly to the principles of substantive justice: an approach somewhat similar to the one chosen by the Czech Constitutional Court.

20.2.4 *The Question of Legal Impossibilism*

In an op-ed published shortly after the 2007 PCT lustration ruling, Krystyna Pawłowicz – who four years later would become a Law and Justice member of parliament and in 2019 a PCT judge – criticized the judgment, calling it an example of the 'judicial review of the ruling party's political programme'. For Pawłowicz, invalidating a provision due to its conflict with a general clause (such as the rule of law) meant that the ruling was not based on strictly legal criteria but rather on an assessment of legislation's goals, subjective and dependent on the 'worldviews and sympathies' of the judges. As most of them were appointed by the opposition, Pawłowicz believed that the PCT could be used to 'overturn any important legislation enacted by a democratically elected majority', thus preventing 'the part of society that won the election from exercising power' and undermining the democratic nature of the Polish political system.[60] This belief in legal impossibilism is echoed in a 2011 book *Poland of Our Dreams*, in which Kaczyński also accused the PCT of illegitimately expanding its authority through the abuse of general clauses.[61] For Kaczyński, this constitutional case law was an aspect of a deeper crisis, in which wide judicial interpretative powers transform the rule of law into the rule of lawyers, and an obligation to base government actions on an explicit statutory basis was a 'specific type of legalism which ultimately leads to impossibilism'.[62] There was a popular belief that transitional justice is one of the spheres in which these limitations were especially strict.

The above analysis does not support this claim. Polish constitutional provisions did not generate any explicit transitional justice restrictions, save perhaps the prohibition of retroactive criminal sanctions. Even though the PCT rulings in lustration cases did create a robust constitutional framework which significantly restricted the scope of lustration, introduced procedural guarantees and created a high evidentiary threshold through the definition of collaboration, in no way did they make lustration impossible. On the contrary, the Court constantly reaffirmed that lustration itself was fully compatible with the rule of law. What is more, the judgments regarding the pre-2015 legislation on the reduction of pensions and the revoking of amnesties were highly permissive and resorted to substantive justice in order to justify these

[60] Krystyna Pawłowicz, 'Konstytucja pozwala na lustrację', *Rzeczpospolita*, 29 June 2007.
[61] Jarosław Kaczyński, *Polska naszych marzeń* (Akapit, 2011), 80.
[62] Ibid., 79.

regulations. Thus, a relative leniency of Polish transitional justice and its general concentration on civil and political rights instead of economic ones – with minor and late exceptions regarding the reduction of retirement privileges and compensation for victims – had more to do with the lawmakers' restraint (and some of the Supreme Court rulings[63]) than the judgments of the PCT.

Official statistics also confirm that transitional justice was possible. Up to 30 June 2021 nearly 125,000 out of circa 466,000 lustration statements were examined, out of which around 13,000 were questioned. Final rulings were announced in 2,144 court cases and in 1,446 of them the statement was proven to be false.[64] As for the 2010 reduction of pensions, 38,563 decisions on their recalculation were issued; in 7,227 cases the pensions remained unchanged.[65] In addition to some early high-profile criminal cases, between 2000 and 2020 exactly 370 criminal proceedings were initiated against 558 people accused of communist crimes, out of which 162 were found guilty.[66] While this last number is arguably low, this had less to do with constitutional limitations and more with the inefficiency of criminal trials in general. Other pre-2015 transitional justice initiatives included the dissolution of the communist secret service, granting the access to its files, rehabilitation of former political prisoners, compensation for victims and memorialization.[67] Thus, Polish reckoning with the communist past was in general rather broad, even if it was also quite lenient.

From this perspective, the popular claim that the transitional justice framework imposed by the PCT was so strict it amounted to legal impossibilism seems more like a myth than an honest and disinterested assessment of Polish *acquis constitutionnel*. In Section 20.4, I argue that the belief in legal impossibilism among the members and supporters of the Law and Justice party stems from a particular (and controversial) interpretation of transition's major objectives. Before I move to this point, I first address another popular claim: that Polish transitional justice framework was simply a copy of standards developed in the West.

20.3 TRANSITIONAL RULE OF LAW FRAMEWORK: INSPIRATIONS

In this section, I use PCT judgments to identify potential inspirations which may have informed the transitional justice framework developed by the

[63] These include a notorious resolution which made it impossible to prosecute judges who, during the martial law, imposed retroactive criminal sanctions, on the grounds that the communist legal system lacked the non-retroactivity principle, constitutional review and clarity as to the status of international treaties. SC Resolution of 20 December 2007, I KZP 37/07 (OSNKW 2007 No. 12, item 86). See also Krotoszyński, 'Transitional Justice', 32–33.

[64] Letter of 7 July 2021 from the IPN prosecutor (on file with author).

[65] K 6/09 (n 46), paras. 530–531.

[66] Letter of 19 February 2020 from the Director of the IPN, no. IP 2.2020 (on file with author).

[67] See, e.g., Frances Millard, *Transitional Justice in Poland: Memory and the Politics of the Past* (Bloomsbury, 2021); Monika Nalepa and Michał Krotoszyński, 'Poland', in Lavinia Stan and Nadya Nedelsky (eds.), *Encyclopedia of Transitional Justice*, vol 2, 2nd ed. (Cambridge University Press, 2023), 927–934.

Court.[68] Contrary to popular beliefs, their minor role and increasingly adaptive use does not support the claim that Polish constitutionalism was a mere imitation of Western rule of law requirements.

20.3.1 *Sources of Inspiration*

In its transitional justice case law, the PCT referred to four kinds of documents which can be regarded as external sources of inspiration: (1) international soft law; (2) foreign legislation; (3) ECHR decisions, ECtHR judgments and rulings of other constitutional courts; and (4) literature on transitional justice and human rights.[69]

In its 2010 ruling on the reduction of pensions, the PCT invoked international soft law – including resolutions and declarations of OSCE, the European Parliament and the Council of Europe Parliamentary Assembly (PACE) – to present a universal condemnation for the crimes of communism and common belief in the need to deal with its legacy in accordance with the rule of law.[70] Legislation of other CEE countries and non-domestic rulings (ECHR decisions, ECtHR and German Constitutional Court judgments) were used by the PCT to provide a wider context of the legislation.[71] In lustration cases, the PCT referred to the ECtHR case law to strengthen its arguments that lustration laws should meet a legislative threshold expected from penal regulations,[72] to argue that lustration of public figures does not violate their right to privacy,[73] to claim that publication of lustration statements without a prior court judgment does not breach the right to fair trial[74] and to comment on the temporary nature of lustration measures.[75] To prove this last point, the PCT also mentioned a Czech Constitutional Court judgment,[76] while a ruling of German *Bundesverfassungsgericht* was used to underline the importance of personal rights protection.[77] Finally, the PCT occasionally quoted transitional

[68] The list presented in Sections 20.3.1 and 20.3.2 is merely a catalogue of external sources that the PCT referred to in its reasoning. Whether these documents really inspired the judges is difficult to assess: some of them may have been invoked in written judgments to support the decisions previously made without them and their use was therefore purely rhetorical; in other cases some actual inspirations might have been missing from written rulings. The reasoning available for analysis belongs to the context of justification, not to the context of discovery: therefore, the list should be regarded only as a non-exclusive catalogue of possible inspirations.

[69] I exclude binding international treaties from my analysis, as the PCT is obliged to take them into account if the petitioners motion the Court to check the statute's compliance with these acts.

[70] K 6/09 (n 46), paras. 272–295.

[71] Ibid., paras. 338–387.

[72] K 2/07 (n 38), para. 328; P 31/12 (n 44), paras. 93, 129, 131.

[73] PCT, Judgment of 5 March 2003, K 7/01 (OTK ZU 2003, No. 3A, item 19), para. 80.

[74] Ibid., paras. 144–148.

[75] P 31/12 (n 44), para. 136.

[76] Ibid., paras. 134–135.

[77] U 6/92 (n 28), para. 35.

justice and human rights literature, mostly to remark on the nature of the implemented mechanisms and the position of victims and perpetrators.[78]

These documents played relatively minor roles in the PCT reasonings and seem to have been used only as additional sources of argumentation. None of them were used in more than two rulings. In this regard, they differ significantly from a 1996 PACE resolution, to which the PCT routinely referred in lustration cases, and which I explore now.

20.3.2 *PACE 1996 Resolution and Guidelines*

On 27 June 1996 the Council of Europe Parliamentary Assembly adopted a resolution on transitional justice in post-communist states.[79] The resolution and the attached guidelines[80] outlined the rule of law requirements that should be met by transitional justice measures, including criminal trials, lustration, restitution and reduction of pensions.

PACE soft law played an important role in the PCT lustration judgments. In 1998, the Court explicitly stated that 'when it comes to lustration, constitutional requirements and, in particular, basic conditions of a democratic state governed by the rule of law, should be interpreted according to, inter alia, the aforementioned Council of Europe Parliamentary Assembly resolution'.[81] In 2007, the PCT explained that, even though the resolution is not legally binding, the Court should take it into account while interpreting both the statutes and the Constitution.[82] The Tribunal also referred to these documents to argue that the goal of lustration measures is to protect democratic institutions and that lustration is therefore a temporary measure.[83] Finally, the PCT relied on the resolution and guidelines to articulate many of the requirements that lustration laws should fulfil: their individual application, protection against political misuse and providing the vetted with full procedural guarantees, such as the right to a fair trial, the right to defence and the presumption of the lustration statement's truthfulness.[84] The PCT reasoning in the 2007 ruling – which, as it was mentioned, is now considered a core of Polish *acquis constitutionnel* with regards to lustration – begins with a list of such requirements. This list, which covers thirteen short paragraphs,[85] is in fact a translation, either

78 Ibid., para. 35; K 6/09 (n 46), para. 561; P 31/12 (n 44), paras. 130, 133.

79 Resolution 1096 (1996) on Measures to Dismantle the Heritage of Former Communist Totalitarian Systems (hereafter also 'PACE 1996 Resolution').

80 'Measures to Dismantle the Heritage of Former Communist Totalitarian Systems' (1996) Report by Adrian Severin (Doc. 7568) (hereafter also 'PACE 1996 Guidelines').

81 K 39/97 (n 33), para. 96.

82 K 2/07 (n 38), para. 337.

83 Ibid., para. 383.

84 K 39/97 (n 33), para. 89; P 31/12 (n 44), para. 85.

85 K 2/07 (n 38), paras. 264–276.

direct or indirect, of fragments of PACE 1996 Resolution and Guidelines, although no footnote is provided by the Court.[86]

However, the resort to these acts is not unproblematic. PACE 1996 Resolution defines lustration as a process which aims to 'exclude persons from exercising governmental power if they cannot be trusted to exercise it in compliance with democratic principles'.[87] Thus, lustration is understood as a mechanism of banning certain groups of people from holding public offices because of their involvement with the previous regime. This is understandable, as in 1996 most lustration laws, including the Czech and German ones, did involve such a disqualification. However, Polish lustration was created a year later as an instrument of historical clarification and did not involve sanctions for work or collaboration with the communist secret service; sanctions were imposed only for a lustration lie. Thus, some parts of the resolution and guidelines quoted by the PCT seem rather ill-fitted when it comes to Polish lustration. For instance, when lustration belongs to a historical clarification model, it seems out of place to claim that a state governed by the rule of law 'has sufficient means at its disposal to ensure that the cause of justice is served and the guilty are punished', that '[p]ersons who ordered, perpetrated, or significantly aided in perpetrating serious human rights violations may be barred from office' and that there is 'a need for an individual, and not collective, application of lustration laws'.[88] On the other hand, these conditions fit perfectly if lustration involves a ban on holding public offices, as in the Czech Republic.

These differences may be the reason why the PCT consciously omitted or modified some of the PACE guidelines to adjust them to Polish circumstances. First, the guidelines suggest that lustration should be administered by a special independent commission, that it should be restricted to non-elective positions of high importance – such as top government offices, law enforcement, security agencies and the judiciary – and that it should not be imposed on people who acted under compulsion.[89] The PCT did not mention these recommendations and Polish lustration does not follow them either: it is conducted by courts (an arguably higher standard), it covers a wider array of public positions, including elective offices, and demands that even individuals who acted under compulsion confess to collaboration. Second, the guidelines recommend a rigorous lustration timeframe: vetting should take into account only acts conducted after 1 January 1980, the disqualification from office should not be longer than five years and lustration measures should end no later than 31 December 1999, as by that time new democratic systems should be consolidated.[90] In its 2007 ruling, the PCT acknowledged

[86] The PCT also referred to PACE 1996 Resolution (n 79) to prove that the reduction of pensions is consistent with European standards. K 6/09 (n 46), paras. 270–271, 488–490.

[87] PACE 1996 Resolution (n 79), para. 11.

[88] Ibid., paras. 4, 12; PACE 1996 Guidelines, pt. H (n 80); K 2/07 (n 38), para. 265, 267, 274.

[89] PACE 1996 Guidelines (n 80), pts. A, D, E and L.

[90] Ibid., pts. G and J.

that lustration should end when a democratic system is firmly established and that sanctions imposed in the process should last only for a rational time, but no specific dates were given.[91] The court also ignored the 1980 threshold and, in fact, Polish lustration covers employment, service and collaboration dating back to 22 July 1944. Finally, the guidelines advise that conscious collaborators should be vetted only if their actions actually harmed others and if this result was predictable.[92] On the other hand, the PCT claimed that lustration is permissible if collaboration is clearly defined by a statute and is verified in a proper procedure.[93] While the collaboration definition was introduced by the PCT in its 1998 ruling, it did not demand that the information provided by the individual cause the others any actual harm. To establish that collaboration took place, its real, genuine character was sufficient.

While some may argue that these differences suggest that the PCT's dedication to the rule of law was selective at best, another interpretation is possible. Restricting the number of those affected by lustration and introducing a rigorous vetting timeframe is arguably more important when lustration involves a ban on holding public offices – an important exception to otherwise equal rights to participate in democratic public life. Yet, these constraints are less crucial when lustration is not a decommunization measure but a transparency mechanism sanctioning only those who lack the integrity to speak openly about their past. Thus, one may argue that, while the PCT took the resolution and its guidelines genuinely into account, the recommendations were adapted to fit a local context: a specific model of Polish lustration.

20.3.3 *Between Imitation and Adaptation*

According to some authors, the lack of knowledge on how constitutionalism, democracy and the rule of law work in practice was the reason why Polish transitional constitutionalism did not create its own independent form based on a local identity, but rather concentrated on a 'mindless imitation of the West' using 'solutions [known] from books' and resulting in 'careless' constitutional transplants.[94] This criticism seems similar to claims made by Kaczyński himself, who believed that legal impossibilism was created inter alia by transplanting conceptions aimed at tempering the communist system to the democratic one,[95] and who scolded Polish academia for its alleged peripherality, lack of intellectual independence and willingness to reproduce foreign ideas.[96]

91 K 2/07 (n 38), para. 273.
92 PACE 1996 Guidelines (n 80), pt. K.
93 K 2/07 (n 38), para. 275.
94 Czarnota, 'Populist Constitutionalism', 53–54.
95 Kaczyński, *Polska naszych marzeń*, 75–76, 103.
96 Ibid., 41, 94–95.

In the field of transitional justice such an imitative approach would surely mean a strict application of all the formal rule of law requirements, in a manner similar to the 1992 Hungarian Constitutional Court ruling. As Wojciech Sadurski points out,

> The universalistic liberal ideal was used as a yardstick to judge the preparedness of the new democracies to join first the Council of Europe, and then the European Union. Western European political elites developed a stake in the integration of the ex-Communist East into the overarching political structures of the continent, not least for the sake of stability and peace in Europe. The criteria of 'normal' democracy, untainted by any extraordinary measures related to its immediate non-democratic past, were instrumental in achieving these aims.[97]

Nevertheless, many Polish scholars were well-aware of the problems faced when the rule of law is applied in a country undergoing a major political change. Suggestions that justice should have been done first, and that the introduction of the rule of law to the Polish legal system was, therefore, premature, were relatively rare.[98] Yet, even among those who believed that the transition (and transitional justice) had to be carried out in accordance with the rule of law, there were scholars who claimed that inconsistencies existing within the transitional legal system may deem fulfilling all the rule of law requirements impossible. This, however, did not release the law-maker from an obligation to respect basic standards of the rule of law.[99] Apart from two radical solutions – to completely reject the rule of law for the time being or to strictly follow all its requirements – a more moderate response was also possible.

The PCT's use of the PACE 1996 Resolution and Guidelines suggests that, in a similar manner, aside from a 'mindless imitation' of the Western constitutionalism and from creating a wholly independent one, there was also a third way: an adaptation of the rule of law framework to local circumstances. It is true that many constitutional ideas and practices were imported to Poland from the West. Yet, the way in which the PCT adapted the PACE resolution and guidelines to local conditions seems to indicate a certain dose of autonomy. It also suggests that, to a certain degree, the Polish transitional justice framework was increasingly adaptive over time instead of merely imitative. This conclusion is further supported by PCT rulings on revoking amnesties and reduction of pensions which have departed far from a formalistic understanding of the rule of law.

More research is needed to verify whether this adaptive technique was also used outside the transitional justice domain. However, if the rule of law requirements are understood as a part of (imported) legal tradition, it may be argued that some level of adaptation is always more probable than sole imitation. Even if an interpreter is dedicated to adhering to the tradition they received (as the PCT definitely was), the

[97] Sadurski, *Rights before Courts*, 232.

[98] In a modern literature this argument was used by Czarnota, 'Populist Constitutionalism', 52.

[99] Sławomira Wronkowska, 'Czy Rzeczpospolita Polska jest państwem prawnym?', in Sławomira Wronkowska (ed.), *Polskie dyskusje o państwie prawa* (Wydawnictwo Sejmowe, 1995), 85–89.

need to apply it to the case at hand is likely to cause modifications and their character may be the result of the local legal tradition.[100] While this process may happen unintentionally, it may also be a conscious one, as in the case of the Polish transitional justice framework.

20.4 TRANSITIONAL JUSTICE ALTERNATIVES: POLITICAL TRANSFORMATION AS AN EXCHANGE OF ELITES

Despite an array of implemented transitional justice measures, there is a widespread belief that reckoning with the past was not possible due to the restrictive constitutional framework created by the PCT through the transplantation of Western rule of law standards. In Sections 20.2 and 20.3, I have argued that legal impossibilism conceived in this way is a myth and that the use of the rule of law framework by the PCT was, to a certain degree, adaptive, instead of purely imitative. However, among the members and supporters of the former government the belief in legal impossibilism in the transitional justice context is based on a specific understanding of the core objectives of political transformation. According to this way of thinking, the process of democratization must also involve a significant change in social hierarchy, including an exchange of elites. To illustrate this way of thinking, I now turn to the alternatives to the Polish transitional justice model, which were possible both at the level of constitutional adjudication and constitutional provisions themselves.

20.4.1 *Dissenting Opinions*

Transitional justice cases are as important, as they are notoriously hard. They involve dilemmas of not only a legal but also a moral and political nature. Therefore, one may expect that many of the constitutional judgments in transitional justice cases will not be unanimous. Table 20.1 proves that this is indeed the case when it comes to the PCT rulings.

Some of the dissenting opinions indicate that, in the case of lustration, harsher reckoning with the communist past was possible. In these opinions judges often referred to substantive values, including justice itself. A separate opinion to the PCT judgment on the 1992 parliamentary resolution questioned the Court's assumption that its application had to violate the personal rights of those included on the list of communist secret service collaborators. According to Judge Łączkowski, this conclusion could not be defended on 'neither legal nor ethical grounds': if information on past collaboration was accurate, it could not harm a good name of former agents – and, even if it would, 'ethical reasons, as well as the principles of justice and equality, suggest that defending the rights of the repressed should be a

[100] See Martin Krygier, 'Law as Tradition' (1986) 5 *Law and Philosophy* 237, 242–243, 254.

TABLE 20.1 *Dissenting opinions in the PCT transitional justice rulings*

Case type	Lustration						Reduction of pensions	Amnesty
Case number	U 6/92	K 39/97	K 7/01	K 44/02	K 2/07	P 31/12	K 6/09	P 2/99
No. of judges deciding the case	10	12	15	14	11	5	14	5
No. of dissenting opinions	1	4	1	4	9[101]	1	5[102]	0
Supporting decisions that would have resulted in harsher transitional justice measures	1	3	–	–	4	1	–	–
Supporting decisions that would have resulted in more lenient transitional justice measures	–	1	1	4	5	–	5	–

priority'.[103] In the 1998 ruling three opinions defended the constitutionality of a provision ordering a removal of a lustration liar from the list of presidential candidates through an administrative act of an election committee. One of the judges argued that a lack of such sanction would violate public morality and the principle of the rule of law. Allowing a lustration liar to become the president would be fatal for the authority of state institutions – 'a principal value in a state governed by the rule of law'. Thus, 'rule of law procedural values' cannot be contrasted with necessary personal virtues: honesty, integrity and respect for the law and fellow citizens. The first virtue is especially important as 'the respect for the government and the law has always relied on truth'.[104]

Four dissenting opinions defended constitutionality of the major part of the 2006 Lustration Law. Some of the judges claimed that the PCT was too eager to interfere with the relative autonomy of the legislator. Even when such an

[101] Four of the dissenting opinions questioned only the constitutionality of the collaboration definition, one claimed that the statute should be entirely invalidated and four defended constitutionality of its various provisions. The latter two are discussed in this section.

[102] Additionally, one separate opinion disagreed with parts of the justification but agreed with the ruling on merits.

[103] Dissenting opinion of Judge Wojciech Łączkowski, U 6/92 (n 28), para. 77.

[104] Dissenting opinion of Judge Marian Zdyb, K 39/97 (n 33), paras. 191–225. Quotes: paras. 200, 214.

intervention was warranted, constitutionality of many provisions could easily be obtained through their binding interpretation.[105] What is more, two opinions demonstrated a more substantive understanding of the rule of law. According to them, a democratic state not only needs appropriate state institutions but it also 'needs to be based on clear axiological and moral standards'.[106] Thus, in such a state, 'the legislator has a duty to deal with a difficult past for the good of society' and to ensure proper operation of state institutions: lustration laws can be instruments of this change, if they are based on virtues such as truth, memory, human dignity and freedom.[107] According to Judge Liszcz, these exceptional transitional circumstances 'justify the need for a gradation and more liberal application of constitutional constraints' designed for stable democracies. This is because, as the time passes, 'dealing with the past in a manner that is fully consistent with all constitutional requirements will be more and more difficult, if at all possible'.[108]

However, dissenting opinions also show that Polish transitional justice could have been much more restricted. A separate opinion to the 1998 PCT judgment claimed that, because of the social stigma associated with the ties to the communist secret service, the need to confess to such connections is equal with self-denunciation and therefore contrary to the rule of law.[109] If this opinion prevailed, the Polish model of lustration would not be possible. Subsequent dissenting opinions questioned overall constitutionality of lustration[110] or that it also covered individuals who did not partake in core activities of the communist secret service.[111] Finally, five dissenting opinions claimed that the 2010 reduction of pensions was unconstitutional. According to the judges, officers who in democratic Poland passed the 1990 vetting and were re-employed in security agencies had a right to expect that their pensions would remain intact. Therefore, the law violated their vested rights, legal security and trust towards the state, which are all protected under the rule of law. The opinions also argued that the act lacked individualization, was disproportionate and infringed on the principle of proper legislation.[112]

The authors of these opinions preferred an even stricter constitutional framework. According to Judge Zdziennicki, transitional justice regulations need to comply with all the rule of law requirements, as 'there are no special constitutional provisions for dealing with people associated with the former system of government'.[113] His own list

[105] Dissenting opinion of Judge Maria Gintowt-Jankowicz, K 2/07 (n 38), paras. 626–657.
[106] Dissenting opinion of Judge Teresa Liszcz, K 2/07 (n 38), para. 758.
[107] Dissenting opinion of Judge Zbigniew Cieślak, K 2/07 (n 38), paras. 583, 623.
[108] Dissenting opinion of Judge Teresa Liszcz, K 2/07 (n 38), para. 766.
[109] Dissenting opinion of Judge Zdzisław Czeszejko-Sochacki, K 39/97 (n 33), paras. 148–164.
[110] Dissenting opinions of Judge Bohdan Zdziennicki, K 44/02 (n 36), paras. 102–140; K 2/07 (n 38), paras. 853–969.
[111] Dissenting opinion of Judge Bohdan Zdziennicki K 7/01 (n 73), paras. 150–176.
[112] Dissenting opinions of Judges: Adam Jamróz, Ewa Łętowska, Marek Mazurkiewicz, Mirosław Wyrzykowski and Bohdan Zdziennicki; K 6/09 (n 46), paras. 617–921.
[113] Dissenting opinion of Judge Bohdan Zdziennicki, K 44/02 (n 36), para. 107.

of acceptable solutions seems relatively short and does not include the politics of memory: in another ruling Zdziennicki claims that 'the law, by its very nature, cannot impose a specific vision of the past and draw legal consequences from such an assessment'.[114] Whether this neutrality is observed or not, the rule of law requirements need to be fulfilled in order to safeguard individual rights. Thus, Judge Jamróz warns against pursuing justice at the expense of the rule of law:

> I do not accept . . . adjudication which relies on 'pure' social justice and is inspired by political and moral convictions, but which disregards constitutional principles developed in the Court's jurisprudence, [the principles] which reflect modern, well-established standards of a democratic state governed by the rule of law. This method creates a risk of turning the Tribunal from a court of law to a court of social justice.[115]

Comparing the number of judges with the number of dissenting opinions suggests that, if the composition of the PCT's adjudicating panels was partially different, some of the Court's pivotal decisions (including the ones in transitional justice cases) may have gone in another direction. This trivial truth explains why altering the personal composition of judicial branch was such an important factor in the Polish rule of law crisis. If one 'sees people rather than institutions' then reshaping the judiciary 'is not an attempt to repair and strengthen the institutions . . . but above all to change the cadres'.[116] As Jarosław Kaczyński himself explained: 'To change Poland, one needs the right people'.[117]

20.4.2 *Alternative Constitutional Provisions*

Transitional justice provisions are not abundant in the 1997 Polish Constitution, and they were similarly absent in its drafts prepared by political actors.[118] One significant exception was Article 29 of the constitutional draft submitted by Kaczyński's Centre Agreement Party, which stipulated that a statute may provide an exemption from the *nullum crimen sine lege* principle with regards to acts which in a particularly severe way violated basic human rights and the rights of the Polish Nation.[119]

On the other hand, the so-called civic draft of the constitution[120] – prepared by experts, financed and managed by the Solidarity trade union and signed by over one

[114] Dissenting opinion of Judge Bohdan Zdziennicki, K 2/07 (n 38), paras. 915, 940.
[115] Dissenting opinion of Judge Adam Jamróz, K 6/09 (n 46), para. 670.
[116] Martin Krygier, 'The Challenge of Institutionalisation: Post-Communist 'Transitions', Populism, and the Rule of Law' (2019) 15 *European Constitutional Law Review* 544.
[117] Kaczyński, *Polska naszych marzeń*, 91.
[118] The drafts available in Polish in: *Komisja Konstytucyjna Zgromadzenia Narodowego: Projekty Konstytucji* (Wydawnictwo Sejmowe, 1993).
[119] Ibid.
[120] Solidarity's Popular Initiative Constitution Draft, *Co Tydzień Solidarność* (30 June 1994), 1.

million of people[121] – included many transitional justice provisions. Article 26(2) ordered lustration of public officials and candidates for office. Article 161(1) stated that the provisions enabling re-privatization should be enacted within a year after the Constitution came into force. The same deadline was set for passing a statute on the vetting of judges (Article 163). Article 164 provided for a transfer of communist secret service files to the IPN and ordered that a law regulating access to them be adopted within a six-month period. However, only one provision made its way to the final text of the 1997 Constitution: Article 22 of the draft stated that there would be no statute of limitations for war crimes and crimes against humanity and that the proscription period would not run when a crime was not prosecuted for political reasons (see Articles 43 and 44 of the Polish basic law).

The popular draft is fondly remembered by the Law and Justice party. In 2017, a conference celebrating the alternative constitutional draft was held in the Polish Senate. In an opening speech, Kaczyński criticized the 1997 Polish Constitution, calling it 'post-communist' and accusing it of petrifying the existing social structure. On the other hand, the Law and Justice leader praised the popular draft. According to Kaczyński, it included 'an ingenious idea' which made it 'fundamentally different' from the current Polish constitution: through its transitional justice provisions, the draft was effectively 'abolishing post-communism', in a way that 'made it impossible to use the law for blocking such changes'.[122]

In fact, two Law and Justice constitution drafts – prepared in 2005 and 2010 – included some similar provisions. They both proclaimed the right to obtain information about the communist regime and individuals involved in its actions, tasked the IPN with fostering this right and provided for lustration. Both drafts also banned individuals who eagerly fought against the democratic opposition from holding public offices, while the later one also explicitly introduced a ten-year period for vetting of judges. Finally, the 2005 draft ordered that a Truth and Justice Commission be created for a period of five years. The task of this commission was to investigate and disclose abuses of public positions occurring after 1989 in the interest of an individual or a group – a striking example of a mistrust towards the early years of the Polish democratic system.[123]

[121] For an overview of the initiative, see Emilia Kowalewska, 'Between Civic and Legal Constitutionalism: Dynamics of Poland's Constitution-making Projects of the 1990s' (2020) 10 *Oñati Socio-Legal Series* 903.

[122] See Jan Majchrowski (ed.), *Konstytucja Solidarności* (Wydawnictwo Sejmowe, 2018), 30–31.

[123] Articles 28, 147 and 166–166 of the 2005 Law and Justice's Constitution Draft and Articles 29, 35, 191 and 192 of the 2010 Law and Justice's Constitution Draft, https://oko.press/images/2017/10/PiS-projekt-konstytucji-2005.pdf and https://oko.press/images/2017/10/PiS-projekt-konstytucji-2010.pdf.

20.4.3 *Tuning the Piano: Transitional Justice and the Transformation of Social Hierarchies*

The 2005 and 2010 Law and Justice drafts suggest that, for this party, 'abolishing post-communism' must involve removing the former elite from important positions in a democratic system. Without such a change, transitional justice is incomplete. Kaczyński makes this point in his 2011 book, describing four aspects of a successful transition: he states that, while Poland was able to build democracy and capitalism, the lack of decommunization meant that it failed to create 'a new state' and 'a new social hierarchy'.[124] Kaczyński describes the Round Table Agreements as the birth of the new post-communist elite, composed of the former members of communist nomenklatura – who during the transition either acquired or remained in control of a large part of national property – and some members of the democratic opposition. According to the Law and Justice leader this meant that, after 1989, the old elite maintained much of their control over Polish political and economic life.[125] Kaczyński seems deeply convinced that the lack of decommunization slowed down crucial reforms: he claims that, if such a vetting would have taken place, 'the GDP would be higher by circa 25 percent', 'more flats would have been built' (he estimates the difference at two million!), the budget for higher education would be a couple of times bigger – and even that 'more children would have been born'.[126] Therefore, for the Law and Justice leader, the lack of thorough screening is one of transition's biggest mistakes and some kind of retrospective vetting is still necessary to reshape the social order.[127]

In order to ensure their effective and fair operation, such a vetting should cover inter alia state offices, security agencies, mass-media, banks and courts.[128] While this does not necessary mean a total purge, in order to induce social change the vetting should be both broad and deep. According to Kaczyński:

> Power is a system of relations between people. If these relations are disrupted and those below are from a different faction than the ones in charge, then it may be said that the keys of the piano cannot reach to the strings. One plays from a new music sheet, but hears an old melody. This is how many institutions, including the television, work today. … This is why until this day it is no difference who plays the piano, because whatever they would play – what we hear is *The Internationale*.[129]

[124] Kaczyński, *Polska naszych marzeń*, 72–73.
[125] Ibid., 42–58; Jarosław Kaczyński, Michał Bichniewicz and Piotr M. Rudnicki, *Czas na zmiany: Rozmowa z Jarosławem Kaczyńskim*, 2nd ed. (Editions Spotkania, 2014), 15–18, 133–194.
[126] Kaczyński, *Polska naszych marzeń*, 82.
[127] Ibid., 108.
[128] Kaczyński et al., *Czas na zmiany*, 133–194.
[129] Ibid., 140.

Thus, for the Law and Justice leader, 'the replacement of personnel is necessary to restore the agency of the state, especially in the judiciary'.[130] For Kaczyński, decommunization is crucial for inducing a transformation of the whole social hierarchy: it is a tool for an essential exchange of the public elite. It is only after such an exchange that political, economic and social transformation is completed.[131]

However, according to the former government, such a transformation was not possible under the 1997 Polish Constitution and the PCT case law. In 2011 Kaczyński claimed that, in order to vet the judges, a constitutional amendment would be necessary[132] and that 'an ostentatious screening' conducted by the Truth and Justice Commission 'could have been easily invalidated by the PCT'.[133] It is therefore no coincidence that the Polish constitutional crisis began with the conflict between the government and the PCT and that, during the same period, many decommunization provisions were also enacted.[134] This is because, under closer scrutiny, legal impossibilism turns out to have a very particular meaning: in the context of political transformation it is understood as a restriction on the fundamental rearrangement of the social hierarchy – an interpretation very much rooted in specific beliefs about the core objectives of democratic transition.

It is true that a widespread disqualification of former communist elites has never been implemented in Poland. However, is the belief that such a process was impossible under Polish transitional justice framework justified? Even though no definite answer can be given, one should note that, in 1990, vetting procedures were carried out with regards to the SC and to the former communist secret service, both resulting in significant personnel changes. While these regulations were not subject to constitutional review, there is no reason to believe the PCT would have held them contrary to the rule of law: in fact, the PACE 1996 Resolution and Guidelines explicitly allowed for such measures. Yet, as the years since the transition go by, it becomes more difficult for such provisions to pass the proportionality test. Thus, when the Law and Justice came to power in 2005 and 2015, it may have indeed been too late to introduce such a disqualification in a way consistent with constitutional requirements. Still, even if this proved to be true (which we shall never know), the lack of decommunization should still be considered mainly a result of the

130 Michał Stambulski, 'Constitutional Populism and the Rule of Law in Poland', in Martin Krygier, Adam Czarnota and Wojciech Sadurski (eds.), *Anti-Constitutional Populism* (Cambridge University Press, 2022), 354.

131 In a similar vein, see also ibid., 351–355; Janusz Reykowski, 'The Massive Exchange of Elites as a Mean of Formation of the Authoritarian Regime', in Jerzy J. Wiatr (ed.), *New Authoritarianism: Challenges to Democracy in the 21st Century* (Verlag Barbara Budrich, 2019), 50–56.

132 Kaczyński, *Polska naszych marzeń*, 104.

133 Ibid., 107. The context suggests that screening is understood here as a disqualification mechanism.

134 Krotoszyński, 'Transitional Justice', 26–27.

lawmakers inactivity, for which the PCT can hardly be blamed. From this perspective, legal impossibilism is, at best, unproven – and possibly a myth as well.

20.5 CONCLUSIONS: LEGAL IMPOSSIBILISM AND POLISH COUNTER-CONSTITUTIONALISM

In her chapter on constitutional sociology, Kim Lane Scheppele describes successful constitutions as ones which 'manage to create their own social life'.[135] Such constitutions reach beyond legal domain and are able to dominate social imaginary: they 'shape social expectations and understandings, and come to be taken for granted'.[136] Scheppele understands constitutions as 'fields of naturalised ideas':[137] as long as they seem obvious and are unquestioned, even a serious economic or political crisis does not threaten the constitutional order. It is when a constitution is 'fundamentally challenged' and its 'reality becomes questionable' that social actors need to adjust the rules 'to rescue its normality': '[i]f they fail – or if they fail to try – constitutions can crumble'.[138]

Constitution can become denaturalized through ideological competition. This competition is caused by counter-constitutions, defined by Scheppele as 'alternative visions of constitutional order, grounded in different understandings of what a constitution is and should be' which 'reject the taken-for-granted constitutional vision already in place'.[139] Scheppele attributes the collapse of Hungarian liberal constitutionalism to the emergence of such a counter-constitutional narrative. This narrative presented the 1989 constitution as foreign, offered an alternative constitutional symbol (the Holy Crown of St Stephen, allegedly a 'true' Hungarian constitution) and created its own politics of memory.[140] Scheppele explains that:

> Had the counter-constitutional ideas not been around to provide a ready-to-hand alternative conceptual frame, the 1989 constitution might have been harder to topple. But once an alternative constitutional conception came to be seen as legitimate by segments of the Hungarian population, it became impossible for the 1989 constitution to naturalise the political space any longer. The dominant constitutionalism ceased to hold, and the post-1989 constitutional order became easy to destroy because it was no longer accepted as real.[141]

In the vast literature on the Polish constitution crisis, theories as to what caused the decline of liberal constitutionalism in this country differ significantly. The answers

[135] Kim Lane Scheppele, 'The Social Lives of Constitutions', in Paul Blokker and Chris Thornhill (eds.), *Sociological Constitutionalism* (Cambridge University Press, 2017), 35.
[136] Ibid., 35.
[137] Ibid., 62.
[138] Ibid., 56.
[139] Ibid., 61.
[140] Ibid.
[141] Ibid.

given by Polish scholars are varied and include factors as different as the need for group identification, globalization and economic disparities, the fear of the migration crisis and the dominance of legal positivism.[142] Many authors agree, however, that the lack of an entrenched democratic culture is one of the reasons of the crisis.[143] While this may well be true, there is also an alternative explanation to consider: that a liberal vision of a political order was well-entrenched but became denaturalized when Polish counter-constitutionalism emerged.

Just like their Hungarian counterparts, Polish conservatives created an alternative constitutional imaginary. An alternate narrative on Polish democratization was formulated, in which the Round Table Agreements and ensuing peaceful transformation were presented not as a historical achievement, but as the original sin of the post-transitional social order: the birth of the new elite, composed of prominent members of the democratic opposition and the former communists. In this vision, the fact that the latter have been able to participate in democratic public life is not a liberal virtue, but proof that the transition was mainly superficial: a true transformation would have to include a fundamental change in social hierarchy, including an exchange of political and economic elites. According to counter-constitutionalists, this was unfortunately not possible, as the 1997 constitution (enacted by the new elite and infused with foreign ideas), the PCT and the rest of the judiciary guarded the post-transitional political, economic and social structure. One of the ways in which they allegedly defended the system was the abuse of general clauses, including the rule of law. In this narrative, the constitutional order was designed to create a state of legal impossibilism, in which social hierarchies would remain intact. Thus, the belief in legal impossibilism which prevented the vetting of public sphere (including the judiciary) is central for this understanding of Polish transition. This interpretation serves to delegitimize liberal constitutionalism and to simultaneously present an alternative, in which the cadres are more important than the institutions and the procedures, and the exchange of elites becomes a prerequisite of a just and efficient state. While the Law and Justice counter-constitutionalism looks for alternative constitutional tokens (such as Solidarity's popular draft) and political symbols (such as the deposition from power of the Olszewski's government), it is ultimately also forward-looking, and promises a new, fair social order.

The role which the PCT and the courts play in this counter-constitutional vision explains why the implementation of the Law and Justice project began with changes in the personal composition of the judicial branch. There is, however, another lesson to be drawn from the analysis of Eastern European counter-constitutionalism – and one especially important for the governments which seek

[142] See, e.g., Matczak, 'Poland: From Paradigm to Pariah?', 9–21; Sadurski, *Poland's Constitutional Breakdown*, 162–191; Skąpska, 'The Decline of Liberal Constitutionalism', 141–143; Stambulski, 'Constitutional Populism and the Rule of Law in Poland', 346–351.

[143] Skąpska, 'The Decline of Liberal Constitutionalism', 142; Sadurski, *Poland's Constitutional Breakdown*, 182–187.

to reinstate the rule of law. While it is tempting to look for straightforward, legal solutions to the constitutional crisis, these may not be sufficient in the long run. If Scheppele's diagnosis is right, then, in order to respond to counter-constitutionalism in a permanent way, its narrative needs to be denaturalized and an alternative constitutional vision has to be present. While this vision may include a return to liberal constitutionalism, its imaginary has to be sufficiently deep to re-inspire and altered enough to make up for its previous deficits; it must also include its own politics of memory. This is a huge and daunting task but, from the perspective of constitutional sociology, a small-scale constitutional project may simply not be possible.

Index

Note
Since the entire book is about 'constitutional imaginaries', the term itself is not listed in the index.

apoliticism
  economic policies, 308
  law, 4, 28, 32, 323
  liberal, 9, 26, 29, 175, 312
Atlanticism, 76, 80
Austria
  constitution in ruins (narrative), 266–70, 275, 279, 289
  Constitution, minimalist compromise, 278–80
  Constitutional Court, 285–6, 289–90
  constitutional identity, 273, 275, 289
  constitution-in-ruins, narrative, 25
  petrification theory, 284–5
  role model constitution (narrative), 26, 267, 286–7, 291
  value neutral constitution (narrative), 25, 266, 275–7, 279, 282, 285
Austria-Hungary
  European Union, comparison, 288–9
  Imperial Court of Justice, 291, 293
  law, integration through, 288
authoritarianism
  constitutionalisation of, 302–3, 374
  descent to, 264, 278, 395
  illiberal, 23
  populism, 174
  societal, 398

belonging, sense of
  Europe, to, 26
  place, to, 24, 92, 227, 232, 239
Bibó, István
  Miseries of East European Small States, the, 86–8, 90

capitalism
  Anglo-American, 315
  ideology, as, 315
  market, 307, 315
Central and Eastern Europe
  authoritarianism, 87
  collective trauma, 90–1, 94, 100
  communism, 89
  constitutionalism, 6, 8, 59, 84, 86, 103, 330, 356
  dissidents, 307–8
  distinctiveness of (*Sonderweg*), 12, 14, 86, 252, 254
  ethno-centrism, 59, 84, 88, 95–7, 252
  Europeanness, 43
  federalism, aversion to, 96
  historical tragedies of, 85, 90–1, 99, 223, 254, 264, 432
  history of, 12, 14, 20, 90
  identity of, 15, 90–1
  illiberalism, 297
  legalism, 303, 322
  misery of, 14, 86, 89, 91–2, 95, 101
  nationalism, 59, 95, 254, 264
  self-victimisation, 87, 211, 251, 271
  small states/nations, 14, 54–7, 85, 87–8, 91–2, 97–8, 105, 251
  state myths, 89, 265
  transformation through courts, 433, 443
Cepl, Vojtěch, 316–17
Čermák, Vladimír, 320–1

communism
  criminalisation of, 181, 183, 200, 432, 439–40, 442
  fall of, 7, 353
  law, legacy of, 322, 324, 329, 331, 355, 431–2
  legal positivism, 338
  othering of, 250
  parliamentary supremacy, 334, 336, 339, 344, 350, 353
  party, leading role of, 301, 303, 339, 347
  reformists, 302, 324, 335, 340, 343, 347
  state power, unity of, 334, 336, 350
constitution
  ancient, 15, 111–13, *See also* United Kingdom
  directive, 34, 379–82, 385, *See also* Portugal
  economic, 34, 309, 378, 382, *See also* Portugal
  historical, 18, 21, 23–4, 181, 193, 195–6, 199–202, 207–9, 224, *See also* Hungary
  invisible, 18, 196, 320, *See also* Hungary
  material, 62
  normative, 33, 375–6, 383, 385, *See also* Portugal
  ordinary law, part of, 110, 118
  value-based, 270, 320
constitution, amendments
  extensive use of, 269
  fragmentation, 268
  political abuse of, 268
constitution, counter
  roots of, 297
constitution, functions of, 202–3, 386
  collective self-representation, 204
constitution, supremacy of, 161–2, *See also* Poland
constitution, symbolism of, 202
  history interpretation, 195
  indifference, 269, 273
  legalism, 276
  pragmatism, 275
  social integration, 202
constitutional aesthetics, 269–70, 274, 293
constitutional claims, 111
constitutional crisis/backsliding, 165, *See also* rule of law
  constitutional restrictions, 432
  constitutionalism, conflict of, 430
  roots of, 8, 26, 391, 407–8, 431, 454–5
constitutional identity
  dark side of, 272
  human rights protection, 272, 376, 385, *See also* patriotism
  public identification, lack of, 391
  sovereignty substitution, 424
  technical, 273–4
constitutional memory, 183
  community building, 201, 204, 206
  constitutional practice, forming, 194–5, *See also* constitutional practice
  critique of, 200, 202
  future aspirations, 210
  glorious past, 9
constitutional moment, 44, 267, 270
constitutional myth, 63, 123, 202
  glorious past, 210–11, 213
  sovereignty, 84
constitutional order, 63, 129
  flexibility of, 391
constitutional practice, 3, 158
  arbitrary, 221
  constitutional law, disjunction between, 120
  constitution-in-being, 110
  emotions, generation of, 203–4, 456
  EU law, concerning, 146
  governing, art of, 111
  scholarly-shaped, 154–8, 169, 267, 293, 392
  society-shaping, 63, 186, 223, 416, 427, 454
constitutional principles, 214, 414
  concurrent, 5, 393–4
  fundamental rights, 270
  liberal market economy, 364
  sovereignty, 156, 223
constitutional reasoning. *See also* legal interpretation
  competing narratives of, 86, 203, 279, 393, 450, *See also* constitution, counter
  constitution-makers, of the, 154
  inner working of, 107
  judicial, 220
  social context of, 271, 279, 354, 386, 395
constitutional reform, 130, *See also* Italy; United Kingdom
  executive strengthening, 79
  modernisation, 126
constitutional review
  acquired rights, doctrine of, 438
  austerity measures, of, 384–5
  authoritarian system, within, 333–5, 341, 344, 350, 352
  constitutional norms, of, 381
  EU law, of, 163, 167, 222
  formalism, 285
  Kelsenian model of, 287, 291–3, 341, 350, 356
  legal certainty, 433, 438, 440
  legitimate expectation, 381, 384
  liberal turn, 433
  mixed model of, 375
  rights-based, 33, 126, 128, 163, 223, 285, 319, 326, 349, 425
  rule of law, 283, 434, 440

constitutional supremacy, 164, 343, 375, *See also* Poland
  constitutional review, 334
  European integration, 17
constitutional traditions, local, 7
Constitutional Treaty (2004), 78
constitutional truth, 28, 414, 454
  contested, 86, 105
constitutionalism
  civic, 305
  communitarian, 391, 394, 396, 399, 404, *See also* Poland
  European. *See* European constitutionalism
  façade. *See* Polish People's Republic (PRL)
  illiberal, 165, 297
  negative, 313, 318, 415, 417, 424
  neoliberal, 309, 313, 357, 371, 392
  Nordic, 33, *See also* Nordics
  political, 28, 417, 422, 429
  popular, 358
  social-democratic, 358, 382–3
  socialist, 334, 338, 340, 343, 350
  societal, 34, 392, 395–6, *See also* Poland
  supranational, 426
  transformative, 380
  transformative nature of, 388–9
  varieties of, 5
constitutionalism, legal
  antimajoritarian, 364, 431
  domination of, 32, 197–8, 297, 430
  formalism, 275–7, 282, 303, 393
  legal impossibilism, 431, 437, 440–1, 445, 447, 455, *See also* Poland
  social engineering, rational, 193, 429
  state organisation, 393, 429
  struggle of, 17
  universalism of, 429
constitutionalism, liberal, 297
  antimajoritarian, 311, 429
  anti-utopian, 370
  civil society, restriction of, 399, 404, 406–7
  community building, 298
  decline of, 6, 26, 454
  domination of, 6, 8, 196, 299, 305, 322, 327, 369, 411
  heterogeneity of, 31, 306
  individual freedoms, protection of, 308, 394, 396, 415, 426
  liberal consensus, 298, 326–7
  origins of, 9
  power limitation, 424, 429
  public support of, 160
  universalism of, 410, 446
constitution-counter, 454
Convention on the Future of Europe, 13, 43, 51–4
corporatism
  associations of professions, 402
  co-governance, 403–4, 408, *See also* Poland
  social model of, 396, 404, 408, *See also* Poland
crisis, refugee, 455
  quotas, 186, 189
culture
  artefacts, 230
  Christianity, 18, 172, 183, 185, 210–11, 358
  conflict, 88, 242
  diversity, 56
  European, 238–9
  governing class, of the, 117, *See also* United Kingdom
  heritage, 113, 238
  imaginaries, 229–33, 237, 240, 246, 248
  independence, 96, 98
  wars, 186, 196
Czechia
  anti-communism, 434
  collective forgetting, 258
  Constitutional Court, 108, 319, 321, 433
  exceptionalism, 25
  legal positivism, 322
  self-victimisation, 25, 93
Czechoslovakia
  collective forgetting, 251
  exceptionalism, 253
  failed state, 25, 253–4
  history, 250
  intolerance, 264
  nationalism, 250, 254
  self-victimisation, 254

democracy
  backsliding, 7, 165
  constrained, 311, 358, 429
  culture, 455
  economic, 368, 374, 377–8, 385, *See also* Portugal, *See also* Nordics
  external threat to, 102
  governance, 377, 387
  illiberal, 168, 170
  liberal, 174, 374
  meanings of, 361
  militant, 272, 294
  minority, protection of, 281, 285, 311
  normative, 197
  participatory, 34, 136, 377
  people's, 334
  procedural, 266, 276, 280–1, 285
  promotion of, 369
  protection of, 435

democracy (cont.)
radical, 310
self-management, 136, 396
separation of powers, 139, 390, 421
social, 385
socialist, 374
domination. *See also* hegemony
identity-framing, over, 178
national, 121
structures of, 4
Dworkin, Ronald
rule of law, 317–18

East and West
cold war, during, 228, 235
cultural dialogue, 236–7
division between, 83, 87, 89, 95, 245
outpost between, 12
East Central Europe. *See* Central and Eastern Europe
East, the. *See also* Central and Eastern Europe
backwardness, symbol of, 227
economy
austerity measures, 383
choices, 4
consultative etatism, 400
crisis, 383, 400
democratic state, separation from, 309, 364
democratically organised, 377–9, 383
emergency rhetoric, 4
free market, 311, 314–15
free zone, 141, 289
independence, 98, 131, 133, 142
property, collective, 419
property, private, 420
redistribution, 4, 309, 368, 378
social dialogue, 400
empire
collapse of, 15, 98, 100, 277
multi-ethnic, 92, 97, 288
protector, as, 97
enemy. *See also* threat
constitutionalised image of, 19, 172, 180–3, 185–7, 211, *See also* Hungary
internal, 185
left-wing politics as, 178, 184
making of, 17, 19, 172, 176–7, 184
political, 173–5, 183
political mobilisation, 17
epiphanies, 414, 425–7
Estonia
Constitution (1992), 11, 50
Estonian SSR, 233, 235
Ilves, Toomas Hendrik, 51, 54, 57–9
imaginary of, 12, 16, 24, 54, 229, 237, 243, 247
Meri, Lennart, 51–2, 54–7
Supreme Court (SC), 11, 51
EU institutions
Court of Justice of the European Union (CJEU), 222, 426
European Court of Justice (ECJ), 127, 387
European Parliament, 58
European President, 53
Euro (single currency), 80, 127, 163
Europe, as the Other, 15
Europe, return to, 6, 18, 24, 147, 151, 244, 356
ideology of, 164
social desire for, 160
European Arrest Warrant, 162
European constitutionalism
constitutional identity, 388, 426
idiosyncrasies, suppression of, 383, 385, 387
multi-level, 162, 164
neoliberal, 378, 382, 411, 426
transformative nature of, 388–9
Western invention, as, 6, 20, *See also* West, the
European Convention on Human Rights, 289–91
individualism, 411, 423, 427
European Court of Human Rights (ECHR)
influence of, 128, 290
neoliberal capitalism, constitutionalisation of, 365
European identity
civilising mission, 410
contested meaning of, 24, 246–7, 249
creation of, 52
lack of, 387
national identity, part of, 223, 238–40
European integration
foundations of, 1
government-strengthening, 404–5
integration clause, 148, 151, 154, 156–8, 164
judicial decisions, through, 77, 127
law, through, 288, 293, 411
limits of, 109, 161–2, 169, 172, 182, 187
market, through, 26, 75, 80
national narratives, challenge to, 5, 8, 17, 410, 423
national reforms, catalyst of, 79, 81, 126, 363, 370, 389, 405
openness towards, 42, 267, 377, 387
rationality of, 409
resistance to, 84, 96, 100, 105, 127, 272, 359, 365, 406
securitisation of, 12, 47, 75, 99, 104, 246, 248
stealth, by, 77–8, 222
WWII resistance, 67
European Union
accession to, 50, 103, 149, 155, 159–60
Common Foreign and Security Policy (CSFP), 54
competences, 53

constitution, 58, 426
diversity of, 55, 388
enlargement of, 7, 46, 56, 83, 102
federalism, 56–7, 61, 67–72, 110, 127, 157, 423
international organisation, as, 103, 157, 423
law, primacy of, 11, 47, 51, 127, 222, 387
law, transposition, 405–6
legal principles, 127
legitimacy, 57, 96, 155, 389, 405–6
periphery, 2, 60, 246
principle of equality, 53
principle of subsidiarity, 58, 388
social model, 193, 389, 406, 408, 426
experts
constitutional practitioners, 153
constitutional scholars, 107, 269, 316–17
economists, 315
law professors, dictatorship of, 373–4
lawyers, late socialist, 322–4, 354
revolutionaries, as, 133–5, 142
technocracy, 310
Western perspective, 6

fascism
dictatorship, 373
France
constitutions, passion for, 417, 427
general will, 36, 416–18, 427
Great Nation, narrative of, 410
indivisibility, narrative of, 36, 418, 423–4
laïcité, 36, 419
law, liberal turn, 423–4
republican imaginary, 35, 411, 416, 422, 425–8
Yellow Vests movement, 426
fundamental rights
collective, 419
constitutional principles, as, 270, 272, 279, 305–6, 376
expansion of, 224
extension of, 213–17
individual rights, 418
neoliberalism, tool of, 365
protection of, 128, 163, 165, 202, 272, 290, 302, 376, 385, 389, 424
regression, prohibition of, 381, 383
right to property, 415, 419
right to vote, 214
socio-economic, 33
struggle for, 299, 302, 307
workers', 377–8, 382

Germany
Basic Law, value-based order, 270, 272
Federal Constitutional Court (BVerfG), 83, 162, 270
Federal Constitutional Court (BVerfG), model court, 320
legal tradition, influence of, 375, 379
globalisation, 209, 423, 455
economic, 313, 363, 370
European integration, 107, 411, 426
neoliberal, 364
government
authority, 119
legitimacy of, 3
technocratic, 310

Hayek, Friedrich A. *See also* neoliberalism
freedom, 315
orders, constructed, 314
orders, spontaneous, 314
republicanism, critique of, 420
rule of law, 314–16, 364
hegemony. *See also* domination
historical bloc, 179
presentism, neoliberal, 369
right-wing, 179, 358, *See also* Hungary
social democracy, of, 362
history
constitutional, 18, 194, 198, 209, 212
continuity of, 213, 217–20
escapism, 20, 265, 271
intellectual, 414
narratives, 18–20, 194–6, 201, 204, 206–7, 230
Hungary
communist legacy, 22
Constitution (2012), 172, 181–4, 198, 200–1, 203, 209–11, 220
Constitutional Court, 18, 187, 196–8, 201, 220–4, 433
constitutional identity, 172, 180, 183, 185, 187, 209, 211, 221, 223
Fidesz, 177–80, 184, 198
Holy Crown of (myth), 85, 200, 203, 205–7, 211, 213–14, 217–20, 224, 454
Horthy-regime, 21, 196, 199, 210, 219
nationalism, 22, 178, 185, 189, 210, 212, 215–17
NER (System of National Cooperation), 19–20, 174

identity
collective, 110, 412
communal, 229
cultural, 46, 121
moral, 180
other, the, 2, 9, 19, 171, 176–7, 180, 183, 229, 242, 412
political, 3, 111, 172, 178
social, 46, 93

identity (cont.)
- sovereignty, through, 46
- subjectiveness of, 412
- vicarious, 41, 43, 48
- *völkish* (ethnic-popular), 87, *See also* Central and Eastern Europe

ideology, 145
- competition of, 454
- constitutional, 84
- language, 142
- liberal, 162
- means of domination, as, 3, 8
- political, 95
- power, 110
- social integration, 204
- transformative function of, 4

illiberalism, 23, 209, 211
- republicanism, 420

imagination
- future, of, 16, 131, 218, 370, 455
- geopolitical, 227, 245, 248

imperialism
- economic, 98
- legacy of, 88, 96, 100, 222
- Soviet Union, 232
- United Kingdom, 122
- United States, 76

Ireland
- colonisation of, 123, *See also* United Kingdom
- independence of, 124

Italy
- Action Party (PdA), 69, 74
- Christian Democratic Party (DC), 70, 73
- Communist Party (PCI), 71–3, 76
- constitution, writing of, 73–5
- Constitutional Court, 78
- EU constitutional irrelevancy, 75–8, 81
- external constraint (*vincolo esterno*), 79–81
- L'Unità, 71
- political parties, 61, 64–6
- resistance, the, 61, 64–72
- self-victimisation, 62, 81–2
- Socialist Party (PSI), 69, 73
- Ventotene manifesto, 68, 75

judicial independence, 165, 167, 407, *See also* Poland
- appointments, political, 430
- lustrations, 437, 453
- safeguards of, 27

judiciary
- other powers, conflict with, 390, 425, 453

juristocracy, 28, 407
- constitutional amendments by, 221
- judicial activism, 285–6, 320–1, 383
- judicialisation of democracy, 197–8, 360, 365, 371, 430, 440

justice
- procedural, 304
- social, 309, 438–9
- substantive, 304, 318, 320, 431, 440
- transitional, 30, 36, 194, 196, 431–3, 437–8, 440–1, 443, 446, 450–2

Kelsen, Hans
- Austrian Constitution, drafting of, 278, 282, 291
- scholar, 280, 282–3, 285, 287, 292, 294
- sovereignty, dogma of, 84

Kis, János, 319

Klokočka, Václav, 319–21

Knap, Viktor, 324–5

Kuisz, Jarosław
- New politics of Poland, the, 94–5, 100–1

Kundera, Milan
- Tragedy of Central Europe, 91–2

law
- administrative, 115–16, 420
- continuity, 217, 219
- crisis jurisprudence, 381, 383
- internationalism, 376–7
- objectivity of, 28
- positivism, 32, 318, 321, 324, 326, 336, 338, 455
- praxis, 45
- pure theory of, 266, 276, 282–3, 356, *See also* Kelsen, Hans
- realism, 358, 362
- social management, tool of, 299–301, 315, 322, 325
- supranational, 426
- supremacy of, 121, 302, 365
- tradition, 446
- unity of, 115, 117, *See also* United Kingdom

legal interpretation. *See also* constitutional reasoning
- concrete-order-thinking, 106
- extra-legal aspects of, 212, 220, 321
- formalism, 284, 294, 322
- originalism, 284
- rule and statute thinking, 107, *See also* normativity/normativism
- *Stufenbau* theorem, 282–3, 342, 344, 375
- systemic, 393

legalism
- dissident, 299, 302, 304
- fascist, 374
- socialist, 300–1, 303–4, 322, 332, 340

legitimacy/legitimation
constitution, of, 148, 161, 198, 394
internal, 47
state power, of, 202, 300, 302, 375, 413
liberalism
Anglo-American, 415–16, 420, 425, 427
anti-totalitarian, 422
critique of, 175, 177
economic, 279, 313, 400, 421
French, 36, 421–3, 427
French republicanism, 416, 420, 425
human rights, 306–9, 311–12, 317, 323
liberal turn, 422
ordo-, 309
political, 223, 307, 421
public support, lack of, 391
liberal-legalism
community building, 193
critique of, 193
post-communist transformation, 298, 305–6, 432
scientific, 26, 29
liberties
civil, 117, 415
French republicanism, 415
negative, 410, 415
political, 87, 314, 415, 417, 427
positive, 410, 415
protection of, 318, 363, 394, 415
restoration of, 125
Lisbon, Treaty of (2007), 78, 107, 159–60, 162
Lithuania
Constitution (1992), 104
Constitutional Court, 108
lustrations
constitutionality of, 433–4, 436, 449, 453
democracy, protection of, 443
historical clarification, 435, 444
PACE guidelines, 443–4
rule of law, compliance with, 435–7, 442–3
temporality, 445, 453

Maastricht, Treaty of (1992), 77, 80, 426
Marxism
ethical superiority of, 342
republicanism, 422
member states/membership (EU), 1
constitutional aspects of, 154, 161, 164
economic benefits of, 108, 166
fundamental rights protection, 382, 385, 387–8
judiciary, 106–8, 127, 168, 222
sovereignty of, 15, 108, 424
transformation into, 7
minorities
persecution of, 22, 252, 264, 342
protection of, 281, 285, 311, 366, 371
minorities, ethnic
discontent of, 88, 215
protection of, 214–16, 289

narratives
constitutional, 63, 110–11, 125, 195, 204, 224, 266–7, 294, 414
political, 61, 201, 416
power of, 63
social, 3
nation
claims, 89
community, 409
culture, defined by, 97
emotions, 193, 207, 409
identity, 93, 122, 178, 180, 184, 214, 229, 412
imagined community, as, 85, 92, 111, 229, 409, 412
interest, 106
myth, 93, 98, 211–12, 409
personification, 92
political, 215–16, 430
representation of, 96, 179–80
social myth, as, 85
survival of, 91–2, 131, 189
nationalism
anti-democratic, 87
civic, 95, 271, *See also* West, the
ethnic, 95–6, 102, 254, *See also* Central and Eastern Europe
imagination, 409
linguistic, 88, 215, *See also* Central and Eastern Europe
neoliberalism
democracy, restriction of, 360
democratic deliberation, outside of, 308, 310
post-communist transformation, 306, 308–11, 313
rule of law, 312–14, 326, 364
Washington consensus, 308
nomocracy, 4
Nordics
corporatism, democratic, 359, 367–9
equality, economic, 368
exceptionalism, democratic, 357, 362, 366, 369–70
neoliberalisation, 361, 364, 366, 368–70
social democracy, hegemony of, 362
social welfare state, 357, 359, 366, 370–1
normativity/normativism
authority, 111
decision, 174
expectations, 3

patriotism
  constitutional, 267, 271–2, 294, *See also* constitutional identity
Poland
  anti-communism, 435, 441, 452
  anti-oligarchy, narrative of, 378
  Civic Platform, 404–5
  Constitution (1997), 103, 144, 164, 168, 397
  constitution, writing of, 148–53, 393, 398, 450
  constitutional compromise, 27, 148, 153, 155, 168, 393
  constitutional drift, 35, 391–2, 398–9, 407
  constitutional identity, 162, 168, 397
  Europeanists, 104
  executive-strengthening, ideology of, 392, 404–5, 407
  Law and Justice Party (PiS), 158, 165, 404–5, 407, 431
  messianic martydom (myth), 85
  partitions of, 94
  societal imaginary, 397–8, 404, 408
  sovereignists, 104, 159, 164–8, 170
Poland, Constitutional Tribunal (PCT)
  case law, inspirations, 442–3
  communist period, 331, 349, 352–4
  European integration, case law, 164, 166–9, 222
  personal changes, 430, 450, 453, 455
  political capture of, 26, 159, 166
  post-communist transformation, 432, 434–7, 439–40, 446–50
  sovereignty, case law, 107, 109
Polish People's Republic (PRL)
  civil society, 347–9, 354
  Constitution (1952), 334, 339
  constitutional review, 333, 336–7, 339–41, 343, 346, 350–2
  constitutionalism, 331
  façade constitutionalism, 335, 338–40, 343, 352
  Small Constitution (1947), 333
  socialism, Polish way, 335
  Supreme Administrative Court (NSA), 347
politics
  action, 3, 61, 65, 81, 94, 416
  alienation of, 128, 173
  anti-communism, 172, 178, 180–4, 211, 431, *See also* Hungary; Poland
  anti-gender, 172, 183, 186–7, 189, 211, *See also* Hungary
  anti-immigration, 172, 182, 184–9, 211, 223, 264, *See also* Hungary
  authority, 48
  claims, 410
  conflict, 88, 175, 374
  consciousness, 89, 106
  consensus, 174, 396
  culture, 101, 134, 417
  decision, 174–5
  emotion, 211
  imaginaries, 83, 230
  independence, 98, 142
  judicialisation of, 362, 365
  law and development, 313, 369
  law, primacy over, 332, 337, 340, 359
  memory, 172, 454, 456
  mobilisation, 78, 135–6, 142
  myth, 94
  organisations, 87, 95
  personalisation of, 404
  pluralism, 377
  policy makers, 399, 402
  praxis, 45
  rule, 3, 8
  struggle, 63, 112, 172, 202
polity
  distrust in, 311, 334
  establishing of, 174, 176, 193, 203, 207, 413
  exclusion from, 180, 184
  integration of, 3, 146, 201, 204, 215
  masses, 179
  polarisation of, 128, 171, 179, 187, 205–6
  post-national, 83
  regional, 91
  tutoring of, 315
  values of, 202, 212, 271, 286, 386, 410
Portugal
  anti-oligarchy, narrative of, 34
  Constitution (1976), 372, 374–5, 377, 379, 382
  constitutional consensus, 374–5
  Constitutional Court, 383–5
  constitutional narratives, 375–8
  Estado Novo, 373
  social question, 372, 381–2
post-communist Europe. *See* Central and Eastern Europe

rationality
  constitution, of, 204, 213, 272
  law, of, 429
Rechtsstaat. *See also* rule of law
  authoritarian, 304
  democratic, 156, 297, 302, 304, 306, 326
  socialist, 299, 302–4, 326, 333, 336
  varieties of, 31
  welfare state, in opposition to, 380
recognition
  external, 47
  international relations, 46
  self-, 46, 230

referendum
constitution, on, 148, *See also* Poland
EU membership, on, 127, 157, 159
EU treaties, on, 426
Scottish independence, on, 129
representation
people, of the, 112, 213, 334, 387
workers', 400
republicanism
citizen, 424
constitution, through, 36, 417, 424, 427
general interest, 36, 418, 420, 423
human rights ideology, critique of, 422
parliament, centrality of, 418–19, 424
powers, balance of, 417
Rome, Treaty of (1957), 75, 126
Rozmaryn, Stefan
constitutional review, 339
constitutional safeguards, 339
legal constitutionalism, socialist, 338
rule of law. *See also Rechtsstaat*
adaptation of, 37, 446–7
constitutional principle, as, 117, 121, 128, 202, 272, 343
crisis/backsliding of, 7, 26, 94, 165, 356, 407, 430
internationalisation of, 313, 363, 369, 423
justice, supremacy over, 433, 449
liberal, 298, 317
meanings of, 117, 302, 312, 325–7
neoliberal, 306, 313
political origins of, 176, 181
power limitation, 308, 312, 325, 415, 424
state based upon, 139
substantive, 317–21, 324, 326, 433, 436, 438, 449
transformation, within, 446, 449
Russia
backwardness, symbol of, 241–3
Europeanness of, 237

Schmitt, Carl
Concept of the Political, the, 173
Schuman Declaration (1950), 22, 76
Scotland
constitutionalism, 122–3
identity of, 122
security
collective, 99
ontological, 49, 59
self-determination, 46, 100, 181
self-management
economic, 16, 133–6
self-sufficiency, as, 140
territorial, 138, 142
self-rule/government, 3
democratic, 429
organisations, professional, 398, 402–3, 408
people, 412
social actors, 396
societal, 377
self-understanding, 3, 176
collective, 410
constitutional, 187
mortality awareness, 50
nation state, as, 88
smallness, perception of, 91
Siemieński, Feliks
constitutional review, 344–5, 351
social imaginaries, 3, 93, 230, 412, 454, *See also* social imagination
elites, hegemony of, 412
social imagination, 63–4, *See also* social imaginaries
society
artefacts, 412–13
autonomy, 395, 397, 402
bureaucratisation of, 399
control, 398, 403
costs, 4
dialogue, 35, 396, 398–401, 403, 406–7
diversity, 395
integration, 202, 206
juridification of, 396
market-based, 306, 308, 361, 367
memory, collective, 409, 412
movements, 78, 398
myth, 412
order, 197
organisations/institutions, 78, 314
participation, 397, 403
pluralism, 139, 395, 397, 415–16
political order of, 63
politicisation of, 395, 407
production and reproduction, 62
revolutionary situations, 132
scientific management of, 301, 310, 352
self-organisation of, 396
systems, 34, 398
society, civil, 398
existence, pre-legal, 397
nonpartisan, 401
political actor, as, 397, 400, 403–4
public funding of, 401, 407
public services, provider of, 401
state, in opposition to, 397, 404
subordination of, 402, 404, 407
trade unions, 399–401, 403

solidarity
  class, 193
  national, 193
Sólyom, László, 320
sovereignism, 14, 59, 84, 95–6, 102, 166, *See also* Central and Eastern Europe
sovereignty
  associated, 48
  conservative notion of, 42
  conundrum, 102–5, *See also* Central and Eastern Europe
  essence of, 109, 162
  external, 47
  indivisibility of, 42, 48, 84, 424
  internal, 47, 131
  international relations theory, 42, 44, 48
  limited, 96, 102, 347, *See also* Central and Eastern Europe; Soviet Union
  losing of, 76, 94, 100, 105, 145, 153, 155–6, 168–9
  meanings of, 10, 14, 45, 103, 136, 156, 424
  national, 9, 46, 85, 209, 214
  people's, 418, 424
  political, 141, 175
  popular, 46, 112, 137, 220, 344, 357–8, 365, 394
  post-imperial, 101, 125, *See also* United Kingdom
  post-traumatic, 94, 100–1, 104
  protection of, 155, 182
  radical, 4
  restrictions of, 13, 99, 108, 386
  right of discretion, 10–11
  semi-, 49
  shared, 48, 108, 424
  symbolic form, 43, 45, 48, 218
  transfer of, 103, 126, 145, 150, 169
  transfer of exercise, 103
  transfer of the exercise of, 149, 155, 160, 162, 167
  vicarious, 13, 43, 47–9, 54, 59–60, *See also* Estonia
Soviet Union
  colonial system, within, 100, 232–3, 235, 248
  Constitution (1977), 136–7
  constitutional theory, 331
  dissolution of, 137, 143
  economic management, 139–40, 233
  parade of sovereignties, 16, 137, 143
  perestroika, 132, 139–40, 302
  satellites of, 100, 102, *See also* Central and Eastern Europe
state
  centrality of, 416
  collapse-built, 90
  continuity, 217
  core-built, 89
  ideology, 228
  nation, 4, 83
  politics, 228
  scientific management of, 9, 26
  shadow, 89
  society, separation from, 416
statehood
  continuity, 224
  national aspiration, 97–8
  protection of, 222
  sovereignty, 97
  transformation of, 2
  unfulfilled desires of, 87

teleocracy, 4
threat. *See also* enemy
  East, from, 12, 246
  existential, 92–4, 101, 129
  external, 9
  imagined, 85
  Russia, 47, 97, 105
  terrorist, 183, 185
transformation, 246
  civic, 21, 398, *See also* Hungary
  constitutional, 6, 128
  decommunisation, 452–4
  democratic, 18, 196, 298, 356, 445, 452
  economic, 27, 139–41, 305–6, 308, 310, 313, 315, 452
  green, 406
  law, through, 297, 305, 375, 379, 385
  liberal, 297, 303, 311, 322, 326, 423
  neoliberal, 29, 297, 360–1, 369
  political, 27, 361, 432, 447
  social, 453, 455
Trianon, Treaty of (1920), 22

United Kingdom
  Brexit, 100, 127–30
  common law, 115–16, 121, 128
  Constitution, 117, 125, 128
  constitutional identity of, 15, 121, 128, 130
  Crown, the, 112, 118–20
  European Communities Act, the (1972), 126
  High Court of Parliament, 116
  imperial past, 100, 110, 122, 126, 130
  local self-government, 15, 113–16
  parliamentary sovereignty, 112, 114–15, 120–1, 123–4, 127–8
  rule of judicature, 114–18, *See also* rule of law
  Union, the, 122–3
  Whig interpretation of history, 113

utopia
alternative future, 131, 370
constitutional, 8, 146
democratic, 374
economic, 136, 142
European constitutionalism, 59
sovereignty, 164, 170
status quo, opposition to, 4

values
conflict of, 393
conservative, 186, 223
constitutional, 392
democratic, 18, 56
European, 56, 168
foundational, 108

welfare state, 380, 384, *See also* Nordics
future of, 385
golden epoch of, 357
political, 366
West, the
constitutional borrowing from, 18, 27, 305, 313, 356, 432, 445, 447
Europeanness, exclusive representation of, 234, 241, 245
Europeanness, symbol of, 242
hegemony of, 6, 306
postmodern, 83
return to, 2
superiority, symbol of, 227, 243, 245, 247
transformation of, 7

For EU product safety concerns, contact us at Calle de José Abascal, 56–1°, 28003 Madrid, Spain or eugpsr@cambridge.org.

www.ingramcontent.com/pod-product-compliance
Lightning Source LLC
LaVergne TN
LVHW011657200926
848484LV00004B/973

* 9 7 8 1 0 0 9 6 0 4 0 7 9 *